Humankind Emerging

Humankind Emerging

The Concise Edition

Bernard G. Campbell

James D. Loy
University of Rhode Island

Allyn and Bacon
Boston ▪ London ▪ Toronto ▪ Sydney ▪ Tokyo ▪ Singapore

Series Editor: Jennifer Jacobson
Editor-in-Chief: Karen Hanson
Senior Development Editor: Mary Ellen Lepionka
Editorial Assistant: Tom Jefferies
Marketing Manager: Judeth Hall
Editorial-Production Service: Omegatype Typography, Inc.
Manufacturing Buyer: Megan Cochran
Cover Administrator: Linda Knowles
Electronic Composition: Omegatype Typography, Inc.

Copyright © 2002 by Allyn & Bacon
A Pearson Education Company
75 Arlington Street
Boston, MA 02116

Internet: www.ablongman.com

Between the time Website information is gathered and then published, it is not unusual for some sites to have closed. Also, the transcription of URLs can result in typographical errors. The publisher would appreciate notification where these occur so that they may be corrected in subsequent editions.

Library of Congress Cataloging-in-Publication Data

Campbell, Bernard Grant.
    Humankind emerging / Bernard G. Campbell, James D. Loy.—The concise ed.
      p. cm.
    "Developed from the eighth edition of ... Humankind emerging"—Pref.
    Includes bibliographical references and index.
    ISBN 0-205-32509-2 (alk. paper)
    1. Human evolution. 2. Prehistoric peoples. 3. Physical anthropology. I. Loy, James.
  II. Title.
    GN281 .C36 2002
    599.93'8—dc21
                                          2001018849

Text and photo credits are found on pp. 389–391 and constitute an extension of the copyright page.

Printed in the United States of America
10 9 8 7 6 5 4 3 2 1   06 05 04 03 02 01

For Susan, Hatty, and Charlie with love

To Fred and Aileen Loy, and
John and Genevieve Woolsey,
with thanks and love

Brief Contents

Contents

Features

Figures

Tables

Preface

Humankind Emerging: The Concise Edition has been developed from the eighth edition of the long-established anthropological text *Humankind Emerging*. We have reduced the text to a shorter length and more approachable format but have retained all the essential facts and theories relating to human evolution. *Humankind Emerging* is the text that generations of students have found useful in physical anthropology, human evolution, and paleoanthropology courses. *The Concise Edition* has been brought fully up to date with some exciting new discoveries and retains all the central features of the bigger book; but, to fit the material into fewer chapters and pages, we have omitted some historical sections and have combined and condensed some geographical and topical sections. For example, australopithecines are here treated in one chapter rather than two or more. What remains is a concise and manageable volume, which nevertheless omits nothing essential to an understanding of human evolution. At the same time, we have given more space to certain essential topics and developments, such as recent advances in bioanthropology and human population genetics.

The Concise Edition has been enhanced for the first time with new instructional features that appear in every chapter:

- **Critical Thinking.** In these features we pose questions that challenge students to apply their learning and then suggest answers that we hope readers will find stimulating as well as instructive.
- **Discoveries and Mysteries.** Here we showcase new discoveries, ideas, and evidence, as well as some continuing puzzles. These features often are illustrated and discuss the curious finds and questions that make paleoanthropology so enthralling.
- **Asking Questions.** Each chapter has a feature anticipating and addressing a significant question that might arise naturally to students as they read. This feature also models questioning as a major first step in the process of scientific inquiry.

Also new to *The Concise Edition* are parenthetical source citations embedded in the narrative for readers' convenience, in addition to a comprehensive References section at the back of the book. The embedded citations call attention to original sources for the most current advances in fields relating to physical anthropology and the study of evolution.

In addition, special banners alert readers to the existence of further information on Allyn and Bacon's content-rich web page for Physical Anthropology at **www. ablongman.com/anthro**. This site contains maps, charts, drawings, photos, links, video clips, and animations pertaining to this subject area.

The following text elements, which students and instructors say they have found especially useful, have been carried over from the eighth edition of *Humankind Emerging* into *The Concise Edition*, where they have been thoroughly updated and augmented:

- *Margin definitions* of key terms and concepts aid the reader, as does the comprehensive end-of-text *Glossary*.

- Both *Mini-Timelines* and expanded *Timelines* are included at the beginning and end of chapters as appropriate. These learning aids summarize our knowledge and understanding of the fossil, technological, cultural, and environmental chronologies relating to human evolution.
- *Review Questions.* Chapters close with questions that test the reader's mastery of chapter content, including the ability to understand and follow arguments in the text.
- *Suggested Further Reading.* At the end of each chapter we list three or four books for student reading—works selected for readability, currency, and interest. Some selections are recent best-selling trade books that help bring the entire subject to life.
- *Internet Resources* and suggested search terms at the end of each chapter have been updated and augmented as aids to learning for students who wish to pursue the subject in greater depth on the World Wide Web. These links also can be accessed directly from the web site.

The Concise Edition continues the same mission that guided the eighth edition of *Humankind Emerging.* The purpose of this book is to set out in simple terms the evidence for human evolution over a period of some millions of years. Many people still believe in a recent creation of the world as described in Genesis and do not accept that the evolution of the earth and its inhabitants has occurred over a period of some 15 billion years. It is important to come to terms with this reality, and we hope that this book will help those who are searching for the truth.

Throughout the world, people of different cultures have passed from generation to generation their myths about the origin of the world and of humankind. It was not until the eighteenth century that anyone seriously speculated that these explanatory creation myths, varied and colorful as they are, were not necessarily reliable and truthful accounts of the creative process. Since the eighteenth century, scientists have slowly built a different story: that the world is very ancient; that its history is long and complex; that the universe is vast and of astonishing and unimaginable antiquity; and that life on earth has developed from a single beginning over a period of at least 3 billion years.

By the nineteenth century, scientists who believed that the Bible contains the word of God—a belief termed *fundamentalist*—faced a difficult intellectual dilemma. How could the new and convincing results of scientific investigation and the text of Chapter 1 of Genesis both be true? One or the other had to be in error. Many people still suffer intellectual anguish over this question. One biologist who thought he had found a solution was Philip Henry Gosse. In his book *Omphalos* (1857) Gosse maintained that the biblical account of the creation is true but that the earth was created to give the *impression* of vast antiquity. Fossils were "planted" to suggest a long evolutionary sequence that never actually occurred. Gosse's book was laughed to scorn, however, by both religious people and scientists. Surely God would never play such a trick on his creation! Nevertheless, this proposal remains the only hypothesis that might allow a person to maintain a fundamentalist belief in the face of scientific fact. But Gosse's hypothesis is improbable and untestable, and therefore is unacceptable to science.

The evidence for the earth's antiquity and for human evolution from simpler forms, in contrast, is overwhelming. Two hundred years of painstaking research offers no evidence to support the veracity of the biblical creation story—and considerable evidence to the contrary. *Humankind Emerging: The Concise Edition* presents the scientific explanation for human evolution. The theory of evolution, scientifically tested repeatedly since Charles Darwin's day, has survived essentially intact; and it is on this theory, and its modern extensions, that this textbook is based.

Acknowledgments

Many thanks to those who have helped us with this edition by sharing their thoughts in careful and detailed reviews. These reviewers included James R. Bindon, University of Alabama; Robert Blumenschine, Rutgers University; James H. McDonald, University of Texas at San Antonio; Ann M. Palkovich, George Mason University; Ann Popplestone, Cuyahoga Community College; and Jon A. Schlenker, University of Maine at Augusta. In addition, *The Concise Edition* reflects the criticisms and suggestions of other reviewers for the larger text on which it is based: George J. Bey III, Millsaps College; George Gill, University of Wyoming at Laramie; Bruce LaBrack, University of the Pacific; Carol Lauer, Rollins College; John Pryor, California State University–Fresno; Mary Sandeford, University of North Carolina at Greensboro; Jeffrey Schwartz, University of Pittsburgh; William A. Stini, University of Arizona; and Ian Tattersall, American Museum of Natural History.

We also want to thank our publishers, Allyn and Bacon, and especially Sarah Kelbaugh, former series editor for anthropology, who first developed the idea of a concise edition, and Mary Ellen Lepionka, senior development editor, who put an enormous amount of effort into guiding us. Mary Ellen's instinct for style and word use and her complete understanding of the world of textbooks were invaluable. Thanks also to the team at Omegatype Typography, Inc., for their superb copyediting and editorial production.

Some of the ideas for this volume came from discussions during a six-month period when our two families were both residing in Cambridge, England. During this time our wives, Susan Campbell and Kent Loy, remained composed as we talked interminably about Darwin, time, and fossils. We are grateful to them for their forbearance!

Bernard Campbell
Jim Loy

About the Authors

Paleoanthropologist Bernard Campbell received his Ph.D. from Cambridge University. He has taught at that institution and at Harvard University and the University of California at Los Angeles, and has conducted field work in South and East Africa and in Iran. Although retired from active teaching, Professor Campbell continues to publish widely on the evolution of human behavior and its ecological setting.

James Loy (shown here with his wife, Kent, and two orphaned patas monkeys being hand-reared) is a professor of anthropology at the University of Rhode Island. After earning a Ph.D. from Northwestern University, Professor Loy conducted research on the sexual behavior of Old World monkeys for more than twenty years.

Humankind Emerging

Paleoanthropology and Evolution

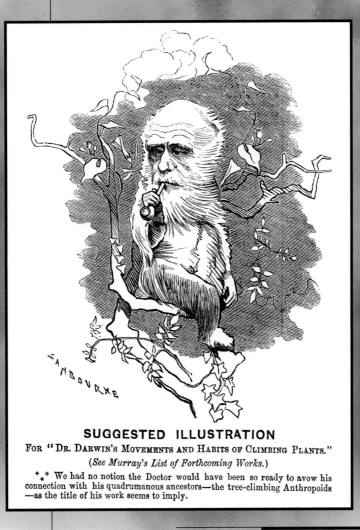

SUGGESTED ILLUSTRATION

For "Dr. Darwin's Movements and Habits of Climbing Plants."

(*See Murray's List of Forthcoming Works.*)

*** We had no notion the Doctor would have been so ready to avow his connection with his quadrumanous ancestors—the tree-climbing Anthropoids —as the title of his work seems to imply.

Paleoanthropology the study of the fossil and cultural remains and other evidence of humans' extinct ancestors.

Physical anthropologists scientists who work in the field of human evolution and human variability.

Biological anthropologists scientists who study human biology and the biology of past and present human populations, human genetics and variability, adaptation including growth, and evolutionary change.

Overview

This book is about the study of the origin of humankind—a science called **paleoanthropology.** It is about our evolution—the slow creation of our bodies and our behavior over millions of years. Most paleoanthropologists can be classified more broadly as **physical anthropologists.** Other anthropological researchers focus mainly on humans' social and behavioral patterns (*cultural anthropologists* if their subjects are living; *archaeologists* if they study extinct societies) or on speech and language (*linguistic anthropologists*); in contrast, physical anthropologists or **biological anthropologists** primarily concern themselves with our biology and its evolutionary development. Today paleoanthropologists pursue the search for human origins within the Western scientific tradition, and therefore some knowledge of that tradition is necessary to understand current theories and discoveries. Toward that end, this opening chapter describes historical

Mini-Timeline: The Meanings of Antiquity

Dates	Historical Concept or Development
1930s–1940s	Modern synthetic theory of evolution
1900	Gregor Mendel's work rediscovered
1866	Mendel publishes his work on heredity
1859	Charles Darwin publishes his theory of evolution by natural selection
1700s and 1800s	Evidence accumulates for "deep time"
1600s and 1700s	Antiquarians begin to recover evidence of ancient humans and stone tools
1650	Bishop Ussher publishes his date of creation
1632	Galileo publishes his *Dialogue on the Two Chief World Systems*
1543	Copernicus publishes *On the Revolutions of the Heavenly Spheres*

Geologic Age (billion years before present)

0.5	First vertebrates
0.7	First animals
3.5	First life
4.5	Earth and moon formation complete
10–15	Big bang (singularity)

Follow links at **http://www.ablongman/anthro** for additional resources in physical anthropology, primatology, biological anthropology, and paleoanthropology.

events and scientific developments that contributed to our modern views on evolution. Beginning with the seventeenth century—when Europeans' opinions were shaped by the biblical creation story and belief in a young earth—we will review briefly the accumulation of geologic evidence for "deep time" (that is, for an ancient earth); the development of Charles Darwin's theory of evolution; and finally, an introduction to the science of paleoanthropology as it is practiced at present, with some detailed discussion of important dating techniques. A short timeline is given on page 2 to help you learn the chronology of these developments. Important concepts in the chapter include deep time, James Hutton's deductions, catastrophism, uniformitarianism, evolution, natural selection, geological terminology, stratigraphy, and relative and absolute dating.

> Check our web site for additional information, photos, drawings, maps, and animations on topics in this chapter.

What Are the Origins of Paleoanthropology?

The history of paleoanthropology is a fascinating story involving the contributions of astronomers, geologists, and biologists. When Copernicus, Galileo, and others claimed that the earth circled the sun, rather than vice versa, these early scientists took the first steps in developing a new worldview. The old view of our place at the center of the universe, based on Greek and Arabic astronomy and accepted as doctrine by the powerful Roman Catholic Church, began to be threatened by the new ideas, which were considered dangerous and revolutionary. Not until 1992 did the Catholic Church issue a retroactive pardon to Galileo for his heretical views.

According to the Scottish geologist James Hutton (1726–1797), in his 1795 book *Theory of the Earth,* the earth showed "no vestige of a beginning, no prospect of an end." It was evidently not created in 4004 BC, as had been claimed by a distinguished Irish divine (Bishop Ussher, 1581–1656). The realization of the earth's antiquity and of **deep time** in the cosmos was the essential basis for a new outlook on the world, which taught us that we could learn more from our own observations of our environment than we could from all the books of antiquity (Gould, 1987). Until the acceptance of the concept of deep time, the discovery of apparently ancient stone tools and animal bones was not taken as evidence of anything significant. Some discoveries were labeled **antediluvian,** meaning that they predated the great flood described in the story of Noah and his sons (Genesis 6–9).

The Discovery of Fossils

Scholarly views on human prehistory changed rather abruptly in the mid-nineteenth century, and the shift was especially clear in England. In 1858, the paleontologist Hugh Falconer (1808–1865) examined a collection of stone tools, made as early as 1830 by Boucher de Perthes (1788–1868) in France, and became convinced of their authenticity. Falconer then persuaded Joseph Prestwich (1812–1896) to examine the geology of the Somme valley—an exercise that resulted in strong proof of the commingling of chipped flint tools and extinct animals' bones on river terraces older than the modern geologic epoch. By 1863 Sir Charles Lyell (1797–1875), then one of England's leading geologists, was sufficiently convinced of the case for ancient humans to write a volume synthesizing the evidence called *The Antiquity of Man.* Finally, in 1865, the naturalist and archaeologist John Lubbock (1834–1913) proposed a classification scheme that separated

Deep time the theory that the earth is billions of years old and thus has a long history of development and change.

Antediluvian relating to a time that preceded the flood described in Genesis.

the oldest and most primitive flaked implements—such as those found by Boucher de Perthes—from younger stone tools attributed to Celtic (pre-Roman) Europe. Lubbock coined the terms **Paleolithic** and **Neolithic** for the respective tool types.

Discoveries and Mysteries

Who Lived in Kent's Hole?

In 1829 a Catholic priest, Father J. MacEnery (1796–1841), excavated a cave called Kent's Hole in southeastern England. Digging through an unbroken layer of stalagmite, and thus into quite old geological deposits, MacEnery found the strange, massive bones of what would later be classified as Pleistocene mammals: mammoth, rhinoceros, and cave bear. He also found what he regarded as several unmistakable flint tools that he felt had to have been shaped by human hands.

At the time of this discovery, however, people were not prepared to view human life as having much antiquity or to see the earth as being very old. When he reported his findings, MacEnery was strenuously opposed by another cleric, the Dean of Westminster, William Buckland (1784–1856). Buckland, himself an amateur archaeologist, confidently announced that the findings in Kent's Hole dated only to some time after the fall of Adam and Eve. Buckland speculated that early Britons dug through the stalagmite layer as they made holes for their ovens and then must have accidentally dropped in some of their own stone tools.

In his own earlier excavation of a site called Goat's Hole in Wales, Buckland found a human fossil skeleton that was recently dated to 25,000 years ago. He insisted that the bones were no older than Roman times. This illustration comes from his 1823 book *Reliquiae Diluvianae* ("Relics from the Flood").

Paleolithic relating to the Old Stone Age; the earliest stage of stone tool making, beginning about 2.5 million years ago.

Neolithic relating to the New Stone Age; a late stage of stone tool making that began about 10,000 years ago.

Georges Cuvier and Catastrophism

At about the same time that James Hutton was publishing his book, French paleontologist Georges Cuvier (1769–1832) and others were discovering the bones of ancient elephants, mammoths, whales, and other exotic and apparently long-dead species in the rocks near Paris.

In all, Cuvier was able to show that at least ninety of the species he had recovered, as well as several genera (groups of similar species), apparently had disappeared entirely from the face of the earth. This was an extremely important discovery, because proving that **extinction** is a common fate of species opened the way for fossils to be used as historical markers in the geologic record. Cuvier enlisted the aid of mineralogist Alexandre Brongniart (1770–1847), and together they began a detailed study of the mechanisms of fossil deposition and the record of ancient environments in the Paris countryside. They studied one geologic column (sequence of rock layers) after another and found the strata (layers) to be variously filled with marine fossils, freshwater or land shells, the bones of terrestrial animals, or no fossils at all. What sense could be made of this bewildering sequence of the comings and goings of life forms? Cuvier concluded that the history of life, in the Paris area and elsewhere, had been disrupted routinely by geologic "revolutions"—earthly convulsions related to buckling of the earth's crust as the world continued to cool down from an originally very hot state. These revolutions sometimes caused the seafloor to be raised and laid dry or, alternately, the dry land to be submerged. Cuvier's theory was dubbed **catastrophism,** and such catastrophes were thought to have occurred suddenly and to have caused great loss of life and extinction of species over quite large areas. Following each catastrophe, Cuvier argued, devastated areas were repopulated by migrations of organisms, some entirely new for that locale, coming in from unaffected regions.

What Did Charles Darwin Discover?

In the middle of the nineteenth century, scholars began to look again at earlier theories of the history of life on earth, and there followed the publication of two revolutionary books by Charles Lyell (1797–1875) and Charles Darwin (1809–1882). Lyell's *Principles of Geology* (published 1830–1833) synthesized the available evidence for deep time and, building on the earlier work of Hutton and others, established a theoretical position called **uniformitarianism.** Unlike Cuvier's catastrophism, uniformitarianism proposed that the earth has changed steadily under constant natural laws. Thus, the processes of erosion, volcanic eruption, and so on that we see today can also explain past changes that occurred slowly over vast eons of time. The idea of organic **evolution** was also in the air at this time. Charles Darwin's grandfather Erasmus Darwin (1731–1802) had written of the evolution of nature; the French naturalist Jean Baptiste de Monet, Chevalier de Lamarck (1744–1829), developed a theory to account for evolutionary change (1801), known then as the transmutation of species. Lamarck had proposed that over time animals change their behavior to meet their needs and that small anatomical changes occurred in response to need, or to use or disuse of organs, and that such acquired characteristics came to be inherited. We now know that his theory was not correct. Charles Darwin's book *On the Origin of Species by Means of Natural Selection* (1859) provided a theory that describes the means by which the evolutionary changes occur: the theory of **natural selection.**

Extinction the loss of a *species* when all its members die as a result of competition or climatic change.

Catastrophism Georges Cuvier's theory that vast floods and other disasters wiped out ancient life forms again and again throughout the earth's history.

Uniformitarianism the belief that the steady changes in the earth's crust that we see today were preceded by similar slow changes throughout geological time.

Evolution changes in the forms of organic life that have occurred throughout time since life first arose on earth.

Natural selection the principal mechanism of Darwinian evolutionary change, by which the individuals best adapted to the environment contribute more offspring to succeeding generations than others do. As more of such individuals' characteristics are incorporated into the *gene pool,* the characteristics of the *population* evolve.

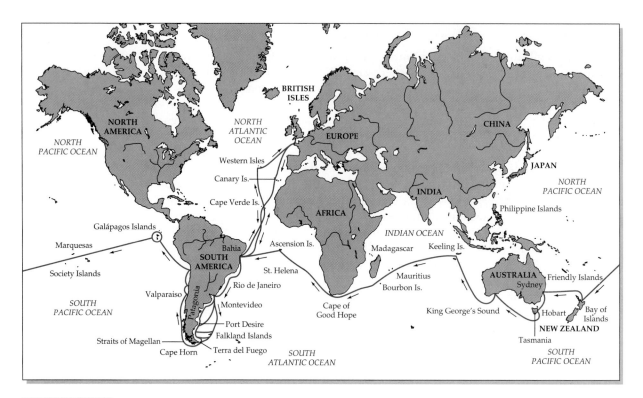

Figure 1.1

Charles Darwin left Devonport, England, in December 1831 and returned to Falmouth in October 1836. Out of the nearly five years spent on the voyage of the HMS *Beagle*, Darwin spent more than three years in South America and its islands. The voyage was completed with visits to New Zealand, Australia, the Keeling (Cocos) Islands, the Cape of Good Hope, and St. Helena. Darwin's experience on this voyage was a rich and fertile source of observation and inspiration in the development of his ideas.

As a young man Darwin traveled extensively, making a round-the-world voyage between 1831 and 1836 (Figure 1.1). His observations on his travels were extremely detailed, his interest in natural history of all kinds insatiable. His theory was based, therefore, not on a moment of inspiration, nor on any ideas he had acquired during his education, but on his own direct observations of all aspects of the changing face of nature, from volcanoes and coral atolls to the beaks of finches. Like Galileo with his telescope, Darwin looked at nature with an open mind and recorded what he saw. What he saw was a world teeming with life of almost infinite variety, but a world that carried a framework of meaning—because all life was ultimately related, was beautifully adapted to its environment, and was an expression of variation and natural selection.

For several reasons, Darwin did not publish his evolutionary theory until many years after his voyage. In the meantime, Alfred Russel Wallace was exploring the tropics of Southeast Asia, collecting specimens for the Natural History Museum in London. In 1858 Wallace wrote to Darwin to propose an evolutionary mechanism similar to Darwin's theory. For this reason, Darwin and Wallace are given joint credit for discovering natural selection. In 1859, Darwin alone wrote *On the Origin of Species*.

How Darwin Developed His Theory of Natural Selection

It turned out that Darwin and Wallace had both read a book by the English clergyman T. R. Malthus (*An Essay on the Principle of Population*, 1798). In this book Malthus pointed out that the reproductive potential of humankind far exceeds the natural resources available to nourish an ever expanding population; the sizes of human populations are therefore limited by disease, famine, and war. A key observation of Darwin and Wallace was that this condition of **superfecundity** is also to be found among all plant and animal species.

The theory of evolution by natural selection is simple and can best be understood by the steps shown in Figure 1.2 (Mayr, 1991). From Malthus, Darwin took the fact of species' superfecundity (Fact 1) and combined it with the observation that most natural populations tend to remain stable in size rather than to expand constantly (Fact 2). This size limitation was clearly the result of limited environmental resources of food and space (Fact 3). From these three facts Darwin (following Malthus) inferred that individual organisms (especially members of the same species) are in strong competition with one

Superfecundity the universal tendency to produce more offspring than required to maintain a population of constant size; more than can possibly survive.

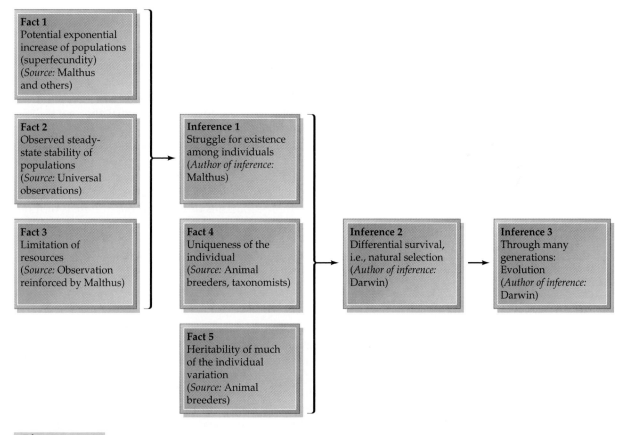

Figure 1.2

Zoologist Ernst Mayr has reduced Darwin's explanatory model of evolution through natural selection to five facts and three inferences.

Source: Mayr, 1991.

another (Inference 1). Combining this inference with the observation that individuals show spontaneous variations in physical and behavioral traits (Fact 4) and the observation that parents often pass their individual variations on to their offspring (Fact 5) allowed Darwin to reach a second inference, that organisms experience differential survival and reproductive success based on the possession of traits that are more or less adaptive in their particular environment (Inference 2; this is the statement that we recognize as natural selection). Finally, Darwin argued that through the action of natural selection over many generations a species could slowly but surely *evolve* (Inference 3).

Thus, natural selection was presented as a process by which adaptive traits are preserved (through the survival and reproduction of their carriers) and maladaptive (or *less* adaptive) traits are winnowed out of species. This process occurs in both plants and animals; and, true to Lyell's uniformitarian principles, Darwin described the evolutionary process as extremely slow and gradual.

Today we recognize that the actual rate of evolutionary change is not constant but can be anything from almost zero (the coelacanth fish has not changed over a period of 200 million years) to what in geological terms is quite rapid—with two new species being evolved within 1 million years (during human evolution). In spite of this apparent speed of evolution, Darwin's principle of gradual change still holds; a million years is a long time. In the 1860s the age of the earth and the time available for the process of evolution was still very uncertain.

The first presentation of the Darwin/Wallace evolutionary model was made at the Linnaean Society in London more than a year before the publication of the *Origin*. On July 1, 1858, a paper entitled "On the Tendency of Species to Form Varieties, and on the Perpetuation of Varieties and Species by Means of Selection" was read and the world has not been the same since that day. Neither Darwin nor Wallace was present.

It is impossible today to recreate the atmosphere of intellectual and moral shock that swept England when Darwin's book was published the following year. It was not that the evolution of plants or animals was so hard to swallow. After all, humans themselves had been responsible, through selective breeding, for the evolution of many domestic animals and of a great variety of crops. Then there were those peculiar dinosaur bones that people had been digging up; they had to be explained, as did the growing evidence that the earth was not simply thousands of years old but hundreds of thousands, perhaps hundreds of millions. No, those things were not really the problem. What was so hard to accept was the implied suggestion that human beings were descended from a bunch of "repulsive, scratching, hairy apes and monkeys."

The Question of Human Origins

The genius of Charles Darwin's evolutionary theory becomes apparent when you consider that he constructed it despite the lack of two critical pieces of information. Darwin knew neither the sources of spontaneous variation within each generation (the basis of Fact 4) nor the mechanisms of intergenerational inheritance (the basis of Fact 5). As it happens, Gregor Mendel was hard at work on those very problems at the time, but Darwin was unaware of Mendel's findings. Furthermore, Darwin was very careful about the way he presented his theory to the world, doing all he could to minimize giving offense to his readers. Of prime importance, in *On the Origin of Species*, Darwin refrained from mentioning the question of human origins with the exception of a single sentence near the end: "Light will be thrown on the origin of man and his history." But, the implication was plain, and nobody missed it.

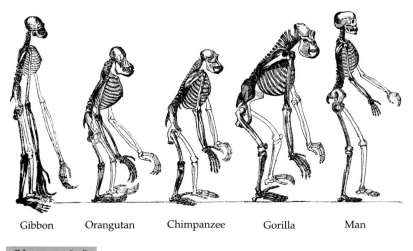

Gibbon   Orangutan   Chimpanzee   Gorilla   Man

Figure 1.3

In 1863 Thomas H. Huxley published this drawing of the skeletons of the four apes and a human to illustrate their extraordinary similarity. He wrote, "Whatever part of the animal fabric might be selected for comparison, the lower apes (monkeys) and the Gorilla would differ more than the Gorilla and the Man." All drawings are to the same scale except the gibbon, which is drawn to twice the scale.

In 1863, Thomas H. Huxley (1825–1895), a friend of Darwin and an ardent supporter of his theory, published *Evidence as to Man's Place in Nature*. This was the first book to address in an orderly and scientific way the problem of human origins. By making many telling anatomical comparisons between humans and the apes, Huxley established that, of all animals on earth, the African great apes—the chimpanzee and gorilla—are most closely related to humans (Figure 1.3). He further stated that the evolutionary development of apes and humans had taken place in much the same way and according to the same laws of natural selection. From this it followed that, if prehuman fossils existed, older and older humanlike fossils would be found, leading eventually to types that would turn out to be ancestral to both apes and humans. Furthermore, these common ancestors probably would be found in Africa.

Darwin concluded that living species were the modified descendants of fossil species. Carrying the case to its full conclusion in *The Descent of Man* (1871), Darwin propounded the theory of an unbroken chain of organisms that began with the first forms of life and evolved into humans. Despite all the logic in Huxley's and Darwin's views, however, they were difficult to support because of a lack of fossils resembling human beings.

At this turning point in the history of human knowledge, there had emerged two great and related ideas about the origin of nature and of humankind: The earth is extremely ancient, long populated by many kinds of plants and animals, some of which are no longer living; and humans themselves, mutable creatures like the animals, have their ancestors far back in time. But how far back and who those ancestors were nobody had even the slightest notion. Almost everything we know about our ancestry we have learned in the past one hundred and fifty years, much of it during the past four decades.

For more on natural selection and fossil evidence, visit our web site.

How Does Natural Selection Work?

Let us look at two examples of the operation of natural selection on variations within breeding populations of animals.

Fur Color in Mice

In 1962 a mutant strain of house mice (*Mus musculus*) was discovered in a farm population in Missouri. Mutant animals had pink eyes and pale yellow fur, in contrast to the dark eyes and dark (agouti) fur of normal mice. Mutants interbred freely with normal mice, and the two strains lived together in a granary used to store corn. The solid construction of the granary prevented the farm's numerous cats from entering.

In order to determine the relative proportions of mutants and normals, researchers periodically live-trapped the granary mice and released them (see Table 1.1). At the first trapping, the mutants accounted for about 28 percent of the population, and their representation increased steadily throughout 1962. In January 1963, because of an increase in the mouse population, the farmer made an opening in the granary wall to provide access for his cats. The cats immediately began to prey on the mice, and the pale yellow animals soon proved to be much more vulnerable to predation than their agouti conspecifics (probably because of greater visibility in the dimly lit corn crib). Percentages of mutants in the population fell to zero soon after the cats began their deadly work.

In September 1963, at the urging of the researchers, the farmer sealed off the cats' entrance, and within three months the pale-colored mice had rebounded to about 5 percent of the population. In this example from nature, heritable differences in fur color were strongly affected by predator pressure (Brown, 1965).

Body Size and Bills in Finches

A species of Darwin's finch (*Geospiza fortis*) was studied on the Galápagos island of Daphne Major between 1975 and 1978. Birds were trapped and measured regularly, and data were collected on their feeding patterns (they ate mostly seeds of various sorts and sizes).

Table 1.1

Predation of Mutant Mice by Cats		
Date	**Total Mice Trapped**	**Mutants as Percentage of Trapped Mice**
Apr. 1962	32	28.1
Aug. 1962	44	40.1
Dec. 1962	58	46.6
(Jan. 1963—cats allowed into granary)		
Apr. 1963	22	0.0
Aug. 1963	29	0.0
(Sept. 1963—cats excluded from granary)		
Dec. 1963	37	5.4

Source: Data from Brown, 1965, pp. 461–465.

Critical Thinking

Natural Selection and the Industrial Age

Imagine a population of moths exhibiting variation in coloration from light with dark speckles to a uniformly blackish hue. The moths rest on the bark of trees. In a preindustrial age this coloring is **cryptic** (it serves to conceal), so the moths are not noticed by predatory birds who recognize them by sight.

Now imagine how the coming of the Industrial Revolution, based on coal burning, might gradually alter the environment to place some of these moths at a selective advantage compared to the others. This actually happened. What do you think was the result? What does the theory of natural selection predict?

Table 1.2

Finch Adaptations to Drought		
Finch Traits	**Predrought Mean**	**Postdrought Mean**
Weight (g)	15.59	16.85
Bill length (mm)	10.68	11.07
Bill depth (mm)	9.42	9.96

Source: Data from Boag and Grant, 1981, pp. 82–85.

In 1977 Daphne Major experienced a severe drought that resulted in a sharp food shortage for the finches. Seeds of all sorts declined in abundance, but small seeds declined faster than large ones, and the result was a strong overall increase in the average size and hardness of the available seeds (averages for the "size-hardness index" for the seeds increased from a predrought figure of just over 4 to about 6 during the drought). In response to these environmental changes, the finches suffered an 85 percent drop in population size. Small birds suffered greater decimation than large ones, apparently because the smaller birds (with their smaller bills) had difficulty cracking and eating large, hard seeds. That is to say, smaller birds were strongly "selected against" because of the drought-related changes in food. Measurements taken after the drought (1978, see Table 1.2) showed the effects of natural selection: Average body size in the population had increased, as had average bill size (Boag and Grant, 1981).

The Science of Paleoanthropology Today

Theories arising from Darwin's arguments in *On the Origin of Species* suggest that human evolution is possible and even probable. But only the fossil evidence can finally demonstrate without question that we do indeed share ancestors with other animals, especially monkeys and apes. A variety of strange fossil finds were made at times when their significance was not understood. The first recorded fossil human skull was discovered in Belgium in 1829 at a place called Engis. Its significance was unclear; such finds were usually labeled antediluvian. Today, however, we have a vast range of fossil evidence from all parts of the world that confirms that humankind has indeed been

Cryptic serving to camouflage, as when coloration allows an animal to blend into its background.

What Skills Are Needed to Study Fossil Sites?

Listed below are the specialists who study fossil sites and their roles.

In the Field

Paleoanthropologists	In charge of investigations from start to finish, they must pick the site, get permission to excavate, obtain financial support, hire the labor, and organize, plan, and supervise the work in progress. Finally, they must integrate the data collected by each of the specialists and publish their conclusions.
Geologists	Often assist in selecting the site. Their knowledge of the geologic history of the region is indispensible in determining the relative ages of fossils. Their study of the strata at the site determines the natural processes—deposition, volcanic action—that laid the strata down and the conditions under which fossilization took place.
Surveyors	Map the general region of the site and the site itself, plotting it in relation to natural landmarks and making a detailed record of its contours before they are obliterated by digging.
Cartographers	Record the exact position of all fossils, tools, and other artifacts as excavated, marking their relationships to each other in both the horizontal and vertical planes.
Photographers	Document fossil remains and artifacts and their associations as they are uncovered, record work in progress and the use of special equipment, and provide overall views of the site as well as of personnel at work.

In the Laboratory

Petrologists	Identify and classify the rocks and minerals found around the site. They can determine the nature of rocks from which tools were made and identify stones that do not occur naturally in the area, which would indicate that the stones were imported by early humans.
Palynologists	Specialize in the study and identification of fossil plant pollen, which may shed light on early humankind's environment and diet and the climate at the time.
Pedologists	Experts on soil and their chemical composition, their findings round out the picture of the environment as it once was.
Geochemists	With geophysicists, conduct chemical and physical tests in the laboratory to determine the absolute age of material found at the site. They may also study the chemical composition of bones and artifacts.
Osteologists	Identify and classify the bone material present, especially the hominid remains. Conserve and reconstruct crushed specimens.

In the Field and Laboratory

Preparators	At the site, preserve and protect fossils and artifacts with various hardening agents and make plaster casts for particularly fragile bones and other organic remains. In the laboratory, preparators clean and restore the specimens, making them ready for study by various specialists.
Paleoclimatologists	Study both faunal and floral remains together with sedimentary evidence to establish the environment and climate of the period of deposition.
Paleontologists	Study the fossil animal remains found at the site. From the finds, they can learn much about the ecology and the eating habits of early humans.
Physical anthropologists	Specialists in the comparative anatomy of apes and humans, they evaluate remains found at the site and the evolutionary status of fossil hominids who lived there.
Taphonomists	Study the condition and arrangement of the fossils in relation to the deposits which carry them, to determine the origin and formation of the fossil assemblage.
Archaeologists	Study humankind's past material culture: tools of stone, bone, and wood; living sites, settlement patterns, and food remains; art and ritual.
Environmentalists	Advise on the excavation and restoration of the site at completion so that the local environment receives the minimum disturbance.

evolving from apelike ancestors during the last 6 million years. The science of paleoanthropology is concerned with the investigation and interpretation of these human and prehuman fossils together with the archaeological evidence of early human culture. Paleoanthropology is no longer a matter of excavation and collection but has joined the scientific revolution and has become a complex undertaking that draws on many disciplines, from biology to physics.

Compared to its humble beginnings, modern paleoanthropology is a complicated field of inquiry. The location, excavation, dating, analysis, and interpretation of hominid fossils requires the combined skills of a team of specialists (see Asking Questions, page 12). Scientists excavate sites with extreme care and plot all fossils, artifacts, and other significant features on maps for further study. Geologists, paleontologists, and other scientists help to reconstruct the ancient landscape and ecosystem in detail. Laboratory analyses of fossils and the publication of results my take several years after the original discoveries.

How Are Fossils Dated?

The proof that evolution has indeed taken place over eons of time depended on the discovery of fossils in ancient geological deposits that could be dated. Thanks to advances in geology, paleontology, and atomic physics, scientists today can often determine the age of deposits and fossils with considerable accuracy. Fossils can be dated through both relative and absolute dating techniques.

Stratigraphy and Relative Dating

Stratigraphy involves interpreting the production and deposition of rock layers, the underwater deposit of sediments, layering by glacial or volcanic action, or the accumulation of windblown soil—and their subsequent rearrangement, if any, as the result of earth movements and weathering (Figure 1.4). Stratigraphic information allows the **relative dating** of any fossils contained in the various rock layers. In undisturbed strata, the oldest layers are the deepest, and both strata and fossils get younger as one nears the surface. Although stratigraphy alone doesn't tell us a fossil's actual age, simply knowing that one specimen is older or younger than another can be critically important for working out evolutionary sequences. Furthermore, because every species has a finite lifetime between its origin and extinction, well-studied fossil lineages—with known sequences of species dated relative to one another—can be used to date other material by **faunal correlation**. For example, a newly discovered prehuman specimen found in the same rock layer as a variety of pig known to be ancient within the pig lineage can properly be assumed to be quite old as well. Better yet, if the actual age of the fossil pig species has been determined, that same age can be attributed to the prehuman material. Scientists can test the claim that fossils from a particular site come from the same rock layer, and therefore are the same relative age, by analyzing their levels of certain chemicals, usually nitrogen (which is lost during **fossilization**) and uranium and fluorine (both of which commonly accumulate in bones from groundwater). Noncontemporaneous specimens will show different chemical levels.

Absolute Dating

Through the constant cross-checking and fitting together of enormous amounts of both rock and fossil evidence, geologists have been able to determine quite a detailed

Stratigraphy the sequence of geologic strata, or layers, formed by materials deposited by water or wind; also, the study of this sequence.

Relative dating estimating the age of geologic deposits (and the fossils in them) by determining their stratigraphic level in relation to other deposits whose relative or absolute age is known. (Compare with *absolute dating*.)

Faunal correlation dating a site by the similarity of its animal fossils to those of another site that may carry a reliable absolute date.

Fossilization the transformation of bones that occurs when they are buried under suitable circumstances. Certain mineral elements are dissolved and replaced by others. The form of the bone is effectively preserved.

Fossils are found in deposits formed by the action of glaciers and rivers or laid down in ancient riverbeds, lakes, estuaries, and seas. Some deposits are windblown and may contain volcanic ash. Fossils are laid down in more or less horizontal beds, or strata, as shown here. Stratigraphy is the science that attempts to understand stratigraphic deposition—its form, its sequence, and its age.

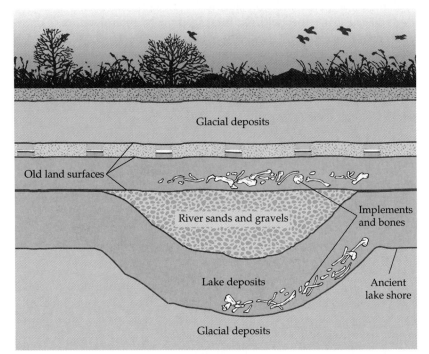

succession of rock formations and fossils from the present back some 650 million years. But this succession provides only the relative dating of fossils. Fortunately, atomic physics provides us with some very valuable techniques for **absolute** or **chronometric** dating of geological formations (and, in some cases, bones), which have revolutionized our study of human evolution (Brown, 1992). We know that certain radioactive elements discharge energy at a constant rate, known as the decay rate. Radium, for example, turns slowly but steadily into lead. Once this steady decay rate is known, we can determine how old a sample is by measuring how much of it is still radium and how much is lead.

Potassium–Argon Dating. One long-lasting radioactive substance used for chronometric dating is potassium 40. This material breaks down into the gas argon at the relatively slow rate of one-half of the original potassium every 1,250 million years; this is known as potassium 40's **half-life.** Because potassium 40 is found in volcanic ash and lava, **potassium–argon dating** (abbreviated K/Ar) can be used to date fossils located in volcanic rock or ash or sandwiched between two layers of volcanic matter. The "clock" starts as the lava or ash cools (argon produced previously escaped while the lava was heated in the volcano), and it continues to run steadily with the breakdown of potassium 40. The age of the rock can therefore be calculated with remarkable precision by determining the ratio of argon gas to potassium 40. Problems arise when the rock sample containing the potassium also contains air (which itself contains small quantities of argon), or if the rock has been reheated by later volcanic eruptions, which may have driven off the argon already produced by radioactive decay. Also, the method can be used to date fossils only from areas where volcanic eruptions occurred at about the same time as the fossils were deposited. Fortunately, many of the most important fossil

Absolute dating determining the actual age of geologic deposits (and the fossils in them) by examining the chemical composition of rock fragments containing radioactive substances that decay at known rates. Also known as *chronometric dating.* (Compare with *relative dating.*)

Chronometric dating an alternative term for *absolute dating.*

Half-life the time taken for half of any quantity of a radioactive element to decay to its fission products.

Potassium–argon dating *chronometric dating* in which age is determined by measurement of the decay of radioactive potassium 40.

sites in East Africa are in areas where volcanic activity was widespread; but in much of Asia, the Americas, and Europe, this method cannot be used.

An important development that supports K/Ar dating is the recognition of ash layers that have been deposited over wide areas. It has been shown that each layer of ash (or **tuff**) can be identified by an analysis of its unique mineral components. Each tuff has its own "chemical signature." Because of this characteristic, it is possible to correlate tuffs from sites as far apart as Kenya, Ethiopia, and the Indian Ocean, where they can be recognized in deep-sea cores. In this way, dated tuffs may be widely mapped, and their K/Ar dates in one area checked against their K/Ar dating in another.

A derivation from K/Ar dating is the Ar^{40}/Ar^{39} procedure. In this test, previously irradiated crystals are melted with a laser beam in order to release argon. The procedure has the advantage of being extremely precise even when very small mineral samples are tested. Together, the K/Ar and Ar^{40}/Ar^{39} procedures can date rocks over a wide span of time, from only a few tens of thousands to many millions of years ago.

Carbon 14 Dating.   Another useful dating technique based on a radioactive element is **carbon 14 dating.** Carbon 14 decays to atmospheric nitrogen. Carbon 14 is present in the atmosphere as carbon dioxide (CO_2) and is incorporated into all plant material. In the plant, the proportion of carbon 14 to the stable atom carbon 12 is the same as the proportion of the two in the atmosphere. The clock starts when the CO_2 is taken into the plant (which animals may feed on) and is buried as fiber or wood, as the collagen in bone, or as charcoal left by a fire. After an organism's death, the carbon 14 it contains breaks down, and the proportion of carbon 12 increases. The laboratory technique measures the ratio of carbon 14 to carbon 12 in these prehistoric samples. Carbon 14 has a half-life of only 5,730 years, and therefore measurements of the age of carbon compounds cover a relatively short period. The method is most useful between 500 and 40,000 years ago, although its range can be extended somewhat farther into the past.

Errors in this method arise from a number of factors. It was originally supposed that the carbon 14 level in the atmosphere was constant, but we now know that it is not. Volcanoes produce CO_2 without carbon 14, which causes local reductions in the level of carbon 14 in the atmosphere. A more serious variation is in the atmospheric level itself, which alters according to variations in the chemical reactions in the upper atmosphere that create the carbon 14 in the first place. Samples also may become contaminated by modern organic compounds (such as the inks with which the fossils are labeled) or by modern CO_2 from the atmosphere. Although these factors somewhat limit the value of carbon 14 dating, the method has great value to paleoanthropologists when it is carefully used.

Other Methods Based on Radioactivity.   Another dating method that depends in a different way on radioactive decay is the **fission-track method.** The rare radioactive element uranium 238 splits spontaneously to create a minute region of crystal disruption in a mineral. The disruption is called a track. In the laboratory, microscopic examination can determine track densities in mineral crystals containing uranium 238 in proportion to total uranium content. Since the rate of spontaneous fission is known, the age of the crystal can be calculated. The clock is started with the eruption of volcanoes, and so this method has the same geographic limitations as the potassium–argon method.

The main value of the fission-track method at present is as a cross-check on the potassium–argon method. The same volcanic samples can often be used, and the

Tuff a rocklike substance formed from volcanic ash.

Carbon 14 dating a method of dating archaeological remains based on the radioactive decay of the element carbon 14 into nitrogen.

Fission-track method method of dating rocks from tracks left by the spontaneous splitting of uranium 238 atoms.

comparison aids in the detection of errors. The fission-track method itself has other problems. With low uranium content and rather recently formed minerals, the track density will be low. Heating eliminates tracks (as you have seen, heating also causes problems in potassium–argon dating). Fission-track dating, however, has proved of great value in dating samples from the beginning of the earth to about 300,000 years ago. It is now being used quite widely in dating early periods of human evolution in volcanically active regions.

Two additional methods of dating that depend on radioactivity are **thermoluminescence** (TL) and **optically stimulated luminescence** (OSL) (Feathers, 1996). Both procedures measure the emission of light from crystalline materials that have been stimulated in some way. In TL the stimulation is by heat; in OSL it is by exposure of the sample to intense light of narrow wavelength. Both types of stimulation release electrons trapped in the sample, and this produces measurable light. To help you further understand luminescence dating, here is how TL works: Over a period of time, electrons become trapped in the crystal structure of buried substances (including pottery and stone tools) as they are irradiated by naturally occurring uranium, thorium, and potassium 40. For accurate dating, the "traps" must have been emptied prior to electron accumulation by a "zeroing event," such as heating by fire. When the irradiated substances are reheated in the laboratory, the electrons are released with a quantity of light proportional to the number of electrons trapped. If the rate of electron accumulation can be established, the amount of light emitted can be used to measure the time elapsed since the test substance was originally heated. TL works best with pottery, but it can also be used on burnt flints and hearth stones. OSL is used to date sediments and works best with windblown deposits, because the OSL zeroing event is exposure to light. Both types of luminescence dating have remaining problems—such as estimating the rate of electron entrapment and controlling for "fading," the natural and gradual loss of trapped electrons—but they have great potential and have been used to establish some important dates. Of particular importance is the fact that the range of usefulness of luminescence dating overlaps those of carbon 14 and potassium–argon (see Figure 1.5).

Paleomagnetism.   Finally, the value of radioactive dating has been greatly increased by its use to date periodic changes in the global magnetic field. It appears that the

Thermoluminescence method of dating pottery and stone tools by heating them to release trapped electrons; the electrons produce measurable light.

Optically stimulated luminescence method of dating sediments by stimulating them with intense light; such stimulation causes the sediments to release trapped electrons and thus measurable light.

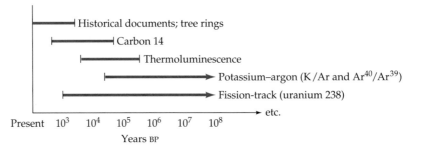

Present 10^3 10^4 10^5 10^6 10^7 10^8

Years BP

Historical documents; tree rings
Carbon 14
Thermoluminescence
Potassium–argon (K/Ar and Ar^{40}/Ar^{39})
Fission-track (uranium 238)
etc.

Figure 1.5

Approximate ranges of time in which dates can be established by the methods discussed in this chapter. Dates at the limits of any method are less reliable than those toward the center. The time scale is logarithmic.

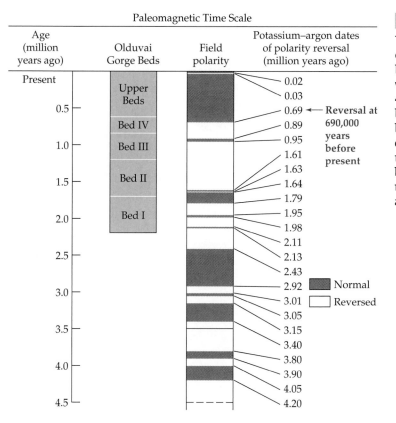

Paleomagnetic Time Scale

Age (million years ago)	Olduvai Gorge Beds	Field polarity	Potassium–argon dates of polarity reversal (million years ago)

Figure 1.6

The left-hand column shows the sequence of beds from Olduvai Gorge; the right-hand column shows known reversals in world magnetic polarity during the past 4.5 million years. The evidence is obtained by measuring the polarity of volcanic lavas, which can also be potassium–argon dated. Deposits that are dated only roughly by relative methods can often be dated more accurately by the measurement of their magnetic polarity and referral to this chart.

north–south magnetic field of our planet has reversed its direction many times during the earth's history. (During periods of "reversal," a compass needle would point south instead of north.) The direction of an ancient magnetic field can be detected by laboratory measurements of the "fossilized" magnetism in rocks, combined with information on how those rocks were oriented (north–south) at the site of their collection. Such **paleomagnetism** dates from around the world have enabled geophysicists to construct detailed time charts of normal and reversed periods (see Figure 1.6). These data help scientists determine the age of sites that lack independent chronometric dates but have known paleomagnetism profiles.

The dating of fossil-bearing deposits has proved a priceless advance in our efforts to understand the processes of plant and animal evolution. Knowledge of a fossil's age allows us to put fossils in a time sequence and so has enabled us to determine the course of human evolution. Paleontologists and geologists have divided the fossil sequence of the earth's fauna and flora—traced back some 650 million years (though primitive life is more ancient still)—into three eras and eleven periods. The names and dates assigned to them are shown in Figure 1.7. We can see from this chart that the first mammals appeared at the beginning of the Triassic, the dinosaurs ruled during the Cretaceous, and only during the Cenozoic era did the mammals flourish and give rise to the primates. This enormous 650 million-year span has allowed the process of evolution by natural selection to give rise to the modern variety of life, including humans.

Paleomagnetism magnetism originally generated by the earth's magnetic field and preserved in rock. Past fluctuations in the intensity and direction of this field allow correlation between strata, a form of *relative dating* that can be used for *absolute dating* because the historic pattern of magnetic fluctuations and reversals is known and dated.

Figure 1.7

The use of fossils as historical markers became possible in the late 1700s and early 1800s, after scientists such as Georges Cuvier proved the reality of extinction. For example, trilobites were marine arthropods that were common on the world's seafloors during the Paleozoic era. After a period of decline, trilobites disappeared completely about 245 million years ago. Thus, trilobite-bearing rock strata are easily recognized as older than those containing the fossilized remains of mammals, here represented by a shrew.

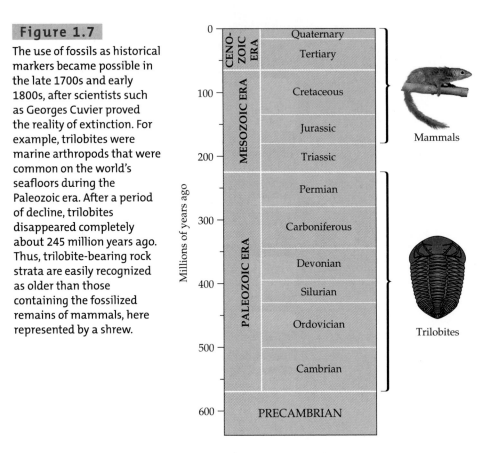

Summary

During the past three centuries, our understanding of the earth's origin—and our own—has changed dramatically. Europeans accepted the Christian belief in a divine creation and calculated the age of the earth in terms of ancient histories and biblical records. The young earth theory fell victim to geological discoveries, however. In 1859 Charles Darwin published a convincing theory of evolution by means of natural selection, and his theory was quickly applied to the question of human origins. Darwin's and his followers' development of the idea of natural selection is the most important scientific advance of the last two hundred years in our understanding of biology and has given us insight into our place in the natural world. Further advances have included the relative dating of fossils through the study of stratigraphy and absolute dating methods such as potassium–argon, carbon 14, thermoluminescence, and paleomagnetism.

Review Questions

1. How did religion influence the development of evolutionary theory and the studies of geologic history and human prehistory? Why was the concept of the earth's antiquity so crucial to establish?

2. What developments and discoveries led to the rise of paleoanthropology as a science? How are fossil sites analyzed?

3. How did the theories of catastrophism and uniformitarianism differ in their explanations of geological and organic change? What evidence supports each explanation? Which view did Darwin embrace?

4. How did Darwin derive his theory of natural selection? How does natural selection work? What are some specific examples of the operation of natural selection in a population?

5. What are the principal methods by which fossils and artifacts can be dated? What are the comparative advantages of relative and absolute dating methods?

Suggested Further Reading

Darwin, C. R. *On the Origin of Species* (facsimile of 1st edition). Harvard University Press, 1996.

Eisley, L. *Darwin's Century: Evolution and the Men Who Discovered It.* Doubleday, 1958.

Mayr, E. *One Long Argument.* Harvard University Press, 1991.

Sackett, J. "Human Antiquity and the Old Stone Age: The Nineteenth-Century Background to Paleoanthropology." *Evolutionary Anthropology* 9, 2000.

Internet Resources

Conveniently access these and other links via our web site at **http://www.ablongman/anthro.**

Darwin
http://www.anselm.edu/homepage/dbanach/darwin.htm
The Charles Darwin Homepage contains links to hypertexts of his classic works, including *The Voyage of the Beagle* and *On the Origin of Species,* as well as to related works on theories of evolution.

Descent of Man
http://www.infidels.org/library/historical/charles_darwin/descent_of_man/
Most of Darwin's comments about human evolution were in this book, published in 1871. Here the book is indexed and annotated by chapter.

Evolution Web Sites
http://www.people.virginia.edu/~rjh9u/evolution.html
A links page listing evolution web sites, including courses, virtual labs, articles, and animations.

National Center for Science Education
http://www.natcenscied.org/
This site contains information about the continuing controversy over teaching evolution and "creation science" in the public schools.

Victorian Science: An Overview
http://landow.stg.brown.edu/victorian/science/sciov.html
Part of the Victorian Web, this site provides background information on Charles Darwin and other nineteenth-century scientists.

Waikato Radiocarbon Dating Laboratory
http://www.c14dating.com
Everything you wanted to know about radiocarbon dating and related topics.

Useful Search Terms:
Charles Darwin
creationism
evolution
history of geology
natural selection

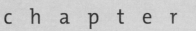

Genetics and Evolution

Overview

When Charles Darwin developed his theory of evolution by natural selection, he was unaware of the actual mechanisms of trait inheritance and the genetic basis of organic change. This understanding began with the work of the pioneer plant breeder and monk Gregor Mendel, who was working at the same time as Darwin. The modern synthesis of evolutionary theory, a combination of Darwin's natural selection and Mendelian genetics, was not formulated until the mid-twentieth century. Key questions had to be answered before evolution could be understood, including: What are the sources of variation on which evolutionary change operates? What biological processes and principles make evolutionary change possible? How do individual organisms, populations, and species contribute to evolution?

 Check our web site for additional information, photos, drawings, maps, and animations on topics in this chapter.

The Mystery of Heredity

Charles Darwin deduced the operation of natural selection even though he was missing two major pieces of the evolutionary puzzle; namely, the sources of variation and the mechanisms of heredity. From personal observations and reading, Darwin knew that all species contain a variety of individuals in every generation and that offspring often inherit parental traits. Folk wisdom in Darwin's day held that blood was intimately involved in the passage of traits from parent to child, a belief that resulted in sayings such as "Blood will tell." Mother's and father's bloods (and therefore, traits) were thought to be blended somehow in each of their children. Logical as it may have seemed, however, this notion of **blending inheritance** raised some formidable problems. After all, if each child is a blend of the parents' characteristics, the long-term effect should be an overall loss of variation within the population. That is, new individuals born should be increasingly alike in each succeeding generation as individual differences are diluted through blending. Yet the opposite is true: In sexually reproducing species, variability is maintained over time and often increases.

Unknown to Darwin, the problems that proved so intractable for him—variation and inheritance—were beginning to yield their secrets to an Augustinian monk named Gregor Johann Mendel (1822–1884). Born in a small village in what is now the Czech

Blending inheritance an outmoded theory stating that offspring receive a combination of all characteristics of each parent through the mixture of their bloods; superseded by Mendelian genetics.

Republic, Mendel was, in his own words, "addicted to the study of Nature" from his youth. After entering the monastery at Brunn at the age of twenty-one, Mendel designed a series of botanical experiments to elucidate the natural laws that control variation and inheritance.

Gregor Mendel's Experiments

Reviewing earlier studies of plant hybridization, Mendel realized that most had been poorly designed and rather haphazardly carried out. He realized that success depended not only on systematic work done on a large scale but also on selecting the right species for study. For his inheritance work, he needed **true-breeding** plants, plants that show little spontaneous variation from generation to generation. He also needed a species whose pollination he could control easily, for otherwise systematic cross-fertilizations would be impossible. Mendel ended up choosing the common garden pea for most of his experimental work.

The garden pea was a good choice because it presents several traits that are easily observed and manipulated. Mendel chose seven characteristics for systematic investigation (illustrated in Figure 2.1), the most important of which, for the following discussion, were pea form and pea color—round or wrinkled, green or yellow. He started with a simple cross between wrinkled-pea and round-pea plants grown from seeds he had bought, taking great care to prevent accidental pollination from plants outside his study and removing the anthers or stigma of each flower (the male and female organs) to avoid self-fertilization. After the necessary time for fertilization, growth, and pea development, Mendel was able to observe the results of his experiment. Upon opening the pods, he found only round peas. The wrinkled trait, which had existed in half of the parent plants, seemed to have disappeared completely! Similar disappearances of

True breeding (breeding true) situation in which the members of a genetic strain resemble each other in all important characteristics and show little variability.

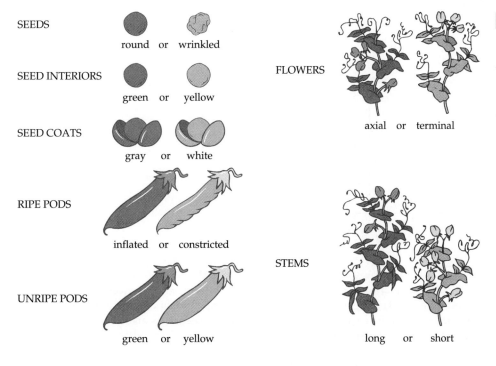

SEEDS — round or wrinkled

SEED INTERIORS — green or yellow

SEED COATS — gray or white

RIPE PODS — inflated or constricted

UNRIPE PODS — green or yellow

FLOWERS — axial or terminal

STEMS — long or short

Figure 2.1

Mendel's pioneering observations of the pea plant were based on a comparison of these seven easily identifiable characteristics.

one variant or the other were found in Mendel's other first-generation hybrids—green pea color disappeared after a green-yellow cross, and short plant height disappeared after a short-tall cross.

After due consideration, Mendel decided to call the characteristic that prevailed (such as roundness) **dominant,** and the one that apparently disappeared, **recessive.** But what, Mendel wondered, would happen to the dominant and recessive traits if the hybrids were allowed to self-fertilize as they would normally? He made the experiments and waited. When at last he could examine the traits of second-generation plants, Mendel found that the recessive characteristics had reappeared! In the round–wrinkled cross, for example, wrinkling was back in about one-third of the peas (Figure 2.2), and round and wrinkled peas could be found side by side in the same pod. In general, dominant traits outnumbered their recessive counterparts by a 3:1 ratio in the second generation.

And there were more surprises in store. When Mendel planted his second generation of peas and then allowed those plants to self-fertilize, he obtained mixed results. Recessive characteristics always bred true; for example, plants grown from wrinkled peas produced only wrinkled peas. Plants with dominant traits, however, came in two types: One-third were true-breeding, but two-thirds acted like hybrid seeds of the first generation and produced both dominant and recessive offspring at a ratio of 3:1 (Figure 2.3). Pondering these results, Mendel drew several conclusions that took him a long way toward solving the riddle of heredity. First, he reasoned that an organism's visible characteristics, now called its **phenotype,** are not always an accurate representation of its set of hereditary qualities, or **genotype.** This discovery not only explained why some plants with dominant traits could produce mixed descendants, but it also forced a second major conclusion: that hereditary qualities are nonreducible *particles.* These particles, which we now call **genes,** are not blended during sexual reproduction, but rather retain their identities as they are passed from parents to offspring. And third, Mendel's mathematical results—his ratios of offsprings' traits—suggested that hereditary particles generally function as pairs, with a particle expressing its trait unless it is blocked (dominated) by its partner.

Dominant expressed in the *phenotype* even when the organism is carrying only one copy of the underlying hereditary material (one copy of the responsible *gene*).

Recessive expressed only when the organism is carrying two copies of the underlying hereditary material (two copies of the responsible *gene*).

Phenotype the observable characteristics of a plant or an animal; the expression of the *genotype*.

Genotype the genetic makeup of a plant or animal; the total information contained in all *genes* of the organism.

Genes primarily, functional units of the *chromosomes* in cell nuclei, controlling the inheritance of phenotypic traits; some genes also occur in *mitochondria*.

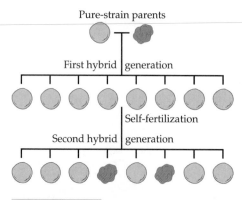

Figure 2.2

The production of a second hybrid generation by self-fertilization showed that the first-generation hybrids had carried the characteristics of both their parents, but with the wrinkled characteristic hidden. The new generation of seeds was made up of both kinds (like the pure-strain parents), but came in the proportion of 3 round ones to 1 wrinkled.

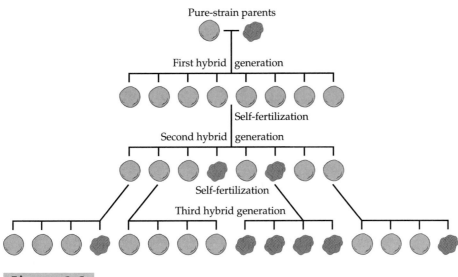

Figure 2.3

Mendel found the explanation of the 3:1 proportion shown in Figure 2.2 when he allowed the second generation plants to self-pollinate. In the third hybrid generation, he found new combinations of characteristics. The wrinkled seeds had bred true (and would always do so); some of the round peas also bred true, while others repeated the 3:1 ratio.

A simple way to visualize the connection between hereditary pairs (genotype) and visible traits (phenotype) is shown in Figure 2.4. Here dominant particles are labeled *A* and recessive ones *a*. With regard to the form of Mendel's peas, hybrids with *Aa* genotypes would be round (of course, so would all *AA* individuals). Crossing two such hybrids could potentially produce three different genotypes (*AA, Aa,* and *aa*) and both possible phenotypes (round and wrinkled). Today, individuals with similar genes for a trait (*AA* and *aa*) are said to be **homozygous,** while those with different genes (*Aa*) are described as **heterozygous.**

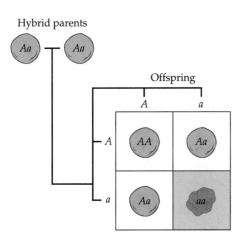

Figure 2.4

The experiment diagrammed in Figure 2.2 was explained by Mendel in this way: Using the letters *A* and *a* for the characters smooth and wrinkled, he accounted for the 3:1 proportion by proposing that *A* is always dominant to *a* in every hybrid.

Homozygous having identical versions of a *gene (alleles)* for a particular trait.

Heterozygous having different versions of a *gene (alleles)* for a particular trait.

Mendelian Inheritance

Mendel eventually looked at much more complex cases than just single contrasting characteristics. As shown in Figure 2.5, simultaneously studying two traits—pea form (round, wrinkled) and pea color (green, yellow)—produced a greatly enlarged set of possible genotypes reducible to four phenotypes with a 9:3:3:1 ratio. In addition, Mendel identified a few traits (for example, flower color in beans) that seemed to be controlled by two pairs of hereditary particles rather than one. In all, his work allowed Mendel to formulate several important biological laws:

1. Heredity is transmitted by a large number of independent, nonreducible particles that occur as pairs in individual organisms. These hereditary particles retain their distinctive identities regardless of the nature of their pair-partners. This is the *principle of particulate heredity,* and it disproved the old notion of heredity as blending.

2. Each hereditary pair is split during the production of sex cells (sperm and eggs, or pollen and ovules) so that a sex cell has only one particle from any pair. This is the *principle of segregation.* New pairs are formed, of course, as a result of fertilization.

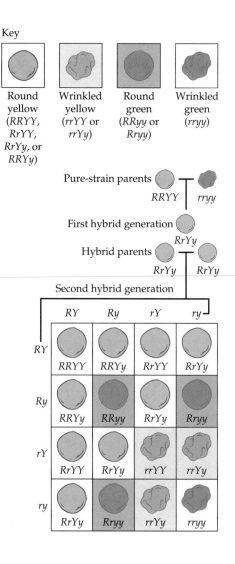

Figure 2.5

The Punnett square shows Mendel's law of independent assortment. A pea with two dominant characteristics (roundness and yellowness, *RR* and *YY*) is crossed with a pea having two recessive characteristics (wrinkledness and greenness, *rr* and *yy*). The hybrid combines all four genes of its parents (*RrYy*). If these hybrids are crossed, their genes produce the combinations shown: four kinds of peas appearing in a ratio of 9:3:3:1.

Key

Round yellow (*RRYY, RrYY, RrYy,* or *RRYy*)

Wrinkled yellow (*rrYY* or *rrYy*)

Round green (*RRyy* or *Rryy*)

Wrinkled green (*rryy*)

3. Hereditary particles for different traits generally are inherited independently of one another. This is the *principle of independent assortment* (see Figure 2.5 for an illustration).

These principles, along with the detailed results of Mendel's long years of work, were read to the Brunn Society for the Study of Natural Science in 1865 and published in that society's proceedings in 1866. Unfortunately, Mendel's work found few interested readers, and virtually no one at the time, including Darwin, recognized how far he had gone toward answering the basic questions about heredity. It would be the turn of the century before Mendel's work was rediscovered; and in the meantime, the man now widely viewed as the "father of genetics" devoted the rest of his life to leadership duties as abbot of his monastery.

Mutations and the Modern Synthesis

The decades following Darwin's and Mendel's deaths in the 1880s found scientists in general agreement about the occurrence of evolutionary change, but at odds concerning such basic questions as the sources of spontaneous phenotypic variation and the effectiveness of natural selection.

Hugo De Vries (1848–1935), a botanist at the University of Amsterdam, accepted Darwin's thesis that descent with modification is the main law of change among organisms, but wondered how large differences between species could ever be produced by natural selection picking and choosing among small individual variations. De Vries had a hunch that **mutations,** spontaneous (and sometimes substantial) changes in an organism's characteristics, are more important than natural selection in directing the path of evolution.

Darwinians recognized the occasional sudden appearance of new traits—so-called *sports of nature*—but gave them only secondary importance. For his studies of mutations, De Vries chose to work with the evening primrose, a plant capable of wide variations in each generation. His observations, carried out for more than a decade, reinforced his confidence in the power of mutations, and also led him to several of the same conclusions that Mendel had formulated thirty-five years earlier, especially the conclusion that hereditary units are "distinct, separate, and independent" particles. As De Vries conducted a literature search in 1900 prior to publishing his primrose data, he came across Mendel's long-lost paper, and only then realized that much of his work had been anticipated by the Moravian monk. (By a remarkable coincidence, Mendel's paper was also rediscovered by two other researchers, one German and one Austrian, in that same year.) Behaving honorably, De Vries gave full credit to Mendel, whose discoveries were at last given the scientific acclaim they deserved.

That natural selection is, in fact, the primary mechanism of evolution was demonstrated in the early twentieth century by Ronald Aylmer Fisher (1890–1962), J. B. S. Haldane (1892–1964), Sewall Wright (1889–1988), and other mathematically inclined biologists. Fisher, in particular, zeroed in on the problem of **mimicry.** This phenomenon, in which one species evolves a striking resemblance to another, is not uncommon in nature. An example is the mimicry of the well-known monarch butterfly by the less common viceroy. The wings of both butterflies have an orange ground with black and white markings. The monarch butterfly is protected from predators by its unpalatability; the viceroy is protected by mimicking the monarch. Fisher proved conclusively that natural selection acting on small variations is the only force that could bring about this

Mutation generally, a spontaneous change in the chemistry of a *gene* that can alter its phenotypic effect. The accumulation of such changes may contribute to the *evolution* of a new *species* of animal or plant.

Mimicry phenomenon in which natural selection brings about the close resemblance of one species to another.

phenomenon. The coincidental occurrence of the same traits in mimics and models due to random mutations is so unlikely as to be mathematically impossible. Besides, said Fisher, the mutation theory explains neither why mimics and models are always found in the same regions and during the same season, nor why mimicry is superficial (involves minimal copying of traits). In the end, the mathematical arguments prevailed and, in accordance with Darwin's original position, natural selection reemerged as the main force driving evolutionary change. Mutation took on the role as the primary source of new genetic material. Thus, mutations contribute to phenotypic variations that then are either rejected or, more rarely, preserved and molded by the action of natural selection.

Progress in the newly formed science of Mendelian genetics continued during the early twentieth century. It was not until the 1930s and 1940s, however, that Darwin's theory of natural selection was finally combined with Mendel's theory of heredity to produce a genetics-based evolutionary model (Fisher, 1930; Huxley, 1942). The new model was dubbed the *synthetic theory of evolution* or, following the title of an important book by Julian Huxley (1887–1975), the *modern synthesis* (it is also occasionally called *neo-Darwinism*). As we enter the twenty-first century, the modern synthesis prevails as the universally accepted evolutionary paradigm. Let us now discuss in more detail the ways populations of organisms evolve.

Population Genetics

The modern synthetic theory of evolution proposes that changes in species' traits are the results of altered frequencies of Mendel's hereditary particles—that is, altered gene frequencies. In strong contrast to the mutationists' theory, which focused on the spontaneous modifications of *individual* organisms as the basis of evolutionary change, the modern synthesis focuses on genetic changes produced by natural selection working within **populations** of plants and animals (Mayr, 1982). Typically, a population is a subunit of a **species**—a geographically localized breeding group of conspecifics. Evolutionary biologist Ernst Mayr (1904–present) has described the emergence of the modern synthesis as a shift to "population thinking."

Although individual organisms contribute fundamentally to evolutionary change, only populations can evolve. That is, only populations can show the sort of intergenerational changes in genes and traits that qualify as evolution. Individuals make their contributions by surviving (or not), reproducing (or not), and getting their genes into the next generation (or not). As certain individuals succeed and others fail, the population itself is modified over time. To understand evolution fully therefore, you must pay attention simultaneously to two levels of biological activity: individual organisms, each trying to survive and reproduce, and populations, each reflecting the cumulative results of its members' efforts. We can identify three types of linkage between individuals and their populations, as shown in Table 2.1.

Population usually, a local or breeding group; a group in which any two individuals have the potential of mating with each other.

Species following the *biological species* concept, a group of interbreeding natural *populations* that are reproductively isolated from other such groups.

Table 2.1

A Framework for Understanding Darwinian Evolution	
Individual	**Population**
Genotype	Gene pool
Phenotype	Collective phenotype
Fitness	Degree of adaptation

Genotypes and Gene Pools

Every living creature is characterized by its genotype or genome, its entire set of genes. Most genes are organized into **chromosomes** and located in the nuclei of the individual's cells (Figure 2.6). A few genes can also be found outside the nucleus within organelles called **mitochondria** (Figure 2.6), where they take the form of closed loops of hereditary material. Nuclear genes are more important in the production of an organism's phenotypic traits; mitochondrial genes seem to be related to the organelles' own functioning and to general cell chemistry. Both nuclear and mitochondrial genes may help scientists date evolutionary events and classify species.

Genes provide a blueprint for the construction, operation, and maintenance of individual organisms. So-called *structural genes* produce particular traits. For example, humans have eye-color genes, skin-color genes, and genes that determine our susceptibility to different diseases. Additionally, *regulatory genes* control the metabolic, energetic, and biosynthetic activities of the body. The genetic blueprint is flexible, however, and the details of which specific traits make up an individual's phenotype are dependent on complex interactions between the genes and the individual's environment. An obvious example is body size. Genes for large body size may not be expressed fully when environmental factors such as poor nutrition or disease during growth are present. As a result, the adult individual may be smaller than its genetic potential might have allowed. The gene-and-environment relationship thus produces the phenotype.

The genotypes of all members of a population constitute the **gene pool.** A full inventory of a population's gene pool would list all the various genes and their frequencies. Though the human genome is now fully mapped, we do not yet have a record of its variability—another momentous task. However, population geneticists usually draw conclusions about the frequencies of a smaller number of well-studied genes such as humans' blood-type genes. If one can show a clear shift in the percentage

Chromosomes coiled, threadlike structures of *DNA,* bearing the *genes* and found in the nuclei of all plant and animal cells.

Mitochondria granular or rod-shaped bodies in the cytoplasm of cells that function in the metabolism of fat and proteins. Probably of bacterial origin.

Gene pool all of the *genes* of a *population* at a given time (summing genes within a species yields the species' gene pool).

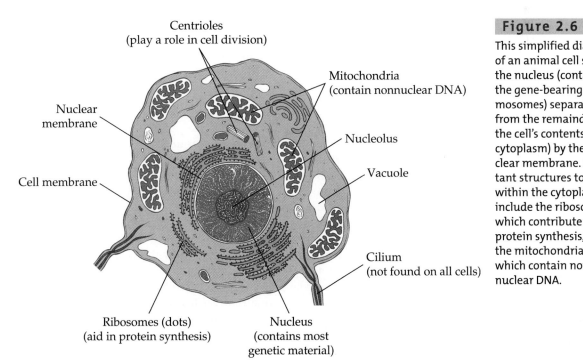

Centrioles
(play a role in cell division)

Mitochondria
(contain nonnuclear DNA)

Nuclear
membrane

Nucleolus

Vacuole

Cell membrane

Cilium
(not found on all cells)

Ribosomes (dots)
(aid in protein synthesis)

Nucleus
(contains most
genetic material)

Figure 2.6

This simplified diagram of an animal cell shows the nucleus (containing the gene-bearing chromosomes) separated from the remainder of the cell's contents (the cytoplasm) by the nuclear membrane. Important structures to note within the cytoplasm include the ribosomes, which contribute to protein synthesis, and the mitochondria, which contain nonnuclear DNA.

Table 2.2

Evolution Shown by Changes in Gene Frequency

This table simulates changes in the frequencies of alleles, two forms of a single gene (labeled *A* and *a*) during 1,000 generations of selection against the recessive form (*a*). Two scenarios are offered: one in which the selection coefficient (*s*) is 0.05 (*aa* individuals have a 95 percent chance of survival compared to 100 percent for *AA* and *Aa* individuals), and another in which the selection coefficient is 0.01 (*aa* individuals have a 99 percent chance of survival compared to 100 percent for *AA* and *Aa*). In each case, what is the outcome of selection?

| | s = 0.05 | | s = 0.01 | |
| | GENE FREQUENCY | | GENE FREQUENCY | |
Generation	*A*	*a*	*A*	*a*
0	0.01	0.99	0.01	0.99
100	0.44	0.56	0.026	0.974
200	0.81	0.19	0.067	0.933
300	0.89	0.11	0.15	0.85
400	0.93	0.07	0.28	0.72
500	0.95	0.05	0.43	0.57
600	0.96	0.04	0.55	0.45
700	0.96	0.04	0.65	0.35
800	0.97	0.03	0.72	0.28
900	0.97	0.03	0.77	0.23
1000	0.98	0.02	0.80	0.20

Source: Adapted from Ridley, 1996, p. 102.

of genes over time, it is strong proof of evolution (Table 2.2). Indeed, documenting change in the composition of a population's gene pool is the best way to show that evolution has occurred.

Phenotypes and Collective Phenotypes

A second way to show that evolution has taken place is to document transgenerational phenotypic change. If we pool the trait data for all members of a population, we can draw conclusions about the population's **collective phenotype.** For continuous traits, such as body weight, statements about the collective phenotype take the form of a mean value plus a measure of standard variation around that mean (e.g., humans' average weight = 128 ± 2 lb [58 ± 1 kg]). For discontinuous traits, such as blood types, collective phenotype statements express percentages of the various phenotypic states shown. For example, among the Quinault Indians, 50 percent of individuals show the MN blood type, just over 38 percent show type M, and 11 percent show type N. When aspects of a population's collective phenotype show clear evidence of change across generations, scientists conclude that evolution has occurred. Such a conclusion is warranted even though we may lack information about a population's genetic makeup—as is usually the case for fossil populations. To summarize, we can document evolution only by demonstrating changes in either gene pools or collective phenotypes.

Collective phenotype the set of phenotypic averages and norms that character-ize a *population* or *species.*

How Does DNA Work?

You now have some idea of how genotypes and phenotypes can help us to understand evolutionary change. But how does the transmission of genetic information occur? And what are the roles of DNA and RNA in that process?

As noted earlier, most genes occur as part of chromosomes, those interesting threadlike structures found in cell nuclei. Each living species has a characteristic number of chromosomes, the so-called **diploid number** (symbolized $2n$). This is the full chromosomal count, and it occurs in all *somatic* cells—that is, all cells except the **gametes** (eggs and sperm). Gametes, or sex cells, in contrast, possess a **haploid number** of chromosomes, or half of the full count (symbolized n). Diploid numbers for some well-studied species include 14 in Mendel's pea plants, 40 in house mice, 42 in baboons, 48 in chimpanzees and gorillas, and 46 in humans. Careful readers will have noticed that diploid numbers are always even. This is because somatic cells primarily contain pairs of **homologous chromosomes**—pairs that resemble each other in shape, size, and their sequence of genes (see Figure 2.7). The pair of **sex chromosomes,** however, is an exception to this rule. The X and Y chromosomes that determine femaleness or maleness are quite different in shape, size, and genetic contents (Figure 2.7). Among mammals, inheriting two Xs results in development as a female; an XY combination results in development as a male. Obviously, in sexually reproducing species, babies' diploid numbers are produced by the union of haploid egg with haploid sperm at conception.

The possibility that the chromosomes might contain the cell's hereditary material was first suggested in 1902 by Walter Sutton in the United States and Theodor Boveri in Germany. Numerous discoveries since then have amply confirmed this suggestion and collectively give us a detailed picture of the chemistry of chromosomes and genes. We now know that chromosomes consist of long, spiraling strands of

Diploid number the full *chromosome* count in somatic cells (all cells except *gametes*)

Gametes reproductive *haploid* cells generated by *meiosis*, which fuse with *gametes* of the opposite sex in reproduction; in animals, eggs and sperm.

Haploid number the number of *chromosomes* carried by *gametes*; one-half of the full count carried by somatic cells.

Homologous chromosomes *chromosomes* that are similar in shape, size, and sequence of *genes*.

Sex chromosomes *chromosomes* carrying *genes* that control gender (femaleness or maleness).

NORMAL MALE

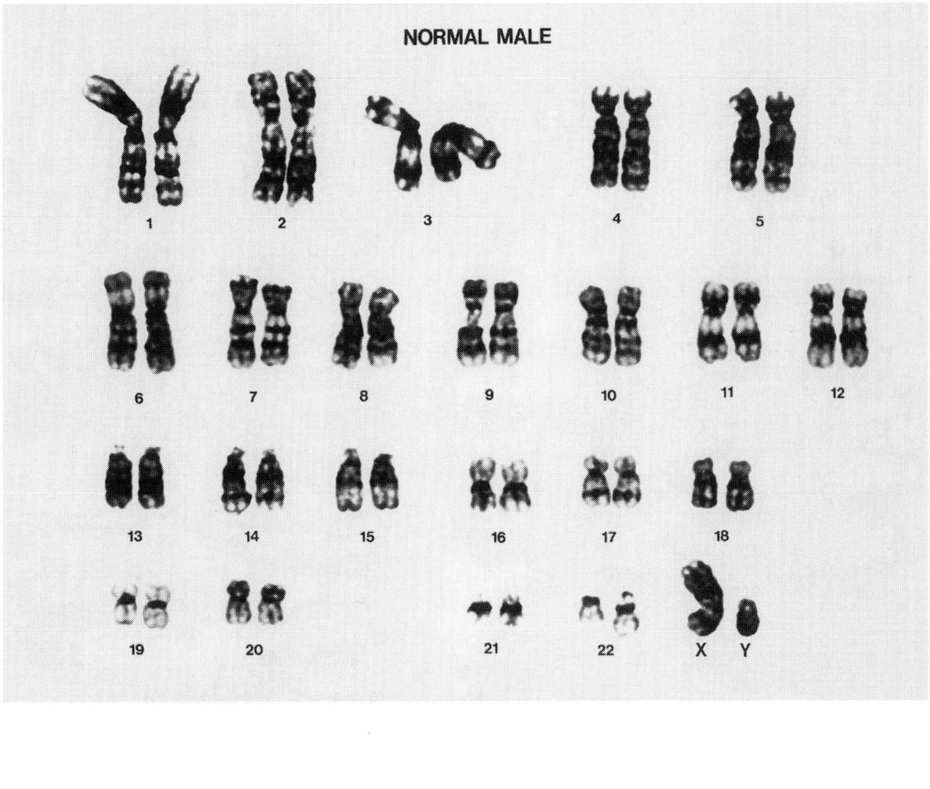

Figure 2.7

Humans have 46 chromosomes as 22 or 23 matching pairs. The sex chromosomes (labeled X and Y) are indicated in this photograph from a male human. Only males have the small Y chromosome, and so in this sex, the twenty-third pair cannot be matched. Females have two similar X chromosomes.

DNA (**deoxyribonucleic acid**), a substance that was first discovered in 1869 by Friedrich Miescher and whose composition and structure were worked out by Francis Crick, Rosalind Franklin, James Watson, and Maurice Wilkins in 1953 (Figure 2.8). Another way to understand genes, then, is to view them as basic functional subunits of DNA—segments of DNA that can be identified with particular phenotypic effects. Each gene tends to occur at a particular chromosomal location or **locus.** But it's a little more complicated than that. A gene at a particular locus may show several different forms, and these variants are called **alleles.** Alleles influence the same phenotypic trait, only differently. Gregor Mendel's work provided several examples of alleles and their pairwise interactions. In Figure 2.5, *R* and *r* represent alleles (variant types) of the gene for pea form. Depending on the combination of alleles that a new plant inherits during fertilization, it can be homozygous dominant (*RR*, producing round peas), heterozygous (*Rr*, also producing round peas), or homozygous recessive (*rr*, producing wrinkled peas). So far so good, but how do genes actually go about producing phenotypic traits? To answer that question, we must literally unravel the DNA molecule.

The Chemistry of Genes

The DNA of a chromosome consists of two long, interlocking polynucleotide chains arranged in a double helix (Figure 2.8). The backbone of each chain is a series of linked sugar and phosphate molecules (deoxyribose phosphates), and each sugar–phosphate unit is bonded to a single **nucleotide** base. These bases come in four varieties—(A) adenine, (T) thymine, (G) guanine, and (C) cytosine—and the two chains are held together in a helical structure by the bonds between complementary nucleotide pairs (A with T, G with C). If the two chains are separated for individual analysis, each can be

DNA (deoxyribonucleic acid) chemical substance found in *chromosomes* and *mitochondria* which reproduces itself and carries the *genetic code.*

Locus the position of a nuclear *gene* on a *chromosome*; each locus can carry only one *allele* of a gene.

Alleles *genes* occupying equivalent positions on paired *chromosomes*, yet producing different phenotypic effects when *homozygous*; alternative states of a gene, originally produced by *mutation.*

Nucleotides organic compounds consisting of bases, sugars, and phosphates; found in cells either free or as part of polynucleotide chains.

Figure 2.8

The DNA molecule is a double spiral (or helix) linked by four interlocking chemical subunits: the base pairs. Replication and protein synthesis take place by the splitting of the double helix: Each separate strand replicates by synthesizing its mirror image from the unit molecules floating in solution, as shown here.

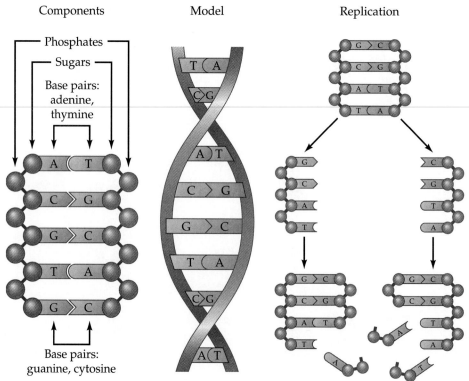

Components   Model   Replication

Phosphates

Sugars

Base pairs: adenine, thymine

Base pairs: guanine, cytosine

described by its sequence of nucleotide bases; for example, ACGTTGCAA. The nucleotides work in groups of three adjacent bases (e.g., ACG). Such a triplet is called a **codon** and codes for the production of particular **amino acids** as part of protein synthesis within the cell (Table 2.3) (this is the first step in the production of phenotypic traits).

Table 2.3

The Genetic Code			
DNA Codon	**Amino Acid**	**DNA Codon**	**Amino Acid**
GCA	alanine	AGA	arginine
GCG	alanine	AGG	arginine
GCT	alanine	CGA	arginine
GCC	alanine	CGG	arginine
		CGT	arginine
GAT	aspartic acid	CGC	arginine
GAC	aspartic acid		
		AAT	asparagine
TGT	cysteine	AAC	asparagine
TGC	cysteine		
		GAA	glutamic acid
CAA	glutamine	GAG	glutamic acid
CAG	glutamine		
		GGA	glycine
CAT	histidine	GGG	glycine
CAC	histidine	GGT	glycine
		GGC	glycine
ATA	isoleucine		
ATT	isoleucine	TTA	leucine
ATC	isoleucine	TTG	leucine
		CTA	leucine
AAA	lysine	CTG	leucine
AAG	lysine	CTT	leucine
		CTC	leucine
ATG	methoinine/**start**		
		TTT	phenylalanine
CCA	proline	TTC	phenylalanine
CCG	proline		
CCT	proline	AGT	serine
CCC	proline	AGC	serine
		TCA	serine
ACA	threonine	TCG	serine
ACG	threonine	TCT	serine
ACT	threonine	TCC	serine
ACC	threonine		
		TGG	tryptophan
TAT	tyrosine		
TAC	tyrosine	GTA	valine
		GTG	valine
TAA	**stop**	GTT	valine
TAG	**stop**	GTC	valine
TGA	**stop**		

Codon a *nucleotide* triplet that codes for the production of a particular *amino acid* during *protein* production.

Amino acids a group of organic compounds that act as building blocks for *proteins*.

Each gene consists of a long sequence of codons (humans' genes range in size from a few hundred to tens of thousands of base pairs) that work together to produce a particular protein.

The DNA double helix actually becomes partially unraveled into two individual chains in two circumstances. First, this occurs as part of chromosomal replication (sometimes called gene replication) during both forms of cell division. During *mitosis,* the normal division process of somatic cells, all of the chromosomes form replicas (thus temporarily doubling the genes in the nucleus) and then the cell divides once. This results in identical twin copies of the original diploid cell. In contrast, during *meiosis,* the process of reduction division that results in gametes, a single act of chromosomal replication is followed by two episodes of cell division. This produces haploid sex cells (see Figure 2.11; meiosis is described in greater detail on pages 37–39 in the section concerned with the sources of phenotypic variation). In any event, during both types of cell division, each polynucleotide chain serves as a template for the formation of its partner from newly synthesized sugar–phosphate–base units (Figure 2.8). The second circumstance of DNA unraveling is during the transcription of DNA information into **RNA** (**ribonucleic acid**) as a step toward protein synthesis. A brief look at protein synthesis reveals more details of the structure of genes and the process of phenotype production.

Protein Synthesis

Proteins are complex molecules composed of long chains of amino acids. They take a variety of forms, and collectively they coordinate and control our basic life processes, being involved in growth, development, reproduction, and bodily maintenance (one researcher has remarked that proteins "breathe life" into the information contained in genes). Examples of proteins include hemoglobin (responsible for oxygen and carbon dioxide transport throughout the body), collagen and keratin (building blocks of connective tissues and hair), the antibodies active within our immune system, and the enzymes that catalyze our biochemical reactions. The cellular process that results in protein synthesis begins with partial unwinding of the DNA helix (Figure 2.9). Transcription of the DNA information then starts as a strand of "messenger RNA" (mRNA) is synthesized by complementary base pairing onto the DNA template. Interestingly, only certain segments of each gene's DNA, called **exons,** actually code for protein production. Long stretches of noncoding DNA, called **introns,** must therefore be removed from the mRNA template after transcription is completed. This is done through a process called *splicing* that leaves the mRNA with only exon information.

Once a gene is completely transcribed, the mRNA strand is released, and the DNA helix re-forms. Messenger RNA is then engaged by particles called **ribosomes** that move along the mRNA chain and catalyze the translation of proteins, triplet codon by triplet codon (Figure 2.10). A key element in this process is the action of another form of RNA—"transfer RNA" (tRNA)—in engaging amino acids and then positioning them on the mRNA template. Bit by bit, amino acids are assembled into long protein chains, all of which will contribute to the formation or operation of the organism's phenotype (Singer and Berg, 1991).

Two final points need to be made before we end this section on the chemistry of genes. First, it bears repeating that by no means all of a cell's nuclear DNA actually contributes to protein (and therefore, phenotype) production. Introns are noncoding sequences; but, surprisingly, they account for much more DNA than do exons. Further-

RNA (ribonucleic acid) a compound found with *DNA* in cell nuclei and chemically close to DNA; transmits the *genetic code* from DNA to direct the production of *proteins*. May take two forms: messenger RNA (mRNA) or transfer RNA (tRNA).

Proteins molecules composed of chains of *amino acids*.

Exons segments of a *gene's DNA* that code for *protein* production.

Introns segments of a *gene's DNA* that do not code for *protein* production (so-called noncoding DNA).

Ribosomes cellular organelles that contribute to *protein* synthesis.

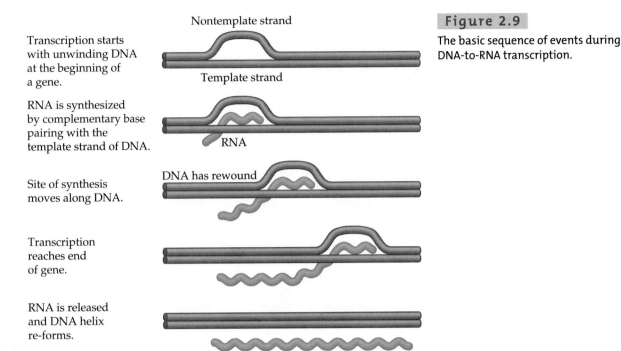

Transcription starts with unwinding DNA at the beginning of a gene.

RNA is synthesized by complementary base pairing with the template strand of DNA.

Site of synthesis moves along DNA.

Transcription reaches end of gene.

RNA is released and DNA helix re-forms.

Nontemplate strand

Template strand

RNA

DNA has rewound

Figure 2.9

The basic sequence of events during DNA-to-RNA transcription.

more, at certain points on chromosomes, tandem repetitions of DNA sequences called **satellite DNA** tend to accumulate, and these are also likely to be noncoding. Current estimates of the total proportion of humans' DNA that is noncoding range from 75 to 90 percent (Ridley, 1996). Just think how much sorting and splicing is required to extract our (relatively few) exon sequences from all of the noncoding material surrounding them! Scientists have yet to learn precisely how and why the "silent" sequences of DNA accumulated, and what functions (if any) they serve. One idea is that the noncoding DNA may have a structural function, to keep the genes correctly spaced within the three-dimensional DNA molecule. Another possibility is that the size of the DNA molecules in the nucleus determines the size of the nucleus and the size of its cell; regardless of the size of the organism, large cells appear to carry more DNA than small ones. Alternately, the extra DNA may just be noncoding "junk." Future studies should lead to the resolution of this issue.

The second point concerns the universal occurrence of the DNA genetic code (Table 2.3). Scientists have found that in virtually all life forms the same sixty-one DNA triplets encode the same twenty amino acids. Furthermore, one triplet (ATG) functions universally as a "start" codon marking the beginning point for a protein coding sequence, while three triplets (TAA, TAG, TGA) function as "stop" markers. This remarkable discovery argues as powerfully as the entire fossil record that all life has evolved from a single ancestral source. If Charles Darwin could come back to life and read these words, he would chuckle and say, "I told you so!"

A resurrected Darwin would also be keenly interested in modern information about the sources of trait variation among conspecific organisms. Today, evolutionary biologists consider two distinctly different processes to be the main sources of phenotypic variation. The first consists of gene mutations. The second involves chromosomal mixing and recombination during gamete production—meiosis and crossing-over.

Satellite DNA tandem repetitions of *DNA* sequences that accumulate at certain locations on *chromosomes* and usually are noncoding.

Figure 2.10

Multiple ribosomes sequentially engage mRNA after transcription and, aided by tRNA (not shown), catalyze the translation of the polypeptide chains that will form proteins. When a ribosome has completed its portion of polypeptide synthesis, it is released from the mRNA chain.

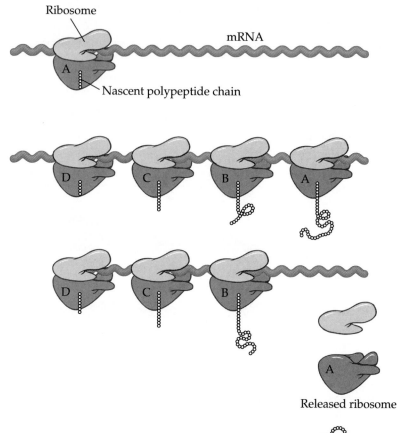

Mutations as a Source of Variation

Modern humans are estimated to carry about 30,000 genes per haploid gamete (Venter et al., 2001), which multiplies into 60,000 alleles per diploid somatic cell. As in all living creatures, spontaneous changes in humans' DNA sequences occur constantly and randomly. Such changes, called **point mutations,** can change the identity of genes and influence an offspring's phenotype if they are carried on gametes and thus inherited. (Mutations in somatic cells also occur, but they cannot be inherited. Somatic mutations may contribute to the development of diseases such as cancer, however.) Although mutations occur constantly, in humans they have a low average rate of about 1 mutation per 100,000 copies of a gene (rates vary for different genes, with some genes mutating at one-third this speed and others ten times as fast). The mutation rate of an organism's genes may be increased, however, through exposure to environmental stimuli such as radiation and certain chemicals; the rate also increases with age.

Point mutations may be as small as the substitution, addition, or loss of a single nucleotide base. Many point mutations are never expressed phenotypically because of DNA's ability for self-repair back to the original condition. Specialized enzymes exist

Point mutation usually the substitution of one *nucleotide* in a single *codon* of a *gene* that affects *protein* synthesis and *genotype*; gene *mutation*.

for DNA repair. Single-strand damage, such as missing or mismatched bases, is repaired using the undamaged strand as a template. Double-strand damage can be repaired after chromosomal recombination (during sperm and egg production) provides unaltered DNA as a template. And even when expressed, mutations do not necessarily produce completely new alleles and monstrous traits. Rather, many mutations alter a gene from one known allele (and trait) to another, as in the case of humans' normal blood-clotting allele mutating into the allele that causes hemophilia, a pathological condition characterized by bleeding due to inadequate clotting. Sometimes, of course, entirely new genetic variants *are* produced, and therefore mutations must be ranked as the primary source of new alleles in a species' gene pool.

Genetic Load

Are constantly occurring point mutations responsible generation after generation for the vast amount of individual phenotypic variation seen in all species? Probably not. First of all, the mutation rates are too low. Second, most new mutant alleles are quickly lost from the gene pool. In some cases mutations are eliminated by natural selection, being selected against because they code for deleterious (harmful) or fatal traits. The term **genetic load** refers to the deleterious genes carried in a population and to the normal mutation rate that commonly reduces fitness. In human populations, genetic birth defects may affect up to 4 percent of births. Most birth defects are due either to inherited genetic factors or to recent mutations in the germ cells. Mutations may lead to chromosomal abnormalities such as Down's syndrome, in which the individual has an extra chromosome (46 + 1); Turner's syndrome, in which the Y chromosome, which determines maleness, is missing (46 − 1); Klinefelter's syndrome, in which individuals are XXY (phenotypic males with two female X chromosomes) and surviving individuals are sterile; or other abnormalities involving multiples of the sex chromosomes.

Given the random nature of mutation, it is unusual for the process to produce beneficial genetic change. Just as a random adjustment inside a computer is unlikely to improve its performance, a random addition to the gene pool of a species is unlikely to be useful to any individual that inherits it. In many cases mutant alleles disappear though chance loss alone. It has been calculated that even mutant alleles with small selective advantages stand a 90 percent chance of disappearing within thirty generations. Mutations do not serve, therefore, as the main sources of phenotypic variation in each generation. A much better candidate exists for that important role: meiosis, the cell division process that produces eggs and sperm.

Meiosis and Crossing-Over

The reduction division process of meiosis is remarkable in many ways. Not only does it reduce the chromosome count of gametes to the haploid number, but it also provides the basis for extensive phenotypic variation in every generation by producing genetically unique sex cells. While mutation stands as the ultimate source of new alleles and allelic variation, meiosis must be viewed as the primary (and proximate) source of genotypic variety among individuals.

Meiosis involves one chromosomal replication and two cell divisions (Figure 2.11). Before the first cell division, each chromosome replicates itself to produce two **chromatids**. The duplicated chromosome with its two elements then pairs with its homologous partner, and this pairing yields clusters of four chromatids called *tetrads*. As the tetrads line up at the equator of the fibrous spindle that stretches between the

Genetic load usually, the *recessive genes* in a *population* that are harmful when expressed in the rare *homozygous* condition.

Chromatid one of the two elements in a duplicated *chromosome*.

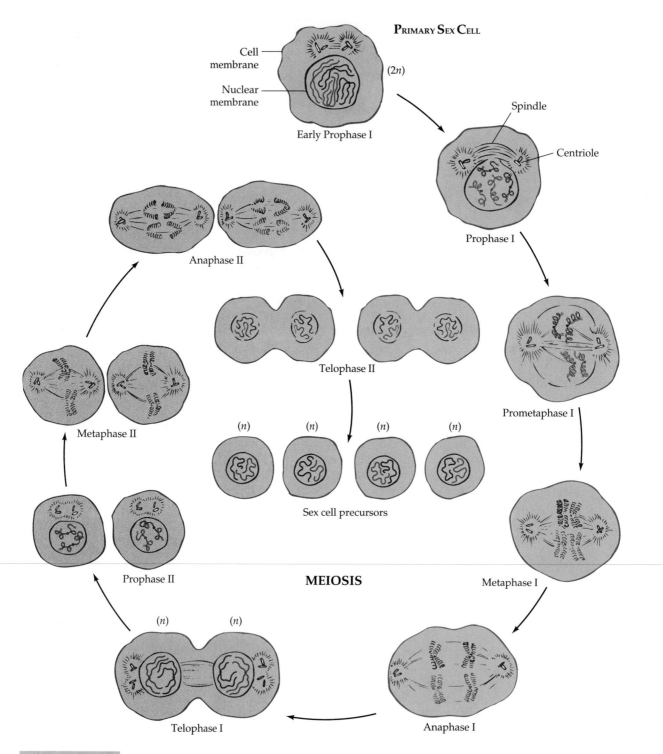

Figure 2.11

Meiosis. The single replication of genetic material occurs in Prophase I. Crossing-over within the tetrad takes place in Metaphase I, producing numerous reconstituted chromosomes. Two cell divisions then follow that (potentially) result in four haploid gamete precursors.

Figure 2.12

A simple example of crossing-over and segment exchange among the chromatids of a tetrad.

centrioles (Metaphase I), the chromatids in each may overlap at points called **chiasmata.** **Crossing-over,** or the exchange of sections between homologous chromosomes, may then take place at these sites (Figure 2.12). During the next stage (Anaphase I), the homologous chromosomes (each still consisting of two chromatids) separate and move toward opposite poles of the spindle. (Technically, the two halves of the dividing cell are now haploid, as we count chromosomes, not chromatids.) At this point, any or all of the four chromatids formerly making up a tetrad may contain a different mixture of genetic material from their original condition.

The first meiotic division is then completed, and the second begins. In females of some species—such as our own—the first division in potential egg cells begins prenatally, is suspended between birth and puberty, and is then completed—along with the second division—by a few cells every month between puberty and menopause. The second meiotic division occurs without further replication of the genetic material and involves the separation of chromatids (Anaphase II). The potential result of meiosis is the production of four haploid "daughter" cells (this term is used for both sperm and egg cells), each genetically unique. This potential is realized in males (four sperm cells from each original parent cell), but in females only one energy-rich egg is produced from every parent cell.

Evolutionary change via natural selection can proceed only if conspecifics vary phenotypically and trait differences are based, at least partially, on genetic differences. Within a population, the proportion of phenotypic variance attributable to genetic variance is referred to as a trait's level of **heritability.** Meiosis, with its genetic and chromosomal mixing, provides the basis for gene-based phenotypic variations. The stage is now set for evolution at the population and species levels.

 For more on genetics and inheritance, visit our web site.

How Do Populations Evolve?

Although individuals' contributions to evolution through the generation of variation are acknowledged, the focus today is on population-level changes in gene frequencies and phenotypic traits. Natural **populations** typically consist of a finite collection of conspecific individuals living in the same area and having the potential of mating with one another. These breeding communities are also called **demes.** Populations are open, however, and have permeable community boundaries that allow communication between neighboring populations through the (occasional or regular) exchange of members.

Centrioles minute granules present in many cells outside the nuclear membrane. The centriole divides in cell division, and the parts separate to form the poles of the spindle.

Chiasmata crossover points where the *chromatids* of a tetrad overlap and segment exchange may occur (singular: chiasma).

Crossing-over the exchange of sections between *homologous chromosomes*.

Heritability a property of phenotypic traits; the proportion of a trait's interindividual variance that is due to genetic variance.

Population usually, a local or breeding group; a group in which any two individuals have the potential of mating with each other.

Deme the community of potentially interbreeding individuals at a locality.

In sexually reproducing creatures, these member exchanges almost always result in the movement of genes between populations. This phenomenon, call **gene flow,** has the obvious result of decreasing differences (both genetic and phenotypic) *between* populations, while increasing variation of both sorts *within* each deme. In other words, thanks to gene flow, populations within a species are homogenized, both genetically and in their traits. If a new and advantageous mutation crops up in one population, sooner or later it will be spread to all of the others. The occurrence of gene flow is what most evolutionary biologists would say binds a set of populations into a species.

What Are Species?

If the presence of gene flow demonstrates permeable population boundaries *within* a species, does its absence reflect relatively impermeable boundaries *between* species? Most biologists would say yes, and this is indeed the basis for the classical *biological species* concept, which defines a species as "a group of interbreeding natural populations that are reproductively isolated from other such groups." Here conspecifics are recognized not from the fact that they look alike (although this is almost always true as well), but from the fact that they mate exclusively (or almost exclusively) with one another. In virtually every case, one or more *isolating mechanisms* have evolved that make organisms unable, or unwilling, to reproduce outside of their own species. Common isolating mechanisms that separate species include morphological differences (body shape, size, coloration, etc.); genetic and chromosomal differences (e.g., distinctive chromosome numbers and shapes); and, perhaps most important of all, behavioral differences. Typical behavioral mechanisms include differences in breeding seasons and courtship patterns. Courtship, in particular, often involves complicated ritualistic behavior that is important in species recognition. (It should be noted that the biological species concept was never meant to apply to species that are naturally separated geographically but can interbreed in captivity. African lions [*Felis leo*] and Asian tigers [*Felis tigris*] may hybridize in zoos to produce "tiglons and ligers," but this does not mean that they are the same species.)

Perhaps the greatest weakness of the biological species definition is that it suggests absolute reproductive barriers between species. In fact, fertile hybridization (crossing) between species is quite common among plants and occurs at least occasionally among animals. About 40 percent of duck and geese species have been known to hybridize; gray wolves (*Canis lupus*) produce fertile hybrids with coyotes (*Canis latrans*); and in the Awash National Park in Ethiopia, primatologists have documented anubis baboons (*Papio cynocephalus anubis*) crossbreeding with hamadryas baboons (*Papio hamadryas*). Even Ernst Mayr, one of the strongest supporters of the biological species concept, has noted the transmission of genes from one species to another through hybridization followed by hybrids back-crossing with one of the original parent species (Mayr, 1996). Mayr argues, however, that despite the fact that reproductive "isolating mechanisms do not always prevent the *occasional* interbreeding of non-conspecific individuals…they nevertheless prevent the complete *fusion* of such species" (emphasis added). Thus, despite occasional cases of "gene leakage" (Mayr's term) between species, most of the time **assortative mating** (the tendency for creatures with similar phenotypes to mate with one another) and other behavioral and genetic mechanisms ensure species' integrity.

A second weakness of the biological species concept, and one that plagues evolutionary biologists, is that it is difficult to apply to fossil species, because we can never be sure about their reproductive behavior. Thus, when scientists try to identify and sort extinct species, they are forced to fall back on trait similarities and differences

Gene flow the transmission of *genes* between *populations,* which increases the variety of genes available to each and creates or maintains similarities in the genetic makeup of the populations.

Assortative mating the tendency of like to mate with like.

as the best indicators of reproductive isolation. Types and amounts of morphological distinctiveness needed for the identification of fossil species are usually based on studies of their closest living evolutionary relatives. For example, knowledge about morphological variation among modern humans, as well as that found among the living ape species, allows anthropologists to make informed decisions about the species of early human ancestors.

How Does Natural Selection Shape Populations?

Despite the impossibility of a precise definition of species, it is clear that they do exist in nature and that they usually can be subdivided into identifiable populations. (Very small species, with limited geographic ranges, may consist of only a single population. In this case, the species and the population are identical.) Presumably, all new species that have resulted from the splitting or branching of an evolutionary lineage began as a single-population species. Once in existence, a species may be stable, or it may change with time. Most species that last for a reasonable period probably experience both stability and change.

Each population consists of individuals that vary in their genotypes and traits (remember the contributions that mutation and meiosis make to variation) and are living under a distinct set of environmental conditions (broadly defined to include physical conditions, food, water, and competing organisms). Individuals simply try to survive and reproduce, and—other things being equal—those lucky enough to possess traits that "work" in that environment succeed. Reproductively successful individuals pass their genes and traits on to the next generation, while nonreproducers obviously do not. Thus, with each passing generation, reproducers' alleles tend to increase in relative frequency, compared to the alleles at the same loci that were carried by nonreproducers. Thus reproducers' phenotypic traits tend to become more common within the population gene pool. The effects of natural selection can be measured as changes in the population's gene pool or as shifts in the collective phenotype (Figure 2.13). Even small differences in the survival rates of different alleles (more correctly, of their carriers) can produce dramatic genetic shifts given enough time. Recent studies of fish, lizards, and even Darwin's Galápagos finches have demonstrated that under sufficiently strong environmental pressures, natural selection can move rapidly on occasion to transform a population or species (Losos et al., 1997; Weiner, 1994). This is referred to as **directional natural selection**.

Natural selection does not always change things, however. Natural selection can act to preserve current gene frequencies and phenotypic distributions. **Stabilizing natural selection** occurs when the environment is relatively constant (unchanging), and it operates by selecting against all individuals that deviate from the prevailing phenotypic norms. Periods of **stasis** in the history of a species, when little or no evolutionary change occurs, generally are periods of stabilizing selection. A striking product of this type of selection is the coelocanth fish, already mentioned, which has remained unchanged in its stable deep-sea environment for two hundred million years—a living fossil.

Founder Effect and Genetic Drift

Although of primary importance, natural selection is not the only force in nature shaping the genes and traits of populations and species. At least five other processes can

Directional natural selection *natural selection* that operates in response to environmental change and produces shifts in the composition of a *population's gene pool* and *collective phenotype.*

Stabilizing natural selection *natural selection* that operates during periods when the environment is stable and maintains the genetic and phenotypic status quo within a *population.*

Stasis a period of evolutionary equilibrium or inactivity.

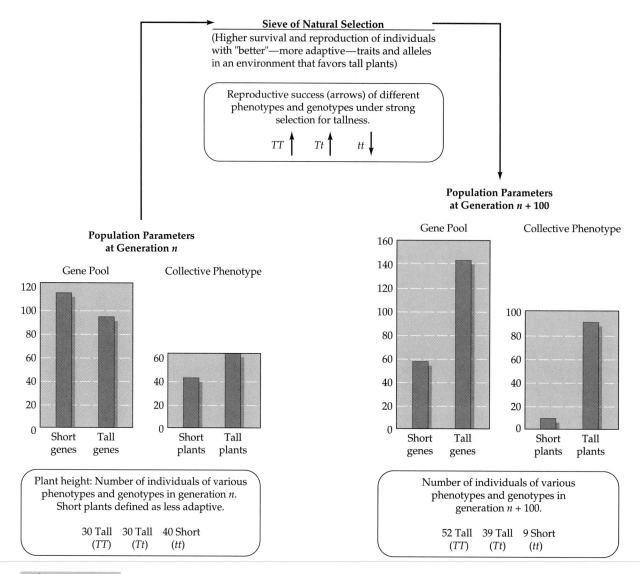

Figure 2.13

A model of evolution by natural selection. In this example, pea plant height has two alleles, *T* (dominant) and *t* (recessive). The effects of selection for tallness from generations *n* to *n*+100 are shown. Population size is held at 100 plants throughout the example.

be identified as non-Darwinian evolutionary mechanisms: mutation, chromosomal recombination during meiosis (crossing over), gene flow, the founder effect, and genetic drift. The first three phenomena—mutation, crossing over, and gene flow—have been described already. These three processes produce random genetic and phenotypic variability within populations—variability that can then be shaped by natural selection. The last two phenomena—founder effect and genetic drift—also affect variability and thus feed natural selection, but may also sometimes produce evolutionary change on their own.

ASKING QUESTIONS

How Did Giraffes Get Long Necks?

Compare the three populations of giraffes illustrated here. Based on the terms and concepts in this chapter, how would you describe the differences?

Now, how would you explain the differences? Which individuals—those with long or short necks—would you say were at a selective advantage over time? How have the frequencies of genes for neck length changed in the population over time? How might that have happened?

In this example, would natural selection be described as directional or stabilizing? If you drew a fourth representation of the giraffe population in the future, what might it look like? Why?

People who are not informed about population genetics might think that individual giraffes grew long necks because they needed them in order to survive and then passed on this trait to their offspring. Why would this explanation be incorrect?

The **founder effect,** like genetic drift, operates in very small populations. These small communities either may be the remnants of larger populations that have gone through size-reducing *bottlenecks* (for example, decimation by disease) or may be *founder populations* started by a few individuals splintering off to establish a new breeding colony. Small, descendant populations often are not typical samples of the parent species. That is, just by chance alone, these populations may, from the very start, carry different gene frequencies and phenotypic norms. In particular, they probably will not contain the full assortment of alleles found among their parents.

Small populations also become good candidates for **genetic drift.** This mechanism involves chance variations in allele frequencies between the generations of small populations (Figure 2.14). In such populations rare alleles may be quickly lost or may be "fixed" (becoming widespread) in the gene pool because of several chance factors. For example, rare alleles may be lost when their few carriers die accidentally. Or perhaps the carriers survive but, because of chance alone, fail to reproduce. Or, finally, perhaps heterozygous individuals with rare alleles are lucky enough to survive and reproduce; but then, just by chance, the alleles are absent from the particular sperm or egg cells involved in reproduction. In the opposite scenarios rare alleles may become fixed by chance alone. Studies suggest that alleles with neutral or weak selective values are good candidates for genetic drift.

Evidence for genetic drift in human populations can be found in the literature on human blood groups. These data are of interest because we believe that during much of human evolution, our ancestors lived in small bands of a few hundred individuals.

Founder effect typically, genetic difference between a newly founded, separated *population* and its parent group. The founding population is usually different because its *gene pool* is only a segment of the parent group's.

Genetic drift genetic changes in *populations* caused by random phenomena rather than by *natural selection.*

Figure 2.14

Computer simulations of genetic drift show how random changes across several generations may lead to either the elimination or the fixation of alleles in small populations. One hundred simulations for two alleles (*A*, *a*) at a single locus were conducted, and the figure shows the randomly generated frequency distribution of one allele (*A*) at generations 1, 5, 10, and 25. Population size was set at five diploid individuals (10 genes) with *A* and *a* equally represented initially.

Source: Data from Cavalli-Sforza and Bodmer, 1971.

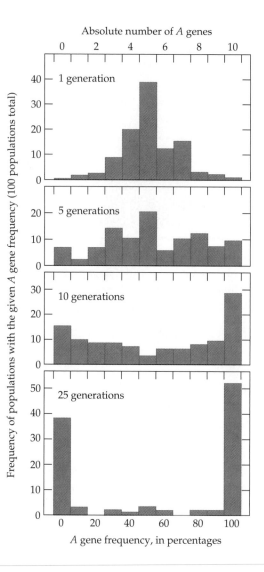

Balanced Polymorphism

The interplay of natural selection and non-Darwinian mechanisms, such as the founder effect and genetic drift, determines the evolutionary potential of populations. Interestingly, however, even these powerful forces acting in combination do not bring populations into perfect genetic and phenotypic harmony with their environments. The nonexistence of perfectly adapted populations is due to several factors, but high on the list is the extreme difficulty of completely eliminating detrimental recessive genes, especially when they are protected through *balanced polymorphism*. In **balanced polymorphism,** two or more alleles of a single gene are expressed in a population in more or less constant proportions because heterozygotes for that gene are somehow at a selective advantage.

    As you have read, all populations of sexually reproducing species carry harmful unexpressed recessive genes as part of their genetic load. These genes are expressed only

Balanced polymorphism maintenance in a *population* of different *alleles* of a particular *gene* in proportion to the advantages offered by each (e.g., sickle-cell and normal *hemoglobin*).

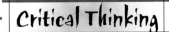

Critical Thinking

Sources of Differences in Human Populations

Years ago, near Thule, Greenland, a small band of "polar Eskimos" (Inuit) became isolated from their parent population. This band, which numbered no more than 271 people at any time, was isolated for generations. A related band from Baffin Island knew of their existence and tried to reach them, but by the time descendants of the Baffin Island band made contact, the descendants of the Thule band had come to believe that they were the only people on earth!

In 1956, American physical anthropologist William Laughlin took blood samples from the Thule band and their parent population and compared the two groups' ABO blood group frequencies. He found significant differences (Laughlin, 1963). What two non-Darwinian evolutionary mechanisms might explain these differences, and why? What are the implications of these mechanisms for understanding human evolution?

in individuals with the comparatively rare double recessive, which may cause a physical malformation or fatal genetic disease. An example of such a phenomenon is **sickle-cell anemia.** Persons who are homozygous for the recessive sickle-cell allele (Hb^S) have anemia, because their red blood cells sickle (become thin and crescent-shaped) to the extent that the cells cannot carry sufficient oxygen. Homozygotes for the normal allele (Hb^A) have normal red blood cells (Figure 2.15).

Sickle-cell anemia is a life-threatening condition in certain populations of West and Central Africa and among their descendants living elsewhere. In some areas 20 to 40 percent of individuals are $Hb^A Hb^S$ heterozygotes; 1 to 2 percent are homozygous recessive ($Hb^S Hb^S$) and usually die soon after birth. The harmful recessive allele persists, however, because heterozygotes have a selective advantage: They possess immunity to malaria (see Discoveries and Mysteries).

Sickle-cell anemia a genetically caused disease that can be fatal, in which the *red blood corpuscles* carry insufficient oxygen.

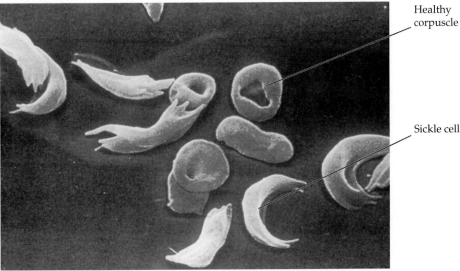

Healthy corpuscle

Sickle cell

Figure 2.15

The sickle-cell trait is due to abnormal hemoglobin, which differs from normal hemoglobin in only 1 amino acid out of nearly 300 that constitute the protein.

Discoveries and Mysteries

Sickle-Cell Anemia

If the sickle-cell gene Hb^S was so undesirable, how did it manage to achieve and maintain such a high frequency in the affected populations? Why didn't natural selection weed it out? A. C. Allison, a British doctor, asked these questions (Allison, 1960). In 1954 he showed scientifically that the sickle-cell trait in its heterozygous state affords protection against malarial infection, and that the distribution of the Hb^S gene coincides with the geographic distribution of the malaria-carrying *Anopheles* mosquito. The Hb^S gene was maintained by selection according to the trade-off it offered to the affected populations: protection from malaria for the more numerous $Hb^A Hb^S$ carriers in exchange for the anemic deaths of the rarer $Hb^S Hb^S$ recipients. Because of balanced polymorphism, about 10 percent of Americans of African descent carry the Hb^S gene today, even though the environment in the United States is free of malaria.

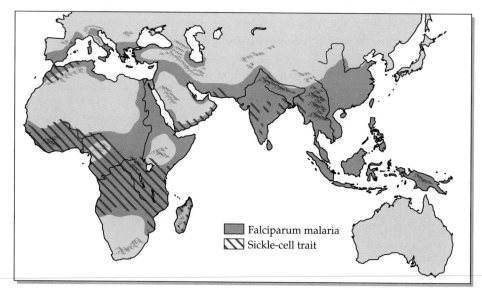

Falciparum malaria
Sickle-cell trait

Coincidence of the sickle-cell trait and malaria in parts of the Old World led us to understand why the abnormal hemoglobin Hb^S appears in these areas. Though disadvantageous elsewhere, in malarial areas the sickling gene gives considerable protection against the dangerous malarial parasite. The two hemoglobin forms are in balance according to the advantages and disadvantages they offer.

As you can see, an allele that provides a lifesaving adaptation in one environment can be part of a population's genetic load in another environment. The survival values of genes are determined by the environment in which they are expressed. Acting on genetic variability, natural selection often will compromise between advantages and disadvantages, so that ordinarily lethal phenotypes are maintained in a population in balance with advantageous phenotypes. At the same time, the genetic load represents a potential for variability that may be necessary for survival in the future, as it may have been in the past. Thus, hidden genetic variability may be insurance against new selective pressures accompanying environmental change.

Summary

Mendel's experiments and insights have unlocked the secrets of inheritance. He recognized that inheritance was particulate and that the traits were sorted independently through the processes of reproduction. Scientists soon located Mendel's particles (genes) on chromosomes and observed them in cell division. The modern synthesis of the theory of evolution incorporated this new knowledge.

Each animal or plant carries a genotype, and its living form is its phenotype. The genes take the form of coded segments of spiral DNA. The codes are a template for RNA, which in turn constitutes a template for protein synthesis. Variation is introduced during meiotic cell division and increased by gene flow.

Populations, not individuals, evolve, and they do so by changes in their gene pool. Species are groups of populations isolated reproductively from other such groups.

The founder effect and genetic drift, along with natural selection, have made important contributions to the evolution of populations and species, including the human species. We are imperfectly adapted to our environment, as natural selection makes compromises between alternative selection pressures; these compromises are often expressed as balanced polymorphisms.

Review Questions

1. What are genes? How do they determine phenotypic traits?

2. What were Gregor Mendel's experiments? What are the principles of Mendelian inheritance?

3. How do point mutations and meiosis (including crossing-over) affect the phenotypic variability seen in all sexually reproducing species?

4. What is a species? How is it best defined, and why is an absolute definition of species impossible?

5. What is "gene leakage"? How does this phenomenon affect our understanding of the biological species concept?

6. What are the roles of DNA and RNA in inheritance?

7. How does natural selection operate on variations in a population to alter its gene pool and collective phenotype?

8. What are some non-Darwinian mechanisms of evolution, and how do they work?

9. What is the relationship between genetic load and balanced polymorphism?

10. What elements were combined to produce the synthetic theory of evolution? How does this theory advance us beyond Charles Darwin's understanding of evolution?

Suggested Further Reading

Henig, R. *The Monk in the Garden*. Houghton Mifflin, 2000.
Price, Peter. *Biological Evolution*. Saunders College Publishing, 1996.
Ridley, Mark. *Evolution*, 2nd ed. Blackwell Science, 1996.
Singer, M., and P. Berg. *Genes and Genomes*. University Science Books, 1991.
Weiner, J. *The Beak of the Finch*. Vintage Books, 1994.

Internet Resources

 Conveniently access these and other links via our web site at **http://www.ablongman/anthro.**

Human Genome Project Information
http://www.ornl.gov/hgmis/project/about.html
This site contains a description of the Human Genome Project and its significance, as well as information on its progress.

Human Population Genetics Links
http://watson.hgen.pitt.edu/~dweeks/teaching.html
Links to articles and tutorials on subjects relating to population genetics.

Natural Selection and Genetic Drift Modeling Exercise
http://fmc.utm.edu/~rirwin/NatSelModIntro.htm
This site allows you to run simulations of evolutionary change in several species, including peppered moths.

Sickle-Cell Information Web Site
http://www.emory.edu/PEDS/SICKLE/
Illustrated information on the inheritance, distribution, diagnosis, treatment, and prevention of sickle-cell disease throughout the world.

The Basic Principles of Genetics
http://daphne.palomar.edu/mendel/
A nicely illustrated introduction to Mendelian genetics, with a practice quiz for each topic.

Your Genes, Your Choices
http://ehrweb.aas.org/ehr/books
Written for the American Association for the Advancement of Science, this short book explores issues raised by genetic research that relate to our daily lives.

Useful Search Terms:
DNA
Gregor Mendel
Human Genome Project
population genetics
RNA
species

Population Genetics, Adaptation, and Variation

Overview

Chapter 3 is a primer on the mechanisms of evolutionary change at the population level and also shows how the survival and reproduction of individuals contribute to the characteristics of the population. For example, individuals contribute through their personal fitness, inclusive fitness through kin selection, and sexual selection.

Changes in gene frequencies in a population both reflect and may cause evolutionary change; and evolutionary change, in relation to environmental pressures, may lead to gradual transformation, speciation through reproductive or geographic isolation, or extinction. The Hardy–Weinberg theorem is a valuable tool for predicting stability or change in the frequencies of genes in a population.

Chapter 3 then focuses on the study of human variability—the diverse anatomical and physiological traits in human populations, such as skin color and blood groups—and on the evolutionary significance of this variability. The concept of race in humans, however, proves to have almost no biological significance. Likewise, the idea of evolutionary progress is a cultural construction with no validity in nature.

 Check our web site for additional information, photos, drawings, maps, and animations on topics in this chapter.

How Do Fitness and Selection Operate in Evolution?

A population's degree of adaptation is related both to the fitness of individuals that make up the population and to mechanisms of kin selection and sexual selection.

Inclusive Fitness

Fitness individuals' relative degrees of success in surviving and reproducing, and thus in gaining genetic representation in succeeding generations.

Traditionally, **fitness** has been measured in terms of individual reproductive success; that is, in terms of how many viable offspring an organism produces and successfully rears to sexual maturity. Because each offspring carries 50 percent of each parent's genes, individual reproduction is a primary path to evolutionary fitness. Surviving

Follow links at **http://www.ablongman/anthro** for additional resources in physical anthropology, primatology, biological anthropology, and paleoanthropology.

without reproducing does not contribute to fitness; nor does simply possessing traits that foster survival, such as strength, stamina, and good health.

Thanks to the work of W. D. Hamilton (1964) and others, however, we know that individual reproductive success is only one component of an organism's **inclusive fitness.** A second important component is the reproductive success of one's genetic kin. After all, in diploid organisms, parents and offspring and full siblings have 50 percent of their genes in common, half-sibs 25 percent, first cousins 12.5 percent, and so on. Assisting a relative to survive and reproduce is therefore a perfectly good way to get copies of one's own genes into future generations. This realization also appears to explain several previously puzzling aspects of animal (and human) behavior. Animals often appear to behave altruistically, doing things that benefit others although inflicting a cost on the actor (there are many examples, such as alarm calling, intervening in fights, and sharing food). But if the recipients of such **bioaltruism** are the actor's kin, then acts that appear to be altruistic may in fact reap a genetic reward for the actor by helping relatives survive and reproduce.

Kin Selection

Bioaltruism is the basis for the evolutionary mechanism known as **kin selection.** Kin selection may be the process by which behaviors evolved that apparently are altruistic but actually serve genetic self-interest. In any event, as individuals possessing advantageous traits (those that contribute to survival and successful reproduction within the prevailing environment) demonstrate their fitness by passing many copies of their genes into the next generation (in the form of offspring, grand-offspring, nieces, nephews, etc.), they drive up the frequencies of good-trait alleles relative to alleles that code for less advantageous traits. Thus, in the next generation, the population's collective phenotype will be shifted (slightly or strongly, depending on selection pressures) toward "good" traits. In other words, the population, viewed as a whole, will be *better adapted* to its environment than before. In this way, the actions of individuals as they face each day's challenges—feeding, survival, reproduction, parenting, aiding kin—contribute to the evolution of their population and species.

Sexual Selection

Another form of selection is **sexual selection,** which occurs when mating between members of the opposite sex of a population or species is not random. In 1871 Darwin described two kinds of sexual selection based on the presence of struggle or choice in mating behavior. The first kind was the result of competition among members of one sex (usually males) for the opposite sex. An example is multimale baboon groups in which the alpha male may have primary sexual access to most females in the troop as they near ovulation. This pattern of reproductive behavior will select the genes for powerful and impressive males.

Darwin's second kind of sexual selection involves differential choice by members of one sex for particular traits (e.g., coloration, body size, specific anatomical features) in members of the opposite sex. In this mating behavior females will usually choose particular preferred males over others, a pattern well known in birds and primates.

The role of sexual selection in human evolution is not yet understood, but it clearly is less significant in a monogamous society with a 50:50 sex ratio than in a polygamous society, in which some individuals have several mates and some have none. The characteristics in humans that may be a product of sexual selection are those that appear to

Inclusive fitness the sum total of an organism's individual reproductive success (number of offspring) plus portions of the reproductive success of genetic kin.

Bioaltruism behavior that appears to be altruistic, but that in fact is believed to benefit the animal indirectly, by increasing its *inclusive fitness.*

Kin selection the selection of characteristics (and their *genes*) that increase the probability of the survival and reproduction of close relatives.

Sexual selection a category including intrasexual competition for mates (usually aggressive and among males) and intersexual mate selection (usually of males by females).

advertise reproductive fitness or sexuality, such as hair pattern, body shape, breast size in women, and penis size in men. In human evolution, the second type of sexual selection (differential choice of mate) probably has been more important than competition among males. Unfortunately, it is difficult to know the mating patterns of early humans, which must be inferred from studies of present-day primates and people.

Other nonrandom mating systems found in animals and humans are inbreeding and outbreeding. **Inbreeding** occurs when sexual partners share a recent common ancestor and therefore are genetically related to some degree. In small, isolated populations, inbreeding may be the typical pattern, but it has costs. It often increases the probability of homozygous pairings of recessive genes and expression of the recessive phenotype. As you have seen, recessive phenotypes often are harmful, and the genotypes tend to become rare unless they are maintained through balanced polymorphism. Increased disease and higher mortality rates have been predicted and observed in inbred animal and human populations.

Outbreeding is characteristic of human groups with extensive **incest taboos** and other rules requiring members to mate or marry outside their kin group. Outbreeding has the opposite effect of inbreeding: Variation within the population increases, lethal recessives remain unexpressed, and the population may show improved health and lower mortality.

How Do Speciation and Extinction Occur?

Inbreeding mating among related individuals.

Outbreeding mating among unrelated individuals.

Incest taboo a sanction against committing incest, found in all human societies.

Speciation the production of new *species*, either through gradual transformation or the splitting or branching of existing species.

Cladogenesis branching *evolution* involving the splitting of a *species* or lineage.

Allopatric speciation *speciation* caused by the geographic isolation of *populations,* which then evolve in different ways.

Sympatric speciation *speciation* among *populations* with the same or overlapping geographic ranges.

Speciation is the process by which new species come into existence. As you read in Chapter 2, the combination of gene flow, accumulating mutations, the founder effect, genetic drift, and natural selection working within different environments can lead to increasing differences between an isolated population and its parent species. When the two have become sufficiently different so that they cannot or will not interbreed should they meet again (due to the disappearance of the reproductive barrier or to migration), then they qualify as different species according to the biological species model. Thus, species are distinct breeding communities in relative reproductive isolation from one another. In conditions of rapid change, speciation might be achieved in several hundred to a few thousand years. There are actually two basic models of speciation: cladogenesis and anagenesis.

Cladogenesis

The model of speciation called **cladogenesis** increases the diversity of life forms through the splitting or branching of existing species, producing the familiar image of evolutionary trees. Branching may occur through **allopatric speciation**—speciation among populations living in different ranges or territories. Allopatric speciation begins with the formation of a physical barrier between a population and the rest of its species. This geographic isolation—perhaps produced by the formation of a new mountain range, volcanoes, glaciers, geologic faults, sea-level rise, change in the course of a river, or some other topographic alteration—leads to reproductive isolation. As gene flow is interrupted, mutations and environmental adaptations on either side of the barrier make the two populations progressively different until speciation can be said to have occurred.

Other forms of cladogenesis include **sympatric speciation,** in which populations living in the same or overlapping ranges separate by adapting to different ecological niches, and **parapatric speciation,** in which populations of sedentary organisms living in adjacent ranges separate.

Anagenesis

The other model of speciation is called **anagenesis** or **phyletic transformation.** The differences between cladogenesis and anagenesis are shown in Figure 3.1. As you can see, anagenesis involves the continuous evolutionary transformation of an entire species into a descendant species, represented by phenotypically different creatures. In this case transformation within an evolving lineage results from the slow accumulation of adaptive changes wrought by natural selection. Anagenesis often is referred to as **gradualism** for this reason.

In phyletic transformation, after sufficient change has built up, a new species or subspecies name may be deemed necessary by scientists studying the lineage, and so they coin one. However, in anagenetic evolution there is no increase in species diversity, because branching does not occur. Thus, phyletic transformation is a problem for taxonomists trying to name a specimen unambiguously—and in fact the identification of successive species in one evolving lineage is largely arbitrary.

Extinction

Extinction, as discussed in Chapter 1, is the process by which species are lost. The term is applied most commonly to the loss of species due to the disappearance of its members. A species becomes truly extinct when all its members die and all their genes die with them. In contrast, when a species is phyletically transformed, its genes do not

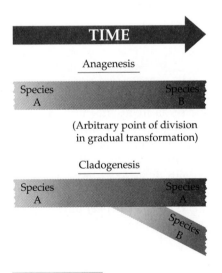

Figure 3.1

Anagenesis (phyletic transformation) involves the gradual conversion (mainly through natural selection) of an entire species into a new species. Although this process occurs in nature, it does not lead to an increase in species diversity. In contrast, cladogenesis involves branching of an existing species (usually due to the isolation of one or more populations) with the result that the total number of species is increased.

Parapatric speciation speciation among *populations* of sedentary organisms with adjacent ranges.

Anagenesis the evolution by *natural selection* of a lineage over time, which may produce changes recognized as a new species.

Phyletic transformation the conversion (mainly through *natural selection*) of an entire *species* into a new species. (See *Anagenesis*)

Gradualism slow and steady evolutionary change in a lineage of plants or animals.

cease to exist but simply end up in a different kind of creature. As you might imagine, the difference between true extinction and phyletic transformation can be extremely difficult to distinguish in the fossil record.

In any event, extinction is the inevitable fate of all species, humans included. While animal species typically last about 4 million years (among humans and our ancestors, the average is closer to 1 million years), it still remains true that the vast majority of all species that have ever lived are now extinct. But why do species become extinct? Is it a matter of bad genes or bad luck (Raup, 1991)? In fact, it appears that, regardless of how well a species is adapted to its normal environment, sooner or later it will be exposed to such extraordinary biological or physical stresses that it will die. Examples of possible extinction-causing stressors include new and intense interspecific competition; extreme environmental changes due to fluctuations in sea level, global climate, and large-scale volcanism; and environmental and ecological disasters resulting from collisions of the earth with extraterrestrial objects (comets and asteroids). The collision hypothesis explains many mass extinction events, particularly the event that killed off the dinosaurs 65 million years ago.

The data on extinction suggest that over geological time the earth is clearly a dangerous and rather unpredictable place, periodically liable to large-scale, devastating environmental fluctuations. The extinctions that result from such fluctuations have played an important part in shaping the history of life on earth, and the existence of each living species is the result of a unique history of adaptation, speciation, and extinction. On the one hand, natural selection has tended to improve species' adaptations to their normal environments and has combined with processes such as genetic drift to produce new species; on the other, extinction has operated to reduce species' diversity and to open up ecological niches. Happily for humans, newly vacated ecological niches tend to open the way for new evolutionary experimentation. Had the dinosaurs not become extinct, mammals might never have diversified, and primates (including humans) might never have evolved.

What Do We Know about Human Variability?

As you can appreciate, variability in a species improves its chances of survival. Variability in behavior and appearance is characteristic of all living organisms as their environment varies. Human populations exhibit much genetic and phenotypic variability: variability due to age and sex, and variability that has evolved in response to different local environmental conditions. Human variations exist both within and between populations, and trait variations correlate with differing environments and susceptibility to certain diseases. These trait variations are of three main kinds: (1) anatomical features, such as skin color, hair form, and body shape; (2) physiological traits, such as metabolic rate and hormone activity, growth rate, color blindness, and genetic diseases; and (3) characteristics of the blood (biochemical traits).

Human Anatomical Traits

Perhaps the most easily noticed physical characteristic of humans is skin color. Depending on the amount of melanin in the epidermis, human skin varies from very light ("white") to very dark (dark brown or "black"). As shown in Figure 3.2, skin color is found to be very closely correlated with latitude when analyzed globally. People with

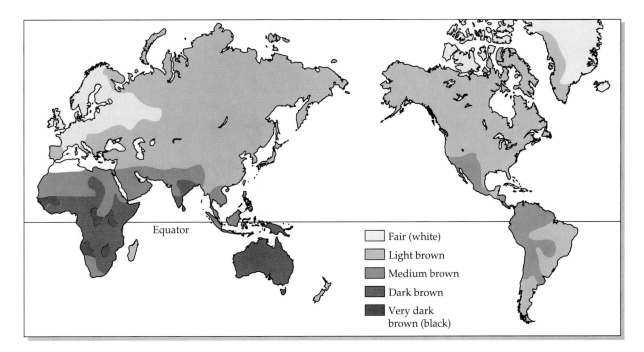

Figure 3.2

This global map shows the distribution of skin colors in indigenous populations. Note the clear correlation between skin color and latitude.

Source: Data from Robins, 1991.

dark skin colors are found nearest to the equator, and lighter populations inhabit higher northern and southern latitudes. This distribution of skin tones seems to reflect a complex pattern of adaptation by our ancestral populations. In equatorial and sub-equatorial regions, people are subjected to intense ultraviolet (UV) radiation, and bombardment by UV rays can be extremely harmful. One relatively short-term effect is sunburn, which may result in an inability to sweat efficiently and thus to reduce body heat. Sunburn-induced impairment of sweating may even lead to hyperthermia and death during heavy exercise by light-skinned individuals with a heavy solar heat load. And of course, prolonged exposure to UV radiation may lead to skin cancer and its sometimes deadly consequences. Heavy epidermal concentrations of melanin help to protect tropical people against the ravages of UV radiation. Among equatorial and subequatorial populations, skin cancer rates are relatively low, and sweat glands are protected from UV-induced blockage. Thus, there has been strong selection for dark skin colors in regions of intense and prolonged sunlight.

The sun-and-skin problem took on a different dimension in those human populations that migrated north and south away from the sunny regions. In the higher latitudes, sunburn damage and skin cancer became less significant threats, while an inability to produce essential vitamins gained in importance. Human populations that inhabited higher latitudes must have experienced selection for lighter skin color (reduced pigmentation) in order to enhance vitamin D production: When exposed to sunlight, humans' skin synthesizes vitamin D. (Insufficient vitamin D causes a condition known as rickets, resulting in bone deficiencies and other problems.) In contrast, in the tropics natural selection would have favored dark skin for the reasons given above and because, despite heavy pigmentation, the intense sunlight would have caused enough vitamin D to be produced. At equivalent latitudes, people in the southern hemisphere are darker skinned than those in northern latitudes. This coincides with higher UV levels in the south (Relethford, 1997). Skin color thus turns out to be a very clear example of evolutionary adaptation among modern people. It is a very striking trait, although very superficial, both literally and figuratively.

Hair and Sweat.   When our early prehuman ancestors started diverging from ancient African apes, they were probably just as hairy as today's chimpanzees and gorillas. In time, their hair must have grown less dense and the sweat glands in their skin more numerous. This change sharply differentiates humans from other primates. Today, human body hair is much shorter, finer, and more sparse than that of apes, and over large areas of our bodies it is almost invisible. Conversely, we have from 2 to 5 million sweat glands, more than are found in any other primate and far more productive of sweat.

Scientists are not sure why this change in body hair and sweat glands took place, but it seems to have been connected with an increasing ability to sustain strenuous physical exertion. When prehumans moved from protective forests onto open savanna and became daytime scavengers, hunters, and gatherers, they solved the problem of avoiding nocturnal predators but created a new problem. They generated a great deal of body heat (metabolic heat), just at the time of day when the temperature of the air was high so that the cooling effect of the air was low. To maintain a constant body temperature, essential to any mammal, these prehumans required a very efficient cooling mechanism. A logical evolutionary adaptation to this biological need was the increased number of sweat glands, producing far more sweat per gland, and the reduction of hair cover. During heavy exertion or in hot weather, the sweat glands bathe the body in moisture. Evaporation of this moisture cools the surface of the skin and the blood just below it. Dense hair would inhibit evaporation and would get matted and clogged by dried sweat. Hence the marked decrease in hair density.

It is possible that other adaptations, such as bipedalism, are also related (at least in part) to metabolic needs; in the tropics walking upright reduces the amount of body surface exposed to the sun and increases the ease of evaporation from the skin.

Body Build.   Another trait with clear adaptive consequences is body build. In 1847 Carl Bergmann, a German physiologist interested in the relationships among body mass, surface area, and heat production in warm-blooded animals, observed that populations occupying the coldest parts of a species' range tended to be bulkier—that is, more compact—than those living in the warmer parts ("Bergmann's rule"). In 1877 the American J. A. Allen added that animals with the largest bodies are found not in the coldest part of the population's range but somewhere in the center. He further stated that the protruding parts of the body, such as limbs, fingers, ears, and tails, tend to be relatively shorter in the cooler parts of the range than in its warmer regions ("Allen's rule"). In cool regions, these adaptations in body build decrease surface area in relation to weight, reducing heat loss. In warm regions, they increase surface area in relation to weight, thus increasing heat loss (Figure 3.3). Human populations follow these rules derived from animal studies, and it seems clear that populations known only from their fossilized remains did the same.

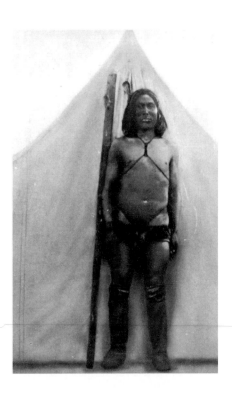

Figure 3.3

These individuals represent populations that demonstrate Bergmann's and Allen's rules. The photographs are of the same scale. The African on the left, tall and slim, has long extremities and a high ratio of surface area to weight. The Inuit on the right has short extremities and low ratio of surface area to weight, which reduces heat loss.

Living humans also show variations in hair form, from tight spirals or coils to curls to waves to straight hair. Although the adaptive significance, if any, of the various hair patterns has yet to be fully worked out, living populations around the world clearly differ in their typical hair form while also showing much intrapopulational variation (Figure 3.4). Similarly, no clear natural selection explanation has yet been proved for the fold of skin that occurs in the upper eyelid of some living people, the **epicanthic fold**. Epicanthic folds are common among Asian people, some Native Americans, and the Khoisan (Bushmen and Hottentot) people of South Africa. Research is continuing on the significance of these and other variable human traits. No doubt, in some cases, differences in selection and adaptation will be the correct explanation; for other traits, variation may be the result of more random processes, such as genetic drift.

One of the neatest demonstrations of environmental adaptation is that relating nose shape to the humidity of the air. Moistening the air when breathing is a prime function of the nasal epithelium; to prevent lung damage, the moisture content of the air must be brought up to 95 percent relative humidity at body temperature before the air enters the lungs. It seems clear that people adapted to areas of dry air (deserts and high mountains) will tend to have narrow noses, while those adapted to moist air

Epicanthic fold a fold of skin above the inner border of the eye; characteristic of Asiatic, some Native American, and Khoisan people.

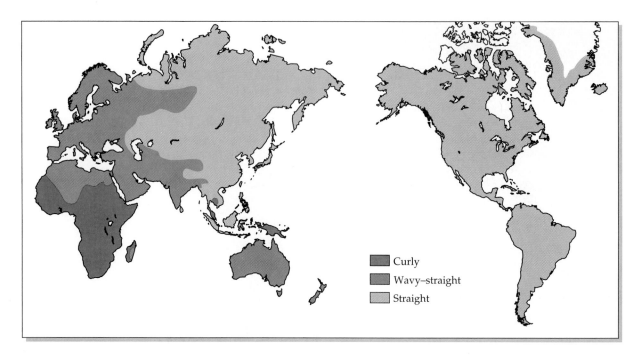

Figure 3.4

Hair form varies both within and between human populations. This map shows the pre-1500 AD distribution of hair form around the globe. Note that hair types overlap geographical race boundaries.

Source: Data from Montagu, 1964.

usually will have broad noses. The correlation can be demonstrated statistically, and the explanation appears empirically valid.

The important thing to remember is that humans' anatomical differences are slight and traits vary continuously: Noses vary from narrow to broad, hair varies by infinitesimal gradations from straight to tightly curled, and skin color varies from very light to almost black. Anthropologists have recognized as many as thirty-six gradations in this color spectrum. These features are determined by numerous genes and are not discretely segregated into just a few phenotypes.

Human Physiological Traits

Physiological traits that vary within and between human populations are probably less well known than the more obvious anatomical differences, but they are also significant and reflect adaptation (see Molnar, 1998, for a general discussion of such traits). The basal metabolic rate, which is related to the level of body heat production, varies, as might be predicted, according to the mean annual temperature. Bone growth rate and maturation age also seem to vary, though both are also greatly influenced by nutrition. The age at which teeth appear and their order of eruption vary significantly. For example, third molars (wisdom teeth), which appear in Europeans between seventeen and twenty years of age, appear in East Africans at age thirteen. Protein structure, keenness of taste, drug sensitivity, balance of urinary substances, color blindness, and sex hormone activity also show measurable differences. Highlanders in the Andes and Tibet are adapted to low atmospheric pressure and oxygen levels (Baker, 1988). And, as you have seen, DNA carries recognizable differences.

Probably the most important physiological differences are those subtle genetic variations that give rise to disease. Because many diseases appear to have simple single- or double-gene explanations, their symptoms are discrete; that is, they are either present or absent. Some genetic diseases are limited to small populations. In the Mediterranean region, there is *favism,* which is a genetically determined allergy to the broad bean (fava bean) and results in severe anemia, and Mediterranean fever, a familial condition causing acute fever and much pain. Other hereditary disorders are much more widespread and occur more commonly in one population than another. One such disorder is *phenylketonuria (PKU),* an inability to develop an essential enzyme, which usually results in brain damage and mental retardation. PKU is most common in some areas of Europe and is rare among persons of African or Asian descent.

Thalassemia, a disease like sickle-cell anemia, appears mostly in the Mediterranean region and parts of Asia. In the homozygous recessive state (two Th^2 alleles), the resulting anemia is so serious that afflicted individuals rarely reach reproductive age. But homozygous dominant individuals who completely lack the Th^2 allele may die early of serious malaria. It is in the heterozygous state that the trait is present but not serious and provides some protection against malaria. Thus, thalassemia persists through balanced polymorphism (see Chapter 2).

Human Blood Groups

The third group of variable traits, the blood groups, have great medical significance. When the possibility of blood transfusions was first investigated during the nineteenth century, it quickly became clear that introducing one individual's blood into another's bloodstream could be fatal. Blood consists of a liquid component, the **blood plasma,** and three main types of cells: the **red blood cells,** which contain the red pigment hemoglobin and carry oxygen to all the parts of the body; the much larger **white blood cells,** or **leukocytes,** which defend against infection; and the smallest cells, the **platelets,** which assist in clotting and maintain the circulatory system as a whole. The liquid remaining after a clot has formed is called the **serum.** The red cells have a protein coat whose molecules function as **antigens;** when introduced into another individual, antigens trigger the production of specific **antibodies,** other proteins that help protect the body against foreign substances. Microscopic examination of the blood of two people mixed together has shown that difficulties with transfusions come from the reactions between antigens and antibodies.

Safe transfusions now rest on biologist Karl Landsteiner's brilliant discovery in 1901 of the existence of different **blood groups.** Transfusions of the wrong kind of blood can cause the recipient's red blood cells to agglutinate, or clump together, and sometimes to burst. The **agglutination** can result in clots that block the blood's flow. Landsteiner discovered that the blood (actually the antigens) of one individual may trigger the production of another individual's antibodies, causing agglutination and clots. Landsteiner labeled with the letter O the blood of individuals that never agglutinated the blood of other persons, but which would in turn be agglutinated by some foreign blood cells. (Modern labels are given here for Landsteiner's groups.) Blood of yet other individuals that was agglutinated he labeled A. The blood that agglutinated A blood and could itself be agglutinated by A blood, he labeled type B. Thus he had three types: A, B, and O. Blood group A carries antigen A and develops anti-B antibodies. Blood group B contains antigen B and develops anti-A antibodies. Group O contains

Blood plasma a clear liquid component of blood that carries the *red blood cells, white blood cells,* and *platelets.*

Red blood cells vertebrate blood cells (corpuscles) lacking nuclei and containing *hemoglobin.*

White blood cells (leukocytes) vertebrate blood cells lacking *hemoglobin.*

Platelets minute blood cells associated with clotting.

Serum the liquid remaining after blood has clotted.

Antigens any organic substances, recognized by the body as foreign, that stimulate the production of an *antibody.*

Antibodies proteins produced as a defense mechanism to attack foreign substances invading the body.

Blood groups groups of individuals whose blood can be mixed without *agglutination* (e.g., group A, B, O, or AB).

Agglutination the clumping of *red blood cells* as a result of the reaction of *antibodies* to an *antigen.*

no antigens but develops both antibodies. Group AB (discovered later) carries antigens A and B but produces neither antibody. Thus type AB people can receive A, B, or O blood, but types A and B can receive only their own groups and type O, and type O people can receive only type O blood. Type O people, then, are universal donors, while type AB people are universal recipients. (The distribution of types A and O throughout the world is shown in Figure 3.5.)

Discovery of the ABO blood groups was followed by the discovery of many others, such as the rhesus (Rh) system (1940), which is responsible for a disease that can kill newborn babies by destroying their blood cells. The cause of the disease is incompatibility between mother and child for the rhesus antigen D. If the mother is Rh-negative (lacks the D antigen) and the child is Rh-positive (possesses the D antigen), then the mother may form anti-D antibodies at the time of the child's birth, when some of the child's blood may enter the mother's bloodstream. In a second pregnancy, this antibody may pass through the placental barrier, coating and destroying the red blood cells of the child if it has Rh-positive blood. This second child will have acute anemia at birth (there is no problem if the second child has Rh-negative blood). The anemia can be treated only with extensive blood transfusions, but doctors can now prevent the disease by giving the mother an injection of powerful anti-D antibody after the birth of the first Rh-positive child. The injection destroys any Rh-positive red cells from the infant remaining in the mother's bloodstream and so inhibits future anti-D antibody production.

Genes and Disease

The study of blood groups, an important medical advance, led to an understanding of their role as adaptations to disease antigens. Carriers of blood allele B have some protection against infantile diarrhea; alleles A_1 and B both protect against plague, and allele O against bronchial pneumonia. (A_1 and A_2 both fall within blood type A.) Those with rhesus gene D are more susceptible to smallpox. Individuals with blood type A seem more susceptible to stomach cancer and pernicious anemia, and gastric and duodenal ulcers tend to affect persons who are homozygous for allele O. Thus, the frequency of blood-group genes may result from selection based on the infectious diseases to which different populations have been exposed. The relation of disease to human genetics is the subject of very active current research, following the mapping of the human genome.

One problem concerns the possibility of a connection between resistance to HIV (the AIDS virus) in some modern human populations and the exposure of these populations' ancestors to the bubonic or Black Plague back in the fourteenth century (Kolata, 1998). Roughly 10 percent of people of European descent, and particularly people from the more northerly parts of the continent, carry a gene that protects them from the AIDS virus. Although common in Europe, the HIV resistance gene becomes scarce around the Mediterranean, and it is absent in modern Africans, Asians, and Native Americans—a distribution that matches the geographic occurrence of the Black Death. Researchers are busy testing the hypothesis that a mutant gene appeared in Europe a few hundred years ago, became a stable part of the regional gene pool because it provided carriers with protection against the Black Plague, and by a stroke of luck also provides their modern descendants with protection against HIV. If future experiments verify the connection between Black Plague survival and HIV resistance, it will provide yet another example of how epidemic diseases can affect the course of human evolution.

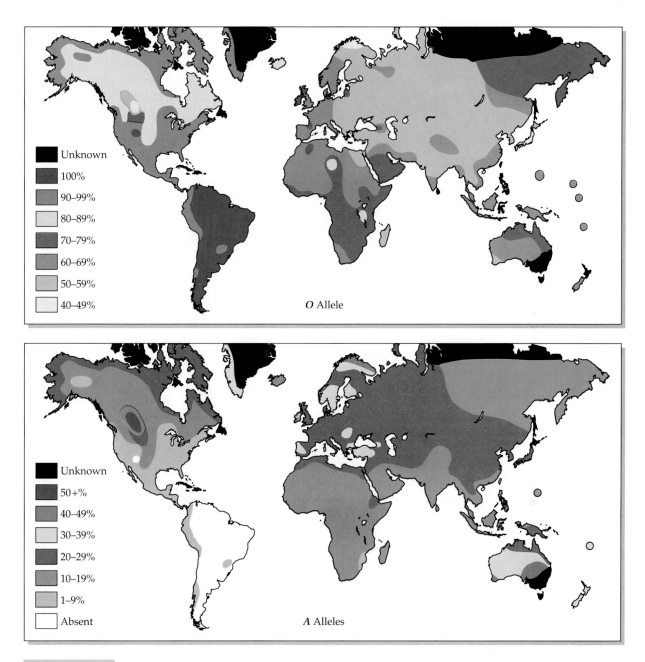

Figure 3.5

These maps give some idea of the distribution and frequency of the most common ABO blood group alleles, *O* and the two *A* alleles (*A₁* and *A₂*, combined for the lower map). This is an example of the kind of genetic data now available for human populations. The upper map charts the distribution of the predominant group O allele, which is common in the New World and especially in South America. The lower map plots the group A alleles, which are reasonably common in the Old World, but rare in many parts of the New World and virtually absent from South America. Remarkable concentrations of the group A alleles are found among the Scandinavian Lapps and the Blackfoot Indians of Western Canada. The latter is possibly the result of a local smallpox epidemic, introduced perhaps by Europeans, in which the alleles were favored.

Source: Data from Coon and Hunt, 1965.

The devastating spread of AIDS throughout sub-Saharan Africa could also generate an example of natural selection in action. Certain women in West Africa have not been infected with HIV despite repeated exposure to the virus over a long period of time. If phenotypes exist that carry HIV resistance or immunity, the genes that confer this trait would be powerfully selected for and would rapidly spread through the evolving population. In this instance, natural selection could also offer scientists a chance to generate a new vaccine.

For more on population genetics and human variation, visit our web site.

Discoveries and Mysteries

The Hardy–Weinberg Calculus for Gene Frequencies

The principle of natural selection describes population change in relation to environmental change. But most of the time populations are in stasis, with little or no change so long as the environment remains constant. How can it be determined whether a population is changing or is in equilibrium for specific traits?

In 1908, English mathematician G. H. Hardy and German physician W. Weinberg independently invented a formula for describing the proportions of any pair of alleles within a stable population. This formula allows scientists to calculate the expected frequencies of genotypes and phenotypes based on information about allele frequencies.

Here's how the formula works. Imagine a trait controlled by a single pair of alleles (A, a). If you symbolize the frequency of the dominant allele (A) as p and that of the recessive allele (a) as q, you get the equation $p + q = 1$, in which 1 represents 100 percent (the total proportion of alleles at any given locus). Now expand the equation to produce the frequencies of the three possible genotypes (AA, Aa, aa) that you would expect in a population at equilibrium:

$$(p + q)^2 = 1$$
$$p^2 + 2pq + q^2 = 1$$

Substituting the genotypes for their mathematical symbols, you get $AA + 2Aa + aa = 1$; that is, the frequencies of the homozygotes (both dominant and recessive) and the frequency of the heterozygotes ($2Aa$) together equal 100 percent of the population for the trait being measured. For single recessive traits, the frequency of q can be determined from the existence of individuals showing the rare (aa) phenotype, and once q is known, p can readily be calculated. Hardy and Weinberg discovered that—all other factors being equal—the allele frequencies p and q will reach equilibrium in one generation and will remain in equilibrium indefinitely until environmental factors change. Theoretically, equilibrium is achieved when there is random mating in a very large population, with no mutation, no selection, and no gene flow.

Thus, most importantly, the **Hardy–Weinberg theorem** can be used to predict *phenotypic* frequencies in a population and to calculate whether trait frequencies—and their underlying genotypes—are at or near equilibrium. This ability has important applications in predicting and possibly eliminating certain rare diseases, such as Tay–Sachs disease.

Hardy–Weinberg theorem
formula that predicts the extent and nature of genetic change in a *population.*

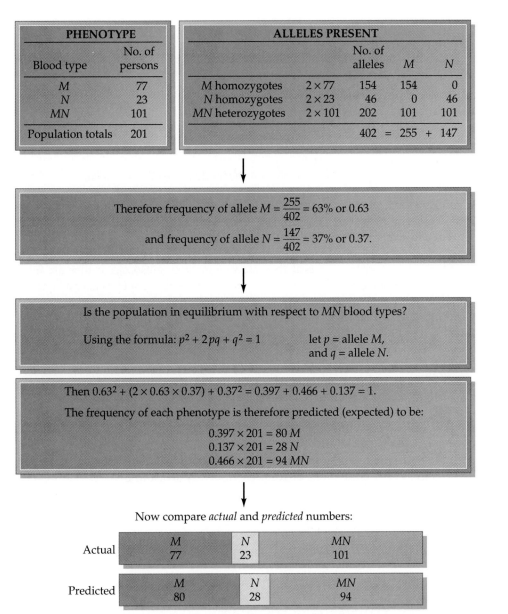

PHENOTYPE		ALLELES PRESENT				
Blood type	No. of persons			No. of alleles	M	N
M	77	M homozygotes	2×77	154	154	0
N	23	N homozygotes	2×23	46	0	46
MN	101	MN heterozygotes	2×101	202	101	101
Population totals	201			402	= 255	+ 147

Therefore frequency of allele $M = \dfrac{255}{402} = 63\%$ or 0.63

and frequency of allele $N = \dfrac{147}{402} = 37\%$ or 0.37.

Is the population in equilibrium with respect to MN blood types?

Using the formula: $p^2 + 2pq + q^2 = 1$ let p = allele M, and q = allele N.

Then $0.63^2 + (2 \times 0.63 \times 0.37) + 0.37^2 = 0.397 + 0.466 + 0.137 = 1$.

The frequency of each phenotype is therefore predicted (expected) to be:

$0.397 \times 201 = 80\ M$
$0.137 \times 201 = 28\ N$
$0.466 \times 201 = 94\ MN$

Now compare *actual* and *predicted* numbers:

	M	N	MN
Actual	77	23	101

	M	N	MN
Predicted	80	28	94

The population is in equilibrium.

Here we see the computation of frequencies of the *M* and *N* blood group genes among the Quinault Indians of Washington State. Genetic stability in these traits is indicated, because the observed frequencies are not significantly different from the predicted frequencies.

Most common in Jews of eastern European descent, Tay–Sachs sufferers experience nervous system degeneration, convulsions, and death at a young age. Although the frequency of Tay–Sachs disease varies strongly between populations, its global incidence is about 1 per 100,000 births, or 0.00001 (= q^2). The value of q is therefore 0.0032, making the frequency of the recessive Tay–Sachs allele 0.32 percent. From these figures

p can be calculated as 0.9968 and p^2 (homozygous dominants) as 99.36 percent of living humans. Finally, of critical importance in the development of programs for the prevention and cure of Tay–Sachs disease, the frequency of unafflicted carriers of the disease (the heterozygotes, $2pq$) can be calculated as 0.0064, or about 1 person in 157 worldwide.

Can Humans Be Classified into Races?

As you have seen, humans, like most animal species, vary anatomically and physiologically in relation to diverse geographical areas with diverse climates. Animal species typically show variation in size and appearance; that is, in superficial (surface) characteristics that respond rapidly to environmental differences. These variations are often described by zoologists as **races** if they are minor, or as subspecies if they are more striking. In the course of human evolution, populations of our species have adapted to just about every ecological zone on the surface of the earth, excluding Antarctica, and have evolved morphological and physiological adaptations to the temperature, solar radiation, humidity, vegetation, and so on of each zone. The degree of visible difference among members of *Homo sapiens* can be striking when we compare, say, Eskimos with sub-Saharan Africans. A zoologist from outer space might well conclude that humans consist of a number of geographic subspecies.

The problem of documenting and classifying human variation fell not to zoologists from Mars, however, but to naturalists and, later, anthropologists here on earth; and it seems fair to say that the whole process has been a struggle from beginning to end. For more than two hundred years, patterns of physical variation have been used by anthropologists (and also by nonspecialists, in the form of "folk concepts") to classify people into races. Typically, races have been viewed as divisions of *Homo sapiens* with two main attributes:

1. **Distinctive sets of physical traits.** Although virtually all racial classifications rest mainly on differences in skin color, other characteristics—nose, lip, and eye shapes, hair color and texture, facial shapes, and so forth—are typically presented as closely correlated with skin color variations.
2. **Distinctive geographic distributions.** Varying from relatively small areas to entire continents, racial distributions are generally described as they were in the days before sea voyages began to have a major influence on the spread of human populations; that is, before about 1500 AD. Since then, human populations have extended their ranges and overlapped, and gene flow (which was never fully blocked except in a few unusual cases of prolonged isolation on islands) has increased.

Early classifiers such as Carolus Linnaeus and the German physician J. F. Blumenbach (1752–1840) believed that racial differences were established by God during the creation of humans. Today, we view racial differences as a consequence of separate evolutionary adaptation to different environments. A typical classification scheme, recognizing the existence of nine geographical races prior to the mixing of the past five hundred years, is shown in Figure 3.6.

The traditional view of human races—as units that are strongly distinctive and thus easily identified, monolithic (showing only insignificant internal variability in traits), geographically separated, and having lengthy independent histories—held sway

Races divisions of a *species,* usually based on physical or behavioral differences and less well marked than subspecies. Many anthropologists reject the concept of biological races of living humans.

Figure 3.6

A polar-projection map showing the nine geographic races of humans envisioned by anthropologist Stanley Garn in 1965.

Source: From Garn, 1965.

for more than two hundred years. Recently, however, traditional racial classifications have begun to break down as information on human genetic variation has accumulated and analytical procedures have improved. The question now is whether or not race is useful or even valid as a biological concept. To this question many anthropologists say no (Littlefield et al., 1982; Shanklin, 1994; but see Gill, 1998). Arguments against the biological race concept rest on accumulating evidence that racial units are neither easily identified nor monolithic, and that racial differences actually account for only a small part of our species' overall genetic diversity.

Augmenting the problem of identifying races is the telling fact that anthropologists have never been able to agree on how human races should be defined. Are presumably diagnostic genetic or physical differences adequate? Is reproductive separation the most important criterion? How can these criteria apply today, given that human populations have spread and mixed so much in the last five hundred years? In addition to debating about which diagnostic tools to use, anthropologists have diverged on the appropriate level for racial subdivisions. Should local populations be recognized as microraces? Or should only large geographic races be named?

Collectively, these problems have led to a bewildering array of racial classifications. Harvard's Earnest Hooton, writing in 1946, recognized three primary races and twenty-one "sub-" or "composite" races. In 1950 Carlton Coon and his colleagues (Coon et al.,

1950) listed six primary races, and in 1965 Stanley Garn identified nine primary races and thirty-two "local" races! This level of disagreement among scientists suggests that there is no finite set of human races out there just waiting to be recognized and named. Rather, judgments about the identity, size, and diagnostic traits of human races are arbitrary and vary from one classifier to the next.

Are There Racial Traits?

Most present-day anthropologists have ceased to search for key "marker" traits that will yield a true or "natural" racial subdivision of humans. Marker traits do not work because of variation within populations and overlaps with other populations, and because marker traits do not correlate well with humans' other physical and genetic characteristics. Consider the familiar example of skin color. Four skin colors (black, white, yellow, red) have been used as markers for racial distinctions throughout human history. As you have seen, however, "black" people are native to many parts of the Eastern Hemisphere (e.g., Africa, South Asia, Australia) rather than to a single geographic homeland; also, "black" skin colors show extensive variation with several underlying color tones. Furthermore, skin shades grade to white or other nonblack colors at the boundaries of the various homelands; and people called "black" exhibit great variety in other characteristics, such as nose forms, hair forms, and blood types. The same results can be demonstrated for each of the other skin-color groupings. Therefore, we must challenge the old notion of historically distinct, monolithic, diagnostically different human races, regardless of how many traits we take into account (see Critical Thinking).

Race and Genetic Diversity

The subject of multivariate analyses brings us to a second major reason why most anthropologists now reject race as a valid biological concept among humans. Ironically, while these studies have failed to identify human races, they have succeeded brilliantly in the other direction: That is, multivariate investigations, particularly of genes, have provided seemingly unequivocal proof that human races do not exist in any biologically meaningful sense. Additional relevant evidence appeared in 1974 when Harvard biologist R. C. Lewontin published the results of a study of genetic diversity within and between several traditionally defined human races (Africans, Native Americans, Mongoloids, Caucasians, South Asian Aborigines, Australian Aborigines, and Oceanians). Lewontin's results, shown in Table 3.1, revealed that just over 85 percent of human genetic diversity, based on genes for physiological character traits, occurs between individuals belonging to the same population (generally, the same nation or tribe). An additional 8.3 percent of genetic variation is accounted for by differences between populations within the same traditional race (for example, between West Africans and Bantus). This leaves only 6.3 percent of genetic diversity accounted for by interracial differences! Thus, even if one is inclined to believe in the existence of biological races among humans, these data argue strongly that such entities make only a trivial contribution to genetic (and phenotypic) variation among humans. As one non-African geneticist is reported to have said, "There could possibly be more genetic differences between myself and my wife [a member of the same skin-color group] than there are between me and a Kalahari Bushman."

What conclusion, then, do most modern anthropologists reach concerning the question of biological races among living humans? Are we asked to deny the proof of our own eyes that people vary physically, sometimes remarkably so? No, of course not. Nonetheless, the majority of anthropologists—though by no means all—conclude that

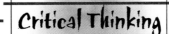

What Can Multivariate Analysis Tell Us about Racial Groupings?

If instead of using single marker traits we used **multivariate analysis,** studying many different characteristics simultaneously—a feat easily done today with computers—could we then divide humans into biologically meaningful and consistent groups? Take a look at the diagram on the left, which presents the results of a multivariate analysis of the occurrence of fifty-eight different human blood-group genes. Looking just at the first fork of the linkage tree, what two major groups of similar (and therefore probably related) populations are formed? In terms of blood factors, who are Europeans' closest relatives, Native Americans or Africans? How does this relatedness compare with other factors, such as skin color? What racial classifications might you propose on the basis of the blood-group data?

Now look at the other diagram, which presents a multivariate analysis of fifty-seven measurements taken on men's skulls. How would you describe the three main groups split out on the basis of these data? Which groups are most closely related to Africans now? How might you classify human races on the basis of this figure, and how would this classification differ from one based on blood groups? Which classification do you think is more accurate or real? What if sex differences in skull measurements changed the branching pattern; would this affect your confidence in multivariate proof of human races? And if blood factors and skull factors show no correlation to each other (show no concordance of occurrence) in human populations, what do these facts suggest about efforts to subdivide humanity into biological races?

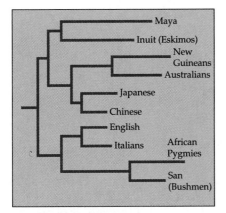

This diagram shows the linkages calculated between living human populations based on an analysis of fifty-eight different blood group genes. Note the association of Europeans with Africans and Australians with Asians.

Source: All data from Howells, 1992.

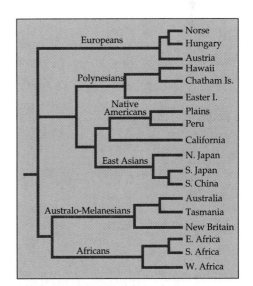

Here linkages are shown between living human populations based on an analysis of fifty-seven measurements of male skulls. Note the separation of Europeans from Africans and the link between the latter and Australo-Melanesians.

the human species cannot be broken down scientifically into monolithic races defined by regularly co-occurring trait clusters. To be sure, striking physical differences can be seen all around us—in skin color, facial features, hair form, and so forth—and they often give us clues to the place and population of a person's ancestry. They are striking and obvious precisely because they are superficial. Nonetheless, when we look beyond

Multivariate analysis method of analysis that makes it possible to compare two or more *populations* using a number of variable traits simultaneously.

Table 3.1

		PROPORTION		
Gene	**Total** $H_{species}$	**Within populations**	**Within races between populations**	**Between races**

Genetic Diversity in Humans

Analyses such as this one indicate that the vast majority of genetic diversity in humans exists *within* so-called races and not *between* them.

Gene	Total $H_{species}$	Within populations	Within races between populations	Between races
Hp	.994	.893	.051	.056
Ag	.994	.834	—	—
Lp	.639	.939	—	—
Xm	.869	.997	—	—
Ap	.989	.927	.062	.011
6PGD	.327	.875	.058	.067
PGM	.758	.942	.033	.025
Ak	.184	.848	.021	.131
Kidd	.977	.741	.211	.048
Duffy	.938	.636	.105	.259
Lewis	.994	.966	.032	.002
Kell	.189	.901	.073	.026
Lutheran	.153	.694	.214	.092
P	1.000	.949	.029	.022
MNS	1.746	.911	.041	.048
Rh	1.900	.674	.073	.253
ABO	1.241	.907	.063	.030
Mean		.854	.083	.063

our superficial differences to the genes that code for our traits, we are confronted by overwhelming genetic similarities. The research results are clear: Most human genetic diversity (in Lewontin's study, well over 90 percent) occurs *within* the traditional skin-color/geographic groupings, not *between* them. Stanford University geneticist Luca Cavalli-Sforza made the same point when he said, "It is because they are external that [so-called] racial differences strike us so forcibly, and we automatically assume that differences of similar magnitude exist below the surface, in the rest of our genetic makeup. This is simply not so: the remainder of our genetic makeup hardly differs at all" (Cavalli-Sforza and Cavalli-Sforza, 1995: 124). Anthropologist Jonathan Marks of Yale University delivers the message even more forcefully: "You may group humans into a small number of races if you want to, but you are denied biology as a support for it" (Marks, 1994: 35). It seems that in order to understand modern human variation, we must study individual traits, their genetic bases, and their evolutionary histories—not arbitrarily constructed biological races.

Ethnic and Other Social Groups

It would be a wonderful world indeed if anthropologists' repudiation of biological races could put an end to divisions between human populations and bring on an age of global unity. Such a world remains a utopian dream, however, because race *as a social construct* is alive and well in most modern cultures. This is undoubtedly linked to humans' tendency to focus on all sorts of differences between people and to divide the world into "we–they" groups. Grouping schemes based on real or imagined differences in behavior, customs, or genealogy (descent) result in the identification of **ethnic groups**. This term, which is much less emotionally charged than "race," is now commonly applied both to huge collections of people (e.g., Asian Americans) and to small populations (e.g., Lakota Sioux). Breaking free of our old fixation on physical differences is difficult, however, and people commonly take phenotype into consideration as they (consciously or unconsciously) make ethnic group distinctions.

Ethnic divisions may foster unity and pride within communities, may serve as the focal point for political solidarity, or may facilitate the preservation of a population's cultural heritage. On the other hand, when either the biological race concept or ethnic divisions are combined with another human tendency, our inclination toward **xenophobia**—fear and hatred of strangers or outsiders—all too often results in **racism**. *Racism* is defined here as the belief that human groups can be ranked as superior or inferior to one another and their members treated accordingly, and is responsible for a multitude of evils ranging from job discrimination to genocide (or, to use a recently created euphemism, *ethnic cleansing*).

A strongly held folk belief—one of the most divisive—is the notion that all other ethnic or racial groups are less intelligent than one's own. In fact, *there is simply no good evidence to support this belief.* Intelligence is such a broad concept that it is impossible to define and measure precisely. So-called IQ tests actually tell us little about intellectual differences between individuals even within the same culture, because a multitude of factors can influence test scores (e.g., genotype, educational history, and family background—particularly parents' socioeconomic status). Furthermore, since none of the IQ tests is culture-free (all operate through linguistic and other cultural modes not shared by all people), none can be used cross-culturally. It is hoped that by demonstrating that human races are basically the products of our imagination, modern anthropologists can begin to dismantle the myths on which racism is based.

Does Evolution Represent Progress?

For most educated people, including the vast majority of scientists, the fact of evolution cannot be denied. Evolutionists often differ considerably, however, in their interpretations of pattern and meaning in the history of life. Among the commonly asked interpretative questions are these: Has evolution shown any broad trends? Has evolution been moving life toward some identifiable goal? Is evolution progressive, producing ever better organisms over time? Interestingly, Charles Darwin would probably have answered "no" to most, if not all, of these questions. Darwin repeatedly expressed the view that natural selection works locally, producing a sequence of adaptive adjustments to changing local environments. Natural selection cannot operate beyond the local level to produce broad trends, thought Darwin, and thus he resisted the notion of progress in life's history. For many people, however, progress and evolution have become synonymous, and they argue that there have been broad increases—progressive trends—in variables such as animals' size and overall organic complexity (including intelligence) throughout life's history.

Unfortunately for believers in evolutionary progress, a close examination of the evidence fails to provide strong support for their position. First, on the issue of size,

Ethnic group a group of people perceived as sharing a common and distinctive culture.

Xenophobia fear and hatred of strangers or outsiders.

Racism the assumption of inherent superiority of certain *"races,"* and the consequent discrimination against others.

ASKING QUESTIONS

Why Are Humans So Prone to Xenophobia and Racism?

Why do we so easily develop attitudes of dislike and distrust toward people we classify—based on superficial traits—as different from ourselves? Answers to this question can be found in humans' sensory systems and in certain evolved ways of thinking and behaving.

First of all, we are overwhelmingly visual animals. Following the ancient anthropoid pattern, humans and prehumans have always relied for survival mainly on the evidence of their eyes, and consequently modern people are masters at noticing visual details. For our early ancestors, among the most important visual details were physical features of conspecifics. Visual clues gave our ancestors important information about group mates, kin relations, age, health, and reproductive condition that helped them make decisions about altruistic investments, mate selection, and alliances. Visual clues would also have allowed the identification of strangers,

a distinction that—judging from observations of monkeys and apes—often would have triggered a hostile reaction. Chimpanzees, for example, can be extremely aggressive toward neighboring communities and are capable of something approaching primitive warfare.

In humans' prehistoric past, when strangers may have spelled trouble more often than they do today, xenophobia could have been an adaptive emotional response. In our modern societies, however, where we are constantly encountering physically and ethnically diverse people, xenophobia has become maladaptive. Happily, because our behaviors are much more strongly shaped by learning than by genes, it should be possible for our species to remove the basis of xenophobia through determined education by parents, peers, and society. This change would lead us into a modern world that accepted and valued diversity.

---

tests of the idea that body size tends to increase in an animal lineage during its evolution have produced mixed results. This premise does not hold true for marine organisms, although fossil mammal species do show a tendency to increase about 9 percent in size over their immediate ancestors (Alroy, 1998). Interestingly, humans have shown a significant decrease in body size over the last 50,000 years (Ruff et al., 1997), a change that cuts against the grain of the general mammalian trend as well as of earlier human evolution. Second, on the issue of organic complexity, studies suggest that the occasional evolution of creatures with increased complexity was predictable from random change alone, given the utter simplicity of the earliest living creatures, the bacteria. That there has been no overall trend toward increased organic complexity is shown by the fact that bacteria are still the predominant form of life on earth.

Finally, concerning the evolution of intelligence, a widely accepted theory is that intelligence (and the correlated trait of brain enlargement) has evolved repeatedly among social animals as an adaptation for remembering and manipulating social relationships. Most mammals are social (that is, group-living) creatures, and this is particularly true for humans and our closest animal relatives, the primates (monkeys, apes, etc.). Therefore, humans' big brains—viewed against a background of big-brained mammalian and primate ancestors—become understandable as an extreme form of a common adaptation for life in a complex society (Dunbar 1992, 1998).

People who believe that humans are the acme of evolution usually find it hard to accept the notion that life wasn't moving from the start toward the production of our kind of creatures. For those who will see, however, the scientific evidence is clear: Like all living species, humans are the result of a series of (for us, happy) contingent events: Despite our many marvelous qualities, in the final analysis, we are the result of chance.

Thus, evolution cannot be described as progressive; the process is characterized by change, the sole result of which is survival. The success of a species can be measured in terms of its numbers, the gross weight of its biomass, its stability and longevity in time, its variety of adaptations, or its geographical range. We humans have a rapidly increasing population and biomass, yet these can hardly be called signs of progress, because these increases put the whole species in danger. Compared with the dinosaurs that ruled the world for more than 100 million years, we are merely upstarts and have no cause for self-congratulation on the basis of stability or longevity. We are a variable and widespread species, but that seems only to make the population explosion more dangerous, for there is now little natural habitat remaining for the survival of many of those other species with which we share the planet and upon which we depend. No, none of these characteristics constitutes evolutionary success for humanity. The dinosaurs appear to have done better, though extinction was their ultimate fate.

So in what way are we special? In what way could we be called the most successful and progressive species in the history of the planet? If we look at *Homo sapiens*, we see, for example, that the species is very complex (especially the nervous system) and is fully self-conscious (which is probably unique in the animal world). The species has also intentionally altered its environment in a drastic manner. But we cannot be sure that it is necessarily progressive to be complex, or to be self-conscious, or to alter the environment; any of these characteristics could prove disastrous to its possessor and so to humankind. But human history does exemplify one evolutionary trend that appears truly progressive: *An increase in the range and variety of adjustments that the organism is capable of making in response to its environment.* This is the secret of our adaptation.

To respond to the environment, animals require a range of sense organs, a powerful brain to process the sensory inputs, and efficient and effective mechanical systems to bring about a whole range of responsive behavior. In *Homo sapiens* we find a greater range of sensory input (we know more about our environment), more analytic processing of that input (a far more complex brain), and a greater range of motor outputs (i.e., of behavior and communication) than in any other species. This much lies in our biology; but our culture has taken this trend much, much farther. Microscopes, telescopes, a variety of sensors and amplifiers of many kinds have vastly increased the range of environmental inputs. Books and computers aid memory, analysis, and prediction. Transportation and tools of every description help us amplify our behavior and satisfy our needs with increasing success. It is in this sense that we are more complex and in this sense that we are more adaptable than other species. If we are more adaptable, we are more likely to survive, and maybe more likely to achieve long-term success. However, we still have some way to travel on the evolutionary journey before we can call ourselves, without qualification, a successful and progressive species.

Summary

This chapter has described some further evolutionary dynamics of populations: inclusive fitness, kin selection, and sexual selection. We have examined two kinds of speciation—cladogenesis and anagenesis—and the balancing phenomenon of extinction, which also occurs in two ways: through extinction of the lineage and through anagenesis.

Like all species the human species is variable, and humans show both anatomical and physiological variations. Anatomical variations such as skin color and hairiness are superficial adaptations to past climates but have given rise to xenophobia and racism. Among physiological variations the blood groups have been widely studied, and we now know that their pattern often is a response to different histories of disease in different regions.

The Hardy–Weinberg theorem is a valuable tool that can actually show the process of evolution happening by calculating changes in gene frequencies.

Race is an important topic that is now well understood. As multivariate analysis demonstrates, humans cannot be classified into biological races in any meaningful way; and traits cannot be used to define races. Prehistoric adaptations to community solidarity have left us with a hangover of xenophobia, but there is far more variation within races than between them. Evolution is in general not progressive, though some evolutionary lines have gained vastly in complexity. Our own special quality is to have an extraordinary ability to adapt to our environment (much of which is cultural), and this alone may result in some ultimate success for the human species.

Review Questions

1. What do we mean when we describe individual organisms as "fit" and populations as well adapted?

2. Why is the Hardy–Weinberg theorem of little use to paleoanthropologists, as opposed to population geneticists? What scientific advances might cause this situation to change?

3. What conditions would promote the production of a new species by phyletic transformation (anagenesis)? By cladogenesis?

4. What circumstances could result in the extinction of humans? Do you think this is a possibility in the near future?

5. Why do most modern anthropologists reject the notion of biological races of humans? What is greater, the amount of genetic and trait diversity *within* human geographic populations or *between* them?

Suggested Further Reading

Cavalli-Sforza, L. L., P. Menozzi, and A. Piazza. *The History and Geography of Human Genes.* Princeton University Press, 1994.
Lewontin, R. *Human Diversity.* Scientific American Library, 1982.
Raup, D. M. *Extinction: Bad Genes or Bad Luck?* W. W. Norton, 1991.
Shanklin, E. *Anthropology and Race.* Wadsworth, 1994.

Internet Resources

Conveniently access these and other links via our web site at **http://www.ablongman/anthro.**

An Introduction to Blood Groups
http://www.umds.ac.uk/tissue/bludgrps.html
This site provides a basic description of the ABO blood groups, with links to other blood systems.

Behavior and Speciation Mechanisms
http://bionet.ucsc.edu/people/barrylab/public html/classes/animal
behavior/SPECIATE.HTM
An introduction to the various ways new species originate, with numerous examples.

Ethnicity and Race
http://daphne.palomar.edu/ethnicity/default.htm
This site and the next provide information about physical and cultural diversity among modern people, as well as discussing the applicability of the biological race concept to humans.

Modern Human Variation
http://daphne.palomar.edu/vary/default.htm
(See the site above.)

The Extinction Files
http://www.bbc.co.uk/education/darwin/exfiles/massintro.htm
Information about the six major extinction events that have been documented in the fossil record.

Useful Search Terms:
ABO blood groups
extinction
Hardy–Weinberg
human races
human variation
speciation

Primate and Human Characteristics

Overview

Classification is central to biology, and Chapter 4 discusses the system of naming, invented by Linnaeus, together with three methods of classification: phenetic, phylogenetic, and cladistic. The chapter describes the Primate order, from the small prosimians to the giant gorillas, and considers primates' origins and characteristics. Then we turn to the human family, the Hominidae, with its own peculiar anatomical specializations: bipedalism, stereoscopic color vision, manipulative skills, and the relatively large and very significant brain. Finally, animal communication is distinguished from human speech, and animal protoculture is distinguished from human symbolic culture. These are the two traits that separate humans profoundly from our animal ancestors.

 Check our web site for additional information, photos, drawings, maps, and animations on topics in this chapter.

How Is Humankind Classified?

Humankind is biologically classified under the Latin name *Homo sapiens; Homo* means "man," and *sapiens* "wise." The human has been called the thinking animal. The human has also been labeled a tool-using animal, a social animal, a speaking animal, a political animal, and the animal that is aware of itself. We are all these things, and more.

The Latin name *Homo sapiens* was coined by the great Swedish biologist Carl von Linné (1707–1778) as part of his classification of all plants and animals. Though a practicing doctor for part of his life, Carolus Linnaeus (the Latinized form of his name, by which he is more commonly known) collected plants and animals in Europe and received specimens from collectors throughout the world. He used a binomial (two-name) system to label each one, choosing Latin for the names because it was a convenient international language. He published his system of names in his famous book *Systema Naturae,* which ran to twelve editions between 1735 and 1766.

Homo sapiens among living *primates,* the scientific name for modern humans; members of the *species* first appeared about 130,000 years ago.

Follow links at **http://www.ablongman/anthro** for additional resources in physical anthropology, primatology, biological anthropology, and paleoanthropology.

Linnaean Classification

Though the evolutionary relationships among different species were not understood, it was already clear to early biologists that some were more similar to one another than to others; they seemed to be created on the same general plan. Linnaeus grouped the similar species in classes and orders to form a hierarchic arrangement based on similarities of **morphology** and anatomy. **Linnaean classification** is still used, because the method has proved to be of immense value. An international system of nomenclature (the rules of naming) has been essential in the development of the biological sciences.

The theory of evolution changed the basis of the system, making it clear that the similarities seen by Linnaeus and others were in many cases the result not of divine creation but of evolutionary, or phylogenetic, relationships. Groups based on anatomical likeness often proved to share a common ancestor. Thus, the form of the system of classification remained, but its meaning altered to reflect the understanding of the process of natural selection and evolution.

Types of Taxonomy

Today classifications reflect the evolutionary process, so the **taxonomy** we use is a **phylogenetic classification.** In cases in which we lack knowledge of evolutionary relationships, classifications can be based only on similarities and differences between species; this approach is called a **phenetic classification** (Linnaeus's original system is an example). Phenetic and phylogenetic classifications provide two different ways of arranging the taxonomy of modern humans and the great apes: chimpanzees, bonobos, gorillas, and orangutans. The basis for each classification scheme is described below.

Phenetic Classification.   Phenetic classification schemes are based simply on overall morphological similarities and differences among organisms. For example, in a phenetic scheme humans are separated from the four ape species, which are clustered together. This arrangement reflects the fact that the apes share such traits as long arms and short legs, grasping feet, projecting canine teeth, and relatively small brains, while humans have short arms and long legs, nonprehensile feet, short canines, and enormous brains. See Figure 4.1 (top).

Phylogenetic Classification.   Phylogenetic or evolutionary systematists routinely place different weights on morphological traits, maintaining that some features are more useful than others in revealing evolutionary relationships. Also, evolutionary systematists do not feel constrained to place sister groups at the same taxonomic level. In this scheme, **sister groups** (groups that are given equal taxonomic rank) often are ranked differently, in a ranking that reflects different amounts of change from the common ancestral condition. Species that show extreme degrees of change from the ancestral condition often are described as having attained a new evolutionary **grade** compared to their near relatives. In the classification scheme favored in this book (Figure 4.1, bottom), humans are placed in a different evolutionary grade from the apes because of their enlarged skull and brain, skeletal adaptations for bipedalism, incisiform canines, a fully **opposable thumb,** and so on. In contrast, ape-grade creatures share smaller brain size, skeletons adapted for some combination of quadrupedalism and suspension, elongated canines, and imperfectly opposable thumbs.

The diagrams shown at the top and bottom of Figure 4.1 demonstrate the contrast between a phenetic classification of apes and humans and one that is phylogentic. A traditional phenetic arrangement based on overall morphological similarity separates

Morphology the study of the form of organisms, especially external appearance.

Linnaean classification hierarchical classificatory system using a binomial terminology and based on morphological similarities and differences.

Taxonomy classification of plants or animals according to their relationships, and the ordering of these groups into hierarchies; taxonomic levels are ranks within these classifications, such as *species* or *genus.*

Phylogenetic classification *taxonomy* that reflects evolutionary descent and is based on the pattern of primitive and derived traits; in traditional evolutionary classifications, traits may be given different weights.

Phenetic classification *taxonomy* based on physical similarities or differences between *species* or other taxa.

Sister groups in *cladistics,* the groups resulting from a dichotomous evolutionary branching event; initially ranked as sister *species,* these groups may change rank due to subsequent branching, but must always maintain the same *taxonomic level.*

Grade arbitrarily defined level of evolutionary development (e.g., *prosimians* vs. *anthropoids*).

Opposable thumb ability to hold thumb and index finger together in opposition, giving a *precision grip.*

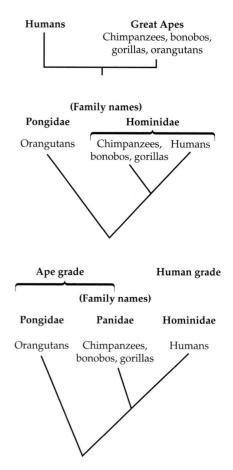

Figure 4.1

Top, a phenetic classification of the great apes and humans. Center, a cladistic classification. Bottom, a traditional phylogenetic classification of the same groups. Note how the groups are composed at family level in the different schemes.

these creatures into two groups: humans on the one hand and the four apes on the other. In contrast, when traits are treated in evolutionary terms and *primitive* features (ancestral and ancient traits, broadly shared) are distinguished from *derived* features (recent innovations, shared by a small number of close species), not only are the two evolutionary grades distinguished, but additionally orangutans are separated from the more closely related quartet of chimpanzees, bonobos, gorillas, and humans.

Cladistic Classification. Not all evolution-based classifications are alike, however. Because characteristics are weighted by the taxonomist, the phylogentic system appears to introduce a factor of subjectivity. For this reason biologists have tried to devise a way of classifying that does not involve weighting characters but treats all as of equal value. **Cladistic classification** is based on a phenetic system, but it does allow the taxonomist to deduce "trees" that indicate the degree of relatedness. Members of a related cluster or **clade** are recognized by the possession of shared derived traits. Sister groups are groups given equal taxonomic rank.

A look at the taxonomy of the great apes in Figure 4.1 shows how this system works. Among the numerous traits shared by humans and the African apes are the following features: a broad nasal opening, square orbits (eye sockets) that are often broader than they are high, and widely spaced eyes. In contrast, the orangutan is characterized by a nasal opening that is higher than it is broad, small oval orbits that are higher than they are broad, and closely spaced eyes. These and many other features support the conclu-

Cladistic classification evolution-based *taxonomy* that gives equal weight to traits and requires *sister groups* to be similarly ranked.

Clade members of an evolutionary cluster (e.g., sister species) plus their common ancestor.

sion that humans and the African apes share a recent common ancestor to the exclusion of orangutans. In cladistic classification the two sister groups (orangutan versus African apes plus humans) must have the same rank and thus are placed at the family level.

The close relationships of humans and the great apes with each other and with the lesser apes (the gibbons) has never been in question. The point was clearly made by T. H. Huxley in 1863 (Figure 1.3). In a phylogenetic classification all these species are placed in the superfamily **Hominoidea.** Linnaeus classified this **taxon,** or group, with the monkeys and some other animals under the name Primates. Linnaeus then grouped the primates with other furry, warm-blooded creatures that suckled their young in the class Mammalia. We mammals have backbones and share an even more general structure with animals such as fish and birds, with whom we constitute the subphylum Vertebrata. Humans' position in the grand hierarchy of the animal kingdom is summarized in Table 4.1.

Hominoidea superfamily of *Primates* that includes *apes* and humans.

Taxon group (*species, genus,* etc.) in a formal system of nomenclature.

Table 4.1

	Classification of Humankind		
Taxonomic Category	**Group Including Humans**	**Primary Characteristics**	**Members**
Kingdom	Animalia	Organisms that move, and that feed by the mouth	Vertebrates and all other animals (e.g., insects)
Phylum	Chordata	Organisms that possess a notochord at some stage of life	All animals with backbones, plus sea squirts, amphioxus, etc.
Subphylum	Vertebrata	Bilaterally symmetrical animals with flexible, internal segmented backbones and other bony skeletal structures	Mammals and all other animals with backbones (e.g., fish, birds, reptiles)
Class	Mammalia	Class of Vertebrates characterized by fur, warm blood, the feeding of live-born young by means of milk glands, and maternal care of young	Primates and all other warm-blooded furry animals that suckle their young (e.g., dogs, elephants)
Order	Primates	Order of Mammalia distinguished by grasping hands and feet, nails on digits, flexible limbs, and highly developed visual sense	Anthropoidea and Prosimii (lower primates; tarsiers, lorises, lemurs)
Suborder	Anthropoidea	Suborder of the Primates with evolved social organization, daytime activity, and notable development of intelligence and ability to learn	Hominoidea, Old World monkeys (e.g., rhesus), and New World monkeys (e.g., spider monkey)
Superfamily	Hominoidea	Superfamily of the Anthropoidea characterized by relatively erect posture, loss of tail, development of arms and shoulders for climbing, and (generally) five-cusped lower molars	Hominidae, Pongidae (orangutans), Panidae (chimpanzees, bonobos, gorillas), and Hylobatidae (gibbons, siamangs)
Family	Hominidae	Family of the Hominoidea characterized by bipedalism, canine reduction, and a trend toward brain enlargement	Genera *Homo, Australopithecus,* and *Paranthropus*
Genus	*Homo*	Genus of the Hominidae characterized by a relatively large brain, skillful hands, and evolving traditions of tool use, toolmaking, and culture	*Homo habilis, H. rudolfensis, H. erectus, H. heidelbergensis, H. neanderthalensis,* and *H. sapiens*
Species	*Homo sapiens*	Species of the genus *Homo* characterized by a large brain, an advanced culture, technology, and language and speech	Modern humans

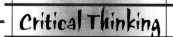

What Does It Matter How Primates Are Classified?

Paleoanthropologists are most interested in the classifications of apes, humans, and prehuman fossils. Collectively, these species provide an example of how taxonomic distinctions can either facilitate or impede effective communication among scientists. Traditionally, the living great apes have been arranged in one or more so-called zoological families (e.g., Pongidae, Panidae) and separated from humans and the extinct species that trace our descent from an ape ancestor. All species on the human lineage, in contrast, were classed in the family Hominidae. The living great apes were referred to as pongids or panids; humans and prehumans were called **hominids**. Under the more recent cladistic system, however, both the great apes *and* humans are placed in the family Hominidae and called hominids. To separate us and our prehuman forebears from the apes, cladists then created the zoological "tribe" Hominini and changed our common name to hominins.

The question then becomes this: Do the new taxonomy and set of common names represent an advance in knowledge sufficiently important to compensate for the confusion in communication that they will initially produce? Or, because most current paleoanthropologists are comfortable with the old classification and common names, because an enormous literature exists that uses these terms, and because arguments can be made against some of the procedural rules of cladistics, should we continue to use the old terms—over the strong objections of some—for the sake of uninterrupted communication? At present the paleoanthropological community is split over this issue, as it is with regard to the classification, characteristics, and boundaries of many individual species. Because taxonomy is as much about promoting effective communication among scientists as it is about reflecting nature, it sometimes seems as much art as science.

What Are the Characteristics of Primates?

The list of animals included in the order Primates has been modified substantially since Linnaeus's time. He had included the bats and *colugos* ("flying lemurs") as primates, but in 1873 these animals were removed by the English scientist St. George Mivart, who also provided a more detailed definition of the order. Mivart defined **primates** as placental mammals that possess the following traits: claws or nails; collarbones; eye sockets encircled by bone; **heterodont** dentition (specifically, having incisors, canines and molars); posterior lobe of the brain that includes a distinctive groove (the calcarine fissure); thumbs or big toes (or both) that are opposable; flat nail on big toe; caecum (pouchlike portion of the large intestine); pendulous penis; scrotal testes; and two nipples (Mivart, 1873).

Mivart also arranged the primates in the two suborders of the Prosimii (or "premonkeys") and the Anthropoidea (monkeys, apes, and humans).

During the twentieth century this anatomical definition of the primates was to some extent superseded by a definition based on the order's *evolutionary trends*. According to the English anatomist W. E. Le Gros Clark (as presented in his influential book *The Antecedents of Man* in 1959), primates are characterized by the retention of **generalized limbs** tipped with five grasping digits; the replacement of claws by nails; retention of a tail; expansion and elaboration of the brain; emphasis on vision; deemphasis on olfaction; fewer teeth than in the ancestral condition; retention of a simple molar cusp pattern; delayed maturation; and reduction of litter size to single infants (Table 4.2).

Today more than 200 species of animals living in Africa, Asia, and the tropical Americas (Figure 4.2) are recognized as primates, and the diversity within the order is

---

Hominids living or fossil members of the human family *Hominidae.*

Primates order of Mammals that includes *prosimians, monkeys, apes,* and humans.

Heterodont having several different types of teeth (incisors, canines, etc.), each with a different function.

Generalized limbs limbs that are not specialized in adaptation to a particular environment and allow a range of locomotion. Compare *specialization.*

Table 4.2

Major Characteristics of Primates

A. Characteristics Relating to Motor Adaptations

1. Retention of ancestral mammalian limb structure, with five digits on hands and feet, and free mobility of limbs with unfused radius and fibula.
2. Evolution of mobile, grasping digits, with sensitive friction pads and nails replacing claws. Palmar surfaces with friction skin.
3. Retention of tail as an organ of balance (except in humans, apes, and a few monkeys) and as a grasping "limb" in some New World monkeys.
4. Evolution of erect posture in many groups with extensive head rotation.
5. Evolution of nervous system to give precise and rapid control of musculature.

B. Characteristics Relating to Sensory Adaptations

1. Enlargement of the eyes, increasing amount of light and detail received.
2. Evolution of retina to increase sensitivity to low levels of illumination and to different frequencies (that is, to color).
3. Eyes that look forward with overlapping visual fields that give stereoscopic vision.
4. Enclosure of eyes in a bony ring in all living groups, and a full bony socket in anthropoids.
5. Reduction in olfactory apparatus, especially the snout.
6. Internal ear structures enclosed within petrosal bone.

C. Dental Characteristics

1. Simple cusp patterns in molar teeth.
2. In most groups, 32 or 36 teeth.

D. General Characteristics

1. Lengthened period of maturation, of infant dependency, and of gestation, compared with most mammals. Relatively long life span.
2. Low reproductive rate, especially among Hominoidea.
3. Relatively large and complex brain, especially those parts involved in vision, tactile inputs, muscle coordination and control, and memory and learning.

staggering. Primates range in size from the gorilla at an average weight of 258 pounds (117 kilograms) to the tiny Demidoff's dwarf bush baby at 2.3 ounces (65 grams). Some primates are exceedingly intelligent creatures; others seem to have run-of-the-mill mammalian intelligence. Most are very social creatures, but some live solitary lives; most are **diurnal,** being active in daytime, but some are **nocturnal.** Dietary specialties range from insects to fruit to leaves. In order to describe all of this diversity, a complex taxonomy based on the Linnaean classification system is required.

The Prosimians

Fossil discoveries indicate that the suborder **prosimians** first evolved at least 60 million years ago (mya) and that this suborder gave rise to the anthropoids some 10 to 15 million years later. Living prosimians shown in Figure 4.3 include the superfamilies Lemuroidea (the lemurs); Daubentonioidea (the aye-aye); Lorisoidea (lorises and bush babies); and, in most classifications, Tarsioidea (tarsiers).

Diurnal active during the day, as *apes,* humans and *monkeys* are.

Nocturnal active during the hours of darkness.

Prosimians a suborder of lower *primates* including lemurs and lorises.

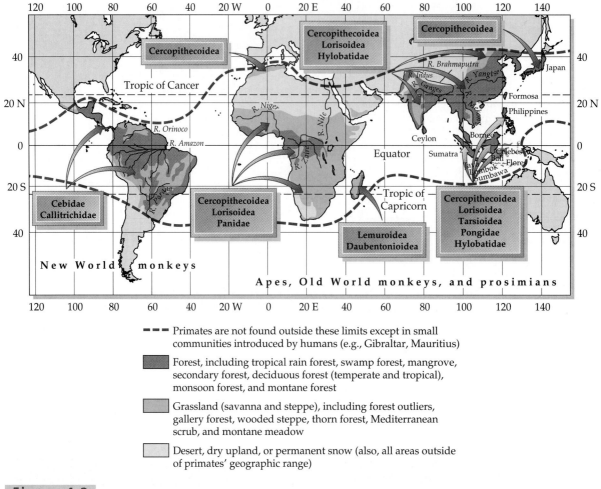

Figure 4.2

Worldwide distribution of nonhuman primates by superfamilies and families, and approximate distribution of principal regions of vegetation within the range of nonhuman primates.

Source: Adapted from Napier and Napier, 1967.

Prehensile adapted for grasping.

Specialization adaptation to a particular environment; may restrict an organism to that lifestyle.

Toothcomb a dental *specialization* of *prosimians* in which the lower front teeth are closely spaced and forwardly inclined.

Quadrupedal moving on all four limbs.

Today prosimians are found only in Africa, particularly on the island of Madagascar, and in Asia, and they are characterized by a suite of primitive traits (Table 4.3). In general, prosimians are small to medium-sized animals with a well-developed olfactory apparatus, visual features that suggest a current or ancestral adaptation to nocturnal activity, claws on some digits, **prehensile** hands and feet (but poor opposability of the thumb), and a dental **specialization** called a **toothcomb** that is used for both foraging and grooming. Prosimians are arboreal animals that move about the forests of the Old World in a **quadrupedal** fashion or by clinging and leaping from one vertical support to another. They are somewhat less social than anthropoids, insofar as many prosimians forage solitarily or form small social groups (often monogamous breeding units). Prosimians also are more committed to insect eating than the average anthropoid—the only specialized primate insectivores are prosimians—although all eat fruit as well.

The ring-tailed lemur (*Lemur catta*) is typical of the varied group of prosimian primates (Lemuroidea) from Madagascar. The most striking features of lemurs are large forward-looking eyes and long separated fingers and toes. The ring-tail stands about 15 inches (38 centimeters) high.

Three species of tarsier occur in Southeast Asia. With their enormous eyes, all are nocturnal, and most are forest living. Their diet consists mainly of insects. They weigh only just over 4 ounces (120 grams), but have long and powerful hind limbs adapted for leaping. They appear to have evolved little in 50 million years.

The loris (*Loris tardigradus*) represents another group of prosimians (Lorisoidea) found in Africa and Asia. Lorises are smaller than lemurs but have very large eyes adapted for hunting insects and other small creatures at night. Lorises' bodies are about 8–14 inches (20–36 centimeters) long.

Hands are among the most characteristic features of primates. One striking primate adaptation is that of nails replacing claws. Both humans and the bush baby (*Galago*), which is just over 6 inches (16 centimeters) long, carry flat nails on their hands.

Figure 4.3

Table 4.3

Distinguishing Characteristics of Prosimians
Long muzzle tipped with moist, sensitive, hairless nose or **rhinarium** (absent in tarsiers)
Tactile **vibrissae** (sensory whiskers)
Frenulum that anchors upper lip (frenulum absent in tarsiers)
Toilet claw on second toe
Postorbital bar only (tarsiers have a virtually complete eye socket)
Two-part frontal bones
Two-part mandible
Mandibular toothcomb in most species

Rhinarium the moist, hairless nose characteristic of all *prosimians* except *tarsiers*, and of most nonprimate mammals.

Vibrissae sensory whiskers present near the mouth of dogs and cats as well as *prosimians*.

Frenulum the flap of skin that tethers the upper lip to the jaw in *prosimians*. It is reduced or absent in *anthropoids* and *tarsiers*.

Orbit eye socket.

Postorbital bar a bar of bone running around the outside margin of the *orbits* of *prosimians*.

In several important ways, living prosimians bridge the anatomical gap between anthropoids and the primates' primitive mammalian ancestors. For one thing, most prosimians lack the extensive eye protection found in anthropoids (Figure 4.4). Monkeys and apes show a complete **orbit,** or bony eye socket, whereas all prosimians except tarsiers display only a **postorbital bar** of bone extending from brow to cheekbone. Second, although both prosimians and anthropoids show a reduction in total tooth count from the ancestral dental formula (Figure 4.5), several prosimian species have retained the ancient three-cusped pattern in their upper molar teeth. Third, prosimians still have claws on some digits, but anthropoids have nails (usually flat, but sometimes

Figure 4.4

Comparative skull anatomy reveals several distinctive primate traits. Lateral views of *(a)* a nonprimate mammal (hedgehog), *(b)* a lemuroid prosimian, and *(c)* an anthropoid (New World monkey). Skulls not drawn to scale.

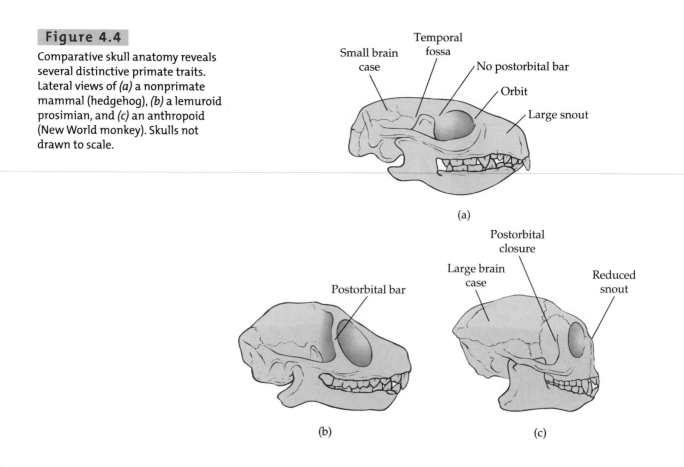

Primate type	Dental formula
Primitive mammals	$\dfrac{3143}{3143}$
Prosimians	
Lemuroidea	$\dfrac{2133}{2133}$
Lorisoidea	$\dfrac{2133}{2133}$
Daubentonioidea	$\dfrac{1013}{1003}$
Tarsioidea	$\dfrac{2133}{1133}$
Anthropoids	
Cebidae	$\dfrac{2133}{2133}$
Callitrichidae	$\dfrac{2132}{2132}$
Cercopithecoidea	$\dfrac{2123}{2123}$
Hominoidea	$\dfrac{2123}{2123}$

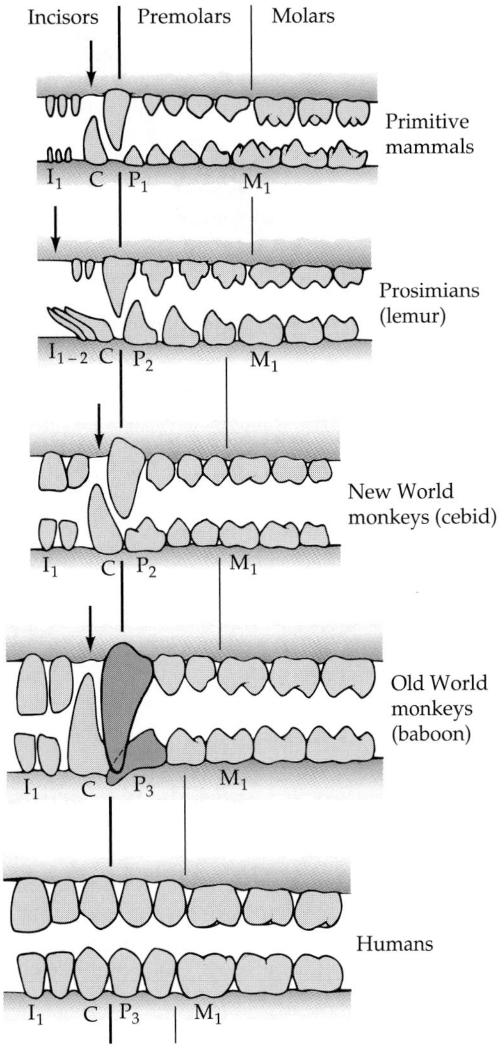

Incisors | Premolars | Molars

Primitive mammals — I_1 C P_1 M_1

Prosimians (lemur) — I_{1-2} C P_2 M_1

New World monkeys (cebid) — I_1 C P_2 M_1

Old World monkeys (baboon) — I_1 C P_3 M_1

Humans — I_1 C P_3 M_1

Figure 4.5

Dental formulae and lateral views of several primate varieties. Dental formulae represent half of the upper dentition over half of the lower and count (from left to right) numbers of permanent incisors, canines, premolars, and molars. In lemurs, I_{1-2} and the lower canines make up the toothcomb. Arrows mark the presence of a **diastema** or gap in the toothrow.

compressed and recurved into "pseudoclaws") on all digits. Fourth, prosimians show much greater divergence of the thumb than nonprimate mammals and have grasping hands and feet, yet they lack the full thumb opposability that characterizes some anthropoids (compare Figures 4.3 and 4.12).

Arboreal Theory.   Despite the retention of some ancestral traits, however, prosimians have the distinctive primate combination of increased emphasis on vision plus grasping hands and feet. This pattern was inherited by the anthropoids, in whom further modifications of the sensory system—such as a reduction of the olfactory sense—took place. But why did the combination of prehension and keen vision evolve among primates? There are two explanations: One, the **arboreal theory,** states that primate characteristics essentially are adaptations to life in the trees. This theory views grasping extremities as having evolved for safe and lively movement through the irregular arboreal habitat. Similarly, keen vision—particularly **stereoscopic vision,** with depth perception for judging distance before leaping—is thought to have evolved to facilitate

Diastema space in the toothrow that accommodates one or more teeth in the opposite jaw when the mouth is closed. (Plural: *diastemata*).

Arboreal theory theory stipulating that early *primates* evolved as an adaptation to tree living.

Stereoscopic vision vision produced by two eyes with overlapping fields, giving a sense of depth and distance; most highly evolved in hunting animals and *primates*.

Tree shrew
(primitive nonprimate mammal)

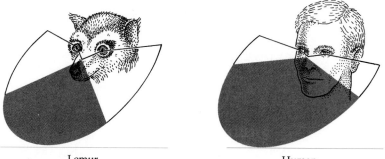

Lemur   Human

Figure 4.6

Stereoscopic vision is of great importance to primates, probably for both arboreal movement and foraging activities. The primitive tree shrew's eyes look sideways, and the visual
fields have small overlap; in the lemur the overlap is greater. In monkeys, apes, and
humans the extent of visual field overlap is great. Upright posture permits easy head
rotation, which compensates for the loss of backward vision. As the eyes moved to the
front of the face in primate evolution and vision became the primary sense, the sense of
smell became less important, the snout was reduced, and the face flattened. Heads not
drawn to scale.

arboreal locomotion and to locate food and danger. In stereoscopic vision the eyes are
on the front of the face and are close enough together to create an overlap of the left
and right visual fields. This overlap increases depth perception and visual distinction
at close range (Figure 4.6).

Visual Predation Theory.   The second explanation was developed in the 1970s by
American anthropologist Matt Cartmill (1974). Cartmill observed that arboreal life
does not necessarily select for primatelike characteristics. Many animals are perfectly
at home in the trees without looking or acting like primates. Gray squirrels are a good
example. Squirrels skitter about in the trees, moving through the branches and making leaps of many times their body length. Furthermore, they successfully locate food
and detect danger in the trees. Squirrels manage all this even though their hands and
feet are relatively nonprehensile and their eyes are much more wide-set and laterally
oriented than those of a primate, producing poorer depth perception.

Thus, the **visual predation theory** holds that grasping extremities and keen vision
originally evolved among the primates as adaptations for vision-directed predation

Visual predation theory
theory that early *primates*
evolved as an adaptation
to hunting insects by sight
and stealth.

on insects; such hunting is still common among some prosimians. In this theory de-emphasis on the sense of smell—and reduction of the olfactory apparatus—is viewed as the result of a migration of the eyes in an anterior (frontal) direction. This could have constricted the olfactory connections between the muzzle and the brain and thus could have led to a reduced sense of smell.

Follow-up studies identified several diurnal visual predators (e.g., mongooses and some tree shrews) that lack convergent, forward-looking eyes, suggesting that the first primates' nocturnal lifestyle also influenced their visual evolution. Because nocturnal creatures have wide-open irises, orbital convergence both enhances their stereoscopic, close-range depth perception *and* improves the clarity of objects directly in front of the eyes. (In diurnal creatures, even those with widely spaced eyes, blurred visual images are focused by constriction of the pupils.) Thus, it was not just hunting but nocturnal hunting that shaped the primates' traits.

A Present-Day Perspective. The two theories—arboreal and visual predation—actually are complementary, with the visual predation theory probably having more explanatory power. After all, the visual predators that were ancestral to primates probably were operating in a tree and bush habitat, and the adaptations for successful hunting would also have satisfied the requirements of arboreal locomotion. Until someone produces evidence to the contrary, it seems that we should tentatively conclude that all living primates—humans included—are the descendants of ancient prehensile, big-eyed, nocturnal insect hunters.

The Anthropoids: Monkeys, Apes, and Humans

The earliest anthropoid fossils are 45 to 50 million years old. From that early beginning, modification and diversification have led to the living representatives of this suborder, including the **Old World monkeys** (Cercopithecoidea), the **New World monkeys** (Ceboidea), and the apes and humans (Hominoidea)(see Figures 4.7 and 4.8).

As shown in Table 4.4, the **anthropoids** possess numerous anatomical differences from prosimians. Among anthropoids the sense of smell has been further reduced as the muzzle has been shortened and the rhinarium (the mammalian moist hairless nose) has been lost. The eyes of anthropoids are close together and directed forward, adapted for diurnal vision, and protected by complete bony sockets. With the exception of the tiny marmosets and tamarins of the New World, anthropoids have flat nails on all their digits rather than claws. The lower jaws of anthropoids are fused at the midline, and their front teeth are implanted vertically (no toothcomb). Finally, anthropoids show increases in the relative size and complexity of the brain. Monkeys, apes, and humans all have a larger and more complex **cerebral cortex** than prosimians, a characteristic related to increased intelligence.

For the purposes of further anatomical comparisons, anthropoids may be grouped into platyrrhines or catarrhines. **Platyrrhines** (the New World monkeys: superfamily Ceboidea) have round nostrils that are widely spaced and directed outward to the sides and have a total of twelve premolars in the adult dentition. **Catarrhines** (the Old World monkeys, apes, and humans: superfamilies Cercopithecoidea and Hominoidea) have compressed closely spaced and downward-facing nostrils, and only eight permanent premolars (see Figure 4.7).

This division of New World versus Old World anthropoids will be useful when we begin to interpret the primate fossil record (Chapter 6), but for now a convenient classification separates all monkeys (Old and New World varieties combined) from all

Old World monkeys *monkeys* inhabiting Africa and Eurasia.

New World monkeys *monkeys* inhabiting the Americas.

Anthropoids suborder of *Primates* that includes *monkeys, apes,* and humans.

Cerebral cortex deeply folded outer layer of the brain, largely responsible for memory and, in humans, reasoned behavior and abstract thought (also referred to as neocortex).

Platyrrhines an infraorder of the *anthropoids* that includes the *New World monkeys;* species have wide-spaced round nostrils.

Catarrhines an infraorder of the *anthropoids* that includes *Old World monkeys, apes,* and humans; species have close-spaced compressed nostrils.

Figure 4.7

Old World monkeys (top): a long-tailed macaque (left) and a mandrill (right), both primarily adapted to terrestrial quadrupedalism. New World monkeys, such as the spider monkey (bottom, left and right), are highly adapted to an arboreal life. Notice the long grasping tail in the New World monkey and its laterally opening nostrils. In contrast, the Old World monkeys' nostrils are downwardly directed.

Figure 4.8

Whereas the orangutan (upper left) and the gibbon (upper right) are still primarily arboreal, the gorilla (lower left) and the chimpanzee (lower right) have developed knuckle-walking as the form of locomotion most practical for their ground-based way of life.

Table 4.4

Distinguishing Characteristics of Anthropoidea
Reduced muzzle with a hairy nose (lack of rhinarium)
Lack of prominent whiskers
Reduced or absent frenulum
Nails (flat or modified) on all digits
Complete bony eye socket
Fused frontal bones
Fused mandible
Lack of toothcomb
Retina that includes a **fovea** (also present in tarsiers)
Cerebral cortex that includes a central sulcus
Generally, extensive thumb and big toe opposability

hominoids (apes and humans combined). Monkeys have long backs, narrow chests, laterally placed scapulae (shoulder blades), and a tail (Figure 4.9). Some ceboids have prehensile or grasping tails, but none of the cercopithecoids is so equipped. Monkeys also have a smaller range of motion at the shoulder than hominoids. These anatomical traits are correlated with habitual quadrupedal locomotion both in the trees and on the ground (Figure 4.9). Generally speaking, monkeys walk, run, and leap about on all fours. This is not to say that monkeys don't or can't do other things—some species do a good deal of hanging and swinging by their arms (or tail)—but the majority of species usually move about quadrupedally along the tops of branches.

The Hominoids: Apes and Humans

As outlined in Table 4.5, the anatomy of hominoids (apes and humans, members of the superfamily Hominoidea) differs significantly from that of monkeys. To start at the top, hominoids have larger brains than monkeys, and this larger brain size is correlated with new functional capabilities. Hominoids also have certain distinctive dental traits. Their lower molars show a characteristic arrangement of five cusps and grooves called the **Y–5 pattern**. Old World monkeys, in contrast, show a molar cusp pattern called **bilophodonty**: four cusps that are arranged in two pairs (front and rear), with each pair connected by a ridge of enamel (Figure 4.10).

With regard to **postcranial** anatomy, all hominoids have broad chests with dorsal scapulae; short, stiff backs; relatively long arms with mobile wrists, elbows, and shoulders; and no tail. These traits probably are adaptations for suspensory locomotion and posture (arm swinging or hanging), behaviors that are shared to some extent by all living apes, though not by humans.

Arboreal and Terrestrial Climbers. A closer look at the variety of hominoid locomotor patterns, and their associated anatomical variations, is instructive. Apes are built for a different mode of travel than that of monkeys. Apes have short, wide, shallow trunks and long, free-swinging arms that rotate at the shoulders. These adaptations allowed apes to reach out in all directions in the trees, climbing arm over arm. From their probable beginning as efficient climbers, the different families of apes have adapted in different ways. The gibbons and siamangs (Hylobatidae), although they climb much

Fovea an area of the *anthropoid* retina that allows extremely detailed vision.

Y–5 pattern an arrangement of the cusps and grooves of the lower molars that is characteristic of living *hominoids*.

Bilophodonty the molar cusp pattern of *Old World monkeys*, featuring four cusps arranged in front and rear pairs.

Postcranial behind the head (in quadrupeds) or below the head (in bipeds).

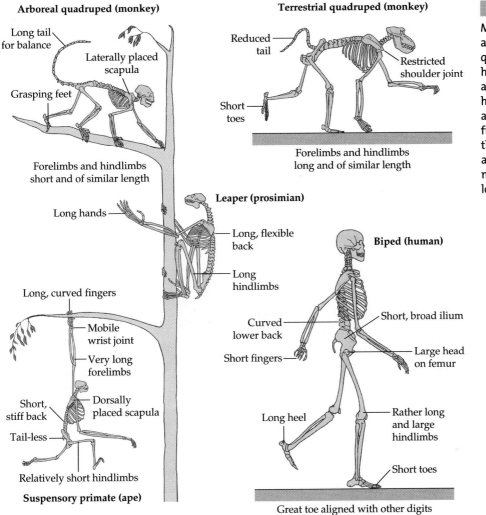

Arboreal quadruped (monkey)
Long tail for balance
Laterally placed scapula
Grasping feet
Forelimbs and hindlimbs short and of similar length
Long hands
Long, curved fingers
Mobile wrist joint
Very long forelimbs
Short, stiff back
Dorsally placed scapula
Tail-less
Relatively short hindlimbs
Suspensory primate (ape)

Terrestrial quadruped (monkey)
Reduced tail
Restricted shoulder joint
Short toes
Forelimbs and hindlimbs long and of similar length

Leaper (prosimian)
Long, flexible back
Long hindlimbs

Biped (human)
Short, broad ilium
Curved lower back
Large head on femur
Short fingers
Long heel
Rather long and large hindlimbs
Short toes
Great toe aligned with other digits

Figure 4.9

Monkeys are generally arboreal or terrestrial quadrupeds, whereas hominoids engage in arboreal suspensory behavior, knuckle-walking, and bipedalism. This figure shows some of the anatomical features associated with each main type of primate locomotion.

Table 4.5

Distinguishing Characteristics of Hominoidea
Lack of tail
Broad chest
Shortened lower back
Dorsally placed scapulae (shoulder blades)
Great mobility at shoulders, elbows, and wrists
Higher ratio of brain size to body size than in other primates
Increased complexity of folding of cerebral cortex
Y–5 cusp pattern of lower molars

Figure 4.10

The cusp patterns of the lower molars enable us to distinguish apes and monkeys with ease. Old World monkeys show four paired cusps (the bilophodont pattern); front and rear cusps are clearly seen in a side view. In contrast, humans are relatively difficult to distinguish from apes on the basis of the molar teeth: Both have five cusps following a Y–5 pattern. In some human lower molars, however, the fifth cusp has been lost, and it is commonly much reduced.

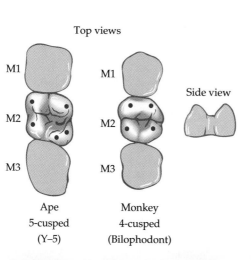

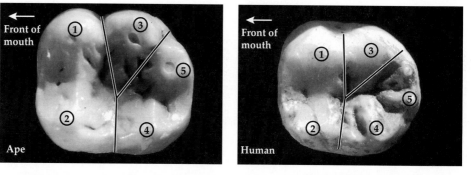

Brachiation an arboreal locomotor pattern featuring manual swinging from branch to branch.

of the time, especially when feeding, have evolved very long arms and hands and are specialized for the horizontal arm-over-arm locomotion called **brachiation.** Swinging under the branches through the treetops, often with their legs tucked up under their bodies, they can travel with considerable speed and extraordinary grace (Figure 4.8).

The orangutan (*Pongo*) moves steadily, climbing through the trees with all four limbs. So flexible are its shoulder and hip joints that its legs are like arms in use: The animal almost appears to be four-armed and four-handed (Figure 4.8). On the ground the orangutan moves quadrupedally with clenched fists and feet, though it occasionally walks on the palms of its hands. Both the gibbons and the orangutans are fully adapted to arboreal life, however, and show no specific terrestrial adaptations.

The African apes (family Panidae), however, do show terrestrial adaptations, and the larger species, especially the mountain gorilla, have almost deserted the trees for the ground, though they still will sleep in trees. Although the smaller chimpanzees are good climbers, all species of panids are adapted to terrestrial quadrupedalism, and they walk on the soles of their feet and the knuckles of their hands. The terrestrial skeletal adaptations are seen in the bones of their wrists and hands, which are modified to support the weight of the animals on their knuckles—on the second phalanx from the tip of the finger (Figure 4.8). Here, normal hairy skin is replaced by hairless friction skin such as we find on the palms of our hands and the soles of our feet.

Thus, the living apes, sharing a common ancestor that was an arboreal climber with a reduction in the tail, have each in their own way modified this original locomotor adaptation together with their skeleton and musculature. The tail was lost because an organ that balances and adjusts the aerodynamics of a leaping animal is not advantageous for a climber. Human ancestors have taken a fourth route—to terrestrial bipedalism. Although we are still quite able as climbers, our lower limbs have undergone profound changes in adaptation to **bipedal** (two-legged) walking on the ground.

The Anatomy of Upright Posture.   The adaptation that gave the apes the ability to climb with their arms and distribute their weight among several branches provided them with an opportunity for increased size. What advantage did the apes win by growing bigger? There was, of course, the competitive advantage that any big animal has over a smaller one when it comes to eating or being eaten. But there is also an extended life span (Table 4.6). Big animals tend to live longer, and their rate of metabolism is slower than that of small animals: Their internal organs simply do not have to work so hard and therefore do not wear out as fast.

Any useful change often begets more change along the same line of development. Climbing prompted a series of further changes in the apes that altered the primate anatomy, providing the potential on the one hand for the development of bipedal and tool-using humans and on the other hand for the specialized adaptations of the modern anthropoid apes. As part of their adaptations for arboreal movement, the apes acquired a whole new complex of characteristics in their shoulders, elbows, and wrists that combined to make their arm movements much more flexible. Apes can swing their arms out in a wide circle from their shoulders. An ape can hang from a branch by one hand and rotate its body completely around, thanks to the flexibility of its arm and wrist joints. Ultimately changes that arose from climbing affected the whole of the apes' upper bodies, giving them their characteristic short, relatively inflexible spine; the wide, shallow trunk with its resultant different arrangement of the internal organs; and a pelvis splayed out to provide additional room for the attachment of muscles for climbing and terrestrial locomotion.

The results of the apes' evolutionary shift from quadrupedalism to climbing and brachiation are profoundly important. If an animal evolves a more upright posture and arm flexibility, it can reach farther and grasp, pluck, hold, examine, and carry with greater ease. The more often a hand performs these acts, the more dexterous it beomes. Despite their short thumbs, chimpanzees have the manual dexterity to strip the leaves from a twig (in other words, to make an implement) and to insert that twig deftly into

Bipedal moving erect on the hind limbs only.

Table 4.6

Hominoid Comparative Anatomy: Size and Longevity						
Trait	Humans (*Homo sapiens*)	Chimps (*Pan troglodytes*)	Bonobos (*Pan paniscus*)	Gorillas (*Gorilla gorilla*)	Orangutans (*Pongo pygmaeus*)	Gibbons (*Hyblobates species*)
Adult body weight: F–M range	100 – 200 lb. (40–70 kg.)	73–132 lb. (33–60 kg.)	73–99 lb. (33–45 kg.)	159–386 lb. (72–175 kg.)	82–179 lb. (37–81 kg.)	11–24 lb. (5–11 kg.)
F body weight as a percentage of M weight	81	78	73	51	46	94
Life span	75 yrs.	>50 yrs.	>50 yrs.(?)	>50 yrs.	>55 yrs.	>30 yrs.(?)

Sources: Data from Fleagle, 1988; Napier and Napier, 1985.

a small hole in a termite mound so that they can lick off the termites that cling to the twig when it is pulled out. This remarkable act of food gathering requires not only careful manipulation but also intelligence. Thus, increased dependence on the hands has an evolutionary effect on the brain. Apes are, as a group, more intelligent than monkeys, whose hands are dexterous enough, but whose quadrupedal way of life limits the use of hands and thus limits the feedback that hand use has on the evolution of the brain.

For more on primate classification and characteristics, visit our web site.

How Do Humans Differ from Apes?

In the traditional phylogenetic classification used in this book, humans are the only living representatives of the primate family **Hominidae;** that is, the only living hominids. An abbreviated list of hominid traits is given in Table 4.7, but this list provides a most incomplete description of the attributes and abilities of modern people. What is it that makes humans different from the other primates? From among all the physical traits that separate humans from all other animals, four have overwhelming significance. The first three are a skeleton adapted for erect bipedalism (upright walking; Figure 4.9); eyes capable of sharp, three-dimensional vision in color; and hands that can both grip powerfully and manipulate things nimbly. These features are found in some degree in many primates; it is their elaboration and combination that distinguishes us. Controlling and making use of this equipment is humans' fourth significant trait: a complex brain with the capacity for rational thought that, with the body, makes possible that other most human of all our abilities—speech.

Bipedalism

The four distinguishing attributes uniquely combined in humans interact with one another. It is impossible to say that one led to the next, or that one is necessarily more important than the others. Each reinforces the others and makes improvements in them possible. Nevertheless, one attribute stands out simply because it is so conspicuous: upright walking. It is a remarkably effective method of locomotion, and no animal can use it as consistently as humans can.

For all its apparent simplicity, walking is an adaptation as specialized as flying is to a bat or swimming is to a seal. True, humans are not the only animals able to stand

Hominidae the taxonomic family that includes *Homo sapiens* and ancestral species.

Table 4.7

Distinguishing Characteristics of Hominidae
Reduced canine length
Nonprehensile big toes
Pelvis and legs reflecting habitual bipedalism (short, wide iliac blades; enlarged iliac spines; close-knee stance)
Extreme brain enlargement and elaboration

on their hind legs; birds, bears, and several other primates occasionally do so. But with the exception of a few flightless birds such as the ostrich, humans are the only animals that depend exclusively on two legs for locomotion. Using two legs, a human has the endurance to outrun a deer and can carry heavier loads, pound for pound of body weight, than a donkey. Only humans can swim a mile, walk several miles, and then climb a tree. Hominid bipedalism is specialized, yet it allows extraordinary versatility in locomotion.

The simple stride is at once the most useful and the most peculiarly human way of getting from one place to another. Probably evolved on the African grassland, or **savanna,** where our early ancestors often covered many miles in a day's food gathering or scavenging, the long, free-swinging stride has taken us to every corner of the earth. Striding is no minor accomplishment. When compared with the way four-legged animals get about, human walking turns out to be a surprisingly complex feat. "Without split-second timing," said John Napier, a British authority on primates, "man would fall flat on his face; in fact with each step he takes, he teeters on the edge of catastrophe"(1970: 165). Human walking is actually a balancing act in which the muscles of the feet, legs, hips, and back are alternately contracted and relaxed according to synchronized orders from the brain and the spinal cord.

The Anatomy of Walking.   As Huxley showed in 1863, the human skeleton is closer in form to that of the African great apes than to that of any other animal. There are nevertheless striking differences between the human and the African ape skeletons— differences almost entirely due to the evolution among hominids of bipedal walking and among apes of quadrupedal knuckle-walking (Figure 4.11; see also Table 4.8). The human foot has lost the ability to grip with the big toe, and the toe itself has become long and robust, forming the ball of the foot—an essential pivot for the act of walking. Human arms are short and legs long, in relation to the length of the trunk; the apes have relatively long arms and short legs, indicating that the arms are more important in locomotion. The human knee has been modified for the transmission of weight and can be locked when extended. Fundamental changes have occurred in the pelvis as well. Compared to apes, our pelvis is shorter (a change that improved bipedal balance) and has a broader blade or *ilium* (giving greater leverage to the muscles that hold the body erect). Additionally, our hip sockets have increased in relative size to match the greater weight they transmit compared to apes. Almost every bone in the body reflects the remarkable evolution of humans' and apes' distinctly different kinds of posture and locomotion.

Disadvantages of Being Bipedal.   Balanced bipedalism is uniquely human and strangely beautiful in its sheer efficiency and its superb adaptation of bone and muscle, brain and nerve, to the tricky problem of moving about on two limbs rather than four. Our adaptations for bipedalism have not been perfected, however. A list of human imperfections related to the switch from quadrupedalism to bipedalism reveals problems that natural selection has not fully corrected (Price, 1996).

First, as an adaptation for a fully upright and balanced stance, humans evolved a strong curvature in the small of the back. The curved shape increases pressure on the lower back, which has to carry the full weight of the upper body. Greater vulnerability to painful conditions such as pulled muscles, slipped discs, lumbago (rheumatism), and scoliosis (lateral curvature of the spine) is the result. Second, expanding brain size in our species has resulted in an increase in the size of a baby's head at birth. Women's average pelvic size has not been able to keep up, however, because pelvic width

Savanna tropical or subtropical grassland, often with scattered trees (woodland savanna).

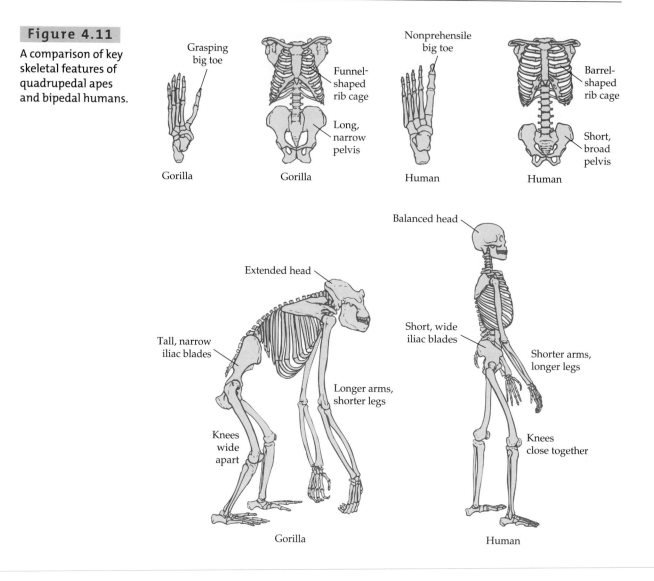

Figure 4.11

A comparison of key skeletal features of quadrupedal apes and bipedal humans.

is constrained by the biomechanical requirements of bipedalism. The ensuing mismatch—newborn head lengths that are slightly bigger than mothers' pelvic widths—has resulted in deliveries that are more difficult than those of other hominoids. Third, humans' upright posture puts much more pressure on the muscles of the lower abdominal wall than is true for quadrupeds; as a result, we commonly rupture those muscles (producing hernias) during heavy lifting or sometimes even as the result of vigorous coughing. Fourth, because the human heart is so far above the ground, the blood can have a hard time overcoming the pull of gravity to make the return trip from the feet. A result: distended and swollen varicose veins, particularly in older people. Fifth, humans' common complaint of hemorrhoids is related partly to our upright posture, which brings extra pressure to bear on the blood vessels supplying the large intestine's lower end. Finally, bipedalism puts the full weight of the body on the feet alone (as opposed to quadrupeds' hands *and* feet). In the course of a human lifetime, this can result in painful calluses and fallen arches (flat feet), conditions that can be exacerbated by poorly designed or ill-fitting shoes.

Table 4.8

Hominoid Comparative Anatomy: Limbs and Hips						
Trait	Humans	Chimpanzees	Bonobos	Gorillas	Orangutans	Gibbons
Arms as % of body weight[a]	8	16	16	?	18	20
Arm length × 100 divided by trunk length[a]	148	172	?	172	200	238
Legs as % of body weight[b]	30	18	24	?	18	18
Leg length × 100 divided by trunk length[b]	169	127	?	124	116	140
Ilium width × 100 divided by ilium length	126	66	?	92	74	49
Width of hip socket × 100 divided by ilium length	30	12	?	15	14	11

[a]Note that humans' arms are lighter and shorter than apes' arms.
[b]Humans' legs are heavier and longer than apes' legs.

Sources: Data from Aiello and Dean, 1990; Schultz, 1968.

The point is that natural selection does not necessarily generate perfection in any trait. If a species survives, natural selection has perpetuated the traits required for survival and reproduction—nothing more.

Color Vision and Depth Perception

Why is it so important to human evolution that we stand erect and walk on two legs? Part of the answer has to do with the human head. The head is where the eyes are, and the taller an animal stands, the more it sees. A dog running through tall grass is forced to leap into the air time and again to get its bearings; and even on a smooth surface where no obstacles obstruct vision, the advantage of height is marked. Eyes that are 2 feet (0.6 meters) above ground level can detect low objects about 6 miles (almost 10 kilometers) away; eyes 5 feet (1.5 meters) above the ground can see 9 miles (14 kilometers) farther.

The advantage of height is especially important because vision is the most important of our five major senses. Scientists estimate that some 90 percent of the information stored in the brain arrives there through the agency of the eyes. Human eyes are attuned precisely to human needs. Most important, humans and their nearest primate relatives have the special combination of full stereoscopic vision (Figure 4.6) and color vision. Human eyes, placed at the front of the head rather than at the sides, can focus together on an object so that it is perceived as a single three-dimensional image in the brain. And within this image, color vision enables us to pick out details by hue as well as by form, relationship, and brightness.

Taken together, color vision and depth perception bring us enormous advantages over most other animals, the majority of which either are color-blind or have a relatively poor capacity to judge visual distances and to focus in fine detail on particular objects. Though it has stereoscopic vision, a dog sees, when it looks out over an open field, little more than what a black-and-white movie might show, and the dog's distance focus is limited. The dog is unlikely to spot a rabbit in the field unless the rabbit moves—one reason rabbits and similar prey react to noises by freezing, which conceals them from their enemies. Human hunters, on the other hand, can scan a scene from their feet to the horizon in a few seconds by focusing sharply and selectively on a succession of images. And they see more images than any dog does because their eyes are raised at least 3 feet (almost 1 meter) higher above the ground and their vision is in color.

Manipulation

Humans stand up partly to see and partly because this posture frees their arms—and particularly their hands—for uses other than locomotion. Hands are free to grab, carry, and manipulate. Not needing hands for support, humans have been able to use them for complicated and creative tasks. With twenty-five joints and fifty-eight distinctly different motions, the human hand is one of the most advanced mechanisms produced by nature. Imagine a single tool that can meet the demands of tasks as varied as gripping a hammer, playing a violin, wringing out a towel, holding a pencil, gesturing, and simply touching and feeling.

Furthermore, although the hand itself is a marvelous tool, it is used to full value only when it manipulates other tools. This capacity is a benefit of upright walking. With our erect posture, our hands are free; with hands free, we can use tools; with tools, we can get food more easily and exploit the environment in other ways to ensure our survival. Humans are not the only animals that use tools, but we are the only ones that have become *dependent* on tools.

There are two distinct ways of holding and using tools: the **power grip** and the **precision grip,** as John Napier termed them (1962). Human infants and children begin with the power grip and progress to the precision grip. Think of how a child holds a spoon: first in the power grip, in its fist or between its fingers and palm, and later between the tips of the thumb and the first two fingers, in the precision grip. All primates have the power grip. It is the way they get firm hold of a tree branch. But only catarrhine primates have thumbs that are long enough or flexible enough to be completely opposable through rotation at the wrist, able to reach to the tips of all the other fingers and thus provide some degree of precision gripping. Apes and Old World monkeys differ in their grips, however—and, unexpectedly, the monkeys are somewhat more like humans. As an adaptation for arboreal arm swinging and arm hanging, apes have evolved greatly elongated fingers, exclusive of the thumb (see the hand length index in Table 4.9). Apes' thumbs are relatively quite short and, despite their potential full opposability, usually produce only an impaired precision grip (Figure 4.12). Humans' long, fully opposable thumbs and the independent control of our fingers make possible nearly all the movements necessary to handle tools, to make clothing, to write with a pencil, to play a flute.

But the fine precision grip of humans would be a much less extraordinary adaptation without the complex brain that coordinates and directs its use. In the human lineage, manipulation, tool use, and the brain may have developed together. The hand carries out some of the most critical and complex orders of the brain, and as the hand grew more skillful so did the brain.

Power grip a grip involving all fingers of the hand equally, as in grasping a baseball.

Precision grip a grip that involves opposing the tip of the thumb to the tips of the other fingers, allowing fine control of small objects.

Table 4.9

Hominoid Comparative Anatomy: Hands						
Trait	Humans	Chimpanzees	Bonobos	Gorillas	Orangutans	Gibbons
Hand length × 100 divided by trunk length[a]	37	49	?	40	53	55
Thumb length × 100 divided by index finger length[a]	65	43	?	47	40	46

[a]Note that humans have relatively short hands, but long thumbs.

Sources: Data from Napier, 1970; Schultz, 1968, 1969.

Changes in the Brain

The human brain is not much to look at. On the dissecting table, it is a pinkish-gray mass, moist and rubbery to the touch. An ape's brain does not look very different. But there is a difference, and it is crucial. It lies in the extent of the gray layer called the **cortex,** the outer layer of the largest part of the brain, or **cerebrum.** The cortex, scientists now know, plays the major role in reasoned behavior, memory, and abstract thought—and also supervises the delicate and accurate muscular movements that control the precision

Chimpanzee   Human

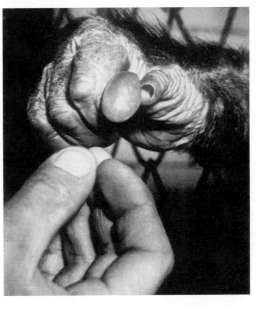

Figure 4.12

Though superficially like a human hand, the hand of a chimpanzee has a relatively short thumb and less independent control of the fingers. As the photograph shows, when the chimpanzee picks up an object between finger and thumb, it does not fully oppose the tip of the thumb to the tips of the fingers as do humans. Thus, compared to humans (and Old World monkeys), the ape's precision grip is somewhat impaired.

Cortex *see* Cerebral cortex.

Cerebrum the large anterior part of the brain.

ASKING QUESTIONS

What's So Special about Brain Size in Humans?

A calculus for comparing relative brain sizes is the **encephalization quotient (EQ),** a measure that relates the actual brain size of a species to the brain size expected for a typical mammal of the same body weight (Jerison, 1973). By definition an average mammal has an EQ of 1.0. If the relative brain size of a species is smaller than that of an average mammal, as in insectivores and rodents, the EQ value is less than 1.0; if the relative brain size is larger than the average, as among carnivores and prosimians, the EQ is more than 1.0. Compare these EQ value ranges and means (Aiello and Dean, 1990; Jerison, 1973). What is distinctive about the average EQ of humans?

SPECIES	EQ
Insectivores	0.2–0.9 (range)
Rodents	0.2–1.2 (range)
Ungulates	0.4–1.7 (range)
Carnivores	0.4–1.7 (range)
Prosimians	0.8–1.9 (range)
Chimpanzees	3.0 (mean)
Gorillas	1.6 (mean)
Orangutans	2.4 (mean)
Gibbons	2.6 (mean)
Humans	7.2 (mean)

EQ compares actual and expected brain size while controlling for the effects of body size. In the following table, do you see relationships between actual brain size and encephalization quotient?

Hominoid Comparative Anatomy: Brains		
	Brain size (sexes averaged)	Encephalization quotient (EQ)
Humans	1,330 cc	7.2
Chimpanzees	383 cc	3.0
Bonobos	?	?
Gorillas	505 cc	1.6
Orangutans	377 cc	2.4
Gibbons	103 cc	2.6

Sources: Data from Aiello and Dean, 1990; Schultz, 1969.

What happens if you simply compare actual brain weight to actual body weight? In terms of this ratio, where do humans fall in the following table?

Ratio of Weight of Brain to Weight of Body in Certain Mammals	
Mammals	Brain–Body Ratio
New World, squirrel monkey	1:12
New World, tamarin	1:19
Porpoise (dolphin)	1:38
Higher primates	
Humankind	1:45
Old World monkey (*Macaca*)	1:170
Gorilla	1:200
Elephant	1:600
Sperm whale	1:10,000

Source: From Cobb, 1965, pp. 551–561.

Notice that humans do not fall at the top of the list; those positions are occupied by two small New World monkeys. Actually, this is not surprising, because a fact of brain development is that small animals within an order have relatively larger brains than large species in the order. For the same reason, large animals within an order have relatively smaller brains. Thus, elephants and whales have the largest brains of any living animals (about 4,000 cc and 6,000 cc respectively), but nonetheless have relatively small brains within their respective orders.

The most surprising ratio describes the porpoise. This group of marine animals has exceptionally large brains, and this ratio is particularly striking in the smaller species. The dolphin brain also has an immense and complex neocortex, and the explanation for this remarkable-looking brain is still one of the great mysteries of modern biology.

grip. The cortex is quite thin, but because it is deeply creased it represents 80 percent of the volume of the human brain and contains most of the brain's estimated 10 billion nerve cells, or **neurons.** If spread out flat, the cortex would be about the size of a large newspaper page. It fits inside the skull only by being compressed like a crumpled rag (the "convolutions" of the brain are the folds and overlaps of the cerebral cortex). This compression suggests that the cortex has all but outgrown its allotted space.

Fossil evidence shows that the cranial capacity of hominids increased threefold (tripled) during the past 3 million years, a very rapid rate of evolution. But to see this in perspective, we need to relate it to body size; increase in body size and a corresponding increase in brain size can occur rapidly in evolution, and this is not an unusual occurrence. Relating brain size to body size involves calculating how large a brain a typical ape would have if it had a human-size body. The answer reveals that the present-day human brain is 3.1 times larger than we would expect in a primate of our build. It appears, then, that our brain's threefold increase in size was accompanied by only a moderate increase in body size. This is perhaps the most significant anatomical fact about the species *Homo sapiens.*

Thus, the unique human potential has been made possible by our large brain. Expansion of a standard primate brain has provided us with behavioral possibilities undreamed of in other, even closely related, species. This brain, absolutely as well as relatively large, with its absolutely large number of neurons (about 10^{10}) and its unbelievably large number of dendritic interconnections (about 10^{12}), gives us the human potential for making tools, talking, planning, dreaming of the future, and creating an entirely new environment for ourselves. The size of the brain, therefore, crudely measured in cubic centimeters, tells us something very profound about human nature. Our brain is not so much different from other brains as it is bigger. We are not a unique evolutionary experiment but a superprimate. Quantitative changes in the evolving hominid brain, however, produced extraordinary qualitative changes in behavior.

Are Language and Culture a Human Novelty?

It is usually supposed that **language** and culture are uniquely human attributes, and that they distinguish us clearly from the animal kingdom. Yet if we look closely at the living primates, we can deduce that both these traits have their roots in our distant past and that some continuity of development can be traced. What is novel and what does separate us from our primate ancestors is the facility of *speech.*

A system of communication is essential to any social animal; and as the social organizations of animals get more complex, so do their communication systems. Living nonhuman primates depend on combinations of gestures, facial expressions, and postures as well as scents and sounds. They are evidently able to lend many shades of meaning to this "body language" vocabulary. This kind of animal communication can be complex and very subtle, and it is characteristic not only of primates but of dogs and other social carnivores—including marine mammals.

Primate Communication

Their wordless communication system serves the nonhuman primates extremely well. As social animals living in troops, they use it to keep in touch with one another at all times. More important, it allows individuals to display their feelings, to recognize

Encephalization quotient (EQ) in mammals, a number expressing observed brain size in a particular *species* relative to expected brain size calculated from body weight.

Neurons nerve cells; the basic units of the nervous system.

Language the cognitive aspect of human communication involving symbolic thinking structured by grammar.

at a glance the intentions and moods of others, and to react appropriately. Many of the signals express the established hierarchy of dominance and submission within the group. A subordinate male chimpanzee, seeing signs of aggression directed at him by a male of superior rank, backs up to the other and presents his rump in a gesture of appeasement—unless he intends to challenge the other male. Different signals, vocal and visual, help individuals stay in contact when moving through the community territory. Still other signals promote mating behavior or foster good mother–infant relations. A mother chimpanzee has been observed to calm her disturbed youngster simply by touching its fingers lightly with hers. So complex and so delicate is this gestural communication in the chimpanzee that it cannot be said to be less evolved than our own. It serves to maintain an extremely complex social system.

Yet for all its complexity, and however well suited it may be to the chimpanzees' needs, such a communication system falls far short of humans' spoken language. As far as is known, nonhuman primates in the wild are limited in the ways they can refer to specific things in their environment and cannot communicate thought through the complex phonetic codes called words that are used by humans. Nor do they seem able to refer easily to the past or future with the aid of their signals. For them, what is out of sight is usually out of mind. The signal system narrowly circumscribes what can be communicated, and vocalizations and facial expressions are under limited voluntary control, at best.

This is not to say that the nonhuman primates' vocal signals are entirely unspecific. Some apes indicate the desirability of the food they are eating by the intensity of their food calls. During normal feeding, chimpanzees emit food grunts, but for a favorite food they give the more excited food bark. They still cannot say "banana," of course, but they communicate something more than simply "food." Even more specialized is the danger-call system of the African vervet monkeys (*Cercopithecus aethiops*), which have three alarm calls for three kinds of predators and a fourth for baboons (Cheney and Seyfarth, 1990). The vervets use a chitter for snakes, a chirp for ground-dwelling carnivores, and a *r-raup* sound to warn of birds of prey. When tape recordings of their alarm calls are played back to them, a chirp sends the vervets scrambling to the tips of branches, well out of reach of ground animals, whereas a *r-raup* launches them from the trees into the thickets below, where predatory birds cannot get at them. As the young mature, they make finer distinctions between the different alarm calls. A cry of "Watch out—eagle!" is beyond their capabilities, but it is also beyond their needs. They do not have to know whether it is an eagle or a hawk diving on them; what matters is that they get the message that the danger is from above, so that they can flee in the right direction.

Limbic and Cortical Communications

In their function, as well as in their causation, the vocal and visual signals used by nonhuman primates can be divided into two kinds. The majority of these signals, probably most of the vocal signals, as we have seen, express inner emotional and physiological states and are under only limited voluntary control. They allow all members of the troop to monitor the emotional status of all other members. All signals of this sort are generated mainly by a group of structures in the brain known collectively as the **limbic system** (the "emotional brain"). These signals come from below the level of conscious awareness, just as the human scream is generated.

In contrast, some communications, particularly gestures, appear to express conscious will or intent. A chimpanzee holds out its hand as a gesture of reassurance; a young baboon anxiously "presents" to a superior male, backing toward him rump

Limbic system lower brain center that generates emotions and their expression.

first. Because of the intentions that they symbolize, and their source in the brain, these expressions are called *cortical communications*. They are generated not by the limbic system but by the higher centers of the brain, just as human language is. It is for this reason that chimpanzees are excellent gestural mimics and can learn some aspects of human sign languages.

Both limbic and cortical communications are seen in human behavior. We, too, have a repertory of wordless signals that universally express emotions. People typically smile to demonstrate friendly intentions, just as chimpanzees do; clenched fists and jaws, scowls, and frowns are unmistakable signs of anger or disappointment; and the laugh, the cry, and the scream are direct expressions of inner psychological and physiological states. Other body motions that humans use, such as shaking and nodding the head, shrugging the shoulders, and clapping the hands, are abbreviated substitutes for spoken language and vary in meaning from one culture to another.

Language and Speech

The evolution of human language and **speech** has involved a number of important anatomical developments that distinguish humans from apes. They are of three kinds and can be summarized as follows:

1. We have evolved a lengthened pharynx (see Figure 4.13). By lowering the **larynx** and so lengthening the pharynx, the human vocal apparatus has developed a tube that makes possible the creation of vowel sounds and has a function analogous to that of an organ pipe. A newborn human baby has an apelike short pharynx and can make only a small range of sounds. The pharynx soon lengthens and enables the baby to babble and eventually to talk. The descent of the larynx—both during the growth of a modern baby and during the evolution of our species—is associated

Speech communication by the human oral mode.

Larynx the voice box; the organ in the throat containing the vocal chords, important in human *speech* production.

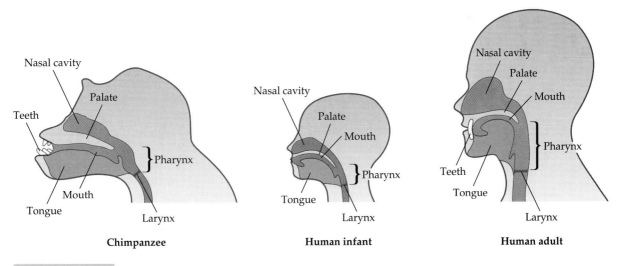

Chimpanzee   Human infant   Human adult

Figure 4.13

Insights into the speaking ability of early hominids have come from comparisons of the vocal apparatus of modern human adults and babies with that of a chimpanzee. To form words, sounds must be modulated by the pharynx, which lies above the larynx. The human newborn baby resembles the chimpanzee with its high larynx and short pharynx. By the age of three, the child's larynx has descended from the level of the fourth cervical vertebra to that of the seventh, and the long human pharynx is complete.

with the flexion of the cranial base. This association means that, where the bones are present, we can trace the evolution of this feature in the fossil record.

2. The tongue also has evolved. The musculature is altered and the nervous system's control of the tongue improved to make rapid articulation possible. The oral cavity is slightly reduced in size compared to that of an ape. These changes make it possible for the human tongue to move around the oral cavity, touching different parts of its roof with astounding speed and accuracy.

3. The musculature of the rapidly moving tongue and the pharynx is controlled by our brain's cortex. Developments in the brain are an essential component of language and speech. Not only has precise and detailed muscular control evolved, but the cortex also houses the speech centers in which lie extensive memory banks and association centers for word storage and meaning. The complexity of the control centers is very great, and this specialized function is restricted to humankind.

Discoveries and Mysteries

What Are the Origins of Spoken Language?

Given the evolution of the anatomical and physiological capabilities for speech, the question remains of when, where, and how humans first used speech for linguistic communication. Did a mutation suddenly give one individual human a language capacity that then spread throughout the population by natural selection? Language certainly would have conferred a huge selective advantage to groups that had it over those that didn't. Just think of the greater efficiency and productivity in daily living that spoken language affords. Cultural selection, too, might have favored individuals with the traits associated with language capacity. And after that, at what point and how did language become a product of cultural transmission rather than just biological inheritance? If only one group in one time and place had language, does that mean that all existing languages are related to one another through a common ancestral language—a mother tongue?

Or did the capacity and tools for language—such as a universal innate grammar—exist for a long time as adaptations of the brain in numerous populations before the advent of spoken languages? Could verbal language capacity, through the evolution of the brain and increasing intelligence, possibly even have preceded the capacity for speech? And if language was a series of preadaptations, slowly accumulating in our species through natural selection and the dynamics of population genetics, what triggered its manifestation? Was a critical threshold reached in environmental and cultural complexity that required spoken language, rather than just signs and gestures, for the optimization of survival? Is it more likely that many groups independently invented languages in different times and places on the basis of widespread preadaptations for language?

Although anthropologists have many theories, human language origins remain a complex mystery. The answer probably lies in some combination of the explanations suggested above. Unfortunately, we cannot (yet) go back to eavesdrop on the first human conversation. So it would seem that multidisciplinary studies—involving the fields of genetics, paleoanthropology, archaeology, linguistic anthropology, and others—are our only way to develop a unified theory of language origins.

Spoken language provides a magnificently efficient and versatile means of communication. It is a complex system of chains of symbols to which meanings have been assigned by cultural convention. The number of meanings that can be so assigned is, in practice, infinite. A coded series of sounds conveys conscious thought at least ten times faster than any other method of signaling can—faster than hand signs, moving pictures, or even other kinds of vocalizations. Through language, humans can step outside themselves and give things and people names, reflect about others and themselves, and refer to the past and the future. Most important of all, language gives people the capacity to share their thoughts. As Sherwood Washburn and Shirley Strum wrote, "It is the communication of thought, rather than thought itself, that is unique to man, makes human cultures possible, and that is the primary factor in separating man and beast" (1972: 477). Through spoken language, discussion, complex bargaining, and democratic processes became a possibility for the first time.

Whenever spoken language evolved, it became the new and extraordinarily efficient means by which humans acquired and passed on from one generation to the next the flexible network of learned, rather than genetically inherited, behavior patterns and the knowledge that allowed them to alter their environment and adapt to new ones. Once language had evolved, culture acquired a symbolic form that changed its whole nature. From this point in human evolution, culture and its medium—language—were necessary for survival.

Protoculture and Culture

Apes and monkeys can be said to have **protoculture**—group traditions and knowledge shared among, for example, different communities of chimpanzees. Much of chimpanzees' daily behavior is learned, and patterns are passed down from generation to generation. Chimpanzees' protoculture includes behavioral traditions such as hunting techniques, food preferences, and material culture such as termite fishing and the use of stones as hammers. Protoculture can include any behavior that does not involve linguistic transmission. Examples include some traditions of stone tool making, subsistence activities, and any social customs not involving symbolic representation.

Humans alone have a symbolic **culture** in which words symbolize objects, actions, and feelings. A culture based on language is necessarily far richer than any protoculture. It is language, and its effects on the flowering of culture, that has lifted humankind above the animals and given us the power to create a very complex material culture and even to learn about our place in nature and in the universe.

Thus, culture can be said to change through the transmission of acquired information. The importance of a cultural way of life cannot be overemphasized. Our reliance on cultural adaptation has set us apart from the other primates. For better or worse, we are the only living primate species that exerts any control over its own evolutionary future.

Protoculture learned patterns of behavior passed down the generations within a social group, not depending on symbols.

Culture system of learned behavior, symbols, customs, beliefs, institutions, artifacts, and technology characteristic of a human group and transmitted by its members to their offspring.

Summary

The first primates evolved at least 60 million years ago. Today the order is represented by more than 200 species and is characterized by extreme physical and behavioral diversity. The most basic primate traits—grasping hands and feet, and stereoscopic vision with depth perception (plus the neural elaborations that go with these developments)—were most likely originally adaptations for predation on insects in an arboreal habitat.

The primate order contains two suborders: Prosimii and Anthropoidea. The prosimians were the first suborder to evolve, and today they are characterized by the retention of several primitive anatomical traits, including a keen sense of smell and relatively unprotected eyes. At present these small (and often nocturnal) creatures are found only in Africa and Asia. The anthropoid suborder, today including monkeys, apes, and humans, first appeared about 45 to 50 million years ago. Compared to prosimians, living anthropoids show a reduced sense of smell, elaborated vision, complete loss of claws, and a more complex brain. Modern monkeys are found in Central and South America (superfamily Ceboidea) and in Africa and Asia (superfamily Cercopithecoidea). Most monkeys show some variety of quadrupedal locomotion in the trees.

The superfamily Hominoidea includes the apes and humans. Humans are found worldwide, but apes are limited to Africa (chimpanzees, bonobos, and gorillas) and Asia (gibbons and orangutans). Apes tend to be large, tailless, arboreal arm-swingers and arm-hangers (or their terrestrial descendants), while humans have evolved into terrestrial bipeds. Hominoids display the largest, most complex brains of all primates. Humans have shown unparalleled brain expansion and elaboration, and they are characterized by language, speech, and cultural adaptation as a way of life. The latter has given humans the ability to influence their evolutionary future.

Review Questions

1. How do the arboreal and visual predation theories differ as explanations of the common characteristics of primates?

2. How does the anatomy of prosimians differ from that of anthropoid primates? Can anthropoids be said to have progressed beyond the prosimian condition?

3. Why are humans classified as hominoids rather than as monkeys? How does human anatomy resemble that of apes and differ from that of monkeys?

4. One can arrange the living primates so that it appears that evolution shaped the creatures to become increasingly humanlike. Does this notion of humans' being the goal of primate evolution have any validity?

5. What are the implications of humans' influence over their own evolutionary future?

6. Some people believe that humans are the result of divine design. What light do the perfections and imperfections of human anatomy shed on this question?

7. How does the brain of a modern human differ from that of an ape? How has brain evolution been related to the appearance of speech and language?

8. Consider the evidence for protoculture among monkeys and apes, and then suggest ways to distinguish protoculture from language-based cultural activities in the archaeological record left by premodern hominids.

Suggested Further Reading

Cartmill, M. "New Views on Primate Origins." *Evolutionary Anthropology,* 1, 1992.

Cheney, D. L., and R. M. Seyfarth. *How Monkeys See the World.* University of Chicago Press, 1990.

Fleagle, J. *Primate Adaptation and Evolution.* Academic Press, 1988.

Smuts, B., et al., eds. *Primate Societies.* University of Chicago Press, 1987.

Internet Resources

 Conveniently access these and other links via our web site at **http://www.ablongman/anthro.**

About the Primates
http://www.primate.wisc.edu/pin/aboutp.html
Authoritative information from the Wisconsin Regional Primate Research Center (WRPRC) about prosimians, monkeys, and apes.

Introduction to Primates
http://www.mc.maricopa.edu/academic/cult sci/anthro/exploratorium/primates/index.html
A well-illustrated introduction to primate anatomy and evolution, with links to numerous subtopics.

Journey into Phylogenetic Systematics
http://www.ucmp.berkeley.edu/clad/clad4.html
This site introduces you to the philosophy, methodology, and implications of cladistic analysis.

Primate Taxonomy
http://www.primate.wisc.edu/pin/taxon.html
Part of the WRPRC Primate Info Net, this site links to lots of material on primate classification.

WRPRC Audiovisual Archive
http://www.primate.wisc.edu/pin/av.html
Numerous links to photographs, videos, and vocalizations of primates.

Useful Search Terms:
apes
cladistics
brain evolution
monkeys
primate evolution
primate conservation
primates
prosimians
taxonomy

Behavior of Living Primates

Overview

The fossilized remains of our extinct ancestors provide important direct information about these hominids' anatomy, but only limited (and indirect) information about their behavior. In order to make reasonable behavioral reconstructions, researchers often rely on analogies drawn from living human cultures (usually hunting-and-gathering peoples) and nonhuman primates. This chapter presents a broad summary of what scientists have learned about the behavior of our nonhuman primate kin, including their diets, grouping patterns, social development, sexuality, dominance systems, and social relations.

Important topics in the chapter include social group type, socialization, dominance, sexual behavior, sexual selection, friendly relations, territoriality, and feeding strategies.

 Check our web site for additional information, photos, drawings, maps, and animations on topics in this chapter.

Why Study Primates?

Fossils can provide a very good indication of the course of evolution, but they are less good at indicating precisely how evolution came about. This limitation has been a source of frustration to anthropologists for many years—so much so that many are now looking for answers elsewhere than in the fossil record. One alternative field that is fruitful is the study of humankind's primate relatives, the monkeys and apes; closely related to us, they are even more closely related to our ancestors.

Recent developments in biochemistry have shown close similarities of DNA, cell proteins, and blood proteins including hemoglobin between humans and the other primates. Now, thanks to numerous studies of monkeys and apes in nature, it is becoming clear that in their social behavior, too, nonhuman primates stand close to us. Many live in highly organized groups in which following routines and sharing knowledge permit a relatively stable social organization. Others, such as chimpanzees, live in more loosely organized groups. Whatever the size or structure of the group, some members are good friends, others dedicated enemies; some are collaborators, others rivals; some are popular, others despised. Infant apes and monkeys, as they grow up, must learn a code of behavior, much as a human child must; and, as you read in Chapter 4, all the

Follow links at **http://www.ablongman/anthro** for additional resources in physical anthropology, primatology, biological anthropology, and paleoanthropology.

members of a group are linked by an elaborate system of communication that uses both sounds and gestures.

The comparison of ape and monkey behavior with human behavior must not be pushed too far, of course. Yet, in their daily routine, and in many aspects of their relationships with their fellows, the nonhuman primates resemble humans in many surprising ways and throw much light on the roots of human behavior.

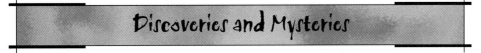

Discoveries and Mysteries

How Primates Behave in the Wild

Early in the twentieth century, casual observation of primates in zoos began to give rise to more serious study of primate behavior. (See Haraway, 1989, and Loy and Peters, 1991, for an overview.) In the 1920s psychobiologist Robert Yerkes observed captive chimpanzees in the United States and was so impressed by what he saw and so astonished by how little was known about the great apes that he sent two students, Henry Nissen and Harold Bingham, to Africa to study the chimpanzee and the gorilla, respectively.

The first systematic investigations of the behavior of apes and monkeys living under natural conditions were made by C. R. Carpenter. In the early 1930s Carpenter journeyed to Barro Colorado Island in Panama to study howler monkeys (*Alouatta palliata*) and then traveled to Southeast Asia to observe gibbons. Later he set up a colony of rhesus monkeys (*Macaca mulatta*) on Cayo Santiago near Puerto Rico and observed them. Carpenter published some revolutionary findings on monkey behavior. The results he obtained by viewing primates in the wild pointed up the limitations of studying primates in captivity, which had been the practice up to that time.

Around the same period, the South African zoologist Solly Zuckerman was studying baboons—first, hamadryas baboons (*Papio hamadryas*) in the London Zoo and then chacma baboons (*Papio cynocephalus*) in South Africa. In Germany, Wolfgang Köhler conducted experiments investigating chimpanzees' capacity to find solutions to problems, such as stacking boxes or using sticks to reach bundles of bananas. In Russia, Nadie Kohts studied chimps' ability to discriminate between objects by size, color, and shape. And in the United States, Harry and Margaret Harlow studied the mother–infant bond in rhesus monkeys.

It became clear that observing apes or monkeys in artificial confinement, including zoos, provides only partial insight into primate behavior. To study normal primate behavior, the best option is to observe monkeys and apes in their natural setting. A major development in field research occurred after World War II, when primatologists in Japan established the Primate Research Group to study native Japanese macaques (*M. fuscata*) under natural conditions. At Takasakiyama, by setting up feeding stations that a macaque colony with approximately two hundred members visited regularly, scientists were able to observe one group of monkeys over an extended period. Other native macaque groups were observed on Koshima Island and elsewhere.

The trend toward studying primates in their native habitats really caught hold in the late 1950s. Led by various anthropologists, a large number of young field workers, including both women and men, began pouring out all over the world from universities and museums in a dozen countries. In the half century since then, field primatologists have obtained naturalistic data on many species of prosimians, monkeys, and apes.

Primates turned out to be much harder to study than anyone had imagined. Many, like the mountain gorilla, live in inaccessible places. Many stay in the tops of trees in dense forest, where they are nearly invisible. Others, like the orangutan, are extremely rare. Most are shy. There is also the problem of what to look for and how to interpret it. Different species act differently in different areas, under different ecological influences, and even in different population densities. Primate behavior is not stereotyped but complex and highly variable.

What Is the Basis of Primate Social Organization?

Monkeys, apes, and humans are all social species (the orangutan is semisocial at best), and their societies are highly organized. What are the advantages of social life? Why are so many mammal and bird species social as well, and why have most hominoid species developed this characteristic to such a high degree?

Social life has four kinds of advantages:

1. Several pairs of eyes are better than one in the detection and avoidance of predators. Defense by a group also is far more effective. Three or four male baboons constitute an impressive display and can frighten many predators. A lone baboon is a dead baboon.
2. Competition for large food patches is more successful when done by groups than when attempted by individuals. In some monkeys, social groups subdivide when food is sparse and widely scattered.
3. Reproductive advantages accrue from social groups, because regular access to the opposite sex is ensured.
4. Social groups permit extensive socialization with both peers and elders, and the young animals have the opportunity to learn from older ones. Among the higher primates, socialization is a factor of great importance.

These advantages are probably the most important in bringing about the selection of social life in animals such as primates. Although considerable variation may occur within a species, especially under different environmental conditions, only a few Old World primate species (including the gibbons and the siamang, a large gibbon) normally live in groups consisting only of an adult male, a female, and their young. The orang is unique in being more or less solitary. Other Old World monkeys and apes all live in social groups that number as many as five hundred individuals but most commonly number between ten and fifty (see Figure 5.1).

But how are these societies organized? Order is maintained in primate societies through a complex interrelationship of several factors. One is the animals' prolonged period of dependence: infant apes and monkeys, like human infants, are far from self-sufficient and maintain a close relationship with their mothers longer than most other animals. During this time they learn some of the roles they will play as adults. Other factors are dominance and hierarchy. In many species the adults of one or both sexes have quite a well-defined social rank within the group. Also important are the other relationships among adults, which to some extent are determined by kinship; friendship; sexual contacts; and competition for food, sleeping sites, and any other limited resources.

Mother + infant; lone males
(e.g., orangutans)

Monogynous family
(e.g., gibbons)

Multimale; unifemale
(e.g., some New World
monkeys [*Saguinus*])

Multimale; multifemale
(e.g., macaques and baboons)

Unimale; multifemale
(e.g., patas monkeys
[*Erythrocebus*] and gorillas)

Multimale; multifemale; dispersed
or "fusion–fission" community
(e.g., chimpanzees and bonobos)

Figure 5.1

Illustrations of the different types of primate societies. Adult males are shown in color. Dotted and dashed lines indicate home ranges or territorial boundaries, depending on the species.

Thinking about these factors, one quickly sees that they are among the most important regulators of human society as well. Thus, for a very long time (we may assume) and for many species—humans, chimpanzees, and baboons—the problem of life has been, and still is, largely the problem of getting along in a group.

Prolonged Dependence and Learning in Childhood

What is meant by a prolonged period of dependence? A kitten has become a cat by the time it is a year old. A comparably-sized ring-tailed lemur takes about twice as long to reach adulthood. A male baboon takes seven to eight years to reach full social and biological maturity, a chimpanzee needs anywhere from ten to fifteen years, and a human even longer. As a result, family ties—and especially those based on **matrilineal kinship**—among higher primates tend to be strong and lasting. This slow development

Matrilineal kinship kinship traced through the maternal line.

among a group of supportive relatives is necessary for a higher primate to learn all the things it must to fit into the complex society into which it is born. It needs time to learn.

For a chimpanzee, childhood imitation and play are the equivalent of going to school. It watches its mother look for food, and looks for food itself. It watches her make nests and makes little nests of its own—not to sleep in, just for fun (Figure 5.2). Later, during a long adolescence, the young chimp picks up from its peers the physical skills it will need as an adult, as well as the more intricate social skills required to get along with others: It learns not only how to interpret the moods of other chimpanzees but also how to respond to other individuals. All this time the learner is finding its own place among its peers, first in play, later in more competitive activity that will help determine its rank as an adult. Thus, two sources of learning and two sets of relationships make up primate society: the family relationship (usually, mother–infant and other matrilineal kin; occasionally, mother–father–infant–siblings) and the larger relationship of the individual to all other members of its social group.

The important role of learned behavior among primates means that the group as a whole has more knowledge and experience than does any one of its individual members. Experience is pooled, and the generations are linked.

Growing Up Langur.   Studies of Hanuman langurs in India have yielded a wealth of information on how the infants of one monkey species learn. These large monkeys live in groups containing several adult females and one or more adult males. The adult females are organized in a **dominance hierarchy** (a ranked society) that is shown by their respective abilities to displace one another from food and other resources. Mothers lavish attention on the distinctively dark new infants, but they also allow other females to hold, carry, and groom the baby—and many females, particularly **nulliparous** youngsters and pregnant adults, are anxious to engage in such "aunting" or **allomothering.** Mothers must be careful, however, as they sometimes have difficulty reclaiming

Dominance hierarchy rank structuring of a primate group, usually based on winning and losing fights. For some purposes, the ranks within a subset of animals, such as the adult males, may be analyzed separately.

Nulliparous never having given birth.

Allomothering typically, care or attention directed toward an infant by a female other than its mother (also called *aunting behavior*).

Figure 5.2

Each night, chimpanzees prepare new nests for themselves by bending tree branches over larger boughs to make a bed.

their infants. When confronted by a high-ranking allomother that refuses to return an infant, a low-status mother can only wait until the "aunt" tires of the baby and deserts it, or watch for an opportunity to snatch back her offspring (Hrdy, 1977).

After the infant reaches the age of about five months, its dark coat lightens to the color of an adult langur. Now the females no longer vie to hold it. It follows its mother about, copying her actions, learning to forage. It also spends much of its time in energetic activity, running, climbing, chasing, and wrestling—skills that will be invaluable as it reaches adulthood. As it plays with its peers, it learns to get along as a member of the group.

Once young langurs are weaned, around the age of fifteen months, they become segregated by sex. The females stay near the center of the group, close to the adults, mixing more and more intimately with the adult females and their infants. Holding the infants and sometimes tending them while the mothers are away, they are gaining experience for their own future role as mothers. The male juveniles, meanwhile, spend most of their free time playing. As they grow older, their play becomes ever more vigorous and wide-ranging, and they drift toward the periphery of the group, away from both the adults and the infants. This is the young males' first step toward eventual emigration.

Growing Up Macaque.   Other monkeys whose development has been studied include the baboons and the macaques. The patterns they follow illustrate interesting social differences in the attitudes of males toward the infants of a group. In a langur group, adult males keep apart from their young. Langur males in captivity do show an interest in newborns, particularly males, but on the whole young langurs grow up in an almost exclusively matriarchal atmosphere. On the other hand, Japanese macaque males have been observed to cradle one- and two-year-old infants during the birth season. In savanna baboon groups, adult males also show an intense interest in infants and associate most closely with the babies of females with whom they share a special relationship. Usually an adult male will approach a mother, smacking his lips to show he means no harm, in order to enjoy the pleasure of playing with the mother's infant.

The Dominance Hierarchy

Part of growing up in most monkey societies is establishing one's place in the group's social hierarchy. The concept of a status or dominance hierarchy, sometimes called a "pecking order," is well recognized among social animals from chickens to gorillas.

Dominance can be defined simply as the relative social status or rank of an animal, as determined by its ability to compete successfully with other individuals for varying goals. Contested goals might include access to resources such as favorite foods or sleeping sites. Social resources, such as mates or grooming partners, are also contested. Dominant animals can direct and control their own and others' aggression. In aggressive encounters, dominant animals consistently defeat less dominant animals.

In some species dominance relationships are clear-cut and static, and a social hierarchy can be recognized. In some species hierarchies are limited to one sex, but in others both males and females are integrated into a general hierarchy within which some animals may share a similar rank. However, dominance hierarchies always are subject to influence by animals' personalities and by social variables, and a particular animal may be dominant or submissive under different circumstances. Successful aggression is not the only behavior that generates high status. Ingratiating behavior can gain allies and lead to high status; in contrast, an ill-tempered, aggressive animal may

---

ASKING QUESTIONS

Why Does Primate Social Behavior Vary?

As you have read, growing up as a macaque or a baboon is a different experience from growing up as a langur. Why is social behavior so different in different primate groups? The answer is that social behaviors are adaptations acquired in the interests of survival and reproductive success in different environments. Comfortable as some langur species are on the ground, no langur ventures far from trees. Females do not require a male's protection, and they usually do not get it. If a langur group is alarmed, it is every monkey for itself (although langur males have been known to defend group mates—particularly infants—against humans and hawks). Baboons, on the other hand, are organized differently, perhaps because they frequently range far from trees. Adult male baboons routinely defend infants against attacks from conspecifics. Furthermore, if a predator approaches the troop, the males *may* (depending on the degree of danger) position themselves between the threat and their group (including the infants). The protective behavior of baboon males may reflect more than a concern for infants. It also is a way for males to maintain relationships with the infants' mothers—relationships that may enhance mating opportunities. Thus, primate social behavior varies according to differences in the environment, such as food distribution (density and clumping), density and type of trees (if any), water resources, and terrain.

---

get little social support (Figure 5.3). Two or three individuals may team up as a coalition to hold a top position that none alone could hold.

High-ranking animals move confidently through their troop, others deferring to them as a matter of course. Supportive relatives are particularly important in maintaining status, and macaque and baboon mothers will pass down their status from generation to generation through the female line. Adult males, however, have to establish their rank from scratch whenever they move from one troop to another. Dominance hierarchies usually are not stable for long. In one baboon troop studied over a long period, male ranks altered on average every two to three weeks; female ranks altered only about every eight weeks or at even longer intervals. Factors that brought about such changes included the movement of males in and out of the troop, births and deaths, and fighting within the troop (Hausfater, 1975).

Long-term observations of baboons and better knowledge of kin relationships within baboon troops have revealed that the long-term stability of the baboon group

Figure 5.3

A dominant male chimpanzee reassures a young male that is presenting his rump in appeasement. As a result, the younger male now feels able to turn and face his superior.

depends not so much on the males as on high-ranking females. Females establish an ongoing aristocracy based on mother–daughter and sister–sister ties (Hausfater, 1975). Once established, this matriarchal aristocracy tends to perpetuate itself, such that the hierarchy of females is much more stable than that of males. Privileged related females groom each other sociably, bringing up their infants in an atmosphere of comfort and security that is denied low-ranking females. The latter are forced to hang about at the edge of the group, alert to the possibility of a bite or a slap if they do not move aside for a higher-ranking animal. Unable to enter permanently into the established matriarchy at the center, they pass on their timidity and generally low self-esteem to their young. Not surprisingly, the young reared by the dominant mothers grow up with a far greater chance of achieving dominance themselves, having learned confidence and assurance from their mothers.

Among rhesus monkeys and Japanese macaques, an individual's rank within its age group is based on its mother's rank. Among baboons, this is also true within each sex, but males of any age consistently dominate females of similar age.

Reproduction and Rank

Several studies of baboons have reported positive correlations between male rank and reproduction. For example, American primatologist Glenn Hausfater found that higher-ranked males clearly outcopulated lower-ranked males within his study group (Hausfater, 1975). To a large extent this success was due to the alpha male's ability to achieve unequaled access to ovulating females, as determined retrospectively from the date of deflation of the female's **sex swellings.** Other studies, however, find no correlation between male rank and reproduction. Because males of many species change ranks frequently, measuring sexual success rates for ranks may not indicate long-term reproductive success of individual animals. In addition, males that live for many years may occupy several ranks and experience many fluctuations in their level of reproduction. It is also important that female choice plays a part in any male's sexual achievements, and many males court females for long periods of time to win their favors. Thus, dominance is not a ticket to unlimited sexual access for males.

In contrast to the baboon studies, analyses of thirty-five years of dominance and reproduction data from the female chimpanzees at Gombe suggest lifetime benefits for high-ranking individuals. In a study that parallels many baboon findings, primatologists report that in comparison to lower-ranked individuals, dominant female chimps have significantly higher rates of infant survival, more rapid production of young, and daughters that mature (and thus begin their own reproductive careers) faster. It appears that high rank enables female chimpanzees to gain access to the best food sources, and being better nourished enhances maternal and infant health as well as daughters' maturation rate (Pusey et al., 1997).

Overall, high rank has been shown at least to produce short-term reproductive benefits for both males and females in many primate species. Lifetime benefits, however, are harder to document, although they do seem to occur among female chimps. In any event, status hierarchies, whether based on conflict and threat (Figure 5.4) or on kinship and personality, represent one means by which natural selection has brought order and organization to primate society. The tendency for an individual to attempt to increase its status is deep-seated and is expressed among most higher primates, and indeed most social animals. Human societies are no exception: Status is just as pervasive and just as variable in its mode of expression as it is among other primates.

Sex swellings hormone-induced swellings on the hindquarters of certain primate females; generally correlated with ovulation.

Male Mating Strategies.   The behavior of chimpanzees shows how flexible the relationship between reproduction and rank can be (Goodall, 1986). Wild chimpanzees have at least three mating strategies. If a male is sufficiently high-ranking, he may try to monopolize a sexually attractive female (a female with large genital swellings) by preventing the approach of other males. Such possessiveness is impossible for lower-ranking males, who usually opt for the strategy of frequent **opportunistic mating,** which can involve the nonaggressive sharing of sexual access to a particular female among males. As a third strategy, a male of any rank may—through skillful social manipulation and sometimes aggressive courting—attempt to form a **consortship** with a female, which he then leads away to the periphery of the community range for several days of exclusive mating. Thus, wild chimpanzee males attempt to exert their dominance rank for reproductive gains whenever possible; but when that strategy is unworkable, they easily shift to other mating patterns, all of which include some likelihood of fathering infants.

Female Choice.   Female preferences remain a powerful factor among chimpanzees, however. Like males, females have sexual strategies shaped by evolution to maximize reproductive success, and in these strategies females may take an active role in mate selection. Some studies suggest that primate females are more sexually assertive than has traditionally been held (Small, 1993). Rather than waiting coyly for a male suitor, females are often sexually aggressive and actively solicit males. Further, females sometimes choose to be **promiscuous,** mating unselectively with the males of their own or other groups. A recent study of paternity among the chimpanzees of West Africa's Taï Forest revealed that despite the resident males' best efforts to control mating within their community, a high proportion of infants (seven of thirteen tested) were fathered by males from neighboring communities (Gagneux et al., 1997). This unexpected discovery was attributed to the Taï females' habit of regularly making surreptitious visits to neighboring groups and mating with stranger males of unknown fitness. These new data show clearly that female choice (a form of sexual selection) and females' interest in

Opportunistic mating mating done whenever and wherever the opportunity presents itself, and with whatever partner is available.

Consortship generally, a period of exclusive sexual association and mating between a female and a male.

Promiscuous having multiple sexual partners.

novel partners must be taken into account for a full understanding of a species' mating patterns.

Grooming and Social Interaction

A common form of social contact between higher primates is **grooming.** One monkey or ape grooms another by picking through its fur to clean out dirt, as well as parasites and salt crystals, which it then eats. Physically, grooming is simply a cleaning mechanism, and it is highly effective, as one can see by comparing lions and baboons that inhabit the same area of the East African savanna. Although lions are clean animals, the backs of their necks, where they cannot reach to clean, are thick with ticks, whereas the baboons' hair is totally free of them.

But to primates grooming is far more than a form of hygiene. It is the most important means of social interaction among members of a group and serves a variety of purposes. For example, grooming reduces tension, as shown by baboons, macaques, and chimpanzees, and serves as an enjoyable pastime when groups are not in search of food. Much as humans gather in conversation groups, monkeys gather in grooming groups. The same function is served: the maintenance of friendly social relations. Being groomed is obviously enjoyable: the groomed animal sits or lies in an attitude of beatific contentment (Figure 5.5). Most grooming is done by females. Mothers regularly groom their young from birth. Equals groom each other in approximately equal amounts; subordinates groom their social superiors much more frequently than they are groomed in turn. As one might expect, dominant males get much grooming and

Grooming cleaning and combing the fur, usually of another animal; an enjoyable pastime.

Figure 5.5

Grooming has two main functions: to remove parasites and keep the fur clean and to establish and maintain social relationships. Here a relaxed female baboon encourages a dominant male to groom her, while a lower-ranking male watches from a proper distance.

give little. The significant function of grooming in monkey society is that it cuts across hierarchical lines, establishing friendly relationships between individuals on various levels of the hierarchy that might not otherwise interact.

Reciprocal Altruism. Chimpanzees and baboons exhibit awareness of individual differences beyond status. These animals show preferences; that is, they prefer to spend time with particular members of the troop, which often are their kin. In both species we see what looks very like friendship. Certain pairs and trios (sometimes of different sexes but more often of the same sex) spend time together and share experiences and food sources. When meat, a rare delicacy, is obtained, chimpanzees will share after the provider has had first pick. Baboons will move aside to make room for a friend to get at the kill. It looks as if these adult primates are in some small way responding to one another's needs even outside of the mother–infant relationship. That is, innate bioaltruism involved in rearing an infant is extended to **reciprocal altruism** between adults. Insofar as the members of a troop help one another and return favors, this behavior has an obvious adaptive value for the social group as a whole.

Group Cohesiveness. As you have read, dominance hierarchies and reciprocal altruism can contribute to the social stability and cohesiveness of primate groups. Also recall the discussion of the social functions of primate communication in Chapter 4. The degree of cohesiveness of a group also seems to vary in relation to danger to its members from the environment. Gorillas live in comparatively little day-to-day danger; and individual male gorillas frequently go off on their own, even for weeks at a time. In a pattern sometimes referred to as a **fusion–fission community,** groups of Gombe chimpanzees, also in little danger, split into small units whose membership constantly changes; individuals often search for food alone, out of sight of others. Chimpanzees seem little concerned about the safety of the group as a whole; when alarmed, an individual chimpanzee often will run off without even giving a warning call! When danger is present, however, group cohesiveness increases in most primate groups, and both adult males and females may move to the forefront to act in defense of the group or of individuals within it.

For more on primate behavior and social organization, visit our web site.

How Do Sexual Characteristics Shape Behavior?

Many aspects of primate social organization relate to the sexual characteristics of species and the role of sexual anatomy and physiology in their behavior. All Old World monkeys, apes, and humans share a basically similar sexual anatomy and physiology. The ovarian–uterine **menstrual cycle** is about twenty-eight to thirty-five days in length, with ovulation occurring near the middle and menstruation (shedding of the uterine lining) at the end. Mapped on top of the menstrual cycle, however, is a pattern of behavioral fluctuation called the estrous cycle.

Estrus in Apes and Humans

In response to the changing levels of sex hormones (mainly the estrogens and progesterone), primate females have monthly **estrous cycles:** cycles in sexual **attractiveness,**

Reciprocal altruism trading of apparently altruistic acts by different individuals at different times; a variety of *bioaltruism*

Fusion–fission community community of primates that splits into subgroups and reunites from time to time.

Menstrual cycle the interval (generally, monthly) from the end of one period of menstrual bleeding to the end of the next; especially characteristic of *catarrhine* females.

Estrous cycle cycle of periods of sexual *attractiveness* and activity of primate females; correlated with ovulation and the *menstrual cycle,* but with great flexibility among *catarrhines.*

Attractiveness in primate studies, the aspect of female sexuality reflected by attention from males.

receptivity, and **proceptivity,** or tendency to initiate mating. A sexually active female—one that is simultaneously attractive, receptive, and proceptive—is said to be in **estrus.** In some species, such as baboons and chimpanzees, females in estrus also display large, colorful sex swellings; but it is sexual behavior and not swelling or color that indicates a female is in estrus. Among monkeys and apes sexual behavior can occur throughout the menstrual cycle and may show a good deal of situational flexibility regardless of a female's hormonal state; but most sex takes place near ovulation, during the period of estrus, which lasts about a week.

One of the primary differences between nonhuman primates and humans is the fact that human females' sexual behavior does not reflect peaks at estrus. Rather, human sexual behavior is highly situational, and mating occurs throughout the menstrual cycle and during pregnancy. For all intents and purposes, the old estrous cycle has been lost in humans, and it is clear that our sexual behavior is controlled by hormones less than that of other primates.

Sexual Dimorphism

Charles Darwin, in his discussion of sexual selection, noted that competition for mates is unequal between the sexes of most species. The more vigorously competing sex tends to be bigger, and male–female differences in body form and color, decorative appendages, and behavioral displays may evolve as well. In many primate species, males compete for females. For all mammals, access to fertile females sets an upper limit on males' reproductive success. This may be the reason that males tend to be larger than females—a form of **sexual dimorphism** that is not uncommon. Great apes, various baboon species, and a number of other monkeys have very considerable differences between the sexes in body size, weight, and size of canine teeth. Shoulder breadth and strikingly handsome hair forms are often well developed in the males (Figure 5.6). Sex differences in size may vary; females average 50 percent the size of males among gorillas and baboons, 78 percent

Receptivity the aspect of female sexuality reflected by cooperating in copulation.

Proceptivity the aspect of female sexuality reflected by inviting copulation.

Estrus the period, usually around ovulation, of sexual *attractiveness* and activity by *primate* and other mammalian females

Sexual dimorphism characteristic anatomical (and behavioral) differences between males and females of a species.

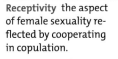

Figure 5.6

Hamadryas female with young, and a male. The male is larger and heavier, and he carries a magnificent mane, which makes him look even larger.

among chimpanzees, 81 percent among humans, and 94 percent—near equality—among gibbons (see Table 4.6, page 93).

It is often claimed that the large, aggressive baboon males are selected as protectors of the troop against predators. If we look at higher primates as a whole, however, we can find a correlation between reproductive system and sexual dimorphism. **Monogynous** species, in which males generally have only one mate and neither sex competes strongly for additional mates (for example, siamangs and gibbons), show little sexual dimorphism. **Polygynous** species (such as savanna baboons), which live in multimale troops and offer greater sexual opportunities to powerful, successful males, are quite dimorphic. It seems that in such a dimorphic species both natural selection and sexual selection are generating large males.

How Does Environment Shape Behavior?

Among the most important functions of primates' communication and interaction systems is the regulation of the animals' use of the landscape and its resources. The relationship between the social group and its environment—its **socioecology**—is ultimately determined by the distribution and density of the natural resources essential to the animals' survival, by the density of competing animals (including humans), and by the pressure of predators. The social group becomes associated with a **home range**—a recognizable area of land or forest—that contains sufficient space, food, water, and safe sleeping sites for all its members. Behavioral mechanisms bring about this spacing, which reduces the possibility of overexploiting the food resources and of having conflict over those resources. The home range of savanna baboons may be partly shared with other groups of the same species; it is always shared with other species, often with other primate species. Within this range, it is usually possible to define smaller **core areas** containing resources absolutely essential for survival, in this case sleeping trees. A core area becomes defended **territory** when it is actively defended against intruders from neighboring groups.

Different primate species use space in very different ways. In many species, such as savanna baboons, some vervet monkeys, orangutans, and gorillas, neighbors simply avoid each other by staying at a distance. At the other extreme, gibbons, chimpanzees, and langur monkeys are among those primates that routinely defend a territory.

Defending a Territory

Why is it that some species defend a territory but others do not? The answer seems to involve the distribution of several essential resources, the most important of which is food.

It appears that if food is unevenly distributed and unpredictable in availability, an optimum feeding strategy is to form large groups and range over large areas of land, as do savanna baboons. Where food is concentrated in space and reliable in supply, smaller groups may occupy a fixed and limited area, as in the case of gibbons; and it is both possible and worthwhile to defend such an area. For these animals, monogyny and a defended territory reduce individuals' competition for food, and each sex is assured a mating partner. Other monogynous species—siamangs in Southeast Asia and marmosets (*Callithrix*) and titi monkeys (*Callicebus*) in South America—also defend territories and show little sexual dimorphism. These species are also characterized by sexual equality of status and a sharing of social roles not found in other species.

Monogynous in zoology, generally having only one mate.

Polygynous in zoology, tending to have regular sexual access to two or more females.

Socioecology the connection between *species'* ecological relations and their social behaviors; also the study of this connection.

Home range the area a *primate* group uses for foraging, sleeping, and so on in a year.

Core area a portion of the *home range* that is used frequently.

Territory the area occupied and defended by individuals or groups of animals against *conspecifics.*

In contrast, savanna baboons and some other monkeys that cover large home ranges are polygynous to promiscuous, having multimale groups. They do not defend their extensive home ranges and are not capable of doing so. The contrast in the use of space, the quality of the environment, and reproductive system is clear and significant.

Thus, troop structure is at least partially a response to troop ecology. Savanna baboons of east Africa, for example, live in large multimale troops of up to 150 individuals and can find sufficient food and sleeping trees in the areas in which they live, without dispersing (Figure 5.7). By contrast, gelada baboons (*Theropitheus,* a related genus) occupy the harsher environment of the Ethiopian mountains. Here, in seasons or areas of poor food supply, the troops break up by day into small wide-ranging polygynous units, each containing a single male, two or more females, and young. This pattern is called **harem polygyny.** When the rains come and food is more plentiful, the one-male groups coalesce into the larger multimale troops. There is reason to believe that the one male group is the ancient catarrhine pattern, and that the multimale units of the savanna baboon and chimpanzee are a more recent adaptation to an abundant food supply.

Feeding Strategies

An important part of a species' socioecology is its feeding "strategy"; that is, the anatomical, physiological, and behavioral characteristics that permit animals to obtain energy efficiently by getting food. The strategy predicted to be favored by natural selection is effective in enabling animals to metabolically convert food into energy while expending the least energy in searching. Thus, a feeding strategy is optimal when it both provides essential nutrients and yields high net energy per unit of time.

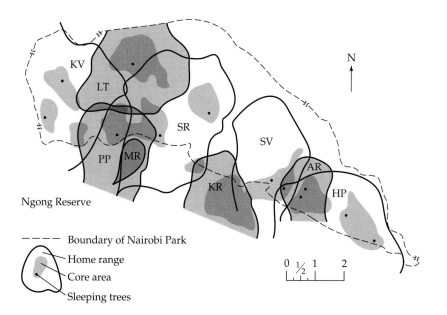

Ngong Reserve

– – – – Boundary of Nairobi Park

Home range
Core area
Sleeping trees

N

0 1/2 1   2

Figure 5.7

This plan shows the home ranges and core areas of the baboon troops in the Nairobi Park in 1960. The home ranges overlap considerably, but the core areas, which contain the baboons' sleeping trees, essential to each troop, are quite distinct. The letters refer to the different troops studied. Scale is in miles.

Source: DeVore and Hall, 1965.

Harem polygyny in zoology, a group structure including one breeding male and multiple females; among humans, a structure involving one male and multiple wives and/or concubines.

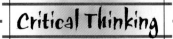

How Do Primate Social Characteristics Interrelate?

As you have seen, many aspects of anatomy, physiology, behavior, and environment all interrelate to produce primate social organization. Consider two different species (take baboons and chimpanzees as examples) and compare the relationships among group size and structure, habitat, and size of home range or territory in these species. What patterns do you see in the multispecies table below? What generalizations might you make?

Some Socioecological Characteristics of Old World Monkeys and Apes

	Japanese Macaques (*Macaca fuscata*)	Savanna Baboons (*Papio cynocephalus*)	Hanuman Langurs (*Presbytis entellus*)	White-Handed Gibbons (*Hylobates lar*)	Eastern Highland Gorillas (*Gorilla gorilla beringei*)	Orangutans (*Pongo pygmaeus*)	Chimpanzees (*Pan troglodytes*)	Bonobos (*Pan paniscus*)
Group size	35–55	10–185	10–65	Adult pair and 1 or 2 offspring	2–34	2 (mother and offspring)	20–105	50–120
Social structure	Multimale; multifemale	Multimale; multifemale	Multimale, unimale, and possibly age-graded; multifemale	Monogamous families	Unimale or multimale with one dominant silverback male; also lone males; multifemale	Mother and infant; lone males	Multimale multifemale; dispersed community	Multimale; multifemale, dispersed community
Habitat	Seasonal, deciduous and evergreen and montane and submontane areas	African acacia woodland, short grass savanna, forest	Deciduous to moist evergreen forests; sea level to high Himalayas	Forest	Lowland and mountain rain forests and bamboo forests	Indonesian jungles; herbivorous (mostly frugivorous) diet	Deciduous woodland; omnivorous (mostly frugivorous) diet	Lowland rain forest and swamp forest; omnivorous (mostly frugivorous) diet
Home range	0.1–10.4 mi^2 (0.27–27 km^2)	0.8–15.4 mi^2 (2.1–40 km^2)	0.04–3 mi^2 (0.1–7.8 km^2)	0.08–0.2 mi^2 (0.2–0.5 km^2)	1.9–3.1 mi^2 (4.9–8.1 km^2)	0.2–2.3 mi^2 (0.4–6 km^2)	2–215 mi^2 (5–560 km^2)	7.7–19.3 mi^2 (20–5- km^2)

Sources: Cheney, 1987; Doran and McNeilage, 1998; Melnick and Pearl, 1987; Nishida Hiraiwa-Hasegawa, 1987; Rodman and Mitani, 1987; Stewart and Harcourt, 1987.

Now add your predictions about the following characteristics:

Food supply (type, availability, and stability of food resources)

Sexual dimorphism (degree of difference in size and weight between males and females)

Reproductive system (male and female mating strategies)

Dominance hierarchy (degree of status differentiation)

Home range and territoriality (habitat use and defense of territory)

1. Do your patterns and generalizations hold?
2. How can you modify them to account for the new variables?
3. How might you describe humans in terms of these variables?

Primate feeding strategies range from the generalist or opportunistic approach to the specialist approach. The generalist–opportunist animal is only selective with regard to the energy value of food. It eats according to availability and eats the most nutritive food available at any particular time. Then it moves on to other, sometimes very diverse, food sources. The South American howler monkey is a good example of a generalist. In some species, opportunism includes the consumption of significant quantities of high-energy insects and meat in addition to plant foods. Baboons, macaques, mangabeys (*Cercocebus*), and chimpanzees have all been observed to eat meat in substantial quantities when the opportunity (sometimes rare) presents itself.

In contrast, specialists concentrate on only a few plant species. These either yield high energy or are abundant enough so that quantity will supplement what may be lacking in calories. Specialist strategies necessarily evolve in relatively stable environments where key foods are always available.

Some dietary specialists have evolved specialized digestive organs, such as the large stomach of leaf-eating Colobine monkeys (*Colobus*), which consists of a forestomach (in which cellulose is digested) followed by a series of saclike chambers. Dietary specializations also tend to be correlated with dental differences (Jolly and Plog, 1986). For example, animals such as tarsiers that commonly eat insects usually have enlarged and pointed incisors and canines for killing prey, and tall, sharp cusps on their molars and premolars for shearing insects into tiny, digestible fragments. Specialized leaf-eaters likewise have high-crowned molars and premolars for slicing up foliage (this aids in the digestion of cellulose), but their incisors tend to be rather narrow. Species that eat mainly fruits (frugivorous species) show yet another combination of traits: large, broad incisors with straight cutting edges (an adaptation for biting off chunks of tough-skinned fruits) and relatively small, low crowned molars (which are adequate, because the inner flesh of fruit is generally soft and needs little chewing). Information on the dental adaptations and feeding strategies of living primates can serve as a basis for inferring the diet and feeding strategies of fossil species—including early hominids.

This account of the basics of primate behavior serves as a background to the description of the behavior of the great apes, which will follow in the next chapter. Because the African apes are our closest relatives in the animal world, knowledge of their behavior is of extraordinary value as we seek to unravel the roots of our own, human, nature.

Summary

Knowledge of the behavior of living primates is an important component in the study of human origins and human nature. Since their beginnings in the early part of the last century, primate studies have produced much useful information about our evolutionary relatives, the monkeys and apes. As shown in this chapter, primates are extremely social creatures whose complex behavioral repertoires are based mainly on learning. Their societies are structured by several types of relationships, especially dominance relations, kinship, and affiliative relations (the last based commonly on grooming). Patterns of sexual behavior vary from species to species, but the levels of reproductive success and the identities of sexual partners are commonly influenced by dominance and female choice. Territorial behavior and its relationship to the ecology of the group influences social organization, and a group's feeding strategy constitutes an important adaptation that enhances survival.

Review Questions

1. Studies of primate behavior are commonly conducted both in the field and in captivity. What are the strengths and weaknesses of research in these two settings?

2. Why do most primates live in groups? What are the advantages and disadvantages of social living? What mechanisms have the animals evolved to cope with the disadvantages of group life?

3. How does the sexual behavior of primate males and females differ? How is sexual behavior affected by rank, age, kinship, and hormonal condition? What is "situation-dependent" sex?

4. How do primates relate to their habitat? Define and compare the following three concepts: home range, core area, territory.

5. What influence, if any, does genetic kinship have on primates' behavior?

Suggested Further Reading

Goodall, J. *The Chimpanzees of Gombe.* Harvard University Press, 1986.
Haraway, D. *Primate Visions.* Routledge, 1989.
Hrdy, S. B. *Mother Nature: A History of Mothers, Infants and Natural Selection.* Pantheon, 1999.
Jolly, A. *Lucy's Legacy: Sex and Intelligence in Human Evolution.* Harvard University Press, 1999.
Loy, J. D., and C. B. Peters, eds. *Understanding Behavior: What Primate Studies Tell Us about Human Behavior.* Oxford University Press, 1991.
Smuts, B., et al., eds. *Primate Societies.* University of Chicago Press, 1987.

Internet Resources

Conveniently access these and other links via our web site at **http://www.ablongman/anthro.**

Lucy's Choice Primate Links
http://www.araneum.mudservices.com/veeder/page2.html
Hundreds (no kidding!) of links to primate sites are compiled here. Like NetVet.Primates, this is a good place to start your own web explorations.

NetVet.Primates
http://netvet.wustl.edu/primates.htm
Multiple links to sites about primates' behavior, biology, evolution, and conservation.

Primate Behavior
http://daphne.palomar.edu/behavior/default.htm
Primates' social structure, adaptations for group living, and communication systems are examined, and each topic is accompanied by a practice quiz.

Primate Behavior & Ecology
http://www.primate.wisc.edu/pin/behavior.html
Provided by the Primate Info Net, this site has links to information on many aspects of primate behavior.

The Primate Gallery
http://www.selu.com/bio/PrimateGallery
Great photographs of primates, including some copyright-free material.

Useful Search Terms:
apes
dominance hierarchy
monkeys
primate behavior
primates
prosimians

Primate Evolution: The Fossil and Living Apes

Overview

This chapter describes the evolutionary beginnings of the primates, a mammalian order that has been around for at least 60 million years and probably much longer. Judging from the fossil record as currently known, the primate order first evolved in Africa during the Paleocene epoch, and its original representatives were prosimian-grade creatures. Anthropoid primates—with their improved vision, reduced sense of smell, and more complex brains—did not appear for perhaps another 10 million years. Around 20 million years ago (mya)—again in Africa—the superfamily Hominoidea made its evolutionary appearance.

These early hominoids fell into two categories: dental apes, which resembled modern apes only in their dental and cranial traits (postcranially, they were more like mon-

Mini-Timeline: Evolutionary Events

Date (Years Ago or Geologic Epoch)	Evolutionary Events	Important Genera
5–7 million	First hominids	*Australopithecus*
Late Miocene	Apes decline strongly	*Oreopithecus, Gigantopithecus*
Mid Miocene	Apes spread and diversify	*Dryopithecus, Kenyapithecus, Sivapithecus*
Early Miocene (20 million)	First apes; first Old World monkeys	*Morotopithecus, Proconsul;* monkey subfamily Victoriapithecinae
27 million	First New World monkeys	*Branisella, Szalatavus*
Oligocene	Anthropoids diversify	*Aegyptopithecus*
Eocene	First anthropoids; prosimians diversify	*Algeripithecus, Eosimias, Amphipithecus, Siamopithecus, Catopithecus;* prosimian families Adapidae, Omomyidae
Late Paleocene	First primates	*Altiatlasius*

Follow links at **http://www.ablongman/anthro** for additional resources in physical anthropology, primatology, biological anthropology, and paleoanthropology.

keys); and suspensory apes, which also showed adaptations for forelimb dominated locomotion (arm-swinging and arm-hanging). After a period of considerable success, when evolutionary diversity increased and geographic expansion carried them into Europe and Asia, the apes began to decline in numbers and variety during a period of late Miocene climatic cooling. It was at this time—some 5 to 7 million years ago—that modern humans' last ape ancestors are thought to have lived, although their precise identity is still unknown. We do know, however, what it took to change those apes into hominids: primarily the remodeling of quadrupedal creatures into bipeds. And because understanding this change is an essential prerequisite to studying the fossil hominid record, one section of the chapter is devoted to a further description of the anatomy of bipedalism.

The last part of the chapter deals with the behavior of the living apes, especially the chimpanzee, and describes their hunting activities, material culture, and aggressive and murderous behavior. The bonobo, in particular, is a smallish chimpanzee species with some remarkably human characteristics. Finally, the chapter presents speculations about the last common ancestor we share with the bonobo and other African apes.

Check our web site for additional information, photos, drawings, maps, and animations on topics in this chapter.

What Were the Earliest Primates?

The oldest known primate fossils are about 60 million years old and are from the late **Paleocene** epoch of geologic time (Table 6.1). Although this date sounds solid enough, it should be taken only as a rough approximation of the first appearance of primates. The reason is the enormous gaps in our knowledge of the fossil record. The 200-plus fossil varieties currently known represent only 2 to 4 percent of an estimated 5,000 to 7,000 extinct primate species. As additional discoveries are made, it seems inevitable that the origin of our order will be pushed millions of years farther back in time—perhaps even into the late Cretaceous period (Martin, 1993).

But for now the late Paleocene marks the origin of primates, and those first members of our order emerged into a world very different from the one we know today. For one thing, the positioning of the continents was different. Studies of **continental drift** have indicated that the Paleozoic supercontinent Pangaea II (Figure 6.1) split during the Mesozoic to form a large northern landmass—including the modern continents of North America, Europe, and most of Asia—and an even larger southern landmass combining Africa, South America, Antarctica, India, Madagascar, and Australia. By the Paleocene, South America and India had drifted away from Africa, and Africa had been separated from Eurasia by high sea levels. In the north, Eurasia and North America were still contiguous and remained so for several million years (Figure 6.1).

Not only was the configuration of the continents different during the Paleocene, but in consequence global climate patterns and habitat zones were different as well. Tropical forests spread much farther north and south from the equator; France and Germany were moist, humid jungles, as was much of Africa and nearly everywhere in between. Parts of North America were similarly forested, and the forest corridor between North America and Eurasia allowed extensive mammalian dispersal.

Within this moist, forested world, the first primates arose from some primitive, semiarboreal mammalian ancestor. Although that ancestor's exact identity remains to be discovered, it may well have resembled modern insectivorous tree shrews (Figure

Paleocene the geologic epoch extending from 65 to 58 million years BP (before present).

Continental drift a theory that describes the movements of continental landmasses throughout the earth's history.

Table 6.1

Geologic Time Scale

Geologic time scales are of such immense duration that it is hard to comprehend fully the great period of time during which nature and humankind have evolved. If the almost 500 million years of vertebrate evolution are symbolized by one hour of time, then primate evolution took seven minutes, and human evolution occurred in the last twelve seconds of that hour. (ME = mass extinction event.)

Years B.P.	Eras	Period	Epoch	Years B.P.	Main Events
		Quaternary	Pleistocene	10,000 to 1.6 million	Humans first learn to use and control fire in temperate zones
			Pliocene	1.6 to 5 million	Genus *Homo* appears Age of *Australopithecus, Paranthropus*
	Cenozoic		Miocene	5 to 25 million	First hominids First apes
		Tertiary	Oligocene	25 to 35 million	Catarrhines and platyrrhines separate
			Eocene	35 to 58 million	First anthropoids
65 million			Paleocene	58 to 65 million	First primates: prosimians
		ME			
		Cretaceous		65 to 135 million	First flowering plants Disappearance of large dinosaurs
	Mesozoic	Jurassic		135 to 180 million	First birds
		ME			
225 million		Triassic		180 to 225 million	First mammals Age of Reptiles begins
		ME			
		Permian		225 to 280 million	
		Carboniferous		280 to 345 million	First coniferous trees First reptiles
Paleozoic		ME			
		Devonian		345 to 395 million	First forests First amphibians, insects, and bony fish
		Silurian		395 to 430 million	First land plants First fish with jaws
		ME			
		Ordovician		430 to 500 million	First vertebrates: armored fish without jaws
570 million		Cambrian		500 to 570 million	First shell-bearing animals
				600 million	First multicellular animals
	Precambrian			3.5 billion	First living things: algae, bacteria
				4 billion	Formation of primordial seas
				4.5 billion	Formation of earth

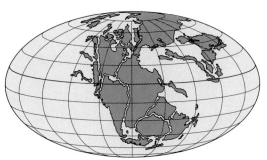

Pangaea II: 200 million years ago

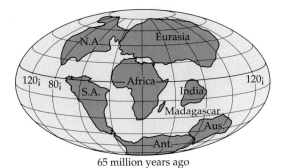

65 million years ago

Figure 6.1

Above, the supercontinent of Pangaea II at 200 mya shows the precursors of most of the modern continents. At about this time, Pangaea II split into a northern landmass, Laurasia, and a southern continent, Gondwanaland. Below, at the beginning of the Paleocene epoch, South America and India had separated from Africa, but North America and Eurasia were still linked.

6.2). In response to the challenges of arboreal living and of visual–manual predation on insects (see Chapter 4), the early primates began the order's evolutionary trajectory toward grasping hands and feet, keen vision, and a reduced sense of smell.

It is to be expected that the earliest primate fossils should be difficult to distinguish from related groups, with the result that their status is often controversial. The earliest fossil primates discovered to date have been found in Morocco at a site named Adrar Mgorn, at the foot of the Atlas Mountains. Here, in late Paleocene sediments, together with remains of twenty-three other mammalian species, have been found ten isolated molar teeth of a very small (2 to 4 ounces; 50 to 100 grams) creature named *Altiatlasius.* Not much to go on, perhaps, but enough to make a case for an African origin for the primate order, for the teeth are undoubtedly the teeth of early prosimians. This claim is supported by later finds from the early Eocene of Algeria, Tunisia, and Egypt. We also have fossils of about this age, or a little later, from Europe, Asia, and North America, but the evidence for an African origin is rapidly accumulating.

Judging from the remains of *Altiatlasius* and many other, more complete fossils, the earliest primates can be classified confidently as prosimians. In clear contrast to nonprimate mammals, they possessed forwardly directed eyes, postorbital bars, grasping big toes, and nails on most digits instead of claws. They have been arranged into two extinct families—the **Adapidae and Omomyidae** (Figure 6.3)—and their diversity during the **Eocene** epoch (we recognize some forty genera) shows that they underwent a strong evolutionary radiation shortly after their origin. Although there is disagreement among paleontologists and more fossil evidence is needed, the adapids appear to be evolutionary predecessors of modern lemurs and lorises, while the omomyids may be ancestral to modern tarsiers and possibly even to anthropoids. *Altiatlasius* has been interpreted as a very early form of omomyid (Martin, 1993).

Altiatlasius the oldest known *primate fossil;* a *prosimian* from the late *Paleocene* of North Africa.

Adapidae and Omomyidae families of *Eocene prosimians,* now extinct.

Eocene the geologic epoch extending from 58 to 35 million years BP.

Figure 6.2

Tree shrews are found in Southeast Asia. They are primitive mammals and are probably similar to the first primates. Their appearance is somewhat similar to that of the squirrel, but they are quite distinct from any rodent. Their bodies are about five inches (thirteen centimeters) long.

The anatomy of the Eocene prosimians indicates that they were agile arborealists that ate a mixed diet of fruit, leaves, and insects. Furthermore, they anticipated one of the main characteristics of modern primates by having larger brains for their body size than most other Eocene mammals.

But working so far in the past, we need information from many more fossils before we can determine with certainty which (if either) of the two prosimian families gave rise to the anthropoids. None of the known adapid or omomyid skulls shows the beginnings of such defining anthropoid traits as complete bony eye sockets or fused frontal bones (Table 4.4, page 90), and all of the Eocene prosimians very likely had a rhinarium. Still, by the middle of the Eocene some prosimian variety had given rise to creatures we can recognize as basal anthropoids, creating a major fork in the primate family tree. As the emerging anthropoids differed more and more from the prosimians, the

Figure 6.3

Representative skulls of early prosimians. Adapid (*Leptadapis magnus*) shown at left and omomyid (*Necrolemur antiquus*) to the right. Both are from European mid-Eocene deposits.

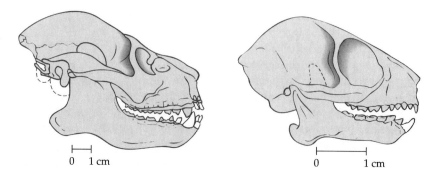

trees became filled with smarter, swifter, defter, altogether abler animals. The surviving prosimians remained nocturnal or died away in many places because they could not compete.

Where Were the First Higher Primates?

Dating the emergence of the anthropoids (higher primates) from prosimian stock is a tricky business (Kay et al., 1997). Anthropoids were clearly well established and diversified by the **Oligocene** epoch (35 to 25 million years ago), but their actual origin was probably much earlier. The oldest fossils likely to be anthropoids come from the site of Glib Zegdou in the North African country of Algeria. These remains (consisting of three molar teeth) have been named *Algeripithecus minutus* and date from the middle or even early Eocene. But although the teeth show a number of anthropoid-like features, the fragmentary nature of the fossil argues for a conservative interpretation. At present the classification of *Algeripithecus* as an anthropoid should be viewed as strictly tentative. If further discoveries—particularly of fossils showing diagnostic anthropoid cranial features—validate the claim, then the appearance of higher primates probably occurred in Africa more than 50 million years ago.

The African case is certainly not airtight, however, and there are some Asian fossils just slightly younger than *Algeripithecus* that also appear to be anthropoids. Among the most exciting are some recent discoveries from mid-Eocene deposits in China. In 1994 a joint American–Chinese research team announced the discovery of a rich deposit of fossil primates near the village of Shanghuang. Dating about 45 million years old, the Shanghuang primates include adapids, omomyids, the earliest known tarsiers, and also fossils assigned to a new genus, *Eosimias* ("the dawn ape")(Beard et al. 1994, 1996). In fact, *Eosimias* was not an ape at all but a generalized creature that showed a strong combination of derived (anthropoid) and primitive (prosimian) traits. A very small primate (body weight of 2.4 to 4.8 ounces, or 67 to 137 grams), *Eosimias* shared certain dental traits with modern anthropoids but still resembled prosimians in its unfused **mandibular symphysis.** Neither a monkey nor an ape, *Eosimias* seems to fill the bill nicely as a basal anthropoid.

Other apparent anthropoids from Asia include *Amphipithecus* and *Pondaungia* from Burma, and the recently discovered *Siamopithecus* from Thailand (Chaimanee et al., 1997). All three species date to the late Eocene. The new fossils from Shanghuang, coupled with evidence from Burma and Thailand, suggest to some researchers that the anthropoid suborder originated in Asia, not Africa. *Eosimias* in particular appears to be only slightly younger than *Algeripithecus*, and the dates for both fossils involve considerable estimation. Although Africa may still hold a slight edge in the contest, theories of an Asian origin of anthropoids must be given careful consideration.

The Oligopithecines

In any case, the anthropoids had become firmly established by the end of the Eocene epoch, and for that story we must return to northern Africa and Egypt's Fayum Depression, a region renowned for its fossil remains. In the Fayum, deposits straddling the Eocene–Oligocene boundary have yielded several undoubted anthropoids belonging to an extinct subfamily called the **oligopithecines** (Rasmussen and Simons, 1992; Simons and Rasmussen, 1996). Located in the desert about sixty miles southwest of Cairo, the Fayum Depression is currently one of the driest places on earth—hardly good

Oligocene the geologic epoch extending from 35 to 25 million years BP.

Algeripithecus minutus tentatively, the oldest known *anthropoid primate* from North Africa's early-middle *Eocene.*

Eosimias probable basal *anthropoid* from the mid-*Eocene* of China.

Mandibular symphysis the midline joint connecting the right and left halves of the lower jaw.

Amphipithecus and *Pondaungia* possible *anthropoids* from the late *Eocene* of Burma.

Siamopithecus the late *Eocene anthropoid* from Thailand.

Oligopithecines late *Eocene anthropoids;* many have been collected from Egypt's Fayum Depression.

anthropoid terrain. In Eocene and Oligocene times, however, the Fayum was a tropical and swampy region lying along the southern shore of the Mediterranean. Heavily wooded in parts and laced with rivers, it was a fine place for early anthropoids to live and evolve—and evolve they did, as the diversity of the oligopithecines attests.

The oligopithecines date to the latest Eocene of northern Africa (about 36 million years ago) and include three genera: *Oligopithecus, Proteopithecus,* and **Catopithecus** (Simons, 1993). All were small-bodied (about 2.2 pounds, or 1 kilogram) forest dwellers that probably ate a mixed diet of fruit and insects. Among the fossils of *Catopithecus* is a well-preserved skull that demonstrates such diagnostic anthropoid traits as bony eye sockets and fused frontal bones. But the oligopithecines were not typically anthropoid in all of their features. Demonstrating that anthropoid traits evolved in mosaic fashion rather than all at once, the oligopithecines still showed a low ratio of brain size to body size as well as some prosimian-like features in their jaws and teeth. *Catopithecus,* for example, had an unfused mandibular symphysis. Interestingly, the oligopithecines varied somewhat in their dental formulae: *Catopithecus* had a total of eight premolars, but *Proteopithecus* had twelve. Although too generalized to be classified as either monkeys or apes, the oligopithecines give us a good view of the anatomy, diet, and habitat of early undoubted anthropoids.

Aegyptopithecus and Other Early Anthropoids

By the early Oligocene epoch, anthropoids were enjoying much success in Africa. Several genera had evolved, including *Parapithecus, Propliopithecus, Apidium,* and **Aegyptopithecus** (Figures 6.4, 6.5). Although these creatures showed some advances over their Eocene ancestors, analyses of their total morphological patterns show that they were still very primitive. *Parapithecus* and *Apidium* are best classified as basal anthropoids that preceded the evolutionary separation of platyrrhines and catarrhines. *Propliopithecus* and *Aegyptopithecus,* on the other hand, can be identified as catarrhines, although both were too primitive to be classified further as either monkeys or apes. A detailed

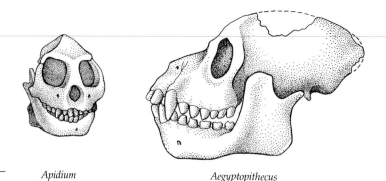

Apidium　　　　　　　*Aegyptopithecus*

Figure 6.4

Catopithecus a particularly well-known *oligopithecine* from the Fayum in Africa.

Aegyptopithecus a basal *catarrhine* from the Fayum in Africa; dated to the *Oligocene* epoch.

The orbits of living primates are surrounded by a ring of bone that constitutes a lateral extension of the frontal bone joining the cheekbone. This structure protects the large, forward-pointing eyes. Fossil anthropoids such as *Apidium* had these laterally bounded orbits and also a full bony socket, as did the more advanced *Aegyptopithecus*. In more primitive nonprimate mammals, the orbit was open at the back and side.

Figure 6.5

Finds of *Aegyptopithecus* bones are now so numerous that a full reconstruction is possible. This drawing of the 12-pound (5.4-kilogram) creature was made under the direction of Elwyn Simons. Notice that this catarrhine carried a long tail.

analysis of the total morphology of *Aegyptopithecus* shows how such a conclusion is reached (Simons, 1972). Although certain dental features suggest that *Aegyptopithecus* had evolved into an ape-grade creature—2123/2123 dental formula, five-cusped molars, rectangular dental arcade (Figure 6.6)—other features are distinctly monkeylike. *Aegyptopithecus* was an arboreal quadruped rather than an arm-hanger or arm-swinger, sported a tail, and had a monkey-shaped skull. Thus, *Propliopithecus* and *Aegyptopithecus* are best regarded as generalized catarrhines that were, however, on or near the ancestral line for all later anthropoids of the Old World. The stage was set for the evolution of the modern superfamilies of monkeys and apes.

New World Monkeys

Humans are catarrhine primates whose evolutionary origins reside in the Old World. That being the case, the history of the New World monkeys is of rather secondary importance to the story being told here. Nonetheless, the evolutionary appearance of these "second cousins" of ours deserves at least a brief description before we move on to fossil apes.

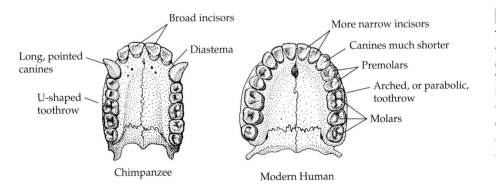

Broad incisors
Diastema
Long, pointed canines
U-shaped toothrow
Chimpanzee

More narrow incisors
Canines much shorter
Premolars
Arched, or parabolic, toothrow
Molars
Modern Human

Figure 6.6

The dentition of the upper jaw of an ape (a chimpanzee) and a human is compared. Notice the ape's more rectangular dental arcade, as well as the ape's large canines and diastemata.

The oldest fossils of platyrrhine monkeys come from late Oligocene deposits in Bolivia. Two genera are recognized—***Branisella and Szalatavus***—and both are about 27 million years old. Thus, on the basis of fossil evidence, anthropoid primates showed up in the New World at least 9 million years later (and possibly as much as 20 million years later) than in Africa. Couple these dates with the present lack of evidence of separate prosimian ancestries for platyrrhines and catarrhines, and one is forced to conclude tentatively that the New World monkeys are descended from African anthropoid stock. But how could they have migrated across the South Atlantic—a sizable span of water even in Oligocene times—to a new neotropical home? The best answer seems to be that they crossed by a combination of island hopping (a series of mid-Atlantic islands may have existed off the coast of Sierra Leone and elsewhere) and rafting aboard floating mats of vegetation. Once in South and Central America, the platyrrhines diversified strongly to produce the great variety of New World monkeys alive today. They made no contribution, however, to the evolution of humankind.

How Did the Earliest Hominoids Evolve?

The earliest known members of the superfamily Hominoidea—that is, the first apes—appear in the fossil record from the early **Miocene** epoch and date to about 20 million years of age (Conroy, 1990). The absolutely oldest genera, *Morotopithecus* and *Proconsul,* are from African sites, as are most of the other early Miocene forms (Table 6.2), making an African origin for hominoids a safe conclusion. Cercopithecoid monkeys apparently evolved at roughly the same time, but details of the evolutionary differentiation of the two living catarrhine superfamilies are unclear at present. The earliest catarrhine monkeys are classed within the extinct subfamily **Victoriapithecinae** (Conroy, 1990), and many species used more open habitats than those favored by the evolving hominoids. Although interesting in their own right, the Cercopithecoidea had little, if any, effect on hominid evolution and therefore they will concern us no further. (Some scientists do speculate that competition from an increasingly diverse and numerous collection of monkeys may have led some African apes to begin adapting to life on the ground, perhaps literally taking the first steps toward hominid status. The idea remains controversial.)

The apes do concern us, however, and during the Miocene they were busy adapting to a warm East African environment covered mostly by forest or woodlands.

The Rise of the Miocene Apes

Miocene apes were forest animals that subsisted on a mixed diet of fruit and leaves, and they ranged from monkey-sized creatures to animals as large as modern chimpanzees. As shown by the genus names in Table 6.2, these early hominoids were a diverse lot, and their evolutionary relationships are not at all clear. Indeed, they were so diverse that many genera (e.g., *Proconsul*) resembled modern apes only in their dental and cranial traits (a fact that brings the proper use of the label "ape" into question). From the neck down, *Proconsul* and several others had more anatomical similarities to monkeys than to today's chimpanzees, orangutans, and gorillas. A few Miocene genera, however—particularly *Morotopithecus,* ***Oreopithecus, and Dryopithecus***—had evolved adaptations for suspensory postures and locomotion (Gebo et al., 1997; Moyá-Solà and Köhler, 1996) and thus looked like modern apes both above and below the neck (that is, cranially, dentally, *and* postcranially). David Pilbeam of Harvard University refers to the first category of creatures (e.g., *Proconsul*) as "hominoids of archaic aspect," and the

Branisella and *Szalatavus* Oligocene platyrrhine monkeys from Bolivia.

Miocene the geologic epoch extending from 25 to 5 million years BP.

Morotopithecus an *ape* from East Africa that lived during the early *Miocene.*

Proconsul an *ape* from East Africa that lived during the early *Miocene* epoch.

Victoriapithecinae extinct subfamily of the earliest *catarrhine* monkeys.

Oreopithecus and *Dryopithecus* ape genera from the mid-to-late *Miocene* of Europe.

Table 6.2

Fossil Ape Genera		
Age	**Genus**	**Location**
Early Miocene	*Proconsul*	Africa
	Morotopithecus	Africa
	Micropithecus	Africa
	Limnopithecus	Africa
	Dendropithecus	Africa
	Rangwapithecus	Africa
	Turkanapithecus	Africa
?	*Dionysopithecus*	Asia
Early to Mid-Miocene	*Afropithecus*	Africa, Saudi Arabia
	Nyanzapithecus	Africa
Mid-Miocene	*Kenyapithecus*	Africa
	Otavipithecus	Africa
Mid- to Late Miocene	*Dryopithecus*[a]	Europe
	Pliopithecus	Europe
	Sivapithecus[a,b]	Africa, Asia, Europe
Late Miocene	*Laccopithecus*	Asia
	Lufengpithecus	Asia
	Oreopithecus	Europe
Late Miocene to Pleistocene	*Gigantopithecus*	Asia

[a] *Rudapithecus* is lumped with *Dryopithecus* by some authors and with *Sivapithecus* by others.
[b] Includes *Ouranopithecus* and the Pasalar fossils from Figure 6.7, and also *Ramapithecus* and *Ankarapithecus*.

Source: With the exceptions of *Otavipithecus, Morotopithecus,* and *Kenyapithecus,* all information from Conroy, 1990.

second as "hominoids of modern aspect"(Pilbeam, 1996). We prefer the shorter terms "dental apes" and "suspensory apes."

Proconsul and the Dental Apes.   Dental apes, such as *Proconsul,* show up right at the very beginning of hominoid history, some 17 to 20 million years ago. As represented by *Sivapithecus, Lufengpithecus,* and others, the dental apes continued until the late stages of the Miocene (Figure 6.7); they are known from Africa, Asia, and Europe. The well-known African genus *Proconsul* (Figure 6.8) serves as a good example of these archaic hominoids. As expected from a catarrhine, *Proconsul's* protruding muzzle showed a dental formula of 2123/2123. In addition, it had projecting and pointed canine teeth, upper canines that sheared against the lower anterior premolars, and postcanine toothrows that were generally parallel. Other features worth mentioning are *Proconsul's* strongly receding forehead and low-vaulted braincase. Despite its apelike teeth and skull, however, *Proconsul* showed few similarities to modern apes from the neck down (Simons, 1992). As summarized in Table 4.5 (page 91) and illustrated in Figure 6.9, modern apes have a broad chest, a short lower back, no tail, and shoulders and arms modified for forelimb-dominated locomotion (arm-hanging and arm-swinging). Although *Proconsul* did lack a tail, the similarities stop there. In contrast to modern apes, *Proconsul* had a long, flexible spine; a narrow torso; and monkeylike limb proportions. Judging from its postcranial remains, *Proconsul* was a rather generalized quadruped, certainly not an animal adapted for forelimb-dominated arboreal movement.

Dental ape a fossil ape having apelike dentition but postcranially more like a monkey.

Sivapithecus a genus of *Miocene apes* that include *Ramapithecus;* probably ancestral to the *orangutan.*

Figure 6.7

Various fossil ape genera are shown here along with their time ranges (solid lines denote well-known ranges; dashed lines indicate probable ranges).

Source: Data primarily from Kelley, 1992.

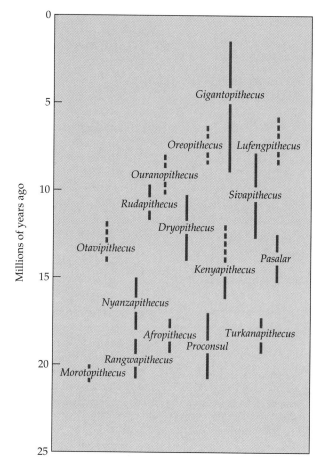

Figure 6.8

The skull of *Proconsul* is a typical ape skull. It combines a low cranial vault, projecting muzzle, and large anterior teeth.

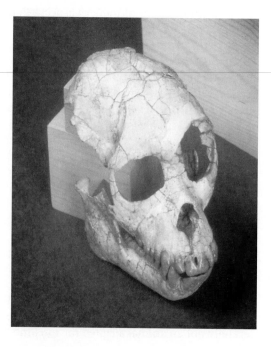

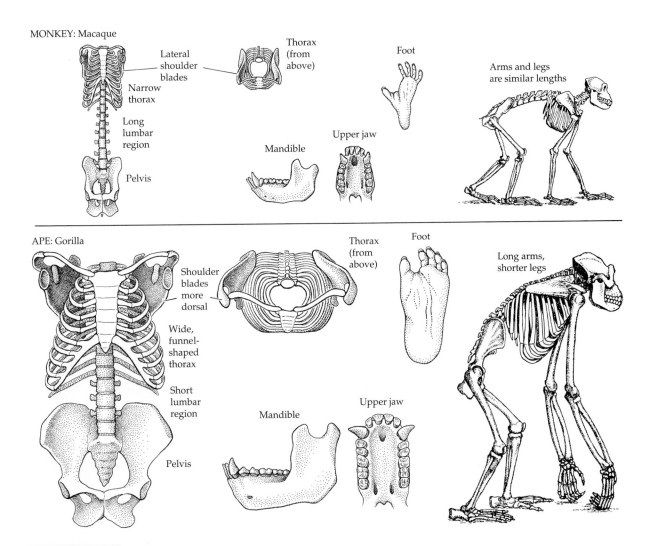

Figure 6.9

Ape and monkey skeletons have much in common. Nonetheless, apes are more like humans than like monkeys in skeletal structure. Note the different proportions of the limbs; the form of the rib cage and shoulder blade; and the use of hands in locomotion. Note that the macaque shown has a relatively short tail.

Dryopithecus and the Suspensory Apes. As regards the postcranially modern apes, it was thought until quite recently that adaptations for forelimb-dominated locomotion (arm-hanging and arm-swinging) were very late developments in hominoid evolution. For example, _Sivapithecus,_ from the mid-to-late Miocene, shows elbow joints apparently adapted for arboreal suspension; but the rest of its skeleton suggests quadrupedal walking. The oldest known full-fledged hanger-and-swinger was once thought to be _Oreopithecus bambolii,_ which inhabited Europe around 8 million years ago. This unique hominoid had a short trunk and a broad thorax, long arms and short legs, and elbow joints like those of living apes (Fleagle, 1988). Unfortunately, the evolutionary relationships of _Oreopithecus_ are extremely obscure. It seems most likely that the line leading to *Oreopithecus* diverged from the main hominoid lineage fairly early, and therefore it is not directly ancestral to modern apes.

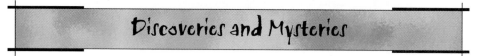

Discoveries and Mysteries

The Ultimate Suspensory Ape

The recent discoveries of two **suspensory apes** have pushed the advent of forelimb-dominated locomotion far back in hominoid history. First, in 1996, Spanish paleontologists Salvador Moyá-Solà and Meike Köhler published evidence that the European species *Dryopithecus laietanus* was an upright climber and swinger 9.5 million years ago. Fossils from the Spanish site of Can Llobateres revealed that, like modern apes, *D. laietanus* had a short back, broad thorax, dorsally positioned shoulder blades, long arms and short legs, and large hands with long, powerful fingers (Figure 6.10). Clearly indicative of suspensory locomotion, these traits have convinced Moyá-Solà and Köhler that *Dryopithecus* is closely related to modern apes (1996).

Figure 6.10

The skeleton of *Dryopithecus laietanus* from Can Llobateres (Spain). Note the long arm, large hand, and long, powerful fingers. All of these traits suggest forelimb-dominated, suspensory locomotion.

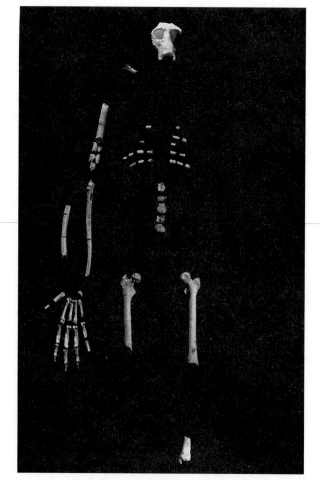

Suspensory ape a fossil ape with an apelike suspensory locomotor adaptation.

The second new find, however, is much older than Can Llobateres and thus even more exciting. In April 1997, a team of researchers headed by Daniel Gebo of Northern Illinois University announced evidence of an upright climber and brachiator dating to 20.6 million years of age. Named *Morotopithecus bishopi* and recovered from a site in northeastern Uganda, this ancient hominoid had a short, stiff back, broadening of the thorax, and modifications of the shoulder that allowed "climbing, a slow to moderate speed of brachiation, . . . quadrupedalism, and . . . an arm-hanging posture" (Gebo et al., 1997: 402). Its discoverers suspect that *Morotopithecus,* which was quite large at about 100 pounds (45 kilograms), is not directly ancestral to modern hominoids, but rather represents a sister taxon that split off early from the lineage of living apes.

In sum, the evidence from *Oreopithecus, Dryopithecus,* and *Morotopithecus,* in combination with that from the dental apes, indicates that hominoids have evolved a variety of locomotor adaptations throughout the superfamily's long history. Most fossil species opted for *pronograde* locomotion (monkeylike quadrupedalism with the spine horizontal), but a few showed *orthograde* (spine upright) suspensory patterns similar to today's arm-hanging and arm-swinging apes. Exactly when and why the pronograde hominoids went extinct, leaving only orthograde locomotors among the living apes, is unknown.

The Spread and Decline of the Miocene Apes

After their evolutionary origin in Africa, the apes began to spread out. By the mid-Miocene they had migrated into Eurasia, where they spread from Spain to Turkey. The recently discovered species called *Otavipithecus namibiensis* shows that meanwhile, back in Africa, apes were living in the southern part of that continent as well as in their old East African haunts (Conroy et al., 1993). Adaptive radiations occurred in both Africa and Eurasia, as well as continued geographic spread, and by the late Miocene there was a tremendous diversity of apes distributed across the Old World as far east as China.

Most of the Miocene apes were moderate to large in body size, although some, such as the 660-pound (300-kilogram) *Gigantopithecus,* were enormous. The favorite habitat of the Miocene apes was dense woods and forests, and their primary foods varied from leaves (e.g., *Oreopithecus*) to fruits to mixed diets including tough, hard items requiring powerful chewing (e.g., *Sivapithecus* and *Gigantopithecus*). As one might expect, enamel thickness on their grinding teeth (molars and premolars) was as variable as their diets. (All living apes have thin molar enamel, with the exception of the orangutan, which shows an "intermediate" thickness.)

Ape diversity declined strongly at the end of the Miocene, however, in association with global climatic changes, principally continental cooling and drying. Forests shrank in size and open habitats expanded. We know that the ancestors of the modern large-bodied apes and hominids were diverging at this time, but we can draw few firm conclusions about evolutionary relationships. The orangutan lineage probably diverged between 13 and 16 mya, and it seems that the fossil genus *Sivapithecus* (now understood to include *Ramapithecus,* a genus once thought to be an ancestor of hominids) may be an evolutionary ancestor of the orangutan (Figure 6.11). The evolutionary histories of the African apes, chimpanzees, bonobos, and gorillas—humans' closest living primate kin—are poorly known at present. One new and interesting suggestion made by Monte McCrossin of Southern Illinois University is that **Kenyapithecus,** a 14-million-year-old

Kenyapithecus a fossil ape from the middle *Miocene* of East Africa and a possible hominid ancestor.

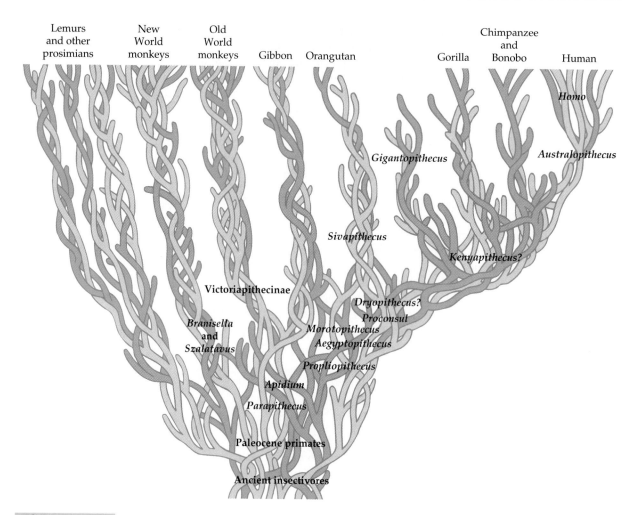

Figure 6.11

Evolutionary trees, or dendrograms, are always greatly oversimplified and in certain ways inaccurate, but they nevertheless give a good indication of the relative ages and phylogenetic relationships of the species shown. The multiplicity of lines indicates that any evolving lineage contains an unknown number of divergent populations that may or may not be different species. Many such populations become extinct. The drawing is highly speculative.

hominoid from East Africa, is "the best, most likely ancestor of humans, chimps, [bonobos,] and gorillas." McCrossin recently advanced this idea based on new fossils he and his colleague Brenda Benefit discovered on Maboko Island in Lake Victoria (McCrossin, 1997a, 1997b). Citing cranial, dental, and postcranial features, these researchers not only link *Kenyapithecus* with humans and the living African apes, but also identify *Kenyapithecus africanus* as the first semiterrestrial hominoid, a species "caught in the act of undergoing the transition from life in the trees to life on the ground." If this is true, further study of *Kenyapithecus* promises to yield great insight into the habitat transition brought about by climate changes at the end of the Miocene and thought to have been critical for the later evolution of hominids.

In any event, we know that the African habitat was strongly affected some 8 million years ago by earth movements that produced the Rift Valley running down the eastern side of the continent (Coppens, 1994) (see Figure 7.1). Because of changes in air circulation and rainfall, the area west of the Rift remained humid and forested; to the east, a drier climate produced open savannas. Biomolecular studies suggest that the gorilla lineage may have branched off around the time the Rift Valley was formed, with hominids separating from the chimpanzee–bonobo lineage shortly thereafter (Table 6.4). It appears that humans' last ape ancestors lived in Africa (as Darwin predicted) during the late Miocene, some 6 to 8 mya. Precisely what those apes were, what they looked like, and how they behaved remains to be discovered. But big changes were afoot: By early in the succeeding **Pliocene** epoch, unequivocal hominids had evolved.

How Are Hominids Differentiated from Apes?

We are now poised to review the fossil record of the human family, the family Hominidae. Indeed, most of the remainder of this book is devoted to that purpose. Before surveying the hominid remains, however, it is important to set out very clearly the minimum criteria for including a fossil species in that category. As reviewed in Chapter 4, living hominids (modern humans) are distinguished by several traits, including short, incisorlike canine teeth; skulls with flat faces and huge brains (Figure 6.12); fully opposable thumbs that give us a fine precision grip; and numerous adaptations of the back, hips, legs, and feet that facilitate bipedal locomotion. Of these traits, only two—the first to evolve—are useful markers of the earliest hominids: reduced canine length and adaptations for bipedalism. But even these two are not equally useful. Some of the late Miocene apes (*Ouranopithecus*, for example) had relatively short canines, and the canines of some early hominids were relatively long in comparison to those of later members of the human family. Therefore, in the final analysis only evidence of habitual bipedalism unmistakably marks a fossil species as hominid.

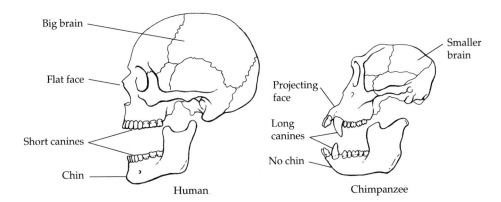

Figure 6.12

The ape and human skulls are quite distinct. The chimpanzee has a large jaw with large canines, especially in the male skull shown here. In humans, the teeth are smaller, and the canines generally project no farther than the other teeth. Humans also show a distinct chin, whereas apes do not. The enlarged braincase of humans brings about a more vertical alignment of the face and jaws.

Pliocene the geologic epoch extending from 5 to 1.6 million years BP.

Wide-knee stance standing position in which the feet and knees are about as far apart as the hip joints.

Iliac blade the broad portion of the *ilium,* one of the bones of the pelvis.

Anterior inferior iliac spine a projection from the *ilium* that serves as an attachment point for certain thigh muscles and also the *iliofemoral ligament.*

Anatomical Criteria

Modern apes are long-armed and short-legged arborealists. They climb, swing, or hang about in the trees using forelimb-dominated movements, and when they come to the ground they walk quadrupedally. As adaptations for these locomotor patterns, apes have evolved (or retained) a distinct suite of postcranial traits. They have short, stiff, straight backs; tall, narrow pelvic bones similar to those of monkeys; widely spaced knees and feet, or a **wide-knee stance** (Figure 6.13); and divergent big toes capable of grasping branches during climbing. Specifically with regard to the pelvis, the following distinctive anatomical traits can be identified in apes (Figure 6.14): (1) The **iliac blade** is tall and narrow and shows no sign of forward curvature into a "pelvic bowl"; (2) the **anterior inferior** (front lower) **iliac spine** is very small and undeveloped; (3) the shaft

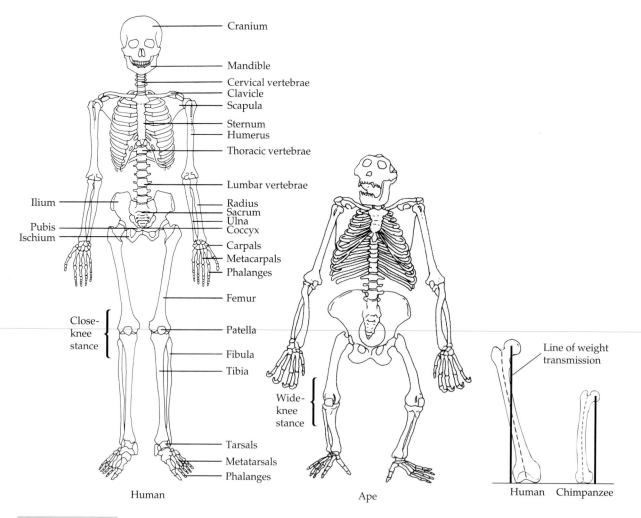

Figure 6.13

Humans (left) have evolved a close-knee stance, while bipedal apes (center) show a wide-knee posture. Postural and locomotor differences are reflected in the ape's lack of an angled femoral shaft in contrast to humans, who have one (right).

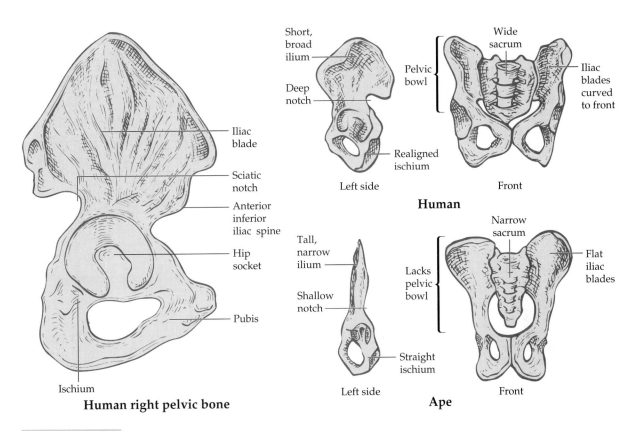

Human right pelvic bone

Human

Ape

Figure 6.14

The right pelvic bone of a human (left) has a broad iliac blade, a deep sciatic notch, and a large anterior inferior iliac spine. The two pelvic bones plus the sacrum form a distinct pelvic bowl in humans (top right), while the iliac blades of an ape show no bowl-like curvature (bottom right). Drawings on right are not to scale.

of the **ischium** lies essentially in a straight line with the main portion of the ilium; and (4) the **sacrum** (the wedge of fused vertebrae that articulates with the pelvic bones) is relatively narrow. Additionally, the ape's wide-knee stance results in the lack of an angled shaft in the **femur** (thighbone) at the knee (Figure 6.13).

Equipped with this set of anatomical features, apes are capable only of energetically expensive, unstable bipedalism. A bipedal ape stands in a bent-hip, bent-knee posture with its center of gravity high above and **anterior** to the hip joints (Figure 6.15). This semiupright posture is needed to produce an angle between the ischium and the femur—an angle that allows the **hamstring muscles** to extend (retract) the thigh—but it is maintained only with considerable muscular effort. When an ape walks, it takes short steps (the knee never passes behind the hip joints), and it balances by swaying its trunk to one side as the opposite leg is swinging forward. This "waddle-and-teeter" bipedalism is the best an ape can do, given its anatomy, but it is a most imperfect means of locomotion.

In contrast to the pelvis in apes, the human pelvis (Figure 6.14) features (1) a short iliac blade that has been widened and bent **posteriorly** (as shown by the deep **sciatic notch**); (2) anterior curvature and lateral flaring of the iliac blades to produce a bowl-shaped pelvic girdle; (3) strong enlargement of the anterior inferior iliac spine; (4)

Ischium one of the bones of the pelvis.

Sacrum the part of the vertebral column that articulates with the pelvis and forms the dorsal portion of the pelvic girdle.

Femur thighbone.

Anterior front, or ventral. In quadrupeds, the forward part of the body.

Hamstring muscles muscles of the hips and the back of the thigh; thigh extensors.

Posterior back, or dorsal. In quadrupeds, the rear part of the body.

Sciatic notch a deep indentation of the dorsal edge of the hominid *ilium*.

Figure 6.15

A bipedal ape (left) stands with its feet wide apart and with a bent-hip, bent-knee posture. The ape's center of gravity (see dot) is located high above and anterior to the hip joints. In contrast, a bipedal human (right) has its feet close together, and the center of gravity is located within the pelvic girdle.

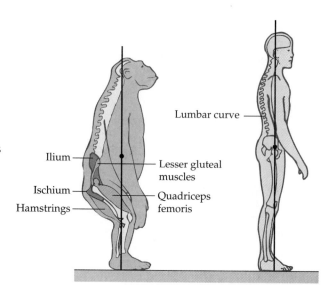

Lumbar curve

Ilium

Lesser gluteal muscles

Ischium

Quadriceps femoris

Hamstrings

Lumbar curve forward curvature of the vertebral column in the lower back that helps bring the hominid trunk over the hip joints.

Gluteus medius and gluteus minimus muscles of the hip; lateral stabilizers of the pelvis in modern humans.

Iliofemoral ligament ligament that prevents backward movement of the trunk at the human hip.

---

realignment of the ischium relative to the ilium; and (5) a wide sacrum. These evolutionary modifications went a long way toward perfecting bipedal walking. In conjunction with the development of a **lumbar curve** in the back, posterior expansion and bending of the iliac blades brought the human trunk over the hip joints and allowed straightening of the legs, while lowering the center of gravity to a point within the pelvic bowl. This greatly increased the energy efficiency of bipedalism and reduced its instability. The evolution of a pelvic bowl with broad, flaring walls allowed the lesser gluteal muscles (**gluteus medius and gluteus minimus**) to function as powerful lateral stabilizers of the trunk during walking—no more teetering to balance the body and free the swing leg (Figure 6.16). Expansion of the anterior inferior iliac spine facilitated pulling the thigh forward (flexion) and also provided space for humans' large **iliofemoral ligament,** an anatomical feature that stabilizes the trunk against backward movement at the hips (Figure 6.16). And finally, the realignment of the ischium relative

Figure 6.16

Left, the lesser gluteal muscles of humans (gluteus medius and gluteus minimus) provide lateral stabilization of the pelvis over the fixed leg during bipedalism. Right, a front view of the pelvis and the femur also shows the position of humans' iliofemoral ligament.

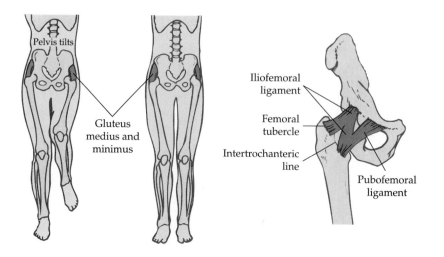

Pelvis tilts

Gluteus medius and minimus

Iliofemoral ligament

Femoral tubercle

Intertrochanteric line

Pubofemoral ligament

to the ilium resulted in an angle between the ischium and the femur that allows the thigh-extending hamstrings to work well with the body fully upright. This last change, in turn, allowed humans to take nice long strides on knees that swing back past the hips (no more waddling).

Two other changes in humans' postcranial anatomy deserve to be mentioned. We evolved a **close-knee stance** that placed our feet nearer the body's midline, making lateral balancing of the trunk much easier than in wide-kneed apes and producing an angled femoral shaft (Figure 6.13). Additionally, we evolved nondivergent and nonprehensile big toes that function to propel our bodies forward during bipedal movement.

The pelvic anatomies of living apes and humans reveal two ends of an evolutionary continuum. We can expect the pelvic remains of early hominids to be intermediate between these extremes, with the very first members of our family resembling apes more than people. But the primary criterion for classifying a fossil species as hominid is clear: evidence of habitual bipedal movement.

Biomolecular Differences

Another criterion of relatedness is biochemical properties. Close evolutionary relationships among humans, apes, and monkeys are demonstrated by our many anatomical similarities, as T. H. Huxley showed in 1863 (Figure 1.3, page 9). Within the last forty years, those close relationships have been verified by studies of anthropoids' biochemistry. For example, Figure 6.17 shows the results of Vincent Sarich and Allan Wilson's work on the evolved differences in one protein, serum albumin, for a select set of primates

Close-knee stance standing position in which the feet and knees are closer together than the hip joints.

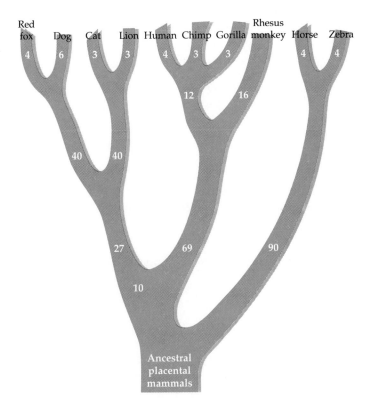

Figure 6.17

This dendrogram shows the molecular differences in serum albumin among various primates and other mammals, drawn to indicate their relationships. There is no time scale.

Source: Data from Sarich and Wilson, 1967.

and other mammals (Sarich and Wilson, 1967). With a total of thirty-two amino acid differences, the serum albumin molecules of humans and rhesus monkeys are quite distinct (32 = 4 + 12 + 16). This suggests that Old World monkeys and hominoids last shared a common ancestor many millions of years ago and thus the monkey–hominoid fork is placed about a third of the way down the primate branch. In contrast, humans only show seven albumin differences from chimpanzees and gorillas, indicating a much more recent evolutionary divergence, as shown by a higher fork. (The two apes are even closer, with only six differences separating them.)

Other biochemical measures have yielded similar results. As shown in Table 6.3, both blood protein immunology and DNA hybridization reveal close evolutionary distances between humans and the African apes, with larger distances separating humans from gibbons (Asian apes), monkeys, and prosimians. (DNA hybridization is a rather complex process that involves splitting a species' double-stranded DNA by heating it, and then comparing the nucleotide sequences on single DNA strands with strands from a second species.) Furthermore, the pooled results of amino acid sequencing studies of several different proteins go beyond the serum albumin evidence and suggest that humans are even closer to chimpanzees than to gorillas. Thus, in Table 6.3 the numbers can be read as measures of *relative evolutionary relationship with smaller numbers reflecting closer relations.*

Finally, although there is some disagreement among specialists, it seems reasonable to assume that molecular changes occur at approximately the same rate in different lineages of organisms. This means that measures of accumulated change can be used to estimate the date when lines leading to different living species diverged from their common ancestor. In other words, accumulated change can be used to construct **molecular clocks.** Table 6.4 lists humans' molecular divergence dates from the African ape lineage, as well as from the lines of several other types of anthropoids. Note that these dates are estimates. Many paleontologists still feel that only fossils can give us conclusive evidence of divergence times.

For more on the evolution of prosimians, monkeys, and apes, visit our web site.

Molecular clocks a variety of molecular measures for estimating the time of divergence of living *species* from their common ancestor.

Table 6.3

				Old World	New World		
Biochemical Marker	**Chimpanzee**	**Gorilla**	**Gibbon**	**Monkey**	**Monkey**	**Prosimian**	**Source**
Protein immunology	8	8	18	40	70	140	V. M. Sarich and J. E. Cronin (1977)
DNA hybridization	2.3	2.4	6.4	9	15	—	R. E. Beneviste and G. J. Todaro (1976)
Amino acid sequencing	0.3	0.6	2.4	3.8	7.5	11.3	M. Goodman (1975)

Relationships between Humans and Other Primates Using Biochemical Markers

Table 6.4

Estimated Times of Evolutionary Divergence among Higher Primates (in millions of years)		
Species	**Time of Divergence Based on Molecular Clock**	**Time of Divergence Based on Fossil Evidence**
Humans and the chimp and bonobo lineage	6–7	6–8
Humans and gorillas	8–10	—
Humans and gibbons	12±3	12–21
Humans and Old World monkeys	20±2	15–20
Humans and New World monkeys	~33	~27

Sources: Dates from Cronin, 1986, pp. 83–85; Sarich, 1992, pp. 303–306; Sibley, 1992, pp. 313–315.

What Are Some Behavior Patterns of the Living Apes?

The anatomical and biochemical characteristics of the apes are important when we try to interpret the fossil remains that are intermediate between apes and humans, but they only tell us half the story of human evolution. As the body of our common ancestor was evolving, so was the behavior of this ancient ape. It is therefore of great importance to know more about the behavior of living apes in order to understand the baseline from which human behavior evolved.

Gibbons and Orangutans

Gibbons (six species including siamangs) and the orangutan are Asiatic apes. By a great number of external and internal measurements, including genetic ones, they are remarkably different from the African apes—chimpanzees, bonobos, and gorillas. These differences indicate separations far back in time, between 12 and 21 million years ago for gibbons and 13 to 16 million years ago for orangutans—long before the separation of human, gorilla, bonobo, and chimpanzee (see Table 6.4).

As we have seen, both gibbons and the orangutan are tree-dwelling animals today. Millions of years of climbing and total reliance on the fruits that grow in rain forest trees have brought them to an extreme point of arboreal specialization. In the trees they move superbly, each in its own way. The gibbon (Figure 4.8, page 89) is an airy flier that hangs from branches, swinging from one to another in a breathtaking arc, grabbing the next branch just long enough to launch itself in the direction of a third. For this brachiator, arms and hands are everything. Its fingers are extremely long, specialized to serve as powerful hooks to catch branches. As a result of this finger specialization, the gibbon has the poorest manual dexterity of any ape. And being the smallest ape, it has the smallest brain.

The orangutan is quite different (Figure 4.8, page 89). It is much larger: Adult males weigh more than 150 pounds (68 kilograms), compared to the gibbons' 11 to 24 pounds (5 to 11 kilograms). Obviously an animal of this size cannot go careening through the branches. Orangutans have developed strongly prehensile hands and feet well adapted to seizing or holding, and their limbs are so articulated that they can reach

---

ASKING QUESTIONS

Can Fossils Yield Biochemical Data?

During the process of fossilization, organic compounds are dissolved from bone and tooth dentine and replaced by inorganic compounds from the ground water. This process, however, takes tens of thousands of years and its speed depends on the geological context of the fossil. Bone that is no more than a few thousand years old will retain its collagen and can be used for carbon 14 dating, but until recently there was little reason to expect other less-stable biochemical compounds to survive for long. It happens, however, that DNA is a surprisingly stable compound and will survive for long periods. We may never be able to obtain the DNA of dinosaurs, but recently researchers have managed to do something almost as fascinating; they have extracted DNA from Neandertal bones, those ancient cousins of *Homo sapiens* who became extinct about 30,000 years ago.

A German–American research project has achieved some significant results (Krings et al., 1997). The extraction of meaningful samples of DNA from fossil bone is complex and the comparison of Neandertal with human and chimp DNA gives fascinating results. Using mitochondrial DNA from these species, a sequence of 379 base pairs was obtained and comparisons were made. Human DNA lineages differed among themselves by 8 ± 3 differences; between humans and Neandertals, the differences amounted to 27 ± 2; between humans and chimps, they numbered about twice this amount. These results have been broadly confirmed by laboratories in Georgia (Orchinnikov et al., 2000).

The data have enabled most paleontologists to conclude that the differences between modern humans and the Neandertal people were sufficient to recognize Neandertals as a separate species from us; closely related, perhaps, but distinct.

How much difference—biochemical or anatomical—do you think is necessary for the recognition of a new species? How do paleoanthropologists reach decisions about recognizing species in the fossil record? Could these new data give us a better understanding of the relationships between ourselves and our more recent ancestors and between those ancestors and the great apes?

---

in any direction. There is almost nowhere in a tree that an orangutan cannot safely go, despite its great bulk, by careful gripping and climbing.

The grouping patterns and mating systems of gibbons and orangutans are very different (see page 124). Gibbons form monogynous families that are usually long-lasting. Adult males and females are **monomorphic** in body size and canine tooth length and, as a result, are often codominant (equally dominant). Both sexes actively defend the family's arboreal territory (0.08 to 0.2 miles^2; 0.2 to 0.5 kilometers^2) against encroachment by neighboring families. Subadults of both sexes disperse from their natal units (often after aggression by their same-sex parent) and start their own families.

This traditional picture of stable and cooperative gibbon families is complicated by recent field studies documenting mate desertion by both male and female gibbons (this usually also involves forfeiture of territory), as well as "extra-pair" (in human terms, adulterous) copulations with neighbors (Palombit, 1994; Reichard, 1995). Within three wild gibbon groups in Thailand, extra-pair matings accounted for 12 percent of all copulations. These new data suggest that gibbons continually assess their mates and that both males and females are prepared to copulate adulterously and/or abandon their families, which may improve their personal reproductive prospects.

In contrast to gibbons, adult orangutans of both sexes live semisolitary lives, and the only real social unit is that of a female and her dependent offspring. Adult males are twice the size of adult females, and males (even as subadults) generally dominate females. Each adult inhabits a large home range (0.6 to 2.3 miles^2, or 1.5 to 6 kilometers^2, for females), with an extensive overlap of males' and females' ranges. Adult males have several mating strategies (van Schaik and van Hooff, 1996; Delgado and van Schaik, 2000). Some inhabit large home ranges and give distinctive "long calls" that deter the

Monomorphic both sexes showing the same trait (e.g., similar body size).

approach of less-dominant males while attracting the attention of receptive females. Other males, both lower-ranking full adults and subadults, simply move over large distances and seek matings opportunistically. Because both males and females have access to multiple sexual partners, the orangutan mating system is best described as promiscuous.

Both gibbons and orangutans are basically frugivorous (fruit-eating) in their diets. Compared to other ape species, gibbons perform very little object manipulation and may be safely classed as non-tool-users (although there was one observation of a leaf being used as a sponge for water dipping) (McGrew, 1992). Wild orangutans, on the other hand, are much more accomplished tool-users (McGrew, 1992; Rogers and Kaplan, 1994; van Schaik et al., 1996). The apes regularly drop twigs and topple snags as part of aggressive displays, and also rub their faces with leaves. Wild Sumatran orangs have been observed to fashion sticks into tools to probe for seeds from partly opened *Neesia* fruits and to extract insects, bits of insect nests, and honey from tree holes. Orangs' stick probes usually are held between the teeth, but occasionally they are hand-held. Finally, female orangutans rehabilitated to the wild in East Malaysia have been seen to arrange several large leaves into "leaf-vessels" into which they spit partially masticated food. They then consume the food gradually from the leaf-vessel. In captivity, orangutans have shown quite extensive and complex tool use.

As noted earlier, among the living apes, gibbons and orangutans are humans' most distant evolutionary kin. Therefore, we must examine our hominoid relatives from Africa in somewhat greater detail.

Gorillas

Much of what we know of the gorilla comes from the work of Dian Fossey, tragically murdered in Rwanda by poachers, who began her extensive observations of mountain gorillas in 1967 and founded a research center in Rwanda (Fossey, 1983). Fossey quickly discovered that, far from being the ferocious beasts of legend, gorillas are generally mild-mannered vegetarians that like to mind their own business.

Whereas the orangutan and gibbon have evolved into specialized tree-dwellers, the gorilla's development has taken the direction of a great increase in size, along with a dietary switch from the fruit and leaves found in trees to a more general menu of terrestrial plants: fresh bark, larger leaves, roots, bamboo shoots, and other plants—herbal as much as arboreal vegetation. These two specializations of size and diet go together; we may suppose size and strength have been selected because other animals will not attack the gorilla while it is on the ground eating. And because the gorilla is so large, it needs a great deal of just the kind of coarse vegetation that it finds in large quantities in the places it inhabits. This great ape retains the equipment for climbing and reaching: long arms, deft hands, and keen vision. Young gorillas are frisky and venturesome in the trees, but their elders are essentially ground animals.

With no predators to fear except humans, and with plenty of food available, the gorillas Fossey encountered lived most of the time in a state of mild and amiable serenity. Most live in groups of two to thirty-four, each group led by a powerful silverback male, so called for the saddle of grizzled silver hair that the males grow when they reach the age of ten. The silverback's dominance over the group is absolute, but normally genial. Occasionally a young gorilla will get too frolicsome and will be silenced by a glare or a threatening slap on the ground by an adult. Sometimes a couple of females will begin to scream at each other until the leader glares at them, when they promptly quiet down. Except for particularly irascible silverbacks, the leaders usually are quite approachable. Females nestle against them, and infants crawl over their huge bodies. When a band of gorillas is at rest, the young play, the mothers tend their infants, and the other adults lie at peace.

Gorilla groups are not territorial; rather, they move about within nondefended home ranges in search of food and other resources. They do not use tools to obtain food or for any other purpose. The gorilla mating system is one of harem polygyny, and a silverback male typically has several sexual partners, while females have only one. Both males and females routinely emigrate from their natal group as adults, and within a harem the strongest social bonds are between females and their silverback leader. Bonds between females are quite weak.

Although normally rather quiet creatures that rarely use their immense strength, gorillas can exhibit strong feelings, especially when they feel threatened. They scream in alarm and as a warning to other members of the group. They toss leaves in the air. They also beat their chests. All gorillas, even very young ones, do this, rising up on two legs on the ground, or popping up amid the foliage of a tree to give a few brief slaps before fading out of sight. The full performance, however, which is given in response to more serious threat or high anxiety, is put on only by the silverback males. It begins inconspicuously with a series of soft, clear hoots that gradually quicken. Already, the silverback expects to command attention because, if interrupted, he is liable to look around in annoyance. As he continues to hoot, he may stop, pluck a leaf from a plant nearby, and place it between his lips. This curiously incongruous and delicate gesture is a prelude to coming violence, and when they see it, the other gorillas get out of the way. The violence is not immediate. First, the male rises to his full height and slaps his hands on his chest or his belly, on his thigh, or on another gorilla, producing a booming sound that can be heard a mile away. The chest beating over, the violence erupts. He runs sideways for a few steps; then he drops down on all fours and breaks into a full-speed dash, wrenching branches from trees and slapping at everything in his way, including any group members that do not have the wits to keep clear. Finally, there comes the last gesture: the silverback thumps the palm of his hand violently on the ground and then sits back, looking as if he is now ready to hear the applause.

Mating Patterns.   Though gorillas usually present a mild demeanor to the outside world, they can be violently aggressive in rivalry between males over females and in other aspects of reproductive behavior. Males reaching full maturity as young silverbacks can form their own family groups only by kidnapping females from other groups, by usurping the position of the dominant silverback male (probably their father) in their own group, or by awaiting the dominant male's death (Fossey, 1983). Sometimes the females support an up-and-coming male against an older one. The group leaders, in turn, must defend their own females against kidnapping and must maintain their authority over their groups. The kidnapping is usually carried out by stealth as much as by overt aggression, but the takeover of a group from an aging male may be a very unpleasant affair. Sometimes two ambitious young silverbacks fight each other. One or more of the older females may be killed, and quite often the youngest infant or infants are killed by the victorious male. The new male then copulates with the females, which will now rear his progeny rather than the young of his predecessor. In this way, the newly promoted dominant male begins mating and starts his own family without further delay.

Here we see one form of sexual selection in action. The intermale rivalry described by Darwin is selecting for sexual dimorphism: Gorilla males are about twice as big as females and have powerful jaws and large canine teeth. Thus, some features of gorilla dentition are associated not only with diet but also with patterns of behavior that have evolved as part of the social structure of the species.

Infanticide. The observation of **infanticide** among gorillas is important. Until 1965 it was believed that the human primate alone had the dubious distinction of sometimes murdering its own infants. In that year, however, the Japanese primatologist Yukimaru Sugiyama (1965) observed the takeover of a langur monkey troop by an outside adult male. First, the incoming male chased away the old adult male; then he asserted his dominant position by threatening the females and other troop members. Finally, he set about killing the dependent infants. After a short time, the bereaved females stopped lactating and came into estrus. He copulated with them in turn, and in due course they raised his offspring in place of those they had been nursing before his arrival.

Similar observations have since been made among several other primate species including gorillas (Hausfater and Hrdy, 1984; Watts, 1989). It has been proposed that such behavior is adaptive for the incoming male, which in this way can ensure the production of a large number of offspring at the expense of other males. His young would presumably be old enough by the time of the next takeover to avoid being killed. In other words, infanticide has been proposed as another component of sexual selection in action, though this explanation remains controversial.

Chimpanzees

Chimpanzees occur in a broad band across West and Central Africa, from Senegal and the Ivory Coast in the west to Uganda and Tanzania in the east. Of all the great apes, the chimpanzee is the least specialized. In size it is a neat compromise: small enough to get about in trees but big enough to take care of itself on the ground against predators, particularly given that it usually travels alone or in subgroups of a larger community. As a result, it is at home in both worlds. Although still a fruit eater whose favorite staple is ripe figs, the chimp is a generalist–opportunist and will eat a wide variety of other fruit and vegetation, together with some meat: birds' eggs or fledglings, insects, lizards or small snakes, and occasionally a young baboon, colobus monkey, or bush pig.

Fusion–Fission Social Organization. Chimpanzee society is not typical of the higher primates. The Gombe animals, whose territories border Lake Tanzania, live in dispersed communities of forty to sixty individuals, loosely bonded to one another. The term *fusion–fission* has been applied to chimpanzee society. Individuals of either sex have almost complete freedom to come and go as they wish. The membership of temporary subgroups is constantly changing. Adults and adolescents may forage, travel, and sleep alone, sometimes for days at a time. An individual rarely sees all the members of the community on the same day and probably never sees them two days in succession. An animal may travel one day with a large, noisy, and excitable gathering and the next day completely alone. Females may spend many days alone or with their young; males tend to be more gregarious. This flexibility of chimpanzee society is one of its most remarkable characteristics (Goodall, 1986).

In addition to their fusion–fission characteristic, chimpanzee communities can be classed as multimale–multifemale, because they contain several adult individuals of each sex. Young females usually emigrate from their natal community to live and breed elsewhere as adults, while males routinely remain in the community of their birth. Although there is considerable variation among chimpanzee populations, this emigration pattern typically results in relatively weak social bonds between females but strong

Infanticide the killing of infants.

bonds (often based on kinship) between males. Heterosexual social bonds also appear to be rather weak, and grooming between the sexes is less common than grooming between males.

Dominance and Density. As noted earlier, male chimpanzees strive to achieve high dominance rank, and within each community one male can be recognized as the alpha animal (Goodall, 1986). Males form strong alliances with one another, and support from allies (often kin) may be crucial to achieving and maintaining high rank. Dominance relations exist among females, but they are not as clear-cut as the male hierarchy, although older females generally dominate younger ones.

The large community of chimpanzees at Mahale, south of Gombe, has a far greater density of males, with the result that there is far more intermale rivalry and a much more marked dominance hierarchy (Nishida, 1990). In place of the more easygoing ways of the Gombe males, we see a situation in which the alpha male dominates the matings of all females in season and plays a more central role in all the group's activities. Interactions generally seem to be more intense and more highly structured. Thus, we see social behavior responding to a difference in population size and density. Chimpanzees have a very flexible and adaptable behavior repertoire.

Hunting. Chimpanzees have been observed to hunt red colobus monkeys (_Colobus badius_) at several study sites including Gombe, Mahale, and the Taï National Park in the Ivory Coast (Boesch-Achermann and Boesch, 1994; Stanford, 1996, 1998). At Gombe chimps may kill up to 150 monkeys during a peak hunting year, and the apes may consume more than 270 pounds (600 kilograms) of meat. This would bring the meat consumption of adult males (who hunt much more frequently than females and thus eat more meat) to a point near the low end of the range for human hunters and gatherers (i.e., to between 5 and 10 percent of the diet).

Observers of the Taï chimps found that red colobus hunts there involve larger groups of chimp males and more complicated strategies than at Gombe. For example, the Taï chimps often take on different roles during colobus hunts: Some males function as drivers, others encircle the fleeing monkeys to keep them from dispersing, and yet others race ahead to block the monkeys' arboreal pathway. The chances of a kill are greatly enhanced by larger hunting parties, and after a successful hunt cooperating males may share meat generously. Such regular sharing of the kill presumably encourages future cooperation. Of course, simpler hunts—arboreal pursuits of monkeys by single chimps or pouncing on piglets and young antelopes when they are discovered hiding in the grass—also occur at all chimpanzee study sites.

Clearly, chimpanzees all across Africa are excited by meat and very fond of it. They chew it long and reflectively, usually with a mouthful of leaves added. Sometimes the carcass is shared in an orderly fashion by the successful hunter(s), with bits of meat being torn off and handed out to begging group mates. Males tend to share with other males (most often with kin, allies, and cohunters) and also with estrous females.

The regularity of chimpanzee males' apparently swapping meat for sex has led to the suggestion that males decide to hunt with an awareness that colobus meat may enhance their access to estrous females. Females with meat almost never share it with other females. It would be incorrect, however, to give the impression that all transfers of meat are nice and orderly. In fact, immediately after a kill fighting may break out around a carcass. Individuals with meat may be attacked or threatened by those without, and sometimes fights occur among the throng of have-nots. Such squabbling is not surprising, given the high value that chimps place on meat.

The revelation that chimpanzees hunt and eat meat—and share it as well, although sometimes reluctantly—has enormous implications in explaining the development of hunting and sharing among hominids. It now becomes possible to speculate that these traits were brought by an omnivorous species from the forest to the savanna.

Tools and Weapons.   One of the most stunning discoveries of the chimpanzee studies is the fact that these apes make and use a wide variety of simple tools (Goodall, 1986; McGrew, 1992) (see Table 6.5). Despite their relatively short thumbs and impaired precision grip, chimpanzees fish for termites with sticks and stems (Figure 6.18), make sponges of wadded leaves, hammer open nuts with stones, and occasionally use natural objects as weapons. Primatologists studying chimpanzees have experienced "aimed throwing" of branches of considerable intensity and accuracy. These chimps had clearly hit on a most effective way of dealing with predators and other intruders—a technique that surely would have been equally valuable to early hominids.

It has been shown that each new generation learns tool-using patterns from the previous one. The youngsters have many opportunities to learn: They watch their elders intently, often copying what they do. In different regions of their range, chimpanzees show "cultural" differences in behavior and tool use. Different kinds of probes are used in "fishing" for termites, and at some sites termite hills are hard and must be broken into with stronger sticks; then the termites are dug out and eaten by hand. The hominid use of digging sticks is foreshadowed by these primates.

In the Taï Forest, chimpanzees have been observed using sticks and stones to break open nuts. Elsewhere, chimpanzees used two stones to smash open palm nuts. They

Table 6.5

A Partial List of Tool-Use Patterns Observed among Wild Apes			
Tool or Behavior Pattern	**Chimpanzees**	**Bonobos**	**Gorillas**	**Orangutans**
Sticks as probes for termite (or other insect) fishing or for honey extraction	X			X
Wadded leaf sponges	X			
Leaf-vessels to hold food				X
Leaves as rain hats		X		X
Leaves wiped, rubbed on body	X	X		X
Branches dragged, torn, dropped in display	X	X	X	X
Branches, rocks as hammers for nut cracking	X			
Roots, rocks as anvils for nut cracking	X			
Leaf petiole of oil palms for pestle-pounding in palm crown	X			
Rocks, branches waved, thrown at opponents	X			

Figure 6.18

Jane Goodall observed chimpanzees fishing with short twigs for termites in mounds. The chimpanzees prepared the twigs by stripping off the leaves and breaking the twigs to a certain length; in fact, they made a tool.

placed the nut in the cavity of one flat stone (platform stone) and smashed it with a hammer stone (Figure 6.19). This behavior is almost identical to that attributed to early hominids, and if these stones had been found in an excavation, they might have been identified as a product of hominid tool use.

Thus, among chimpanzees we have evidence of the use of tools as weapons, digging sticks, and nutcrackers, and as implements for the collection of social insects such as termites and ants. Even the use of stone tools—so important in hominid evolution—is seen in chimpanzees' hammer-stone-and-anvil nut processing. But an additional interesting and suggestive observation must be made: Female chimpanzees appear to use tools more often and more efficiently than do males. Can sex differences in chimpanzee tool use be applied to early hominids?

Murder and War. Observations have revealed that encounters between chimpanzee communities sometimes are sought and may become very aggressive. The best data come from observations at Gombe (Goodall, 1986). Here it was observed that parties of up to ten adult males, sometimes accompanied by females and young, might patrol peripheral areas near the boundary of the community territory and actively search for signs of neighboring groups. Contact might result in displays until one or both groups gave up or fled and returned to the core area of their range. When single chimpanzees or very small parties were encountered, they might be chased and even attacked, often brutally. Males have been observed setting out as a small group with the clear intention

Figure 6.19

Chimpanzee using a hammer stone and an anvil to crack open oil palm nuts.

of stalking a neighbor. They silently moved through the forest, avoiding the crackle of branches or leaves underfoot. Such behavior is known to have resulted in what can only be called brutal murder, clearly cold-blooded and calculated. Jane Goodall has described one four-year period at Gombe as essentially a war, during which an entire community was annihilated so that the victorious males and their females were able to move into the unoccupied territory. This behavior looks all too familiar, and the whole question of intercommunity relations and aggression among chimpanzees is now a subject of active research. Understanding it is important to those studying the evolution and nature of human violence.

Bonobos

One ape species remains to be described: *Pan paniscus,* the **bonobo,** or pygmy chimpanzee (Stanford, 1998; de Waal and Lanting, 1997; White, 1992). Bonobos are found in Central Africa, in the lowland rain forests and swamp forests south of the Zaire River. They are about the size of the smallest subspecies of chimpanzees (*Pan troglodytes*), although bonobos are somewhat more slender, with narrower shoulders and longer legs. In addition, bonobos have smaller brow ridges and ears and lighter-colored lips than chimpanzees, and the hair on their heads is parted down the center. As in the other African apes, sexual dimorphism in body size is significant among bonobos, and females' body weight is about three-quarters that of males.

Bonobo small chimpanzee of the species *Pan paniscus.*

Contrasts with Other Chimpanzees.   Bonobos live in multimale–multifemale communities characterized by the fusion–fission subgrouping already described for chimpanzees: Females appear to emigrate from their natal communities, but males do not. Interestingly, the tendency of bonobo males to remain in their natal communities is not correlated with strong male–male relationships or clear-cut male dominance, as it is among chimpanzees. The strongest social bonds among adult bonobos are (depending on the study population) either between females or between males and females. Adult males tend not to develop close relations with one another but rather remain strongly bonded to their mothers, associating with them frequently.

The Role of Sex in Bonobo Society.   Newly immigrated females use affiliative and sexual interactions (genito-genital rubbing) to establish friendly relationships with resident females, and coalitions of bonded females dominate males and limit males' access to preferred feeding sites. Bonobo females develop distinct dominance relationships, and the support of a high-ranking mother can enhance an adult son's rank among the males. In general, bonobo females have much more influence within their communities—and bonobo males have less—than is true for their chimpanzee counterparts.

A community of bonobos includes between 50 and 120 animals and inhabits a range of about 8 to 19 miles^2 (20 to 50 kilometers^2). The apes spend most of their time in the trees foraging for fruits, a diet supplemented with other plant parts, insects, and some meat. Food is regularly shared. Unlike chimpanzees, bonobos apparently do not use tools to obtain or process either plant or animal foods (Ingmanson, 1996). Among the few tool-use patterns recorded for bonobos are making rain hats from leafy boughs, wiping feces from their bodies with leaves, and dragging branches in display. In another contrast to chimpanzees, bonobo communities show extensively overlapping home ranges and often fail to defend their ranges as true territories. Thus, there is much less territorial patrolling than in chimpanzees. When subgroups from different bonobo communities meet in the forest, they initially display hostility but may soon begin to interact in a friendly and sexual fashion. First, females from the two communities engage in genital rubbing and then grooming. Youngsters from the different groups begin to play. Finally, adult males may participate in scrotal rubbing with their counterparts from the other group. Amazingly, even copulations between males and females from different communities can take place during these relatively relaxed encounters—something no chimpanzee male would ever allow.

Among the similarities claimed for bonobos and humans, most are sexual, but one is postural. Studies of captive animals have suggested that bonobos stand and walk bipedally more often (and with greater ease) than chimpanzees or gorillas (Figure 6.20). While this may be true, no one is claiming that bonobos are habitual bipeds. Field studies have shown that bipedalism represents less than 2 percent of the total locomotion of wild bonobo subjects.

The similarities in sexual behavior, however, are more striking and possibly more important. Bonobo females show unusually long sexual cycles of thirty-five to forty-nine days, and between menstrual flows they may be maximally sexually swollen for up to 49 percent of the time (Dahl, 1986; Stanford, 1998). This is a longer period of sexual attractiveness and mating activity than is recorded for chimpanzees, whose females are maximally swollen for 27 to 40 percent of their menstrual cycle. Humans, of course, engage in sexual behavior throughout all or most of the menstrual cycle, rather more like bonobos.

But the sexual similarities take two more interesting twists. First, while virtually all chimpanzee copulations are ventrodorsal (the male mounts the female from the rear),

Figure 6.20
Bonobos stand and move bipedally much more often than chimpanzees.

some 25 to 30 percent of bonobo matings are ventroventral. Of the two sexes, female bonobos seem to be particularly fond of face-to-face sex; several instances have been recorded of females interrupting ventrodorsal copulations in order to change their position and embrace the male ventrally. And second, bonobos are without doubt the most inventive of all the apes in their sexual variations (de Waal and Lanting, 1997). Bonobos show all of the possible combinations of sexual partners: opposite-sex, same-sex, and old and young. Pairs of females frequently embrace ventrally and rub their genitals together, while males mount one another and occasionally "fence" (mutually rub) with their erect penises. Sex is used by bonobos to reduce tension and in postconflict reconciliations. As has been remarked about this make-love-not-war species, "the chimpanzee resolves sexual issues with power; the bonobo resolves power issues with sex" (de Waal and Lanting, 1997: 32). Indeed, some researchers believe that frequent female–female and male–female sexual contacts explain why these relationships are stronger among bonobos than among chimpanzees.

Studies of bonobos are in their infancy. Assuming that humans allow (and assist) bonobos to avoid extinction, this species promises to yield critical information for interpreting human evolution.

What was involved in the evolutionary transformation of our last ape ancestor into a hominid? To begin to answer that question, we need to focus on the fossil record of the earliest hominids, the australopithecines.

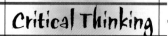

What Was the Common Ancestor of Chimps and Humans Like?

Studies of chromosomes and DNA are beginning to allow fine distinctions among humans' evolutionary relationships with the African apes. Most molecular research suggests that humans, bonobos, and chimpanzees are a clade with a common ancestor that lived about 5 to 7 million years ago. These studies further suggest that the chimp and bonobo lines may have separated from each other only within the last 2.5 to 3 million years, so they are extremely close sister species. Based on data from living humans, chimpanzees, and bonobos, therefore, we can speculate cautiously about the probable characteristics of their last common ancestor, an ape-grade creature whose exact identity has yet to be established.

Study the table here, comparing the behavior of living chimpanzees, bonobos, and humans. Notice that the last column in the table has been left blank. Based on what you have read, what do you predict were the behavioral characteristics of our last common ancestor with the chimps and bonobos? On what empirical grounds and inferences do you base your predictions?

Trait	Chimpanzees	Bonobos	Humans	Common Ancestor
Social group[a]	MM–MF community; fusion–fission	MM–MF community; fusion–fission	MM–MF community; fusion–fission	
Females or males change groups?	Females	Females	Females more often	
Male–male bonds	Strong	Weak	Strong	
Female–female bonds	Weak	Strong	Weak to moderate	
Male–female bonds	Weak	Strong	Strong	
Territorial defense?	Common, by males	Occasional, by males	Common, by males	
Mating system	Promiscuity	Promiscuity	Mild polygyny to promiscuity	
Sexual swelling?	Yes	Yes	No	
Sexual activity[b]	27–40%	35–49%	Near 100%	
Hormonal control of female sexuality	Moderate	Moderate to low	Low	
Copulation pattern	Ventrodorsal	Ventrodorsal > ventroventral	Variable	
Paternal investment by males	Slight	Slight	Moderate to strong	
Tool use?	Frequent and variable	Rare	Very frequent and variable	
Meat eating?	Yes	Yes	Yes	
Food sharing?	Routine	Routine	Frequent	
Bipedal stance?	Rare	More common than in chimps	Habitual	

Characteristics of Chimpanzees, Bonobos, Humans, and Their Common Ancestor

[a] MM, multimale; MF, multifemale.
[b] Percentage of menstrual cycle with mating.

Did you deduce that humans' last ape ancestor probably formed multimale–multifemale communities characterized by fusion–fission subgrouping? Female emigration from the natal community probably was the prevalent pattern, and territorial defense by males probably occurred at least occasionally. Sexual behavior probably was variable and situational; that is, hormonal control of sex was moderate to low, and mating occurred throughout much of the menstrual cycle. Did you conclude that males almost certainly had access to multiple mates, and that the same may have been true for females? The common ancestor probably engaged in some tool use, included meat in its diet, and shared food. Finally, bipedal standing and walking almost certainly occurred occasionally though not habitually. What are some behavioral patterns that you might add to this inventory?

Timeline: Primate Evolution

The time scale of primate evolution is immense. The first part of the 60 million years of primate history was the age of the prosimians, which occupied much of the Old and New Worlds. By 20 million years ago the apes were established in Africa, and for this reason we too find our origin on this continent. By about 15 million years ago the apes had spread into Eurasia.

	YEARS B.P.	FOSSIL RECORD	PRIMATES
CENOZOIC	Pleistocene ♦		
Early prosimians	2 million —	Early *Homo*	*Homo*
65 million	Pliocene ♦	*Australopithecus* and *Paranthropus*	
	5 million —	Earliest *Australopithecus*	
Basic insectivores			
		Earliest hominids?	Australopithecines
		Sivapithecus in Asia and Europe	
MESOZOIC			
	Miocene ♦	*Kenyapithecus* in Africa	
		Morotopithecus and *Proconsul* in Africa	Apes
First mammals			
225 million			
	25 million —		
	Oligocene ♦		Catarrhines and Platyrrhines
		Propliopithecus and *Aegyptopithecus* at Fayum	
	35 million —		
PALEOZOIC		Oligopithecines in Africa	
		Amphipithecus and *Pondaugia* in Burma *Siamopithecus* in Thailand	
	Eocene ♦		Prosimians and early anthropoids
		Eosimias in China	
		Algeripithecus in Algeria	
First vertebrates			
	58 million —		
		Altiatlasius in Morocco	First primates
570 million	Paleocene ♦		
PRECAMBRIAN	65 million —		

BACK BEYOND THE APES

163

Summary

As currently known, the fossil record indicates that the primate order originated about 60 million years ago (during the late Paleocene epoch) in Africa. This date is an approximation, however, based on very incomplete evidence, and future discoveries are likely to push the actual point of origin several million years back in time.

Despite the uncertainty on dates, the earliest primates can be classified confidently as prosimians—not enormously different from today's lemurs, lorises, and tarsiers. By perhaps 45 to 50 mya, the ancient prosimians had given rise to the first anthropoids, although whether this occurred in Africa or in Asia is hotly debated. By the Eocene–Oligocene boundary (35 million BP) the anthropoids were well established. Too primitive to be classified as either monkeys or apes, the early anthropoids nonetheless had such distinctive features of higher primates as bony eye sockets and fused frontal bones.

The Oligocene epoch saw anthropoids differentiate into catarrhines and platyrrhines, and by 20 mya (the early Miocene), the first hominoids (apes) had evolved in Africa. Two distinct types of early apes can be identified: dental apes and suspensory apes. Dental apes resembled living hominoids (chimpanzees, etc.) in many dental and cranial traits, but they had monkeylike bodies and moved through the trees in a pronograde, quadrupedal fashion. In contrast, as their name implies, suspensory apes from the Miocene not only showed dental and cranial similarities to modern species, but also possessed postcranial adaptations for orthograde, forelimb-dominated locomotion (arm-hanging and arm-swinging).

Finally, during the very late Miocene epoch, the Hominidae—the human family—evolved from an as yet undiscovered African ape ancestor. Marked primarily by distinctive adaptations for bipedal locomotion, the first hominids began the evolutionary journey that would culminate in modern humans.

The behavior of the living great apes contributes to our understanding that chimpanzees and bonobos are our closest evolutionary relatives and provides some insights about the likely traits of both our last common ancestor and the earliest hominids.

Review Questions

1. What fossil evidence do we have for the origin of the order Primates? Is the date of that event known with certainty?

2. When and where did the suborder of the anthropoids arise? Describe the fossil evidence for the appearance of anthropoids.

3. How do fossil apes compare with living apes with regard to postcranial anatomy and locomotor behavior?

4. What do we know about the age, location, identity, and behavior of humans' last ape ancestor?

5. What are hominids' anatomical adaptations for habitual bipedalism?

6. What sort of tool use is seen among chimpanzees, and what implications do the chimp data have for the evolution of tool use among hominids?

7. Why do some anthropologists think that bonobos make a better model for hominid evolution than chimpanzees? What are some questions about hominid evolution to which one could apply a bonobo model?

8. What are the (speculative) characteristics of the chimpanzee–bonobo–human common ancestor?

Suggested Further Reading

Conroy, G. C. *Primate Evolution.* W. W. Norton, 1990.
Deacon, T. W. *The Symbolic Species: The Co-Evolution of Language and the Brain.* W. W. Norton, 1997.
Fossey, D. *Gorillas in the Mist.* Houghton Mifflin, 1983.
Galdikas, B. M. F. *Reflections of Eden: My Years with the Orangutans of Borneo.* Little, Brown, 1995.
Stanford, C. B. *The Hunting Apes: Meat-Eating and the Origins of Human Behavior.* Princeton University Press, 1999.
Tobias, P. V. *The Brain in Hominid Evolution.* Columbia University Press, 1971.
Waal, F. de. *Chimpanzee Politics: Power and Sex among Apes.* Harper & Row, 1982.

Internet Resources

Conveniently access these and other links via our web site at **http://www.ablongman/anthro.**

Chimpanzee Hunting Habits Yield Clues about Early Human Ancestors
**http://www.usc.edu/ext-relations/news_service/chronicle_html/
1995.02.06.html/chimp.html**
A report of chimpanzee hunting behavior at Gombe National Park, with implications for hominid evolution.

Chimps.org
http://www.chimps.org/
Billing itself as The Chimp Database, this site has information about chimpanzees and bonobos, as well as links to other related web sites.

Evolution of Hominid Locomotion: A Bibliography
http://www.primate.wisc.edu/pin/loco.html
A useful list of books and scientific journal articles about the evolution of bipedalism (no web links, however.)

Fact Sheets about Primates
http://www.primate.wisc.edu/pin/genifo.html
A collection of thumbnail sketches of the living primate species, including the apes.

NetVet.Primates
http://netvet.wustl.edu/primates.htm
Look for links to particular living apes: gibbons, orangutans, gorillas, chimpanzees, bonobos.

Primate Evolution
http://www.primate.wisc.edu/pin/evolution.html
Links to web sites concerning primate and human evolution and fossils.

Useful Search Terms:
apes
bipedal locomotion
bonobos
chimpanzees
gibbons
gorillas
hominid evolution
orangutans
primate evolution
primate fossils

Australopithecus

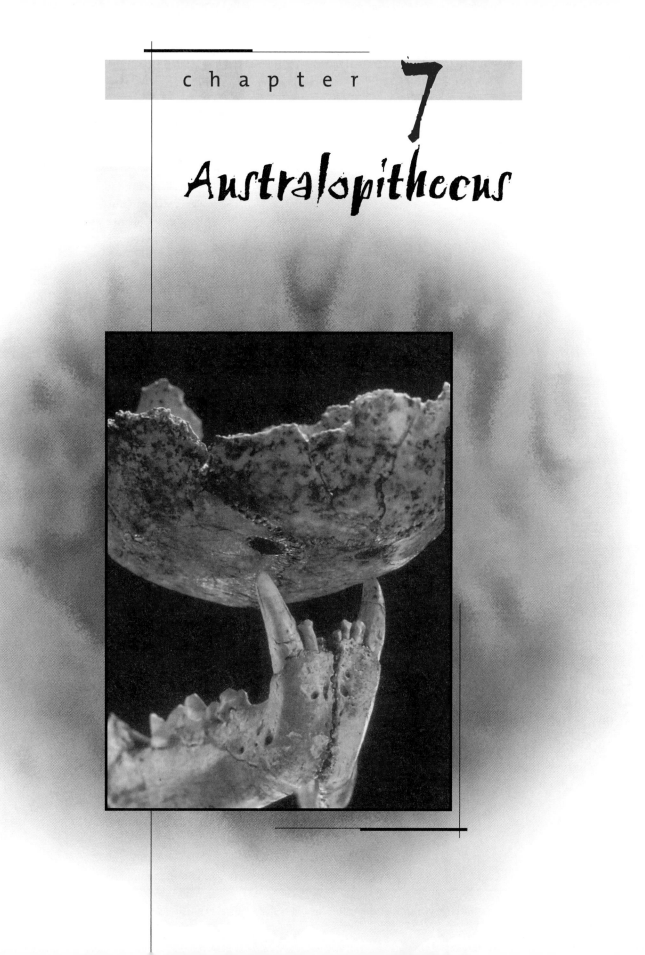

Overview

Hominid fossils have been discovered at numerous locations in East, Northeast, and North-Central Africa as well as in South Africa. To date, paleoanthropologists have recovered the remains of two australopithecine genera (*Australopithecus* and *Paranthro-*

Mini-Timeline: The Australopithecines

Date or Age	Fossil Discoveries or Evolutionary Events
(A) Date (years AD)	
1999	*Australopithecus garhi* announced
1995	*Australopithecus anamensis* and *A. bahrelghazali* discovered
1994	*Australopithecus ramidus* announced
1978	*Australopithecus afarensis* announced
1968	*Paranthropus aethiopicus* named (originally, *Australopithecus*)
1959	*Paranthropus boisei* discovered at Olduvai Gorge (originally named *Zinjanthropus*)
1950	Le Gros Clark classifies australopithecines as hominids
1938	Broom discovers first *Paranthropus*
1924	Dart discovers first *Australopithecus*
(B) Age (million years BP)	
2.0–1.0	*Paranthropus robustus* inhabits South Africa
2.3–1.3	*P. boisei* inhabits East Africa
2.5	*Australopithecus garhi* inhabits Northeast Africa
2.7–2.3	*P. aethiopicus* inhabits East Africa
3.5?–2.5	*Australopithecus africanus* inhabits South Africa
3.5–3.0	*A. bahrelghazali* inhabits North-Central Africa
4.2–2.5	*A. afarensis* inhabits East Africa
4.2–3.9	*A. anamensis* inhabits East Africa
4.4	*A. ramidus* inhabits Northeast Africa
5.6	Lothagam fossil and *Orrorin tugenensis* (oldest known hominid remains)

 Follow links at **http://www.ablongman/anthro** for additional resources in physical anthropology, primatology, biological anthropology, and paleoanthropology.

pus) and nine species. Although specialists disagree somewhat on species and genus names and on the assignment of particular fossils, the following list of australopithecines from the **Plio–Pleistocene** seems reasonable: *Australopithecus ramidus; Australopithecus anamensis; Australopithecus afarensis* (including the "Lucy" fossil); *Australopithecus bahrelghazali* (a provisional species from Chad); *Australopithecus garhi* (announced in 1999); *Paranthropus aethiopicus* (the oldest member of the robust lineage); *Paranthropus boisei;* and from South Africa, *Australopithecus africanus* (the initial australopithecine discovery by Raymond Dart in 1924) and *Paranthropus robustus.*

All of the australopithecines appear to have walked upright, but with their ape-sized brains, they almost certainly lacked speech and language. Questions about australopithecine material culture remain open, although there is no conclusive evidence for tool use or toolmaking by these hominids. A consensus reconstruction of australopithecine phylogeny suggests that *Australopithecus* gave rise to both *Homo* and *Paranthropus* (specialists disagree about the exact ancestor–descendant relationships); and *Paranthropus* then went extinct without descendants some 1.0 million years ago. The South African fossils show an evolutionary sequence somewhat similar to those known from East Africa.

Important topics in Chapter 7 include the various australopithecine species and their characteristics; the first fossil evidence of habitual bipedalism; the selection pressures (including habitat type) that resulted in bipedalism; problems involved in the recognition and naming of extinct species; the varying lifestyles of the australopithecines; and the ancestor–descendant relationships binding the australopithecines to one another and to the genus *Homo.*

Check our web site for additional information, photos, drawings, maps, and animations on topics in this chapter.

African Fossil Hominids

Fossil and living species of the family Hominidae can be divided into two subfamilies: Australopithecinae and Homininae, colloquially known as the **australopithecines** and **hominines** (Table 7.1). Dating from about 5 million years ago, the fossils placed in the subfamily Australopithecinae are exclusively African and the earlier group of hominids, though some species survived until about 1 mya. They survived long after the more human hominines split from the australopithecine stem and began to evolve unmistakable human characteristics. This chapter will describe the earliest australopithecines, which have been discovered in East, Southeast, and Northeast Africa and which constitute the long sought link to our apelike ancestors. (Chapter 8 will introduce the hominines.)

The fossil hominids from East Africa are overwhelming in their species diversity. In all, East Africa may have yielded the remains of as many as nine australopithecine species representing two genera as well as four species of pre-sapiens hominines (see Table 7.2). Some of the australopithecines are referred to generally as **gracile** (the genus *Australopithecus*) and others as **robust** (the genus *Paranthropus*). Within the australopithecine subfamily this chapter will present various species in the chronological order of their antiquity. The probable evolutionary relationships among the East and South African hominid species, including those between subfamilies, will be discussed at the end of this and the subsequent chapter.

Plio–Pleistocene a combination of the last two epochs of the Cenozoic era; the Pliocene lasted from 5 to 1.6 million years BP and the Pleistocene from 1.6 million to 10,000 years BP.

Australopithecines members of the subfamily Australopithecinae, which includes *Australopithecus* and *Paranthropus.*

Hominines members of the subfamily Homininae, which includes just one genus—*Homo.*

Gracile small, fine-boned, lightweight; lightly built.

Robust heavy; heavily built.

Table 7.1

Hominid Taxonomy

Family Hominidae (Common Name: Hominids)

Subfamily Australopithecinae (Common name: australopithecines)

Genus *Australopithecus*	Species	*Australopithecus afarensis*
		Australopithecus africanus
		Australopithecus anamensis
		Australopithecus bahrelghazali (provisional)
		Australopithecus garhi
		Australopithecus ramidus
Genus *Paranthropus*	Species	*Paranthropus aethiopicus*
		Paranthropus boisei
		Paranthropus robustus

Subfamily Homininae (Common name: hominines)

Genus *Homo*	Species	(Paleoanthropologists recognize between three and seven species of hominines. The taxonomic controversies will be discussed in later chapters.)

Table 7.2

A Record of Australopithecine Fossils			
Species	**East African Sites**	**South African Sites**	**Age (million years)[a]**
Australopithecus ramidus	Aramis		4.4
Australopithecus anamensis	Allia Bay		3.9
	Kanapoi		4.2–3.9
Australopithecus bahrelghazali	Bahr el Ghazal (Chad)		3.5–3.0
Australopithecus afarensis	Omo		3.0–2.5
	Hadar		3.3–2.8
	Laetoli		3.8–3.6
	Maka/Belohdelie		4.0–3.4
	Allia Bay		4.0
	Fejej		4.2–4.0
Australopithecus garhi	Bouri		2.5
Australopithecus africanus		Taung	2.8–2.6
		Makapansgat	3.0–2.5
		Sterkfontein	3.5?–2.5
Paranthropus aethiopicus	Omo, Lomekwi, and Kangatukuseo		2.7–2.3
Paranthropus boisei	Peninj		1.5
	Olduvai		1.8
	Koobi Fora		2.0–1.3
	Omo		2.3–1.5
Paranthropus robustus		Swartkrans	1.8–1.0
		Kromdraai	2.0–1.8

[a]Dates attributed to South African sites often are based not on chronometric procedures, but on comparative analyses of fauna. Nonetheless, these dates probably do bracket the times of existence of the various fossil species. Most of the dates for sites in East and North-Central Africa are based on chronometric procedures and are therefore quite accurate.

Before considering the traits of *Australopithecus,* it may be useful to review quickly the anatomical expectations that we have of the first hominids. The biochemical and fossil data together indicate that the Hominidae diverged from the chimpanzee–bonobo lineage quite recently—probably only 5 to 7 million years ago. Given this recent evolutionary descent from ape ancestors, we expect the oldest members of the human family to show a clear mixture of ape traits and human traits. Apes have small brains, big canines, and bodies (particularly arms, hands, and feet) adapted for arboreal movement. In contrast, modern humans have huge brains, small canines, and bodies (particularly pelvic girdles, legs, and feet) specialized for bipedal locomotion. If we are correct in concluding that modern humans are descended—via the australopithecines—from a long extinct species of ape, then our early australopithecine ancestors should be strongly intermediate between the two evolutionary grades.

The East African Australopithecines

The most ancient hominid fossils come from sites in East Africa: Ethiopia, Kenya, and Tanzania. They are mostly quite recent discoveries, and they indicate that the split from our ape ancestors, which gave rise to the hominid line, probably occurred in East-Central Africa, not far from the present range of the African apes (Figure 7.1).

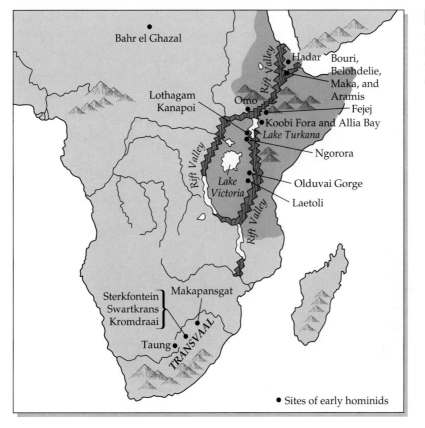

Figure 7.1

Southern, Eastern, and North-Central Africa showing some of the many sites in which australopithecine fossils have been discovered.

Australopithecus ramidus

Between 1992 and 1993 an international team of anthropologists focused its collecting efforts on early Pliocene deposits at the Aramis site, in the middle of Ethiopia's Awash River drainage system (Figure 7.2). Over the two field seasons, a total of seventeen fossil specimens were collected, all of which date back to about 4.4 mya. Among the ancient remains were several teeth, a mandible fragment, and a few arm bones (including the rare discovery of all three bones from the left arm of a single individual).

After preliminary analysis of the Aramis fossils—and comparisons with living and fossil apes, modern humans, and several extinct hominid varieties—it became apparent to the discovery team that they had recovered a new species of australopithecine. Initially the new species was called *Australopithecus ramidus* (with *ramidus* based on *ramid*, the local Afar word for "root"; White et al., 1994). After only a few months, however, the discoverers rethought that designation and placed the fossils in a genus of their own: *Ardipithecus* (*ardi* means "ground" in Afar; White et al., 1995). At present anthropologists (including the authors of this text) are split over which genus name to use, and the situation will not be fully resolved until a final analysis of the fossils—including those found during subsequent field seasons—is published. In this book the Aramis fossils are conservatively placed within the genus *Australopithecus,* with recognition of the genus name *Ardipithecus* pending the publication of additional information.

The most important anatomical features of *Australopithecus ramidus* are summarized in Table 7.3. This species had canines that were shorter and more incisorlike than those of apes but larger (relative to the premolars and molars) and less incisiform than those of certain other early australopithecines. *A. ramidus* also had mandibular anterior premolars lacking **sectorial** function (not shaped for cutting action), unlike those of apes; but, like chimpanzees, it had thin enamel on canines and molars. Like other australopithecines, *A. ramidus* had its **foramen magnum** positioned forward on the base of

Australopithecus ramidus species of *Australopithecus* known from Ethiopia and dated 4.4 mya.

Sectorial evolved to cut fibrous material by shearing action.

Foramen magnum hole in the base of the skull through which the spinal cord passes.

Figure 7.2

Important hominid remains have been recovered from the extensive stratified deposits at Aramis, Hadar, and other sites in the drainage system of the Awash River of northeastern Ethiopia.

Table 7.3

Characteristics of *Australopithecus ramidus*	
Trait	**Australopithecus ramidus (provisional)**
Height	At least 3.3 ft (100 cm; upper height limit and sexual dimorphism unknown)
Weight	At least 66 lb (30 kg; upper weight limit and sexual dimorphism unknown)
Brain size	Unknown
Cranium	Forwardly positioned foramen magnum; small occipital condyles; very flat surface of jaw joint
Dentition	Canines shorter and more incisiform than those of apes, but less incisiform and larger (relative to the postcanine teeth) than those of certain other australopithecines; lower anterior premolars (P3s) lacking evidence of sectorial functioning; thin enamel on canines and molars; apelike anatomy of lower first deciduous molar
Diet	Unknown (thin molar enamel may rule out "hard object feeder")
Limbs	Arm bones showing a mosaic of hominid and ape traits; elliptical shape of the head of the humerus and the anatomy of the elbow joint resembling those of later hominids; pelvic and lower limb anatomy unknown
Locomotion	Bipedalism? (classification tentative; knuckle-walking can be ruled out)
Known dates (million years BP)	4.4

the skull rather than at the back of the skull, suggesting upright posture. Furthermore, features of its arm bones, including the shape of the head of the humerus (upper arm bone) and the anatomy of the elbow, resemble those in later hominids, not in apes. One characteristic that strongly distinguishes *A. ramidus* from other australopithecines is the apelike lower first **deciduous molar** (temporary tooth) found at Aramis.

It seems safe to conclude that the Aramis fossils are hominids and australopithecines, especially as shown by their dentition (particularly the canines and lower first premolars), the positioning of the foramen magnum, and the elbow anatomy. To its discoverers, *A. ramidus* fulfills virtually all the theoretical expectations of a species occurring immediately after an ape–hominid split. This conclusion will be tested by the detailed analysis of additional fossil specimens discovered in 1994. During that field season at Aramis, 45 percent of an adult individual was recovered, including parts of the skull, arms, vertebral column, pelvis, and legs. For these new fossils to reveal their secrets, however, they must first be extracted from blocks of stone, reconstructed, and analyzed, a lengthy process that may take years to complete. When the new finds have been analyzed and published, they may or may not justify the naming of a fourth hominid genus.

If *A. ramidus* does prove to have been a biped, it could yield important information about the environmental conditions that originally selected for bipedalism. It has long been thought that this distinctly hominid way of getting around began as an adaptation to life on the African savanna—the implication being that the earliest hominids changed quickly from their ape ancestors' forest-based existence to terrestrial life in an environment of broad grasslands dotted with occasional trees. In stark contrast to this theory, however, geologists working at Aramis have suggested that the environment of *A. ramidus* was relatively flat, closed woodland. They base this description on the occurrence of preserved wood and seeds, as well as on discoveries of the bones of woodland antelopes

Deciduous molar temporary tooth or "milk tooth" that is lost and replaced by a permanent tooth during the early years of life.

and colobine (leaf-eating) monkeys. The origin of bipedalism in the forest? Such a notion stands conventional anthropological wisdom on its head, but the australopithecine evidence suggests that it may be time to take the possibility seriously.

The Lothagam Jaw

In 1967 paleoanthropologist Bryan Patterson led a fossil-hunting expedition to northern Kenya. At a location called Lothagam, just southwest of Lake Turkana, Patterson and his team hit pay dirt and unknowingly kicked off a controversy that has lasted more than thirty years. In this case, pay dirt consisted of a rather scrappy lower jaw, broken off in front of the first molar and preserving that tooth along with the roots of lower molars M2 and M3 (Patterson et al., 1970). A battery of different dating procedures indicated that the fossil was probably in the neighborhood of 5.6 million years of age—possibly a million years older than *A. ramidus.*

Unfortunately, the **Lothagam jaw** is so old and fragmentary that it is very difficult to classify accurately. Some scientists have concluded that it is an ape jaw, others 'that it is an ancient hominid, and still others that it is too fragmentary to be given a name at all. Some analyses (e.g., Hill et al., 1992), however, support Patterson's initial impression that Lothagam is the remains of an australopithecine, albeit species unknown. At present this mysterious and extremely old fossil must sit on the shelf and await further research before its role in hominid evolution can be understood.

Australopithecus anamensis

Another species of *Australopithecus* is *Australopithecus anamensis,* whose remains have been gathered from river deposits at Allia Bay and from lakeside deposits at Kanapoi. The two sites lie some 90 miles (145 kilometers) apart and on opposite sides of Kenya's Lake Turkana (see Figure 7.1 on page 171; Leakey et al., 1995). The Allia Bay fossils occur as a "bone bed," and each fragment was rolled and weathered as it was swept into position by a precursor of the modern Omo River. Among the Allia Bay fossils are aquatic animals (fish, crocodiles, and hippopotamuses) as well as the bones of leaf-eating monkeys and woodland antelopes—remains that collectively suggest a gallery forest habitat along the river. In contrast, the Kanapoi site probably combined "dry, possibly open, wooded or bushland conditions [with] a wide gallery forest" (Leakey et al., 1995: 571). The remains of kudus, impalas, hyenas, and a semiterrestrial monkey called *Parapapio* (an early ancestor of today's baboons) confirm the somewhat more open conditions at Kanapoi. Meave Leakey and her team believe that the early hominids who lived at the two sites utilized a wide range of habitats.

So what sort of hominid was *Australopithecus anamensis*? As one might expect of a 4-million-year-old species, it was bipedal but still had many apelike traits, as listed in Table 7.4. The list of fossils recovered so far includes numerous teeth, upper and lower jaw fragments (Figure 7.3), part of an elbow, a piece of temporal bone from the skull that includes a distinctively narrow and elliptical external acoustic meatus (ear opening), and the top and bottom portions of a right tibia (shinbone). The tibia fragments clearly show that *A. anamensis* was habitually bipedal. Unlike the shinbone of an ape, the tibia of *A. anamensis* showed a distinctively hominid knee joint, extra spongy bone just below the knee to absorb the shock of upright walking, and a bony buttress at the ankle to facilitate weight bearing. Furthermore, according to Leakey and Walker (1997), the elbow joint seems to indicate that *A. anamensis* was not a knuckle-walker;

Lothagam jaw a mandibular fragment found at Lothagam in Kenya and dated about 5.6 mya.

Australopithecus anamensis an early species of *australopithecines* found in Kenya and dated between 4.2 and 3.9 mya.

Table 7.4

Characteristics of *Australopithecus anamensis*[a]	
Trait	***Australopithecus anamensis***
Height	Unknown
Weight[b]	104–121 lb (47–55 kg)
Brain size	Unknown
Cranium	Mandibular symphysis slopes strongly down and back, suggesting facial prognathism; external acoustic meatus (ear canal) is small and apelike in outline
Dentition	U-shaped toothrows; all canines have long, robust roots; lower canines are larger than those of *A. afarensis*; lower P3 is very asymmetrical, with a centrally positioned and blunt main cusp (semisectorial?); thick molar enamel
Diet	Fruit and foliage; thick enamel suggests a diet including some hard items
Limbs	Elbow anatomy seems to rule out knuckle-walking; condyles of tibia differ from those of apes in both size and shape; top of tibia shows extra spongy bone for shock absorption; bottom of tibia shows extra bony buttressing at ankle
Pelvis	Unknown
Locomotion	Bipedalism (probably primitive; unknown whether accompanied by arboreal climbing)
Known dates (million years BP)	4.2–3.9

[a]Values for anatomical measurements may change with additional fossil discoveries.
[b]Weight estimated for one (presumably male) individual.

although whether it showed any other apelike locomotor patterns—such as arboreal climbing—remains an open question.

In contrast to its hominid-type lower body, several features of the face and jaws of *Australopithecus anamensis* were strongly apelike. For example, *A. anamensis* showed a primitive U-shaped toothrow, a mandibular symphysis that sloped strongly backwards, and upper canines with enormous roots. (Those same canines wore flat at the tip, however, rather than remaining pointed as in modern apes; see Figure 7.3.) More modern dental traits included thick tooth enamel, a feature that suggests some adaptation to a diet including hard food items.

In summary, *Australopithecus anamensis* is known to have lived between 4.2 and 3.9 mya. It moved bipedally through the habitats of East Africa, apparently using both open bushland and forested terrain.

Australopithecus bahrelghazali

The dust had barely settled from the Leakey group's naming of *A. anamensis* in August 1995 before another new hominid hit the press. In November 1995, a team led by Michel Brunet of the University of Poitiers announced the discovery of an australopithecine mandible from the site of Bahr el Ghazal in Chad (Figure 7.1, page 171; Brunet et al., 1995). The find excited tremendous interest among paleoanthropologists, because it extended the known range of the australopithecines to some 1,500 miles (2,500 kilometers) west of the Rift Valley. Brunet and his colleagues gave the fossil from Chad its own species name: *Australopithecus bahrelghazali*.

Australopithecus bahrelghazali provisionally, a new *species* of *australopithecine* known from Chad and dated 3.5 to 3.0 mya.

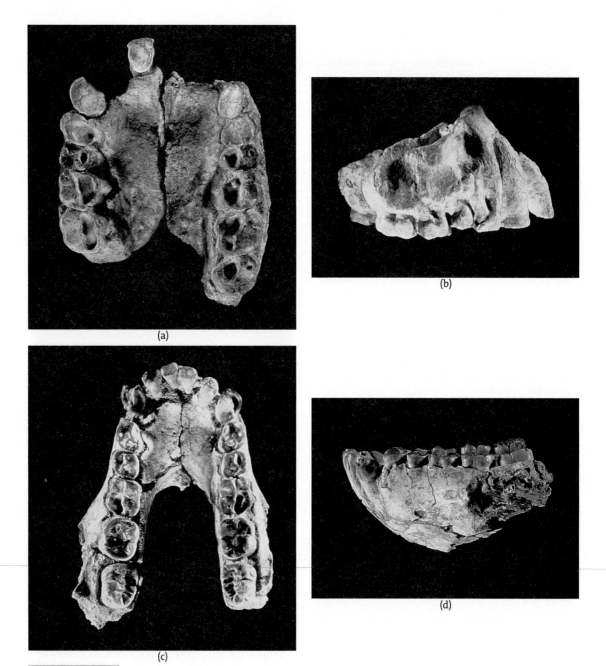

(a)

(b)

(c)

(d)

Figure 7.3

The upper dentition of *Australopithecus anamensis* (a and b) shows a U-shaped toothrow and massive canine roots. The same toothrow configuration is present in the mandible (c and d), which also shows a strongly sloping symphysis at the midline of the lower jaw, where a chin would be in humans.

The Bahr el Ghazal mandible, which has been dated by faunal correlation with Hadar deposits at 3.5 to 3.0 mya, preserves only the front portion of the jaw (from the symphysis back to the last premolar). Included in the jaw are all of the canines and premolars, and one lateral incisor. As indicated in Table 7.5, very little can be con-

Table 7.5

Characteristics of *Australopithecus bahrelghazali*[a]	
Trait	***Australopithecus bahrelghazali* (provisional)**
Height, weight, and brain size	Unknown
Cranium	Mandibular symphysis shows a unique outline, particularly on the lingual (internal) surface
Dentition	Short, pointed lower canines; bicuspid (nonsectorial) lower first premolars (this implies short upper canines); three-rooted lower premolars; premolar enamel thicker than in *A. ramidus*, but thin compared to other australopithecines
Diet	Few hard items in the diet? Mostly fruit and foliage?
Limbs and pelvis	Unknown
Locomotion	Bipedalism (assumed)
Known dates (million years BP)	3.5–3.0

cluded about the anatomy and adaptations of this hominid because of the limited fossil sample. *Australopithecus bahrelghazali* had short, but pointed, canines; bicuspid (non-sectorial) lower first premolars; and a unique outline of the mandibular symphysis. Furthermore, it differed from other *Australopithecus* and *Paranthropus* species in its three-rooted lower premolars (theirs were two-rooted) and its thinner premolar enamel. Collectively, these traits support at least the provisional listing of *A. bahrelghazali* as a new australopithecine species.

Like many of the other australopithecine species, *A. bahrelghazali* apparently inhabited a lakeside environment that included both gallery forest and wooded savanna with open grassy patches. Judging from its thin enamel, this early species apparently subsisted rather exclusively on soft foods—undoubtedly mostly fruits, foliage, and vegetables. *Australopithecus bahrelghazali*'s main claim to fame, however, is its extreme western location.

Australopithecus afarensis

The 1973–1976 discoveries from Hadar in the Afar region of Ethiopia (Figure 7.2) are among the most important in East Africa (Johanson and Edey, 1981; Johanson and White, 1979). Dating from the period 3.3–2.8 mya, they constitute a small population of the gracile australopithecines and give us clear evidence of bipedalism at this early date. The characteristics of *Australopithecus afarensis* in Table 7.6 show that these fossils constitute a critically important link between an ancestral ape and modern humans. This species had workable but primitive bipedalism, a mixture of humanlike and apelike dental traits, and a brain that was a little larger than that of an ape. A more perfect evolutionary link could hardly be imagined.

Lucy and the Hadar Fossils.   The body size of *Australopithecus afarensis* varied considerably both within a sex and between sexes (sexual dimorphism); females like "Lucy," the best-preserved skeleton (Figure 7.4), may have been just over 3 feet (about 1 meter) tall, whereas large males may have been as much as 5 feet (1.5 meters) tall. Weight probably varied from 66 to as much as 154 pounds (30 to 70 kilograms). The individuals,

Australopithecus afarensis gracile australopithecine species that inhabited East Africa from 4.2 to 2.5 mya.

Table 7.6

Characteristics of *Australopithecus afarensis*[a]	
Trait	*Australopithecus afarensis*
Height	F: 3.3–3.4 ft (100–105 cm) M: 5.0 ft (151 cm) (F is 68% of M)
Weight	F: 66 lb (30 kg) M: 99–154 lb (45–70 kg) (F is 52% of M)
Brain size (sexes combined)	433 cc mean (400–500 cc range)
Cranium	Prognathic (protruding) face; low, flat forehead; low-vaulted braincase; large brows; unflexed cranial base

Dentition	U-shaped toothrow; relatively large anterior teeth (incisors and
	  canines); moderately large molars; canines that project somewhat;
	  upper jaw diastemata; lower P3s at least semisectorial

Diet	Fruit and other plant foods; some meat (?)
Limbs	Long arms relative to legs; curved finger and toe bones (adaptations for arboreal movement?); close-knee stance

Pelvis	Short, broad iliac blades; incomplete pelvic bowl; weak iliofemoral
	  ligament; ischial shaft relatively shorter than in apes, but not yet
	  realigned in modern fashion; pelvis wide between hip joints

Locomotion	Bipedalism (probably primitive) and possibly arboreal climbing
Known dates (million years BP)	4.2–2.5

[a]Mean values, and ranges of values, for anatomical measurements may change with additional fossil discoveries.

though small, were powerfully built: The bones were thick for their size and carried markings suggesting that they had been well muscled. The evidence of the knee joint makes it clear that, like all other hominids, these creatures were habitually bipedal (Figure 7.5).

In the upper body *A. afarensis* shows signs of continuing arboreality, including relatively longer arms and shorter legs than those of modern humans, rather apelike wrist bones, and curved fingers (another apelike trait). The pelvis of *A. afarensis*, however, shows unmistakable adaptations for habitual bipedalism (Figure 7.6). First, the iliac blades are short and broad, and deep sciatic notches indicate the extent of backward expansion and bending. Thus the center of gravity of *A. afarensis* was considerably lower than that of an ape; as a consequence, bipedal balancing was much more stable and energy-efficient. Second, the iliac blades of *A. afarensis* are curved toward the front of the body, producing a partial pelvic bowl. Third, the anterior inferior iliac spines are well developed and mark the upper attachment of powerful **rectus femoris** muscles that flexed the thigh and extended the lower leg during bipedal walking. And finally, the ischial shaft is short compared to the shaft of an ape. Despite these humanlike features, however, there are clear pelvic indications that the evolutionary transformation was not complete and that *A. afarensis* probably did not have fully modern bipedal locomotion. These indications include the incomplete pelvic bowl, the lack of modern realignment of the ischial shafts, the extreme width (hip joint to hip joint) of the pelvic girdle, and evidence that the iliofemoral ligaments may have been small and weak. This combination of traits has convinced some anthropologists and anatomists

Rectus femoris one of the muscles that flexes the hominid thigh.

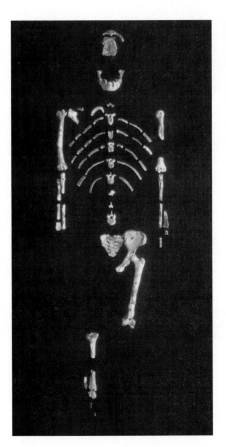

Figure 7.4

"Lucy," discovered by Donald C. Johanson and his team in 1974, lived by a lake about 3 million years ago. She was just over 3 feet (about 1 meter) tall and died in her early twenties. Based on this and other discoveries, Johanson and his colleagues named a new species, *A. afarensis*.

that *Australopithecus afarensis* had a more primitive kind of bipedalism than modern humans, perhaps with apelike balancing and more twisting of the trunk.

The skull bones of *Australopithecus afarensis* reveal a rather primitive mixture of traits. The face was **prognathic,** the forehead receded strongly from behind large brows, and the braincase was low-vaulted—a distinctly apelike cranium indeed. Furthermore, *A. afarensis*'s average **cranial capacity** of 433 cubic centimeters (range 400–500 cc) was only slightly larger than that of a chimpanzee (383 cubic centimeters mean).

Finally, the *A. afarensis* dentition is of great importance: It is apelike in many respects. In particular, the upper canine is somewhat pointed, with a large root, and is reminiscent of that of an ape; it also shows noticeable sexual dimorphism (Figure 7.7). The lower canines are associated with small diastemata in the upper jaw. At the same time, the first lower premolar (P3) is also remarkable in lacking or having only a small internal (lingual) secondary cusp; yet the tooth is not truly apelike, for the apes have no second cusp, but only one single large one. It is, as Johanson says, "a tooth in transition" (Johanson and Edey, 1981:210). The molar teeth show the kind of wear we associate with modern humans and suggest the grinding of grit-laden foods. However, the shape of the toothrow is more apelike than human, as is the profile of the face (Figure 7.7).

Altogether, the *A. afarensis* fossils show a remarkable set of traits that place them squarely in the family Hominidae, yet reveal many similarities to apes. Two and a half decades' work has made *A. afarensis* one of the best known of all fossil hominid species. The species *A. afarensis* also includes more than the Hadar fossils. In addition, there are recently reported 4-million-year-old remains from Allia Bay, east Turkana; equally

Prognathic having a protruding jaw.

Cranial capacity the capacity of the cranium or skull, measured in cubic centimeters (cc).

Figure 7.5

The critical feature of the evolving knee is the plane of the **condyles** of the knee joint (horizontal lines in the drawing) in relation to the shaft of the femur. The photograph of knees shows that in the ape (left) the alignment is such that the leg is straight when extended. In humans (right) and in *A. afarensis* (middle), the leg is angled at the knee (see drawing and photo). The lower drawings show that the bearing surfaces of the condyles are broadened in bipedal species as an adaptation to the greater weight transmitted through the knee (drawn circles indicate rounded and broadened condyles).

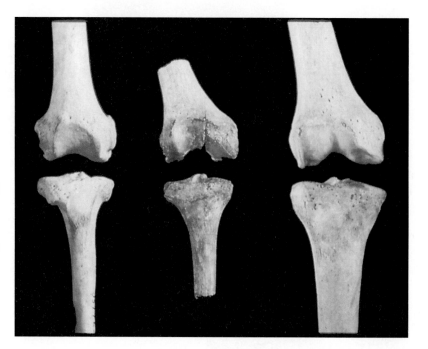

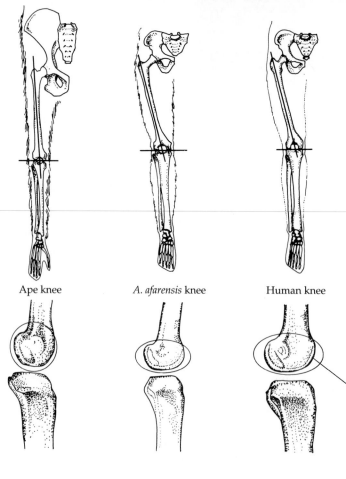

Ape knee   *A. afarensis* knee   Human knee

Condyle

Condyles bearing surfaces on bones, such as mandibular condyles or condyles of leg bones.

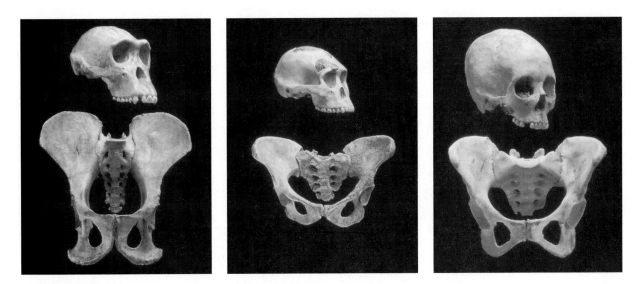

Figure 7.6

The restored pelvic girdle of *A. afarensis* (center) compared with that of a modern human (right) and a chimpanzee (left). Note the shorter, broader ilia and more bowl-like pelvis of *A. afarensis* compared to that of the ape. Also visible are the deep sciatic notches and extreme pelvic width (hip joint to hip joint) of *A. afarensis*. A typical skull for each species is shown with the corresponding pelvis.

ancient Ethiopian fossils from Middle Awash sites such as Maka and Belohdelie; and 4.2-million-year-old specimens from Fejej in the Omo River basin. Finally, among the most important *A. afarensis* fossils are the remains from a remarkable site in northern Kenya called Laetoli.

Laetoli. In 1974, archaeologist and fossil hunter Mary Leakey returned to Laetoli, a site in Tanzania that she and her husband, Louis Leakey, had first visited in 1935. She collected more than twenty fragmentary hominid jaws from eroding Pliocene strata in this area. The fossils represented eight adults and three children, and they were conveniently sandwiched between two volcanic ash strata dated 3.6 and 3.75 million years BP. They have a striking affinity with the Hadar fossils, and it is claimed by Johanson and White (1979) that they belong to the same species; indeed, Johanson and White chose one of the Laetoli jaws as the **type specimen** of the species *Australopithecus afarensis*. Others believe, for several reasons, that the Laetoli finds should be classified separately from the Hadar fossils. First of all, the Laetoli fossils carry some unique traits, and they have features in common with *A. africanus* (to be described later) and with the early hominine *Homo habilis* from nearby Olduvai Gorge, though they are much older than either. Second, some researchers, such as anthropologist Sigrid Hartwig-Scherer (1993), are troubled by the extreme degree of sexual dimorphism in body weight attributed to *A. afarensis*. Were there really two species, rather than one species with very large males and very small females? And third, the Hadar and Laetoli sites are a little more than 1,000 miles (1,600 kilometers) apart—a considerable distance for combining fossil assemblages to produce a single species.

Although many of these issues have yet to be settled, new discoveries and analyses have provided some light. Regarding the issue of sexual dimorphism in body size, fossil discoveries at the Ethiopian site of Maka (just south of Hadar) have shown that a single

Type specimen the *fossil* specimen that serves as the basis for identifying all other individuals in a *species*; usually the original specimen to be found.

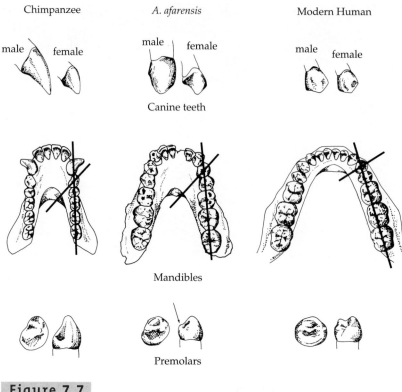

Chimpanzee   *A. afarensis*   Modern Human

male   female   male   female   male   female

Canine teeth

Mandibles

Premolars

Figure 7.7

Comparison of *A. afarensis* with chimpanzee and modern human dentitions. At the top, a comparison of the male and female upper canines of each species. Notice the pointed ape canines and the blunt human teeth, and the considerable sexual dimorphism in the ape and *A. afarensis* teeth. Below this, the three mandibles are illustrated. Notice the intermediate traits of the *A. afarensis* mandible. The lines show the alignment of the first lower premolar in relation to the rest of the molars. At the bottom, a typical first lower premolar is illustrated. The ape premolar is one-cusped; the human premolar two-cusped. The *A. afarensis* premolar illustrated has a small lingual cusp (arrow) and is intermediate in form.
Source: Johanson and Edey, 1981.

A. afarensis site can produce the same amount of intraspecific variation in tooth and body size as the combined Hadar–Laetoli assemblage (White et al., 1993). Furthermore, statistical analyses have shown that the degree of size dimorphism in *A. afarensis* does not exceed that of gorillas and orangutans. It seems entirely possible, therefore, that the original interpretation of (relatively) huge *A. afarensis* males and much smaller females was correct. And this is an important point, because it may well give us a critical clue about the mating system of these early hominids.

Similarly, the problem of combining the Hadar and Laetoli samples into one, extremely widespread species has been eliminated by the discovery of new *A. afarensis* sites in between Fejej (Ethiopia) and Allia Bay (east of Lake Turkana, Kenya) fall almost exactly halfway between Hadar and Laetoli (Figure 7.1), and the demonstration of *A. afarensis* material from these localities should put an end to geographical qualms about the species' validity. For now, most anthropologists (including the authors of this book) are following Johanson and White and treating *Australopithecus afarensis* as a single, widespread, anatomically variable species.

Discoveries and Mysteries

Hominid Footprints at Laetoli

Paul Abell, a geochemist working at Laetoli, made another discovery that was, if possible, more remarkable than the fossil finds. Sandwiched in layers of volcanic ash were the preserved footprints of a whole range of animals, including elephants, rhinoceroses, many types of antelope, three kinds of giraffe, a saber-toothed cat, and many other species, all now extinct. One of these other species was a hominid: Clearly impressed in the ash layer, hominid tracks cover a distance of more than 150 feet (45 meters). Portions of the tracks are slightly eroded; but, as shown in the photo here, several intact prints are preserved. The pattern and form of the footprints are like those made in soft sand by modern humans and suggest (like the other evidence) an evolved bipedalism. The smaller and larger footprints (on the basis of modern people's foot size) suggest a stature ranging from about 4 to 5 feet (1.2 to 1.5 meters). This discovery is a most remarkable one, and it is unique in paleontology for the number of mammalian species represented: A large proportion of the Laetoli Pliocene fauna have left their imprint. Above all, it is quite clear that *Australopithecus afarensis* was walking very nearly like a human almost 4 million years ago—and perhaps earlier.

The Laetoli site has produced a unique record of the footprints of animals dated from about 3.6 million years BP. The footprints of a large proportion of the fossil species are present, including those of *Australopithecus afarensis* as shown in this picture.

Interestingly, adopting bipedalism apparently did not require forsaking the trees completely—at least not initially. *A. afarensis* and some other australopithecines show anatomical evidence of both the derived trait of terrestrial bipedalism and the continuation of some arboreal climbing and suspension. Indeed, australopithecine bipedalism has been described as "facultative" (optional, dependent on conditions), as opposed to the "obligatory" bipedalism of modern humans. And while the australopithecines' hips and legs were evolving relatively quickly in response to conditions favoring bipedalism, other parts of their anatomy were lagging behind. For example, new evidence from CT (computerized tomography) images of australopithecine skulls has revealed that these early hominids had **semicircular canal** morphologies like those of apes, not of modern humans (Spoor et al., 1994). This means that, although routinely bipedal, the australopithecines were not yet fully adapted to upright balance and coordination. As is so often the case with evolution, natural selection moved the early hominids toward full bipedalism through a mosaic of adaptive changes.

Australopithecus garhi and the Awash

In April 1999 the newest hominid species was announced (Asfaw et al., 1999). Recovered from 2.5-million-year-old sediments at the Bouri site west of Ethiopia's Awash River, the cranial and dental remains of *Australopithecus garhi* show the following set of features (Table 7.7): a prognathic face fronting a low-vaulted skull that housed a 450-cc brain; a **sagittal crest** atop the skull (note that the single known skull may be a male) and a marked constriction behind the brows; broad anterior teeth (compared to other early hominids); and very large premolars and molars (comparable in size, but not cusp complexity, to those of *Paranthropus*, to be described shortly). Apelike traits retained in the *A. garhi* dentition include a U-shaped toothrow and small diastemata in the upper dentition, the latter present despite the fact that the canines appear to have been thick but short.

Table 7.7

Characteristics of *Australopithecus garhi*	
Trait	**Australopithecus garhi**
Height	Unknown
Weight	Unknown
Brain size	450 cc mean (one specimen measured)
Cranium	Prognathic lower face; marked postorbital constriction; sagittal crest in males; low-vaulted braincase
Dentition	Short upper canines; anterior dentition very broad compared to that of other australopithecines; postcanine dentition similar to *Paranthropus* in size; incisors procumbent; U-shaped dental arcade with slightly divergent toothrows; thick enamel; diastemata in upper jaws; absence of facial "dishing"
Diet	Unknown
Limbs	Unknown
Pelvis	Unknown
Locomotion	Bipedalism (predicted)
Known dates (million years BP)	2.5

Semicircular canals fluid-filled canals of the inner ear that control balance and coordination.

Australopithecus garhi australopithecine species known from Northeast Africa (Ethiopia) and dated 2.5 mya.

Sagittal crest bony ridge that arises on the midline of the skull in response to extreme muscle development; typical of gorillas and some *Paranthropus*.

The discoverers of *A. garhi* suggest that it might be a direct ancestor of the homi-nines (i.e., of early forms of *Homo,* in the subfamily of Homininae), but this remains speculative. Of considerable interest is the fact that about 300 to 400 meters from the *A. garhi* skull, and in the same-aged sediments, researchers found hominid postcranial remains that show lengthening of the leg compared to arm length—a significant step toward modern humans' limb proportions—and animal bones bearing stone-tool cut marks. Asfaw and his colleagues (1999) are careful to say that neither the postcranial remains nor the butchered animal bones can be attributed conclusively to *A. garhi.* The postcranial material may come from an entirely different hominid, and the cut-marked bones from that (more modern?) creature's food-gathering activities. Nonetheless, the proximity of the various remains is suspicious, and Bouri will no doubt be the site of continued intensive fossil hunting.

For more on the australopithecines, visit our web site.

The South African Australopithecines and Australopithecus africanus

The species of *Australopithecus* first to be discovered and named, **Australopithecus af-ricanus,** was found in 1924 in a box of bones collected from the old limeworks at Taung, in the Cape Province of the Republic of South Africa. Anatomist Raymond Dart real-ized that the fossil skull of a "child" (three to four years of age) was that of an apelike creature with a near human dentition and an upright posture (Dart, 1959). The im-portance of this fossil today is mainly historical, but it is still the finest specimen of an *Australopithecus* child's skull in our possession.

It was nearly ten years before further discoveries were made in the Transvaal, when the intrepid collector and retired doctor, Robert Broom, collected more material from the limeworks at Sterkfontein, between Johannesburg and Pretoria (Broom, 1950). The discoveries fell into two groups: relatively small and gracile fossils, now classed as *Aus-tralopithecus africanus,* and a more robust and heavily built species, which was put into a separate genus and named *Paranthropus robustus.* Although Broom also coined other names for these species (*A. transvaalensis* for the gracile form and *P. crassidens* for the robust forms), the two first mentioned names have priority and have been retained by most scholars.

The Transvaal fossils appear to represent offshoots from the earlier East African populations, and we can observe that as time passes, the more gracile forms (the oldest here dated at 3.5 to 2.5 mya) appear to be evolving into the more robust forms (dated 2.0 to 1.0 mya). The more robust forms are less humanlike than the earlier gracile forms; and, as we shall see, they eventually became extinct.

A. africanus is a very well known species that has been found mainly at the site of Sterkfontein in the Transvaal. We have a magnificent skull (Figure 7.8) and many mandibular fragments. There are also limb bones, foot bones, ribs, and a pelvis. Alto-gether these remains point quite conclusively to a small-brained (about 450 cc) bipedal hominid living in a mixed savanna and woodland environment. The bipedalism, as we might expect, shows some prehuman characteristics reminiscent of those seen in this hominid's apelike ancestors. The foot bones (possibly 3.5 million years of age) show adaptations for bipedalism at the rear of the foot along with the clear presence of an

Australopithecus africanus gracile australopithecine species that inhabited South Africa 3.5–2.5 mya.

This magnificent skull of *Australopithecus africanus* was found at Sterkfontein by Robert Broom in 1947. Although the teeth and jawbone are missing, the skull is otherwise complete and undistorted—a rare find.

apelike grasping big toe at the front (Clarke and Tobias, 1995). A shinbone (tibia) shows evidence of apelike mobility at the knee joint (Berger and Tobias, 1996). Furthermore, the forelimbs may be longer in relation to the hind limbs than we find in modern humans—distinctly apelike body proportions. This evidence from the limbs suggests that *A. africanus,* though bipedal, was also equipped for arboreal climbing—exactly the situation that we might predict for an early hominid at this time period.

Raymond Dart also found fossils of *A. africanus* at a site farther north called Makapansgat, but his discoveries there have only supported the deductions made on the basis of the Sterkfontein finds. Characteristics of *A. africanus* are listed in Table 7.8.

Altogether, the Transvaal discoveries have added much to our understanding of the genus *Australopithecus*. Its widespread distribution is clear, and its morphological and ecological range is becoming understood. As the accuracy of the dates given to the fossils improves, we may be able to trace a possible phylogenetic line from the earlier East and Northeast African discoveries to the Central and South African fossils.

The Robust Australopithecines: Paranthropus

Paranthropus genus of the Australopithecinae with robust characteristics.

Paranthropus robustus species of *Paranthropus* from the Transvaal of South Africa dated between 2 and 1 mya.

As mentioned earlier, fossils of **Paranthropus,** a more robust australopithecine species, were discovered in South Africa by Robert Broom and named *Paranthropus robustus* and *P. crassidens.* Further finds of this genus were made in 1959 at Olduvai Gorge in Tanzania. Louis and Mary Leakey had been working at Olduvai for nearly thirty years before they found fossil hominids. During that period they had discovered a great variety of stone tools made from pebbles (what became known as the Oldowan tool industry; see Chapter 8) together with a vast range of animal bones.

When the Leakeys eventually found the hominid skull, it was at the very bottom of the gorge (in Bed I) lying on what had been the margin of a lake, surrounded by stone

Table 7.8

	Characteristics of *Australopithecus africanus*
Trait	***Australopithecus africanus***
Height[a]	F: 3.8 ft (115 cm) M: 4.5 ft (138 cm) (F is 83% of M)
Weight	F: 55–66 lb (25–30 kg) M: 90–132 lb (41–60 kg) (F is 54% of M)
Brain size (sexes combined)	454 cc mean (405–515 cc range)[b]
Cranium	Prognathic face; no sagittal crest; low, flat forehead; low-vaulted braincase; lacks flexure (arching) of cranial base[c]
Dentition	Parabolic toothrow; small incisorlike canines; no diastemata; lower P3s have two cusps; smaller grinding teeth than *P. robustus*
Diet	Mostly fruits and leaves; also, possibly grasses, sedges, some meat
Limbs	Longer and larger arms and shorter legs than modern humans; apelike tibia; grasping big toes
Pelvis	Short, broad ilia; pelvic bowl nearly complete; short ischial shafts realigned in modern manner; pelvis wide between hip joints
Locomotion	Bipedalism (probably primitive) and arboreal climbing
Known dates (million years BP)	3.5(?)–2.5

[a]Mean values for height, weight, and brain size are sometimes based on small samples and may change with additional fossil discoveries.
[b]The brain size of Sterkfontein fossil 505 is controversial. It is taken here as 515 cubic centimeters.
[c]A fully flexed (arched) cranial base would suggest the presence of the throat anatomy that allows modern speech.

tools and the bones of small animals: mice, rats, frogs, lizards, birds, snakes, tortoises, young pigs, and parts of small antelopes. But there were no remains of large animals. Nearly all these bones were broken, but the near-human skull and tibia and fibula (the two bones of the lower part of the leg) that appeared at the same site were not. It seemed to the Leakeys that the hominid had killed the other animals.

The skull that took shape from the fragments uncovered at the campsite was that of a nearly mature male (Figure 7.9). That the wisdom teeth were unworn and that the suture joining the two halves of the skull, the **sagittal suture,** had not yet closed indicated that it was a young adult. In brain size and in general appearance, the young male broadly resembled *Paranthropus robustus* of the south. The molars were extraordinarily large and heavy, but detailed study confirmed that they were, in their structure, undoubtedly hominid teeth. The skull had the characteristic massive face and teeth and rugged low cranium of *P. robustus* but was even larger and more specialized. These differences led Louis Leakey to set up a new genus for what he believed was the earliest tool user, and he named it ***Zinjanthropus boisei.*** (*Zinj* means "Eastern Africa" in Arabic; *boisei* honored Charles Boise, who had helped to finance the Leakeys' search for early humans.) Today the skull is classified as ***Paranthropus boisei.***

Age of *Paranthropus*

Fortunately, the approximate age of the Leakeys' Bed I fossil could be determined because the skull had been found sandwiched between layers of volcanic ash. Geologists

Sagittal suture the line of union joining the two main side bones of the braincase.

Zinjanthropus boisei original name for the *australopithecine species* now called *Paranthropus boisei*.

Paranthropus boisei robust *species* of *Paranthropus* that lived in East Africa 2.3 to 1.3 million years ago.

Figure 7.9

Zinjanthropus, the immense skull found by Mary Leakey at Olduvai in 1959. It is now classified as *Paranthropus boisei.*

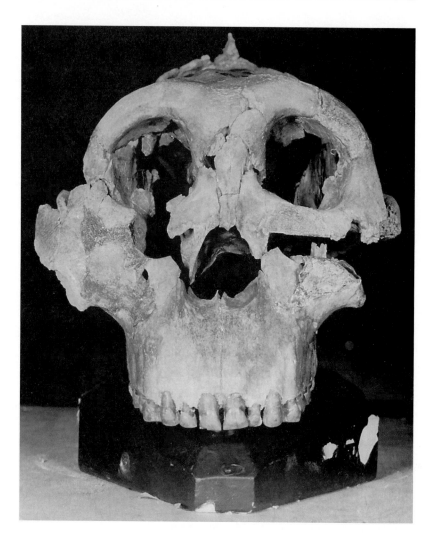

extracted minerals containing potassium from the volcanic ash covering the fossils and also from an older volcanic bed that underlaid the site. When they analyzed these layers by the then new method of potassium–argon dating, they were able to fix the startling age of about 1.75 million years. This date was repeatedly confirmed by later potassium–argon tests.

But several important questions remained unanswered, despite firm information about the antiquity of the *P. boisei* fossils from Olduvai. Chief among those questions was whether or not *Paranthropus* was responsible for the Oldowan flake and chopper tools. Initially the Leakeys thought that was probably the case; but later they changed their minds, following the recovery of hominine (early *Homo*) remains from the same rock layer. Today most paleoanthropologists agree with the Leakeys' second thoughts and attribute the Bed I tools to hominines with larger brains than that of *Paranthropus.* In any event, by the mid-1960s the hominid fossil record in Africa was already becoming complex. South Africa had produced the remains of two genera of australopithecines—*Australopithecus* and *Paranthropus*—as well as fossils of early hominines—and East Africa had yielded evidence of *Paranthropus* coexisting with "early *Homo*" fully 1.75 million years ago.

Finds Near the Omo River

Africa's Rift Valley is an unstable area where the earth's crust is still moving. It has long been a center of volcanic activity and is pockmarked by cones and craters. Because of neighboring volcanic activity, Olduvai has invaluable layers of datable volcanic ash; so does Omo, in extreme southwestern Ethiopia. Both places supported more life in the past than they do now. Laced with rivers, much greener, carrying a far larger animal population than they do today, each provided the lush water-edge environments, gallery forests, and woodland savannas that the early hominids are believed to have preferred.

At Omo the strata, investigated between 1967 and 1974, are more than 2,000 feet (600 meters) thick and span more than 2 million years. Moreover, they contain volcanic ash at varying intervals, some only 100,000 years apart, some more widely spaced, and each datable by chronometric methods. Together, these layers of ash enable scientists to step backward into time and into the earth, determining an approximate date at each step. You do not have to dig at Omo to go deeper into time: The strata have been heaved up in the past and now lie at an angle to the earth's surface. You need only walk along to find successively older layers revealing themselves.

The Omo deposits date from more than 4 million years ago and continue to about 1.5 million years BP (before present). This date conveniently overlaps with the fossil deposits at Olduvai, which begin about 1.9 million years BP, so that between them the two sites give us an almost unbroken story for 4 million years.

In addition to many useful animal fossils found at Omo, traces of hominids have appeared. Paleoanthropologists first found a robust jaw that they felt was sufficiently different from known material to warrant a new name: *Australopithecus aethiopicus* (now referred to as *Paranthropus*). They also found teeth, jaw fragments, parts of two skulls, and several arm and leg bones. It was an enormously significant haul for several reasons. First is the age of the oldest specimens, more than twenty teeth: 3.0 million years. These teeth are almost certainly those of a small gracile australopithecine whose identity was not clarified until years later—as *A. afarensis*. Also of significance was the fact that remains of this small hominid were found along with robust fossils similar to, but much older than, *P. boisei* found at Olduvai. Furthermore, robust specimens continued to turn up in various layers, dating right up to 1.5 million years ago. *P. boisei* apparently lived at Omo for almost a million years.

Robust Hominids at Koobi Fora

The results of work near Lake Turkana between 1969 and 1976, directed by Richard Leakey and Glynn Isaac, were sensational. At the sites east of the lake, named Ileret and Koobi Fora, they discovered three superb skulls, more than two dozen mandibles or parts of mandibles, some arm- and leg-bone fragments, and isolated teeth, amounting to more than a hundred specimens in all. Much of this material is of the robust *P. boisei* type and dates from about 2 to 1.3 million years ago. These East Turkana fossils, combined with the Omo finds, provide enough material in the way of young and old individuals, both males and females, and enough variation in dentition to describe a variable population of the robust *Paranthropus boisei*.

The Robust Hominid from West Turkana

In 1985 the number of robust australopithecine species increased by one because of discoveries made at the sites of Lomekwi and Kangatukuseo on the west side of Lake Turkana. From deposits dating about 2.6 million years of age, an excavating team headed

Australopithecus aethiopicus original name for the robust *australopithecine species* now called *Paranthropus aethiopicus*.

ASKING QUESTIONS

Why Is It Important to Study a Fossil Population?

Having a population to study instead of an individual fossil is extremely important. No two people today are exactly alike; no two australopithecines were, either. For that reason, drawing conclusions from a single fossil is risky. Measurements can be taken of a single fossil, and theories can be built up as a result of those measurements; but this information may be misleading, because the fossil may not be typical. Only when a large number of specimens is available can variations be taken into account. If visitors from outer space were to describe and name *Homo sapiens* by examining one skeleton—for example, that of a short, heavy-boned Inuit—they certainly might be excused if they thought they had another species when they discovered a second skeleton of a 6.5-foot (2-meter) slender-boned Watusi from central Africa.

---

by Alan Walker and Richard Leakey recovered a nearly toothless cranium (dubbed the Black Skull because of its coloration) and a partial mandible (Walker et al., 1986). Although much larger, the mandible is otherwise similar to the jaw found years earlier by French scientists at Omo and named *Australopithecus aethiopicus*. The west Turkana cranium is massively built and quite prognathic (Figure 7.10). It features a low fore-

Figure 7.10

The Black Skull (museum number KNM–WT 17000) represents a new species of australopithecine, *Paranthropus aethiopicus*. Although a member of the robust australopithecine clade, it resembles *Australopithecus afarensis* in several traits.

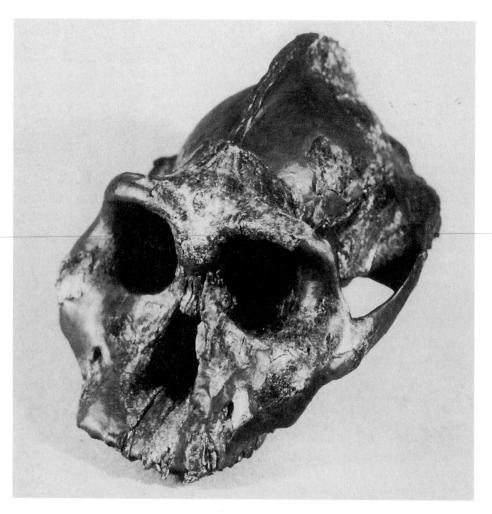

head and a small braincase (410 cc) and is topped by a sagittal crest that would have anchored large jaw muscles. The **zygomatic arches** flare widely to the side, and the face is somewhat "dished" (concave) in appearance. The few measurable teeth and tooth roots indicate that the grinding teeth were as large as those of *Paranthropus boisei*.

Naming the west Turkana skull and jaw has proved difficult. In many ways the fossils resemble *P. boisei,* and indeed, many paleoanthropologists view them as early remains of that species. In this text, however, the Black Skull is classified as ***Paranthropus aethiopicus,*** a third variety of robust australopithecine (Table 7.9). The *A. aethiopicus* jaw found earlier at Omo is also included here and thus renamed *Paranthropus*.

Zygomatic arches
bony arches extending backwards from the cheekbone in higher primates

Paranthropus aethiopicus species of *Paranthropus* found in east Africa and dated 2.7–2.3 mya.

Table 7.9

Characteristics of the Robust Australopithecinae[a]			
Trait	***Paranthropus boisei***	***Paranthropus aethiopicus***	***Paranthropus robustus***
Height	F: 4.1 ft (124 cm) M: 4.5 ft (137 cm) (F is 90% of M)	Unknown	F: 3.6 ft (110 cm) M: 4.3 ft (132 cm) (F is 83% of M)
Weight	F: 75–88 lb (34–40 kg) M: 108–176 lb (49–80 kg) (F is 57% of M)	Unknown	F: 71–88 lb (32–40 kg) M: 88–176 lb (40–80 kg) (F about 60% of M)
Brain size (sexes combined)	487 cc mean (410–530 cc range)	410 cc mean (range unknown)	530 cc mean (range unknown)
Cranium	Tall, broad, "dished" face; sagittal crest; low forehead; low-vaulted braincase; some flexure of cranial base	"Dished" face; sagittal crest; low forehead; low-vaulted braincase (compared to *P. boisei:* unflexed cranial base; shallow jaw joint; extreme facial prognathism; parietal bones flared strongly at the mastoid)	Face is wide, flattish, and "dished"; sagittal crest; low, flat forehead; low-vaulted braincase; some flexure (arching) of cranial base
Dentition	Parabolic toothrow; small incisors and canines; huge grinding teeth; lower P3s often have 3+ cusps	Grinding teeth appear to be as large as those of *P. boisei*	Parabolic toothrow; short, incisorlike canines; small anterior teeth; no diastemata; lower P3s have two or more cusps; very large grinding teeth
Diet	Hard, tough, fibrous vegetable foods; some meat	Unknown	Harder, tougher items than *A. africanus* (more nuts? gritty tubers?); some meat?
Limbs	Longer arms and shorter legs than modern humans	Unknown	Longer arms and shorter legs than modern humans; humanlike (nongrasping) big toes
Pelvis	Short, broad ilia; short ischial shafts (?); pelvis wide between hip joints	Unknown	Short, broad ilia; weak iliofemoral ligaments (?); shortening of ischial shaft (?); pelvis wide between hip joints
Locomotion	Bipedalism (primitive?)	Bipedalism predicted)	Bipedalism (more primitive than modern human walking?)
Known dates (million years BP)	2.3–1.3	2.7–2.3	2.0–1.0

[a]Mean values, or range of values, for anatomical measurements may change with additional fossil discoveries.

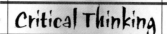

Tracing the Evolution of the Australopithecines

There are many ways of constructing a phylogenetic tree to indicate the evolution of the australopithecines. In the diagram below, key species have been omitted. According to this chapter, where would the authors of this text place *A. ramidus*? Where would *A. afarensis* appear? According to the text, what is the significance of these two species in the story of hominid evolution?

Where in the diagram do you think the authors of this text would place *P. aethiopicus*?

According to the text, why might *A. africanus* represent a South African evolutionary side branch that did not contribute to the ancestry of humankind (*Homo*)? Do you think any living humans carry the genes of any of the individual fossils on which this phylogenetic tree is based? Why or why not? If you wanted to show an alternative interpretation of the fossil record for the australopithecines, how would you draw the diagram, and what evidence would you use to support your view?

Here is the authors' construction of the evolution of the australopithecines. Were you correct?

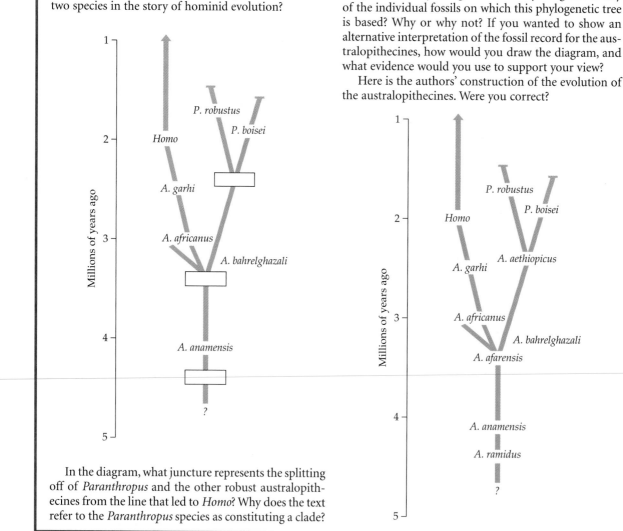

In the diagram, what juncture represents the splitting off of *Paranthropus* and the other robust australopithecines from the line that led to *Homo*? Why does the text refer to the *Paranthropus* species as constituting a clade?

The limited fossil material known to date allows only an incomplete picture of *Paranthropus aethiopicus*. Many more specimens, especially of the postcranial skeleton, must be described for us to understand the species' adaptations, including its diet and locomotion. Interestingly, some new information about *P. aethiopicus* has been gained recently from the continuing analysis of fossils (mainly teeth) collected decades ago at Omo (Suwa et al., 1996). First, the dental remains from Omo extend the time range for *P. aethiopicus* an additional 100,000 years into the past, back to 2.7 mya. *P. aethiopicus* was in residence at Omo until about 2.3 million years ago, by which time it apparently had given rise to *P. boisei*. Second, comparisons of the teeth of *Paranthropus aethiopicus* from Omo with those of *P. robustus* from South Africa suggest an ancestor–descendant relationship between these two species as well. It thus appears entirely possible that *P. aethiopicus* was ancestral to all later members of the *Paranthropus* clade.

New Fossil Finds from Africa

As we go to press, exciting new discoveries are pushing back the date of hominid origins and enlarging the inventory of hominid types. First, in October 2000, researchers recovered apparent hominid remains from 6-million-year-old deposits in Kenya's Baringo district. Put in a new genus and species called *Orrorin tugenensis*, the fossils show small canines and adaptations for bipedalism, but also some signs of arboreality (Senut et al., 2001). If verified, *Orrorin* will be the oldest known hominid. Second, in March 2001, Meave Leakey's team announced another new genus and species, *Kenyanthropus platyops*, from Lomekwi on the west side of Lake Turkana and dating to 3.5 mya (Leakey et al., 2001). Combining small grinding teeth with a big flat face, *K. platyops* resembles not only *Australopithecus*, but also *Homo rudolfensis*. Indeed, Leakey et al. suggest that it might be appropriate to transfer *rudolfensis* to *Kenyanthropus*. However the taxonomic niceties and phylogenies are finally worked out, hominids' evolutionary bush has just gotten bushier and the dynamic nature of paleoanthropology has been demonstrated.

Summary

Since the discovery of *Paranthropus boisei* at Olduvai Gorge in 1959, East Africa has produced the remains of a variety of Plio–Pleistocene hominids that collectively have established that continent as the birthplace of the human family. At present, the oldest of the named East African species is *Australopithecus ramidus* dating from 4.4 million years ago. Fossils have recently been found that take the hominid line back to 6 million years ago. Although the bipedalism of these finds (and therefore their hominid status) requires further confirmation, the new fossils constitute a good candidate for the base of the hominid evolutionary tree.

Later East African representatives of *Australopithecus* included *A. anamensis, A. afarensis, A. bahrelghazali,* and *A. garhi*. The first two of the later australopithecines confirmed the evolution of terrestrial bipedalism; *A. bahrelghazali* extended the range of the genus 1,500 miles (2,500 kilometers) west of the Rift Valley; and *A. garhi* may have been ancestral to the genus *Homo*. In South Africa *Australopithecus* was represented by only one species: *A. africanus*.

Sometime before its disappearance around 2.5 million years ago, the genus *Australopithecus* gave rise to two very different genera of descendants: *Homo* (the first hominines) and *Paranthropus* (a lineage characterized by enlargement of the grinding teeth, apparently an adaptation for a hard and tough diet). Many paleoanthropologists believe the three *Paranthropus* species constitute a monophyletic clade, the last member of which died without descendants about a million years ago, leaving *Homo* as the sole surviving hominid genus.

Timeline: Hominid Evolution

Epoch / Era		
HOLOCENE		
10,000		
PLEISTOCENE		
1.6 MILLION		
PLIOCENE		
5 MILLION		
MIOCENE		
Dryopithecus		
Kenyapithecus		
Proconsul		
25 MILLION		
OLIGOCENE		
Apidium, Parapithecus, *Aegyptopithecus,* and *Propliopithecus*		
35 MILLION		
Amphipithecus		
Siamopithecus		
Eosimias		
EOCENE		
58 MILLION		
PALEOCENE		
Early prosimians		

CENOZOIC

YEARS AD — DISCOVERIES

Year	Discovery
2000	*Orrorin tugenensis* hominid discovered at Baringo
1999	*A. garhi* discovered in the Middle Awash
1998	*Australopithecus* skeleton found at Sterkfontein
1995	Discoveries of *A. anamensis* and *A. bahrelghazali*
1994	Discovery of *A. ramidus*
1985	Skull of oldest *P. aethiopicus* from west side of Turkana
1981	Middle Awash finds of oldest *A. afarensis*
1974	Hominids found at Laetoli
1973	Hominids first found at Hadar
1969	First Koobi Fora expedition
1967	First Omo expedition
1959	Discovery of *P. boisei (Zinjanthropus)* at Olduvai
1950	Definitive assessments by Le Gros Clark published
1948	*Paranthropus* found at Swarkrans
1947	*A. africanus* found at Sterkfontein
	Dart discovers *Australopithecus* at Makapansgat
1939	First hominids found at Laetoli
1938	*P. robustus* found by Broom at Kromdraai
1936	Broom's first adult *Australopithecus* found at Sterkfontein
1931	First Leakey expedition to Olduvai
1925	Dart's work on *A. africanus* published
1924	Dart discovers *A. africanus* from Taung

YEARS BP — FOSSIL RECORD

Time	Fossil Record
Pleistocene	Later *Homo* species
1 million	Most recent *P. boisei* at East Rudolf
	Most recent *P. boisei* at Omo
	P. robustus in South Africa
	P. boisei at Olduvai
2 million	*Homo* in South Africa
	Oldest *P. boisei* fossils at Omo
	P. aethiopicus west of Turkana
	A. africanus in South Africa
2.5 million	*A. garhi* at Bouri
Pliocene	
3 million	*A. afarensis* at Hadar
	A. bahrelghazali in Chad
4 million	*A. afarensis* at Fejej
	A. anamensis at Kanapoi
	A. ramidus at Aramis
5 million	
Miocene	Lothagam jaw
6 million	Ancient apes, *Orrorin tugenensis*
	?Origin of bipedalism
10 million	

Review Questions

1. What are the grounds for classifying the species *aethiopicus, boisei,* and *robustus* within the single genus *Paranthropus*? What do these species have in common? How do they differ from one another and from *Australopithecus*?

2. What is the evidence for bipedalism in *Australopithecus ramidus, A. anamensis,* and *A. afarensis*?

3. How do the cranial traits of the australopithecines compare with those of living apes?

4. How do the dental traits of the australopithecines compare with those of living apes? What conclusions can you draw about the australopithecines' diet on the basis of their dental anatomy?

5. What are the main points of australopithecine phylogeny? In particular, what were the evolutionary fates of the two genera?

6. Why is it so difficult for paleoanthropologists to determine how many hominid species and genera they have discovered and how they relate to one another evolutionarily?

Suggested Further Reading

Conroy, G. C. *Reconstructing Human Origins.* W. W. Norton, 1997.
Howells, W. *Getting Here.* Compass Press, 1993.
Johanson, D. C., and B. Edgar. *From Lucy to Language.* Simon & Schuster, 1996.
Tattersall, I. *The Fossil Trail.* Oxford University Press, 1995.

Internet Resources

Conveniently access these and other links via our web site at **http://www.ablongman/anthro.**

AMNH Anthro Bulletin
http://www.amnh.org/enews/anthro.html
Information on AMNH anthropology and evolution exhibits, including a phylogenetic tree of hominids with skulls that can be examined in 3-D.

Ardipithecus ramidus
http://www.uea.ac.uk/~x9706887/Aramidus.html
This site profiles *A. ramidus* as well as the other australopithecine species.

The Australopithecines
http://www.ants-inc.com/inhandmuseum/LA/aust.html
Descriptions by Dr. Meave Leakey of the gracile and robust australopithecines.

The Genesis of Man
http://cybrfair.gsn.org/adelaar/index.htm
Information and pictures of the South African australopithecines and sites.

The Talk Origins Archive—Fossil Hominids
http://www.talkorigins.org/faqs/fossil-hominids.html
Click on Hominid Species in the table of contents for information on the australopithecines and other hominid species.

University of Minnesota Duluth: Australopithecines
http://www.d.umn.edu/cla/faculty/troufs/anth1602/pcaustr.html
Lots of links to interesting sites about australopithecines and hominid evolution.

Useful Search Terms:
Ardipithecus
australopithecines
Australopithecus
fossil hominids
human evolution
Paranthropus

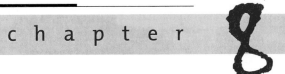
The Coming of Homo

Overview

Between 4.4 and about 2.5 million years BP, the hominid family was represented in Africa by *Australopithecus*. To start this chapter we shall look briefly at what we have deduced about the lifestyle of the *Australopithecus* species.

Around 2.5 million years ago, for reasons not yet well understood, *Australopithecus* disappeared and was replaced by its successors, *Paranthropus* and *Homo*. Two species of the earliest hominines can be identified: *Homo habilis* (2.3 to 1.6 million years BP) and *Homo rudolfensis* (2.4 to 1.6 million years BP). Both were terrestrial bipeds (although not necessarily walking exactly like modern humans), and both had significantly larger brains than their australopithecine forebears. Furthermore, one or both of these "early *Homo*" species apparently made Oldowan stone tools—a development that paleoanthropologists believe signals increased meat in the diet. Early *Homo* spread from Northeast to South Africa and survived until 1.6 mya. By 1.8 mya, at the latest, early *Homo* (most likely, *Homo habilis*) had given rise to *Homo erectus*.

Mini-Timeline: First Appearances of *Homo*

Date or Age	Fossil Discoveries or Evolutionary Events
(A) Date (years AD)	
1997	2.5-million-year-old Oldowan tools found at Gona
1994	*Homo habilis* (?) found associated with Oldowan tools at Kada Hadar
1960	Discovery of first *Homo habilis* fossils at Olduvai Gorge
(B) Age (million years BP)	
1.0–1.3	*Paranthropus* goes extinct
1.8	Oldest definite *Homo erectus* fossils
2.3?—1.6	*Homo habilis* inhabits first East, then South Africa
2.4–1.6	*Homo rudolfensis* inhabits East Africa
2.5 million	Oldest Oldowan choppers and flakes

Follow links at **http://www.ablongman/anthro** for additional resources in physical anthropology, primatology, biological anthropology, and paleoanthropology.

Check our web site for additional information, photos, drawings, maps, and animations on topics in this chapter.

Lifestyles of the Australopithecines

From a study of the geological, paleontological, and botanical context of hominid fossils, as well as of their anatomy, we are able to build up a limited picture of the environment and lifestyle of these early creatures.

Australopithecus

As we saw in Chapter 7, *Australopithecus ramidus* is the oldest and least known species. Still, what clues we have about its environment are of considerable interest. *A. ramidus* appears to have inhabited East Africa's closed woodland environment, and within that environment it probably survived on a standard hominoid diet of ripe fruit, leaves, insects, and—if its tastes were like those of modern chimpanzees—the occasional small animal. Certainly, judging from its thin dental enamel, it does not appear to have eaten very many things that were hard to open or tough to chew.

The few fossils of *A. ramidus* described to date suggest that it moved bipedally throughout its habitat (White et al., 1994). Whether or not it still climbed about in the trees is unclear, although this seems likely given its recent descent from ape stock. Equally unclear is exactly what *A. ramidus* was doing as it stood and moved in an upright posture. A clue on this point, however, comes from evidence that the Aramis habitat was not quite as closed as the label "closed woodland" implies (WoldeGabriel et al., 1994). Along with the remains of forest creatures, the Aramis deposits contain the bones of such open-country animals as giraffes and rhinos. This suggests the presence at Aramis of (extensive?) grassy spaces and raises the possibility that *A. ramidus* was moving bipedally across open country from one wooded food patch to another. Other possibilities, judging from observations of modern chimpanzees, are that *A. ramidus* might have stood bipedally to threaten other animals, to carry or brandish various objects, or to see over long distances. And that's really about all we can say about the oldest known hominid species until more fossils are described.

Australopithecus is represented by five other species: *A. afarensis*, *A. anamensis*, *A. africanus*, *A. garhi*, and *A. bahrelghazali*. These members of the so-called gracile lineage of australopithecines ranged from modern South Africa to Ethiopia and west to Chad. All of the gracile australopithecines used a mixed bag of habitats, including gallery forests at the edge of rivers and lakes and wooded savanna with open grassy patches. Within those habitats, the various species were mainly terrestrial bipeds, although both of the best known types—*A. afarensis* and *A. africanus*—appear to have retained adaptations for arboreal climbing (shown in their upper bodies and feet, respectively). Furthermore, given the grasping big toes of some and the wide pelvises of all of the gracile forms, it seems likely that their bipedalism was rather primitive and somewhat apelike, with some twisting of the trunk as the lead leg swung forward and with different balancing mechanisms. Exactly how the *Australopithecus* species used their bipedalism is unclear; threatening, carrying things, making long-distance observations, and moving between dispersed food patches all remain possibilities. Interestingly, there is no direct evidence that *Australopithecus* stood and moved erect so it could use tools. As shown in Table 8.1, none of these species has been found in direct association with stone tools, although it is always possible that they used perishable tools, like the

Table 8.1

Association between Australopithecine Fossils and Tools		
Species and Site	**Found in Association with Stone Tools?**	**Found in *Sole* Association with Stone Tools?**
Australopithecus ramidus Aramis	No	—
Australopithecus afarensis Hadar and elsewhere	No	—
Australopithecus anamensis Kanapoi and Allia Bay	No	—
Australopithecus africanus Sterkfontein and elsewhere	No	—
Australopithecus garhi Bouri	No	—
Paranthropus aethiopicus Omo and elsewhere	No	—
Paranthropus boisei Olduvai Gorge Elsewhere	Yes No	No (*Homo habilis* also present) —
Paranthropus robustus Swartkrans	Yes	No (*Homo erectus* [?] also present)

termite-fishing sticks of modern chimpanzees. With regard to food, and as judged by their moderately sized molars, the gracile australopithecines seem to have depended primarily on a soft diet of ripe fruit and foliage. Additionally, based on studies of the carbon (C^{13}) content of teeth from Makapansgat, it has been suggested recently (Sponheimer and Lee-Thorp, 1999) that *Australopithecus africanus* (at least) ate grasses and sedges—or, alternatively, insects and small mammals that had eaten C^{13}-enriched plants. Such insectivory and small-scale meat-eating, of course, has been seen in modern chimpanzees and bonobos. Finally, except for *A. ramidus* and *A. bahrelghazali*, the *Australopithecus* species all had thick dental enamel, suggesting that they were also beginning to eat some harder foods.

With regard to reproduction, the moderate to extreme sexual dimorphism in body size shown by *A. africanus* and *A. afarensis* suggests to some paleoanthropologists (on the basis of studies of living primates that show extreme sexual dimorphism) that these early hominids had polygynous mating systems characterized by fairly high levels of male–male breeding competition that favored increased male size. This suggestion has not gone unchallenged, however; other researchers remain skeptical that mating systems can be inferred accurately from the size differences between australopithecine females and males. A second possibility, and one that agrees with behavioral data from living hominoids, is that the australopithecines were promiscuous. At present, neither mating pattern can be either proved or conclusively rejected.

Paranthropus

The *Paranthropus* species were all habitual bipeds, although some paleoanthropologists question whether or not they were fully modern in their locomotion. The robusts' long arms and short legs may reflect the continuation of arboreal activities, although this is difficult to determine with certainty; their limb proportions could also simply be the result of recent ape ancestry. And finally, the moderate to marked sexual dimorphism in body size found in the *Paranthropus* species may indicate polygyny, but other mating systems such as promiscuity cannot be ruled out.

P. aethiopicus, P. boisei, and *P. robustus* also used a variety of habitats. *P. robustus* was adapted to the open grasslands of South Africa, whereas to the north *P. boisei* seems to have preferred well-watered sites such as the gallery forests along rivers. The massive grinding teeth of the robusts suggest that, in contrast to their gracile cousins, they ate large amounts of predominantly tough, fibrous, and/or gritty vegetable foods. That the robusts may have supplemented their vegetable diet by eating some amount of meat has recently been indicated by the strontium-to-calcium ratio in their bones (Stewart, 1992). Tool use by the robust australopithecines is problematic. These species overlapped in time and space with the earliest stone tools (Oldowan choppers and flakes), but because nowhere are they found *exclusively* associated with such tools, they often are regarded as "nontechnological." Nonetheless, Randall Susman's argument (Susman, 1994) that *Paranthropus robustus* made some or all of the tools at Swartkrans is plausible, though lacking strong proof. At the very least, as with the other australopithecines, chimpanzee-type toolmaking should have been well within the capabilities of *Paranthropus.*

Homo habilis

The beginning of the hominid story consists exclusively of tales of the australopithecines. The subfamily Australopithecinae enjoyed at least 3 million years of existence in Africa without competition from more advanced hominid types (roughly 5.6 to 2.4 million years BP). Then, about 2.5 million years ago, a critical (for us) evolutionary development took place: One of the australopithecine species gave rise by cladogenesis to a different sort of creature, one that was bigger-brained than its ancestors and definitely produced material culture. Paleoanthropologists classify these new creatures as *Homo,* the first representatives of the subfamily Homininae (Table 8.2); and the rest of this chapter is devoted to the story of their discoveries, adaptations, and accomplishments.

You will recall that in 1959 Mary and Louis Leakey hit paleontological pay dirt in Bed I at the bottom of Olduvai Gorge. That was the year they discovered the skull of

Table 8.2

Hominid Taxonomy		
Subfamily Australopithecinae (see Table 7.1 for species names)		
Genera		
Australopithecus		
Paranthropus		
Subfamily Homininae (Common name: hominines)		
Genus *Homo*	Species	*Homo rudolfensis*
		Homo habilis
		Homo erectus
		Homo heidelbergensis
		Homo neanderthalensis
		Home sapiens

Zinjanthropus (now *Paranthropus*) *boisei,* a creature that they suspected was responsible for the numerous Oldowan stone choppers and flakes also found at the site. Their suspicions were short-lived, however, because just the next year the bones of a better candidate for the office of stone toolmaker showed up: a hominid with a much bigger brain than *Zinjanthropus.*

Though these new bones were found at broadly the same stratigraphic level as *Paranthropus boisei* and not far away, Louis Leakey realized that they represented a creature far closer to modern humans than was *P. boisei,* with its huge molars and sagittal crest. The new fossil showed much smaller grinding teeth and relatively larger front teeth than *Zinjanthropus,* as well as a larger braincase. By 1964 a thorough analysis, plus the discovery of additional and confirming specimens, convinced Leakey and his coworkers that the Bed I toolmaker was not *P. boisei* but a previously unknown species. They named it **Homo habilis** ("handy man").

Homo habilis remains have now been recovered from Olduvai Gorge, from Omo in extreme southwest Ethiopia, and from Koobi Fora in Kenya (Table 8.3). In addition, a recently discovered maxilla (upper jaw) from Hadar may well turn out to be *Homo habilis.* The known time range for the species currently stands at 2.0 to 1.6 million years BP (this extends back to 2.3 million years ago if the Hadar jaw is included). Among the most important specimens discovered thus far is a partial foot from Olduvai (Figure 8.1), a very fragmented skull from the same locality, and a much more complete skull from Koobi Fora that dates to 1.9 million years of age (Figure 8.2). Finally, in the mid-1980s, Donald Johanson and Tim White worked at Olduvai Gorge for four seasons and recovered a fragmentary skeleton that has been attributed to *Homo habilis.* This find is particularly important because it provides critical information about body size, limb proportions, and other aspects of the postcranial anatomy of this species.

The Question of Classification

The taxonomic validity of *Homo habilis* is now widely accepted, although this was not the case initially. Indeed, over the years so much variable fossil material was attributed to *Homo habilis* that many scientists started to believe that specimens from more than one species were being included. Splitting the *H. habilis* bone collection led to the recent naming of a second early hominine, **Homo rudolfensis** (Wood, 1992). Together, the two species are commonly referred to as "early *Homo.*" In any event, the main characteristics of *Homo habilis,* as adjusted after the removal of the *H. rudolfensis* material, are summarized in Table 8.4. Comparisons with Tables 7.6 and 7.8 show that *Homo habilis* had

Homo habilis one of the two *species* of "early *Homo*"; inhabited East Africa 2.3 to 1.6 million years ago.

Homo rudolfensis one of the two *species* of "early *Homo*"; inhabited East Africa 2.4 to 1.6 million years ago.

Table 8.3

	A Partial Record of Early *Homo* Fossil Sites			
Species	**South African Sites**	**Age (million years)[a]**	**East African Sites**	**Age (million years)**
Homo habilis	Sterkfontein	2.0–1.8	Olduvai Gorge	1.9–1.6
			Omo and Koobi Fora	2.0–1.8
			Hadar (?)	2.3
Homo rudolfensis			Omo and Koobi Fora	2.0–1.6
			Uraha (Malawi)	2.4

[a]As noted in Table 7.2, the East African sites are dated more accurately than those from South Africa.

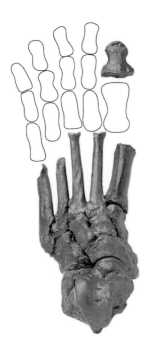
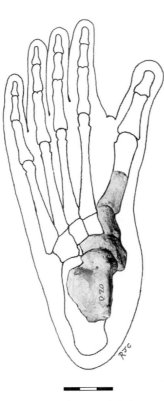

Figure 8.1

Small clues of great significance, the foot bones of *Australopithecus* and *Homo habilis* give us important information about the evolution of bipedalism and the grasping capability of the great toe. At left, the foot of *Homo habilis* shows slight evidence of a grasping toe but in other respects is modern. In the fragments of the *A. africanus* foot, right, the interpretation suggests an almost apelike configuration of the great toe. This fossil may date from 3.5 mya. Not to scale.

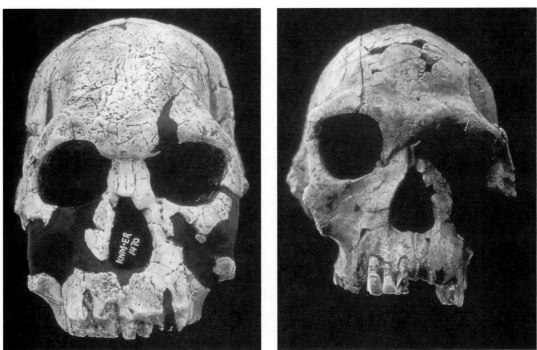

Figure 8.2

At left, *Homo rudolfensis* (museum number KNM–ER 1470); at right, *Homo habilis* (KNM–ER 1813). Note the differences in size of braincase and brows between these two early *Homo* species both from Koobi Fora.

Table 8.4

Characteristics of *Homo habilis*[a]	
Trait	***Homo habilis***
Height	F: 3.3 ft (100 cm) M:?
Weight	F: 71 lb (32 kg) M: 82 lb (37 kg) (F about 86% of M)
Brain size	612 cc mean (509–674 cc range)
Cranium	Somewhat prognathic face; incipient brow ridge; foreshortened palate; no sagittal crest; rounded mandibular base
Dentition	Narrower lower grinding teeth than in *Homo rudolfensis*; mostly single-rooted lower premolars
Limbs	Longer arms and shorter legs than modern humans; feet retaining adaptations for climbing
Locomotion	Bipedalism (probably almost modern, but with a few remaining apelike characteristics)
Known dates (million years BP)	2.0–1.6 (2.3–1.6 if Hadar jaw is included)

[a]Mean values for anatomical measurements may change with additional fossil discoveries.

much in common with East Africa's *A. afarensis* and South Africa's *Australopithecus africanus*. For example, body size was very similar in the three species; all showed rather apelike limb proportions (relatively long arms and short legs); and all showed some indication of continuing arboreal activity. The dentition of *Homo habilis* was much more modern than that of *A. afarensis,* but only marginally more so than that of *A. africanus*. It is immediately clear that the main factor differentiating *Homo habilis* from the australopithecines was brain size. With an average of 612 cubic centimeters, *Homo habilis* had a bigger brain than apes and the various australopithecines, but a much smaller brain than modern people or the well-established hominine **Homo erectus** (Table 8.5). But what do these differences say about taxonomy? Specifically, do the brain size data help us decide whether *habilis* is a hominine or an australopithecine?

Homo rudolfensis

Early in the work at Koobi Fora (early 1970s), it became clear that the Lake Turkana region contained fossils of hominids other than robust australopithecines. Over time, searchers found several specimens of larger-brained, gracile creatures that did not fit well into either *Australopithecus* or *Paranthropus*. One of the finest fossils carries the museum number KNM–ER 1470; it is an almost complete cranium and face, but with the skull base and jaw missing (Figure 8.2). ER 1470 combines a large face with strongly built zygomatic arches and molars that are relatively large (although much smaller than in *Paranthropus*). The skull is relatively lightly built, and the braincase is considerably larger than any australopithecine's at 775 cubic centimeters.

As the search for fossils continued at Koobi Fora, several other specimens of relatively large-brained hominids were discovered, including the splendid skull labeled ER

Homo erectus *hominid species* that inhabited much of the Old World between 1.9(?) million and at least 300,000 years BP; successor to "early *Homo*."

Table 8.5

Cranial Capacities for Apes and Certain Hominid Species[a]		
Species	Range of Cranial Capacity (cc)	Average Cranial Capacity (cc)
Chimpanzees	282–500	383
Gorillas	340–752	505
Australopithecus ramidus	Unknown	Unknown
Australopithecus afarensis	400–500	433
Australopithecus africanus	405–515	454
Australopithecus garhi	Unknown	450
Paranthropus robustus	Unknown	530
Paranthropus boisei	410–530	487
Paranthropus aethiopicus	Unknown	410
Homo habilis	509–674	612
Homo rudolfensis	752–810	781
Homo erectus	750–1,251	994
Modern humans	1,000–2,000	1,330

[a]Measurements of cranial capacity are always given in cubic centimeters (cc; a cubic centimeter equals about 0.06 in³); the size of the brain itself is usually somewhat smaller, because the cranial cavity also contains other structures. The above figures are approximate: For the two African apes they are based on rather small samples; and in the case of the fossil groups, the samples are extremely small and may prove to be misleading. Furthermore, a recent study by Conroy et al. (1998) suggests that cranial capacities measured using traditional techniques may well be inflated compared to those done with modern CT scans and computer imaging. For modern humans, rare extremes exceeding even the approximate range given above have been found; the average figure is based on a limited number of samples. Slight variations in these figures will be found in other authors' works. As a general rule, and within an order, species of animals with larger brains are more intelligent than those with smaller brains, but this does not hold among species of different body sizes. Within a species, variations in brain size are not believed to be related to intelligence among normal individuals.

Sources: Aiello and Dean, 1990; Brown et al., 1993; Tobias, 1985; Walker et al., 1986. Fossils are attributed to *Homo habilis* and *Homo rudolfensis* following Wood, 1992. West Turkana fossil KNM–WT 17000 is classified as *P. aethiopicus.*

1813 (Figure 8.2). But what to call the nonaustralopithecines from Koobi Fora? Initially they were lumped with similar specimens from Olduvai Gorge and classified as *Homo habilis.* This is still the classification endorsed by South African anthropologist Phillip Tobias, who prefers a single-species interpretation of all early *Homo* material. Others disagree and have argued that there is too much variation in the combined Olduvai and Koobi Fora assemblage for these creatures to be contained in a single species—even a species with marked sexual dimorphism in body size (Rightmire, 1993; Wood, 1992). It now seems increasingly likely that *Homo habilis,* as traditionally defined, probably contained at least two species. In this text we retain the name *Homo habilis* for the Olduvai material and some of the fossils from Omo and Koobi Fora (including ER 1813); we classify ER 1470 and certain other Omo, Uraha, and Koobi Fora specimens as belonging to the new species *Homo rudolfensis* (Wood, 1992).

If the early *Homo* fossils from Olduvai and Koobi Fora are sorted in this way, interesting differences appear between the two resulting species (compare Tables 8.4 and 8.6). *Homo habilis,* as now narrowly defined, has the more primitive-looking skull, with some prognathism, an incipient brow ridge, and a much smaller brain (although brain size is increased by about one-third over the australopithecine average). Additionally, the postcranial anatomy of the newly defined *Homo habilis* includes small body size,

ASKING QUESTIONS

What Is the Meaning of Brain Size?

Because all creatures are bundles of characteristics (including brain size), many of which may be evolving at different rates, drawing a line that is based on such characteristics always causes trouble. Early in the twentieth century, the British anatomist Arthur Keith chose to draw the line marking the appearance of humanity where the brain capacity touched 750 cubic centimeters (1948). Anything below that, according to Keith, was not human; anything above it was. To measure brain size Keith used mustard seed; he poured the seeds in (via the foramen magnum) to fill the cranium, then emptied them into a measuring cylinder. Today the finer millet seed is often used. Most modern people have brains in the 1,200 to 1,600 cc range (mean 1,330 cc), although smaller and larger brains regularly occur (see Table 8.5). Reviewing the problem, Le Gros Clark has implied that a boundary of about 700 cc would be more appropriate (Clark, 1959, 1967), but it has been on the move ever since.

Homo habilis laid this problem on the scientists' doorstep. The great difficulty in deciding whether this creature was human (i.e., a hominine) lay in the fact that the "type specimen," the first one to be found and named *Homo habilis* by the Leakeys, had a brain capacity estimated to be about 657 cubic centimeters—just under Clark's limit. Since then, five other *H. habilis* skulls have been measured by two experts: Phillip Tobias and Ralph Holloway. They came up with surprisingly uniform figures for these skulls. They range in capacity from 509 to 674 cc and average about 612 cc. Too small-brained for a human? Perhaps, but probably too large-brained for a typical gracile *Australopithecus*, whose mean cranial capacity was only about 450 cc.

What is the meaning of brain size? How significant is the steady increase in cranial capacity that we find in human evolution? Large brains are found in large animals generally, and the brains of elephants and whales are very much larger than those of humans. As a general rule, brain size among mammals can best be interpreted when it is related to body size, and a doubling of body size during the evolution of a lineage usually results in a considerable increase in brain size. When we look at the figures in Table 8.5, therefore, we should consider the size of the animal itself. For example, the stature of *A. afarensis* varied from 3.3 to 5 feet (1 to 1.5 meters), while that of modern humans varies from approximately 4.5 to over 6 feet (1.4 to 1.8 meters). The difference in *relative* brain size is therefore not quite as great as the table might suggest. It should not be forgotten, however, that many human populations—of pygmies, for example—fall into the range of stature for *A. afarensis* and yet have brains in the region of 1,200 to 1,350 cubic centimeters: three times as large. A consideration of stature is therefore not going to alter very seriously the significance of the figures for the Hominidae listed in Table 8.5.

australopithecine-like limb proportions, and some adaptations of the feet for climbing—features that suggest the continuation of arboreal activities in addition to terrestrial bipedalism. On the progressive side, however, the teeth of *Homo habilis* seem more like those of later hominids than do the teeth of *Homo rudolfensis*.

For its part, *Homo rudolfensis* has a larger body, a flatter face, and a larger brain than *H. habilis* (showing about a two-thirds increase in brain size over the australopithecine average); but these are combined with broad grinding teeth that remind one of *Paranthropus*. And although the limb proportions of *Homo rudolfensis* are currently unknown, certain features of the foot and the thigh are quite similar to those of later *Homo* species. The few pelvic remains of early *Homo* suggest that these hominids showed an almost modern form of bipedalism, but with a few remaining apelike characteristics.

These two species of early *Homo* overlapped temporally for 400,000 years or more; and, at least at Koobi Fora, they overlapped geographically as well. *Homo rudolfensis* was apparently the first to evolve and may have been strictly an East African form. Recent discoveries at the Uraha site west of Lake Malawi have set the earliest date for *Homo rudolfensis* at about 2.4 mya. *Homo habilis*, as newly defined, ranged from Koobi Fora and Omo (and perhaps Hadar) in the north to Sterkfontein in the south.

Table 8.6

Characteristics of *Homo rudolfensis*[a]	
Trait	***Homo rudolfensis***
Height (sexes combined)	4.9 ft (150 cm) (?)
Weight	F: 112 lb (51 kg) M: 132 lb (60 kg) (F about 85% of M)
Brain size (sexes combined)	781 cc mean (752–810 cc range)
Cranium	Flat face; no brow ridge; large palate; no sagittal crest; everted mandibular base
Dentition	Broader lower grinding teeth than *Homo habilis*; multirooted lower premolars
Limbs	Limb proportions unknown; feet more like those of later humans than was true for *H. habilis*
Locomotion	Bipedalism probably almost modern, but with a few remaining apelike characteristics
Known dates (million years BP)	2.4–1.6

[a]Mean values for anatomical measurements may change with additional fossil discoveries.

Phylogeny of the Hominidae

The phylogenetic relations among the australopithecines, as well as the evolutionary connections between that subfamily and the hominines (the genus *Homo*), rank near the top of the list of controversial topics in paleoanthropology. Using different methodologies and emphasizing different aspects of the fossils, researchers have come up with a wide variety of evolutionary trees for the earliest hominids. Some of that variety is illustrated in Figure 8.3, which shows phylogenetic schemes recently published by prominent researchers.

Hypothesis A was published by Bernard Wood in 1994. In his view, *A. ramidus* was ancestral to all later hominids, *A. anamensis* was ancestral to *A. afarensis*, and *A. afarensis* in turn gave rise to *Homo*. *Paranthropus* is shown as a dead-end genus, possibly with multiple origins (i.e., not as a monophyletic clade): *P. aethiopicus* is descended from *A. afarensis*, and *P. robustus* is possibly descended from *A. africanus*. *Australopithecus africanus* is shown as a descendant of *A. afarensis*, but the South African form is given no direct link at all with *Homo*.

Hypothesis B is the product of Meave Leakey and Alan Walker (1997). From *A. ramidus* through *A. afarensis* the scheme is similar to the first hypothesis, but at that point the two phylogenies begin to differ. First of all, Leakey and Walker agree that *A. africanus* was the descendant of *A. afarensis*; but, in contrast to Wood, they believe the South African species might have been ancestral to *Homo*. Furthermore, Leakey and Walker classify all of the robust forms as members of the genus *Australopithecus* rather than *Paranthropus* (i.e., *A. robustus*, *A. boisei*, *A. aethiopicus*), and they too reject the theory that the three species constitute a monophyletic clade. Agreeing partially with Wood, they see *aethiopicus* as most likely descended from *A. afarensis*, and *robustus*

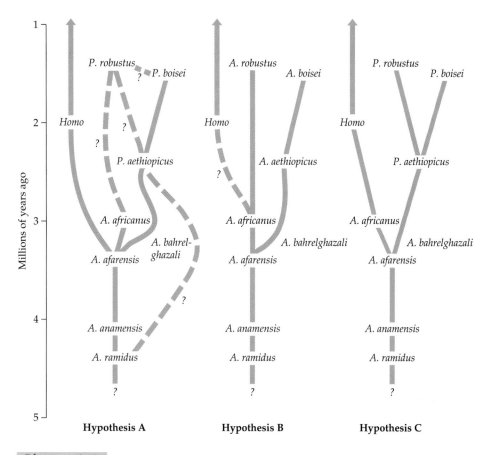

Figure 8.3

Three evolutionary trees for hominids. The various australopithecine species are identified individually, while the hominines are lumped into a single *Homo* lineage for simplicity (later chapters will expand on hominine phylogeny). Solid lines show ancestor–descendant relationships that seem conclusive to the particular researcher(s); dotted lines show questionable relationships. Hypothesis A is from Wood (1994), hypothesis B is from Leakey and Walker (1997), and hypothesis C is from Tattersall (1995a). Although its evolutionary connections are unknown, *A. bahrelghazali* has been added to each hypothesis for completeness. Additionally, due to its recent discovery, *A. garhi* is not shown in any of the hypotheses. The figure is not drawn to scale and does not attempt to depict accurately the divergence dates for the various branches. The hominine branch of the tree is shown in streamlined form.

definitely descended from *A. africanus* (all three evolutionary trees conclude that *boisei* descended from *aethiopicus*).

The third hypothesis, by Ian Tattersall (1995a), has a straightforward tree trunk in agreement with the other models. It then differs from Wood and Leakey/Walker by arranging the three *Paranthropus* species in a monophyletic clade and by hypothesizing a clear-cut (as opposed to possible) ancestor–descendant link between *A. africanus* and *Homo.*

Which—if any—of these phylogenies is correct? Only time and further research will tell. The hominid fossil record has only begun to be discovered (witness the recent rush of new species), and thus our "family trees" must be flexible enough to accept new evolutionary relatives and revised positions for old ones. Despite the confusion, however, a few broad conclusions can be drawn. First, the fossil and molecular data agree that the family Hominidae has been separated from the African apes for 6 million years or more. Second, as a genus, *Australopithecus* preceded and was ancestral to both *Paranthropus* and *Homo*. And third, the *Paranthropus* forms were not on the direct evolutionary line to modern humans; indeed, the last representatives of that lineage went extinct about 1 million years ago without leaving any descendants.

In contrast, the gracile lineage (*Australopithecus*) was much luckier. It almost certainly gave rise near the end of the Pliocene to more humanlike hominids of the genus *Homo*. Many of the genes we carry about today were inherited from gracile australopithecine forebears.

But how do scientists decide that early *Homo*—*H. habilis* and *H. rudolfensis*—were members of our genus and not simply advanced australopithecines? What derived traits do these species share with later varieties of *Homo* that mark the genus boundary? As it turns out, this is not an easy question, and the answer has become more complex as the fossil record around the Plio–Pleistocene dividing line has become better known. One trait stands out above all others, of course, and that is *Homo*'s increased brain size. In addition, thanks to modern cladistic analyses, we can expand the defining criteria for *Homo* using the following list (traits 2 through 9 are taken from Wood, 1992). Compared to the australopithecines, *Homo* shows the following:

1. larger brain (roughly 600 cubic centimeters and up)
2. thicker bones of the braincase
3. reduced postorbital constriction (narrowing of the skull at the temples)
4. occipital bone that makes an increased contribution to the cranial **sagittal arc** length
5. higher cranial vault
6. foramen magnum farther forward
7. flatter lower face
8. narrowed tooth crowns (especially the lower premolars)
9. shorter molar toothrow

One final trait is ineligible for inclusion in anatomical lists but cannot be dissociated from our image of *Homo,* and that is the presence of a stone culture. Modern humans and our immediate ancestors, *Homo erectus,* are characterized by dependence on a cultural lifestyle. The widely accepted view that the hominids labeled early *Homo* made the Oldowan stone tools to a simple but recognizable pattern suggests to many anthropologists that these hominids had taken the first steps toward a cultural way of life and therefore, in addition to their anatomical distinctions, deserve to be included in our genus.

Hominid Adaptations

As you have seen, hominids are characterized by a rather distinctive set of evolving traits that include habitual bipedalism, canine reduction (shortening and blunting), brain enlargement, speech and language, and technology (i.e., the development of material culture, especially tools). The fossil record makes it clear that these traits evolved individually and in a mosaic fashion rather than monolithically. Bipedalism and canine reduction appeared early; brain enlargement, speech and language, and complex tools

Sagittal arc the distance around a skull from defined points at the base to the front, around the median sagittal line.

emerged later. It is also true that these traits were interrelated and either limited or facilitated the development of one another.

Since the mid-nineteenth century scientists have theorized about the course of hominid evolution, developing sometimes elaborate scenarios about the environmental conditions that selected for our package of traits and the sequence of trait development. Furthermore, since early in this century, it has been common practice to explain the most basic hominid traits (particularly bipedalism) as adaptations for terrestrial life on the African savanna. Recent discoveries have challenged this point of view, however, and the evidence from Aramis, Kanapoi, and elsewhere now has some paleoanthropologists theorizing that hominid evolution probably began in more wooded circumstances. But whether on the savanna, in the woodland, on the floodplain or in gallery forest, the specifics of hominid origins and the development of our distinctive traits remain speculative. The following sections will focus primarily on hypotheses about the advent of bipedalism and the related canine reduction, and about stone tool technology. Discussions of the evolution of human society and of our enlarged brains, including linguistic communication, follow.

 For more on the characteristics of the first humans, visit our web site.

Bipedalism

A survey of the fossil record thus far demonstrates that hominids diverged from apes sometime between 5.6 and 7 million years ago. Although the exact identity of our ape forebears remains to be discovered, our own postcranial anatomy—and more especially, that of the australopithecines and early hominines—provides clear evidence that those ancestral apes were arboreal creatures that engaged in arm-swinging, hanging, and especially quadrupedal climbing. If modern chimpanzees and bonobos are accurate models, our ape ancestors were rather generalized in their locomotion, their food tastes, and their pattern of habitat use. Ready to eat a variety of foods, capable of moving about in or across a variety of habitats, and living in or near the mosaic environment of the forest–woodland–savanna **ecotone,** our ape ancestors lived in a world full of opportunities—they could go in any of several directions.

About 5 to 7 million years ago, tropical forest extended through a good part of Central Africa as it does today. Of course, there also existed a comparably large amount of forest edge and open woodland, with opportunities for tree-dwellers to descend to the ground and eat the berries, roots, insects, and other food that abounded in the open. Such a place, where multiple ecological zones meet, presents new opportunities for survival; for if an animal adapts to the mixed habitat, it can exploit the food found in several zones. Advanced apelike creatures thronged the late Miocene and early Pliocene forests, probably as a variety of species, some of which must have lived on the forest edge. Like a good many monkeys and apes today, some of these creatures (among them our ancestors) undoubtedly came to the ground when opportunities for feeding presented themselves.

Opportunity and aptitude went together. No one decision by one ape or one group of apes had any evolutionary meaning whatsoever. But in places that, century after century, provided a better living on the ground for apes able to exploit it, the animals best adapted to living and feeding on the ground were the ones that spent the most time there and whose descendants became still better adapted to that environment and lifestyle.

Ecotone the area where two ecological communities, or biomes (e.g., woodland and savanna), meet.

Tool Use

In *The Descent of Man,* Charles Darwin wrote, "The free use of arms and hands, partly the cause and partly the result of man's erect position, appears to have led in an indirect manner to other modifications of structure.… As they gradually acquired the habit of using stones, clubs or other weapons, they would use their jaws and teeth less and less. In this case the jaws, together with the teeth, would become reduced in size" (1871; I: 144). Thus Darwin believed that bipedalism led to tool and weapon use and then to smaller jaws and teeth.

In contrast, the American anthropologist Sherwood Washburn (1963) suggested that tool using might have preceded walking on two legs; more than that, it probably helped to develop walking. He pointed out that apes, unlike monkeys, were characteristically upright even before they left the trees. Whereas monkeys ran along branches on all fours or jumped about in them, apes climbed hand over hand. They swung from branches, sat upright in them, and sometimes even stood on them. Their arms were well articulated for reaching in all directions; and the important interrelated development of stereoscopic eyesight, a larger brain, and improved manual dexterity had already evolved. Apes, in short, had the physical equipment and the dawning brain potential to use their hands in new and useful ways. That certain of them did so is suggested by the knowledge that chimpanzees, humans' nearest relatives, are simple tool users today.

Like Darwin, many authors have believed that hominids were bipedal from the time they first stepped away from the trees, and that it was this characteristic that gave them the opportunity to become tool users and toolmakers. If hominids found it technologically advantageous to walk on two legs from the beginning, the argument goes on, then, to make it easier for them to get about in that way, natural selection would inevitably improve their pelvis, leg bones, foot bones, and muscles.

As seen from the fossils of *Australopithecus anamensis* and more recent discoveries, habitual bipedalism can be demonstrated clearly from 4.2 mya, if not earlier. With their ape-sized brains and with hands at least as dexterous as those of modern apes, it seems probable that *A. anamensis* used tools to some degree. Modern chimps, however, show us not only that apes can be tool users, but also that it's possible to be an occasional tool user and remain a quadruped. Therefore, chimp-type tool use might or might not have been sufficient to select for habitual bipedalism in the protohominids.

What about stone tool manufacture and use? Here the answer seems easier: Because the appearance of *A. anamensis* predates the oldest stone tools by at least 1.7 million years, stone tool technology can be confidently ruled out as the stimulus for bipedalism in that species. In summary, the tools-and-bipedalism question remains something of a riddle. However, because the earliest hominids do not appear to have exceeded a chimpanzee level of technology, Washburn's argument that tool use was the trigger for locomotor change remains unconvincing.

Energy Efficiency

Another theory about the origin of hominid bipedalism is the **energy efficiency hypothesis:** the proposal that bipedalism was favored by selection because it was more energy-efficient than the terrestrial quadrupedalism of our last ape ancestor. The energy efficiency of different locomotor patterns is usually measured by standardized oxygen consumption. Modern humans show the greatest energy efficiency when they are walking at a moderate pace; indeed, our walking bipedally is slightly more efficient

Energy efficiency hypothesis proposal that the increased energy efficiency of *bipedal* walking brought about the selection of bipedalism.

than an average mammal's ambling along quadrupedally at the same speed. (We are not very efficient runners, however, using about twice as much energy as a running quadrupedal mammal of the same body size. This fact suggests that, if energy efficiency played a role, bipedalism probably evolved to allow us to walk, not run.)

Energy studies of chimpanzees have shown that these apes consume oxygen at the same rate whether they are moving bipedally or quadrupedally. Regardless of how they are moving, however, chimps' energy efficiency compares poorly with that of other same-sized quadrupeds; in fact, chimps use about 150 percent more energy. Therefore, given that bipedal humans have a slight energy advantage over the average nonprimate quadruped, there is no doubt that human walking is *significantly* more efficient than chimpanzee quadrupedalism.

Results such as these have convinced several paleoanthropologists that selection for energy-efficient walking was probably an important factor in the evolution of hominid bipedalism, the main idea being that our ancestors were moving long distances each day as they traveled between widely separated food sources. But is there anything about our efficient ambling that identifies it as a savanna adaptation rather than an adaptation to the forest–woodland–savanna ecotone? Not really. Both the mixed-habitat ecotone and the open savanna by itself were probably characterized by patchily distributed food sources, some occurring on the ground and some in the trees (groves of trees commonly dot the African plains). As long as the distances between food patches were equivalent, upright walking would have had the same energy advantages whether the early hominids were moving through the woods or across the grasslands between food sources.

Primatologist Lynne Isbell and her colleague Truman Young (1996) have argued that, faced with Miocene–Pliocene forest shrinkage and patchy food distribution, the earliest hominids had to evolve either energy-efficient locomotor abilities or smaller group sizes. Smaller groups (with fewer mouths to feed and thus a reduced need for travel to find the necessary food) would have been at a disadvantage in intergroup competition, however. Instead, our ancestors opted for energy-efficient movement. Bipedalism allowed them to maintain large group size, move rapidly and with minimal energy expenditure between distant food patches, and then drive away rival foragers once they got there.

Not everyone is convinced, however. At present anthropologists are split on the question of energy efficiency as a selection pressure for the evolution of hominid bipedalism.

Body Temperature

Body temperature control has been suggested as another selective mechanism. Proponents of the **body temperature hypothesis** point out that two key variables affect the accumulation of heat from direct solar radiation: the amount of body surface exposed to the sun's rays and the intensity of those rays. Scale models of australopithecines in various postures (Figure 8.4), demonstrated that when the sun is near the horizon or about 45 degrees above it (thus emitting cool to moderately warm rays), quadrupeds and bipeds have similar amounts of body surface exposed and accumulate equivalent heat loads. At noon, however, when the sun is directly overhead and its rays are the most intense, the heat load buildup of a biped is 60 percent less than that of a quadruped because of the biped's minimal surface exposure (Wheeler, 1993).

Bipeds also are farther from the hot ground surface than are quadrupeds, and thus a biped's skin contacts cooler and faster-moving air currents; this contact aids in heat loss through convection. Such convectional cooling would, of course, be enhanced by the loss of thick body hair; the loss would allow an essentially naked surface to be held aloft in the

Body temperature hypothesis proposal that reduction in body surface area exposed to sunlight brought about the selection of bipedalism.

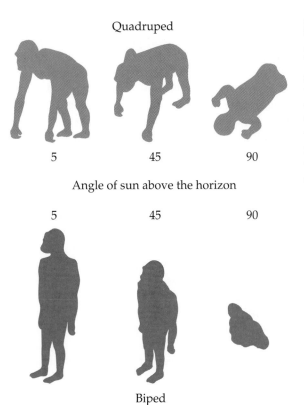

Quadruped

5   45   90

Angle of sun above the horizon

5   45   90

Biped

Figure 8.4

Models of hypothetical early hominids show how much body surface is exposed to direct solar radiation by quadrupeds (top) versus bipeds (bottom). From left to right, the sun is low on the horizon, 45 degrees above the horizon, and directly overhead. Note the small amount of body surface exposed by a biped at midday.

cool breezes. Thus, the temperature regulation model may help to explain the reduction of human body hair. In this way early hominids might have increased their convectional heat loss by as much as one-third by adopting bipedalism (Wheeler 1991b).

The combination of lower heat buildup and easy heat dissipation could have reduced the early hominids' dependence on shade and allowed them to remain active throughout much of the equatorial day and at relatively high temperatures. Furthermore, if heat loss could be accomplished mainly through convectional cooling, rather than by evaporative cooling through sweating, hominids' dependence on water would have been lowered. If true, this would have freed the early hominids to range widely across the savanna as they foraged (Wheeler 1991a).

Tool use, energy efficiency, and temperature regulation—combined with habitat variability—are three of the many explanations that have been offered for bipedalism. Other hypotheses, less popular than these three, include the possibility that bipedal displays fostered social control in early hominid groups. It seems reasonable and probable that some combination of selection pressures, rather than a single evolutionary factor, led to erect walking. One thing is quite clear: Regardless of what selection pressures led to habitual bipedalism, evolution worked through the enhanced reproductive success of those individuals that were best suited for upright locomotion.

The Birth Canal

American anthropologist Wenda Trevathan (1987, 1988) and others have speculated on the possible effects of bipedalism on childbirth and, by extension, on hominid sociality.

As shown in the preceding chapters, the evolution of bipedalism involved a good deal of remodeling of the hominid pelvis. In particular, in *Australopithecus* the shape of the **birth canal** changed from the ape's long oval, becoming quite wide transversely (from side to side) but shallow sagittally (from front to back) (Figure 8.5, center). Later, in *Homo,* the canal regained a relatively long sagittal dimension—particularly at the exit, or outlet—producing a more rounded shape (Figure 8.5, right). A modern human baby, with its large skull, negotiates the birth canal by entering with the head oriented transversely. It then rotates 90 degrees into a sagittal position before exiting the canal facing the sacrum, that is, with its back toward the mother's face. A human mother is therefore in a bad position to assist in delivery, since her infant is exiting "down and back," away from her helping hands. Furthermore, pulling an emerging human infant up toward the mother's breast would bend it against the normal flexion of its body and would possibly result in injury. Interestingly, the human delivery pattern is very different from that of nonhuman primates, in which there is no fetal rotation (babies are sagittally oriented throughout birth) and newborns exit the canal face-to-face with their mothers. In this pattern, mother monkeys and apes routinely assist in delivery by reaching down and pulling emerging infants up and toward their chests in a curve that matches the normal flexion of the babies' bodies.

Trevathan has speculated that, at some point in human evolution, with the introduction of fetal rotation and down-and-back delivery, hominid mothers would have benefited significantly from the assistance of "birth attendants," and thus the behavior of seeking companionship at birth would have been selected for. In turn, seeking and giving assistance at births is viewed as contributing to the development of empathy, communication, and cooperation among the evolving hominids—that is, to the evolution of social relationships. Although speculative, this theory seems logical enough; but a major problem involves determining when the "human birth pattern"—possibly including the first birth attendants—originated. Trevathan thinks this pattern might have developed early, perhaps among the australopithecines. Other researchers, how-

Birth canal the passage through the mother's pelvis through which infants are born.

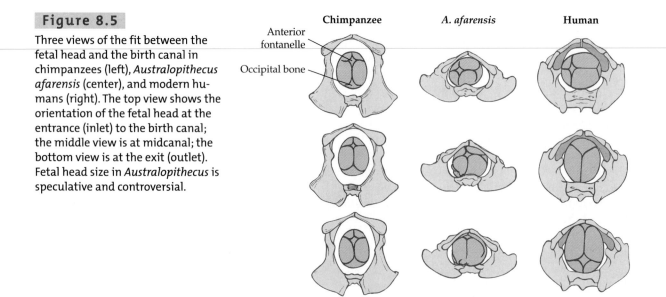

Figure 8.5

Three views of the fit between the fetal head and the birth canal in chimpanzees (left), *Australopithecus afarensis* (center), and modern humans (right). The top view shows the orientation of the fetal head at the entrance (inlet) to the birth canal; the middle view is at midcanal; the bottom view is at the exit (outlet). Fetal head size in *Australopithecus* is speculative and controversial.

Chimpanzee   *A. afarensis*   Human

Anterior fontanelle

Occipital bone

ever, think that australopithecine births were as fast and trouble-free as those of living apes and argue that down-and-back human deliveries, with big-brained babies twisting and turning through a constricted birth canal, are probably the result of strong brain expansion within the genus *Homo*. If the latter view is correct, as seems most probable, the human birth pattern is probably not much more than 2 million years old.

Canine Reduction

Discussing the connection between bipedalism and canine anatomy, Sherwood Washburn, champion of the theory that tool use preceded and possibly stimulated bipedalism, called attention to the fact that the australopithecines had relatively small canine teeth that would have been of little value in aggression or defense. In contrast, in all other large ground-dwelling primates—chimpanzees, gorillas, and particularly baboons—the male's canines are enormous teeth, true fangs. Among their uses are self-defense against both conspecifics and the large and dangerous predators to which ground-dwelling primates are exposed. As part of his scenario for early hominid evolution, Washburn argued that the loss of large canines must have been balanced by some other means of self-defense; namely, the use of various objects as weapons (Washburn and Moore, 1974).

As noted earlier, however, the hypothesis that tool use triggered bipedalism is unconvincing. But if canine reduction was not related to tool use, what caused it? Clifford Jolly of New York University suggested an answer to that question. Jolly (1970) proposed that the evolution of hominids was marked by a shift from ape-type frugivory to a diet that included a significantly higher proportion of small, hard objects, such as seeds, nuts, and tubers. Such tough, hard-to-chew items would presumably have been plentiful in the forest–woodland–savanna habitat to which the early (and newly terrestrial) hominids were adapting. The evolutionary scenario proposed by Jolly became known as the **seed-eating hypothesis.**

Jolly's hypothesis of hominid canine reduction was based on two types of evidence. First, he presented comparative data from savanna baboons and gelada baboons that suggested the presence of shorter canines in the more seed-dependent geladas. And second, Jolly argued that long, interlocking canines (such as those shown by apes) limit the range of movement of the lower jaw during chewing (particularly side-to-side grinding movements), and thus that long canines would have been *selected against* as early hominids adopted a small-object diet. Finally, according to Jolly, the need for an upright posture during small-object harvesting could have selected for habitual bipedalism. And so, in contrast to Washburn's theories, the seed-eating hypothesis explains the primary hominid characteristics as being the results of a dietary change. In this scenario, tool use followed diet-induced dental and postural changes, rather than serving as the primary trigger for **hominization.**

Jolly's theory has been received with a mixture of support and disagreement. A very recent discovery that tends to weaken his model is the evidence that *Australopithecus ramidus*—claimed by its discoverers to be the oldest hominid and to show some anatomical signs of bipedalism—had thin enamel on its canines and molars, a finding that is hard to reconcile with a hard-object diet.

One of Jolly's most vigorous critics is American anthropologist Leonard Greenfield, who believes that flawed assumptions about dental mechanics underlie the seed-eating model. Greenfield (1992) has suggested as a substitute his **dual-selection hypothesis.** This model proposes that two forms of selection shaped canine tooth

Seed-eating hypothesis proposal that seed eating brought about a change in canine shape and body posture, which in turn led to bipedalism.

Hominization the evolutionary transformation from ape to human.

Dual-selection hypothesis proposal that the canine tooth evolved under selection either as a weapon or for incisorlike functions.

anatomy: selection for use as a weapon and selection for incisorlike functions. These selective forces tended to move canine anatomy in mutually exclusive directions and therefore can be viewed as competing with one another. If the weapon-use function prevailed, the canines would be long, fanglike teeth; but if incisorlike selection was stronger, the canines would be short and would have broader cutting edges. The dual-selection hypothesis assumes that if selection for weapon-use functions diminished, canines *automatically* would shift toward an incisorlike anatomy.

Greenfield's model leaves a critical question unanswered: Did the canines of early hominids get shorter and broader because they were no longer needed as weapons or because they were *strongly* needed as additional incisorlike teeth? And, to get back to Washburn, if selection for use of the canines as weapons diminished among the first hominids, was it because some sort of biodegradable implements were being used instead? Not all anthropologists agree that the dual-selection hypothesis will help to answer these questions.

Clearly, definitive answers to "how" and "why" questions about the evolution of bipedalism, short canines, and numerous other traits of the human lineage await the efforts of future researchers. There seems little doubt, however, that once hominids had some of the major behavioral and anatomical traits in place, particularly bipedalism and simple technology, a complex **positive feedback** system could have developed. A speculative model of one such feedback system is shown in Figure 8.6.

Positive feedback a process in which a positive change in one component of a system brings about changes in other components, which in turn bring about further positive changes in the first component.

Figure 8.6

Numerous feedback systems occur in nature and are often interlocking. Negative feedback maintains stability, whereas positive feedback brings about major adaptive changes that constitute evolution. Shown here in simplified form is a positive feedback system that may have been important in hominid evolution.

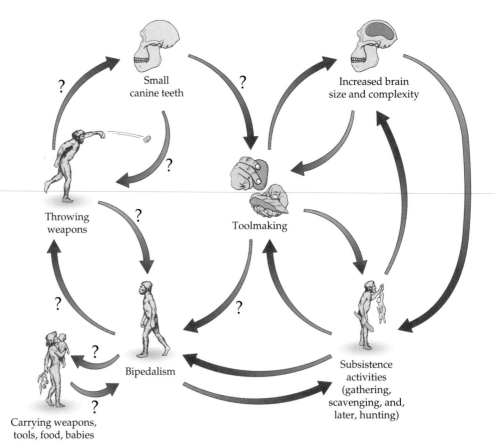

What Are the Characteristics of Early Technology?

The origin of tools in human evolution must have occurred through trial and error. The nearest we can come to reconstructing that process is to remind ourselves that there must have been a time when our ancestors started with fewer tools than chimpanzees use today.

A group of not-too-large apes will seem more formidable standing erect because they appear larger; in fact, the erect posture is sometimes used by nonhuman primates as a gesture of threat. The brandishing of sticks or branches enhances that effect and may have been enough, on occasion, to swing the balance to the hominids—for example, in a set-to with hyenas over the possession of a kill. The earliest use of objects by our ancestors, probably then ground-dwelling scavengers and gatherers, may have received its strongest impetus from its value in threat displays against competing species. For an immensely long time, the only type of implement was the found object, picked up and then thrown away when its immediate use was over. But there must have come a stage at which early hominids began to recognize more and more clearly the usefulness of certain objects and, as a result, tended to hang onto them longer, finally carrying them around much of the time. The great abundance of wood, and the fact that it is softer and easier to work than stone, suggests that the earliest hominids may have used wood a great deal, probably for digging. They may also have used the horns and long bones of some of the larger animals. But the great triumph of our ancestors as creators of culture came much later and is seen most clearly in the legacy they have left us of worked stone. All the oldest surviving artifacts are implements for cutting and chopping, not weapons. We can therefore recognize a clear succession: tool use, tool modification, and toolmaking.

Oldowan: The Earliest Stone-Tool Industry

The oldest known stone tools have been recovered from the site of Gona, in the Hadar region of Ethiopia, and they are dated at 2.5 million years of age (Semaw et al., 1997). Consisting of simple **cores,** whole **flakes,** and flaking debris, the Gona assemblage is a clear example of the **Oldowan industry** identified by the Leakeys many years ago at Olduvai Gorge (Figure 8.7). At Gona, sharp flakes were struck off cores and then used as cutting implements. The cores themselves apparently were used as hammerstones and multipurpose pounders; this can be detected from the way the cores are pitted and battered. Other ancient Oldowan assemblages have come from Omo (2.4 to 2.3 mya), the Semliki River Valley in the western Rift (2.3 mya), and, of course, Olduvai Gorge (1.9 to 1.7 mya). Although absolutely conclusive proof that the various Oldowan assemblages were made by early *Homo* is still lacking, one recent discovery was very nearly the smoking gun that archaeologists are seeking. At the Kada Hadar site in Ethiopia, an upper jaw of early *Homo* (most likely *H. habilis*) was found "closely associated" with 2.3 million-year-old Oldowan tools (Kimbel et al., 1996). Pending the discovery of a skeleton with tool in hand, we find this sort of sole association of early *Homo* with Oldowan tools to be convincing. Therefore, for the remainder of this discussion (and this book), we treat the first hominines as stone toolmakers without further qualifying remarks.

The question of what early *Homo* was doing with Oldowan tools remains unanswered. A hint comes, however, from Kada Hadar, where a piece of bovid (cattlelike animals of the mammalian family Bovidae) shoulder blade was found bearing what

Cores worked stones from which *flakes* have been removed.

Flakes sharp-edged fragments struck from a stone; the flake may then be used as a cutting tool.

Oldowan industry earliest stone-tool tradition; appeared about 2.5 mya in Northeast Africa.

An Oldowan chopper, which early hominids made by striking some flakes from a rounded cobble to obtain a cutting edge. This is one of the simplest stone implements.

appears to be a cut mark from a stone tool (Kimbel et al., 1996). Most paleoanthropologists conclude that Oldowan tools signal an increased reliance on meat in the early hominines' diet, although whether that meat was the result of scavenging or active hunting is unclear. The Oldowan flakes were probably used for butchering carcasses; the cores were used to batter open bones so the marrow could be consumed. Beyond that, only one other statement concerning the diet of early *Homo* is possible. The relatively larger, multirooted grinding teeth of *Homo rudolfensis* suggest that members of that species ate more tough and hard food items (nuts, roots, seeds, etc.) than *Homo habilis.*

The magnet that drew Louis and Mary Leakey back to Olduvai Gorge year after year was the large number of extremely primitive stone implements. Mary Leakey made the study of these objects her special province. Her first monograph on the stone culture at Olduvai (1971) covers material taken from the gorge's lowest strata, known as Beds I and II, representing a time period that extends from 1.2 to 2.2 million years ago (Table 8.7).

Certain details of the lives of the creatures who lived at Olduvai so long ago have been reconstructed from the hundreds of thousands of bits of material that they left behind—some stone, some bone, some large, some extremely small. No one of these things, alone, would mean much; but when all are analyzed and fitted together like a gigantic three-dimensional jigsaw puzzle, patterns begin to emerge that speak across the gulf of time.

Mary Leakey found that there were two stoneworking traditions at Olduvai. One, the **Acheulean industry,** appears first in Bed II. The Oldowan industry, older and more primitive, occurs throughout Bed I, as well as at other early African sites. Its signature implements are what anthropologists for a long time called *pebble tools,* but what Mary Leakey preferred to call **choppers.** The word *pebble* suggests something quite small, and her term was an improvement—for many of the chopping tools at Olduvai are of hen's-egg size or larger, some of them three or four inches (eight to ten centimeters) across. In addition to the choppers, Oldowan sites typically contain numerous stone flakes.

An Oldowan chopper typically was made from a cobble, a stone that had been worn smooth by sand and water action. The stone selected was often a close-grained, hard, smooth-textured type such as quartz, flint, or chert. Many cobbles at Olduvai are of hardened lava that flowed out of the volcanoes in the region.

Acheulean industry stone-tool tradition that appeared 1.7 to 1.4 million years ago in Africa and originated with *Homo erectus.*

Choppers small, generally ovoid stones with a few *flakes* removed to produce a partial cutting edge.

Table 8.7

Stratified Beds and Fossils at Olduvai Gorge		
Approximate Age (years)[a]	Bed	Fossils and Industry
620,000–100,000	Upper beds	*Homo sapiens*
840,000–620,000	Bed IV	Fossils of *Homo erectus* Late Acheulean hand axes and cleavers
1.2 million–840,000	Bed III	No fossils Few artifacts
1.7–1.2 million	Bed II	*Homo erectus* and early Acheulean tools *Homo habilis* and Oldowan tools
2.2–1.7 million	Bed I	*Paranthropus boisei* and *Homo habilis*
	Volcanic lava	Oldowan choppers
2.2 million		

[a]The ages of the upper beds are still rather uncertain. Bed I fossil sites date 1.9–1.7 mya.

Oval or pear-shaped, and small enough to fit comfortably in the hand, such a water-rounded stone could be gripped firmly without hurting the palm. What an early toolmaker had to do to turn it into a tool was simply to smash one end down hard on a nearby boulder, or to balance it on the boulder and give it a good whack with another rock. A large chip would fly off. Another whack would knock off a second chip next to the first, leaving a jagged edge or perhaps a point on one end of the stone. There are large choppers and small ones. The tool was presumably held as one would hold a rock while banging downward, with a direct hammering or chopping motion. The small chips knocked off during the manufacture of choppers are the fragments known as flakes. Sharper than choppers, flakes often may have been more useful than the core. They undoubtedly became dull very quickly, however, for although stone is hard, its edges break easily.

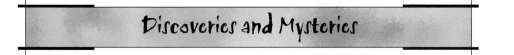

Discoveries and Mysteries

How Were the Oldowan Choppers and Flakes Used?

How were the Oldowan choppers and flakes used? What do they tell us about the lifestyle of their makers? American archaeologists Kathy Schick and Nicholas Toth have made an in-depth study of these questions, and their discoveries are revealing. In order to extract the maximum information from the ancient stone implements, Schick and Toth have used a combination of traditional and innovative techniques. Of course, they have followed traditional archaeological procedures, studying the occurrence and distribution of Oldowan tools at the various African sites as well as the fossil bone assemblages associated with the tools. In addition, they have conducted numerous field experiments, using newly made flakes and choppers to butcher animals that have died naturally and to smash animal long bones for marrow. Finally, they have utilized data from electron microscope studies of cut marks on fossil bones and of **microwear** on

Microwear the microscopic pattern of scratches, pits, and polish produced during the use of a stone tool.

tool surfaces: The microwear pattern of chips, pits, and polish can provide excellent clues as to how a tool was used.

Based on all of their various analyses, Schick and Toth (1993) have concluded that the principal reason for the emergence of stone-tool technology was to enable hominids to butcher animal carcasses quickly and efficiently before eating them on the spot or carrying them elsewhere for later consumption. Flakes were found to be excellent implements for skinning, defleshing, and dismembering animal carcasses—even better than choppers, so often thought of as the premier Oldowan tools. Indeed, many choppers may be nothing more than **débitage,** or waste cores left after flake manufacture. Using simple flake tools, Schick and Toth were able to skin even an elephant with its inch-thick hide! Choppers were useful for dismembering carcasses and, along with unmodified cobbles, for bone breaking, as shown in the photo here. One should not conclude that Oldowan tools were used only for meat processing, however. Microwear analyses have identified tools used for cutting soft plants and others used to work wood; hammer stones were no doubt used to crush nuts; and the use, if any, of **manuports** (unmodified stones brought from elsewhere to the site by hominids) is unknown. Nonetheless, based on their work, Schick and Toth believe that the primary message of the oldest stone tools is a significant increase in meat eating by early hominids.

The use of a stone chopper and an anvil to crack a limb bone in order to expose the marrow.

Débitage debris produced during stone-tool manufacture.

Manuports unmodified stones that could not have occurred naturally at an archaeological site and must have been carried there; how manuports were used is unknown.

Identifying Stone Tools

As we go back in time, we depend more and more on the ability of archaeologists to identify stone tools reliably—that is, to distinguish between them and naturally occurring rocks. There is no sure way of identifying individual primitive artifacts occurring alone; but if one or more of the following conditions is satisfied, the ancient presence of hominid toolmakers usually can be safely inferred:

1. The tools occur on an ancient land surface in reasonable numbers and conform to a regular and recognizable pattern.
2. The tools are made of a kind of stone that is not present locally and that therefore must have been brought there. The evidence of transport of materials is a very important feature of many stone-tool assemblages. The possibility of their arriving in position as a result of being washed by a river or glacier must be ruled out.
3. The tools are associated with bone fragments showing cut marks.
4. The tools occur with other signs of human habitation (e.g., with hearths or the foundations of a shelter).
5. The tools are of such sophisticated manufacture that they could not possibly have been generated naturally.
6. Tools are made of a rock suitable for bashing or cutting bones or flesh (i.e., not a soft sandstone), usually flint (also called *chert*). Primitive tools might be made of various kinds of hard rocks, but the materials from which advanced tools could be made are very much more limited in number.

Given that hominines and australopithecines were contemporary in Africa for 1.4 million years, and given that their remains occasionally occur together at sites that also include stone tools, it is sometimes extremely difficult to know for certain who made the Oldowan tools. In the past, most researchers have attributed stone tools from mixed-species sites to the larger-brained hominines (early *Homo*). To a great extent, this continues to be done—although some paleoanthropologists have begun to question this practice, arguing that if australopithecine remains are more abundant at a particular site than hominine remains, then the australopithecines were probably responsible for any tools that are found. Of course, a third possibility—that *both* the early hominines and certain australopithecines were toolmakers—must be considered as well. And numerous additional questions about mixed-species sites are beyond our ability to answer at this time. For example, did one species scavenge off the food supplies of the other? Did one species prey on the other?

In any event, in the final analysis Mary and Louis Leakey were quite certain they knew who had made the 1.8-million-year-old tools from Bed I at Olduvai Gorge: namely, the hominid type whose brain so greatly exceeded that of the other candidate for toolmaker, *Paranthropus* (*Zinjanthropus*) *boisei*. And it was primarily these two factors—brain size and stone tool culture—that ultimately led the Leakeys to name the large-brained species *Homo habilis*.

Occupation Sites at Olduvai Gorge

During their decades of work at Olduvai Gorge, Mary and Louis Leakey and their sons and coworkers laid bare numerous ancient hominid sites. Sometimes the sites were simply spots where the bones of one or more hominid species were discovered. Often, however, hominid remains were found in association with concentrations of animal fossils, stone tools, and debris. In some places it appeared that the bones and stones had been gently covered without much disturbance by blown dust, encroaching vegetation, rising water, and mud. Other sites, however, revealed signs of disturbance by water and wind. Although many of the sites originally were called **occupation levels** or **floors** (Leakey, 1971) suggesting that the hominids found there actually camped on the spot, we are now wary of jumping to that conclusion. Only after a team of experts—archaeologists,

Occupation level (floor) land surface occupied by prehistoric *hominids*.

geologists, paleontologists, paleoanthropologists, and taphonomists—has thoroughly studied a site can its true nature be understood.

The oldest sites at Olduvai come from Bed I and date between 1.9 and 1.7 million years old. Sites at this level have produced Oldowan stone tools in abundance and also (sometimes at the same location) fossils of both the robust australopithecine *Paranthropus boisei* and an ancient representative of our own genus, *Homo habilis.* For many anthropologists, Olduvai Gorge is particularly fascinating because of what we think it tells us about the lifestyle of the latter species.

During the 1970s and early 1980s, many workers, including Mary Leakey and archaeologist Glynn Isaac, used an analogy from modern hunter-and-gather cultures to interpret the Bed I sites. They concluded that many of the sites were probably camps, often called **home bases,** where group members gathered at the end of the day to prepare and share food, to socialize, to make tools, and to sleep (Isaac and McCown, 1976). The circular concentration of stones at the DK-I site (Figure 8.8) was interpreted as the

Home bases camps where *hominid* groups gathered at evening for socializing, food sharing, and sleeping.

Figure 8.8

This plan of an ancient land surface shows the distribution of bones and stones discovered at the DK-I site in Bed I of Olduvai Gorge by Louis and Mary Leakey. The dense concentration of rocks suggests to some the remains of a hut or a windbreak; to others it is merely broken lava rocks produced by the roots of an ancient tree. Stones are shown here in black; bones are outlined. Labels for objects other than bones and teeth identify stone tools using the scheme devised by Mary Leakey. Important implement types include choppers (CH), scrapers (SC), hammer stones (H), discoids (DC), heavily utilized material (UTH), and débitage (unmodified flakes, D).

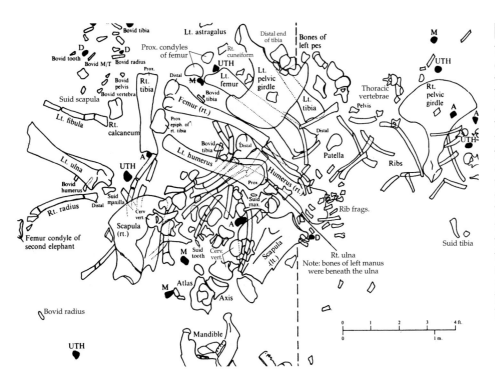

Figure 8.9

This plan shows part of the ancient occupation level of a possible butchery site in Bed I of Olduvai Gorge. Stone tools (solid black) are mixed in with almost the entire skeleton of an elephant, together with other food remains. Implement labels are as given in Figure 8.8, with the additional important occurrence of several manuports (unmodified rocks brought from another locality, M).

remains of a shelter or windbreak similar to those still made by some African people. Other concentrations of bones and stones were thought to be the remains of living sites originally ringed by thorn hedges for defense against predators. However, more recent studies suggest that the majority of these sites were temporary butchery sites, and that the hominines were most probably scavengers rather than hunters (Blumenschine, 1995; Potts, 1996; Figure 8.9). It seems likely that our *Homo* ancestors would have slept in trees, away from these sites, which no doubt attracted other dangerous scavengers such as hyenas.

It is difficult to imagine the lifestyle of these creatures, neither apes nor modern humans but something in between. But we know for a fact that they existed in the East African plains, that they had a mixed diet, and that they lived in a dangerous environment surrounded by a rich community of large mammals. We also know that they survived in their risk-laden hostile world.

Evolution of the Human Brain

It seems reasonable to ask whether the various interpretations of the lifestyles of early *Homo* provide any insights into their rather remarkable brain expansion compared to *Australopithecus*. Certainly, once bigger brains were in existence, they would have allowed various other advances—increasingly sophisticated material culture and communication patterns, for example. But what might have triggered the evolution of bigger brains in the first place?

Along with certain of our colleagues, the authors of this text think the key elements in hominine brain expansion may have been group size, complex subsistence patterns, and the high nutritional value of meat. Anthropologist Robin Dunbar (1992)

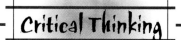

What Feedback Loop Could Account for Brain Expansion?

What factors and pressures selected for bigger, more intelligent brains in early *Homo*? On the basis of information in this chapter, try your hand at drawing feedback loops suggesting how the following variables may have interrelated in the evolution of the hominine brain. (Use the feedback loops in Figure 8.6 as a model.)

group living
larger group size
omnivorous diet
larger home ranges
brain expansion

social intelligence
subsistence intelligence
increased meat consumption
cooperative scavenging

has produced good evidence that among the living primates there is a strong positive relationship between brain size and the size of a species' social groups. The implication is that the original function of big brains was to keep track of a complex network of social information: group-mates' identities, dominance relationships, alliances and friendships, grudges and debts. Remembering and manipulating social relationships and socially important information has clear effects on primates' chances of survival and reproduction, and there is every reason to believe that this was true among the early hominines just as it is today. Using an equation that related brain size to group size for primates, Dunbar plugged in *Homo habilis*'s brain size and came up with an estimated group size of eighty-two individuals for that species. (Dunbar notes that these are "cognitive groups," including individuals about whom one has social knowledge, but not necessarily with whom one lives on a daily basis.) So, if Dunbar is right, early *Homo* lived in a complex social environment within which a big brain would have been a great help in dealing with the soap opera of everyday life.

A second variable involves subsistence and ranging patterns. Various studies have shown that among primates large brains also are correlated with diet. For example, omnivores are thought to have large brains partly because their lifestyle requires complex strategies for extracting high-quality foodstuffs. Similarly, primates with large home ranges seem to have bigger brains so they can handle a sophisticated "mental map" of their feeding area. This pattern seems to hold true for frugivores (fruit eaters) as compared to **folivores** (leaf eaters). The archaeological record supports both points for early *Homo*: The first hominines ate a complex, omnivorous diet including plant and animal products, and they apparently ranged over wide areas in the process of locating food and also raw stone for toolmaking. If early *Homo* not only lived in groups but also actively scavenged for meat in groups, the hominines could have increased their odds for success by cooperatively driving predators away from kills and cooperatively defending kills against other hominids (Rose and Marshall, 1996).

This brings us to a third evolutionary variable. Big brains are metabolically expensive organs (Aiello and Wheeler, 1995), and meat is an energy-rich food. If the early hominines successfully increased their meat intake—as is suggested by studies of Oldowan tools—this would have allowed brain expansion, because the enhanced diet could nourish a larger brain.

In any case, something happened around two and a half million years ago that propelled the early hominines beyond their australopithecine ancestors in both intelligence and material culture. But early *Homo* was also due to be outstripped by a descendant—*Homo erectus*.

Folivore a leaf-eating animal (compare frugivore).

Timeline: The Coming of *Homo*

The earliest hominines (members of the genus *Homo*) have been recovered from sites in Northeast and East Africa. At least one variety of early *Homo*—*H. habilis*—also inhabited South Africa around 2 million years ago.

HOLOCENE		
10,000		
PLEISTOCENE		
1.6 MILLION		
PLIOCENE		
5 MILLION		

MIOCENE

Kenyapithecus
Dryopithecus

25 MILLION

OLIGOCENE

Apidium, Parapithecus,
Aegyptopithecus, and
Propliopithecus

35 MILLION

Amphipithecus
Siamopithecus

EOCENE

CENOZOIC

58 MILLION

PALEOCENE
Early Prosimians

YEARS AD	DISCOVERIES
1997	2.5-million-year-old Oldowan tools discovered at Gona
1995	2.4-million-year-old *Homo rudolfensis* jaw discovered at Uraha
1994	*Homo habilis* (?) found associated with Oldowan tools at Kada Hadar
1983	2.5-million-year-old Oldowan tools found at Hadar
1969	First Koobi Fora expedition
1967	First Omo expedition
1960	Discovery of first *Homo habilis* fossils at Olduvai Gorge
1931	First Leakey expedition to Olduvai Gorge First Oldowan tools found

YEARS BP	FOSSIL RECORD	HOMINID SPECIES
1 million	Most recent *Paranthropus* fossils at Swartkrans and Koobi Fora	More advanced *Homo*
1.3 million		
	Most recent *Homo habilis* fossils at Olduvai Gorge; most recent *H. rudolfensis* fossils from East Africa	
1.6 million		*Homo erectus*
1.8 million	*Homo habilis* at Sterkfontein	? *Paranthropus*
2 million		*Homo habilis*
2.3 million	Probable *Homo habilis* fossil at Hadar	*Homo rudolfensis*
2.4 million	Oldest *Homo rudolfensis* remains at Uraha	
		Australopithecus
3 million		
4 million		
		A. ramidus
5 million		
		First hominids
6 million		?

225

Summary

Around two and a half million years ago, for reasons that are not well understood, the African family Hominidae experienced a significant evolutionary shake-up: The last representatives of *Australopithecus* died out, and two new genera appeared, *Paranthropus* and *Homo*—the latter marking a new evolutionary grade for hominids. Shortly after its evolutionary appearance, *Homo* was present in at least two forms, *H. habilis* and *H. rudolfensis*, both bipeds (although apparently not fully modern in that locomotor pattern) and one or both making Oldowan stone tools. With significantly larger brains than the australopithecines, the two early *Homo* species were undoubtedly somewhat smarter than their predecessors, which would have facilitated toolmaking, and probably had more complex communication systems. Stone-tool manufacture and use probably points to more meat in the early hominines' diet; but anthropologists are undecided about how additional meat was obtained, whether by scavenging or by active hunting. In any event, along with the *Paranthropus* forms (with which early *Homo* had a long temporal overlap and even spatial overlap at some sites), the first hominines haunted the gallery forests, woodlands, and savannas of both East and South Africa for very nearly a million years. And although the early *Homo* species were not quite at the point where most anthropologists are comfortable calling them human (admittedly, this is a matter of taste; there are no established criteria for the use of that term), one of them (probably *H. habilis*) gave rise to a species that clearly deserves that label: *Homo erectus.*

The primary hallmark of hominids is bipedalism; and yet, as this chapter has demonstrated, we have only an imperfect understanding of the selection pressures that produced our characteristic form of locomotion. Increased energy efficiency (compared to ape quadrupedalism), body temperature control, and adaptations to variable and unstable habitats appear to be among the best explanations for the evolution of bipedalism. Still, there are several other suggestions that cannot be discounted entirely, (such as the benefits of freeing the hands for tool use and carrying things, and of adopting an upright posture to harvest small food items). Furthermore, the connection between bipedalism and canine tooth reduction remains unclear. Undoubtedly, several variables—both anatomical and behavioral—were involved in a complex feedback system throughout hominid evolution.

The presence of stone tools made to a regular pattern—the Oldowan culture—is the most significant archaeological fact of the Late Pliocene and enables us to say that *Homo* was becoming skilled in hand and brain. Technologists had made their appearance on the world stage, and an irreversible feedback loop had been triggered. Nevertheless, our present knowledge of early *Homo* limits these hominids to the very beginning of culture and the first seeds of modern humanity.

Review Questions

1. What evidence supports the idea that tool use stimulated the beginnings of habitual bipedalism? If this hypothesis is valid, what type and frequency of tool use do you think were involved?

2. What are the various hypotheses about the origin of hominid bipedalism? Can you arrange the hypotheses in order from the most to the least likely, and then present evidence to support your ordering system?

3. How do *Homo habilis* and *Homo rudolfensis* differ physically from each other and from their *Australopithecus* ancestors?

4. What are the difficulties in identifying the makers of the various Oldowan tool assemblages? What sort of evidence do you think is needed before a conclusive identification can be made?

5. Describe the possible evolutionary relationships of the early *Homo* species. Which australopithecine type do you think gave rise to them, and which early hominine variety do you think gave rise to *Homo erectus*?

6. Should the earliest hominines (or even the australopithecines) be called "humans"? What criteria would you establish for the use of this term?

7. What were the forms and functions of Oldowan tools? What do these tools suggest about the subsistence patterns of their makers? What conclusions can we reach about the sexes of their makers?

8. What sort of group structure and mating pattern do you think characterized the australopithecines? What about early *Homo*? Present evidence to support your conclusions.

9. What can be concluded about the lifestyles of the australopithecines—*Australopithecus* and *Paranthropus*? Be sure to include information about habitat, locomotion (i.e., the variety, if any, of locomotor patterns), diet, and material culture.

Suggested Further Reading

Aiello, L., and R. I. M. Dunbar. "Neocortex Size, Group Size, and the Evolution of Language." *Current Anthropology,* 34, 1993.

Falk, D. *Braindance.* Henry Holt, 1992.

Potts, R. *Humanity's Descent.* William Morrow, 1996.

Trevathan, W. *Human Birth: An Evolutionary Perspective.* Aldine de Gruyter, 1987.

Wheeler, P. "Human Ancestors Walked Tall, Stayed Cool." *Natural History,* 102, 1993.

Internet Resources

Conveniently access these and other links via our web site at **http://www.ablongman/anthro.**

Early Transitional Humans
http://daphne.palomar.edu/homo/homo-1.htm
Basic information on *Homo habilis* and *Homo rudolfensis,* with a practice quiz.

Hominid Origins: Ecology, Changing Social Patterns, and Bipedalism
http://www.as.ua.edu/ant/bindon/ant101/syllabus/hom_orig/hom_orig.htm
A listing of the various hypotheses regarding the evolution of bipedalism.

Stone Tool Technology: Explore the Potentials
http://www.mc.maricopa.edu/anthro/origins/stone_tools.html
This site describes the various types of stone tools and explains in detail how they were made.

The First Stone Tools: The Great Advantage
http://www.mc.maricopa.edu/anthro/exploratorium/hominid_journey/oldowan.html
Discussion of the beginnings of lithic technology.

World's Oldest Stone Tools
http://www.archaeology.org/9703/newbriefs/tools.html
A short report of the discovery of 2.5-million-year-old Oldowan tools in Ethiopia.

Useful Search Terms:
bipedal walking
brain evolution
Homo habilis
Home rudolfensis
Oldowan tools
stone tools

Homo erectus

Overview

The earliest fossil of *Homo erectus* was found in Java in 1891 and named *Pithecanthropus*. Today we group this fossil with others from China (including those from the great cave of Zhoukoudian), Europe, and Africa as *Homo erectus*, a species that has a geographical range much greater than that of early *Homo*. In this chapter we describe these *Homo erectus* discoveries and discuss their age. We devote considerable attention to the possible phylogeny of the species. We also examine evidence for the geographical dispersion of *H. erectus* and describe its characteristic anatomy. The chapter considers

Mini-Timeline: The Earliest Humans

Date or Age	Fossil Discoveries
(A) Date (years AD)	
1996	Dates for fossils from Ngandong and Sambungmacan revised
1994	Dates for *Homo erectus* fossils from Sangiran and Modjokerto revised
1984	Nariokotome *H. erectus* skeleton found
1929	First skull of *Sinanthropus* discovered
1891	Eugene Dubois discovers first *Pithecanthropus* fossils

(B) Age (years BP)	**Evolutionary Events**
400,000–300,000	First regular use of fire; oldest shelter construction
1.5 million	Nariokotome *Homo erectus* skeleton
1.7–1.4 million	First Acheulean tools (Africa); establishment of a hunting-and-gathering way of life
1.8–1.6 million	*Homo erectus* at Dmanisi, Republic of Georgia
1.8–1.7 million	Oldest (?) Asian *H. erectus* fossils at Sangiran and Modjokerto
1.8 million	Oldest African *H. erectus* fossils at Koobi Fora
1.9 million	Oldest known *Homo erectus*(?) from Longgupo Cave, China

the environment and culture of *Homo erectus*, including their use of hand axes, biodegradable tools, fire, and shelter. These early humans' ability to hunt is controversial, but the evidence for meat-eating is clear. Their culture and lifestyle enabled them to expand into the cool north temperate biomes and to survive winter temperatures.

Check our web site for additional information, photos, drawings, maps, and animations on topics in this chapter.

The Discovery of Pithecanthropus

Eugene Dubois is one of the most famous names in paleoanthropology because of his remarkable discovery of **Pithecanthropus.** Dubois set out from Holland in 1887 with the single intention of finding the "missing link." A. R. Wallace had noted in his travels that gibbons and orangutans lived in Borneo and Sumatra; so, as Java and Sumatra were at that time under Dutch rule, Dubois chose these islands for his project. He enlisted in the army as a doctor and arranged to be sent to Java. In 1891, at a site named Trinil on the Solo River in Eastern Java (Figure 9.1), he found a skullcap or *calvaria* of an "extinct manlike ape" together with a femur. Dubois named the new species *Anthropopithecus erectus* (erect man–ape). In 1893, after further study, he changed the name to *Pithecanthropus erectus* (erect ape–man) (Theunissen, 1989). Today we believe the skull dates from 1.0 to 0.8 million years ago; the femur, however, is thought to be relatively modern and unrelated.

Pithecanthropus the original genus name given by Eugene Dubois to fossil material from Java now classified as *Homo erectus.*

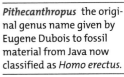

Figure 9.1

During glacial periods, when far more water was locked up in the polar and continental ice sheets than today, the world sea level fell. During the coldest periods, the maximum lowering of the sea appears to have been more than 330 feet (100 meters), which would have enlarged considerably the landmasses available for occupation by plant and animal life. Throughout the Pleistocene, the sea level fluctuated extensively.

[Map showing Asian sites: Zhoukoudian, Jian Shi, Hexian, Longgupo, Gongwangling (Lantian), Yuanmou, Sunda Shelf, SUMATRA, BORNEO, JAVA, Sangiran, Sambungmacan, Ngandong, and Trinil, Modjokerto]

• Sites of Asian
Homo erectus fossils

Landmass exposed when sea level was lowered during ice age.

Dubois's discovery was unfortunately followed by years of controversy. Scholars in Europe could not accept that this was the skull of a missing link. The problem was exacerbated by the 1912 appearance of the fraudulent but supposedly very ancient Piltdown skull in England, which—being in fact modern—led scientists to expect a large-brained human ancestor (Walsh, 1996). *Pithecanthropus,* whose brain was relatively small compared to that of Piltdown, was therefore dismissed as a possible ancestor. It was either a rather human-looking ape or an apelike human. But we now know that Dubois was right regarding both the evolutionary position of *Pithecanthropus* and its erect posture.

The years following Dubois's discovery saw several important additions to the hominid fossil record. The Mauer mandible (now thought to be *Homo heidelbergensis*) was discovered near Heidelberg, Germany, in 1907; and Dart's baby *Australopithecus africanus* from Taung was described in 1925. None of the finds, however, shed much light on Dubois's *Pithecanthropus erectus* fossils.

Discoveries and Mysteries

The Beijing Fossils

New light came in 1927 with the discovery of more Asian fossils at the Chinese site of Zhoukoudian, near Beijing (Peking). The discovery of **Peking Man,** as the fossils were named, involved a piece of scientific detective work almost as remarkable as Dubois's exploit in Java (Jia and Huang Weiwen, 1990). This ancestor was added to the human family tree simply because a small band of scientists had gone to China determined to hunt it down. A Canadian physician, Davidson Black (1884–1934), was sure that he would unearth a human ancestor in China if only he looked long and hard enough. And so in 1919, when he was offered an appointment as professor of anatomy at Peking Union Medical College, he eagerly accepted.

Black's conviction was based both on geologic evidence showing that the ancient climate and geography of China were quite suitable for primitive humans, and on the theory that patterns of evolution are closely related to climatic conditions. Also supporting his feeling was a single tantalizing piece of fossil evidence suggesting that some early primate had once inhabited China. In 1899, a German physician, K. A. Haberer, had chanced on an unusual fossil tooth among some "dragon bones" about to be ground up for medicine in a druggist's shop in Beijing. The tooth was among more than a hundred fossils the doctor had picked up in various Chinese drugstores and sent to paleontologist Max Schlosser. Schlosser identified the tooth as a "left upper third molar, either of a man or a hitherto unknown anthropoid ape" and predicted hopefully that further searching might turn up the skeleton of an early human.

Zhoukoudian

Peking Man traditional name for *Homo erectus fossils* from Zhoukoudian, near Beijing (Peking).

While Davidson Black was teaching anatomy in Beijing, a group led by John Gunnar Andersson, a Swedish geologist, began to dig at a site twenty-five miles (forty kilometers) southwest of the city, near the village of Zhoukoudian (see Figure 9.1). The Chinese had been digging "dragon bones" out of this spot and others like it for hundreds of years, and no one will ever know how many powdered fossils have passed harmlessly through the alimentary canals of dyspeptic Chinese. Whatever the losses may have been to paleoanthropology, some of the limestone caverns in the hillside were still richly packed with interesting material. There were bits of broken quartz among the limestone deposits around an ancient cliffside cave. The quartz would not naturally be associated with limestone, Andersson knew; it must have been brought there—perhaps by some toolmaking peoples of the past.

A great many fossils were dug out of the rock and shipped back to Sweden for study. Twenty different mammals were identified, many of them extinct species. But Andersson's toolmaker was not easily found. Finally, in 1926, when one of Andersson's associates had given up and returned to Sweden and the digging had stopped, a closer study of a fossil molar and another tooth found later suggested that they might indeed be human. The teeth were sent back to Andersson, who turned them over to Davidson Black for his expert appraisal. Preoccupied though Black was with medicine, he had never lost interest in the Zhoukoudian site. He was certain that the teeth came from a human of great antiquity, and he persuaded the Rockefeller Foundation to support a large-scale excavation of the site.

Work started in 1927, and on October 16 the searchers found a human molar tooth that Black named *Sinanthropus pekinensis* (Chinese man of Peking). In 1928 more human teeth and bone fragments were found, and in 1929 a skullcap (calvaria). Following this development, work continued at a great pace; the whole hillside was sliced off, revealing deposits 160 feet deep. By 1937 parts of more than forty women, men, and children had been discovered, including 9 fragmentary skulls, 5 calvariae (Figure 9.2), 6 facial fragments, 14 lower jaws, 152 teeth, and numerous other skeletal fragments.

Davidson Black died in 1934 and was succeeded in his post by Franz Weidenreich (1873–1948), who made a thorough study of the material and concluded that *Sinanthropus* was an early human with upright posture, bipedal locomotion, and a cranial capacity of about 1,000 cc. The teeth were human and the skull rounded. And the material was associated with extensive cultural remains.

Sinanthropus pekinensis the original name given by Davidson Black to ancient *fossils* from Zhoukoudian, near Beijing. These remains are now classified as *Homo erectus*.

Figure 9.2

Although not the first to be discovered, this is one of several skullcaps of "Peking Man" (*Homo erectus*) recovered from Zhoukoudian.

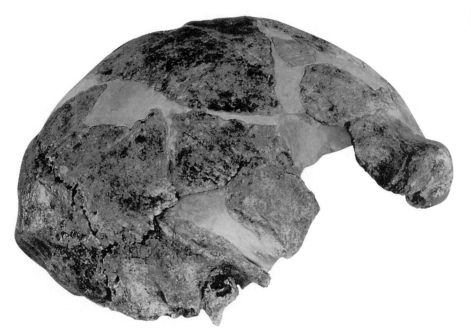

Material Culture at Zhoukoudian

At Zhoukoudian continuing excavations produced thousands of stone tools. Many were simple choppers with only a few chips removed, but they were made to a rough pattern. In the largest cave that was explored, 100,000 stone tools and fragments, most of quartz, were found. Some of them lay with charred bits of wood and bone. From this it was concluded that *Sinanthropus* had mastered the use of fire.

The bones and antlers of thousands of animals also were present in the deposits. Nearly three-quarters of them belonged to deer; there were also bones of giant sheep, zebra, pigs, buffalo, rhinoceros, monkeys, bison, elephant, and even river-dwellers such as the otter. Among these were scattered the bones of predators; bear, hyena, wolves, fox, badger, leopard and other cats, and humans. All these bones came from species that are now extinct.

The possibility that some of the bones and antlers were shaped and used as tools was put forward by the distinguished French prehistorian Abbé Henri Breuil. Years later, Raymond Dart used Breuil's work to support his thesis that a somewhat similar "osteodontokeratic" (bone, tooth, and horn) culture had been produced by australopithecines at Makapansgat, South Africa. But could all these so-called tools have been produced by nonhuman agencies? Pei (1939) discussed this question and pointed out the effects on bone of predators and rodents. Binford and Ho (1985) have shown that the evidence for such a bone-and-horn culture at Zhoukoudian is not conclusive; all the so-called tools made of these materials could have been produced naturally.

About twenty feet (six meters) below the lowest outer threshold of the big cave, the expedition found what may have been *Sinanthropus*'s garbage dump, a stony amalgam of thousands of scraps of bone, stone chips, and hackberry seeds. All in all, by their handiwork as well as by their bodily structure, the specimens found in China indubitably established their right to a place in the human genus. Recent Chinese research places the human occupation of the cave between 230,000 and 500,000 years BP (Table 9.1).

Pithecanthropus and *Sinanthropus*

Weidenreich's assessment of the fossils at Zhoukoudian corroborated Black's earlier conclusion that *Sinanthropus* was humanlike. Black had compared his Zhoukoudian skull with Dubois's detailed description of *Pithecanthropus*. He concluded that the skulls were two specimens of the same type of creature. In each, the bones of the skull were thick, the forehead was low and sloping, and massive brow ridges jutted out over the eye sockets.

In 1931 Dutch geologists resumed the search for fossils in Java and found eleven somewhat more recent skulls at a site called Ngandong. Further finds were made by the German paleontologist G. R. H. von Koenigswald (1902–1983) between 1936 and 1939 (von Koenigswald, 1956). Comparison of the skulls from China and Java again made it clear that they were very closely related, and today all these fossils are classified as *Homo erectus* (Howells, 1980, 1993; Rightmire, 1990; Figure 9.3).

Homo erectus in Africa

Since the 1950s the continent of Africa has yielded numerous fossils of *Homo erectus* from a variety of locations (Figure 9.4 and Table 9.1). In 1954 *Homo erectus* mandibles dating 650,000 to 450,000 years BP were discovered at the northwest African site of

Table 9.1

A Partial Record of *Homo erectus* Fossils		
Continent	**Site**	**Age (years BP)**
Africa	Salé	300,000–200,000
	Sidi Abderrahman	300,000–200,000
	Thomas Quarries	350,000–240,000
	Lainyamok	600,000
	Ternifine	650,000–450,000
	Melka Kunturé	900,000
	Olduvai Gorge	1.2 million–600,000
	Omo	1.4 million
	Nariokotome	1.5 million
	Swartkrans[a]	1.8–1.5 million
	Koobi Fora	1.8–1.6 million
Asia	Ngandong [Solo](?)[b]	46,000–27,000
	Sambungmacan(?)[b]	53,000–27,000
	Jian Shi	300,000–200,000
	Zhoukoudian	500,000–230,000
	Hexian	700,000–250,000
	Gongwangling [Lantian]	700,000
	Yuanmou	900,000–500,000
	Trinil	1.0–0.8 million
	Sangiran	1.7 million–500,000
	Modjokerto	1.8 million
	Longgupo[c]	1.9–1.7 million
Europe	Ceprano	800,000
	Dmanisi	1.8–1.6 million

[a]Some argue that the *Homo* fossils from Swartkrans do not fit easily into *H. erectus* and require their own species designation.
[b]Classifications for the Ngandong and Sambungmacan fossils are problematic. Some researchers assign them to *Homo erectus,* while others believe they belong in a more advanced species (perhaps *Homo heidlebergensis* or even *Homo sapiens*). They are included here provisionally, and their equivocal status is explained in the text.
[c]Although its discoverers claim the Longgupo Cave fossils may represent *H. habilis,* a more conservative view is that they are best assigned to early *Homo erectus.*

Ternifine, Algeria. The next year another jaw was recovered from slightly younger deposits at the coastal Moroccan site of Sidi Abderrahman, and in 1971 cranial fragments of late *Homo erectus* also were reported from Salé, Morocco.

Fossils from South and East Africa have pushed the species farther and farther into the past. The Swartkrans site has produced remains dating between 1.8 and 1.5 million years of age that *may* represent *Homo erectus.* In 1960 Louis Leakey recovered undoubted *Homo erectus* remains dating 1.2 million years BP from Tanzania's Olduvai Gorge—and since then, younger *H. erectus* fossils, circa 600,000 to 700,000 years of age, have also been found at Olduvai. Just north of Olduvai, the Kenyan site of Lainyamok has yielded *Homo erectus* teeth and limb bones dating around 600,000 years BP. The central Ethiopian site of Melka Kunturé has produced a cranial fragment that may go back 900,000 years.

Figure 9.3

The reconstruction of the skull and jaw of *Homo erectus* is based on numerous fossil finds. The general form of the face can also be reconstructed with reasonable accuracy, but we have little information on such important features as nostrils, lips, and hair.

The distinction of producing the most ancient remains of East African *Homo erectus*, however, belongs to the Omo region of extreme southwestern Ethiopia and the east and west shores of Lake Turkana in Kenya. Relevant Omo fossils date to 1.4 million years ago, and discoveries in east Turkana's Koobi Fora region carry *Homo erectus* all the way back to 1.8 million years BP. Among the Koobi Fora fossils is a superb skull whose owner boasted a cranial capacity of 850 cc some 1.7 mya.

But of all the African specimens, the *Homo erectus* boy from the west Turkana site of Nariokotome is perhaps the most exciting (Walker and Leakey, 1993). Initially discovered in 1984 by the veteran fossil hunter Kamoya Kimeu, the specimen consists of a nearly complete skeleton that lacks only the left humerus (upper arm bone), both radii (lower arm bones), and most of the bones of the hands and feet (Figure 9.5). Dated to 1.5 million years BP, the Nariokotome boy was about twelve years old when he died (perhaps from the septicemia of a gum infection after the loss of a lower milk molar) and came to lie in a shallow swamp that was probably replenished seasonally by the floodwaters of the Omo River. After death the body lay relatively undisturbed in the quiet water as it gradually decomposed. Small portions of the body were very likely eaten by scavenging catfish, and the skeleton was dispersed and damaged somewhat as large wading animals trampled and kicked the bones. Most of the skeleton, however, settled quietly into the mud and began the long wait until its discovery a million and a half years later.

The nearly complete nature of the Nariokotome skeleton has allowed detailed studies of *Homo erectus* anatomy never before possible. The boy was about 5.3 feet (160 centimeters) tall at death and would very likely have grown to be a big man of about 6.1 feet (185 centimeters) and 150 pounds (68 kilograms). His boyhood cranial capacity of 880 cc would probably have expanded to about 909 cc when he became an adult (68 percent of the modern human average). He had long arms and legs and a slender torso—bodily

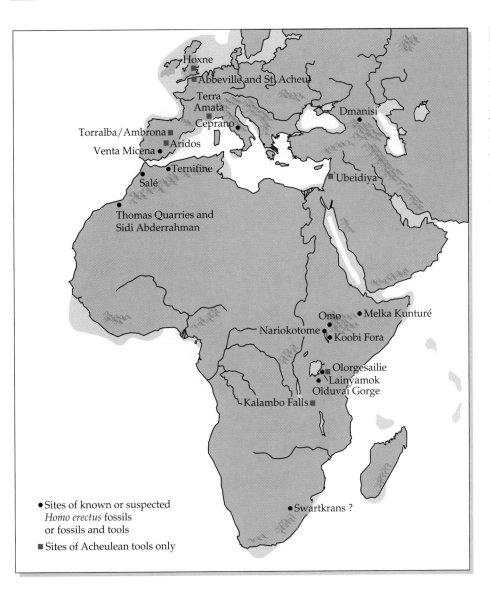

Figure 9.4

Since the earliest discoveries in East Asia, a number of sites in Europe and Africa have yielded fossil remains of *Homo erectus* or Acheulean tools. On this map, the coastline is shown as it might have been during a period of glaciation when the sea level fell.

proportions identical to those of modern people who are adapted to hot, dry climates. His estimated adult pelvic dimensions, if characteristic of the species, suggest that *Homo erectus* newborns had relatively small brains (perhaps about 200 cc) and that, as in modern humans, rapid brain growth then continued for the first part of an infant's life. And finally, details of his thoracic (rib cage) vertebrae suggest that *Homo erectus* may have lacked the fine muscular control over breathing that is required for speech.

Homo erectus in Europe

After about 1.5 mya, *Homo erectus* people in Africa, parts of Europe, and western Asia produced a new and distinctive type of stone tool industry called the Acheulean (Schick and Toth, 1993). In addition, *H. erectus* populations everywhere continued to make

Figure 9.5

The most complete early hominid skeleton ever found was discovered at Nariokotome, west of Lake Turkana, Kenya, in 1984 and was excavated from sediments that are dated close to 1.5 million years ago. The skeleton, known as KNM–WT 15000, belongs to a twelve-year-old *Homo erectus* boy who would have grown into an adult more than 6 feet (1.8 meters) in height.

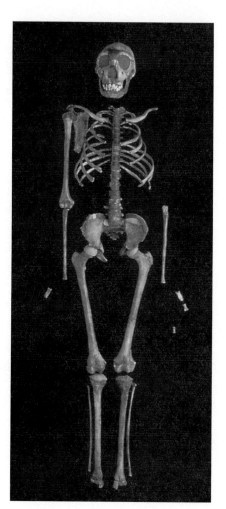

and use Oldowan flakes and choppers, and in eastern Asia these were their only stone implements. Both Acheulean and Oldowan sites attributed to *Homo erectus* have been excavated in Europe, but only a handful of *H. erectus* fossils have come from that continent. By far the most interesting site is that of Dmanisi, in the Caucasus mountains of Georgia, in extreme southeastern Europe (see Figure 9.4). First a jaw and then two crania have been found in the same strata, dated quite securely at about 1.7 mya (Brauer and Schultz, 1996; Gabunia et al., 2000). The mandible is in quite good condition, with all its teeth; the crania are equally rewarding, and one is surprisingly complete. Although full descriptions are not yet available, the skulls are reported to be reminiscent of the East African specimens of *Homo erectus* that are called *Homo ergaster* by some researchers, and they were found in association with Oldowan-type choppers and flakes. The evidence suggests strongly that this population was the progenitor of Asian *Homo erectus*. We now have an impressive geographical and temporal link between Africa and Asia and a reliable date before which the first hominid exodus from Africa must have occurred.

The single other European specimen of *Homo erectus* comes from the site of Ceprano, Italy (see Figure 9.4), and was discovered in 1994 (Ascenzi et al., 1996). This fossil is a calvaria with a sloping forehead, large brows, and a cranial capacity of more than 1,000 cc. Estimated from geological studies to be about 800,000 years old, the Ceprano fossil (like the Dmanisi jaw) apparently was associated with an Oldowan-type chopper and flake tool assemblage.

Although these two are the only definite fossils of *Homo erectus* to come from Europe, we would be remiss if we ended this section without mentioning the exciting (and controversial) material from Venta Micena near Orce in southern Spain (Borja et al., 1997; Palmqvist, 1997) (see Figure 9.4). Dated by paleomagnetism and faunal studies to about 1.6 million years ago, Venta Micena has produced Oldowan tools; the remains of several immigrant animal species from nearby Africa (including hippos, ancestral zebras, and ancestral hyenas); and three bones—a skull fragment and two arm bones—that some workers attribute to *Homo* (species indeterminate, but probably *erectus*). If the latter remains prove to be human, they will represent the oldest western Europeans. Their hominid status has been challenged, however. None of the bones is distinctively human anatomically, and the cranial fragment in particular cannot be distinguished from that of a horse (genus *Equus*). On the other hand, immunospecificity studies of residual proteins recovered from the Venta Micena skull fragment have produced reactions characteristic of human, not horse, material. Unfortunately, these offsetting results leave the Venta Micena remains in taxonomic limbo at present. Nonetheless, the site is tremendously exciting because of its extreme age and undoubted stone tools. At 1.6 million years of age, Venta Micena is clearly the oldest hominid site in western Europe, matching Dmanisi in its antiquity. Furthermore, the Spanish material shows that the first documented human exodus from Africa occurred at both ends of the Mediterranean simultaneously (perhaps also in the center via Sicily?), rather than simply through the Middle East.

Homo erectus in Asia

World War II caused a temporary break in paleoanthropological research in Asia, but during the second half of the twentieth century exploration resumed and more *Homo erectus* specimens were discovered (Howells, 1980; Jia and Huang Weiwen, 1990). In China, intermittent work was resumed at Zhoukoudian during the 1950s and 1960s and new dental, cranial, and postcranial material was recovered. Additionally, Chinese workers found *Homo erectus* remains at several new sites, including Gongwangling (where the finds included a partial skull with an estimated cranial capacity of about 780 cc), Yuanmou, and Hexian (Figure 9.1). The Hexian material, which is no older than 700,000 and perhaps as young as 250,000 years BP (Table 9.1), represents at least three *H. erectus* individuals and was discovered in 1980–1981. Finally, and most intriguing of all, excavations carried out between 1985 and 1988 at the Longgupo Cave site in Sichuan Province (Figure 9.1) may have produced the very oldest evidence of hominids in Asia (Wanpo et al., 1995). The Longgupo fossils include a partial mandible with the left P4 and M1 and an upper incisor. Found in association with two apparent Oldowan tools, the teeth show similarities to both *Homo erectus* and *Homo habilis* and carry a paleomagnetic date of 1.9 to 1.7 million years ago. For simplification, and because of their early date and lack of diagnostic traits, the Longgupo fossils are treated as early *Homo erectus* in this text. Nonetheless, some researchers (including the fossils' discoverers) think the teeth, and thus the first Asians, are best classified as a pre-*erectus* hominid type.

Java, too, has continued to produce *Homo erectus* fossils since Indonesia's independence in 1945. Included in the new discoveries are calvariae and postcranial fossils from

Ngandong (found between 1976–1980); a partial skull from Sambungmacan (1973); and an exceptionally complete cranium from Sangiran, found in 1993 and estimated to have a cranial capacity of 856 cc (Rightmire, 1990). A joint American–Indonesian research team has recently redated two of Java's classic *H. erectus* sites (Swisher et al., 1994). Using an Ar^{40}/Ar^{39} dating technique, the team—headed by geochronologists Carl Swisher and Garniss Curtis—determined in 1994 that *Homo erectus* inhabited the Sangiran region more than 1.66 million years ago and the Modjokerto region as early as 1.81 million years BP! If these new dates are valid—and, like all scientific findings, they require verification—then the evidence of *H. erectus* is equally old in Asia, Africa, and Europe.

Two sites in Java have yielded much more recent material: the skulls from Ngandong dated at 46,000–27,000 BP and a skull found at Sambungmacan dated at 53,000–27,000 BP (Swisher et al., 1996). These fossils show a distinct affinity with *Homo erectus* but carry many features of *H. sapiens;* their classification is controversial. The best interpretation at present is that they represent a relict population of very late *H. erectus* that survived in Java long after *H. sapiens* was established throughout the rest of the Old World. Whether they contributed to the modern gene pool is uncertain, but it has been claimed that they anatomically resemble some early Australian skeletal material, believed to be ancestral to the modern Australian aborigines.

For more on *Homo erectus,* visit our web site.

The Anatomy of Homo erectus

Fossils attributed to *Homo erectus* cover an enormous time span (1.9 million to at least 300,000 years BP) and an equally impressive geographic range (from South Africa to southeast Asia). As a consequence of its longevity and geographic spread, *Homo erectus* has been traditionally understood to display a good deal of anatomical variability (Figure 9.6).

Indeed, some researchers think there is too much variability to be contained within one species. They argue that we should divide the material classified as *H. erectus*, retaining the name *Homo erectus* for the Asian fossils from Java and China, and classifying the early African remains from Lake Turkana and the Nariokotome boy as a separate species called **Homo ergaster.** Supporters of this scheme view *Homo ergaster* as more closely related (and more likely to be ancestral) to modern humans than was Asian *Homo erectus.* Other scientists disagree with the proposed taxonomic split. Some paleoanthropologists, such as G. Philip Rightmire (1990, 1992) conclude that there is insufficient anatomical difference to justify the recognition of two separate species, arguing that *Homo erectus*'s anatomical variability matched its geographic spread. Rightmire and other members of the single-species group point out that many of the traits claimed to be distinctive, derived features of Asian *Homo erectus* also can be identified on some of the early African specimens. For example, **sagittal keeling** of the frontal and/or parietal bones is common among the Asian fossils, but it is also present on specimens from East Africa (Figure 9.6, left). At least for the moment, the authors of this book agree with the Rightmire camp and thus retain the traditional classification scheme and treat *Homo erectus* as one variable and widespread species.

In many important ways, *Homo erectus* had reached anatomical modernity. On average, these people were as tall and as heavy as modern humans. They seem to have

Homo ergaster species name given by some paleoanthropologists to certain African *fossils* regarded by most workers as being early *Homo erectus.* The authors of this book side with the majority.

Sagittal keeling appearance of a slightly raised ridge running down the center of a skull; smaller than a *sagittal crest.*

ASKING QUESTIONS

How Did *Homo erectus* Disperse So Widely?

During the last half of the twentieth century, paleoanthropologists' explanation of hominines' development in and migration from Africa seemed straightforward and conclusive: *Homo erectus* originated there and began to spread north and east around 1.0 million years ago. However, the discovery of ancient hominine fossils from Longgupo, Dmanisi, and Java have shown that the migration (or migrations) must have begun much earlier than originally thought, and some researchers suggest that the first transcontinental travelers weren't *Homo erectus* at all. If the discoverers of the Longgupo Cave hominid are correct in identifying their find as belonging to a pre-*erectus* species, it would go far toward proving that early *Homo* (possibly *H. habilis* or *H. rudolfensis*) was the first hominine species to migrate from Africa, not *Homo erectus*. This development would open up the possibility that *Homo erectus* originated in Asia and not in Africa.

On the other hand, if a slightly older African *Homo erectus* specimen turns up in the future, enormous amounts of time probably aren't needed for the traditional Africa-to-Asia expansion. For example, an African origin for *H. erectus* at 2.0 mya, followed by a leisurely spread of 1 mile (1.6 kilometers) every 10 years, would have put hominids at Longgupo Cave and in Java 100,000 years later. In any event, only time and further discoveries will help to answer these questions. As things stand at present, none of the possible points of origin—Africa, Asia, or somewhere in between—can be ruled out for *Homo erectus*.

had a modern body build, with a distinct waist instead of the potbelly that probably characterized earlier hominids; this finding has implications for the diet of *Homo erectus* (Aiello and Wheeler, 1995). Furthermore, the limb proportions of *H. erectus* were similar to those of modern humans, in contrast to the longer arms and shorter legs of early *Homo*. There can be no doubt that *Homo erectus* stood and moved in a fully modern, upright fashion.

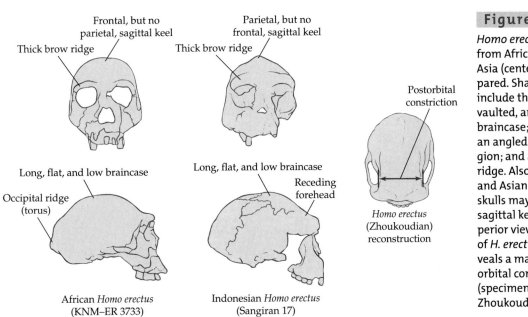

Frontal, but no parietal, sagittal keel
Thick brow ridge
Long, flat, and low braincase
Occipital ridge (torus)

African *Homo erectus*
(KNM–ER 3733)

Parietal, but no frontal, sagittal keel
Thick brow ridge
Long, flat, and low braincase
Receding forehead

Indonesian *Homo erectus*
(Sangiran 17)

Postorbital constriction

Homo erectus
(Zhoukoudian)
reconstruction

Figure 9.6

Homo erectus skulls from Africa (left) and Asia (center) are compared. Shared traits include the long, low-vaulted, and wide braincase; large brows; an angled occipital region; and an occipital ridge. Also, both African and Asian *Homo erectus* skulls may show some sagittal keeling. A superior view of the skull of *H. erectus* (right) reveals a marked postorbital constriction (specimen from Zhoukoudian).

Changes in Cranium and Brain

Despite their modern postcranial skeletons, however, *Homo erectus* individuals differed greatly from modern people in their brain size and cranial anatomy. Including Ngandong and Sambungmacan, the average brain size for *Homo erectus* was 994 cubic centimeters (range 750 to 1,251 cc; Table 9.2)—some 27 to 62 percent bigger than early *Homo*, but still only two-thirds the modern average. Without the recent Javanese skulls, the *H. erectus* average drops to 937 cc (range 750 to 1,225 cc). But because brain expansion in *Homo erectus* was matched by increased body size, the species' relative brain size (brain size controlling for body weight) was not significantly greater than that of early *Homo*. Furthermore, the enlarged *H. erectus* brain was still encased in a primitive-looking container. The skull of *Homo erectus* was constructed of thick cranial bones, and it was long, low-vaulted, and widest at the base, a combination of traits labeled **platycephalic.**

The front of the cranium was topped with huge brow ridges, and behind those brows the skull showed a distinct postorbital constriction at the temples. Often, particularly in the Asian specimens, the top of the skull showed a distinct sagittal keel (the function of this feature, like many others, is unknown). And finally, at the back the skull of *Homo erectus* had an **occipital torus,** or ridge, and angled sharply toward the cranial base; the cranial base itself tended to be rather flat and unflexed, lacking the arched configuration characteristic of modern humans.

Several researchers have attempted to determine whether *Homo erectus* showed any significant evolutionary changes in anatomy during its long period of existence, and here again opinions differ. David Begun and Alan Walker (1993) present evidence that little, if any, expansion of the brain occurred from early to late *Homo erectus*. Simi-

Platycephalic long, low-vaulted, and widest at the base; describes a skull.

Occipital torus a ridge running side-to-side across the occiptal bone at the back of a skull.

Table 9.2

Trait	Characteristics of *Homo erectus*	
	Homo erectus (including Ngandong and Sambungmacan)	*Homo erectus* (excluding Ngandong and Sambungmacan)[a]
Height (sexes combined)	4.8–6.1 ft (145–185 cm)	—
Weight (sexes combined)	123–128 lb mean (56–58 kg) (range up to 150 lb, or 68 kg)	—
Brain size (sexes combined)	994 cc mean (750–1,251 cc range)	937 cc mean (750–1,225 cc range)
Cranium	Long, low-vaulted (platycephalic) braincase, widest at the base; large brow ridges; some sagittal keeling common; thick skull bones; unflexed cranial base; occipital torus	—
Dentition	Both anterior and posterior teeth smaller than those of early *Homo*	—
Limbs	Relative arm and leg lengths within modern human range of variation	—
Locomotion	Bipedalism (fully modern)	—
Distribution	Africa, Asia, Europe	—
Known dates (years BP)	1.9 million to ca. 27,000	1.9 million to ca. 300,000

[a]Adjusted trait descriptions are given only as needed.

larly, Walker and others have argued that *Homo erectus* showed no significant temporal changes in stature, dental dimensions, or skull shape. The weight of the evidence at present seems to indicate that *Homo erectus* experienced a rather long period of anatomical stasis. Its characteristic anatomy remained essentially stable for more than a million years, then disappeared upon the evolution of later *Homo*.

Evidence of Speech?

A crucial question that so far has defied our attempts to find an answer concerns the beginnings of those uniquely human traits, speech and language. The australopithecines all seemed too small-brained and behaviorally primitive to have had language and speech. Early representatives of *Homo* showed a strong increase in brain size and the beginnings of stone-tool technology, but most paleoanthropologists hesitate to regard them as linguistic creatures. But what about *Homo erectus*? Surely, with all we know about the anatomy of this species, we can draw some clear conclusions about its linguistic capacities.

Unfortunately, additional anatomical knowledge has exacerbated rather than reduced the problem. Certainly *Homo erectus* had an absolutely larger brain than its evolutionary predecessors, but this fact does not prove conclusively that they produced spoken language. An examination of the brain's so-called language areas (Figure 9.7) can be made from the impressions of the brain on the inner surface of the cranium; and **Broca's area,** in the inferior frontal lobe, is well developed in *Homo erectus*. Research on modern humans has shown that this cortical region supports both the hierarchical organization of grammar and the manual combination of objects, including tool use (Greenfield, 1991)—but it is not known if this was true for *Homo erectus*. Furthermore, **Wernicke's area,** in the temporal lobe, appears to be extremely difficult to assess for most ancient skulls—including those of *Homo erectus*—because of distortion during fossilization. And finally, **hemispherical asymmetry** in the cerebrum—demonstrable in the Nariokotome boy (Begun and Walker, 1993) and very likely associated in that specimen with right-handedness—cannot be trusted as a guide to language abilities, because asymmetry (including left-hemisphere dominance for vocalizations) has also been documented for monkeys and apes (Falk, 1992).

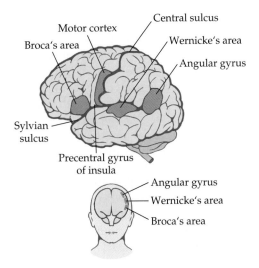

Figure 9.7

Areas of the brain cortex (surface layer) involved in speech production. Wernicke's area and the angular gyrus are also involved in the decoding of speech.

Broca's area part of the human *cerebral cortex* involved with the hierarchical organization of grammar and the manual combination of objects.

Wernicke's area part of the human *cerebral cortex* essential in comprehension and production of meaningful speech.

Hemispherical asymmetry the condition in which the two cerebral hemispheres differ in one or more dimensions. In most modern humans, the left hemisphere is somewhat larger than the right.

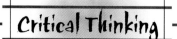

How Can the Phylogeny of *Homo erectus* Be Interpreted?

The figure here shows two interpretations of the evolution of *Homo erectus*. In phylogenetic scheme A, the African species *Homo ergaster* gives rise first to the Asian species *Homo erectus* and later to the new and bigger-brained worldwide species **Homo heidelbergensis.** This view would successfully explain why modern humans show few of the anatomical specializations of Asian *H. erectus*. However, scheme A splits the mid-Pleistocene hominids into two different species. (In both schemes the letter S represents a speciation event.)

Phylogenetic scheme B, on the other hand, retains all the mid-Pleistocene hominids in the single widespread species *Homo erectus*. Scheme B's speciation event takes place in Africa, which also explains the stronger resemblances of *H. heidelbergensis* to the African *H. erectus* than to the Asian *H. erectus*.

Based on information in this chapter, which scheme do you think is favored by the authors of this text? Do you favor the view that *H. erectus* was one widespread species directly ancestral to modern humans? Or do you

agree with the view that *H. erectus* was an Asian species that went extinct without descendants, and that modern humans ultimately descended from African *H. ergaster*? What evidence and interpretations support your view?

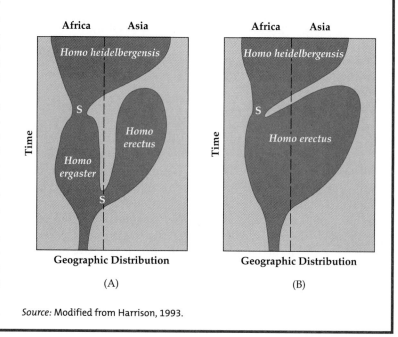

Source: Modified from Harrison, 1993.

Two negative bits of anatomical evidence argue against spoken language in *Homo erectus*. First, although there is some variation among specimens, the cranial base generally is flat and unflexed. This suggests a short **pharynx,** or throat, and an inability to produce the full range of modern vowel sounds (Figure 4.13). Second, analyses of the vertebral canals of the Nariokotome boy (MacLarnon, 1993) have revealed dimensions similar to those of monkeys and apes in the thoracic (rib cage) region. In contrast, modern humans have enlarged canals in their thoracic vertebrae, possibly to accommodate increased nerve connections with the rib cage muscles that control this part of the breathing apparatus. The small thoracic canals found in *Homo erectus* suggest that this species lacked the fine control of breathing that is essential for modern speech.

After a thorough review of the evidence, Alan Walker thinks that modern speech and language probably appeared rather late in hominid evolution and that archaeology may be a better guide to these capacities than is anatomy (Walker, 1993b). However, speech had a beginning, and evolution is a slow process. It seems therefore quite possible that *H. erectus* used a very simple form of speech with a limited range of vowels and consonants, but which was useful enough to render a distinct advantage to those who used it. This protolanguage may then have helped trigger the relatively rapid and late development of modern speech.

Homo heidelbergensis successor to *Homo erectus*, first appearing about 800,000 to 600,000 years BP; ancestral to both *Homo sapiens* and the Neandertals.

Pharynx the throat, above the *larynx*.

Evolutionary Relationships of Homo erectus

Our interpretation of the fossil evidence is that *Homo erectus* evolved from some form of early *Homo* around 1.9 million years BP. As explained previously, it is impossible at present to pinpoint the place of origin of *H. erectus*, although an East African homeland still seems most likely. Following its advent, *Homo erectus* spread across the face of the Old World—eventually occupying portions of Africa, Asia, and Europe—and survived until at least 300,000 years BP (and perhaps as late as 53,000 to 27,000 years BP, if one includes Ngandong and Sambungmacan).

At some point in the mid-Pleistocene—roughly, sometime around 800,000 to 600,000 BP, judging by fossils discovered in southern Europe and Africa—*Homo erectus* gave rise to a new and bigger-brained descendant that many paleoanthropologists call *Homo heidelbergensis* (although some still interpret *Homo erectus* as evolving into "archaic *Homo sapiens*"). This speciation event probably occurred in Africa. Undoubtedly more intelligent than their ancestors and with a more complex culture, *Homo heidelbergensis* lived on eventually to give rise to both modern humans and the Neandertals.

Those are the bare bones of the *Homo erectus* story. They appeared, they survived, they begat descendants, they became extinct. But many questions remain unanswered. What adaptations—cultural as well as biological—enabled them to survive for the better part of two million years? To understand *Homo erectus* more completely, we must now turn to the archaeological record.

Environment and Culture of Homo erectus

What sort of world did these early people with their smallish brains and primitive skulls inhabit? Clearly, the answer to that question varies from one *Homo erectus* population to another, given that the species lived a long time and was spread from the tropics to the cold–temperate zones. Traditionally, we might have said that *H. erectus* preceded and then overlapped the beginnings of the Ice Age. It is now known, however, that the Ice Age began much farther back in time and involved a more complex pattern of glacial advances and retreats than thought originally (Figure 9.8).

The first important Plio–Pleistocene glaciation occurred around 2.4 million years ago, and there were additional important pulses on both sides of the 2.0-million-year BP mark. Granted, there was an intensification of the climatic swings in the mid-Pleistocene that resulted in a series of very strong glacial advances, but it is no longer accurate to describe the Ice Age simply in terms of the traditional four-stage Alpine glaciation series. During periods of glaciation, worldwide temperatures would have fallen significantly, and parts of the Northern Hemisphere would have been bitterly cold. Rainfall patterns would have been altered, probably producing more extensive grasslands in North Africa and other parts of the Old World. In addition, with so much water locked up in the glaciers, ocean levels would have dropped some 330 feet (100 meters) or more, exposing continental shelves and creating land bridges between locations now separated by the sea (Figures 9.1 and 9.4).

All these factors—temperature, rainfall, land bridges, and the distribution of grasslands and forests—would have affected hominids' abilities to spread beyond the continent of Africa. As noted earlier, we prefer the traditional assumption that *Homo erectus* was the first species to take advantage of the changing conditions and extend its geographical range. Nonetheless, environmental conditions would have allowed geographic

Figure 9.8

Plio–Pleistocene glacial and interglacial cycles extended much farther into the past than was originally believed based on evidence from the European Alps (a). Oxygen isotope measurements from deep-sea cores (b) show evidence for Northern Hemisphere glaciations starting about 2.4 million years ago (point X) with an intensification following the mid-Pleistocene (point Y).

Source: Data from Roberts, 1992.

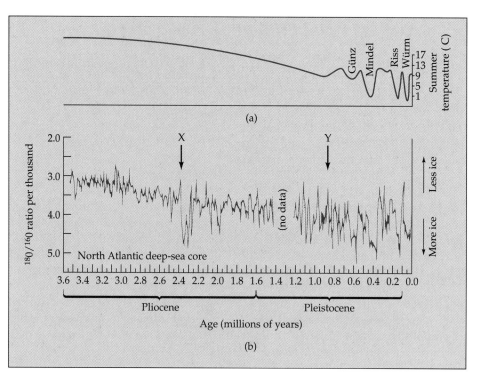

expansion during the time of early *Homo* (at about 2.4 to 2.0 mya) and a pre-*erectus* exodus from Africa cannot be disproved conclusively at present.

Stone Tools

As described in Chapter 8, stone-tool technology probably got its start with early *Homo;* and by the time *Homo erectus* appeared, Oldowan choppers and flake tools had been in use for at least half a million years. For another 100,000 to 400,000 years, Oldowan tools continued to be the top-of-the-line implements for early *Homo erectus* in Africa. The same may have been true in Asia, although the association of early Asian (i.e., Javanese) *Homo erectus* with stone tools of *any sort* remains questionable. In any event, between 1.7 to 1.4 million years BP, Africa witnessed a significant advance in stone-tool technology: the development of the Acheulean industry of flaked tools and its premier implement, the **hand ax.** Named after a much later French site at St. Acheul, where hand axes were found in abundance, the Acheulean tool kit included not only hand axes, picks, and **cleavers** (Figure 9.9), but also an assortment of Oldowan-type choppers and flakes, suggesting that the more primitive implements continued to serve important functions.

To understand this advance in **lithic technology,** we need to take a closer look at how stone tools are made. First of all, not all stones are suitable for use in tool production. Rocks of a coarse, granular composition, such as granite, are almost useless for making chipped tools; they do not fracture along smooth, clean edges but tend to crumble. Certain other rocks, such as common feldspar, tend to break only along certain fracture lines and hence cannot be controlled by the toolmaker. As explained in Chapter 8, the ideal stone from the point of view of the toolmaker is one of flint or chert: hard and tough, with smooth, fine-grained consistency. Stone of this type behaves somewhat like glass; it fractures rather than crumbles, and cone-shaped flakes

Hand ax a bifacially flaked stone implement that characterized the *Acheulean industry.*

Cleaver an *Acheulean* stone implement with a straight cutting edge at one end; probably used for butchering animal carcasses.

Lithic technology stone-tool technology.

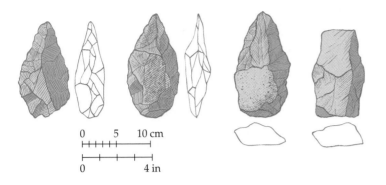

Figure 9.9

These early Acheulean artifacts are from Olduvai Gorge and date to approximately 1.5 million years BP. Shown from left to right are three hand axes (the right one is quite crude in its chipping) and a cleaver. Note the cleaver's straight bit.

can be knocked off that are razor-sharp. Flint was the most common of the desirable tool stones in western Europe, and the typical Acheulean implement there was a flint hand ax. In Africa, Acheulean tools were often fashioned from large lava flakes.

Combining various kinds of stone with various ways of working them produces a surprising variety of results. The finer-grained the stone, the flatter and more leaflike the flakes can be. The size and shape of these flakes can be further controlled by the manner in which they are separated from the original stone. They may be knocked loose by a hammer or pried loose by a pointed stick or bone. The angle at which the hammer blow is struck can be changed to produce either a small, thick flake or a large, thin one. Also, different kinds of hammers produce different kinds of flakes. Relatively soft hammers of wood or bone produce one kind, hard stone hammers another. A wooden point pressed against the edge will produce a different edge. Even the way a tool is held while it is being made will affect the kind of flake that can be struck from it: when it is held in the hand, the results are not the same as when it is balanced on a rock that serves as an anvil.

Every toolmaker must have had a good deal of skill based on necessity, on years of practice, and on an intimate knowledge of the nature of different stones. For each stone has its own qualities, which vary further depending on whether the stone is hot or cold, wet or dry.

The Acheulean Industry

Despite all the variations in techniques and materials, there are still only two basic categories of lithic tools: core tools and flake tools. To make a core tool, take a lump of stone and knock chips from it until it has the desired size and shape; the core of stone that remains is the tool. A flake tool, as its name implies, typically is a chip struck from a core. It may be large or small, and its shape may vary, depending on the shape of the core from which it was struck. It may be used as it is, or it may itself be further flaked or chipped, somewhat in the manner of a core tool. In any event, the flake itself, and not the core from which it was struck, is the tool, and it can be very sharp.

The Acheulean industry is noted for its use of a prepared core in the production of its characteristic implement, the **biface,** a hand ax whose cutting edge has been flaked carefully on both sides to make it straighter and sharper than the primitive Oldowan chopper. This may seem like an awfully small improvement, but it was a fundamental

Biface a stone tool in which the edge is created by convergent flaking from two surfaces to produce a sharp cutting edge.

one and made possible much more efficient tools. The purpose of the two-sided, or bifacial, technique was to change the shape of the core from essentially round to flattish, for only with a flat stone can one get a decent cutting edge. The first step in making an Acheulean hand ax was to rough out the core until it had somewhat the shape of a turtle shell, thickest in the middle and thinning to a coarse edge all around. This edge could then be trimmed with more delicate little scallops of flaking (Figure 9.10). The cutting surfaces thus produced were longer, straighter, and considerably keener than those of any Oldowan chopper.

During the Acheulean period different kinds of hammers came into use. In earlier times, it appears, the toolmaker knocked flakes from the stone core with another piece of stone. The hard shock of rock on rock tended to leave deep, irregular scars and wavy

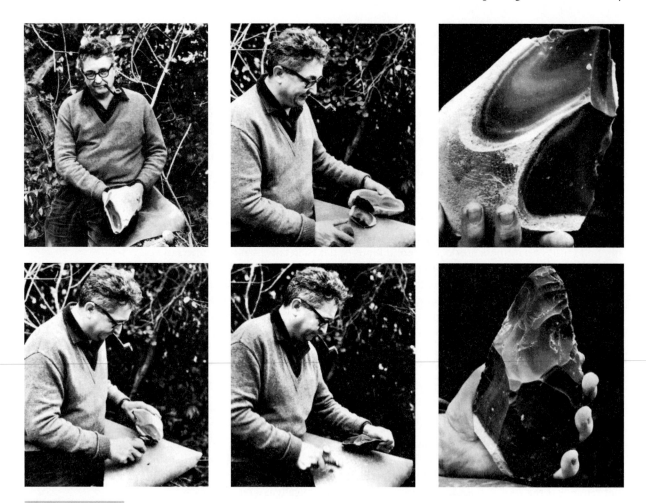

Figure 9.10

Making a hand ax is more difficult than making a chopping tool, as shown by these photographs of Francois Bordes. Having knocked the end off a large flint nodule, Bordes has prepared a striking platform (upper left). Using a hammer stone, he proceeds to strike off several large flakes, roughing out the general shape (upper center, upper right, and lower left). He then switches to an antler hammer, working both sides of the tool to thin out and retouch the edge (lower center). The final product, with long, straight, sharp edges (lower right), is one of the tools used for thousands of years by *Homo erectus* and *Homo heidelbergensis*.

cutting edges. But a wood or bone hammer, being softer, gave its user much greater control over flaking. Such implements left shallower, cleaner scars on the core and produced sharper and straighter cutting edges. In time, the use of stone was pretty much restricted to the preliminary rough shaping of a hand ax, and all the fine work around the edges was done with wood, antler, and bone.

Acheulean hand axes usually were pear-shaped or pointed and were somewhat larger than chopping tools. Some have been recovered that were more than 2 feet (0.6 meters) long and weighed more than twenty-five pounds (eleven kilograms). Obviously these were far too heavy and cumbersome to have been used for the kind of cutting and scraping that the smaller ones were designed for. One suggestion is that they may have been fitted to traps, set to fall and split the skulls of animals.

Another type of implement that appears for the first time in the Acheulean industry is the cleaver. A cleaver had a straight cutting edge at one end and actually looked much more like a modern ax head than the pointed hand axes did (see Figure 9.9 on page 247). It was probably used for heavy chopping or for hacking through the joints of large animals.

The Movius Line

As noted earlier, Acheulean tools originated in Africa between 1.7 and 1.4 million years ago. They were then produced continuously (along with a few Oldowan choppers and flakes) throughout *Homo erectus*'s long African residency and beyond, finally disappearing about 200,000 years BP. Acheulean tools were being made in the Middle East by 1.0 mya, as shown at the site of Ubeidiya in Israel; they were present in Europe as early as 500,000 to 780,000 years BP, and in northeastern Pakistan by 400,000 to 730,000 years BP. Several later sites in Africa and Europe show that the Acheulean tradition survived *Homo erectus* in some areas and was continued for a time by their descendants. Generally, Acheulean tools from sites clearly older than 400,000 to 500,000 years BP are attributed to *Homo erectus*, even in the absence of confirming fossils. At several important Acheulean sites, however, the toolmakers' species identity remains ambiguous because the sites lack hominid fossils and they date to a period when *Homo erectus* and *Homo heidelbergensis* overlapped in time. Examples of Acheulean assemblages that could have been produced by either late *H. erectus* or *Homo heidelbergensis* include Africa's Kalambo Falls; Torralba and Ambrona in Spain; Abbeville, St. Acheul, and Terra Amata in France; and Hoxne in England (Figure 9.4, page 237).

Wherever they are found, Acheulean hand axes and cleavers generally are interpreted as implements for processing animal carcasses. True, the cleavers could have been used to chop and shape wood; but according to archaeologists Kathy Schick and Nicholas Toth (1993), the wear pattern on cleaver bits is more suggestive of use on soft material, such as hides and meat. Schick and Toth believe that Acheulean tools represent an adaptation for "habitual and systematic butchery, [and] especially the dismembering of large animal carcasses" (Schick and Toth, 1993: 260), as *Homo erectus* experienced a strong dietary shift toward more meat consumption. Schick and Toth leave unanswered the question of whether meat was obtained primarily by scavenging or by hunting.

You may have noticed that no sites in China or Southeast Asia are included in the inventory of Acheulean locales. In fact, there is strong evidence that Acheulean tools were never produced in much of the Far East. As first pointed out in 1948 by Hallam Movius (then of Harvard University), Acheulean sites are common in Africa, the Middle East, Europe, and much of western Asia, but they are strangely absent in far eastern and southeastern Asia. The line dividing the Old World into Acheulean and non-Acheulean regions became known as the **Movius line** (Figure 9.11). Hand-ax cultures flourished to the west and south of the line, but in the east only choppers and flake tools were found. Today we know the actual situation wasn't quite as clear as first described. There are a few examples of crude hand axes from sites in South Korea and China, although nothing that is clearly Acheulean. Also, there are some African and European sites contemporaneous with the Acheulean that produced only chopper and flake assemblages.

But why were there no Acheulean hand-ax cultures in the eastern extremes of Asia? Traditionally this has been a hard question to answer. Researchers believed until quite recently that *Homo erectus*'s departure from Africa postdated the invention of Acheulean tools by some 400,000 years. If *Homo erectus* left Africa with Acheulean technology, why didn't the tradition arrive in eastern Asia? Was it discarded or forgotten along the way? The revised dates from Java help solve this riddle somewhat, because they place *Homo erectus* in Southeast Asia at least 100,000 years *before* the earliest possible advent of the Acheulean in Africa (Swisher et al., 1994). It thus appears that even if, as traditionally thought, *Homo erectus* turns out to be a native African species that spread to Asia, its initial migration certainly predated the development of Acheulean tools. Thus, a chronological barrier might have prevented the introduction of Acheulean technology to eastern Asia.

Schick and Toth (1993) have listed several other possible explanations for the absence of the Acheulean tradition from eastern Asia. Perhaps it was due to a paucity of suitable raw stone; coarse quartz is common in the East, but fine-grained flints, cherts, and lavas are rare. This distribution of raw materials would lend itself to the production of Oldowan choppers, but not to bifacial hand axes requiring extensive chipping. Alternatively, the absence of the Acheulean tools may be related to different functional requirements in Asia compared to the West. If the Acheulean developed as an adaptation for meat processing by African hunters-and-gatherers operating in open country, it may have been distinctly less useful in the closed and forested habitats of Asia, where large prey animals were probably less common and vegetable foods easier to harvest.

Biodegradable Tools

Certainly the most intriguing of the explanations offered for the "missing Acheulean" is the suggestion by anthropologist Geoffrey Pope (1989, 1993) and others that in far eastern and southeastern Asia, bamboo tools were used in place of stone implements to perform a variety of tasks. According to Pope, many useful tools such as cooking and storage containers, projectile points, and knives can be made from bamboo. When a bamboo stalk is split, it produces razor-sharp "stick knives" that can be used to butcher animals or perform other hacking and scraping jobs. Such bamboo utensils are still used in some parts of the world today; and, as Pope has pointed out, the natural distribution of bamboo coincides closely with those Asian areas that lack Acheulean tools (Figure 9.11). Pope's conclusions remind us that *Homo erectus*, like its ancestors, almost certainly used a variety of biodegradable tools (whether bamboo or some other material) of which we have no evidence. Such tools would always have been of great importance, and their development could have been of as great value to the evolving hominids as was their stone industry.

We can conclude, therefore, that although the Acheulean tradition with its hand axes and cleavers was an important lithic advance by *Homo erectus* over older technologies, it constituted only one of several adaptive patterns used by the species. Clever and behaviorally flexible, *Homo erectus* was capable of adjusting its material culture to the local resources and functional requirements. Nonetheless, the Acheulean tradition clearly reflected significant cognitive progress by *Homo erectus* people over their evo-

Movius line geographic dividing line between the Acheulean tradition in the West and non-Acheulean lithic traditions in eastern and southeastern Asia.

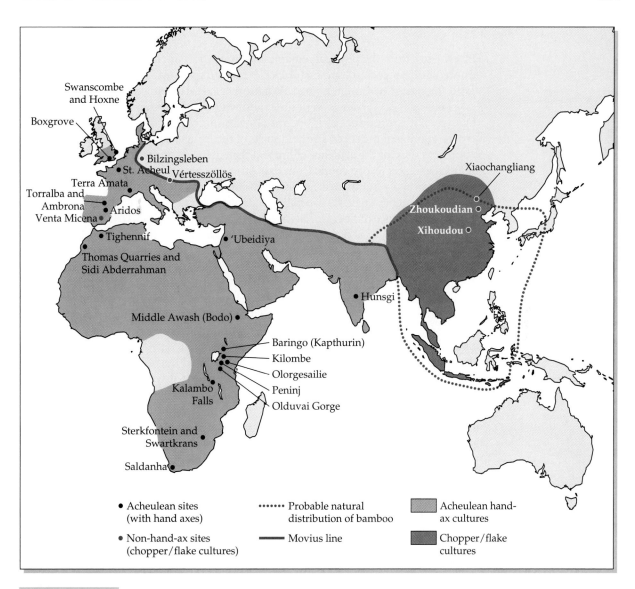

Figure 9.11

The "Movius line" divides the world of *Homo erectus* and its immediate descendants into Acheulean hand-ax cultures to the west and chopper/flake cultures to the east. Note that in eastern and southeastern Asia, the absence of hand-ax cultures coincides closely with the presence of bamboo.

lutionary predecessors. As American anthropologist A. J. Jelinek remarked, Acheulean tools were the first "fully conceived implements whose final form is regularly patterned and in no way suggested by the shape or exterior texture of the stone from which they were made. This is certainly a significant step in conceptualization" (1977: 29). Interestingly, once in existence, the Acheulean tradition showed very little overall change during perhaps 1.5 million years. Harvard's William Howells (1993) has referred to this lack of change as a "general stagnation" in material culture, and he has attributed it to a long period of stasis in intelligence and communication skills—a stasis that apparently was interrupted only by the evolution of *Homo heidelbergensis*.

Fire

The evidence from the physical remains and stone tools of *Homo erectus* shows us that this was a widespread and successful species that survived throughout much of the Old World for nearly two million years. What other adaptations does the archaeological record reveal? The answer is, very little; and where such evidence exists, we often do not know if it is a product of *H. erectus* or of its successors.

The coming of the successive cold spells of the ice ages suggests that we should look to northern sites for the evidence of fire and shelter. In fact the earliest evidence of fire in the archaeological record comes from East Africa (Koobi Fora) and dates from 1.6 to 1.4 million years ago—but there is no clear association with any hominid, and it seems that the evidence merely suggests naturally occurring bush fires; that is, there is no hearth. The earliest evidence of fire associated with a hearth and stone tools comes from Menez-Dregan in France and is dated 465,000 to 380,000 BP. At the sites of Torralba and Ambrona in Spain, there also is extensive evidence of both fire and human activity; but again natural fire seems the more likely explanation, as there are no hearths and charcoal is scattered widely. There are recognized hearths at Terra Amata in southern France dated 300,000 BP, but we do not know which hominid species created them.

One of the most impressive sites is that of Vértesszöllös in Hungary, where several small hearths have been excavated together with burnt bones and an industry of Oldowan choppers together with human skull fragments, all dated to 475,000–250,000 BP. Finally there is evidence of the use of fire (charcoal and burnt bone) in the great cave at Zhoukoudian; but although we do know for sure that it was occupied—if intermittently—by *H. erectus,* the dates could be anytime between 500,000 and 230,000 BP. On the basis of what we know at present, there is little reason to believe that fire was an essential adaptation in the dispersion northwards of *H. erectus*. Common sense tells us, however, that in the cooler periods of *H. erectus*'s tenancy of north temperate regions, fire would have been a very valuable, if not essential, adaptation. We should not underestimate the capabilities of *H. erectus*—especially in the species' later years—merely because reliable and associated archaeological evidence of hearths is lacking at the present time.

Shelter

The evidence for shelters and cave dwelling is less convincing. We know that at Zhoukoudian the cave was occupied intermittently by *Homo erectus,* cave bears, and hyenas. There is no reason to doubt that *H. erectus* groups would have occupied caves wherever they could do so, because caves offered invaluable shelter, especially in the higher latitudes. The earliest evidence of artificial shelters comes again from the site of Terra Amata, which may not have been an *H. erectus* site. Here we find evidence of postholes, indicating the presence of several oval huts measuring about fifteen by forty feet (de Lumley, 1969). The hut roofs appear to have been supported by two or more posts, and the walls to have been made of saplings and branches. Such huts are made to this day by some hunter-gatherer people. With a date of 400,000–300,000 BP, this site suggests a beginning of architectural knowledge that may or may not have been shared by the later generations of *Homo erectus*.

Was Homo erectus a Hunter?

Early discoveries of *Homo erectus* fossils in association with stone tools and animal bones suggested a hunting-and-gathering way of life—an interpretation that anthropologists eagerly embraced. The *Homo erectus* inhabitants of Zhoukoudian in China were described as deer hunters who consumed (cooked?) meals that combined venison with local plant products such as hackberries. At Torralba and Ambrona in Spain, the archaeological evidence—primarily the presence of Acheulean tools—was believed to indicate that *Homo erectus* hunters had systematically killed and butchered elephants on the spot, possibly after driving them into a marshy area by using fire. And in Africa, the Olorgesailie site was interpreted as showing that *Homo erectus* hunters occasionally preyed on fellow primates, including giant gelada baboons. These bits of data were combined into an elaborate picture of the society and lifestyle of *Homo erectus* that generally tended to portray these Plio–Pleistocene hominids as an early version of modern human hunters-and-gatherers.

This picture of *Homo erectus* as a hunter-and-gatherer has come under intense criticism (Binford and Ho, 1985; Binford and Stone, 1986). For example, Lewis Binford and his colleagues have reexamined the material from the late *H. erectus* site of Zhoukoudian and concluded that there is very little *conclusive* evidence of systematic hunting. Comparisons of the Zhoukoudian animal bones with faunal remains from both carnivore (especially hyena) dens and undoubted hunting sites (such as the 105,000-year-old European site of Combe Grenal) convinced Binford that the Chinese assemblage was primarily the result of animal activity rather than hunting-and-gathering. A few of the deer and horse bones at Zhoukoudian showed cut marks from stone tools that overlay gnaw marks by carnivores, suggesting that *Homo erectus* was not above scavenging parts of a carnivore kill.

Although Binford and his coworkers acknowledged that *Homo erectus* certainly used the Zhoukoudian cave site, they were forced to conclude that at Zhoukoudian "all the positive evidence is consistent with what is believed to be evidence for hominid scavenging [and] there are *no positive indicators* of hunting in the available data" (Binford and Stone, 1986: 468; italics in the original). In a similar fashion, archaeologist Richard Klein (1989) has shown that the bone and stone assemblages at Torralba and Ambrona fail to provide conclusive proof of *Homo erectus* hunting. Both sites could be nothing more than lakeside or streamside assemblages produced by regular animal use for feeding and drinking, predation by carnivores, and scavenging by Acheulean tool-producing people. At both sites, the archaeological evidence for scavenging by hominids is much more convincing than is that for actual hunting.

Evidence for Meat

Nevertheless, there are at least two sorts of evidence showing that *Homo erectus* people were consuming so much more meat than their evolutionary predecessors that hunting was almost certainly a regular subsistence pattern. First, there is the matter of their advance in stone-tool technology. As noted earlier, Acheulean hand axes and cleavers probably were used primarily for dismembering and butchering large animal carcasses. This conclusion is based on studies of the artifacts' design and wear patterns, as well as on experimental studies of how they could have been used most effectively. It appears, therefore, that the development of the Acheulean tradition is a clear indicator of a distinct shift toward greater reliance on meat by *Homo erectus*.

The second sort of evidence of hunting by *Homo erectus* involves anatomy; specifically, the size and shape of these early people. *Homo erectus* was a species of big individuals, comparable to the top 17 percent of modern human populations in height and within the modern range with regard to weight (Walker, 1993a). Compared to early *Homo* (*H. habilis* and *H. rudolfensis*), *Homo erectus* showed an increase in body size of about one-third—which is difficult to explain simply as the result of increased scavenging activities.

Brain and Belly

As for *Homo erectus*'s body shape, two aspects concern us: the enormous enlargement of the brain and the coincidental reduction of the gastrointestinal tract. As noted earlier, *Homo erectus* (including Ngandong and Sambungmacan) showed a 27 to 62 percent increase in brain size compared to the two species of early *Homo*. Furthermore, as shown by analyses of the Nariokotome skeleton, *Homo erectus* probably was the first hominid type with a barrel-shaped thorax and a distinct waist, similar to modern human anatomy (Jellema et al., 1993). Earlier species apparently possessed funnel-shaped rib cages and potbellies, like living apes. This modification in the shape of the *H. erectus* thorax suggests significant reduction in the size of the gastrointestinal tract.

Both brains and intestines are metabolically expensive organs: Brains have a mass-specific (i.e., organ or part-specific) metabolic rate about 9 times higher than the average mass-specific rate for the body as a whole, and the intestines and liver together have a mass-specific rate that is 9.8 times higher than the bodily average (Table 9.3). Researchers Leslie Aiello and Peter Wheeler (1995) believe there were only two ways to accommodate the increased energy demands of the big brain of *Homo erectus*: Either raise the overall basal metabolism rate of the body or compensate for brain growth by reducing the size of some other metabolically expensive organ(s). All indications are that our forebears evolved down the second path. Modern humans show a standard basal metabolism rate for mammals our size, but we have much bigger brains and smaller gastrointestinal tracts than expected (Figure 9.12). Furthermore, the energy savings realized by reducing the digestive system are approximately the same as the added costs of a larger brain. Beginning with *Homo erectus*, humans experienced an evolutionary trade-off of intestines for brains.

Reducing the digestive system has dietary implications, of course, which brings us back to the question of *Homo erectus*'s subsistence patterns. Animals that depend on poor-quality (low-energy) and hard-to-digest diets (folivores and, to a lesser extent, frugivores) consume large quantities of food and then process it slowly in their large stomachs and intestines. More carnivorous animals, on the other hand, eating higher-

Table 9.3

Mass-Specific Organ Metabolic Rates in Humans[a]	
Organ	Metabolic Rate in Watts per Kilogram
Brain	11.2
Heart	32.2
Kidney	23.3
Liver and gastrointestinal tract	12.2
Skeletal muscle	0.5
Lung	6.7
Skin	0.3
Whole body	1.25

[a]Mass-specific organ metabolic rates are those for a 143-pound (65-kilogram) human male with a bodily basal metabolic rate (BMR) of 90.6 watts.

Source: Data from Aschoff et al., 1971, as reported by Aiello and Wheeler, 1995.

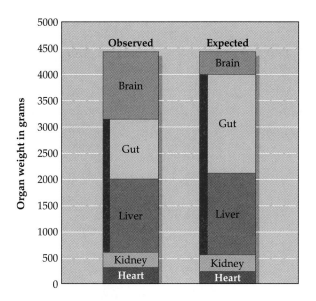

Figure 9.12

The right-hand column shows the organ weights predicted (expected) for a 143-pound (65-kilogram) human with typical primate organ sizes. The left-hand column shows the actual (observed) organ weights found in 65-kilogram modern people. The modern human brain is almost three times larger than expected, while the gut is 40 percent smaller.

Source: From Aiello and Wheeler, 1995.

quality (higher-energy) and more digestible diets, need both less food and smaller digestive organs. The anatomical evidence places *Homo erectus* in the latter group. By becoming active and effective hunters, *Homo erectus* people were able to tap into an extremely energy-rich food source. Their meat-intensive diet required less digestive effort than was true for earlier hominids—thus allowing gastrointestinal organ reduction—and simultaneously provided plenty of energy for their expanding brains. As discussed in Chapter 8, several factors have been suggested as triggers for brain expansion among hominids, with the pressures for increased social intelligence and subsistence intelligence being high on the list. The evolution of a hunting-and-gathering lifestyle by *Homo erectus* would have simultaneously relaxed the metabolic constraints on brain growth and intensified the selective pressure for further brain expansion.

The Significance of Culture

Homo erectus evolved sometime in the late Pliocene, and the species spread to extreme southeastern Asia from eastern Africa by 1.8 million years ago. What enabled this phenomenal geographic spread? Was it increased intelligence? Certainly this must have played a part, as *Homo erectus* showed a significant jump in overall brain size compared to early *Homo*. But precisely how increased intelligence aided the species' spread and longevity is unclear.

But what of culture? Surely there were key cultural advances that set *Homo erectus* apart from early *Homo* and enabled its success. Unfortunately, we are limited primarily to statements about the material culture of *H. erectus;* that is, about their tools and

Table 9.4

A Distribution of the Technological and Subsistence Innovations of *Homo erectus* to Early, Middle, and Late Stages of the Species' Span[a]		
Stage	**Bracketing Dates (million years BP)**	**Technological or Subsistence Innovation**
Early *Homo erectus*	1.9–1.2	Acheulean industry (Oldowan continues as well). Hunting-and-gathering lifestyle likely (more meat).
Middle *Homo erectus*	1.2–0.6	No clear innovations. Acheulean continues west of Movius line, Oldowan to the east.
Late *Homo erectus*	0.6–0.03	Shelters (possibly). Control and use of fire (possibly).

[a] Stages were arbitrarily defined as approximately 600,000-year periods. Ngandong and Sambungmacan are excluded.

other artifacts. Social and behavioral traits, such as group composition, level of social organization, territoriality, and cooperation in (and/or division of) subsistence activities, do not fossilize and can only be inferred. And inferred cultural advances must be considered only as hypotheses for investigation, not as reliable explanations.

As summarized in Table 9.4, only one technological advance can be attributed undeniably to *Homo erectus*, and that is the early development of the Acheulean lithic tradition with its bifacial tools, particularly hand axes and cleavers. As discussed, this innovation in stone-tool technology probably signaled a shift from scavenging-and-gathering to hunting-and-gathering—an extremely important change in subsistence patterns that helped catapult *Homo erectus* to the top of the Plio–Pleistocene food chain and enabled intense exploitation of energy and nutrient-rich animal products. Other cultural innovations frequently attributed to *Homo erectus*, such as shelter construction and the control and use of fire, probably came so near the end of the species' life span that many researchers feel they are better assigned to later humans, most likely *Homo heidelbergensis*. But the lithic and subsistence data are of little help in our understanding of the Old World spread of *Homo erectus* because Acheulean tools and hunting-and-gathering apparently both postdate hominines' initial exodus from Africa. The very earliest dates given for Acheulean technology are 1.7 million years ago, and many archaeologists prefer 1.5 to 1.4 mya. In view of the fact that *Homo erectus* people (or their ancestors?) *had* to have left Africa before 1.8 million years BP, the conclusion seems inescapable that they did so as *scavengers* and gatherers, and with tools no more complex than Oldowan choppers and flakes. That conclusion makes their successful colonization of Eurasia all the more impressive.

Summary

Compared to its evolutionary predecessors, *Homo erectus* had achieved considerable modernity in its anatomy. These people were as tall and as heavy as modern humans, and they showed modern limb proportions. Average brain size had increased to more than 900 cubic centimeters, but these big brains were still contained in rather primitive-looking skulls that were long, low-vaulted, and widest at the base. Despite their large

Timeline: *Homo erectus*

Discoveries of *Homo erectus* have been made throughout the Old World since the first Java finds in 1891. *Homo erectus*'s predecessors, early *Homo,* were intermediates between the ancestral *Australopithecus* and themselves.

HOLOCENE	
10,000	
PLEISTOCENE	
1.6 MILLION	
Earliest Oldowan tools at Omo and Hadar	
PLIOCENE	
5 MILLION	
Earliest australopithecines	
10 MILLION	
15 MILLION	
MIOCENE	
Proconsul	
20 MILLION	
25 MILLION	
OLIGOCENE	
Apidium, Parapithecus, and *Aegyptopithecus*	

CENOZOIC

YEARS AD	DISCOVERIES
1994—	*H. erectus* at Ceprano
1991—	*H. erectus* at Dmanisi
1984—	*H. erectus* skeleton found at Nariokotome, west of Lake Turkana
1975—	*H. erectus* at Koobi Fora
1960—	*H. erectus* at Olduvai
1955—	*H. erectus* at Ternifine
1953—	Piltdown finds shown to be a hoax
1936—	New finds in Java
1929—	First skull of *Sinanthropus*
1921—	Excavation begins at Zhoukoudian
1894—	Dubois's treatise on *Pithecanthropus*
1891—	Dubois discovers *Pithecanthropus* skull in Java

YEARS BP	FOSSIL AND BEHAVIORS	LITHIC AGES
53,000–27,000—	Ngandong and Sambungmacan fossils	Upper Paleolithic (40,000 BP)
100,000—		
200,000—		Middle Paleolithic (200,000 BP)
300,000—	Regular use of fire; oldest shelters	
400,000—	*H. erectus* at Zhoukoudian, China	
500,000—		Lower Paleolithic
600,000—		
700,000—	*H. erectus* at Gongwangling (Lantian), China and Ceprano, Italy	
800,000—		
900,000—	*H. erectus* at Trinil, Java	
1 million—		
1.1 million—		
1.2 million—		
1.3 million—		
1.4 million—		
1.5 million—	Nariokotome boy	
1.6 million—	Beginnings of Acheulean tradition and beginnings of hunting-and-gathering lifestyle	
1.7 million—		
1.8 million—	*H. erectus* in Africa, the Caucasus, and Java	
1.9 million—	Hominids at Longgupo Cave, China	
2 million—	Hominids spread out of Africa (?)	

brains, however, there seems to be little anatomical evidence that *Homo erectus* had spoken language. *Homo erectus* survived for more than one and a half million years, and most populations seem to have gone extinct about 300,000 to 200,000 years ago. If one includes Ngandong and Sambungmacan as relict populations of the species, however, its final disappearance was as recent as 53,000 to 27,000 years BP.

Homo erectus has been found in southern Europe and Asia as well as in Africa. It is believed to be the first hominid species to disperse out of Africa. In Africa *H. erectus* is accompanied by the Acheulean industry; in eastern Asia we find Oldowan choppers only, though it is believed that the use of bamboo and some other biodegradable tools may have characterized this species. Although we have only limited evidence of cultural advances, *Homo erectus* did manage eventually to penetrate into the cooler temperate regions of the Old World. *H. erectus* were certainly scavengers and ate meat, and we believe, but do not know for certain, that they hunted. Toward the end of their time span, they may have begun using fire as well as building shelters; their cultural advances were critical factors in their survival.

Review Questions

1. What were the anatomical differences between *Homo erectus* and early *Homo*? How did *Homo erectus* differ anatomically from modern humans?

2. Where did *Homo erectus* first evolve? When did it go extinct, and did it leave any descendants? Is there any evidence of an overlap in time between *H. erectus* and modern humans?

3. What were the innovations in material culture attributed to *Homo erectus*? Which ones are we sure of, and which are we not? Where do these innovations fall within the species' time span?

4. What evidence is there that *Homo erectus* had language? How do you think the species communicated? How would a lack of modern language have affected the species' potential for geographic spread?

5. How do you feel about referring to *Homo erectus* individuals as "people" and "early humans"? What criteria do you think must be met before a hominid is labeled a "human"?

6. Why have so few Acheulean hand axes been found in eastern and southeastern Asia? Suggest as many explanations as you can for their absence.

7. What were the probable relationships among brain size, digestive system size, and diet of *Homo erectus*? How might brain enlargement have been both the result of evolutionary pressures and the trigger for further evolution?

Suggested Further Reading

Pope, G. G. "Bamboo and Human Evolution." *Natural History,* 98, 1989.
Rightmire, G. P. *The Evolution of Homo erectus.* Cambridge University Press, 1990.
Schick, K., and N. Toth. *Making Silent Stones Speak.* Simon & Schuster, 1993.
Theunissen, B. *Eugene Dubois and the Ape-Man from Java.* Kluwer, 1989.
Walker, A., and P. Shipman. *The Wisdom of Bones: In Search of Human Origins.* Knopf, 1996.

Internet Resources

 Conveniently access these and other links via our web site at **http://www.ablongman/anthro.**

Georgian *Homo erectus* Published
http://www.archaeology.org/0001/newsbriefs/georgia.html
Information about the hominid skull from Dmanisi, Republic of Georgia.

Homo erectus
http://daphne.palomar.edu/homo/homo_2.htm
Basic information about the discovery, anatomy, and evolutionary relations of *Homo erectus*.

Peter Brown's Australian and Asian Palaeoanthropology
http://www~personal.une.edu.au/~pbrown3/palaeo.html
An introduction to hominid fossils from the Far East, with lots of good skull photos.

Seafaring *Homo erectus*
http://www.utad.pt/~origins/erectus.htm
A report on *Homo erectus* discoveries in Indonesia and on the species' apparent potential as seafarers.

The African Emergence and Early Asian Dispersal of the Genus *Homo*
http://www.sigmaxi.org/amsci/articles/96articles/Larick.html
An interesting and important paper about the fossils—including those from Longgupo Cave in China—that have some paleoanthropologists questioning whether *Homo erectus* was the first hominid to expand its range out of Africa.

The Fossil Evidence for Human Evolution in China
http://www.cruzio.com/~cscp/index.htm
This site contains an extensive catalogue of Chinese human fossils, useful photos and maps, and links to other interesting sites about evolution.

Useful Search Terms:
Acheulean tools
hand axes
Homo erectus
Homo ergaster
Pithecanthropus
Sinanthropus

chapter 10

Middle to Late
Pleistocene Homo

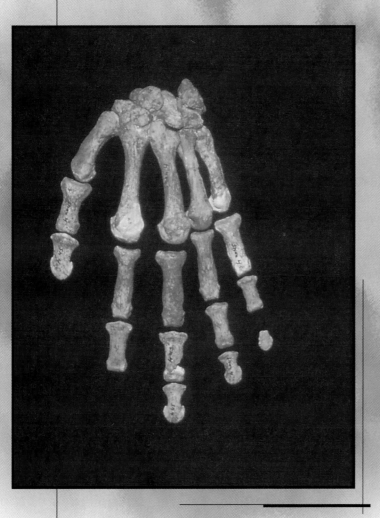

Overview

Deciphering the hominid fossil record from the middle to late Pleistocene is quite difficult at present. The human types that came after *Homo erectus* were geographically widespread and anatomically variable; as a consequence, paleoanthropologists disagree

Mini-Timeline: Middle to Late Pleistocene Fossil Discoveries and Evolutionary Events

Date or Age

(A) Date (years AD)	Fossil Discoveries
1997	Genetic evidence suggests Neandertals were a distinct species
1976–1997	*H. heidelbergensis* and *H. neanderthalensis* fossils found at Atapuerca
1978	Dali skull discovered in northern China
1976	Bodo fossil found in Ethiopia
1921	Kabwe skull found in Zambia
1907	Mauer jaw (type specimen: *H. heidelbergensis*) found in Germany
1913	Boule's monograph on the La Chapelle Neandertal remains
1848–1856	Neandertal discoveries in Gibraltar and Germany

(B) Age (years BP)	Evolutionary Events
30,000	Approximate date of Neandertals' extinction; last known Neandertals in southern Spain
34,000	Carved bone and ivory ornaments among late Neandertals
50,000	Shanidar flower burial
82,000–43,000	Bone flutes possibly carved by Neandertals
90,000–30,000	Period of the classic Neandertals
250,000	Approximate beginning of the Middle Paleolithic
300,000–200,000	Levallois flaking technique invented
300,000	Oldest Neandertals at Sima de los Huesos (Atapuerca)
400,000	Oldest evidence for wooden spears (attributed to *H. heidelbergensis*)
800,000	Oldest *Homo heidelbergensis* at Gran Dolina (Atapuerca)

on the number of post-*erectus* species and their relations to one another. Although many of us currently recognize three such species—*Homo heidelbergensis,* **Homo neanderthalensis,** and *Homo sapiens*—no two experts agree on the exact allocation of fossils to these taxa. Some researchers also argue that additional post-*erectus* species should be recognized. Nonetheless, despite the confusion, a reasonable (but clearly provisional) interpretation of the later stages of hominid evolution has *Homo erectus* as the immediate ancestor of *H. heidelbergensis,* who, in turn, gave rise (at different times and in different places) to both the Neandertals (*H. neanderthalensis*) and modern *Homo sapiens.* The present chapter utilizes this evolutionary scheme as it describes the two premodern but post-*erectus* species, *Homo heidelbergensis* and the Neandertals.

Homo heidelbergensis and the Neandertals (henceforth collectively referred to as "archaic humans") differed from their *Homo erectus* forebears in a number of significant ways. Not only were they considerably brainier, but in addition—and perhaps as a consequence—they showed several important cultural advances. This chapter describes the cultural innovations that allowed these archaic people to inhabit not only the hospitable tropics and subtropics of the Old World, but also the considerably more challenging **periglacial** northern regions.

> Check our web site for additional information, photos, drawings, maps, and animations on topics in this chapter.

Homo heidelbergensis

By about 800,000 BP, humans who were larger-brained and smaller-jawed than *Homo erectus* had evolved in Africa or western Eurasia. It was not long before similar humans were living in present-day Spain, Germany, and England; and by perhaps 600,000 years ago they could be found in eastern Asia as well (see Figure 10.1). These various populations are grouped here into the species *Homo heidelbergensis*—a taxon thought by many researchers to be ancestral (at different times and in different places) both to the Neandertals and to *Homo sapiens.* A partial record of *H. heidelbergensis* sites is given in Table 10.1.

Homo neanderthalensis a *species* of humans that inhabited Europe and the Middle East from about 300,000 to 30,000 BP. Descended from *Homo heidelbergensis,* the species' common name is usually spelled Neandertal.

Periglacial bordering a glacial region

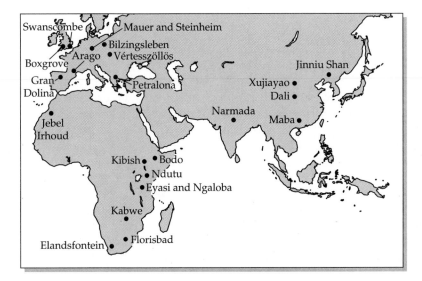

Figure 10.1

Fossils of *Homo heidelbergensis* have been found in Africa, Asia, and Europe. This map shows only a sample of all known sites.

Table 10.1

A Partial Record of *Homo heidelbergensis* Sites		
Geographic Area	**Site**	**Age (years BP)**
Africa	Singa (Sudan)	97,000
	Jebel Irhoud	125,000–90,000
	Eyasi	130,000–35,000(?)
	Omo Kibish 2	130,000(?)
	Ngaloba (LH18)	150,000–125,000
	Kabwe	250,000–130,000
	Florisbad	260,000
	Elansfontein	350,000–130,000
	Ndutu	400,000–200,000
	Bodo	600,000
Asia	Xujiayao	125,000–100,000
	Narmada	150,000
	Maba	150,000
	Dali	300,000–200,000
	Jinniu Shan	300,000–200,000
	Diring Yuriakh(?)	300,000
	Yunxian	600,000(?)
Europe	Vértessöllös	210,000
	Steinheim	250,000
	Swanscombe	250,000
	Bilzingsleben	340,000–230,000
	Petralona	400,000–200,000
	Arago	400,000
	Boxgrove	500,000
	Mauer	700,000–400,000
	Atapuerca (Gran Dolina, TD6)	800,000

African Fossils

In 1921, laborers mining lead and zinc ore in Zambia uncovered a skull and other human bones in a cave in a knoll called Broken Hill, which rose above plateau country just north of the Zambesi River, at a place called Kabwe. The presence of stone tools and extinct animal bones indicated considerable age, and indeed the skull currently is dated at 250,000 to 130,000 years BP. The fossil human from Kabwe had a large, heavy skull (1,285 cubic centimeters), a heavy bar of bone over the eyes, and a receding forehead and was given the name **Rhodesian Man** (Figure 10.2).

Further discoveries followed. A cranium found in 1953 at Elandsfontein, South Africa, on an open site near Saldanha Bay has turned out to be very similar to the Kabwe skull, though less complete. It is probably about the same age, though it may be older, possibly dating to 350,000 years BP. In 1973 a crushed human skull was found near Lake Ndutu in Tanzania; it has turned out to be of the same general type but even older (400,000 to 200,000 years BP). A cranium found in 1976 at Bodo, Ethiopia, carried the African fossil record of *Homo heidelbergensis* all the way back to 600,000 years BP

Rhodesian Man the skeleton of an archaic human found at Kabwe in Zambia in 1921.

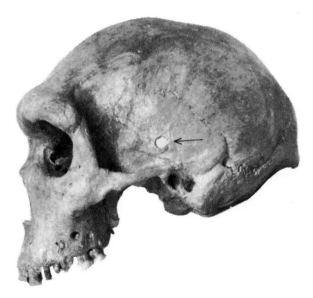

Figure 10.2
Homo heidelbergensis people flourished for 500,000 years in Africa. This skull from Kabwe, in Zambia, is exceptionally powerfully built. The hole in the temporal bone (arrow) was probably caused during life by a small tumor.

(Figure 10.3). Although discovered in association with Acheulean artifacts, the Bodo fossil has a much larger cranial capacity (1,300 cubic centimeters) than expected for *Homo erectus* and also shows a more modern skull shape. In particular, Bodo shares a number of facial traits with the Kabwe skull and with more modern humans (Rightmire, 1996).

Figure 10.3
The Bodo cranium is the oldest African *Homo heidelbergensis,* dating to 600,000 years BP.

Asian Fossils

Homo heidelbergensis remains, some quite ancient, have also been found in Asia. They include the fossil from the Narmada Valley, near Hoshangabad in central India, where Indian paleontologist Arun Sonakia made the first discovery of a Pleistocene hominid from the subcontinent (Kennedy, 1999). In 1982 Sonakia unearthed a heavy skullcap (without a jaw) from alluvial river deposits of the late middle Pleistocene epoch—probably in the region of 150,000 years BP. The skull is heavily built and reminiscent of the Beijing *Homo erectus* fossils; it also bears some resemblances to European forms of *H. erectus*. The Indian fossil is associated with hand axes, cleavers, scrapers of quartzite, and some small flint artifacts. Its considerable importance lies in the way it links Europe and China both geographically and anatomically.

China has produced several fossils of *Homo heidelbergensis,* including some with impressively early dates. From the site of Dali in north China, a nearly complete skull dating 300,000 to 200,000 years BP was discovered in 1978. The Dali fossil resembles *Homo erectus* in its long, low, thick-walled cranium and large brow ridges, but it seems more modern in the higher placement of maximum cranial width and reduced postorbital constriction. Furthermore, the midfacial dimensions of the Dali fossil seem most similar to certain *H. heidelbergensis* specimens from the West: Steinheim, Arago, and Jebel Irhoud (Conroy, 1997). With a cranial capacity of 1,120 cubic centimeters, Dali seems best classified as Chinese *Homo heidelbergensis,* as do fossil remains from the sites of Xujiayao (125,000 to 100,000 years BP), Maba (150,000 years BP), Jinniu Shan, and possibly Yunxian. The Jinniu Shan site has yielded a probable *Homo heidelbergensis* skull with an impressive cranial capacity of 1,390 cubic centimeters that dates from about 300,000 to 200,000 years ago. Yunxian has produced two crania that are even older—possibly as much as 600,000 years of age, according to recent paleomagnetic analysis; but the mixture of *erectus*-like and more modern traits makes these skulls hard to classify. The Yunxian skulls are tentatively included in *Homo heidelbergensis* pending further information.

New and tantalizing archaeological evidence suggests that the geographic range of *Homo heidelbergensis* may have extended as far as northern Siberia (Wilford, 1997a). In 1982 stone choppers and flakes were discovered by Russian archaeologists at the site of Diring Yuriakh, located on the Lena River south of the town of Yakutsk, some 1,500 miles (2,400 kilometers) north of Beijing, China, and 300 miles (480 kilometers) south of the Arctic Circle. No human fossils were found with the stone tools, but their thermoluminescence date of 300,000 years BP is comparable to the ages of the Jinniu Shan and Dali fossils, suggesting that the Siberian implements probably were made by *Homo heidelbergensis.* (Although late *Homo erectus* probably was still alive in Asia 300,000 years ago, it seems unlikely that this species produced the Diring Yuriakh tools, as it probably had not achieved the level of cultural sophistication necessary to survive the bitter Siberian winters.)

European Fossils

Several European sites have produced fossils of *Homo heidelbergensis,* including the oldest known remains of that taxon. In a 1907 discovery, quarry workers found a primitive-looking mandible at the site of Mauer near Heidelberg, Germany (Figure 10.1). This fossil was the first to carry the name *H. heidelbergensis* (given to it by the paleontologist Otto Schoetensack), and it has become the type specimen for the species. The **Mauer jaw** is between 700,000 and 400,000 years old and shows similarities both to its *Homo erectus* ancestors (in its overall robustness) and to *Homo sapiens* (in its molar size).

Mauer jaw *fossil* mandible found at Mauer in Germany in 1907 and named *Homo heidelbergensis.*

Interestingly, it shows few traits that anticipate the Neandertals except for certain details of the teeth.

Another interesting fossil was discovered in the mid-1930s in Thames River gravel deposits near the English village of Swanscombe. At that site a human skull was unearthed that was dated, by means of geologic information and faunal correlation, to approximately 250,000 years BP. The partial skull consists only of three bones: both parietals and the occipital—the face is missing. Its fragmentary condition makes the Swanscombe skull difficult to classify, and therefore the taxonomy is somewhat controversial.

A very similar skull—this time with a face—was discovered at Steinheim, Germany, in 1933. Approximately the same age as Swanscombe, the Steinheim fossil has a braincase that is more or less similar to the English specimen and that held a 1,100-cc brain. The Steinheim skull also shows rather heavy brows and a low forehead. Unfortunately, like Swanscombe, the Steinheim fossil is hard to classify. Both fossils are anatomically intermediate between *Homo erectus* and modern humans, and neither is clearly a Neandertal. Steinheim and Swanscombe are treated in this text as representatives of *Homo heidelbergensis,* although it is possible that they were early members of the Neandertal lineage.

The oldest hominid fossil known from England was excavated in 1993 at the site of Boxgrove in West Sussex (Figure 10.1). The fossil is a fragment of a massive left tibia, or shinbone, and is between 524,000 and 478,000 years old (roughly the same age as the Mauer jaw). Analyses of the bone suggest assignment to *Homo heidelbergensis.* Besides being the earliest evidence of hominid occupancy of the British Isles, the Boxgrove tibia is exciting because it is accompanied by Acheulean stone tools. As noted in Chapter 9, a critical absence of hominid fossils leaves the identity of the toolmakers uncertain at several Acheulean sites in Europe; particularly at sites that fall within the period of *Homo erectus–Homo heidelbergensis* overlap. At Boxgrove, however, it seems likely that a half million years ago *H. heidelbergensis* made and used Acheulean tools (Pitts and Roberts, 1998; Roberts et al., 1994). This discovery will no doubt have implications for interpreting other sites.

In 1960 the Greek site of Petralona (Figure 10.1) produced a large-brained (1,230-cc) skull that may be *Homo heidelbergensis.* Dating from approximately 400,000 to 200,000 years BP, the Petralona skull shares some features with its *Homo erectus* ancestors and others with the more modern specimen from Kabwe in Africa. Certain features of the Petralona face and braincase suggest links to the later Neandertals. Also resembling *Homo erectus* to some extent, but with a projected brain size that is too large and a date (210,000 years BP) that is too late, are some scrappy dental and cranial remains from Vértesszöllös in Hungary.

In 1971 a discovery was made of fossil humans from approximately 400,000 years BP. Henry and Marie-Antoinette de Lumley excavated a cave at Arago near Tautavel in the Pyrenees. Along with stone implements, the de Lumleys found the partial skull of a man about twenty years old and two partial jaws of other individuals. The man had a forward-jutting face, heavy brow ridges, a slanting forehead, and a braincase somewhat smaller than the modern average. The two jaws were massive and somewhat resembled the Mauer jaw of much greater antiquity; they seemed well suited to chewing coarse food. Altogether classified here as *Homo heidelbergensis,* the fragments appear to be more primitive in form—that is, closer to *Homo erectus*—than to the Swanscombe and Steinheim remains.

But of all the European specimens we are classifying here as *Homo heidelbergensis,* perhaps those from the Gran Dolina site in Spain's Atapuerca mountains are the most remarkable. Located just a short distance from the ancient Neandertal site of Sima de los Huesos (to be described later), the Gran Dolina cave site has produced the oldest known human fossils from Europe. From a deep level called the Aurora stratum, or TD6, researchers at Gran Dolina have recovered human fossils dated by paleomagnetism to more than 780,000 years of age (roughly 800,000 BP). Found in association with a pre-Acheulean chopper-and-flake tool assemblage, the TD6 fossils show smaller jaws and teeth than *Homo erectus;* a cranial capacity of more than 1,000 cubic centimeters; separated brow ridges; and, in at least one specimen—a juvenile designated ATD6–69—modern-looking midfacial features. Indeed, the facial features of ATD6–69, along with certain other cranial and dental traits, have convinced the Spanish team excavating the site that the TD6 materials constitute a new species of premodern humans. In May 1997 they named that species *Homo antecessor* (Bermudez de Castro et al., 1997; Carbonell et al., 1995). Initial reactions to the new species designation are mixed, however; many anthropologists prefer to keep the TD6 fossils in *Homo heidelbergensis,* at least for the time being. The argument to reject *H. antecessor* as a valid taxon revolves mainly around the danger of assuming that one juvenile's modern midfacial features accurately reflect the general condition of its population. The authors of this text agree that at present a conservative approach is best and support lumping the TD6 fossils into *Homo heidelbergensis.* Exciting things are happening at Gran Dolina, however, and future discoveries there may justify changing the taxonomy.

In summary, discoveries from Africa, Asia, and Europe indicate that by 800,000 to 600,000 years ago, *Homo erectus* had given rise to a more modern human type, *Homo heidelbergensis* (Rightmire, 1998b). The precise location of that transition is unclear at present, but Africa or western Eurasia seems most likely. After spreading widely across the Old World, *H. heidelbergensis* lasted until perhaps 100,000 years BP, and maybe even later.

The Anatomy of *Homo heidelbergensis*

Compared to their *Homo erectus* ancestors, *Homo heidelbergensis* people were modern in several points of anatomy (see Table 10.2 and Figure 10.4). Perhaps the most significant change was in their brain size, which now averaged 1,283 cubic centimeters—almost a 30 percent increase over the most inclusive *Homo erectus* average (compare Table 9.2). Increased brain size was accompanied by a rise in the height of the cranial vault (the

Table 10.2

Characteristics of *Homo heidelbergensis*	
Trait	***Homo heidelbergensis***
Height (sexes combined)	Essentially modern? 4.9–6.1 ft (150–185 cm)?
Weight (sexes combined)	Essentially modern? 110–165 lb (50–75 kg)?
Brain size (sexes combined)	1,283 cc mean (1,100–1,450 cc range)
Cranium	Compared to *Homo erectus:* smaller and separated brows; higher cranial vault; less prognathic face; incipient chin on some specimens; variability in degree of cranial base flexure
Dentition	Similar to *Homo erectus,* but with smaller teeth overall
Limbs	Modern arm and leg proportions; massive construction suggests a powerful body
Locomotion	Bipedalism
Distribution	Africa, Asia, Europe
Known dates	800,000–100,000(?) years BP

Homo antecessor proposed new *species* name for certain fossils from the site of Gran Dolina, Spain; *taxon* not recognized in this book.

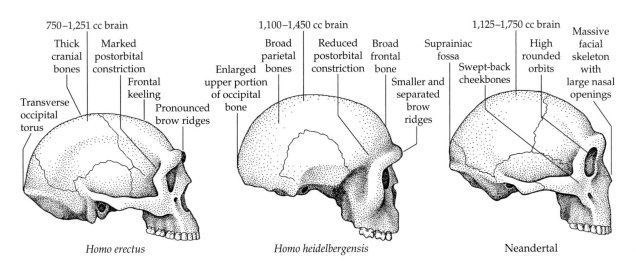

750–1,251 cc brain

Thick cranial bones

Marked postorbital constriction

Frontal keeling

Transverse occipital torus

Pronounced brow ridges

Homo erectus

1,100–1,450 cc brain

Broad parietal bones

Reduced postorbital constriction

Broad frontal bone

Suprainiac fossa

Enlarged upper portion of occipital bone

Smaller and separated brow ridges

Homo heidelbergensis

1,125–1,750 cc brain

Massive facial skeleton with large nasal openings

High rounded orbits

Swept-back cheekbones

Neandertal

Figure 10.4

Compared to *Homo erectus, Homo heidelbergensis*—represented here by the Steinheim fossil—and the Neandertals showed much larger brains and more modern cranial anatomies, but retained such primitive traits as relatively large brows. Several distinctive anatomical traits are listed for each species.

bones of which were still generally quite thick); also, brow size, facial prognathism, and tooth sizes all declined. Brows showed a change in shape from the straight, shelflike structures of *Homo erectus* to curved prominences above the separate eye sockets. Most *Homo heidelbergensis* individuals (e.g., the Mauer and Arago fossils) continued to lack a distinct chin, but some specimens do show incipient development of this feature. Equally variable is the degree of flexure of the cranial base (an important indicator of how the vocal apparatus was configured), with some specimens (e.g., the Kabwe skull) approaching the modern condition. Finally, *Homo heidelbergensis* faces were sometimes quite broad, with rather large noses (e.g., those from Bodo and Kabwe).

Few conclusions can be drawn about the postcranial skeleton of *Homo heidelbergensis* because of a paucity of relevant fossils. It seems likely that these people were essentially modern in their overall height and weight, but there are some tantalizing hints that they might have been much more powerfully built than modern humans. For example, the fragmentary tibia from Boxgrove, England, has very large midshaft dimensions and thick walls (Roberts et al., 1994). Similarly robust femoral and tibial fragments were found at Kabwe. Modern humans have apparently experienced a significant reduction in bodily robustness compared to their *H. heidelbergensis* forebears.

Not surprisingly, given the species' wide range and the likelihood of interpopulation differences in adaptations, *Homo heidelbergensis* shows not only temporal but geographic variability. Nonetheless, there appears to be enough internal consistency to consider it a valid taxon, at least until further discoveries.

Homo neanderthalensis

The present evidence suggests that within the confines of Europe, *H. heidelbergensis* gave rise to the even larger brained Neandertals around 300,000 years ago (Arsuaga et al., 1993, 1997a, 1997b). And some 100,000 to 170,000 years later in Africa, a different

Homo heidelbergensis population apparently evolved into anatomically modern people (*Homo sapiens*). This three-part division of the successors of *Homo erectus*—into *Homo heidelbergensis, Homo neanderthalensis,* and *Homo sapiens*—is accepted by many, but not all, paleoanthropologists, however. The species names given to particular fossils are controversial, origins and extinctions of individual species are hard to identify, and the possibility exists that additional species from the mid- to late Pleistocene will be named in the future.

Of all the prehistoric peoples, those who project the clearest image are the Neandertals. For many they are *the* Stone Age humans; shambling, beetle-browed louts who prowled the earth during the time of the glaciers. The Neandertals got a poor reputation among the general public because they were grievously misjudged by the experts. Previously, many paleoanthropologists regarded Neandertals as a brutish breed that at best represented an insignificant side branch of the human family tree. Only recently has this misjudgment been remedied. It now seems clear that the Neandertals were members of a distinct and accomplished species. From perhaps as early as 300,000 years ago to about 30,000 years ago, they expanded the regions occupied by humans into arctic climates, devised ingenious stone tools to exploit nature, developed a relatively complex society, and possibly opened the door to the world of the supernatural. Clearly they were people of great achievements (Stringer and Gamble, 1993; Tattersall, 1995b).

The first Neandertal to be recognized as a primitive human was discovered in 1856, not far from the city of Düsseldorf, Germany, where a tributary stream of the Rhine flows through a steep-sided gorge known as the Neander Valley, *Neanderthal* in nineteenth-century German (see Figure 10.5). In 1856 the flanks of the gorge were being quarried for limestone. During the summer, workers blasted open a small cave about sixty feet (eighteen meters) above the stream. As they dug their pickaxes into the floor of the cave, they uncovered an assortment of ancient bones. But the quarriers were intent on limestone; they did not pay much attention to the bones, and most of what was probably a complete skeleton of a Neandertal was lost. Only the skullcap (Figure 10.6), ribs, part of the pelvis, and some limb bones were saved.

Meanwhile, a second skull had been brought to England from the Natural History Society collections in Gibraltar, where it had been discovered in a cave in 1848. When this skull was exhibited at the meetings of the British Association for the Advancement of Science in 1864, it was seen quite clearly to be a second example of a human with the unique and recognizable shape of the Neandertal skull.

William King, professor of anatomy at Queen's College in Galway, Ireland, accepted the German fossil as an extinct form of humanity. In 1864 King suggested that the specimen be placed in a separate species, *Homo neanderthalensis*. In giving the fossil the genus name *Homo*, King was acknowledging a general similarity to humankind; but he believed that he could not add the species name for modern humans, *sapiens*, because, as he wrote, "The Neanderthal skull is eminently simian...I am constrained to believe that the thoughts and desires which once dwelt within it never soared beyond those of the brute" (Trinkaus and Shipman, 1993: 88).

The Caves of Europe

In 1886 additional primitive-looking fossils appeared. A cave near a town called Spy in Belgium yielded two skeletons. One skull, probably from a female, was reminiscent of the original fossil from the Neander Valley, although the cranium was higher and the forehead somewhat less slanted. The other skull was virtually identical to the German

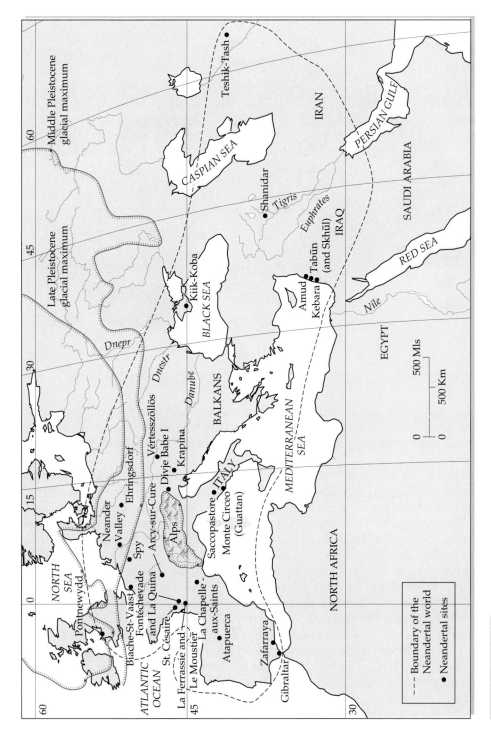

Figure 10.5

The Neandertals' world extended over Europe, the Middle East, and portions of western Asia. Only a few of the known Neandertal sites are shown.

Figure 10.6

The skullcap from the Neander Valley is possibly the most famous fossil discovery ever made. Following its discovery in 1856, it was thought by many to be the skull of some pathological idiot. Today we know that it belonged to an early, but by no means excessively primitive, variety of humans.

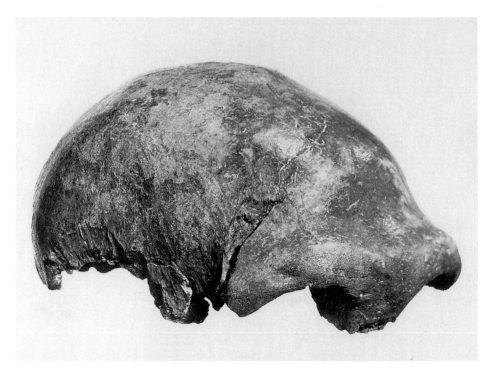

find. These fossils were definitely very old: Along with them were found primitive stone tools and remains of extinct animals. Most scientists were obliged to admit that an archaic people, distinct from modern humans, had indeed lived in Europe during some bygone era.

Based on the fossil skeletons at Spy, the Neandertals were short and thickset. Their heads were long and low, with large brow ridges. Their faces were massive and protruding, with a heavy jaw but a receding chin. Could these have been our ancestors? Nearly all scientists said no. They were willing to give Neandertal a place on the human family tree, but not on any branch shared by modern humanity.

Finds in France both enriched and complicated the picture. In the first decade of the twentieth century, archaeologists were at work in the Dordogne region of southwestern France. From the 1860s on, countless stone tools had been found in the region, proof that the Dordogne had been a population center in ancient times. Beginning in 1908, a magnificent series of Neandertal fossils also was discovered. One was the skeleton of an old man in a cave near the village of La Chapelle-aux-Saints (Figure 10.7). A nearby cave at Le Moustier, from which quantities of stone implements had been excavated earlier, yielded the skeleton of a Neandertal youth. A rock shelter at La Ferrassie produced adult male and female Neandertals and later the remains of several children. Another rock shelter at La Quina held parts of several Neandertal skeletons.

The great value of this material was its completeness. The bones from Spy had given only a rough portrait of the Neandertal people that could lead to extremes of interpretation. In contrast, the wealth of skeletal material from southwestern France now seemed to promise enough data to set the most vivid anthropological imagination to rest. Now scientists would be able to reconstruct what a Neandertal looked like and study the physical resemblances—or lack of them—between Neandertals and modern humans.

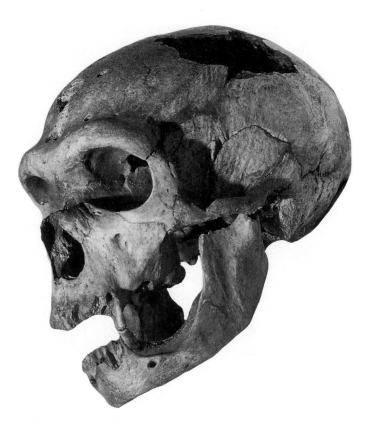

Figure 10.7

The skull of the old man of La Chapelle-aux-Saints shows he lost many teeth during life. He was less than 5 feet (1.5 meters) tall and bent by arthritis, but he had a large cranial capacity of about 1,625 cubic centimeters. The average modern human capacity is 1,330 cc.

Discoveries in Israel

Israel has proved a gold mine of fossil remains. Since the 1930s, finds have been made at cave sites on the slopes of Mount Carmel at Mugharet et-Tabūn (a female skeleton and male mandible) and Mugharet es-Skhūl (remains of ten individuals); at Amud (north of the Sea of Galilee); at Kebara; and at Qafzeh (south of Nazareth). The variation exhibited is striking, from remains that are fully Neandertal (as at Tabūn, Amud, and Kebara) to almost modern-looking skulls (Skhūl and Qafzeh; Figure 10.8). The sites span the period 120,000 to 40,000 BP.

The initial impression left by the Skhūl and Qafzeh people was that they occupied an evolutionary middle ground between the Neandertals and modern humans. They were certainly extremely variable in form. Today, both the Skhūl and Qafzeh specimens are classified as early representatives of *Homo sapiens* (Stringer, 1993; Tattersall, 1995b).

The latest dates for the Middle Eastern cave-dwellers are surprising and have changed our understanding of human occupation in that region. Although scientists originally believed that more modern-looking people lived only after the Neandertals, new dates based on uranium analyses, thermoluminescence, and electron spin resonance indicate that Neandertals and early moderns may have been contemporaries in the Middle East for thousands of years. The Neandertal remains from Tabūn are now known to date to approximately 110,000 years BP, and the early moderns from Qafzeh and Skhūl date to 120,000 to 90,000 and 100,000 to 80,000 years BP, respectively. Neandertals continued to use the region until at least 41,000 years ago, based on the dates from Amud; but by 37,000 years ago modern humans probably were the only people in the Middle East.

Figure 10.8

Shown here is the skull of an early *Homo sapiens* fossil from the cave of Skhūl on the slopes of Mount Carmel. This skull shows several modern features, including a chin and a relatively steep forehead.

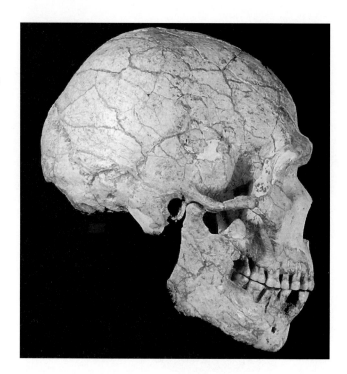

Other Mid-Eastern/Western Asian Neandertal sites are worth mentioning. First, the site of Shanidar in the Zagros Mountains of Iraq yielded several Neandertal skeletons during excavations carried out between 1951 and 1960. Dated about 50,000 years BP or a little earlier, the Shanidar skeletons show fully developed and typical Neandertal traits and also a very high incident of antemortem (predeath) trauma, including broken ribs, scalp wounds, apparent stab wounds, and degenerative joint disease. As paleoanthropologist Glenn Conroy of Washington University (1997: 446) remarked, the "Neandertals clearly had a tough time of it" as they hunted and gathered and perhaps also fought with one another. Second, the easternmost Neandertal remains showed up in 1938 during work at the cave site of Teshik-Tash located in the Bajsun-Tau Mountains of Uzbekistan, about 78 miles (125 kilometers) south of Samarkand. At this rugged high-altitude site, a nine-year-old Neandertal boy was found buried, and it appeared that some care had been given to the interment.

The Last Neandertals

For the most exciting recent fossil finds of Neandertals, however, we return to Europe and to the country of Spain. Here researchers have uncovered evidence not only of the very oldest members of the Neandertal lineage, but also of what may have been the final survivors (Arsuaga et al., 1993, 1997a, 1997b; Bischoff et al., 1997; Tattersall, 1995b). The most ancient material comes from the site of the Sima de los Huesos (Pit of Bones) in the Sierra de Atapuerca, some 150 miles (250 kilometers) due north of Madrid. You will recall that fossils designated by their discoverers as *Homo antecessor* were found in these mountains. In addition, the remains of more than thirty-two early humans have been found deep in a cave, scattered about a small chamber at the bottom of a narrow shaft forty feet (thirteen meters) deep. Intermingled with the bones of bears and other animals, the human remains in the Pit of Bones apparently accumulated as

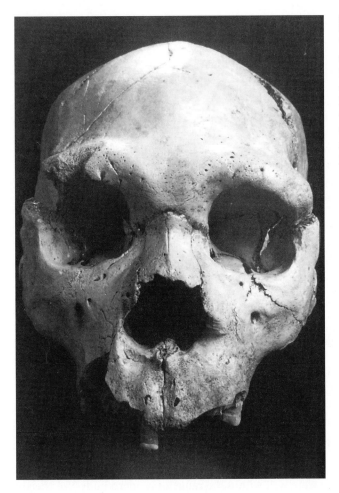

Figure 10.9
This skull from the Spanish site of Sima de los Huesos in the Sierra de Atapuerca displays several evolving Neandertal traits, including large brows and mid-facial prognathism. Cranial capacity was 1,125 cubic centimeters.

people living near the cave's mouth disposed of their dead by dumping them down the shaft. Carrying a minimum age of 200,000 BP, but probably closer to 300,000 years old, the Sima de los Huesos fossils share many traits with *Homo erectus*; but the majority of their anatomical characteristics—including the shape of the brows, projection of the face, and the shape of the back of the braincase (see Figure 10.9)—are shared with undoubted Neandertals, and thus they are classified here as the oldest known members of that lineage.

The Neandertals seem to have made their evolutionary exit about 270,000 years later in the same region that witnessed their origin. The southern Spanish cave site of Zafarraya has produced typical Neandertal stone tools dating to 27,000 years BP. From slightly older deposits at the same site have come Neandertal fossils. In Portugal, at a site in the Lapedo Valley, north of Lisbon, a recent discovery of a four-year-old child's skeleton may bring the date of the last Neandertals down to 24,500 BP (Duarte et al., 1999). The child, however, appears to carry not only Neandertal characteristics (short stocky limbs and trunk) but some features of *Homo sapiens* in its teeth and chin. Furthermore, it is accompanied by an Upper Paleolithic industry. Duarte and his colleagues (1999) claim that this child represents a cross between Neandertal and *Homo sapiens*—and indeed, this is not impossible, although, as we shall see, the two species do appear to be genetically distinct. If this Lapedo skeleton is that of a Neandertal, then it is the last known. Following this time, it seems that Neandertals disappeared from the face of the earth.

Classification and Distribution of the Neandertals

For the better part of the twentieth century, the classification of the Neandertals and their place in hominid evolution was in dispute. Some paleoanthropologists followed William King's lead of 1864 and gave them a separate species designation, *Homo neanderthalensis*. Others opted to include the Neandertals within *Homo sapiens,* but as a distinct subspecies, *H. sapiens neanderthalensis.* As a result of this uncertainty, there has been continuing controversy about whether the Neandertals made a genetic contribution to modern people. As we shall see, however, the extraction and analysis of Neandertal DNA have suggested that the Neandertals belonged to a different species from modern people, and thus it is unlikely that we carry many (if any) of their genes.

In any event, archaeological studies and fossil discoveries have shown that the Neandertals were a capable and successful species that spread widely across Europe and western Asia. As shown in Figure 10.5, Neandertal remains and artifacts have been recovered from the western extremes of Europe (from Gibraltar and possibly Pontnewydd in Wales); and to the east as far as Israel, Iraq, and Uzbekistan (Teshik-Tash is one of the easternmost sites). The world of the Neandertals was quite extensive, covering an area some 4,000 miles (6,400 kilometers) east to west and 1,500 miles (2,400 kilometers) north to south. The fossil record shows that they inhabited that world for some 270,000 years, and biomolecular estimates may increase that figure to as much as 500,000 years (Krings et al., 1997). Table 10.3 lists several of the more important Neandertal sites, along with their ages.

The Anatomy of *Homo neanderthalensis*

Several of the more important anatomical features of the Neandertals are summarized in Table 10.4. As shown, they were well within the range of modern body size (height and weight), although on average they were shorter and considerably more stocky than most living people (Tattersall, 1995b). The Neandertals were built to withstand the extreme cold of the European ice ages. Their broad bodies and relatively short limbs helped to conserve heat. They were also built for strength, with thick limb bones, broad shoulder blades that anchored powerful arm muscles, and massive hands.

Atop their ruggedly built bodies, the Neandertals carried large and distinctive heads. Their skulls showed a long and rather low-vaulted braincase; midfacial prognathism; cheekbones that were swept back rather than laterally flaring; a large nose; large brow ridges; and variability in the degree of cranial base flexure. Additionally, the Neandertal occipital bone at the back of the skull tended to protrude somewhat and featured a characteristic depression or pit for the attachment of neck muscles, the **suprainiac fossa.** Within their big skulls, the Neandertals possessed equally large brains. Average brain size calculated over their entire 300,000 to 30,000 BP time period is 1,410 cubic centimeters—some 6 percent greater than modern humans' average size (1,330 cubic centimeters) and 10 percent greater than that of the Neandertals' immediate ancestors, *Homo heidelbergensis.* Furthermore, brain size seems to have increased from early to late Neandertal times. Pre–classic Neandertals from the period of 300,000 to 100,000 BP showed an average cranial capacity of 1,275 cubic centimeters, while so-called **classic Neandertals** (90,000 to 30,000 BP) showed an average of 1,519 cubic centimeters—a 19 percent intraspecific increase in brain size.

Suprainiac fossa a characteristic depression on the occipital bone of Neandertals.

Classic Neandertal the type of Neandertal *fossil* originally found in western Europe.

Table 10.3

	A Partial Record of Neandertal Sites	
Geographic Area	**Site**	**Age (years BP)**
Europe	Zafarraya	30,000–27,000
	St. Césaire	36,000–32,000
	Le Moustier	41,000
	La Chapelle-aux-Saints	47,000
	Gibraltar	50,000
	Monte Circeo	52,000
	La Quina	64,000
	Spy	68,000
	La Ferrassie	70,000
	Neander Valley	100,000–30,000
	Krapina	100,000
	Fontéchevade	115,000
	Saccopastore	120,000
	Biache-St.-Vaast	180,000–130,000
	Ehringsdorf	225,000
	Pontnewydd[a]	225,000
	Atapuerca (Sima de los Huesos)	300,000
Middle East and Western Asia	Amud	41,000
	Kebara	64,000–60,000
	Shanidar	70,000–50,000
	Teshik-Tash	75,000–30,000(?)
	Tabūn	110,000

[a] The Pontnewydd specimens are linked to the Neandertal lineage only by shared dental traits.

Table 10.4

	Characteristics of the Neandertals[a]
Trait	***Homo neanderthalensis***
Height (sexes combined)	4.9–5.6 ft (150–170 cm)
Weight (sexes combined)	110–143 lb (50–65 kg)
Brain size (sexes combined)	1,410 cc mean (1,125–1,750 cc range)
Cranium	Occipital depression (*suprainiac fossa*); occipital torus; large nose; midfacial prognathism; variability in degree of cranial base flexure; modern hyoid bone
Dentition	Large incisors: gap behind lower M3
Limbs	Robust, stocky physique as adaptation to cold; short legs; powerful hands
Locomotion	Bipedalism
Distribution	Middle East, Europe, Western Asia
Known dates (thousand yrs)	300,000–30,000 years BP

[a]Mean values for anatomical measurements may change with the addition of new fossil discoveries.

Retromolar gap the space between the M3 and the mandibular *ramus*; characteristic of Neandertals.

Ramus the vertical portion of the *mandible,* as opposed to the mandibular body, which bears the teeth.

The Neandertals' jaws and teeth also had certain distinctive features. The mandible usually lacked a chin, although some individuals showed incipient development of this trait. Midfacial prognathism resulted in the lower toothrow being moved forward, producing a characteristic **retromolar gap,** or space between the last molar (M3) and the **ramus** of the mandible. Finally, many Neandertal fossils show extreme wear of the front teeth (Figure 10.10), a feature thought to reflect the use of the teeth as tools (Figure 10.11).

Figure 10.10

Lateral view of the dentition of a Neandertal from Shanidar, Iraq. The retromolar gap is obvious at the left, and strong wear can be seen on the upper front teeth (right).

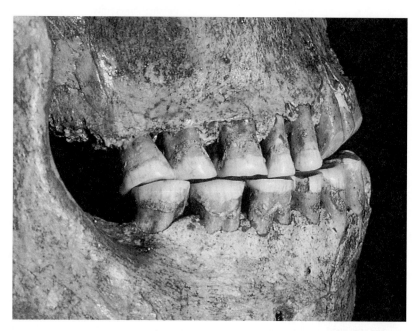

Figure 10.11

American Museum of Natural History reconstruction of a classic Neandertal group. Note how the woman in the center is anchoring an animal skin with her teeth as she scrapes it with a stone tool. Such use of the teeth would have caused the wear seen in Figure 10.10.

In summary, the Neandertals were somewhat short but powerful and rugged people who thrived for some 270,000 years in Europe and certain adjacent areas. Although the latest studies show that they probably were not us—that is, not *Homo sapiens*—but rather a distinct species, *Homo neanderthalensis,* they were a remarkable offshoot of hominid evolution and produced a complex culture.

> For more on the Neandertals and other extinct humans, visit our web site.

Evolutionary Relationships to Homo sapiens

The effort to decipher the evolutionary connections of mid to late Pleistocene humans was facilitated recently by genetic analyses suggesting strongly that the Neandertals were a distinct and dead-end species. Before this genetic breakthrough, the Neandertals' classification and their place in hominid evolution—including the question of whether they were ancestral to modern people—had been matters of chronic dispute among anthropologists; standard anatomical and archaeological studies had proved unable to decide the issues. In July 1997, it was announced that a team of German and American scientists had succeeded in extracting mitochondrial DNA (mtDNA) from the original (1856) Neandertal fossil and comparing it with mtDNA from modern humans (Krings et al., 1997). After determining that the fossil (which dates to between 100,000 and 30,000 years BP) contained sufficient DNA for analysis, the researchers extracted genetic material from an arm bone and then cloned it using the **polymerase chain reaction** (PCR). This procedure involves heating DNA to separate the two intertwined strands (see Chapter 2) and then using a particular enzyme, DNA polymerase, to induce the replication of each strand's missing partner. PCR enables researchers to make an infinite number of copies of small amounts of DNA, and in the case at hand it allowed the ultimate assembly of a mitochondrial DNA sequence 379 base pairs in length. When the Neandertal sequence was compared with modern human mtDNA samples, an average of 27 differences (substitutions) was found, with modern Africans, Europeans, Asians, Native Americans, and Australian/Oceanic people being equally distant from the Neandertal sample. In contrast, variation among those same modern populations was found to average only about 8 substitutions for this particular mtDNA sequence. Finally, the differences between humans and Neandertals were found to be half as great as those between humans and chimpanzees (which show an average of 55 substitutions) for the cloned sequence. These genetics data have been confirmed recently by the analysis of a second Neandertal specimen (Orchinnikov et al., 2000).

How can the mtDNA differences between modern people and Neandertals best be explained? Without doubt, the simplest tentative interpretation is that the Neandertals belonged to a distinct species that deserves its own designation (*Homo neanderthalensis*); that their evolutionary line separated long ago from that leading to modern humans (lengthy separation would allow the accumulation of numerous mtDNA differences); and that little or no interbreeding occurred between the two evolutionary lineages. However, as we have seen, the Lapedo child could represent a cross between the two. The result of DNA studies of this skeleton are eagerly awaited.

With the central Neandertal question apparently resolved, interpreting the rest of mid to late Pleistocene human evolution might seem simple; but that is not the case. Many researchers prefer the scheme illustrated in Figure 10.12(A), in which *Homo erectus* (or, for some, *H. ergaster*) gave rise to *Homo heidelbergensis* (probably in Africa or southwest Asia), who in turn was ancestral (at different times and probably in different

Polymerase chain reaction technique for making an infinite number of copies of a *DNA* molecule from a single precursor; known as the PCR.

Critical Thinking

The Neandertal Question

It now seems likely that the old view of the Neandertals as a geographic race of "archaic *Homo sapiens*" should be discarded. What data confirm that Neandertals were a separate species and a dead end in human evolution? An estimate of the date of the evolutionary origin of the Neandertals can be derived from the magnitude of mtDNA differences, which suggests separation from the line leading to *Homo sapiens* between 690,000 and 550,000 years ago. How does this molecular data compare with the archaeological and anatomical data? Based on your knowledge of human population genetics (Chapters 2 and 3), how would you explain the discrepancy between molecular data and other data regarding dates for Neandertal origins? What other "questions" about the Neandertals remain to be resolved?

places) to both the Neandertals and *Homo sapiens.* An alternative scheme, suggested by the Spanish discoverers of the Atapuerca fossils, is shown in Figure 10.12(B). Here a newly named species, *Homo antecessor,* represented by the 800,000-year-old Gran Dolina specimens, is shown arising in Africa from *Homo erectus* (for some, *H. ergaster*). *Homo antecessor* then serves as the common ancestor of *Homo heidelbergensis* (who ultimately gave rise to the Neandertals) and *Homo sapiens* (modern humans). The basis of this alternative point of view is the claim that *Homo antecessor,* who shares numerous traits with both *H. heidelbergensis* and *H. sapiens,* is in fact more like modern humans than is the more recent species, *H. heidelbergensis.* At present the most straightforward view of mid to late Pleistocene human evolution is probably scheme A. As always, however, the picture may be changed significantly by future discoveries.

Figure 10.12

Two alternative schemes for mid to late Pleistocene human evolution are shown. (A) Here *Homo erectus* gives rise to *H. heidelbergensis,* who is the common ancestor of modern humans and the Neandertals. (B) Alternatively, *Homo erectus* gives rise to *Homo antecessor,* who is the common ancestor of modern humans and *H. heidelbergensis,* with the latter being ancestral to the Neandertals. The authors of this text favor phylogeny A, although the evidence for neither scheme is conclusive.

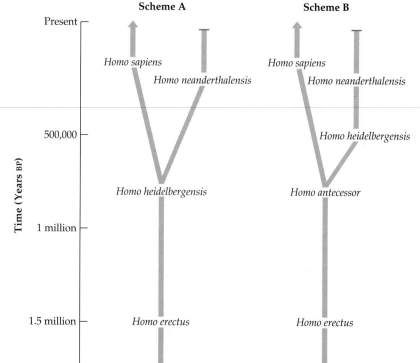

The Environment of Late Pleistocene Homo

Two hundred and fifty thousand years ago, the archaic human population (including both *Homo heidelbergensis* and the Neandertals) was probably less than 3 million. But this unimpressive total is deceptive, for even then humankind occupied far more of the earth's surface than any other mammalian species. Most of Europe was then woodland, frequently interrupted by lush meadows, with temperatures so warm that water buffalo thrived in central Germany and monkeys chattered in dense woodlands along the northern Mediterranean coast. Most of Asia was less hospitable, and archaic human bands apparently generally avoided the heartland and far north of that continent because of harsh winters and/or dry, blistering summers (see Figure 10.1). But human groups were scattered around the entire southern perimeter of Asia, from the Middle East to Java and northward into central China. In all probability the most densely populated continent was Africa. This sprawling landmass may have contained more people than the rest of the world put together.

The lands settled by these various people reveal much about their ability to deal with nature. They almost invariably chose grasslands, savannas, or partially wooded country. These regions supported the herds of grazing animals that provided much of the meat in the human diet. Even though vegetable foods probably still provided the bulk of a group's diet, wherever animals were lacking, humans stayed away. The unoccupied areas included the deserts, the rain forests, and the dense evergreen woods of the north—a substantial portion of the earth's surface. A few herbivorous animal species did exist in the forests of north and south; but they tended to wander alone or in small groups, because the scantiness of forage and the difficulty of moving through the thick growth of a forest made herd life impractical. It seems likely that humans were not attracted to these areas for the same reasons.

Another environment that resisted human invasion for a long time was the **tundra** of the far north. Here, obtaining meat was not the problem. Enormous herds of reindeer, bison, and other large, vulnerable animals found ready forage in the mosses, lichens, grasses, and shrubs of the nearly treeless tundra country. Archaic people, however, would have had difficulty coping with the extreme cold of the region. Consequently, archaic humans stuck primarily to the same lands that had supported their *Homo erectus* ancestors: the savannas and open thorn woodlands of the tropics and the grasslands and open deciduous woodlands found in the temperate latitudes.

The Ice Ages

Just after 200,000 years ago, the weather in the Northern Hemisphere began to grow colder (Conroy, 1997; Stringer and Gamble, 1993). Glades and meadows in the deciduous woodlands of Europe broadened at an imperceptible rate; the tangled, lush woodlands along the Mediterranean gradually withered; and the expanses of spruce and fir in eastern Europe slowly yielded to the expanding steppe, or grassy plain. Similar changes occurred in China and North America. The increasing cold did not necessarily mean that the basic patterns of human life were about to change. Because the archaic humans' way of life was nomadic to begin with, they had simply to follow wherever the herd animals led or perhaps adopt a different mix of hunting, scavenging, and gathering. But certainly the pressure to develop a different material culture was felt by groups that had formerly had no pressing need for fire, clothing, or artificial shelter. These groups now had to develop skills in cold-weather survival.

Tundra treeless, low-vegetation arctic or sub-arctic plain, swampy in summer, with permanently frozen soil just beneath the surface.

Snow was falling in the mountain ranges of the world, more snow than could melt during the summer. Year by year it piled up, filling deep valleys and compacting into ice. The stupendous weight of the ice caused its lower layers to behave like very thick putty, sliding outward from the valleys as the ever accumulating snow pressed down from above. Inching through the mountain ranges, the great fingers of ice plucked boulders from cliffsides and used them like a giant's scouring powder to grind the once green land down to bedrock. In the summer, torrents of meltwater carried the debris of sand and rock dust out in front of the advancing ice, where it was later picked up by winds and blown across the continents in great yellowish-brown clouds. And still the snow continued to fall, until in some places the ice sheets grew more than a mile thick, burying the mountains and causing the very crust of the earth to sag under the load. At their fullest extent, the great glaciers covered more than 30 percent of the world's land surface, compared to a mere 10 percent today. North America was covered by ice from the Arctic regions to a point south of today's Great Lakes. Continental ice sheets existed in the mountains and highlands of central Asia, and along the extreme southern tip of South America. Europe was almost entirely icebound. The surrounding ocean and seas offered a limitless source of moisture for snow, which fed separate glaciers that spread outward from the Alps and the Scandinavian ranges to cover vast stretches of the continent (see Figure 10.5 on page 271).

This glacial age, which lasted from about 186,000 to 128,000 years ago, was one of the worst climatic traumata in the 5-billion-year history of the earth. Although many similar glaciations are believed to have occurred during the last 700,000 years, some of which undoubtedly affected such early European arrivals as the *Homo heidelbergensis* people of Mauer, Boxgrove, and Bilzingsleben, the glaciation of 186,000 to 128,000 years ago was the first ice age to try the endurance of *Homo neanderthalensis*. The Neandertals survived 60,000 years of bitter cold, interspersed with mild spells, before the northern part of the earth warmed up again—for a time.

Global Climatic Changes

The effect of the climatic changes was enormous. During the cold periods, the wind patterns of the world were disrupted. Rainfall increased in some places and diminished in others. Patterns of vegetation were greatly altered. Many animal species died out or evolved new, cold-adapted forms, such as the cave bear and the woolly rhinoceros in northern latitudes.

During some particularly severe phases of the glaciation 186,000 to 128,000 years ago, what is now England and other parts of northern Europe, which had been so pleasant a few thousand years earlier, became so bitterly cold that midsummer temperatures often were below freezing. The temperate woodlands of central and western Europe were transformed into tundra or steppe. As far south as the shores of the Mediterranean, trees gradually died and were eventually replaced by grassland. Few hominid fossils are known from Europe during the coldest phases of this glaciation, and it seems likely the climate was too cold for humans.

What happened in Africa is less clear. In some places, reduced temperatures apparently were accompanied by greater rainfall, allowing trees or grass to grow on formerly barren parts of the Sahara and the Kalahari. Woodland may have increased at the expense of savanna. At the same time, changing wind patterns had a drying effect on the dense Congo rain forest, causing it to give way in parts to open woodland or grassland. Thus, while Europe was becoming less habitable, Africa was probably becoming more so, favoring an expansion of people through much of that continent.

The land resources available to human groups during the glaciation also were increased by a worldwide lowering of sea levels. As discussed in Chapter 9, so much water became locked up in the huge ice sheets that the level of the oceans dropped, exposing to the elements large areas of the continental shelves—those shallow submarine plains that reach outward from the continental margins, in some places for hundreds of miles, before dropping off steeply to the ocean floor far below. The baring of formerly submerged land gave humans access to millions of square miles of new territory, and there is no doubt that they took advantage of this dividend of the ice ages. Each year, bands of people and their game must have wandered farther into newly drained land.

Selection for Intelligence and Ingenuity

During the 60,000 years of glaciation, surviving inhabitants of the northern latitudes suffered enormous hardships. These hardships may have had a stimulating influence on intelligence, cultural inventiveness, and subsistence creativity.

At Lazaret, near Terra Amata in southernmost France, Henry and Marie-Antoinette de Lumley made a spectacular find that seems to reflect that inventiveness and creativity: remnants of shelters that had been constructed *inside* a cave. These simple shelters, dating to about 125,000 years ago, were tents, probably consisting of animal hides anchored by stones around the perimeter. The entrances of the tents faced away from the cave mouth, a fact suggesting that the winds blew cold and hard even at this spot close to the Mediterranean.

Finally, around 128,000 years ago, the long glacial agony began to taper off, and another period of relative warmth began. It was to last almost 60,000 years. Glaciers shrank back into their mountain fastnesses, the seas rose, and northern latitudes all across the world once again became an inviting place for humans. By 90,000 years ago, the "classic" stage of the western European Neandertals had begun.

The classic Neandertals were characterized by a set of cold-adapted traits that had served their ancestors well throughout the glaciation and that benefited their descendants during the final Pleistocene glacial period (Holliday, 1997; Stringer and Gamble, 1993; Tattersal, 1995b). As noted earlier in this chapter, the classic Neandertal body was stocky and had short limbs; the jaw was massive and chinless; the face was out-thrust; and the skull was still low, with a sloping brow. But the volume of the braincase equaled or exceeded that of present-day humans.

The Final Glaciation

After a respite of warmer weather between 128,000 and 71,000 years ago, the glaciers once again began to grow. This last major glacial cycle of the Pleistocene produced cold weather that lasted until about 13,000 years ago. It was not overly severe at first; initially it brought snowy winters and cool, rainy summers. Nevertheless, open grassland spread, and formerly wooded portions of Germany and northern France were transformed into tundra or into a forest–tundra mixture where open areas of moss and lichens alternated with groups of trees.

During preceding ice ages, the archaic human bands had pulled back from such uncongenial lands. Now, in the summer at least, the northern populations stayed, subsisting on the herds of reindeer, woolly rhinoceros, and mammoth. They had to be creative scavengers and hunters, for tundra country offered little vegetable food to tide them over in lean times. Evidence from Russia shows that settlements extended right up to the Arctic Ocean northwest of the Ural mountains. Here there are indications of huts or windbreaks built with mammoth tusks and skins and warmed by small fires, together with remains of polar bears, which evidently were hunted. No doubt the death toll was high on the northernmost frontier, and bands remained small and scattered. Away from the frigid border of the ice sheets, populations were denser.

To understand the extent to which these populations depended on cultural adaptations, we must remember that hominids are biologically adapted to a tropical climate. Hominids had evolved an efficient system of perspiration to prevent overheating in the tropics, but they lacked a counterbalancing system effective against overcooling. Such changes require a long time to evolve. Archaic humans did not have to depend solely on such evolutionary changes to cope with the cold, however: They were intelligent enough to deal with the problem mainly through cultural means. They generated extra heat with well-controlled fires, almost certainly put on hide clothes, and either took shelter in caves or, where there were no caves, constructed their own shelters.

Selection for Lighter Skin Color

One noteworthy physical change that very likely coincided with humans' expansion into northern lands was associated with the use of clothing and with the scarcity of sunlight during winter in the higher latitudes. Their skin probably got lighter. There is no certain evidence, but it seems likely that the australopithecines—and early, tropical *Homo* as well—had been quite dark-skinned. In equatorial regions, dark brown skin has an advantage. Overexposure to ultraviolet (UV) rays of the tropical sun is harmful to skin, and many experts believe that as the hominid skin became less hairy and more exposed, the melanocytes (the cells that produce the skin-darkening pigment melanin) compensated by producing extra pigment, which blocked the ultraviolet rays. This UV blockage could have prevented potentially lethal skin cancers.

But the presence of a screen of pigment also inhibits the beneficial UV-induced synthesis of vitamin D in the skin. When people settled permanently in regions with less sunlight, they did not produce enough vitamin D; pigment was no longer a protection but a drawback. Animal hides worn against the cold further decreased the amount of sunlight that could fall on the skin. In these conditions a level of pigmentation that could enhance the contribution of vitamin D to the body's chemistry was better for survival, and lighter skin evolved. Skin color is simply an evolutionary response to the intensity of UV light and the extent of clothing required in different geographic regions. The Neandertal people may have been fair.

The significance of vitamin D in the lives of archaic populations was probably considerable. Today we know that, in the absence of adequate sunlight, humans can obtain the vitamin only from milk and fish oils. Further, we have learned that deficiency in the vitamin causes the bone-bending disease rickets. It is no surprise, therefore, that we find many skeletons of early northern peoples, especially children, showing direct evidence of a deficiency in the vitamin. And it is equally unsurprising that, among the first modern people who followed archaic humans in these icy regions, and whom we know to have had fishing tackle, the incidence of the disease is greatly reduced: Fish consumption served as a substitute for exposure to sunlight. The importance of sunlight to the survival of archaic human inhabitants in northern lands, and the limitations that it placed on their further expansion, cannot be exaggerated.

ASKING QUESTIONS

How Was Fire Created?

Following the onset of the last ice age, hearths became very common in European Neandertal sites; in fact, their absence is more surprising than their presence. It appears that by this time fire was used wherever it was required—far more in Eurasian sites than in Africa. The Neandertal people certainly had control of fire.

We know that by Upper Paleolithic times, people created fire by percussion, using hard stone on **iron pyrites,** and by friction, using a fire or twirl drill on wood or bone. But during the earlier period of the Middle Paleolithic, we have no direct evidence of either technique for making fire. The number of hearths found makes it quite clear that fire was made regularly by one means or another, and the most probable is by percussion. To date, however, iron pyrites have been found at only one Neandertal site (Arcy-sur-Cure, France).

During the last ice age, fire would surely have become an essential cultural asset for the Neandertal people. It offered warmth and light during long and very cold winter nights, and would no doubt also have been used for roasting food. It was also invaluable for keeping dangerous animals out of caves and might have been used to drive game. Magical rites may have been associated with fire, once people had achieved mastery of it. The earliest monotheistic religion in western Asia, Zoroastrianism, was centered on the symbolic significance of fire.

Archaeologists are beginning to unravel the history of fire. Although iron pyrites are not preserved in wet or alkaline deposits, the evidence of charcoal, burnt bone, and stone is accumulating. We should soon learn more about the early mastery of this vital resource, which became so important in the development of metallurgy.

Technological Adaptations of Late Pleistocene Homo

Both *Homo heidelbergensis* and the Neandertals showed significant cultural elaboration compared to *Homo erectus.* The stone-tool industries of *Homo heidelbergensis* bridge the gap between the Lower Paleolithic (characterized by Oldowan choppers and flakes and Acheulean hand axes) and the next lithic stage, the **Middle Paleolithic.** Recognized mainly by declining numbers of hand axes and the invention of the **Levallois technique** for the production of prepared flakes, the Middle Paleolithic is reckoned by many archaeologists to have begun around 250,000 years ago and lasted until about 35,000 years BP.

The Levallois technique emerged as a significant advance in stone-tool technology at the start of the Middle Paleolithic and can be attributed to *Homo heidelbergensis.* Before that time, early *Homo* and *H. erectus* toolmakers had produced flake tools by simply banging away at a large core with various hammers. The resulting flakes were unpredictable in their sizes and shapes, but they served well enough as butchering implements. Some 300,000 to 250,000 years ago, however, some particularly ingenious stone-knappers developed a sophisticated new technique for making flake tools.

Called the Levallois technique after the Parisian suburb where such tools were first discovered by archaeologists, the procedure involves carefully preparing a stone core and then producing a finished implement with a single blow (see Figure 10.13). First, a nodule of flint or other stone is chipped around the sides and on the top. This procedure produces a prepared core that looks something like a tortoise and removes most of the nodule's original surface. Then the prepared core is given a well-aimed blow at a point on one end. This detaches a flake of predetermined size and shape, with long, sharp cutting edges.

Much less wasteful of raw material than earlier flaking methods, the Levallois technique also represents a remarkable insight into the potential of stone, for no tool is visible until the very end of the process. (In contrast, in the making of a hand ax, the tool

Iron pyrite a mineral substance (iron disulfide) that, when struck with flint, makes sparks that will start a fire.

Middle Paleolithic a period of stone-tool manufacture in the Old World (mainly Europe, Africa, and western Asia) that lasted from about 250,000 to 35,000 years BP.

Levallois technique stone-knapping method in which a core is shaped to allow a *flake* of predetermined size and shape to be detached; originated about 250,000 years BP.

Figure 10.13

The Levallois flake has a distinctive predetermined shape. The toolmaker first prepared a nodule by trimming its sides (top right). This core was then further refined by the flaking of small chips from the front and back surfaces. This is known as a *tortoise core* because of its appearance. A final brisk blow at one end removed the finished flake (bottom right), already sharp and in need of no further retouching.

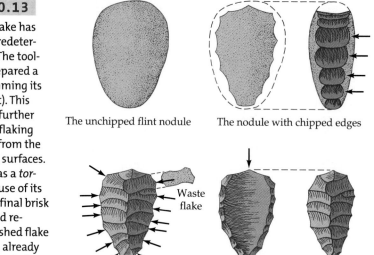

The unchipped flint nodule   The nodule with chipped edges

Waste flake

Top surface flaked   Finished tool

gradually and reassuringly takes shape as the stone-knapper works.) The oldest known Levallois flakes are from the La Cotte site on the English Channel island of Jersey and date to 238,000 years BP. The actual invention of the technique is thought to have taken place in Africa by at least 250,000 years BP, and possibly as early as 300,000 years ago.

Tool Kits of *Homo heidelbergensis*

As expected, given the postulated descent of *Homo heidelbergensis* from *H. erectus,* the oldest tool kits of *H. heidelbergensis* continue the Acheulean hand ax tradition. For example, the Bodo skull from Ethiopia—which dates to 600,000 years BP—was found in association with Acheulean hand axes and cleavers. The same is true for other early African fossils such as Ndutu and Elandsfontein, as well as remains from the 500,000- to 400,000-year-old European sites of Boxgrove (England) and Arago (France). The easternmost Acheulean assemblage that can be attributed to *Homo heidelbergensis* comes from Narmada in India and dates to 150,000 years BP. Interestingly, the oldest fossil remains of *Homo heidelbergensis,* those 800,000-year-old bones from Gran Dolina in the Atapuerca mountains, are accompanied not by Acheulean tools but rather by a flake-and-chopper assemblage that lacks hand axes.

A second feature of the Middle Paleolithic industries produced by *Homo heidelbergensis* is their diversity. This is not unexpected, of course, given the wide geographic spread of *H. heidelbergensis* and the fact that *Homo erectus*'s tool kits also showed regional distinctions. As shown in Table 10.5, *Homo heidelbergensis* people in eastern Asia continued the local tradition of producing nondescript flake tools and pebble choppers (implements that may have been used in combination with bamboo tools). The Levallois technique apparently never spread to that part of the Old World. In contrast, African and western Asian Middle Paleolithic assemblages included Levallois flake tools and a variety of implements including scrapers, choppers, and **denticulates.** In East and Central Africa, *Homo heidelbergensis* people made stone tools attributed to the

Denticulates stone implements made with toothed or notched edges.

Table 10.5

A Partial Record of *Homo heidelbergensis* Lithic Cultures			
Geographic Area	**Site/Fossil**	**Age (years BP)**	**Tool Kit**
Africa	Jebel Irhoud	125,000–90,000	Mousterian, Levallois-flaked tools
	Eyasi	130,000–35,000(?)	Acheulean tools (probable)
	Kabwe	250,000–130,000	Sangoan tools
	Elandsfontein	350,000–130,000	Acheulean tools (probable)
	Ndutu	400,000–200,000	Acheulean tools
	Bodo	600,000	Acheulean tools
Asia	Xujiayao (China)	125,000–100,000	Flake tools (no hand axes)
	Narmada (India)	150,000	Acheulean tools
	Dali (China)	300,000–200,000	Flake tool (no hand axes)
Europe	Vértessöllö	210,000	Flake tools, choppers, (no hand axes)
	Swanscombe	250,000	Flakes, choppers, and Acheulean tools
	Bilzingsleben	340,000–230,000	Flake tools (no hand axes)
	Arago	400,000	Acheulean, including small flake tools
	Boxgrove	500,000	Acheulean hand axes
	Gran Dolina	800,000	Flake tools, choppers (no hand axes)

Sangoan industry. The Kabwe fossil, dated to 250,000 to 130,000 years BP, was found in association with several such implements. Although the Sangoan included some hand axes and scrapers, its most distinctive tools were long, narrow, and heavy stone picks that may have been used for woodworking by archaic populations adapted to forested environments.

In addition to their stone tools, *Homo heidelbergensis* people left a few other artifacts that help archaeologists decipher their adaptations. For example, 400,000-year-old wooden spears were recently recovered at Schöningen, Germany (Thieme, 1997). (A similarly aged spear fragment was discovered at the Clacton site in England some years ago.) Made of spruce, six to seven feet long, and balanced like a modern javelin, the Schöningen spears were designed for throwing, not close-range jabbing, and they would have required a strong-armed hunter. Further evidence that *Homo heidelbergensis* hunters used such implements comes from the 500,000-year-old Boxgrove (England) site, where researchers found a horse scapula with a circular hole precisely like that expected from a thrown spear (Pitts and Roberts, 1998).

Evidence of other adaptations of *H. heidelbergensis* people is sparse. As noted in Chapter 9, they may have been responsible for the shelters and hearths found at Terra Amata and others of similar age; the likelihood that *H. heidelbergensis* people controlled and used fire is strengthened by the report of a possible hearth at Schöningen and by ash deposits and human remains at the 210,000-year-old Vértesszöllös site in Hungary. With regard to clothing, it seems most unlikely that humans would have been able to inhabit the cold northern regions of Europe 500,000 to 250,000 years ago without at least the rudiments of bodily coverings, but conclusive evidence has yet to be discovered. Finally, at present we simply have no information about any belief systems, burial practices, or artistic products of *Homo heidelbergensis*. For mid to late Pleistocene evidence on those topics, we must leave *Homo heidelbergensis* and turn to a better-known species, the Neandertals.

Sangoan industry *Middle Paleolithic* tool industry from East and Central Africa; associated with *Homo heidelbergensis*.

Mousterian Culture and the Neandertals

The Neandertals' ability to survive and spread throughout the northern latitudes must have been due, at least in part, to cultural advances—and chief among these were new stone-knapping techniques and a variety of new tools. Early in the final glacial cycle, these people invented a new stoneworking method that made flake tools vastly superior to core implements. Fine flake tools had now been made for a long time by the Lavallois technique, but the new method—the **disk–core technique**—was far more productive. People began to trim a nodule of stone around the edges to make a disk-shaped core; then, aiming hammer blows toward the center of the disk, they repeatedly rapped at its edges, knocking off flake after flake until the core was almost entirely used up. Finally, they further trimmed the unfinished flakes to create sharp edges for work on wood, carcasses, or hides.

The great virtue of the new technique was twofold. It permitted the production of large numbers of usable flakes with little effort; and, because flakes can be retouched easily so that they have a shape or an edge, the new technique ushered in an era of specialization in tools. Neandertal tool kits were far more versatile than those of earlier peoples. Francois Bordes, at one time the world's foremost expert on Neandertal stonecrafting, listed more than sixty distinct types of cutting, scraping, piercing, and gouging tools. Different bands of Neandertals probably used differing tool kits.

New weapons may also have been made at this time. Spears probably were improved when pointed flakes were attached to long pieces of wood by being wedged into the wood or tied with thongs. With such an arsenal of tools, the Neandertals could tap natural resources as never before. Confirming this point, recent archaeological and taphonomic studies conducted in the Middle East confirm that the Neandertals were active and vigorous hunters (as opposed to mainly scavenging for meat) and that in that region they regularly preyed on herd-dwelling species such as dromedaries, wild horses, and ibexes (Marean and Kim, 1998; Shea, 1998).

Everywhere north of the Sahara and eastward as far as Teshik-Tash, retouched flakes became the preeminent tools. The tools made within this broad area are collectively placed in the **Mousterian industry** (see Figure 10.14), named after the French site of Le Moustier, where such tools were first found in the 1860s. The makers of this wide-ranging culture were usually Neandertals; but in the Middle East, Mousterian tools have also been found in association with early anatomically modern people, and at Jebel Irhoud in Morocco they were made by *Homo heidelbergensis*. Complete with Levallois-flaked implements, the Jebel Irhoud tool assemblage is unusual because the human remains from this site show no Neandertal affinities. No good explanation for this archaeological puzzle is known at present.

The abundance and variety of scrapers in the Neandertals' tool kits confirms our suspicions that these people must have spent enormous amounts of time preparing animal hides for use as loose-fitting clothing and possibly in the construction of shelters. Furthermore, we can assume that the geographically widespread Neandertals—and *Homo heidelbergensis* people as well—were clever enough to modify their resource use to fit the locally available raw materials (e.g., in treeless areas, to use bone in place of wood for various purposes) and were always alert to the value of local specialties. A good example of this flexibility comes from the sun-baked Negev region of Israel, where ostrich eggshells have been unearthed along with Mousterian tools. The strong implication is that Neandertal people used the locally available eggshells as water containers, thus enabling a band to survive a journey across the parched hills from one water hole to another.

Disk–core technique Neandertal stone-knapping method in which a core is trimmed to disk shape and numerous *flakes* are then chipped off; the flakes are then generally retouched.

Mousterian industry a *Middle Paleolithic* tool industry from Europe and the Middle East; primarily associated with the Neandertals.

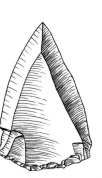

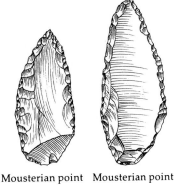

Convex side-scraper   Levallois point   Mousterian point   Mousterian point

Figure 10.14

Flint tools of the typical Mousterian. The points are carefully worked, and retouching is expertly done, usually on two sides.

Mousterian point   Canted scraper   Transversal scraper

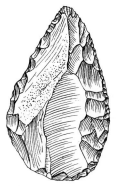

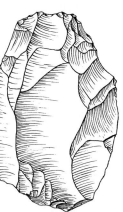

Convergent scraper   Double scraper   Levallois flake

Hunting Rituals, Magic, and Art

Discovery after discovery has suggested that the Neandertals probably started some of the activities and beliefs that are considered most characteristic of humankind (Stringer and Gamble, 1993; Tattersall, 1995b). They possibly attempted to control their own destiny—particularly their success in hunting—through magical rites. They buried their dead (at least occasionally) and may have conceived of a life after death. They may even have taken (albeit late in their existence) the first hesitant steps into the realm of art.

And they cared for aged and disabled individuals. In fact, it seems that the Neandertals may have been among the first people to display nearly the complete spectrum of behavior that constitutes modern human nature.

Evidence from some sites suggests the existence of magical cults among the Neandertal people. In one cave, pellets have been thrown at an animal-shaped stalagmite; in another, bear skulls seem to have been collected and stored. In another Neandertal cave a deer was apparently buried, sprinkled with red ochre. And in Regourdou in France, a rectangular pit held the skulls of more than twenty cave bears. However, the interpretation of these sites is questionable, especially because (with the exception of the deer burial) they were not immediately associated with Neandertal tools or other remains. We can guess that the Neandertals may have practiced magic to assist in their hunts, but we cannot yet prove it conclusively.

Evidence of art among the Neandertal people is slight but tantalizing. Red, yellow, and black mineral pigments were certainly used as colored powders. Pencil-shaped pieces that show signs of having been rubbed on a smooth surface, such as skin, have been found at some sites together with Neandertal remains or a Mousterian industry. Also found have been a few perforated teeth that might have formed part of a necklace. A small stone has been claimed to be a figurine reminiscent of the Venus of Willendorf, but the evidence is not convincing.

In 1955 a small piece of cave bear bone was discovered in a Slovenian Neandertal site with four round holes along one side. It is claimed that it was part of a flute. There is a second flutelike fragment from Libya (Wilford, 1996). Again, the evidence that the Neandertals enjoyed music and dance is suggestive but not convincing. More discoveries might allow us to attribute to some of the Neandertals cultural developments that are universally characteristic of *Homo sapiens*. Meanwhile, one way in which the Neandertals certainly foreshadowed modern people was in their occasional practice of burying their dead.

Death and Burial

The original Neandertal bones taken from the cave in the Neander Valley of Germany may have belonged to someone who was buried by members of the group, although no one suspected so when the bones were found in 1856. The two fossils discovered at Spy in Belgium in 1886 had indeed been buried; apparently fires had been lighted over the bodies, perhaps in an effort to counteract the chill of death. But no one guessed in 1886 that Spy had been the scene of an ancient burial. Then, in 1908, the cave of La Chapelle-aux-Saints in France almost shouted its evidence of a Neandertal funeral rite. The excavators found an ancient hunter who had been laid out carefully in a shallow trench. A bison leg may have been placed on his chest, and the trench was filled with broken animal bones and flint tools. These various articles could have been interpreted as provisions for the world beyond the grave, for it was well known in the early 1900s that many modern cultures bury their dead with food, weapons, and other goods. But most experts failed to make the connection.

Far to the east, on the Crimean peninsula that juts into the Black Sea, the graves of two individuals were found in a cave at Kiik-Koba in 1924. One trench held the remains of a one-year-old child resting on his side with his legs bent. This skeleton was in poor condition, because later inhabitants of the cave had dug a pit for their fire directly over the grave and inadvertently disturbed the bones. Three feet (0.9 meters) away from the child was the grave of a man, also lying on his side with his legs tucked up. The body was oriented east to west—as were the Spy fossils and five out of six of the Neandertal burials from La Ferrassie in France. Possibly the orientation had something to do with the rising or setting sun.

Even farther to the east, at Teshik-Tash in Uzbekistan, the partial skeleton of a Neandertal boy was found in a shallow grave surrounded by several pairs of mountain goat horns. The horns may have served some ritual function, but this point is unclear, since goat horns are found throughout the Teshik-Tash deposit and not just in association with human remains.

There is little doubt then, that archaic humans, and perhaps the Neandertals in particular, performed deliberate burials. But does this prove that they were the first hominids to ritually dispose of deceased group mates? Probably, but the case rests on negative evidence and is therefore inconclusive. Burial is only one of several types of funeral rite, but it is the one most likely to preserve remains for discovery by later archaeologists. Other funeral patterns, such as ritual exposure of the body to the elements, could have been practiced before the advent of burial customs, leaving no traces. Burial may simply have been an esthetic method of corpse disposal and may tell us little about spirituality. But with the evidence of grave goods such as were found at La Chapelle, it does indeed look as if there was a belief in life after death.

The Neandertal people had weapons to hunt and kill game, and it is perhaps not surprising if occasionally, in their sparsely occupied world, they turned their weapons on one another. A skeleton showing spear wounds is known from Shanidar, and the Neander Valley man himself was severely wounded before his death.

In the Krapina site in Croatia, bones of some twenty men, women, and children are split and broken and carry cut marks that indicate that flesh has been removed. Although the cut marks were originally interpreted as evidence of cannibalism, we must also bear in mind that they may signify some sort of preburial preparation of corpses. For the present, though cannibalism is by no means improbable, we must wait for further evidence before we attribute this behavior of *Homo sapiens* to the Neandertal people (Turner and Turner, 1999).

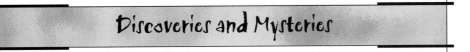

Discoveries and Mysteries

Funerary Flowers at Shanidar

Perhaps the most amazing Neandertal burial of all was found in the Shanidar cave in Iraq (see photo on page 292). There Ralph Solecki (1971) dug down through compressed deposits to uncover a total of nine burials. At the back of the cave, in a layer estimated to be 50,000 years old, he found the grave of a hunter with a badly crushed skull. As a routine procedure, Solecki collected samples of the soil in and around the grave and sent them to a laboratory at the Musée de l'Homme in France. There his colleague Arlette Leroi-Gourhan checked the pollen count, hoping it would provide useful information on the prevailing climate and vegetation.

What she found was completely unexpected. Pollen was present in the grave in unprecedented abundance. Even more astonishing, some of it appeared in clusters, and a few clusters had been preserved along with the parts of the flowers that had supported them.

Microscopic examination of the pollen indicated that it came from numerous species of bright-colored flowers related to grape hyacinth, bachelor's button, hollyhock, and groundsel. Some of these plants are used in poultices and herbal remedies by contemporary peoples in Iraq. Perhaps the mourners, too, believed that the blossoms possessed medicinal properties and added them to the grave in an effort to restore the fallen hunter to health in the afterlife. On the other hand, the flowers may have been put there in the same spirit that moves people today to place flowers on graves and gravestones.

Kurdish shepherds, shown here helping with the excavations at Shanidar, still use the cave to shelter themselves and their animals during the cold winters, much as their predecessors did thousands of years ago.

These are powerful speculations, suggesting as they do the beginnings of modern reactions to death. But not all researchers agree with Leroi-Gourhan's interpretation. Some prefer instead a completely naturalistic explanation for the pollen distribution patterns such as the action of burrowing animals. The case of the Shanidar flower burial remains problematic but highly suggestive.

Summary

At least two, and possibly more, species of archaic (premodern) humans existed during the mid to late Pleistocene. The most straightforward evolutionary reconstruction views *Homo erectus* as giving rise to *Homo heidelbergensis* around 800,000 to 600,000 years ago. Bigger-brained and smaller-jawed than their ancestors, *Homo heidelbergensis* people then spread from their (probable) African homeland to inhabit portions of

Timeline: *Homo heidelbergensis* and the Neandertals

Epoch / Period	YEARS BP	Industry	FOSSILS AND ARTIFACTS	YEARS AD	DISCOVERIES AND PUBLICATIONS
HOLOCENE 10,000				1997	Neandertal mtDNA report
UPPER PALEOLITHIC				1992	Atapuerca Neandertals
40,000					
MIDDLE PALEOLITHIC	30,000		Last Neandertals in Spain	1976	At Bodo
			St. Césaire		
200,000			Le Moustier	1971	At Arago
			La Chapelle		
	50,000		Shanidar flower burial	1965	At Hortus
			Shanidar fossils	1964	Swanscombe report
		Mousterian Industry in Middle East and Europe	Charred skulls at Hortus	1961	At Amud
			Neandertal bone flutes	1957	At Shanidar
LATE PLEISTOCENE			La Quina, La Ferrassie, Spy fossils		La Chapelle reconsidered by Strauss and Cave
			Teshik-Tash goat horn burial		
Homo erectus at Zhoukoudian			Disk–core technique of toollmaking originated		
500,000			Kiik-Koba burials	1939	At Monte Circeo
			Classic Neandertals		Full publication of finds at Tabūn and Skhūl
	100,000		⎰ Skhūl, Qafzeh burials, Maba Fontéchevade skull Tent shelters in caves at Lazaret Tabūn	1938	At Teshik-Tash
				1935	First Swanscombe discoveries
	150,000		Ngaloba, Narmada	1933	First Qafzeh discoveries; at Steinheim
	200,000	Sangon Industry in Africa;	Ehringsdorf and Kabwe	1931	At Skhūl, and Tabūn
			Levallois technique originated	1928	Monograph on Rhodesian finds
1 MILLION	250,000		Swanscombe, Steinheim, Dali fossils	1926	Gibraltar child
Paranthropus extinct				1924	At Kiik-Koba
	300,000		Sima de los Huesos fossils	1921	At Kabwe (Broken Hill)
			Elandsfontein		
	350,000			1914	At Ehringsdorf
LOWER PALEOLITHIC		Acheulean Industry		1913	Boule's monograph on La Chapelle finds
	400,000		Arago fossils; oldest wooden spears		
			Petralona	1909	At La Ferrassie
	450,000			1908	At La Chapelle, Le Moustier, and La Quina
	500,000		Boxgrove, Mauer		
Acheulean industry originated	550,000			1886	At Spy
1.5 MILLION					
	600,000		Bodo	1864	King creates species *Homo neanderthalensis*
			Yunxian		
	650,000			1863	Huxley's report on the Neandertal skull cap
	700,000			1859	Darwin's *On the Origin of Species*
H. erectus in Africa, the Caucasus, and Java				1856	In Neander Valley
	750,000				
1.8 MILLION					
	800,000		Gran Dolina	1848	In Gibraltar

Europe and Asia as far east as modern China. *Homo heidelbergensis,* in turn, apparently gave rise to the Neandertals—a powerfully built variety of archaic people centered in Europe and western Asia—about 300,000 years ago or earlier. The Neandertals went extinct without descendants about 30,000 years BP, despite the fact that they were rugged people with the largest average brain size recorded for any hominid species. Recent studies involving the extraction and analysis of Neandertal mtDNA support the view that these people constituted a distinct species and that they probably made little, if any, genetic contribution to *Homo sapiens.* The other species that descended from *H. heidelbergensis,* namely modern humans (*Homo sapiens*), has not only survived but thrived since its evolutionary appearance between 200,000 and 130,000 years ago.

Regardless of their increased brain sizes, both *H. heidelbergensis* and the Neandertals characteristically showed a set of rather primitive skull traits: large brows, some facial prognathism, relatively low-vaulted skulls, and little development of the chin. Flexure of the cranial base was variable, with some specimens reaching the modern human condition—a development that suggests concomitant improvements in linguistic skills.

Both *Homo heidelbergensis* and the Neandertals clearly surpassed their *Homo erectus* ancestors in lithic technology and cultural complexity. Indeed, their cultural accomplishments, in combination with a few key biological adaptations, allowed them to exploit a wide range of climatic zones, including challenging periglacial regions. In the area of lithic technology, the archaic humans showed an increase in tool types and stone-knapping techniques. In eastern Asia, *Homo heidelbergensis* people continued their traditional production of nondescript chopper-and-flake assemblages, possibly supplemented by bamboo tools. In contrast, African and European *Homo heidelbergensis* populations showed a continuation of the Acheulean hand-ax tradition early on, and later produced Levallois-flaked tools. For their part, the Neandertals developed a varied tool culture called the Mousterian, which was widely spread across Europe and the Middle East.

Clear evidence exists that archaic people, especially the Neandertals, occasionally buried their dead. Questions remain, however, about the frequency of this practice and the elaborateness of the burial rites. Few conclusions can be drawn at present about the state of spirituality, religious beliefs, and rituals among the archaics.

Overall, both *Homo heidelbergensis* and the Neandertals (*Homo neanderthalensis*) showed considerable progress toward modernity compared to *Homo erectus.* And yet in some ways they were still hovering at the edges of what we today understand as human behavior and culture. One final transformation remained before fully modern people would walk the earth.

Review Questions

1. What were the anatomical differences between *Homo heidelbergensis* and *Homo neanderthalensis*? How did each of these species differ from *Homo erectus*?

2. The role of *Homo heidelbergensis* in human evolution during the mid- to late Pleistocene is a matter of current controversy. What are the various possibilities?

3. How complex was the material culture of *Homo heidelbergensis* people, especially their lithic technology and hunting implements? Can you detect any improvements over the material culture of *Homo erectus*?

4. How complex was the material and behavioral culture of the Neandertals? Do you think the Neandertals were behaviorally human in the modern sense?

5. How did the Neandertals treat their dead? Were they actually practicing burial rites, or were they merely disposing of corpses? Do you think the Neandertals' treatment of the dead reveals a developing spirituality?

6. In 1913 the French paleontologist Marcellin Boule described the Neandertals as "bestial" creatures who represented "an inferior type [of hominid] closer to the apes than to any other human group." Based on your knowledge of Neandertal anatomy and culture, how would you respond to Boule?

Suggested Further Reading

Pitts, M., and M. Roberts. *Fairweather Eden.* Fromm International, 1998.
Stringer, C., and C. Gamble. *In Search of the Neandertals.* Thames and Hudson, 1993.
Tattersall, I. *The Last Neandertal.* Macmillan, 1995.
Trinkaus, E., and P. Shipman. *The Neandertals.* Knopf, 1993.

Internet Resources

Conveniently access these and other links via our web site at **http://www.ablongman/anthro.**

A New Species?
http://www.archaeology.org/online/news/gran.dolina.html
A report of the mid-Pleistocene fossils that some researchers classify as *Homo heidelbergensis* and others as *Homo antecessor.*

Archaeological Excavations at Boxgrove
http://www.ucl.ac.uk/boxgrove/
In 1993 a 500,000-year-old *Homo heidelbergensis* tibia was found at this English site. Details of the fossil and the location are given here.

Evolution of Modern Humans
http://daphne.palomar.edu/homo2/
Although retaining the outdated label "archaic *Homo sapiens,*" this site has lots of useful information on mid to late Pleistocene premodern humans (*Homo heidelbergensis* and the Neandertals) and their cultural achievements. Each section includes a practice quiz.

Grupo de Paleontología Humana Universidad Complutense (UCM)
http://atapuerca.geo.ucm.es/
This nicely illustrated site describes the excavations conducted since 1978 in the Sierra de Atapuerca in northern Spain, a region that has produced both *Homo heidelbergensis* and extremely early Neandertals.

Homo neanderthalensis
http://www3.cybercities.com/h/humanorigins/neanderthalensis.html
An extremely detailed description of Neandertal anatomy and the fossils from specific sites. Good photos of individual specimens.

Some Neanderthals Practiced Cannibalism...
http://www.eurekalert.org/releases/aaas-snp092499.html
Description of recent evidence for cannibalism at a Neandertal site in France.

Useful Search Terms:
Atapuerca
Homo antecessor
Homo heidelbergensis
Homo neanderthalensis
Ice ages
Mousterian tools
Neandertals

Evolution of Modern Humans

Overview

It appears that fully modern people (*Homo sapiens*) evolved from *Homo heidelbergensis* stock around 130,000 years ago, but the details—biological, cultural, and geographic—of that transformation are matters of considerable controversy. Two major evolutionary scenarios are currently being debated. The "regional-continuity" hypothesis holds that modern humans evolved more or less independently in several geographic regions, the species' unity being maintained by gene flow. In contrast, the "rapid-replacement" hypothesis holds that anatomically modern people evolved only once, most likely in Africa or the Middle East, and then spread quickly across the Old World, replacing all nonmodern hominids. This chapter discusses the evidence—cultural, anatomical, molecular, and fossil—supporting these competing evolutionary models. In addition, the chapter describes the spread of modern humans to the Americas and to Australia. Important topics and concepts include the anatomy of fully modern people; the emergence of the Upper Paleolithic; fossil evidence supporting the regional-continuity and rapid-replacement models; the fate of the Neandertals in the

Mini-Timeline: The Emergence of Modern Humans

Date (Years BP)	Evolutionary Events and Cultural Developments
12,500	Native Americans at Monte Verde (Chile)
40,000–10,000	Upper Paleolithic in Europe
40,000–20,000	Possible time of first human migration into the Americas
55,000	Humans present in northern Australia
130,000	Oldest fossils of anatomically modern humans
200,000	Possible start of *Homo heidelbergensis–Homo sapiens* speciation event

transformation to modernity; genetic and chromosomal evidence of the geographic origin of modern people; and the colonization of the Americas and Australia.

> Check our web site for additional information, photos, drawings, maps, and animations on topics in this chapter.

Discoveries of Early Homo sapiens

In recent years prehistorians have begun to seek the origins of modern humankind in diverse parts of the globe: Africa, Asia, and Australia. But the story of the discovery of early modern people begins in the Dordogne region of France (Figure 11.1), where archaeologists from many countries have excavated and analyzed and argued since 1868, when the first site was laid bare. This important discovery takes us back again to the nineteenth century, twelve years after the first Neandertal find, but still long before anyone really understood its implications or the full meaning of human evolution.

The first discovery of modern human fossils was made by a gang of railway workers cutting into a hillside just outside the village of Les Eyzies, France. They dug out the earth from an overhanging rock shelter in one of the many limestone cliffs that loom over the village, and with the dirt came bones and what looked like stone tools. Scientists summoned to the site soon uncovered the remains of at least four human skeletons: a middle-aged man, one or two younger men, a young woman, and a child two or three weeks old (Figure 11.2). The skeletons were similar to those of modern humans and were buried with flint tools and weapons, seashells pierced with holes, and animal teeth similarly perforated, probably to make ornaments.

The name of the rock shelter was Cro-Magnon, in garbled recognition of a local hermit called Magnon who had lived there. And so the name **Cro-Magnon** was affixed to these newfound humans. In the succeeding years the name was broadened to include all anatomically modern people inhabiting Europe between about 40,000 and 10,000 years ago, during a period technically known as the Upper Paleolithic.

An advantage of the Dordogne region was the extraordinary natural riches it offered its prehistoric inhabitants. The Massif Central, a mountainous plateau that covers most of central France, begins about fifty miles (eighty kilometers) east of Les Eyzies. Its high plains would have been a fruitful summer hunting ground that provided reindeer, horses, and bison in abundance. West of Les Eyzies, the coastal plain stretching toward the Atlantic was also good grazing ground. The Vézère River ran then in much the same course as it does now, providing water and, to the successors of those who learned to take advantage of it, a ready supply of fish. Many of the caves and shelters face south, offering warmth and protection from the cold winds of winter. Although many peoples around the world 30,000 to 20,000 years ago probably were nomadic, following game through seasonal migrations, it seems likely that the hunters who lived in this fortunate region were able to stay there for the greater part of the year.

Archaeologists believed that there was no cultural connection between the Neandertal and the Cro-Magnon peoples. The stone tools of the Cro-Magnons seemed markedly more sophisticated than Neandertal implements. And when archaeologists dug down through successive layers in caves, they sometimes found sterile layers between the Neandertal deposits and the deposits left by Cro-Magnons, indicating that no one had occupied the cave for a time. These layers containing no sign of human occupation were interpreted as proof that the Neandertals had become extinct without having given rise to their successors in western Europe.

Cro-Magnon anatomically modern humans living in Europe between about 40,000 and 10,000 years ago.

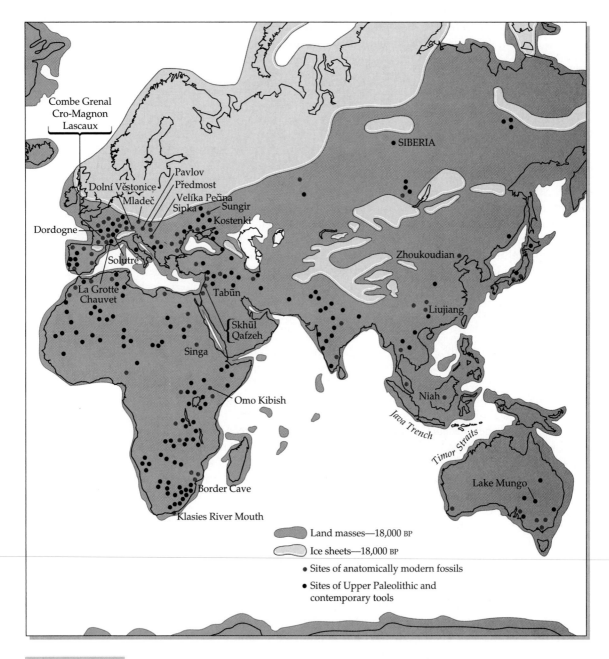

Figure 11.1

Anatomically modern fossils and related archaeological sites are today being discovered in many regions of the Old World. Modern humans lived in many places and varied environments, and their population and technology rapidly developed.

In the years since the discovery of the fossils in France, the ancient skeletal remains of anatomically modern people have been turning up all over the world: in Hungary, Russia, the Middle East, North and South Africa, China and Southeast Asia, and even in Australia and North and South America. Not all the fossils are complete, of course, and some are no more than fragments, but everywhere they are anatomically modern.

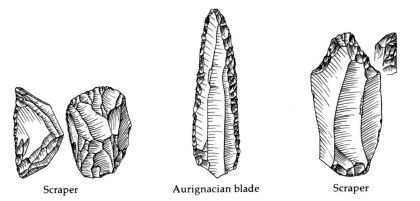

Scraper   Aurignacian blade   Scraper

Figure 11.3

Typical Aurignacian tools of the Upper Paleolithic. The Aurignacian appears to have developed in the East, probably in western Asia. The most typical Aurignacian tool was the blade, much longer and narrower than any scraper. The Aurignacian retouching was very fine. The tools were made from a specially prepared core.

The **Aurignacian industry** (Figure 11.3), with its finely retouched blade tools, was so completely unlike any typical Middle Paleolithic style that it almost certainly was imported into western Europe, apparently from the east. Although the physical identity of the very earliest Aurignacians (circa 40,000 years BP) remains undetermined, by 30,000 years ago they were fully modern Cro-Magnons. At most European sites, the Aurignacian replaced the preceding Mousterian culture more or less abruptly, a fact suggesting to many anthropologists the rapid replacement of the Neandertals by fully modern humans.

In contrast, the **Chatelperronian industry** (Figure 11.4) seems to have been an indigenous development that originated in Spain and France from a variant of the Mousterian (the Mousterian of Acheulean tradition). In addition to side-scrapers,

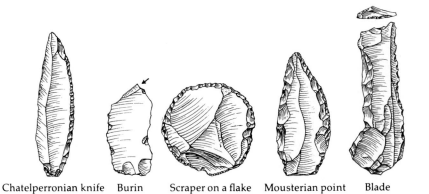

Chatelperronian knife   Burin   Scraper on a flake   Mousterian point   Blade

Figure 11.4

Typical Chatelperronian tools of the Upper Paleolithic. This tradition began with strongly marked Mousterian features and included Mousterian points, flakes, and other tools. Later tool kits contained a high proportion of burins and points.

Aurignacian industry an *Upper Paleolithic*, mainly European, tool culture that existed from about 40,000 to 27,000 years ago.

Chatelperronian industry an *Upper Paleolithic* tool culture of western Europe, largely contemporaneous with the *Aurignacian* culture (40,000 to 27,000 years BP).

denticulates, and Mousterian points, the Chatelperronian included blades, burins, end-scrapers, and numerous bone artifacts. This is the industry associated with Neandertal remains at St. Césaire and Arcy-sur-Cure. The question is: Do these sites really reflect Neandertal involvement in the development of the European Upper Paleolithic? Although there are sharp differences of opinion on the subject, many paleoanthropologists agree with Richard Klein (1992) that the Chatelperronian is best explained as being the result of traits diffusing from the Aurignacian into an otherwise Mousterian cultural context. In other words, the Chatelperronian probably reflects cultural diffusion from modern humans to Neandertals and need not imply any ancestor–descendant relationship between the two.

Thus, the Upper Paleolithic probably started in Europe, western Asia, and Africa about 40,000 years ago (thus overlapping briefly with the end of the Middle Paleolithic) and primarily as the result of cultural innovations by *Homo sapiens.* Klein and others think that the Upper Paleolithic transformation resulted from a "biologically based [advance] in human mental and cognitive capacity" (Klein, 1992:12); that is, from the achievement of full modernity of the human brain.

Fossil Evidence for the Origin of Homo sapiens

Fossils, provided enough could be found, should give us a more direct line of inquiry into the fate of the archaic humans than assemblages of tools can do. With a complete series of fossils from all over the world dated from about 200,000 to 30,000 years ago, it should be easy to study the remains and tell what happened to the archaics. Regrettably, the trail of humanity through this period is not yet well enough marked by well-dated bones to provide a conclusive picture of the transition.

The oldest known remains of anatomically modern humans (*Homo sapiens*) come from sub-Saharan Africa. Some specimens, such as Omo Kibish 1 and the remains from Klasies River Mouth, may date back to 130,000 years BP. Additionally, moderns from around 100,000 years BP have been discovered at sites in the Middle East (e.g., Skhūl and Qafzeh in Israel).

The next oldest *Homo sapiens* fossils come from sites in Asia. A cave in south China, at Liujiang, has yielded anatomically modern remains dated at 67,000 years BP, and similar fossils found at a place called Salawuzu have a date of 50,000 to 37,000 years BP. A skull from Niah in Sarawak on the island of Borneo carries an early (but questionable) date of 40,000 years BP, but is supported by Australian evidence from two skeletons with a date of 25,000 years BP. There is also impressive archaeological evidence from Australia going back beyond 40,000 years BP.

Interestingly, in contrast to Africa and Asia, dates from Europe suggest that that continent was not significantly involved in the archaic-to-modern transition. In Europe, Neandertals gave way to *Homo sapiens* between 40,000 and 30,000 years BP. Judging from sites such as Zafarraya, Spain; St. Césaire, France; and the Lapedo Valley in Protugal, the Neandertals held out the longest in western and southwestern Europe. Upper Paleolithic cultures, most of which can reasonably be assumed to indicate the presence of modern humans, date back some 10,000 years before the Neandertals' ultimate demise. Somewhat younger is the fossil evidence of European *Homo sapiens*, which dates back to slightly more than 30,000 years (e.g., at Velíka Pečina in Croatia). There is some possibility that barriers of glacial ice kept Europe out of the mainstream of the last stages of human evolution (Figure 11.1, page 300).

The main landmasses of the Old World were probably fully, if sparsely, populated by archaic humans at 200,000 years BP. But from about 130,000 years BP onward, and especially after 40,000 years BP, we find increasing evidence of anatomically modern people more or less indistinguishable from the present populations of these lands. They were modern from head to toe, talented as artists, and skilled in a wide range of technology. We must now ask ourselves how, where, when, and why the arachaic-to-modern transition occurred.

The Regional-Continuity Hypothesis

All specialists agree that the transition of archaic humans into *Homo sapiens* involved elevation and rounding of the cranial vault (which produced a fairly steep forehead); full flexion of the cranial base; reduction of the brows; development of a distinct chin; and probably some decrease in the size of the face and teeth (Table 11.1). Average brain size may have gone up or down a bit, depending on whether one believes we evolved only from *Homo heidelbergensis* or from all archaics generally, but such changes in volume probably were insignificant. Whether there were important advances in the internal organization of the brain is another question, however, and some researchers (e.g., Klein, 1989, 1992) believe that a fully modern brain appeared only with the evolution of *Homo sapiens*. Despite general agreement on the biological modifications of modernity, however, paleoanthropologists have recently disagreed sharply on the specifics of *Homo sapiens*'s evolution. Two primary hypotheses (as well as several intermediate schemes) have been proposed.

The first model, the **regional-continuity hypothesis,** suggests that modern humans evolved more or less simultaneously across the entire Old World from several ancestral populations (Wolpoff, 1996). As illustrated in Figure 11.5 (top), this scheme envisions a broad-scale transformation of *Homo erectus* into modern humans via several, geographically varying, archaic populations. In other words, all or most archaic humans from around the Old World—including the Neandertals and *Homo heidelbergensis*—

Table 11.1

Characteristics of Anatomically Modern People (*Homo sapiens*)	
Trait	**Homo sapiens**
Height (sexes combined)	ca. 5 to 6 ft (140–185 cm)—extremely variable (F is 90%—95% of M)
Weight (sexes combined)	ca. 100 to 200 lb (40–70 kg)—extremely variable (F is 90%—95% of M)
Brain size (sexes combined)	1,330 cc mean (1,000–2,000 cc range)
Cranium	High-vaulted, globular skull with widest point high on the sides; small brows; high forehead; little facial prognathism; flexed cranial base
Dentition	On average, smaller front and rear teeth and more lightly built jaws than *Homo erectus* and some archaics; definite chin
Limbs	Relatively long legs and short arms overall; body build that varies strongly with climatic conditions
Distribution	Africa, Asia, Europe, Australia, Americas
Known dates	ca. 130,000 years BP to present

Regional-continuity hypothesis proposal that *populations* of archaic humans throughout the Old World evolved more or less simultaneously into *Homo sapiens*.

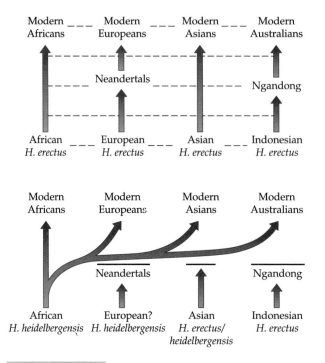

Figure 11.5

The hypothesis of regional continuity (top) proposes that *Homo erectus* people on each continent evolved through various archaic types into modern humans. In this model, intercontinental gene flow is shown by horizontal dashed lines. In contrast, the hypothesis of rapid replacement (bottom) envisions modern *Homo sapiens* evolving once—in Africa from *Homo heidelbergensis* ancestors—and then migrating throughout the Old World replacing their archaic predecessors. Note that detailed theories about the evolutionary connections between *Homo erectus, Homo heidelbergensis,* and the Neandertals are not shown in the bottom model, but can be found in Figure 10.12.

Source: Redrawn after Stringer and Gamble, 1993.

are hypothesized as having contributed to the modern gene pool. In order for this sort of transformation to work, its supporters propose that there was extensive gene flow among the various populations of *Homo erectus* and later populations of archaic people. (Gene flow is shown as dashed lines in Figure 11.5.) Africa is viewed as exchanging genes with Eurasia, which in turn shared alleles with East and Southeast Asia and Australia. Because of gene flow, regional-continuity supporters argue, new traits evolving in one region would have been carried inevitably to all other regions, and thus all of humanity would have evolved together from the level of *H. erectus* to full modernity. Let us examine some of the fossil evidence for this evolutionary model.

Evidence for Regional Continuity. In the Middle East, an ancestral relationship between archaic and modern people seems possible, with the fossils from Zuttiyeh, Skhūl, and Qafzeh somewhat bridging the evolutionary gap. The oldest of these three sites is Zuttiyeh cave in Israel (Sohn and Wolpoff, 1993). Found there in the mid-1920s was a distinctly archaic partial face plus frontal bone that has been dated to 350,000 to 250,000 years BP. Unfortunately, the fragmentary nature of the Zuttiyeh fossil and its mosaic of traits allow numerous comparisons but very little certainty with regard to its phylogenetic connections. With its large brows (centrally thickened and thinning laterally), receding frontal, and gracile zygomatic bones, the Zuttiyeh face shows some similarities to the archaic skull from Steinheim, Germany. Looking eastward, it has also been noted that Zuttiyeh's flat upper face and frontal contours resemble the *Homo erectus* population from Zhoukoudian, China. Finally, considering only possible Middle East connections, some think Zuttiyeh was ancestral to the Skhūl and Qafzeh people; in sharp contrast, others regard it as a member of the Neandertal lineage. For their parts, the Skhūl (100,000 to 80,000 years BP) and Qafzeh (120,000 to 90,000 years BP) fossils look somewhat transitional, because each includes some primitive features, even though on balance both fall within the modern category. For example, Skhūl 5 shows moderate brow ridge development, and Qafzeh 9 shows rather significant facial prognathism. Taken together, Zuttiyeh, Qafzeh, and Skhūl *may* document a gradual archaic-to-modern transition in the Middle East, but other interpretations also are possible.

In eastern Europe, although clear intermediates are missing, regional continuity has been postulated based on the fact that the most recent archaic specimens anticipate modern features and the oldest true moderns appear rather primitive. In the latter category are the specimens from Mladeč and Předmost (both sites in Moravia) and Velíka Pečina (in Croatia), all probably more than 30,000 years old and therefore among the oldest European *Homo sapiens* fossils, and all showing a mosaic of traits that include some Neandertal-like features (e.g., thick cranial bones and large brow ridges among the Mladeč people). The possibility that the Neandertals were ancestral to modern Europeans, long promoted by regional-continuity supporters, has had to be given less importance because of recent evidence from DNA.

Arguments for regional continuity in China are based on claims that certain dental and cranial traits show long histories of evolutionary occurrence in that area. In particular, evidence for a broad and flat face is claimed to link fossil and modern inhabitants of the Far East. The proposed continuity sequence in China views the archaic fossils from Dali, Jinniu Shan, Maba, and Xujiayao (all dated to 300,000 to 100,000 years BP) as evolutionary descendants of the Zhoukoudian *Homo erectus* people, and as the probable ancestors of modern populations such as that from Liujiang (67,000 years BP).

In the Indonesian/Australian region, a medley of cranial features has been used to argue that modern Australian Aborigines are descended from Javanese *Homo erectus* via intermediate populations such as Ngandong, Java, and (later) Willandra Lakes, Australia (same location as Lake Mungo in Figure 11.1)(Wolpoff, 1996). Among the traits claimed to show evolutionary continuity in this part of the Old World are well-developed brow ridges, a receding forehead, and facial prognathism. As explained in Chapter 9, however, evidence that the Ngandong fossils are quite young may bar them from a role as the Aborigines' ancestors. Furthermore, although regional-continuity proponents maintain that several anatomical traits link the late Pleistocene specimen from Willandra Lakes (WLH 50) with Ngandong on the one hand and modern Aborigines on the other, a 1998 analysis of eleven skull measurements offers differing evidence. In the new study, Chris Stringer (1998) has found WLH 50 to be no closer metrically to the Ngandong population than to a sample of African archaics (e.g., Jebel Irhoud, Ngaloba, Singa, Omo Kibish 2). Additionally, Stringer's study suggests that with regard to its modern traits, WLH 50 is somewhat closer to the Middle Eastern specimens from Skhūl and Qafzeh than it is to modern Australian Aborigines.

Finally, certain fossils in Africa from the period between 400,000 and 50,000 years BP may constitute an evolutionary series of humans from fully archaic to intermediate to anatomically modern (see Table 11.2). Very robust archaic skulls include the Kabwe

Table 11.2

Selected Human Fossils from Africa Dated between 400,000 and 50,000 Years BP			
Site	Anatomical Type	Approximate Age	Date of Discovery
Ndutu, Tanzania	Archaic[a]	400,000–200,000	1973
Elandsfontein, RSA[b]	Archaic	350,000–130,000	1953
Ileret, Kenya	Intermediate?	ca. 270,000	1992
Florisbad, RSA	Intermediate	260,000	1932
Kabwe, Zambia	Archaic	250,000–130,000	1921
Singa, Sudan	Intermediate	200,000–100,000	1924
Omo Kibish 2, Ethiopia	Archaic	ca. 130,000	1967
Ngaloba, Laetoli, Tanzania	Intermediate	ca. 130,000	1978
Omo Kibish 1, Ethiopia	Modern	ca. 130,000	1967
Klasies River Mouth, RSA	Modern	130,000–120,000	1972
Border Cave, RSA	Modern	85,000–50,000	1941
Die Kelders Cave, RSA	Modern	75,000–60,000	1976
Equus Cave, RSA	Modern	75,000–60,000	1985
Dar-es-Soltan, Cave 2, Morocco	Modern	70,000–50,000	1975

[a] Most of the archaic and intermediate fossils listed here are tentatively classified as *Homo heidelbergensis*.
[b] Republic of South Africa.

fossil from Zambia and the Elandsfontein skull fragments from South Africa. These two skulls date to at least 130,000 years BP, and may go back a quarter of a million years or more. Omo Kibish 2 and the Ngaloba fossil are more lightly built archaics from East Africa and both date around 130,000 years BP. Additionally, the Ileret cranium from Kenya, recently dated to about 270,000 years BP, has been described as showing anatomical traits that approach modernity. Lastly, the fossil remains of fully modern humans who lived 130,000 years BP have been recovered from the South African site of Klasies River Mouth on the Tsitsikama coast of Cape Province. Somewhat younger modern populations have been documented at Border Cave on the Swaziland border and elsewhere in South Africa, as well as at the north African site of Dar-es-Soltan.

Evidence against Regional Continuity. This overview of the fossil evidence for the regional-continuity model has been brief and selective, but it gives a general sense of the database used by those researchers who argue for a broad-scale phyletic transformation of *Homo erectus* into modern humans via various archaic populations. An extreme version of the regional-continuity hypothesis remains the minority opinion among present-day paleoanthropologists, however, for a variety of reasons. First, many researchers prefer to interpret hominid evolution—including its final stages and the appearance of modern humans—as primarily involving repeated cladogenetic (branching) speciation, not widespread phyletic change within a single variable species or a series of connected **chronospecies** (time-defined species). Second, even the experts disagree on the diagnostic usefulness of many of the traits claimed to show regional continuity. Third, there is a marked lack of simultaneity in the first appearances of modern humans in the different regions of the Old World. The very oldest modern fossils are from Africa, whereas elsewhere moderns appear much later. Fourth, as detailed in the next section, there is a growing body of genetic and molecular evidence for our species' cladogenetic evolution in Africa or the Middle East, followed by widespread migration.

Chronospecies a paleospecies defined by the temporal extent of its existence.

Fifth and finally, two recent studies have weakened key elements in the regional-continuity argument. As noted in Chapter 10, mtDNA data collected from the Neandertal specimens (Krings et al., 1997; Orchinnikov et al., 2000) suggest that these people belonged to a distinct and dead-end species that made little, if any, contribution to modern humans' gene pool. These results reduce the likelihood of an evolutionary link between the Neandertals and modern Europeans (see Figure 11.5, top). Furthermore, the possibility that the Ngandong (Solo) population was ancestral to modern Australians (Figure 11.5, top) has been reduced by new studies (Swisher et al., 1996) showing that the Ngandong people lived so late in time (46,000 to 27,000 years BP; see Chapter 9) that they were in fact the contemporaries of anatomically modern Indonesians and Australians who had migrated into the region from elsewhere (see below).

At present, therefore, the hypothesis of regional continuity across the entire Old World is an embattled, minority opinion, but one that certainly still has its supporters. We now turn our attention to an alternative hypothesis that is more popular among anthropologists as an explanation for the origin of modern humans: the rapid-replacement, or "out-of-Africa," hypothesis.

The Rapid-Replacement Hypothesis

Without doubt, one of the strongest pieces of evidence for the **rapid-replacement hypothesis** is the clear occurrence of anatomically modern humans in the adjacent regions of Africa and the Middle East long before they showed up in Europe, Asia, and Australia—a pattern that strongly implies a single, branching origin. As shown in Table 11.2, modern humans were apparently living in South and East Africa as early as 130,000 years ago. Relevant fossils come from Omo Kibish and the Klasies River Mouth. The archaic and transitional populations that were likely to have given rise to these early moderns have been discovered at Elandsfontein, Kabwe, Ngaloba, and Singa, and in North Africa at the Moroccan site of Jebel Irhoud. By 120,000 to 80,000 years ago, essentially modern people were inhabiting such Middle Eastern sites as Skhūl and Qafzeh.

In comparison, the appearance of anatomically modern humans outside Africa and the Middle East was much later. Cro-Magnon people first appeared in Europe sometime after 40,000 years ago; and, as shown by the skull from Liujiang, anatomically modern humans were present in China by 67,000 years BP. In addition, Niah Cave in Sarawak has produced modern fossils dating to 40,000 years BP, just slightly older than the modern material from the Upper Cave at Zhoukoudian (about 25,000 years BP). And finally, there is evidence of the occupation of northern Australia—presumably by modern people—by 55,000 years BP. A brief survey of the fossil record, therefore, can be interpreted as providing solid evidence in favor of an African–Middle Eastern birthplace for anatomically modern people.

Comparative Analyses. Detailed comparative analyses of the known fossils also seem primarily to support the rapid-replacement hypothesis. For example, anthropologist Marta Mirazon Lahr (1994) took a close look at the cranial traits claimed to reflect morphological continuity from *Homo erectus* to modern people in East Asia and Australia. She concluded that the features in question "are not exclusive to these regions, either spatially or temporally, and some occur at a higher incidence in other populations" (Lahr, 1994: 49). Based on her studies, Lahr favors the hypothesis of a single African origin for modern humans. In a similar vein, American paleoanthropologist Diane Waddle (1994) conducted a matrix correlation test of the regional-continuity and rapid-replacement hypotheses. Using more than 150 different cranial traits and

Rapid-replacement hypothesis proposal that *populations of Homo sapiens* from Africa rapidly dispersed and displaced archaic humans on other continents.

measurements, Waddle calculated and compared overall "morphological distances" between groups of fossils arranged by region (West Europe, East Europe, Southwest Asia, Africa) and age (600,000 to 125,000, 125,000 to 32,000, and 32,000 to 8,000 years BP). Waddle ran her comparisons several times, varying the hypothetical place of initial appearance of modern humans and the amount and pattern of gene flow between regions. In the end, she concluded that the study "support[ed] a single African and/or [Middle Eastern] origin for modern humans" (Waddle, 1994: 452).

"African Adam."   Several genetic or molecular studies bear on the regional-continuity versus rapid-replacement question. For example, a team of researchers led by A. M. Bowcock of the University of Texas analyzed diversity in humans' polymorphic **microsatellite** alleles, reasoning that the oldest populations should show the greatest amount of genetic variation. (Satellites are usually noncoding DNA sequences that accumulate at certain points on chromosomes.) Using genetic information from 148 people representing fourteen indigenous populations and five continents, Bowcock and colleagues found that the "diversity of microsatellites is highest in Africa, which … supports the hypothesis of an African origin for [modern] humans" (Bowcock et al., 1994: 455). Similar results have come from studies of genetic variation in certain regions of the Y chromosome; that is, variation that is inherited only through the male line (Hammer, 1995; Hammer and Zegura, 1996). When diversity in the YAP (Y Alu polymorphism) region of that chromosome was examined, African populations were found to contain more variation than non-African groups, a finding that supports the idea that humans have been living in Africa longer than elsewhere. In fact, researchers estimate that the first man to show the pattern of Y chromosome mutations since inherited by all men worldwide—an individual dubbed our "African Adam"—lived around 185,000 years ago. Interestingly, however, the Y chromosome data also showed evidence of some Asian patterns occurring among modern Africans, rather than strictly the reverse. It appears, likely, therefore, that initial movements of early modern humans from Africa to Asia were probably followed at some later time(s) by back-migrations in the opposite direction.

The conclusion that the first anatomically modern Asians were migrants from Africa—rather than the results of an independent evolutionary origin *in situ*—recently gained strong support from a study of the genetic profiles of twenty-eight present-day Chinese populations. Chinese geneticist J. Y. Chu and colleagues used genetic information to work out the most likely ancestral migration routes into and throughout Asia. As they noted in a 1998 paper describing their work, "[I]t is now probably safe to conclude that modern humans originating in Africa constitute the majority of the current gene pool in East Asia" (Chu et al., 1998: 11766).

"African Eve."   Without doubt, however, the best-known genetic studies probing the place and date of modern humans' origin are those focused on **mtDNA** (the DNA in the *mitochondria* of cells). This work has attracted tremendous media attention to the possibility of an "African Eve." Analyses of mtDNA were pioneered by the late Allan Wilson of the University of California, Berkeley, working with numerous colleagues (Cann et al., 1987). In the late 1980s, Wilson's research team set out to measure the variations in mtDNA in people from several living populations. Because mtDNA is found only in the cytoplasm of the cell and because sperm provides almost no cytoplasm to the fertilized egg, no mtDNA is inherited from the father (that is, fertilization involves the combination of only the *nuclear* DNA of egg and sperm). Thus, the genetic codes carried by a cell's mtDNA come from the mother alone, and each of us

Microsatellites short sequences of *DNA* believed to carry no functional code.

mtDNA genetic material found in the *mitochondria* of cells.

carries the mtDNA that we inherited from our mother, her mother, our maternal great-grandmother, and so on along a single genealogical line. This is quite a different mode of inheritance from that of nuclear DNA, which comes from an expanding network of grandparents of both sexes. Our ancestral mtDNA lineage converges with that of others with whom we share female grandparents, to produce an expanding inverted tree of relationships. Using identifiable differences in the mtDNA of their subjects—differences that presumably accumulate through mutations at the rate of 2 to 4 percent per million years—the Wilson team attempted to construct a branching dendrogram or tree. Their results led Wilson and his coworkers to the following set of conclusions:

1. The mtDNA structure of the female common ancestor of all modern humanity was closer to that of most living Africans than to any other geographic group. Therefore the common female ancestor of modern humanity was most probably a woman living in Africa.
2. The amount of genetic change (0.6 percent) recorded between the most different individuals tested (calibrated on the basis of 5 million years BP for the chimpanzee–hominid split) suggests a period since that common ancestor lived of between 150,000 and 200,000 years; to take a rough mean, say 175,000 years. This was roughly the time of late *Homo heidelbergensis* and just prior to the appearance of anatomically modern humans.
3. It follows that the population to which Eve belonged gave rise to all living humans through a process of successful diversification, adaptation, and expansion out of Africa and throughout the world. It does not mean that Eve was the only woman alive at that time, but that her female progeny alone gave rise to the existing human race. She was undoubtedly a member of an interbreeding population, but the female progeny of other individuals living at that time must have eventually died out.
4. It also follows that other populations of *Homo* that lived before about 250,000 years BP in places other than Africa (that is, European and Asian *Homo erectus* and archaic humans) could not have contributed to the mtDNA of modern humankind unless there were migrations back into Africa before the critical date of origin.

Criticisms of mtDNA Studies. These broad and sweeping conclusions, wrapped in the scientific sophistication of molecular studies, seemed to provide proof positive of a common African ancestor for all living humans. But to survive in science, research results must withstand the challenges of skeptics, and in this the mtDNA studies have not been entirely successful. Indeed, critics have uncovered serious flaws in the original mtDNA research. For one thing, the validity of these studies depends on the ability of modern computer programs to produce accurate ancestor–descendant trees, and the geographic identity of "Eve" is affected by the order in which individual subjects' mtDNA types are entered into the computer for analysis. Enter the data in one sequence, and the computer says "Eve" was African. Enter the same data in another sequence, and the computer may well put "Eve" in an entirely different location. Other criticisms strongly challenge the selection of subjects for the original mtDNA studies, claiming that the researchers did not control adequately for recent (historic, as opposed to prehistoric) interbreeding between representatives of different geographic populations.

Problems such as these have led some anthropologists to dismiss the validity of mtDNA studies altogether. Nonetheless, in a review article on the subject, mtDNA researcher Mark Stoneking (1993) urged against throwing the baby out with the bathwater. While admitting that there were serious problems with the first mtDNA analyses, Stoneking maintained that "an African origin still appears to be the best explanation for the [original and other] mtDNA datasets" (1993: 64). Stoneking also noted that a second measure of mtDNA variation—information on sequence changes by nucleotide bases (presumably a reliable indicator of accumulated mutations)—also points to African populations as the oldest on earth.

One other small but important piece of evidence from genetic studies tends to support the rapid-replacement model and argues against the regional-continuity hypothesis. Genetic studies often allow estimates of humans' global population size at various points in the past, and they suggest that around the time when modern humans originated, our ancestors numbered only between 5,000 and 10,000 individuals worldwide (Hammer and Zegura, 1996). These numbers are significant because they seem too small to allow the extensive gene flow required for the regional-continuity model to work.

To summarize, the mtDNA controversy notwithstanding, the combined evidence currently favors the rapid-replacement hypothesis rather than the regional-continuity model. As diagrammed in Figure 11.5 (bottom), anatomically modern people probably first evolved by branching speciation in Africa or the Middle East around 130,000 years ago and then spread throughout the world, replacing all of their archaic predecessors. Whether or not this was a rigid replacement with no interbreeding between moderns and archaics is difficult to say. The Neandertal mtDNA data suggest little, if any, interbreeding between moderns and Neandertals in Europe. On the other hand, other genetic data, plus the 1998 discovery in Portugal of a 24,500-year-old skeleton claimed to show both Neandertal and modern traits, suggest to some researchers that some interbreeding may have occurred (Kunzig, 1999). This possibility in turn suggests a replacement-and-hybridization phenomenon. Overall, however, African genes and traits drove humans' final evolutionary transformation, and the genetic contributions by non-African archaic people to the modern gene pool are likely to have been small. The message is clear: The biological core of every living person is overwhelmingly African.

 For more on the evolution of *Homo sapiens,* visit our web site.

Transformation to the Modern Human Skull

Our discussion to this point has focused mostly on the who, when, and where of humans' final evolutionary transition. But what sorts of selection pressures could have produced the extensive remodeling of the human skull from the forms characteristic of *Homo erectus* and the archaics to that of living people?

Among the most striking changes in the skull is a reduction in the masticatory apparatus. This process seems to have begun toward the end of *Homo erectus* times—say, 0.8 million years ago—and to have continued until about 70,000 years ago, with our present head shape. The **masticatory apparatus** includes the jaws, the teeth, the associated musculature, and the supporting structures on the cranium to which the muscles are attached. The skull responds in its shape to the stresses placed on it by the jaws, and these stresses are caused not just by the action of the jaw muscles, but also by the weight of the entire apparatus. Thus, the heavy jaws of *Homo erectus* and, later, of archaic humans were balanced by a relatively large occipital bone, which sometimes projected backward as a bunlike torus. Well-developed nuchal (neck) muscles held the head up and balanced the weight of the jaws.

Masticatory apparatus the entire apparatus involved in chewing: lips, jaws, teeth, tongue, and the associated musculature.

Critical Thinking

Where, When, and Why Did the Archaic-to-Modern Transition Occur?

How do you evaluate the two major hypotheses regarding the origins of modern humans? How has recent scientific evidence from genetics forced changes in both these models? Based on the information presented in this chapter, where and when do you think the archaic-to-modern transition occurred? What role might environmental changes have had on this transition? What anatomical and cultural characteristics of *Homo sapiens* do you think might explain the selective pressures that led to the transition to modern humans?

Numerous explanations for the reduction of the jaws and teeth among anatomically modern people have been proposed. The first and most obvious is that changes had occurred in diet and food preparation that reduced the requirement for very powerful jaws, and it is significant that this change was accompanied by a marked development in technology. We can only guess that by grinding grain, chopping vegetation and meat, and eventually cooking food, early moderns reduced their need for heavy jaws.

Second, the size of the front teeth was a sort of "technological" adaptation for some archaic people, who regularly used their front teeth as a built-in tool. Teeth may have served as pliers to hold one end of some material such as wood or hide so that one hand would be free to cut, scrape, or pierce the material with a stone implement (see Figures 10.10 and 10.11). Patterns of wear on the incisors of some fossils suggest that archaics softened animal hides by chewing them and twisted plant fibers or straightened wooden shafts with the aid of their teeth. Improvements in stone implements gradually allowed people to rely less and less on their front teeth, and this then possibly led to a gradual reduction in tooth and jaw size—which in turn permitted reduction in the face and other features of the skull, giving rise to people with heads like ours.

The Shortened Sphenoid

The **sphenoid** is a small bone in the base of the skull, but the changes that it has undergone during the final stages of our evolution are extremely important. Daniel Lieberman of Rutgers University, using CT scans and radiographs of modern and fossil specimens, has suggested that a single evolutionary change—namely, the shortening of the sphenoid in the cranial base—probably triggered the final steps in the modernization of the human skull (1998). Lieberman has shown that the sphenoid of modern humans is shorter than that of either Neandertals or *Homo heidelbergensis,* or of their predecessors.

A shortened sphenoid accounts for the shorter skull base and for bringing about the retreat of the masticatory apparatus from its former out-thrust position. With the face thus pulled in, the whole brain case would have become higher to contain the same amount of brain tissue. As these changes occurred, the brow and sides of the skull would have become more vertical. Thus, the ancient low-vaulted skull would have been transformed into the modern *Homo sapiens* skull. Archaic and modern skulls are different ways of packing the same quantity of brain tissue.

As was originally proposed by David Pilbeam (1975), Lieberman believes that these changes in the skull are responsible for the evolution of the modern vocal tract, because the shorter sphenoid lies higher in the base of the skull and this results in a longer

Sphenoid a bone of complex shape in the floor of the skull.

pharynx (see Figures 11.6, this page, and 4.13, page 103). The longer pharynx made possible a full range of vowel sounds and the development of modern speech.

Speech was an incredibly important—indeed, formative—adaptation for *Homo sapiens*. This is not to say that the Neandertals, *Homo heidelbergensis*, or possibly even *Homo erectus* were completely incapable of speech. But what we see in the evolution of anatomically modern people is the final, very significant, step. Natural selection may have worked at maximum speed to weed out the slow talkers and to foster better speaking ability. It is almost impossible today, tens of thousands of years later, to sense the

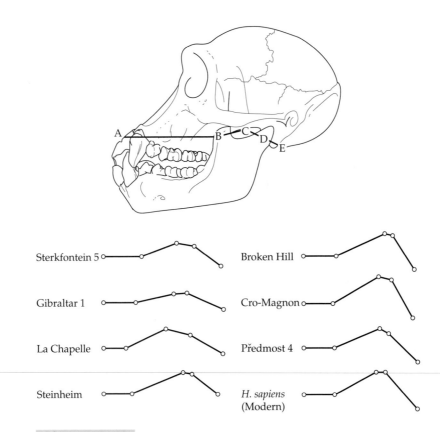

Figure 11.6

Cranial base profiles from fossil hominids and modern humans document the recent development of full basicranial flexion and modern throat proportions. As shown here on the skull of a female chimpanzee (top), profiles are measured by connecting five midline points: A, prosthion (most anterior point on the alveolar process—toothbearing ridge—of the upper jaw); B, staphylion (near the posterior edge of the hard palate); C, hormion (near the posterior edge of the vomer, one of the internal bones of the face); D, sphenobasion (a point on the sphenoid/occipital articulation); and E, basion (midpoint of the anterior margin of the foramen magnum). At the bottom of the figure, cranial base profiles are shown for an australopithecine (Sterkfontein 5), two Neandertals (Gibraltar and La Chapelle), two *Homo heidelbergensis* specimens (Steinheim and Broken Hill [=Kabwe]), two fossil *Homo sapiens* (Cro-Magnon and Předmost 4), and modern humans.

Source: Modified from Laitman, Heimbuch, and Crelin, 1979.

powerful evolutionary pressures that may have been launched when this new element was introduced into the vocal tract. The development of a modern pharynx and associated changes, with its enormous potential for communication, may very well explain a leap in physical and cultural evolution.

Evolution of the Chin

The shortening of the skull base, as described previously, tucked the face and jaws of newly modern humans downward and backward into close proximity to the neck. This shift in position not only affected a set of dwindling structures (teeth, jaws, and supporting facial bones) but also led to the evolution of that distinctive modern trait, the chin. Analyses of the mechanics of chewing have revealed how and why the chin was produced. During chewing the mandible is subjected to bending and twisting stresses as the jaw muscles pull it backward and forward and from side to side. Furthermore, lateral grinding on the molars concentrates stress specifically at the mandibular symphysis (the midline of the lower jaw). Symphyseal stresses continue to be an issue for living people—because, although we have small jaws and teeth, we can still generate powerful grinding by the molars. Typically, skeletal stresses like those on the mandible are counterbalanced by thickening of the bone in question, and in earlier hominids (as in nonhuman primates) lower jaw reinforcement usually involved internal thickening. This option was not open to modern humans, however, because tucking an internally buttressed mandible up against the neck could have constricted vital soft structures such as blood vessels, the windpipe, and the larynx, or voice box. Given these anatomical constraints, natural selection found a compromise—the lower margin of our lightly buttressed symphysis was everted slightly (turned outwards). This simple modification produced an externally reinforced jaw that was adequately spaced from the neck, and in the process gave us a chin.

The Dispersion of Homo sapiens

The most probable answer to our question of why modern head and jaw forms evolved is that all the factors that have been mentioned were at work: The pharynx certainly increased in length, and the jaws, teeth, and associated bony structures were indeed reduced in size.

Whenever and wherever it began, the evolutionary transition transformed humankind. By about 30,000 years ago the changes were largely complete, and the world was populated with people who looked like ourselves. People were living in larger bands than they ever had before. Cultures were branching and rebranching along countless idiosyncratic paths, like a plant that has lived long in the shade and is suddenly offered the full strength of the sun. Successful initiatives in technology or art or symbol making brought on more initiatives, and cultural change steadily accelerated.

Like people living today, the first modern people developed characteristic physical types from region to region, and possibly even from site to site within a region (Figure 11.7). Their diverse environments, climates, and food supplies account for some of the variations. Such physical characteristics as tallness and shortness, dark skin and light skin, straight hair and curly hair, had formed and would continue to evolve during the millennia when the human body had to accommodate itself to both heat and cold and to the variations of sunlight and humidity in different latitudes.

Four anatomically modern European skulls show some of the variation we would expect to find in a population the size of the one that occupied Europe. These are from Chancelade and Combe Capelle in France (top, left and right); from Grimaldi in Italy, near the border with France on the Mediterranean coast (bottom left); and from Předmost in Moravia (bottom right). All are dated at about 25,000 to 20,000 years BP.

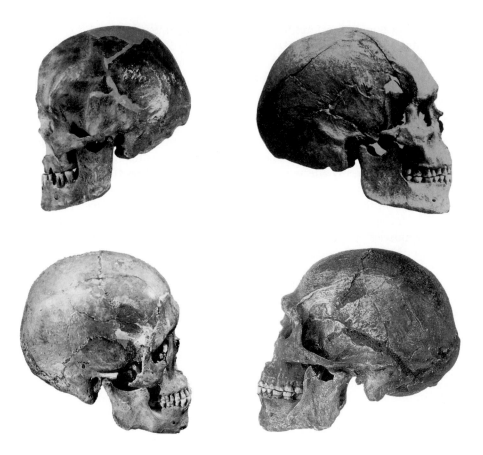

Advantages of the Large Gene Pool

That peoples varied in physical type from one location to another may be related as much to demography as to geography, for there was a great increase in numbers of people and a continued division of human populations into many fairly isolated groups. The gene pool grew with the expanding total population, but its division into small breeding populations still partially inhibited gene flow.

When the population of a species is relatively small, the genetic material available to it is relatively limited in scope, and trait variation may be similarly limited. But as the population increases, it also begins to vary more, simply because greater numbers provide more opportunities for variations to appear. When gene flow within a large population is limited, as it may have been by around 20,000 years ago, the variations may become specialized, adapting to local environments according to the dictates of natural selection and perhaps the chance consequences of the founder effect (Chapter 2).

Entry to the Americas

The first anatomically modern people lived through the last ice age. Warm and cold periods followed one another in close succession—close at least in geologic time. With each cold interlude the glaciers advanced, and with each warm interlude they withdrew. Islands rose and fell, and natural causeways and corridors appeared, making new traffic routes for the coming and going of humans. Along one of these ancient routes, *Homo sapiens* moved northward from central or southern Asia into the chilly reaches of Siberia. From Siberia they migrated across the wide land bridge of Beringia—now covered by the Bering Sea—into the continent of North America and then south along the Pacific coast or possibly by way of an ice-free inland corridor (Figure 11.8).

All indications are that *Homo sapiens* were the first humans to enter the Americas, but it may well have been a near thing. As noted in Chapter 10, stone tools from the Russian site of Diring Yuriakh suggest that *Homo heidelbergensis* people had advanced well into the depths of northeast Asia some 300,000 years ago. Judging from the available evidence, however, these archaic humans did not then proceed to cross the Beringia corridor. The land bridge from Asia was open only intermittently, although migration by boat may have been possible at other times. Furthermore, current evidence suggests that both the inland corridor leading south through the Canadian Rockies and coastal routes were made impassable by the glaciers between 20,000 and 13,000 years BP. Finally, although it seems clear that all immigrants were anatomically modern people (*Homo sapiens*), accumulating physical and archaeological evidence suggests that the New World was peopled not by one but by at least two or more migratory waves.

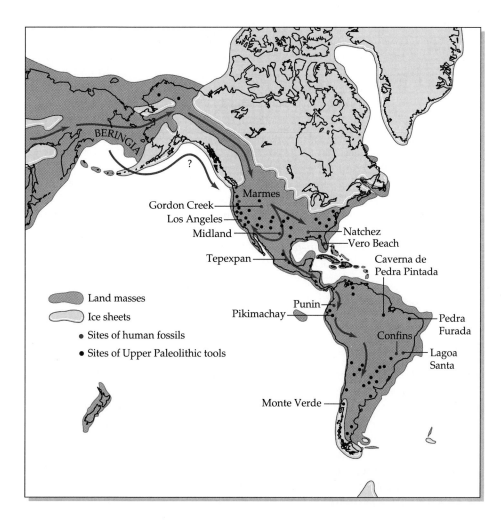

Figure 11.8

Much is still to be learned about the arrival of humankind in the New World. This map gives an idea of the migrants' most probable routes and of the extent of the landmass during the last glaciation. Carbon 14 and other dates from many sites suggest that humankind entered North America before 20,000 years BP and possibly as early as 40,000 years BP.

Discoveries and Mysteries

The First Americans

Exactly when humans first entered the Americas is still quite uncertain (Dillehay, 1999; Frison, 1993; Lahr, 1995: Meltzer, 1997). It has been believed for many years that the oldest evidence for the first Americans did not predate 10,000 years BP, and there was no sure evidence of tool traditions of very much greater antiquity. Today we have good evidence of stone spear points from North America, called **Clovis points**, back to 11,500 years BP. These points were produced by big-game hunters who were most accomplished, as their butchery sites make clear. But radiocarbon dates are beginning to accumulate from much earlier times than the Clovis cultures.

One important—but controversial—early date from the New World comes from Brazil, at Pedra Furada in the state of Piaui. Here the French archaeologists Niede Guidon and Georgette Delibrias excavated a cave site, with remarkable results. They obtained a series of radiocarbon dates from well-stratified deposits, with hearths and a stone industry, which apparently take human occupation at the site back to more than 32,000 years BP. There is even evidence of rock painting estimated at 17,000 years BP, as spalls of paint that have fallen from the painted cave walls are present in the deposits. The Pedra Furada dates are still considered tentative by many archaeologists; but if confirmed, they will support other claims of early dates from South and Central America, such as Pikimachay (Peru) at 19,000 years BP, the Alice Boer site (Brazil) at 14,200 years BP, and the Caverna da Pedra Pintada site (Brazil) at 16,000 to 9,500 years BP. Additionally, in Mexico the site of El Cedral may be older than 30,000 years BP, and deposits at Hapacoya may date to 24,000 years ago. And finally, there is a site in Chile, Monte Verde, that has yielded a very reliable date of 12,500 years BP and evidence of at least semisedentary living.

The various extremely early dates from New World habitation sites are exciting, but difficult to interpret. A conservative view, based on the solid date of 12,500 years BP from Monte Verde, suggests an initial entry into North America by *at least* 20,000 years BP, followed by movement farther south. An even earlier entry—perhaps 42,000 to 21,000 years ago—has been suggested by the results of genetic (mtDNA) studies. Greater precision in dating is needed, and the final answer may not be long in coming.

The First Australians

Although the vast ice caps of the last glaciation locked up enough of the world's water to drop sea levels more than 330 feet (100 meters), adding great expanses of dry land to the continents, such extensions never joined Australia to the mainland of Southeast Asia. The subsidence of waters from the comparatively shallow Sunda Shelf united Borneo, Java, and Sumatra to the mainland of Southeast Asia and probably exposed enough small islands to make a good deal of island-hopping feasible. But between Australia and the shelf at the edge of the Asian mainland still remained the waters of the Timor Trough, 10,000 feet (3,050 meters) deep and 60 miles (97 kilometers) wide. How did humankind manage to get across it?

Clovis point distinctive spear points of early native North Americans, dating from 11,500 BP.

ASKING QUESTIONS

What Accounts for the Diasporas of Modern People?

The geographic scattering of people with a common origin, typically through migration, is termed a **diaspora.** What were the reasons for the diasporas of modern human groups? Like the migrations of all the peoples who had gone before them, the movements of modern *Homo sapiens* probably were activated by a search for food. But in the means *Homo sapiens* used to achieve this end—in their implements, their techniques, their social organization, and their choice of habitation—they went far beyond what anyone had done before. Their diet included almost every sort of food the earth provided, and they became enormously adept at acquiring those foods. Indeed, in living off the land, and living well, they must have been far more successful than anyone before their time.

When early hominids developed their skills as hunters, they tapped a source of food energy unavailable to their mainly vegetarian predecessors. When they began to hunt migratory grazing animals and an occasional predatory animal whose territory extended beyond their own, their intake of food energy began to draw on a still wider range of resources. Thus, when territorial expansion took humans into the temperate zone, where grazing herd animals sometimes migrate between winter and summer feeding grounds, the humans' food intake tapped nutritional energy from distant sources that were sometimes extremely different from the resources supplied by their own immediate environment. Cro-Magnons, harvesting the reindeer of the Dordogne region, were benefiting from the nutrients of the northern pastures and coastal plains where the reindeer herds did some of their grazing, but where people seldom, if ever, ventured. Anthropologists call this kind of long-distance nutrient collection living on **unearned resources.** Of all the ways in which organisms had adapted to and drawn sustenance from their environment (short of actually controlling it), this was the most sophisticated. Not until pastoralism and agriculture were developed did humans' exploitation of nature become more effective.

It was long assumed that humans did not reach this major island continent until the ancestors of the modern Aborigines migrated there by boat, probably from Southeast Asia, some 10,000 to 8,000 years ago. Then, in the 1930s, finds indicated an earlier human arrival; and in 1968 archaeologists digging near Lake Mungo in New South Wales discovered a 25,000-year-old skeleton of a woman, unmistakably modern in her anatomy, and artifacts dating back as far as 32,000 years BP.

A site from Arnhem Land in Australia's Northern Territory, called Malakunanja, has recently yielded artifacts and dates that stretch the evidence for human occupation back to 55,000 years BP. Most researchers are skeptical of suggestions for an earlier arrival of humans in Australia (Klein, 2000; O'Connell and Allen, 1998). Such an early date is supported by dates from northeast Papua New Guinea of 40,000 years BP and from southern Australia of 38,000 years BP. Although there are no human remains from any of these sites, the evidence from artifacts makes it clear that humans were present in Australia at this early time. If the first Australians settled there as early as 55,000 years BP, they would have had considerably greater problems than if they had arrived as late as 30,000 years BP during the last glaciation, because the sea level at 55,000 BP was only about 98 feet (30 meters) below its present levels. This means that people would have had to cross far wider straits and far more ocean by watercraft than if sea levels had been lower. There was, however, a cold spell between 70,000 and 60,000 years ago, and during this time the sea level dropped 195 to 225 feet (60 to 70 meters). On the present evidence, this might have been the opportunity that made it possible for this historic human migration. Even then, the first Australians must have crossed seas as wide as 250 miles (400 kilometers), an extraordinary undertaking.

It is very hard to imagine either the means or the motivation for such a remarkable journey. The earliest clear archaeological evidence of any form of watercraft dates from

Diaspora migration and dispersion of people with a common origin.

Unearned resources resources that are outside a predator's range, but to which it nonetheless gains secondary access by preying on migratory herds moving between summer and winter pastures.

only 5,500 years ago. At this time the predynastic Egyptians depicted sailing boats in their rock carvings. The Chinese may well have developed the junk at an earlier date, but the evidence is lacking. There is even a recent suggestion that Asian *Homo erectus* built watercraft some 0.9–0.8 million years ago (Morwood et al., 1998). In any event, excavations in Australia show that people from Southeast Asia must have mastered to a remarkable degree the arts of sea travel and navigation at an extremely early point in our prehistory. Was their craft simply a raft of bundled bamboo and reeds, meant for offshore fishing? Or was it perhaps a primitive version of the dugout canoe used today by Melanesians? Even more intriguing is the question of how the voyagers happened to journey to Australia. Were they carried there inadvertently by a wayward current—or, according to one far-out speculation, by a massive tidal wave like the one that rolled out from the island of Krakatoa during a volcanic eruption there in the nineteenth century? Or did they go to Australia purposefully? If so, what drew them? We do not know.

Summary

The oldest fossils of anatomically modern people (*Homo sapiens*) date from about 130,000 years ago and come from Africa. Modern fossils that are only slightly younger have been found in the Middle East. The complete replacement of archaics by modern people took quite some time, however, and was not completed until perhaps 30,000 years BP. During this period the Middle Paleolithic stone tool industries (Acheulean, Mousterian) were slowly replaced by quite different blade tool industries (Aurignacian, Chatelperronian), and this industrial transformation broadly accompanied the human transformation.

Precisely how the evolutionary transition occurred is a matter of much debate among paleoanthropologists, but there seem to be two primary possibilities. The rapid-replacement hypothesis holds that modern people evolved once, by cladogenetic branching, in Africa and/or the Middle East. Once in existence, modern people spread all across the Old World, replacing archaic humans everywhere. This rapid-replacement model is well supported by the fossil record as well as by anatomical, genetic, and molecular studies. A second, and less likely, hypothesis holds that modern people evolved more or less simultaneously in several regions of the Old World. This model, dubbed the regional-continuity hypothesis, envisions broad-scale phyletic transformation of *Homo erectus* into archaic humans and then into *Homo sapiens*. As noted, the weight of the evidence strongly favors rapid replacement, but it is important to remember that some slight hybridization (gene leakage) between *Homo sapiens* migrants and indigenous archaics cannot be ruled out completely. Thus, some non-African archaic populations may have contributed to the *Homo sapiens* gene pool.

The physical changes from archaic people to modern humans involved mainly a remodeling of the cranium and the face. Skulls became more rounded and higher-vaulted; foreheads became more vertical; faces and teeth were reduced in average size; the chin was added; and, of particular importance, the cranial base became sharply flexed. The last change may well have allowed the full development of modern speech, which may have facilitated rapid cultural progress.

Once anatomical modernity had been achieved, humans did not waste much time spreading to Australia and the Americas. Modern people were living in Australia some 55,000 years ago, and they may have entered the New World via the Bering Strait between 42,000 and 21,000 years BP.

Timeline: The Modern Transformation

This chart shows the approximate chronology of the Middle to upper Paleolithic sequence. Many dates are approximate.

NEOLITHIC AND MESOLITHIC		YEARS BP	EMERGENCE OF MODERN HUMANS	TYPES OF HOMININES
10,000			Iron Age	
UPPER PALEOLITHIC			Bronze Age: pottery	
40,000	Aurignacian and Chatelperronian industries		Copper Age New Stone Age (Neolithic)	
MIDDLE PALEOLITHIC		10,000—	Mesolithic First Agriculture: domestication of plants and animals	
	Archaics in Europe, Asia, and Africa Mousterian industry		Monte Verde, Chile	
		20,000—	Lake Mungo, Australia: skeletons	
200,000			Předmost: robust modern skulls	
	Swanscombe and Steinheim; Levallois technique		Most recent Mousterian tools; Zafarraya Cro-Magnon, Dordogne	MODERN HUMANS (*Homo sapiens*)
		30,000—	Lake Mungo, Australia artifacts	
400,000	Arago		Velíka Pecína, Předmost: robust modern skulls	
			Le Moustier	
500,000		40,000—	Possible entry into Americas	
			Amud	
			La Chapelle	
		50,000—	Sipka jaw fragment: blend of archaic and modern features	
			Monte Circeo, Shanidar: all clearly archaic skulls	
	Gran Dolina fossils		Malakunanja, Australia	
		60,000—	Possible entry into Australia	
			La Quina, La Ferrassie, and Spy	
1 MILLION	*Paranthropus* extinct		Border Cave	
		70,000—		
LOWER PALEOLITHIC		80,000—		ARCHAICS AND MODERNS
		90,000—		
1.5 MILLION	Acheulean industry			
			Skhūl and Qafzeh: modern features	
		100,000—		
	Homo habilis at Olduvai	110,000—		
1.8 MILLION	*Homo erectus* in Africa, the Caucasus, and Java			
		120,000—		
2 MILLION	Oldowan industry			FIRST MODERN HUMANS IN AFRICA AND WESTERN ASIA
		130,000—	Omo Kibish and Klasies River Mouth	

Review Questions

1. What is the fossil evidence supporting the rapid-replacement hypothesis of the appearance of anatomically modern people? What weaknesses do you see in the model?

2. What is the fossil evidence supporting the regional-continuity hypothesis of the appearance of anatomically modern people? What weaknesses do you see in the model? How could wide-scale phyletic transformation of early humans have taken place?

3. Do genetic and other molecular studies suggest that modern people evolved by rapid replacement or by regional continuity?

4. How does the anatomy of *Homo sapiens* differ from that of archaic humans? What are some functional explanations for the changes? What anatomical features, if any, are unique to our species?

5. When did humans first arrive in the Americas and Australia? How were these regions first entered, and by whom?

6. Does the archaeological (cultural) record support the rapid-replacement model or the regional-continuity model of modern human origins?

Suggested Further Reading

Meltzer, D. J. "Pleistocene Peopling of the Americas." *Evolutionary Anthropology*, 1, 1993.
Stoneking, M. "DNA and Recent Human Evolution." *Evolutionary Anthropology*, 2, 1993.
Stringer, C., and R. McKie. *African Exodus*. Henry Holt, 1996.

Internet Resources

Conveniently access these and other links via our web site at **http://www.ablongman/anthro.**

Evolution of the Skull
http://abcnews.go.com/sections/science/Daily News/hominidskulls980513.html
This site reports on the research of Professor Daniel Lieberman into the evolutionary development of modern human skull anatomy.

Human Anatomy Online
http://innerbody.com/htm/body.html
Details of the skeletal and soft tissue of modern humans.

The Great DNA Hunt
http://www.archaeology.org/9609/abstracts/dna.html
Abstracted from *Archaeology* magazine, this site presents evidence from mtDNA, Y chromosome DNA, and other molecular studies on the question of modern human origins.

The Great DNA Hunt, Part II: Colonizing the Americas
http://www.archaeology.org/9611/abstracts/dna.html
The application of genetic data to the problem of human migrations into the New World.

The Origins of Modern Humans: Multiregional and Replacement Theories
http://www.linfield.edu/~mrobert/origins.html
Maintained by biologist Michael Roberts, this site provides extensive information on the two primary hypotheses on the evolution of modern people.

Useful Search Terms:
Clovis
Homo sapiens
Mitochondrial DNA
Modern human origins
Native Australians
Paleoindians
Rapid-replacement (or out-of-Africa) hypothesis
Regional-continuity (or multiregional) hypothesis

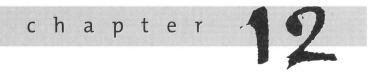

The Longest Journey

Overview

A significant upswing in cultural complexity followed the evolution of anatomically modern humans—*Homo sapiens*—and this chapter describes that cultural surge. People gained increased control over the production and use of fire; improved gathering, fishing, and hunting techniques ensured a dependable food supply and allowed a degree of sedentary living; and technology broadened through the invention of new stone tool types and the use of bone, antler, and ivory as raw materials. Striking improvements in artistic endeavors and skill resulted in beautiful rock shelter and cave art, carved ivory and bone implements, and clay sculptures. Elaboration of funeral rites very likely reflected in the development of religion. Humankind had become modern not only anatomically but intellectually as well.

Important topics and concepts in this chapter include new fire-making techniques; technological innovations and the use of new raw materials; improvements in subsistence

Mini-Timeline: Cultural Adaptations of *Homo sapiens*

Date (years BP)	Evolutionary Events and Cultural Development
10,000	End of Upper Paleolithic
16,500–11,000	Magdalenian culture (blade tools and harpoons)
20,000	Probable first use of bow and arrow
21,000–16,500	Solutrean culture (laurel-leaf blades)
27,000–21,000	Perigordian culture (female figurines)
33,000–30,000	Oldest cave art (La Grotte Chauvet)
40,000–27,000	Aurignacian culture
40,000	Start of Upper Paleolithic
130,000	Oldest fossils of *Homo sapiens*

activities; the development of art and ritual, human altruism, plant and animal domestication; the beginnings and effects of settled living; physical variation among living humans; human traits as evolutionary adaptations; human population growth; and humans' control over their evolutionary future. The chapter concludes with a discussion of some of the challenges that await humans in the future, including the limiting of global population size and the wise use of our growing control over our own evolution.

> Check our web site for additional information, photos, drawings, maps, and animations on topics in this chapter.

How Did Human Life Change after the Pleistocene?

During their 30,000 or so years, Upper Paleolithic people made more technological progress and gained more control over their environment than had been made or gained in all the preceding million-plus years of human experience. They were master stoneworkers, improving old techniques to produce stone tools of greater effectiveness and variety; and they used bone, antler, and ivory to fashion not only new tools but domestic inventions and decorative objects as well. They learned to build better fires more easily and to use them for new purposes. Some Upper Paleolithic shelters were only a step away from real houses; they were more durable than earlier shelters and afforded more protection against the elements. And when the climate changed, these people invented ways to deal with it. Technological innovation and cultural adaptation increasingly reduced the need for physical evolution, and humans' links to their animal past were weakened. People still depended on nature, but nature's control was lessened.

The Upper Paleolithic Home and Hearth

As the last ice age people learned to help themselves more efficiently to nature's bounty, they also found ways to protect themselves more effectively from nature's rigors. Carefully sewn, fitted clothing was part of the equipment that enabled them to conquer the far north and eventually to penetrate North America. The hide clothing of these people was probably much like that of today's Inuit. A tunic or pullover with tightly sewn seams to keep heat from escaping, pants easily tucked into boots, and some sort of sock, perhaps of fur, would have been warm enough in all but the coldest weather. For frigid days, outer clothing consisting of a hooded parka, mittens, and high boots would have kept a person from freezing. What is our evidence that the people had clothing of this sort? Female figurines from Stone Age Russia look as if they are clothed in fur. Furthermore, even in more moderate climates, well-sewn clothing seems to have been an advantage; the earliest eyed needles discovered to date were fashioned by Stone Age Europeans between 21,000 and 16,500 years ago.

Humans also left proof of their ability to strike a fire quickly whenever they needed one. A cave site in Belgium yielded a beautifully rounded piece of iron pyrite (Figure 12.1), one of the few natural materials from which flint will strike sparks that will set dry tinder on fire. Sparks struck from two flints or two ordinary rocks are not hot enough to do so. Furthermore, the Belgian pyrite has a groove showing where it was struck again and again. Because iron pyrite is not easy to find lying about on the ground, each "firestone" was undoubtedly a cherished item, carried wherever a band roamed.

The growing mastery of fire is also seen at sites in Russia and France where shallow grooves were dug into the bottom of a hearth with a channel curving away from the

Figure 12.1

The oldest known firestone, this iron pyrite is from a Belgian cave, Trou-du-Chaleux. The Upper Paleolithic Magdalenian people were apparently the first to discover that flint and iron pyrite used in combination yielded sparks hot enough to ignite tinder.

hearth like a tail. The grooves and channels in these prehistoric fireplaces allowed more air to reach the fuel; fires would thus burn hotter, the first small step toward the blast furnaces of modern steel mills. The people who built these special hearths needed them because of the type of fuel they used. In an area where wood was scarce, they had to turn to a material that normally does not burn well: bone. Although bone is hard to ignite and burns inefficiently, being only about 25 percent combustible material, it gives off adequate heat. That these people did burn it is proved by the lack of charred wood and the considerable quantities of bone ash found in their specially vented hearths.

Roasting of meat and roots may have been common and would have enhanced the nutritional value of the food. The tenderizing effect of cooking also would have reduced demands on the dentition and may have led to a reduction in the size of humans' jaws and indeed of their entire masticatory apparatus.

The hearth was home, and the Upper Paleolithic people who changed so much else also changed the concept of home. Though some lived in the same caves and rock shelters that had protected their predecessors, they seem, in some places at least, to have kept cleaner house than those earlier tenants; litter was thrown outside instead of being allowed to pile up inside.

It was in regions that offered no ready-made habitations that the home improvements were most noticeable. Particularly in central and eastern Europe and in Siberia, remnants of many sturdily built shelters made of bone, stone, hide, and sod have been found in open country.

Nomadism and Sedentism

In the fertile valleys of Egypt, on the frigid plains of Siberia, and along the seacoast of Africa, Upper Paleolithic people were demonstrating that they not only could stay alive but also could actually prosper under conditions of extraordinary diversity. Cold was no barrier to their existence; when meat was scarce, their food became fish; and in at least one area we have evidence that with foresight and planning they harvested natural grains. After centuries of **nomadism,** of moving from place to place in pursuit of game or fresh supplies of plant food, humans were finally able to stay in one place and systematically exploit the seasonal resources of one locality. They were, in short, gaining ever increasing control over their relations with the natural world.

As modern human groups learned to tap the potential of rivers and seas, they met the challenges of climatic changes. The rising sea level associated with the retreat of the ice submerged the Atlantic continental shelf and increased the area of warm, shallow sea in which many species of fish could breed. The systematic exploitation of the waters' abundant protein resources—including great quantities of shellfish—was highly significant, not only because it broadened the base of the human diet, but also because it helped lead humans toward the next great step in cultural evolution: settled living. With fish and shellfish as a dependable supplement to their regular meat and plant food, people did not have to move around so much in quest of sustenance. With nets they could gather more food with less effort than they could as nomadic hunters-and-gatherers, and thus one place could support a greater number of people.

The change to **sedentism** (a sedentary way of life) and the changes in subsistence that it accompanied amounted to a minor revolution in human society and lifestyle. More efficient exploitation of resources and the permanence of living quarters brought a rapid increase in the human population. The skeletal evidence also suggests that the life span was extended (perhaps exceeding the Neandertals' life expectancy by 20 percent), which enabled people to accumulate more knowledge and to pass on more of that knowledge to their children and grandchildren.

How Did People Make Their Living?

Along with increasing population, people's sedentary living and their efficiency as food producers allowed them to accumulate more material goods, which in turn made providing food and shelter easier. Central to this growing efficiency was toolmaking technology that attained new levels of sophistication.

Solutrean Culture

Improvement in stone tools was crucial to the developing Paleolithic technical mastery. It is ironic that, despite all efforts to decipher them, no one really knows what purpose was served by the most beautiful examples of this new skill. Anyone who has ever held and examined a tool such as the magnificent "laurel-leaf" blade (Figure 12.2) must eventually wonder how this implement could have been used. Too delicate for a knife, too big and fragile for a spearhead, so beautifully crafted a piece of flint seems to be a showpiece. Clearly, to produce an object of such daring proportions required craftsmanship bordering on art, and many archaeologists think this masterpiece and others like it may have been just that: works of art that served an aesthetic or ritual function rather than a utilitarian one, and that may even have been passed from one person or group to another as highly prized items.

If the large laurel-leaf blades were made for no useful purpose, they were clearly an instance of technology transcending itself. The smaller, everyday implements on which such showpieces were modeled had strictly practical functions. They are known in the thousands and come in various styles from sites all over the world. Stone points in various sizes have been found in western and central European excavations at cultural levels called **Solutrean**—a style typified by finds from Solutré in France. There is

Nomadism lifestyle involving continual traveling between different pastures or other resources.

Sedentism a way of life marked by the lack of migratory movements and by the establishment of permanent habitations.

Solutrean an *Upper Paleolithic* culture existing in western Europe between 21,000 and 16,500 years BP. Best known for its "laurel-leaf" blades.

Figure 12.2

A laurel-leaf blade is so delicate that it could have served no practical purpose. This blade—11 inches (28 centimeters) long but only 4/10 inches (1 centimeter) thick—may have been a ceremonial object or even the proud emblem of a master toolmaker. These finely chipped blades are part of the Solutrean tool industry.

no doubt that many of these points could have served most effectively as spear points or knives with razor-sharp edges. They were significant items in the armory of a people who depended for their existence less and less on the simple strength of their biceps and more and more on their brainpower and the efficacy of their tools.

The small stone blades were unquestionably sharp and efficient. Modern experiments have shown that well-made flint projectile points are sharper than iron points of a similar type and penetrate more deeply into an animal's body. Flint knives are equal, if not superior, to steel knives in their cutting power. The only drawback of flint is that, because of its brittleness, it breaks more easily than metal and has to be replaced more often.

The importance of such blades in the lives of hunters lends authority to the theory that the large, nonutilitarian examples, of which at least several dozen have been found, may have been ritualistic objects representing the quintessential spear point. They may, too, have been used as a primitive currency for trade. On the other hand, it has also been suggested that a magnificent laurel-leaf may have simply been a tour de force tossed off by a virtuoso toolmaker as a demonstration of talent. The laurel-leaf is without doubt a splendid creation, and fewer than a handful of people in the world today are skilled enough in the ancient craft to produce one.

Tool Specialization

However different the various tool industries of this period may have been in style, in character they had much in common. Human groups everywhere produced tools more specialized than any used before. Archaeologists identify sixty to seventy types of tools in the kits of some Neandertals: scrapers meant to be held horizontally, knives with blunted backs, others with double edges, and so on. But they count more than a hundred types in the tool kits of Upper Paleolithic humans: knives for cutting meat, knives for whittling wood, scrapers for bone, scrapers for skin, perforators, stone saws, chisels, pounding slabs, and countless others. Among the innovations are two-part **composite tools.** These people are believed to have begun putting bone and antler handles on many of their stone tools, such as axes and knives. By providing users with a firmer grasp and enabling them to use much more of the muscle power in their arms and shoulders, the handles, through leverage, could double or triple the power the users could put into a blow with a tool.

One of the most important tools developed was the cutter called a burin (see Figure 12.3). It is tempting to say that Upper Paleolithic people invented the burin, but it had existed in a few Neandertal tool kits, and a few burinlike tools are sometimes found in the tool assemblages of *Homo erectus.* In the hands of early anatomically modern people, however, the burin was gradually improved and became more important and much more prevalent. As you read in Chapter 11, a burin was a kind of chisel. Today the name is given to a fine steel cutting tool used by engravers in preparing copper plates. In the Stone Age, a burin was a tool with a strong, sharply beveled edge or point used to cut, incise, and shape other materials such as bone, antler, wood, and some types of stone. It differed from most other stone tools of prehistory in that it was not used by itself to kill animals, cut meat, clean hides, or chop down saplings for tent poles. Rather, like the **machine tools** of the modern age, the burin's chief function was the manufacture of other tools and implements. With a tool that made other tools, technology could expand many times faster than ever before.

The burin probably helped produce many wooden implements, but only fragments of these have survived. The best record of the object's effectiveness is in the tools it shaped that have come down to us. Besides wood, three organic raw materials—bone, antler, and ivory—helped supply the needs of an ever expanding economy, and the burin made possible the widespread exploitation of these materials. At a typical Neandertal site, perhaps 25 out of 1,000 tools were made of bone and the rest are stone. In some Upper Paleolithic encampments, however, the mix included as much as half or an even greater proportion of bone.

Bone, antler, and ivory were the wonder materials of those times, much as plastics are today. Less brittle and therefore more workable than flint, much stronger and more durable than wood, they could be cut, grooved, chiseled, scraped, sharpened, and shaped. They could be finely worked into tiny implements like needles, or they could be used for heavy work. A deer antler makes an excellent pick. A mammoth's leg bone cracked lengthwise needs only minor modifications and a handle to become an efficient shovel. Ivory could be steamed and bent, processes adding yet another dimension to toolmaking.

Figure 12.3

This Upper Paleolithic burin is an early chisel, which was a new and important technological development. Its main use was perhaps to make other tools of wood or bone.

Composite tools tools made from more than one material or part; for example, bone-handled ax.

Machine tools tools used to make other tools, such as *burins.*

Best of all, the very animals Stone Age people hunted and depended on for food provided these materials in abundance. Many large animals—red deer, reindeer, mammoth—have antlers or tusks as well. Antlers, shed every year, lie on the ground for enterprising humans to find. Because reindeer and red deer were at one time the most abundant game animals in western Europe, antler was used there more than bone or ivory. In parts of eastern Europe and Siberia, where wood was relatively scarce, the skeletons of giant mammoths were a source of tools. A mammoth tusk might measure more than 9 feet (2.7 meters) and weigh more than 100 pounds (45 kilograms); a lot of implements could be made from that much ivory.

With its strong chisel point, the burin could easily scratch or dig into ivory or bone without breaking. To cut up a bone, the toolmaker could incise a deep groove around the bone and then, with a sharp blow, break it cleanly at the cut, just as a glazier today cuts a groove in a glass pane before breaking it. To get slivers for needles, points, and awls, it was necessary only to draw a burin repeatedly lengthwise down a bone to score two parallel grooves deep enough to hit the soft center. Then the piece of hard material between the grooves was pried out and ground to shape (Figure 12.4). Other pieces of bone could be turned into spatulas, scrapers, beads, bracelets, digging tools, and more.

In addition to domestic utensils, bone and antler provided spear points, lances, and barbed harpoon tips, with which the hunters took advantage of bountiful supplies of game. Probably at no time since have there been so many grazing animals roaming the earth: Europe and Asia had mammoths, horses, red deer, pigs, reindeer, and bison. Africa had all the animals known there today, as well as a great many others that are now extinct: enormous relatives of buffalo, hartebeest, and zebra. The scene was set for hunting-and-gathering humans to reach the peak of successful adaptation. Full exploitation of these rich resources gave an extraordinary amount of control over their environment and formed the stable basis for still further cultural developments.

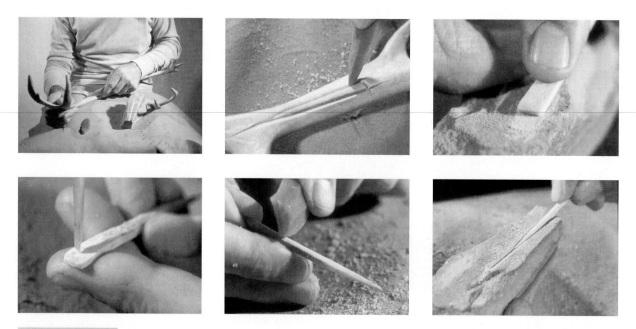

Figure 12.4

The slow process of making a needle out of an antler can be broken down into six steps.

Upper Paleothic Hunters

Two dazzling examples of Upper Paleolithic hunting success have been unearthed by archaeologists in Europe. Near the town of Pavlov in the Czech Republic (Figure 11.1), excavations have revealed the remains of more than 100 mammoths in one giant bone heap; near Solutré, in France, an even more staggering bone pile contains the fossils of an estimated 10,000 wild horses lying in a tangled heap at the bottom of a high cliff. The mammoth bones are apparently the remains of the giant beasts trapped in pitfalls; the horses had perhaps been stampeded off the cliff over many years, even generations, by intelligent hunters who were familiar down to the last detail with the terrain of the region and the behavior of their prey.

It is likely that the people of this period all across the world understood as much about hunting large herd animals as any humans in history. They undoubtedly knew just which plants the animals preferred to eat; when seasonal migrations began and how fast the animals traveled; what panicked them and what soothed them. They knew how to drive the animals into pit traps; how to snare them with baited thong nooses; and how to guide them into natural or human-made corrals, either by stampeding them or herding them quietly from a discreet distance. Once trapped, the animals could be killed with spears or knives and butchered on the spot. The meat was then taken back to camp, perhaps in processed form, possibly cut up in strips and smoked or sun-dried.

These hunters also knew a great deal about the anatomy of their victims and the virtue of eating certain of their organs. Today the inland native Alaskans save the adrenal glands of slaughtered caribou to give to young children and pregnant women. Chemical analysis of the gland reveals an astonishingly high content of vitamin C, an essential element but one hard to come by in the standard circumpolar diet. It can be assumed that Upper Paleolithic hunters, too, knew exactly which parts of the animals they hunted were good, and also which parts were good for them.

Spear Throwers and Points.   The people's profound understanding of their prey, combined with significant technical advances in their hunting equipment, paid off in increased food supplies. Hunters had long had wooden spears with fire-hardened tips or sharp stone heads to thrust or throw at their prey; but the effectiveness of a thrown spear against even a young deer, to say nothing of a thick-skinned giant auroch (a kind of extinct wild ox), must have been limited, especially if the animal was in full retreat. Upper Paleolithic hunters made the spear a more effective weapon by inventing the spear thrower—a weapon commonly referred to today by its Aztec name, the **atlatl.**

The spear thrower is, in the simplest explanation, an extension of the arm. It is one to two feet (thirty to sixty centimeters) long, with a handle at one end and a point or hook at the other that engages the butt end of the spear. Hunters hold the atlatl behind their shoulder, hook the spear, and lay it along the thrower so that the spear points forward and slightly upward. During the throw they keep hold of the thrower, which may be attached to the wrist with a thong. When throwing, they swing the arm forward and snap the wrist, launching the spear with great velocity from the end of the thrower at the top of its arc—thus taking advantage of the centrifugal force generated. The spear travels faster than if hand thrown, because the extension of the throwing arm provides more leverage; the spear thrower's end moves faster than the hand holding it.

The oldest tangible evidence of the atlatl dates from about 14,000 years BP, from the cave of La Placard in France. Here several fragments of spear throwers were discovered, including a length of bone with a hooked end resembling an oversized crochet needle. More than seventy reindeer-antler spear throwers have turned up in southwestern France

Atlatl Aztec name for the spear thrower, a rodlike device used as an extension of the arm that greatly increases both distance and impact of throw.

and near Lake Constance along the northeastern border of Switzerland. They are absent elsewhere in the Old World, perhaps because they may have been made of perishable wood and rotted away. By about 10,000 years ago, the wooden spear thrower was being used by the Indians of North and South America. The Inuit used it until recently, and some Australian Aborigines still use it today, calling it a *womera* (Figure 12.5).

Modern experiments have demonstrated the great advantages a spear thrower gives (Hutchings and Bruchert, 1997). A 7-foot (2-meter) spear can be thrown no more than 180 to 210 feet (55 to 65 meters) when launched directly from a hunter's hand, but it can be projected up to 450 feet (135 meters) with a spear thrower, and it can kill a deer at 90 feet (25 meters). Increased distance of throw may not have been the primary benefit, however. Experimental archaeologists W. K. Hutchings and L. W. Bruchert (1997) suggest that most hunting with the atlatl was done at distances of 50 to 65 feet (15 to 20 meters) from the prey, with experienced hunters hitting their target almost half of the time. Of particular importance, hits often would have been fatal or disabling, because atlatl-thrown spears generate enormous kinetic energy and highly lethal impact. (Surprisingly, the atlatl produces more kinetic energy than arrows shot from either traditional or modern bows.) The combination of greater range (compared to hand-thrown spears) and greater impact undoubtedly worked to the Upper Paleolithic hunters' advantage.

The first spear throwers undoubtedly were of wood, as the Australian *womeras* are today, but soon they also were being made from antler. People of the late Upper Paleolithic **Magdalenian** culture embellished many of their throwers with carved figures and designs and may even have painted them. One ancient Magdalenian thrower bears traces of red ocher in its hollows, and some have black painted into the eyes. Other throwers display exquisite renderings of animals, including horses, deer, ibex, bison, birds, and fish. At least three show an ibex defecating—depicted by the art of the engraver at a vulnerable moment when a kill may be made.

Other functional advances were in the spear itself. Hunters had come to realize that a barbed point does more damage than a smooth one. Harpoon-style points, fashioned from bone or antler, often had several barbs on one or both sides. Another development

Figure 12.5

The method of throwing a spear has not changed since spear throwers were introduced in Magdalenian times, about 14,000 years ago. Here an Australian is shown poised to throw his stone-tipped spear. The *womera*, or spear thrower, can be clearly seen.

Magdalenian *Upper Paleolithic* culture existing in western Europe from about 16,500 to 11,000 years BP. Produced many *blade tools* and prototype harpoons.

stemmed from the difficulty of killing an animal outright by one spear wound alone; hunters would have to follow their wounded prey for a while until loss of blood made it weak enough for them to kill. To speed this process, some hunters carved bone spear-heads with grooves along each side—runnels apparently designed to increase the flow of blood from the wound.

Bows and Arrows. An interesting puzzle is the use of the bow and arrow. There is no clear-cut archaeological evidence that people used such a weapon until the very end of the Upper Paleolithic (Klein, 1989). But because bows are normally made of wood and sinew or gut, it would be a lucky accident indeed if any had survived the last ice age; so the lack of evidence cannot be taken as conclusive. A couple of bows have been uncovered in Denmark that date back approximately 8,000 years, and a larger number of stone-tipped wooden arrow shafts, perhaps 10,000 years old, have been found at the campsites of ancient reindeer hunters in northern Germany. In a cave in La Colombière, in France, small stones have been found that are possibly more than 20,000 years old. Pictures scratched on them may represent feathered projectiles; whether these were ar-rows or dartlike spears, however, is uncertain. Among the best early evidence of the bow and arrow are approximately 20,000-year-old microliths and bone foreshafts from Africa. These artifacts closely resemble historic arrow points and foreshafts from the region.

Certainly the bow would have given hunters the advantage of increased stealth. The spear thrower, no matter how valuable an aid, required hunters to break cover and stand out in the open where they could be spotted by their prey; an unsuccessful launch would scare off the target. But with the bow, hunters could remain hidden. If they missed with the first arrow, likely they could shoot again. Moreover, the arrow was swifter than the spear and it could be shot at a variety of animals—big and small, standing, running, or on the wing—with a good chance of hitting them.

Fishhooks and Weirs. Another invention that helped Upper Paleolithic people ex-pand their food supply and make a living in varied environments was their develop-ment of fishing gear. Before the Upper Paleolithic, some human groups had earlier availed themselves of the bounty offered by streams, rivers, and the sea. At Blombos Cave on the South African coast, for example, there is some evidence for spear fishing approximately 70,000 years ago (Gore, 2000). During the Upper Paleolithic, however, fishing became a way of life for some settlements.

The oldest known bone fishhooks come from European sites about 14,000 years old. A slightly younger development (about 12,000 years BP) was a device called the **leister:** a tridentlike spear with a point and two curving prongs of bone that held the fish securely after it had been lanced. Another was the fish gorge, a small sliver of bone or wood, perhaps two inches (five centimeters) long, with a leather or sinew line tied around its middle. When the baited gorge was swallowed by a fish, it cocked sideways in its throat in such a way as not to come out easily, and the catch was made.

From a slightly later date, we have evidence suggesting that in South Africa and perhaps in Europe, people began catching fish in much greater numbers than ever before. Small, grooved cylindrical stones found in South Africa may have been weights on nets made of thongs or plant fibers. With a net, two or three people could catch a whole shoal of fish on one sweep.

The **weir,** a stone corral for trapping fish still used by some modern peoples, was probably also used at this time. This technique would have been especially effective on rivers such as the Dordogne and the Vézère in France, where spawning salmon swarm upstream in great numbers. It seems likely that at the spawning season parties went to

Leister a three-pronged spear used for fishing.

Weir barrier or dam made of stones or sticks set out in a stream or river and used as a fish trap.

the fishing grounds to lay in a supply of salmon for the whole band, which may have had its home base miles away. The fish may have been cleaned and perhaps sun-dried or smoked where they were caught, then carried to camp. At Solvieux, in France, a large rectangular area carefully paved with small stones has been excavated; its placement and design strongly hint that it was a fish-drying platform.

The Middle Stone Ages in Africa and Europe

In southwest, south, and east Asia and in many parts of Africa, small stone blades were fashioned into minute arrowheads, barbs, and adzes. These **microliths** are examples of the miniaturization of tools, a sign of progress in any technology. Microliths also appeared ultimately in Arctic America and Australia.

The Middle Stone Age in Africa dates from about 35,000 BP and was marked by a wide range of tool types that differed from the Upper Paleolithic cultures of the Eurasian continent. The varied tool kits of the African Middle Stone Age reflect the continent's vast range of environments, especially its forests and savannas, which required different adaptations. African tool kits featured microliths and tools of bone, ivory, and wood.

The Middle Stone Age in Europe occurred later, after the last retreat of ice. In forested northwest Europe an advanced hunting-and-fishing culture with compound artifacts based on microliths, wood, and bone, the **Maglemosian,** developed between 10,000 and 2,700 BP. This period of cultural development in Europe is termed the **Mesolithic,** which means "Middle Stone Age," and represents a significant break with the Paleolithic past. The European Mesolithic was characterized by a great diversification and specialization of technology in response to post-Pleistocene climatic changes. The warming of the climate resulted in a sea-level rise, productive lakes and rivers, a greater variety of food sources, the spread of forests and edible plants, and different kinds of game, especially deer, aurochs, and elk, requiring different hunting techniques. In addition to the diversification and specialization of material cultures to adapt to and exploit the new environments, changes among human groups included the greater stabilization of populations in more permanent or seasonal settlements.

Even before the beginnings of the European Mesolithic, however, a revolutionary new type of economy—the Neolithic, or New Stone Age—developed in other parts of the world, starting 11,000 or 12,000 years ago in southwest Asia. Plants and animals suitable for domestication were especially abundant in that area. Neolithic economies were based on entirely new elements: the cultivation of cereals and domesticated animals, the defense of permanent settlements, the control of water resources, the creation of trading networks, the accumulation of wealth, and record keeping.

What Are the Origins of Art and Magic?

Our discussion of Upper Paleolithic peoples has centered on their improvements in working stone and particularly bone, and on the lifestyle changes furthered by these technological improvements.

Even more important than material wealth was the evolution of social behavior—a base for the full development of language, art, and religion and for the complex forms of social and political organization that are the hallmark of all human cultures. It is the intellectual and spiritual achievements of Upper Paleolithic people that make them so impressive to us today. Particularly striking is their astounding artistic ability, a talent that seems to have sprung full-blown out of nowhere.

Microliths small, geometrically formed stone tools made from flakes, usually *Mesolithic.*

Maglemosian Mesolithic hunting-and-fishing culture of the north European plain (stretching from the UK to the Urals) with a composite microlithic culture.

Mesolithic a Stone Age period recognizable at some European sites and characterized by the use of small stone tools called *microliths;* the Mesolithic followed the *Paleolithic* and preceded the *Neolithic.*

Cave Paintings

There are dozens of examples of cave art in France alone (Breuil, 1952; Clottes et al.,1999; Laming, 1995; Leroi-Gourhan, 1967). These date from more than 30,000 to 10,000 years BP and are attributed primarily to the Solutrean and Magdalenian peoples. Equally ancient rock art sites have been found in Tanzania and in the southern African nation of Namibia. At the Namibian site of Apollo Cave, rock slabs painted with the outlines of animals have been recovered that date to between 28,000 and 19,000 years BP (Deacon, 1999). Similarly dated paintings have come from Australia. Red paint from the Sandy Creek site in Queensland is reported to date back 26,000 years. Additionally, sticklike figures from the Kimberley region in western Australia have recently been dated by optically stimulated luminescence to more than 17,000 years BP (Roberts et al., 1997). By the latest Pleistocene, rock art had also appeared in India and the Americas. All of these sites show that Upper Paleolithic peoples and their contemporaries outside Europe were close observers of the animals they hunted as well as magnificent artists. More than that, the record they left behind shows that they had a sufficiently sophisticated way of life to be able to appreciate and encourage their own talents and to work them into their rituals.

Reports suggest that the art in the recently discovered cave of La Grotte Chauvet in Ardèche, France, may surpass even that of the famous caves of Lascaux and Altamira (Clottes, 1999). It is estimated that the cave, which consists of at least four huge halls, contains more than 300 paintings by Upper Paleolithic artists. Included in the vivid images are human hands, bears, mammoths, woolly rhinos, lions, and hyenas, as well as the first known images of owls and a panther. In addition to its artworks, the cave is said to contain stone tools, hearths, and numerous bones, including the skull of a cave bear that may have been deliberately displayed amidst a group of bear paintings. This cave exemplifies the majesty and mystery of Paleolithic art.

Traditionally, Upper Paleolithic paintings and carvings have been interpreted as closely associated with people's spiritual life. One strong indication is seen in the places the artists chose to put wall paintings.

The caves in the Dordogne are basically of two kinds. The rock overhangs, more or less open and facing out over the valleys, could be made livable if people added barriers of brushwood or animal skins to keep out the wind and snow. These shelters are full of the signs of many generations of occupancy; tools lie in all strata in their floors, together with buried skeletons. Hearths abound, tending to become bigger as they become more recent. Some fragments of wall decoration have been found in the open shelters, although perhaps originally there were more that have since been destroyed by exposure to the elements.

But the most spectacular wall art is confined to true caves: deep underground fissures with long galleries and passages. These caves have their own subterranean pools, rivers, and festoons of stalactites and stalagmites. They are dark, mysterious, and very cold; they could be entered only by people holding stone lamps or torches. Certainly these caverns were inappropriate as dwelling places, and they contain little or no evidence of having been lived in. By nature removed from day-to-day life, these caves may well have been used as shrines and for the performance of certain rites.

Important observations about the location of cave art were made by the late Abbé Henri Breuil (1952), a French priest who devoted his life to the study of prehistory, and by Johannes Maringer, who also intensively studied this art. The paintings or engravings were often made in the places least convenient for viewing: in narrow niches, behind protrusions of rock, sometimes in areas that must have been not merely difficult but actually dangerous for the artist to work in. Maringer (1960) maintains that it is simply impossible that this art should have been invented, in these locations, to give pleasure to the eye of the beholder; the intention must always have been to veil it in mysterious secrecy.

ASKING QUESTIONS

What Was the Real Purpose of Cave Art?

What was the purpose of cave paintings, if they were not meant to be seen and enjoyed? The traditional explanation, accepted by Maringer (1960) and numerous other experts, is that cave art was a vehicle for magic—more specifically, a vehicle for a form known as **sympathetic hunting magic.** Upper Paleolithic people were strong and intelligent, and they were well equipped with all kinds of weapons, from spears and knives to slings. They knew how to make traps for small animals and pitfalls for large ones. They could ambush animals and stampede them. And, as we have seen, they left behind them impressive records of their prowess. Nevertheless, despite their formidable powers, they walked always in the shadow of unpredictable and incomprehensible events, which they may have seen as malign forces. Doubtless they felt it necessary to try to forestall misfortune and injury—and perhaps death, for some of the animals they came up against were extremely dangerous. Doubtless, too, they believed, like so many people living today, that magic could help them not only dodge misfortune but also gain control over the animals they wanted to kill. By painting the animals' pictures, they became, in effect, the animals' masters and strengthened their chances of dealing the prey a mortal wound during the hunt. Even today, people of many societies believe that creating the likeness of a person or thing gives the maker of the likeness some supernatural power over the subject.

This interpretation of the paintings as hunting magic has a variety of evidence to support it. First, and most direct, is the large number of animals painted with spears lodged in them or marked with the blows of clubs, as though the artists intended to illustrate what they hoped would be the outcome of a chase; see the photo here. Less obvious are the drawings of rectangular enclosures with animals seemingly trapped in them. The most frequently seen example of these is in a cave at Font-de-Gaume near Les Eyzies, where a magnificent painted mammoth seems to be caught in a pitfall even though its enormous tusks thrust beyond the snare.

There is also a hint of hunting magic in the practice of superimposing one picture over another. This phenomenon has been observed over and over again in the caves. In one spot at Lascaux in France, the paintings are four layers deep, even though there is plenty of empty wall space nearby. If the painters had meant simply to express themselves or give pleasure to others, they probably would have started with a clean wall surface for each animal depicted. The concentration of paintings in one spot, one atop another, suggests that the placement of the painting was somehow important and that the overpainting was done for a purpose. Certain areas of the cave were favored for some reason, and it would be logical to suppose that paintings that had previously brought hunters good luck came, in themselves, to be regarded as good hunting magic. Because all ritual depends on duplicating as closely as possible a procedure that has proved successful in the past, certain spots in the cave may have come to be regarded as lucky.

In some instances, entire caves seem to have been imbued with an aura of good fortune. In Les Combarelles in southwestern France, nearly three hundred animals crowd onto the cave walls. Perhaps it was this

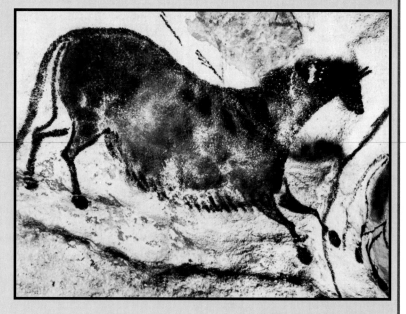

A pregnant horse gallops across the limestone ceiling of Lascaux. The slash marks above its shoulders may indicate spears. Lascaux, among the finest of all the painted caves of southwestern France, is a Magdalenian masterpiece, dated about 17,000 years BP. The newly discovered cave of La Grotte Chauvet may surpass even Lascaux in its works of art.

crowding that produced still another phenomenon of wall art: the tendency to overpaint one animal's head on another's body. Where space was at a premium, it would have been more provident to use the magic already available than to start afresh. Or perhaps artists simply looked for a less arduous way of working magic, for many of the cave paintings obviously took time and effort to execute. It is not difficult to imagine wishful hunters contemplating a beautifully painted bison and deciding to take a magical shortcut by substituting a deer's head for the bison's.

Hunting magic may also explain the occasional human–beast figures found in caves, strange-looking creatures with human bodies and animal or bird heads called *therianthropes*. According to South African archaeologist David Lewis-Williams, these creatures represented **shamans** or sorcerers, who must have played an important part in the lives of the artists. Lewis-Williams (1983) believes that many of the paintings were created by shamans in deep trance, and he has made a good case for this supposition. Such a hypothesis would account for many of the curious features of cave art that have no other obvious explanation. His ideas certainly reinforce the belief that the paintings carried powerful magical connotations.

But despite the logic and the long-term popularity of the hunting-magic hypothesis, some researchers believe that it is not the only—and perhaps not even the best—interpretation of cave imagery. For example, Margaret Conkey, of the University of California at Berkeley, and others have pointed out that the cave paintings and sculptures are generally of animal species *other* than those that predominated in Upper Paleolithic diets (Conkey, 1993). Roughly 65 percent of the European cave images depict either horses or bison, but two other species—red deer and reindeer—actually dominate the food refuse. Thus, if the images were intended to ensure success in the hunt, they didn't work very well—at least as reflected by the remains of ancient meals. Furthermore, the idea that many of the cave sites were shrines whose images accumulated over long periods has been called into question. Recent analyses of pollen in cave sediments and of paint composition ("pigment recipes") suggest that in some cases complex images, including depictions of groups and/or superimposed animals, were painted quickly and on one occasion. Results such as these tend to weaken the traditional notion that the caves were used over thousands of years by many generations of hopeful hunters.

Fertility Symbols and Other Uses of Art

Some paleoanthropologists believe that the animal paintings and geometrical signs are sexual and represent fertility magic. Pairs of animals are often shown together, sometimes in the act of mating. Horses, does, and cows are painted with swollen bellies (as in the photo on page 338) interpreted as advanced pregnancy. Other paintings show enlarged udders, as if to emphasise the rich supply of milk available to nourish any newborns.

The fertility of prey animals was a natural concern of the hunters. Scarcity of food must have been a periodic problem in many regions. During the colder episodes of the last glacial period, Magdalenian hunters killed mammoths, woolly rhinoceros, ibex, steppe horses, and particularly reindeer, which flourished in large numbers in the tundra environment. When the climate warmed from time to time, they undoubtedly hunted the deer, bison, and wild cattle that replaced the cold-adapted species; but the need to feed increasing numbers may well have led these people to encourage the natural productiveness of their game with fertility magic.

Other authorities think that cave art, though sexual in content, was far less utilitarian in its purpose. Instead of fertility magic, they see it as an attempt to express in visual symbols the dual forces in human nature: male and female. The most notable spokesperson for this point of view is French anthropologist André Leroi-Gourhan (1967), who charted the frequency of occurrence of the various kinds of animals and signs, along with their locations in the caves and their positions in relation to each other. He thinks that most of the paintings and drawings have specific sexual connotations—that

Sympathetic hunting magic the use of rituals (and associated artifacts) that practitioners believed would ensure success and safety in the hunt.

Shaman a priest of primitive religion who claims contact with spiritual forces.

deer and bear are masculine, as are signs such as spears and clubs, whereas cattle and bison, and figures of entrapment, are feminine.

Taking an entirely new approach, Alexander Marshack (1972) has examined the smaller portable items of Upper Paleolithic art under a low-powered microscope. A beautiful horse 2.5 inches (6 centimeters) long, carved in mammoth ivory and from the site of Vogelherd in Germany, is the earliest known example of animal sculpture, dating from about 30,000 years BP. The carefully carved ear, nose, mouth, and mane have been worn down by persistent handling. At some time during this use, a fresh angle or dart was engraved in its flank, apparently symbolizing an act of actual or ritualized killing. The object was touched and used often and seems to have served some important purpose.

A second example described by Marshack is the image of a horse engraved on a horse's pelvis from the site of Paglicci in Italy. Microscopic examination of the image indicated that the horse had been symbolically killed twenty-seven times. Twenty-seven feathered darts or spears were engraved on and around the horse, each made by a different engraving point and in a different style, possibly over a considerable period of time. This horse was clearly a symbol that could be used in an appropriate way when required.

A large painted horse from the cave of Pech-Merle proves to have somewhat similar characteristics: The black and red dots on its body are made of many pigments and ochers, suggesting that they were applied over a period and that the horse was used continually as an important symbol.

But Marshack has noticed other details. On some portable items he has found small marks, often in series, made at different times by different tools, which seem to indicate some sort of notation or numerical record. One particularly interesting antler fragment, from La Marche in the Dordogne, shows both a pregnant horse (which has been "used" a number of times) and a lengthy notation consisting of small notches in rows made from the tip downward, in lines of eleven (Figure 12.6). Marshack points out that eleven is the number of months in the gestation of a horse. Other notations on other fragments suggest that the phases of the moon were being logged.

Marshack's work has opened our eyes to the fact that these people were very much more sophisticated than anyone had supposed, and that they were not only great artists but also possibly on the brink of developing arithmetic, and even perhaps the beginning of very primitive writing.

Sculpture and Portable Art

Upper Paleolithic people were proficient as sculptors and engravers. In early examples of their skill, they incised the outlines of animals on cave walls. Later artists went on to develop the more advanced technique of carving subjects in high relief, often using the contours of the walls. Le Cap Blanc, near Les Eyzies, has a marvelous set of horses done in this way. The entire frieze is about forty feet (twelve meters) long; the largest horse is seven feet (two meters) long. As the bulging sides of the horses' bodies reveal, the artists incorporated the natural curves of the rock into their work with great skill. Apparently more than one artist was guided by the formation of the rock in carving this frieze, for the animal figures appear to have been worked on at various times.

Portable art objects of art, such as small sculptures, that can be carried from place to place.

These artists also made small complete statues in the round—objects known as **portable art.** In doing so, they left us a means of gaining further insights into Stone Age life and thought. The statues are usually of stone, bone, or ivory, although some were carved out of a mixture of clay and ground bone that had been hardened by firing.

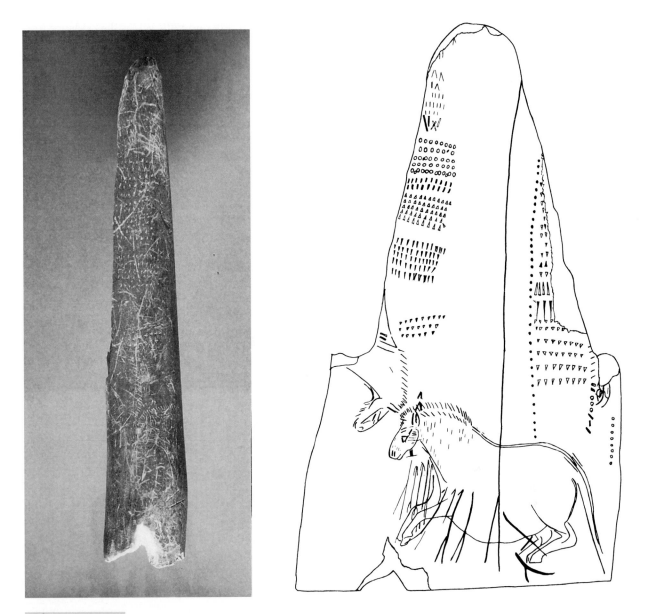

Figure 12.6

Fragment of an antler tool from La Marche, France. This is the earliest known artifact containing two types of notations: cumulative markings and naturalistic sketches. The markings may be related to the gestation period of a horse. The line drawing shows the entire surface of the antler fragment.

Ceramics. The first evidence of firing comes from the site of Dolní Věstonice in the Czech Republic (Figure 11.1, page 300). At a settlement dated about 27,000 years BP is a kiln where the bone and clay mixture was fired into a new, rock-hard material. This is the first example in technological history of synthesizing—a process that became widespread and would eventually be used in producing glass, bronze, steel, nylon, and countless other materials of present-day life. It was another 15,000 years or so before other people, living in Japan, learned to turn clay into pots; yet, as the evidence from Dolní Věstonice attests, **ceramics** had already been invented. When the kiln hut was first investigated in 1951, its sooty floor was littered with fragments of ceramic figurines. There were animal heads: bears, foxes, lions. In one particularly beautiful lion head was a hole simulating a wound, perhaps intended to help some hunter inflict a similar wound on a real lion. The floor was also cluttered with hundreds of scrap pellets that were probably pinched off the lump of unbaked clay when sculpting began and that still bore the artisan's fingerprints. There also were limbs broken from little animal and human figures. They may have cracked off in the baking or when the ancient ceramist tossed aside a failed work.

Female Figurines.   More intriguing than any waste fragments of clay animal figures on the hut floor at Dolní Věstonice are the human statuettes found there, particularly the female figures. Unlike the animals, these are not naturalistic but almost surreal. Such figurines have a very wide distribution at Upper Paleolithic sites over much of Europe and eastward as far as western Siberia and Ukraine. Although they vary a good deal in appearance, they have some significant things in common, the most obvious being that the sculptors' interest was focused on the torso. The arms and legs are extremely small in proportion to the trunk, and in some cases they are merely suggested (see Figure 12.7). The heads are also small and typically show little attempt to portray facial features, although the famous Venus of Willendorf, a four-inch (ten-centimeter)

Figure 12.7

This Czech clay figure from Dolní Věstonice shows the Venus's typical traits: huge breasts and belly and shapeless arms. This figure's legs are now broken, but they probably had no feet.

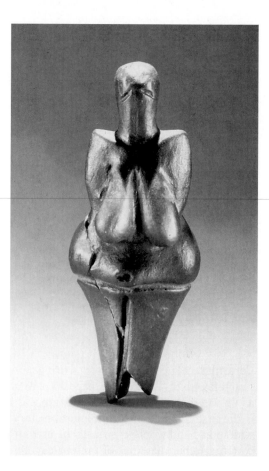

Ceramics objects of hard material made by mixing different substances (including clay) and heating them in an oven.

figurine made of limestone, does have a wavy hairdo executed with considerable care. All the emphasis is on the bodies, with their female characteristics—breasts, belly, and buttocks—greatly exaggerated in size. These **Venus figurines** look like tiny earth goddesses or fertility figures, and a good deal of informed speculation suggests that this is what they were. Many of them show the polish of long use and some the remains of red ocher, which indicates that they were symbolically painted.

Some evidence supporting the idea that they were fertility figures is based on where the statuettes were found and when they are believed to have been made. The majority of them come from the period of the Upper **Perigordian** (or Gravettian), a Paleolithic culture of western Europe that existed between 27,000 and 21,000 years ago. During this period the weather ranged from cool to very cold. In the cold periods it was bitter in the extreme, especially on the eastern European plains; nevertheless, many people continued to live there. Some made their homes in shallow pits that they dug in the ground and then roofed over with hides or other material. The vague outlines of the walls of many of these sunken huts may still be seen. The interesting thing is that these sites contain abundant examples of these female figurines, and they are often found lying right next to the walls or buried near hearths. The figurines themselves often taper to a point at the bottom, as if they had been designed to be stuck into the earth or into a base of some sort.

On this evidence, it is fairly clear that the figurines were closely associated with the daily life of the peoples who made them and have a significance utterly unlike that of the wall art created in secret, deep in underground caves. Speculating on their purpose, several authorities have proposed various theories. To Johannes Maringer (1960) the figurines seem to point to an enhancement in the status of women, possibly as a result of harsh climatic conditions and a relatively sedentary way of life. When people settle down in one place for considerable periods, the home becomes important, and homemaking usually is the woman's work. In the cold of the windswept eastern steppe, it was perhaps the women who had the critical jobs of planning, rationing, storing, and using supplies so that the group could get through the winter. Storage pits were found at many sites, some with animal remains. Women probably were sometimes responsible for making the fur clothing that the people are thought to have dressed in.

But the role of women would also have been important because of their procreative function. The mysteries of fertility and birth made women the guardians not only of hearth and home but of life itself. In the minds of some modern experts, the female figurines are cult objects. They represented the tribal ancestresses from whom the group was descended, assuring them of continuity as a group and increasing their population and the populations of the animals they hunted. Whether the little figures were worshiped as goddesses or simply venerated as good-luck charms is not known.

For more on the cultural transformations of modern humans, visit our web site.

Religion, Ritual, and Other Social Institutions

Upper Paleolithic people were concerned about death as well as life, and their treatment of the dead was careful and thoughtful. The bodies often were placed in graves dug in the ashes of previously occupied living sites, and in many places it was a common practice to sprinkle the deceased with red ocher, perhaps in an effort to bring the flush of life back to pallid skin. The practice of including grave offerings, probably begun by

Venus figurines small sculptures of women, probably fertility symbols or objects of veneration.

Perigordian *Upper Paleolithic* culture of western Europe dating 27,000 to 21,000 years BP.

archaic humans, was expanded by their successors in Eurasia to extraordinary heights of funerary luxury.

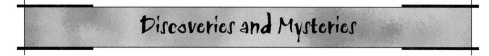

Discoveries and Mysteries

The Buried Boys of Sungir

An example of Upper Paleolithic funerary rites is the grave of two boys shown here, excavated during the 1960s in a Paleolithic settlement about 130 miles (210 km) northeast of Moscow, at Sungir. The grave suggests either that the boys were very important or that the settlers who lived at Sungir 23,000 years ago had some fairly elaborate ideas about an afterlife. The boys—one seven to nine years old, the other twelve or thirteen—were laid out in a line, skull to skull. Both had been dressed from head to toe in clothing decorated with ivory beads carved from mammoth tusks, and they wore bracelets and rings of the same material. On the older boy's chest lay a disk of mammoth tusk carved into the shape of a horse, and both boys were equipped with an assortment of ivory weapons, such as lances, spears, and daggers. The lances had been formed from a split mammoth bone that had been warmed over a fire in order to be straightened, a technique that requires considerable sophistication.

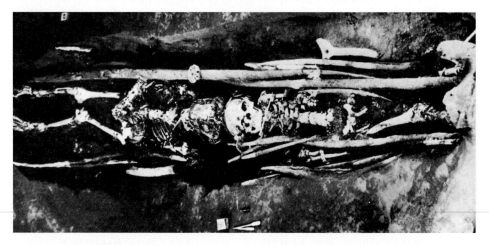

The skeletons of two boys who died 23,000 years ago lie head to head in a grave at Sungir in Russia. The elaborateness of their grave suggests that the boys were laid to rest amid solemn ritual, perhaps with a view to an afterlife.

American archaeologist D. Bruce Dickson (1990) has recently synthesized all of the available evidence on European Upper Paleolithic burial practices and art, and he has reached a set of interesting conclusions. Dickson believes that the elaborate burials of the Upper Paleolithic indicate a more complex and socially differentiated society than that of the Middle Paleolithic. Furthermore, because complex societies are supported by complex institutions, religious institutions in the Upper Paleolithic probably exceeded the simple shamanistic cult with its part-time religious specialist. Dickson believes that religious rituals, conducted fundamentally in "an attempt to control nature and society by supernatural means" (Dickson, 1990: 203), involved shamanistic direction of a community of participants.

Community rituals, according to Dickson, were likely to be performed seasonally when, following the rhythms of their subsistence activities, Upper Paleolithic groups aggregated at the painted caves that served as their ceremonial centers. Annual visits to such ceremonial centers may account for the evidence that the caves were used, and their art added to, repeatedly. Seasonal aggregations and societywide rituals would have fostered group integrity and continuity, and shared religious beliefs may even have promoted friendly interactions and information sharing among widely separated cultures. Finally, Dickson believes that woven into the ritual practices of Upper Paleolithic people were concepts about the passage of time and about human sexuality, "especially the periodicity and fecundity of women" (Dickson, 1990: 215). Thus, the Venus figurines and also artifacts suggesting notation systems are seen as facets of a larger, and quite elaborate, belief system.

Social institutions developed around these elaborated belief systems and their underpinnings in the realities of daily life. Other than religion, art, and medicine, emergent human social institutions included kinship, marriage and family, economic, political, and communication systems. These social institutions both reflected and facilitated people's adaptations to their environments and ways of making a living.

What Conditions Led to the First Civilizations?

When food surpluses became possible through the domestication of wild plants and animals, and technologies were developed for food preservation and storage, permanent settlements developed rapidly. As mentioned earlier, the development of agriculture constituted a revolution in the way humans extracted resources from the environment—the **Neolithic revolution.** For example, food surpluses supported people who could be freed from food-getting to work full time in specialized occupations in urban centers; such people included crafters, artists, weavers, metalsmiths, priests, and merchants. Complex divisions of labor and differential accumulations of wealth and power led in turn to social inequality and systems of social stratification. Eventually, population increases contributed to large-scale migration and wars of expansion or conquest.

Growing villages, such as Jarmo and Jericho, became the first cities. The most ancient city known to us is Jericho, which lies on the west bank of the Jordan River. This city was first built about 10,000 years BP and was no doubt a smaller settlement before then. Trade flourished at Jericho; hematite, greenstone, obsidian, seashells, and salt all passed through the city, together with much else of which we have no trace. The north–south trade route on which the city lay was an important stimulus to its development. But civilization probably would not have grown from these early roots without improvements in agriculture. The greatest cities grew in areas of rich agricultural land, where the productivity was greatest; they reflected the agricultural foundation on which they necessarily were based.

Cultivation and Domestication of Wild Plants and Animals

Identification of the first evidence of the domestication of animals presents problems (Diamond, 1997): The process of turning wild animals into tame ones will generate few identifiable archaeological remains, though after a considerable period of selective breeding, new breeds can be recognized by changes in skeletal structure. Dogs, sheep, goats, and cattle were probably the first animals to be bred selectively, and probably at an approximate date of 10,000 years BP in the Middle East (Figure 12.8). By 9,000

Neolithic revolution revolutionary developments in human culture that took place between 15,000 and 10,000 years ago.

Figure 12.8

This map of the Middle East shows the Fertile Crescent, where the domestication of certain plants began about 10,000 years ago. During the past 5,000 years, the rainfall of this region has diminished. Now much of the area is no longer suitable for agriculture. The reduction of rainfall was accompanied by the development of the earliest known system of irrigation in the valleys of the Tigris and Euphrates Rivers. The earliest villages and towns also developed in this region of agricultural wealth.

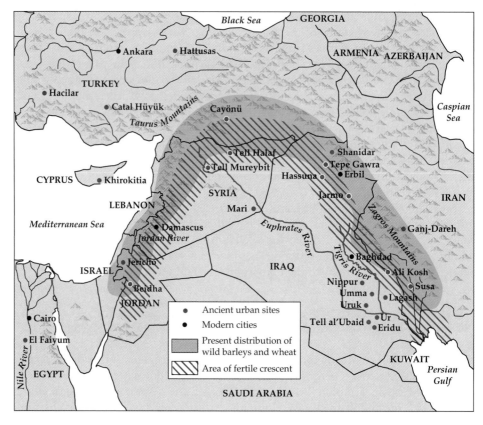

years BP, the domestic goat and sheep had become the principal source of meat and raw materials for the people of this region, and cattle and pigs were almost certainly undergoing domestication at this time. One of the most significant sites is that of Lukenya Hill, near Nairobi, Kenya, where cattle bones dated 4,000 years BP are present on human occupation floors. Earlier sites (circa 6,500 years BP) are known from Algeria. Cattle are not indigenous to sub-Saharan Africa, so these animals must have been driven in from Eurasia—which proves that they had reached a certain level of domestication by this time. Indeed, from that date on, domesticated cattle, sheep, goats, and horses are found widely throughout the Old World.

The first evidence of agriculture—of sowing, harvesting, and selecting wild barleys and wheats—dates from about 10,000 years BP and again comes from the Middle East (Diamond, 1997). Agriculture also appeared about this time, or soon after, in north China and Mexico, and somewhat later in Peru. The cultivation of rice—a crop that supports an enormous percentage of modern humans—was an early occurrence in eastern Asia. The independent development of agriculture in these different regions is one of the most remarkable events in human prehistory. The plants and animals domesticated in each area were different (Table 12.1), but the techniques were the same: The farmers collected and sowed seeds, then selected the high-yielding varieties for continued planting.

Hunting persisted in many areas; and in some regions, where humans herded animals and **pastoralism** became a way of life, agriculture did not follow until much later, even though the land and the climate were suitable. Clearly the development of agriculture must have been slow, involving a number of steps. Some researchers believe that

Pastoralism a way of life, often nomadic, that involves herding domesticated animals for milk and meat.

Table 12.1

Some Wild Vegetables and Animals Domesticated in the Three Primary Zones of Agricultural Development		
Zone	**Plants**	**Animals**
Middle East	Almonds	Cattle
	Apricots	Dogs
	Barley	Goats
	Dates	Horses
	Figs	Pigs
	Grapes	Sheep
	Lentils	
	Olives	
	Peas	
	Rye	
	Wheat	
India, China, and Southeast Asia	Bananas	Banteng (Javanese wild cow)
	Coconuts	Dogs
	Millet	Pigs
	Rice	Yak
	Soybeans	Geese
	Sugarcane	
South and Central America	Avocados	Alpaca
	Beans	Guinea pig
	Chili	Llama
	Cocoa	
	Corn	
	Gourds	
	Peanuts	
	Potatoes	
	Squashes	

the development of agricultural techniques brought with it a rapid increase in population; others contend that the increase in population came first (following sedentism) and that the resulting pressures for food stimulated the development of agriculture and animal husbandry ("necessity is the mother of invention"). Whichever the order of events, it seems clear that the two factors would soon have come to interact in the manner of positive feedback, which would have resulted in a period of relatively rapid change in both population and culture. Certainly the increase in population that we believe accompanied sedentism would have triggered the need for an even greater and more reliable food supply.

Resource domestication occurred only where the appropriate plants and animals existed and the climate was right. One such environment was the Fertile Crescent in the Middle East. Robert Braidwood of the University of Chicago, who worked during the 1960s in northeastern Iraq, described how some 10,000 years ago the climate and plant and animal life were ideal for the innovation of agriculture. Braidwood pointed out that within that zone there occur in nature a remarkable constellation of the very plants and animals that became the basis for the food producing pattern of the Western cultural tradition. Nowhere else in the world were the wild wheats and barley, the wild sheep, goats, pigs, cattle, and horses to be found together in a single environment (Braidwood, 1967). The rainfall was right for agriculture without irrigation, but not sufficient to encourage the dense growth of forest, which would have been a stumbling block to primitive farmers.

The Spread of the Neolithic Revolution

On the heels of the Neolithic revolution in the Fertile Crescent, extending from present-day Turkey to the Caspian Sea, similar developments followed in the Indus Valley in India; in the Nile Valley in Egypt; in the river valleys of China and Southeast Asia, such as the Yangtze and the Mekong, where wet and dry rice production were pioneered; and in Mexico and Peru. In the Tigris and Euphrates basin, the Indus valley, and other centers, extensive irrigation works were undertaken and they led to extraordinary agricultural productivity. Strong central governments arose to manage irrigation and dam projects; to organize labor to build terraces and canals; to settle disputes over the distribution of land, water, and other resources; and to organize food storage and surplus trade. As intensive agriculture developed, the fortunes of urban centers rose and fell according to the strength of political unity and leadership.

The control of land and water resources was the primary concern of agriculture-based economies. Desertification through overgrazing and erosion or through natural changes affecting rainfall, rivers, and water tables often determined the survival of agricultural communities. The Neolithic thus spread east and west along latitudes and waterways that would support domesticated plants and animals. Only much later did these developments move north to Eurasia and North America and south to southern Africa and Australia.

What Are Some Challenges to Humans' Future?

Animals have always faced challenges from their environment, and *Homo sapiens* has been no exception. Instead of undergoing a slow biological adaptation to make the necessary adjustments, humans have come to face the challenges of life consciously and have developed cultural responses to them. The challenges today are no fewer in number and more varied than ever before, and most of them result from our technological success over the centuries. It seems that as we respond to one challenge, we create another for ourselves. For instance, as medical science, driven by compassion, saves lives, so we face a population explosion. As we enter the twenty-first century, we face some awesome challenges to our survival.

Economic and Demographic Challenges

Physically and culturally diverse, humans are today spread throughout all regions of the globe. Yes, we appear to be a grand evolutionary success; and yet, ironically, our very success may contribute to our undoing. Consider the issue of human population size. Edward S. Deevey (1964) estimates that the hominid population of the earth 2 million years ago was little more than 100,000 individuals. By 300,000 years ago, at or near the end of *Homo erectus*'s tenancy, the human population had climbed to 1 million; and by 25,000 years ago, during the Upper Paleolithic, it had jumped to perhaps more than 3 million. (Note that there may have been significant bottlenecks within the broad trend of population growth. Modern humans—*Homo sapiens*—may have numbered between 5,000 and 10,000 shortly after their evolutionary origin.) The world population has risen at an increasingly steep pace since the Upper Paleolithic (Figure 12.9). Deevey brings home the extraordinarily rapid mushrooming of today's human population when he shows that more than 3 percent of all humans who have ever lived are alive today.

The population, according to Deevey, has not risen in a steady curve. Rather, the increase in the world's population has had a series of surges, reflecting the great cultural innovations associated with hominid evolution. The first cultural innovation, of course, was the development of stone tools. This advance allowed a population increase in two ways: Stone tools enabled hominids to venture out into a vast number of environments that people without such tools could not have survived in; it also made populations more efficient, enabling them to exploit those various environments more intensively. The population density of Africa 2 million years ago, in the days of the crude Oldowan industry, has been estimated at only one individual per 100 square miles (260 square kilometers). By the end of the Paleolithic, humans had spread around the world, and their density had probably risen tenfold. Likewise, human **life expectancy** has increased further, challenging our ability to support ballooning populations (see Table 12.2).

The second cultural innovation was the double discovery of how to grow crops and how to domesticate animals. About 10,000 years ago, this event enabled people to settle permanently for the first time, and for the first time to live together in large numbers. Even nomads herding animals could exist in far greater concentrations on a

Life expectancy the average age at death of individuals born into a particular *population*.

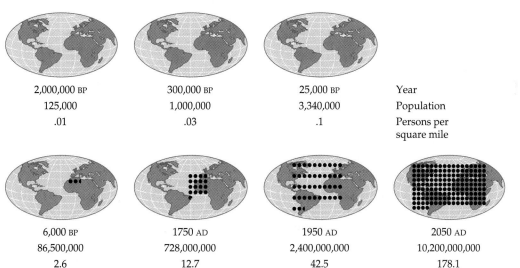

2,000,000 BP	300,000 BP	25,000 BP	Year
125,000	1,000,000	3,340,000	Population
.01	.03	.1	Persons per square mile

6,000 BP	1750 AD	1950 AD	2050 AD	Year
86,500,000	728,000,000	2,400,000,000	10,200,000,000	Population
2.6	12.7	42.5	178.1	Persons per square mile

Figure 12.9

Until about 25,000 years BP, humankind was a stable part of the equilibrium existing among animals and plants. With better hunting technology, animal domestication, and agriculture, humans began to increase dramatically and to destroy the wilderness of which they had been a part. The figures given for the populations of the distant past are, of course, estimates. The figure for 2050 AD is a projection that might be reduced by an effective worldwide population-control policy or by extensive famines.

Source: Based on Deevey, 1964.

Table 12.2

Changes in Average Human Life Expectancy	
Hominid Group	**Life Expectancy in Years**
Australopithecus	15 to 20
Homo erectus	20 to 30
European Neandertals	29
Upper Paleolithic Europeans	32
Bronze Age Austrians	38
Fourteenth-Century English	38
Present Day United States	76.7

Source: For U.S. figure, Centers for Disease Control and Prevention and the National Center for Health Statistics, 2000.

given area of land than could hunters. The effect on world population was extraordinary. In 4,000 years, it jumped from an estimated 5 million to more than 86 million.

The third innovation was the industrial age. It had its beginnings about 300 years ago, when the human population of the world was in the neighborhood of 550 million. World population has been ballooning ever since and today has passed 6 billion. If it continues at its present rate of increase, it will double within fifty years.

Although these figures are impressive, even more impressive is the *acceleration* in population growth. It took 2 million years to get through the first phase; the second took only 10,000 years; and the third has been going on for only a few hundred. How long it will continue or what the human population of the earth will ultimately be is anybody's guess. But we can be sure that, because the surface of the earth is finite, as are its resources, present rates of increase will bring us to the limit very soon. How will all those people be fed, housed, educated, and provided with decent lives?

Environmental Challenges

Interestingly, even the changes in environment brought about by the very earliest farmers often were fatal to the people who initiated them. Gary Rollefson and Ilse Köhler-Rollefson of San Diego State University have uncovered strong evidence that deforestation caused a collapse of early civilization in the Levant (present-day Israel, Jordan, and southern Syria) around 9,000 years BP (Rollefson and Köhler-Rollefson, 1992). The area was rapidly depopulated at this time, and evidence suggests clearly that this depopulation was due not so much to a change in rainfall as to the extensive felling of woodland. Trees were used as fuel for, among other things, the production of lime plaster. As time passed, houses were built with smaller and smaller timbers, and the final destruction of the woodland habitat was completed by the herds of goats that ranged over the onetime forest lands and consumed the tender saplings. Then the steep hills eroded rapidly, the soils were lost, and the flourishing communities disappeared, replaced by scrubland and desert.

This is just one very significant example of how humans have changed and, in doing so, destroyed their own productive environments. Such changes have occurred in many parts of the world since the coming of animal husbandry and agriculture brought our ancestors to the doors of civilization. The pattern has been repeated the world over, but it was especially devastating around the Mediterranean basin and in the Middle East, where the goat had been so widely domesticated, and in parts of Africa.

Changing the environment was humankind's unique achievement, and it constitutes a central theme in the last phases of human prehistory. But the continuing expansion of agriculture and animal husbandry cannot be taken to the ultimate limits of the earth's landmass without destroying all the natural wilderness and the miraculous array of wild plants and animals that occupy it. Continued destruction of the tropical forests poses a serious and immediate threat of extinction for many plant and animal species and indigenous ways of life. The further expansion of agriculture and industry promises to be destructive to the quality of life.

Technological Challenges

Humans have used technology to tame and control the environment. Machines have been devised to do most kinds of human work. The success of the machine age has been breathtaking, and technological progress is accelerating. The Stone Age lasted 2.5 million years; the agricultural age has lasted for 10,000 years or so; and the industrial age began a mere 300 years ago. What will be the impacts of rapid technological change on humans as a species?

Today we are launched into an electronic age in which the computer is an extension of a modern human's intelligence, just as the atlatl was an extension of an Upper Paleolithic hunter's arm. Will the results of these two examples of greater efficiency and productivity be comparable? Today direct communications among all the people on earth are becoming possible. Information and ideas and products are shared globally on the Internet. Satellites watch our every move—meaning that, among other things, preparations for war can be monitored. Governments find it increasingly difficult to keep secrets. How will these new realities change us? Will there be a merged panhuman culture with globally shared knowledge and skills? Could a megaculture replace all the other evolutionary forces in the human story?

Genetic Challenges

Like information technology, medical technology is having a profound effect on human life. Nevertheless, the evolutionary processes described by Charles Darwin and later biologists will, of course, continue to operate in the future. Mutations and new gene combinations will continue to provide the raw material for natural selection. According to British geneticist Steve Jones (1992b), the mutation rate due to external agents will probably remain stable in the near future. Mutations due to delayed reproduction, however, may be expected to rise. This rise will be related to the fact that modern people are having children later than has been true during most of human evolution.

This predicted rise in mutations will coincide with the medical and scientific communities' increased ability to deal with genetic problems. By using procedures such as amniocentesis, we can already learn not only the sex but also a great deal about the genotype and health of a developing fetus. How will this information be used? Will we limit ourselves to curing (through such procedures as gene therapy) or preventing diseases? Or will our desire for perfect children result in increased abortions and genetic engineering for cosmetic effects?

And, looking beyond parents and offspring, how will society use additional genetic information? With our already sophisticated medical knowledge, humans have taken

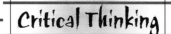

Critical Thinking

Are Humans a Third Kingdom?

Unlike any other animal on earth, humans are capable of self-conscious symbolic interaction through language. Some other primates can sign and manipulate symbols—but not without human tutors, and they lack the ability to speak. Does language set humans apart from the animal kingdom?

Unlike any other animal on earth, humans are capable of *disinterested* altruism, in which no reward is expected for behavior that benefits the group. Like humans, nonhuman primates may practice *reciprocal* altruism between individuals, in which one good turn deserves another (Trivers, 1971). It can be shown that such altruism contributes to individual and group selection. Reciprocity is an important basis of much of hu-

man social life, and there are strong sanctions against cheating. In fact, human societies have developed reciprocal altruism to the point where there are sanctions against the failure to act altruistically; that is, against selfishness. Does the additional capacity for disinterested altruism set humans apart from the animal kingdom?

Have we in some sense escaped from the constraints of our animal ancestry? Are we different in kind? We have language, technology, complex society, even civilization. Yet some have proposed that ethical behavior—behavior motivated by disinterested altruism, as contrasted with our capacity for unethical behavior—is the characteristic that most clearly divides human from beast. What do you think? What exactly are we?

several steps down the path of artificial selection within our own species. Increased knowledge of human genetics and improved ability to manipulate the genotype will take us even farther down that path. Many people are very concerned about these developments, and the issue will become even more pressing in the near future. Natural selection, genetic drift, mutation, and other natural processes got us where we are today. Are we wise enough to meddle with the selection systems of the future? Jeremy Rifkin of the Foundation for Economic Trends and other opponents of genetic engineering believe that the answer is no. According to Rifkin, "Perhaps none of us is wise enough, has the clairvoyance, the wisdom, to dictate basic changes in millions of years of genetic evolution. I don't think any of us should have that power. I think it's an unwarranted power and should not be exercised" (Levin and Suzuki, 1993: 218–219).

Behavioral Challenges

The hominid story is important because it gives us a clear picture of modern human equality—and thus allows us to look to the future with a degree of optimism. Optimism is sometimes a rare commodity.

Your authors are optimistic because of our deep belief in the unity of humankind. The fossil record shows that all modern people are the descendants of African or Middle Eastern ancestors who lived a short 100,000 to 150,000 years ago. Although in the intervening years people have spread all over the globe, have adapted to a variety of environments, and have developed substantial genetic and physical diversity, that diversity is eclipsed by our overwhelming similarities. Recent common ancestry and overwhelming genetic similarities—from these two facts flows the inescapable inference of *human unity*.

We are certainly not the first to make this inference, nor will we be the last. Human unity is a principle that we need to discover and describe over and over, in the hope that humanity will finally get the message and move from genocide and international confrontation to peaceful coexistence and cooperation. The challenges facing humankind in the twenty-first century will put a premium on human unity and cooperation

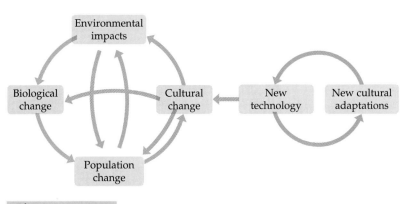

Figure 12.10

The relationship between humans and their environment can be shown as a web of positive feedback loops. Change in each factor brings about change in every other, and the rate of change is accelerating. Only biological change (evolution) is necessarily slow, and biological change will increasingly lag behind cultural change, as it already does. The most effective way to begin to slow down these accelerating feedback loops is to stabilize the human population.

as never before. In order to make any significant headway against population growth, resource depletion, and human misery, we must act as a global community (Figure 12.10). But the development of such a community clearly hinges on our acceptance of one another as absolute equals.

Humans have certainly come a long way: in life span, in efficiency in extracting resources, in population density, in technological complexity, and in increased physical comfort. Whether we are really better off as a species, and whether our progress will continue, remains to be seen. Our species, whose survival depends on culture (which is based on knowledge), must find ways to use all available knowledge and understanding to achieve better adaptation to a changing environment. *Homo sapiens*'s 130,000 years is nothing in universal and geologic time, and millions of species have evolved and become extinct in earth history. Compared with most mammals, we are evolutionary infants. From this point of view, our apparent present success can continue only if we can achieve some sort of stability in our relationship with the earth's resources. Otherwise we shall surely perish as a species.

Summary

By 30,000 years BP the sedentary lifestyle was becoming more common, with increased control of the environment. People had learned to make fire and had developed a wide range of specialized stone tools. With these they created objects made of wood, bone, antler, and ivory—all invaluable materials available in reasonable quantities. They made beads and bracelets and a whole range of hunting weapons, including spears, spear throwers, spear points, fishing gear of different kinds, tailored clothing, and eventually the bow and arrow.

Ritual life became very important, and with it art and magic. Cave paintings may have served to influence hunting success and the fertility of game. Sculpture (female figures) and the first ceramics may have been involved in fertility rites. At Magdalenian sites we find the first evidence of numeracy, and an artistic eye can be seen in the design

Timeline: Technology, Magic, and Art

Many of the dates given to finds are estimates based on indirect evidence; the brackets shown for cultural phases are approximations.

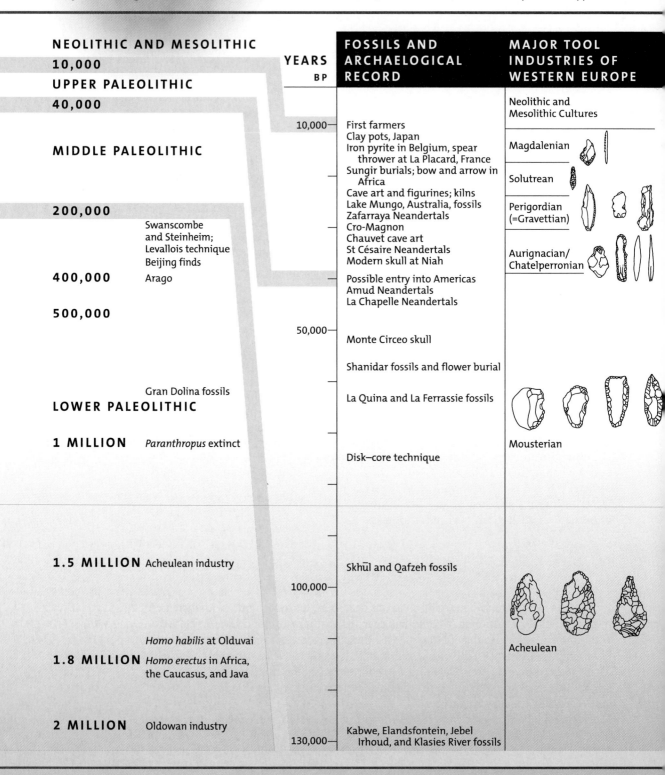

		YEARS BP	FOSSILS AND ARCHAEOLOGICAL RECORD	MAJOR TOOL INDUSTRIES OF WESTERN EUROPE
NEOLITHIC AND MESOLITHIC 10,000				Neolithic and Mesolithic Cultures
UPPER PALEOLITHIC 40,000		10,000	First farmers Clay pots, Japan Iron pyrite in Belgium, spear thrower at La Placard, France Sungir burials; bow and arrow in Africa Cave art and figurines; kilns Lake Mungo, Australia, fossils Zafarraya Neandertals Cro-Magnon Chauvet cave art St Césaire Neandertals Modern skull at Niah	Magdalenian Solutrean Perigordian (=Gravettian) Aurignacian/ Chatelperronian
MIDDLE PALEOLITHIC			Possible entry into Americas Amud Neandertals La Chapelle Neandertals	
200,000	Swanscombe and Steinheim; Levallois technique Beijing finds	50,000	Monte Circeo skull	
400,000	Arago		Shanidar fossils and flower burial	
500,000			La Quina and La Ferrassie fossils	
	Gran Dolina fossils			
LOWER PALEOLITHIC				Mousterian
1 MILLION	*Paranthropus* extinct		Disk–core technique	
1.5 MILLION	Acheulean industry	100,000	Skhūl and Qafzeh fossils	
				Acheulean
	Homo habilis at Olduvai			
1.8 MILLION	*Homo erectus* in Africa, the Caucasus, and Java			
2 MILLION	Oldowan industry	130,000	Kabwe, Elandsfontein, Jebel Irhoud, and Klasies River fossils	

of the artifacts. Considered collectively, the evidence of Upper Paleolithic burials and art suggests an extremely elaborate belief system and complex religious institutions. Clearly, Upper Paleolithic peoples were modern both anatomically and intellectually.

Cultural developments have proceeded at an ever accelerating pace since the evolutionary appearance of anatomically modern humans. Plant and animal domestication was under way by 10,000 years BP, and the establishment of civilization soon followed. These developments facilitated or accompanied a strong surge in human population growth around the world. Human evolution did not stop with the attainment of modernity, however, and differential adaptation (very likely combined with genetic drift) led to physical diversity within and between human populations.

The primary challenges for humankind in the twenty-first century include the needs to gain control over global population growth; restrict our runaway use of the earth's finite resources; and deal with the technological, genetic, and medical advances that allow us an ever increasing measure of control over our evolutionary future.

Review Questions

1. Many researchers argue that Upper Paleolithic people were more sedentary than their Middle Paleolithic predecessors. What sorts of technological and subsistence innovations and/or environmental changes would have allowed the development of sedentism? What sorts of cultural change may have resulted from a less mobile lifestyle?

2. Some of the world's most beautiful flaked stone artifacts were made by Upper Paleolithic artisans, but some seem too delicate or the wrong size for practical use. What are some of the possible functions of such "showpiece" artifacts?

3. What is the evidence for increases in hunting efficiency in the Upper Paleolithic?

4. How might cave paintings and sculptures have been incorporated into Upper Paleolithic rituals? Compare your speculations with the use of icons in modern religions.

5. What can we conclude about the relative status of women and men in Upper Paleolithic societies? Which sex do you think made the greater contribution to subsistence activities? To toolmaking? To art? To religion?

6. Do you think there is a connection between humans' genes and human culture—specifically, human moral systems?

7. The global human population is currently burgeoning. What are some of the developments over the course of human evolution that have allowed massive population growth?

8. What evidence is there to suggest that future human evolution will be controlled mainly by self-directed artificial selection, not by natural selection?

9. What, if anything, can we draw from the study of human evolution for guidance in our individual and societal decisions in the future?

Suggested Further Reading

Campbell, B. G. *Human Ecology: The Story of Our Place in Nature from Prehistory to the Present,* 2nd ed. Aldine de Gruyter, 1995.

Clottes, J., and D. Lewis-Williams. *The Shamans of Prehistory: Trance and Magic in the Painted Caves.* Abrams, 1999.

Diamond, J. *Guns, Germs, and Steel.* W. W. Norton, 1997.
Dickson, D. B. *The Dawn of Belief.* University of Arizona Press, 1990.

Internet Resources

Conveniently access these and other links via our web site at **http://www.ablongman/anthro.**

New Perspectives on Agricultural Origins in the Ancient Near East
http://www.mc.maricopa.edu/academic/cult_sci/anthro/lost_tribes/agriculture.html
This site discusses the development of farming and herding in the Khabur Basin of ancient Mesopotamia.

Rock Links!
http://www.geocities.com/Tokyo/2384/links.html
Links to more than two hundred rock art home pages.

Self-Representation in Upper Paleolithic Female Figurines
http://cmsu2.cmsu.edu/~Idm4683/l.htm
An illustrated paper by Professor Le Roy McDermott exploring the hypothesis that the Upper Paleolothic Venus figurines are women's views of their own bodies.

Stone Age Man Wasn't So Dumb
http://cogweb.english.ucsb.edu/EP/Blombos.html
As described here, South Africa's Blombos Cave may have produced evidence of complex culture that predates the European Upper Paleolithic.

The Chauvet-Pont-d'Arc Cave
http://www.culture.fr/culture/arcnat/chauvet/en/gvpda-d.htm
A nicely illustrated site describing the recently discovered painted cave in the Ardèche region of France.

Year 2000 World Population Data Sheet
http://www.prb.org/pubs/wpds2000/
Maintained by the Population Reference Bureau, this site provides current information on the global human population and projections of growth.

Useful Search Terms:
Animal domestication
Cave art
Paleolithic art
Plant domestication
Population explosion
Upper Paleolithic

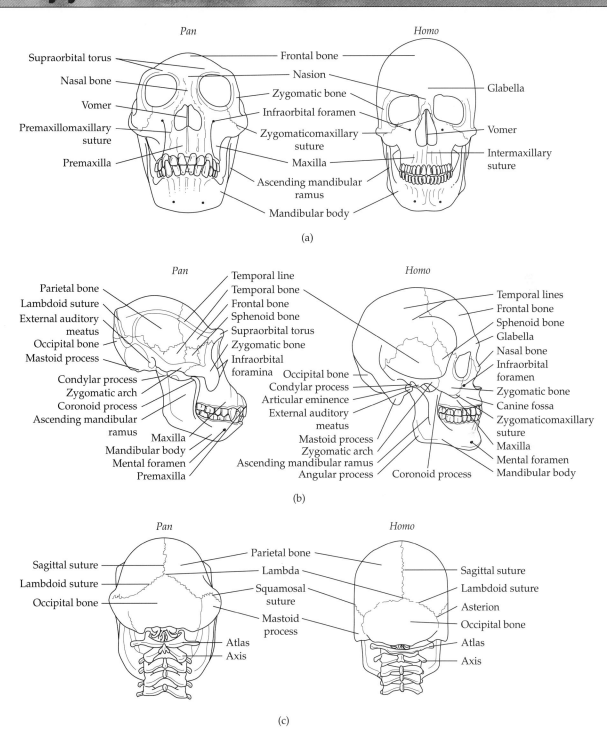

Comparison of the skull in chimpanzees (left) and modern humans (right) with the major bones and bony landmarks identified. (a) Frontal view. (b) Lateral view. (c) Posterior view.

Source: Conroy, 1997

Glossary

Note: Words in *italics* are defined elsewhere in the glossary. Several terms are included that are not defined in text.

Absolute dating: determining the actual age of geologic deposits (and the fossils in them) by examining the chemical composition of rock fragments containing radioactive substances that decay at known rates. Also known as *chronometric dating.* (Compare with *relative dating.*)

Acheulean industry: stone-tool tradition that first appeared 1.7 mya in Africa and originated with *Homo erectus.*

Adapidae and Omomyidae: families of *Eocene prosimians,* now extinct.

Adaptation: an evolutionary change, generally resulting from *natural selection,* which better suits a *population* to its environment, thus improving its chances of survival; a characteristic resulting from such a change.

Aegyptopithecus: a basal *catarrhine* from the Fayum in Africa; dated to the *Oligocene* epoch.

Agglutination: the clumping of *red blood cells* as a result of the reaction of *antibodies* to an *antigen.*

Algeripithecus minutus: tentatively, the oldest known *anthropoid primate,* from North Africa's early-middle *Eocene.*

Alleles: *genes* occupying equivalent positions on paired *chromosomes,* yet producing different phenotypic effects when *homozygous;* alternative states of a gene, originally produced by *mutation.*

Allomothering: typically, care or attention directed toward an infant by a female other than its mother (also called *aunting behavior*).

Allopatric speciation: *speciation* caused by the geographic isolation of *populations,* which then evolve in different ways.

Altiatlasius: the oldest known *primate fossil;* a *prosimian* from the late *Paleocene* of North Africa.

Altricial: the state of being born helpless and requiring parental care.

Alveolar: referring to the toothbearing portion of the jaws.

Amino acids: a group of organic compounds that act as building blocks for *proteins.*

Amphipithecus: possible *anthropoids* from the late *Eocene* of Burma.

Anagenesis: the evolution by *natural selection* of a lineage over time, which may produce changes recognized as a new *species.*

Angular gyrus: part of the human *cerebral cortex* that associates information received from different senses.

Antediluvian: relating to a time that preceded the flood described in Genesis.

Anterior: front, or ventral. In quadrupeds, the forward part of the body.

Anterior fovea: a *mesially* positioned depression on the surface of a tooth.

Anterior inferior iliac spine: a projection from the *ilium* that serves as an attachment point for certain thigh muscles and also the *iliofemoral ligament.*

Anthropoids: suborder of Primates that includes *monkeys, apes,* and humans.

Anthropoidea (Anthropoids): suborder of *Primates* that includes humans, *apes,* and *monkeys.*

Anthropology: the science of humankind; the systematic study of human evolution, human variability, and human behavior, past and present.

Antibodies: proteins produced as a defense mechanism to attack foreign substances invading the body.

Antigens: any organic substances, recognized by the body as foreign, that stimulate the production of an *antibody.*

Ape: among living animals, a large, tailless, semierect mammal of the order *Primates.* Living types are the *chimpanzee, bonobo, gorilla, gibbon, siamang,* and *orangutan.*

Aphasia: the loss or distortion of speech.

Apidium: primate of the *Oligocene* epoch found in Egypt; possibly a basal *anthropoid.*

Arboreal: adapted for living in or around trees, as are most *monkeys* and *apes.*

Arboreal theory theory stipulating that early *primates* evolved as an adaptation to tree living.

Archaeology: the systematic study of prehistoric human cultures; finding and interpreting the cultural products of prehistoric people.

Archaic humans: collectively, *Homo heidelbergensis* and the Neandertals (*Homo neanderthalensis*).

Arcuate fasciculus: a bundle of nerve fibers in the human brain transmitting signals from *Wernicke's area* to *Broca's area,* making possible vocal repetition of heard and memorized words.

Articular eminence: a swelling of the zygomatic arch just anterior to the jaw joint.

Articulation: in anatomy, the joint between two bones; in linguistics, the action of the tongue and lips to form the consonants of speech.

Asterion: juncture of the temporal, parietal, and occipital bones.

Artifact: a purposefully formed object.

Assortative mating: the tendency of like to mate with like.

Atlatl: Aztec name for the spear thrower, a rodlike device used as an extension of the arm that greatly increases both distance and impact of throw.

Attractiveness: in *primate* studies, the aspect of female sexuality reflected by attention from males.

Auditory bulla: a bulbous bony development that houses the middle ear region.

Aurignacian industry: an *Upper Paleolithic,* mainly European, tool culture that existed about 40,000 to 27,000 years ago.

Australopithecines: members of the subfamily Australopithecinae, which includes *Australopithecus* and *Paranthropus.*

Australopithecus aethiopicus: original name for the robust *australopithecine species* now called *Paranthropus aethiopicus.*

Australopithecus afarensis: *gracile australopithecine species* that inhabited East Africa from 4.2 to 2.5 mya.

Australopithecus africanus: *gracile australopithecine species* that inhabited South Africa 3.5–2.5 mya.

Australopithecus anamensis: an early *species* of *australopithecines* found in Kenya and dated between 4.2 and 3.9 mya.

Australopithecus bahrelghazali: provisionally, a new *species* of *australopithecines* known from Chad and dating 3.5 to 3.0 mya.

Australopithecus garhi: *australopithecine species* known from Northeast Africa (Ethiopia) and dated 2.5 mya.

Australopithecus ramidus: *species* of *Australopithecus* known from Ethiopia and dated 4.4 mya.

Autosome: a chromosome other than the sex chromosomes.

Baboon: a large *monkey* with a long, doglike muzzle; most baboons have short tails and live on the ground in troops. They live close to the trees in East and Central Africa and in rocky deserts in Ethiopia. (See also *gelada* and *hamadryas.*)

Balanced polymorphism: maintenance in a *population* of different *alleles* of a particular *gene* in proportion to the advantages offered by each (e.g., sickle-cell and normal *hemoglobin*).

Band: a small, economically independent group of primates, smaller than a troop.

Basicranium: base of the skull.

Beijing man: see *Sinanthropus pekinensis.*

Biface: a stone tool in which the edge is created by convergent flaking from two surfaces to produce a sharp cutting edge.

Bilophodonty: the lower molar cusps pattern of *Old World monkeys,* featuring four cusps arranged in front and rear pairs.

Bioaltruism: behavior that appears to be altruistic, but that in fact is believed to benefit the animal indirectly, by increasing its *inclusive fitness.*

Bioethicist: a person who specializes in exploring the ethical dimensions of biological decisions.

Biological anthropologists: scientists who study human biology and the biology of past and present human populations, human genetics and variability, adaptation including growth, and evolutionary change.

Biomass: the total weight of living material of a species or population.

Biome: an area characterized by a broadly uniform climate and consisting of a distinctive combination of plants and animals.

Bipedal: moving erect on the hind limbs only.

Biretia: a late *Eocene anthropoid* from Algeria.

Birth canal: passage through the mother's pelvis through which infants are born.

Blade tools: slender, razor-sharp *flake* tools that are at least twice as long as they are wide.

Blending inheritance: an outmoded theory stating that offspring receive a combination of all characteristics of each parent through the mixture of their bloods; superseded by Mendelian genetics.

Blood groups: groups of individuals whose blood can be mixed without *agglutination* (e.g., group A, B, O, or AB).

Blood plasma: a clear liquid component of blood that creates the *red blood cells, white blood cells,* and *platelets.*

Body temperature hypothesis: proposal that reduction in body surface area exposed to sunlight brought about the selection of bipedalism.

Bola: two or more stones connected by thongs or a cord and used as a weapon.

Bonobo: small *chimpanzee* of the *species Pan paniscus.*

Brachiation: an arboreal locomotor pattern featuring manual swinging from branch to branch.

Branching: the splitting of a family tree into separate evolutionary lines: The *monkeys, apes,* and living *prosimians* diverged from a common prosimianlike ancestor; the hominid line diverged from the apes.

Branisella: Oligocene platyrrhine monkeys from Bolivia.

Broca's area: part of the human *cerebral cortex* involved with the hierarchial organization of grammar and the manual combination of objects.

Brow ridge: a continuous ridge of bone in the skull, curving over each eye and connected across the bridge of the nose. An extremely prominent brow ridge is characteristic of the *Neandertal* people.

Buccal: within the mouth, toward the cheek. (See also *lingual.*)

Budding: the gradual expansion of a species into new areas, accomplished by a group splitting off from a prospering *population* to set up in an unexploited area near the original territory.

Burin: a chisel-like tool used to shape other materials such as bone, antler, and wood; a tool for making tools.

Calvaria: a braincase; that is, a skull minus the facial skeleton and lower jaw (plural, *calvariae*).

Canines: pointed teeth in the front of the mouth between the incisors and the premolars. In monkeys and apes, canines are usually large, projecting beyond the other teeth, and are used for tearing up vegetation and for threats and fights. Hominid canines are much smaller.

Canine fossa: concavity in the maxilla just behind the *canine jugum.*

Canine jugum: vertical ridge or bulge in the maxilla caused by a large canine root (plural, *juga*).

Carbon 14 (C14): a radioactive form of carbon present in the atmosphere as CO2 that disintegrates at a predictable rate. The amount of carbon 14 remaining in fossils indicates their age.

Carbon 14 dating: a method of dating archaeological remains based on the radioactive decay of the element carbon 14 into nitrogen.

Carotid foramen: opening for the carotid artery.

Catarrhines: an infraorder of the *anthropoids* that includes *Old World monkeys, apes,* and humans; species have close-spaced compressed nostrils.

Catastrophism: Georges Cuvier's theory that vast floods and other disasters wiped out ancient life forms again and again throughout the earth's history.

Catopithecus: a particularly well-known *oligopithecine* from the Fayum in Africa.

Cenozoic: geologic era that began about 65 mya.

Centrioles: minute granules present in many cells outside the nuclear membrane. The centriole divides in cell division, and the parts separate to form the poles of the spindle.

Cephalic index: a skull measurement sometimes used by anthropologists; defined as skull breadth divided by length multiplies by 100.

Ceramics: objects of hard material made by mixing different substances (including clay) and heating them in an oven.

Cerebral cortex: deeply folded outer layer of the brain; largely responsible for memory and, in humans, reasoned behavior and abstract thought (also referred to as the *neocortex*).

Cerebrum: the large anterior part of the brain.

Chain of Being: pre-Darwinian theory of a hierarchy ranking living things from lowest to highest, with humankind at the top; the chain was thought to have been fixed forever at Creation, which meant that no species could change into other forms.

Chatelperronian industry: an *Upper Paleolithic* tool culture of western Europe, largely contemporaneous with the *Aurignacian* culture (40,000 to 27,000 years BP).

Chemical signature: unique chemical nature of a geologic deposit; for volcanic rocks, it is usually determined by an analysis of the ash and lava content.

Chiasmata: crossover points where the *chromatids* of a tetrad overlap and segment exchange may occur (singular: chiasma).

Chimpanzee: African great *ape* thought to be somewhat like the ancestor from which apes and humans are descended. In the trees it climbs; on the ground it usually moves by *knuckle walking.*

Choppers: small, generally ovoid stones with a few *flakes* removed to produce a partial cutting edge.

Chordata: the *phylum* of animals characterized by the possession of a notochord (a gelatinous dorsal stiffening rod) at some stage of life.

Chromatid: one of the two elements in a duplicated *chromosome.*

Chromosomes: coiled, threadlike structures of *DNA,* bearing the *genes* and found in the nuclei of all plant and animal cells. (See also *meiosis* and *mitosis.*)

Chronospecies: a paleospecies defined by the temporal extent of its existence.

Chronometric dating: an alternative term for *absolute dating.*

Cingulum: shelf of enamel running around the periphery of a tooth (plural, *cingula*).

Clade: members of an evolutionary cluster (e.g., sister *species*) plus their common ancestor.

Cladistic analysis: the grouping of *species* by their shared derived traits, with the aim of identifying groups of organisms descended from a common ancestor.

Cladistic classification: evolution-based *taxonomy* that gives equal weight to traits and requires *sister groups* to be similarly ranked.

Cladogenesis: branching *evolution* involving the splitting of a *species* or lineage.

Class: a *taxonomic* rank in biology. Humans belong to the class *Mammalia.*

Classic Neandertal: the type of Neandertal *fossil* originally found in Western Europe.

Cleaver: an *Acheulean* stone implement with a straight cutting edge at one end; probably used for butchering animal carcasses.

Cline: the gradual change in frequency of a trait or gene across a geographic range.

Clivus: see *nasoalveolar clivus.*

Clone: a genetically identical organism asexually reproduced from an ancestral organism.

Close-knee stance: standing position in which the feet and knees are closer together than the hip joints.

Clovis point: distinctive spear points of early native North Americans, dating from 11,500 BP.

Cobble: stone worn smooth by sand and water in running streams or on a rocky seashore. Often used as a core for making a stone tool.

Coccyx: the bones at the end of the human and ape spine, the remnants of an ancestral tail.

Codominant: alleles that, in heterozygous combination, produce a phenotype distinct from either type of homozygote.

Codon: a *nucleotide* triplet that codes for the production of a particular *amino acid* during *protein* production.

Collective phenotype: the set of phenotypic averages and norms that characterize a *population* or *species.*

Colugos: nonprimate mammals from Asia known for *arboreal* gliding; misnamed "flying lemurs."

Composite tools: tools made from more than one material or part; for example, bone-handled ax.

Condyles: bearing surfaces on bones, such as mandibular condyles or condyles of leg bones.

Consortship: generally, a period of exclusive sexual association and mating between a female and a male.

Conspecifics: members of the same *species.*

Continental drift: a theory that describes the movements of continental landmasses throughout the earth's history.

Cores: worked stones from which *flakes* have been removed.

Core area: a portion of the *home range* that is used frequently.

Core tool: implement made from the core of a rock nodule. (Compare with *flakes.*)

Cortex: see *cerebral cortex.*

Coronal plane: any plane that divides the body into front and rear portions.

Cranial capacity: the capacity of the cranium or skull, measured in cubic centimeters (cc).

Cranium: the skull without the jaw.

Creationism: the belief that humans and all life forms were specially created by God or some other divine force.

Creation myth: a story describing the origins, usually supernatural, of the earth and life (including humans).

Cro-Magnon: anatomically modern humans living in Europe between about 40,000 and 10,000 years ago.

Crossing-over: the exchange of sections between *homologous chromosomes.*

Cryptic: serving to camouflage, as when coloration allows an animal to blend into its background.

Cultural evolution: changes in human *culture* resulting from the accumulated experience of humankind. Cultural evolution can produce *adaptations* to the environment faster than organic evolution can.

Cultural swamping: overwhelming of one *culture* by a technologically more powerful one, often leaving the culture with the weaker technology extinct or nearly so.

Culture: system of learned behavior, symbols, customs, beliefs, institutions, artifacts, and technology characteristic of a human group and transmitted by its members to their offspring.

Cusps: conical projections on the biting surfaces of teeth. On the molar teeth of primates these include mainly the metacone, hypocone, protocone, and paracone (upper molars), and the metaconid, hypoconid, hypoconulid, entoconid, and protoconid (lower molars). (See also *molars*).

Cytoplasm: the contents of a cell excluding the nucleus.

Darwinian fitness: see *fitness.*

Deciduous molar: temporary tooth or "milk tooth" that is lost and replaced by a permanent tooth during the early years of life.

Débitage: debris produced during stone-tool manufacture.

Deep time: the theory that the earth is billions of years old and thus has a long history of development and change.

Deme: the community of potentially interbreeding individuals at a locality.

Demography: study of the size, density, distribution, and other vital statistics of *populations.*

Dental ape: a *fossil ape* having apelike dentition but postcranially more like a monkey.

Dental formula: the numbers of incisors, canines, premolars, and molars in half of the upper and lower toothrows.

Denticulates: stone implements made with toothed or notched edges.

Deoxyribonucleic acid: see *DNA.*

Derived traits: recently evolved characteristics shared by a small number of closely related species.

Diaspora: migration and dispersion of people with a common origin.

Diastema: space in the toothrow that accommodates one or more teeth in the opposite jaw when the mouth is closed. (Plural: *diastemata.*)

Differential reproduction: the effect of *natural selection* that individuals with certain traits are less *fit* than those with other traits.

Diploid number: the full *chromosome* count in somatic cells (all cells except *gametes*). (Compare with *haploid* number.)

Directional natural selection: *natural selection* that operates in response to environmental change and produces shifts in the composition of a *population*'s *gene pool* and *collective phenotype.*

Disk–core technique: Neandertal stone-knapping method in which a core is trimmed to disk shape and numerous *flakes* are then chipped off; the flakes are then generally retouched.

Distal: further away from a point of reference; in the jaw, further away from the anterior midline and toward the back of the mouth (see also *mesial*).

Diurnal: active during the day, as *apes, humans,* and *monkeys* are.

DNA (deoxyribonucleic acid): chemical substance found in *chromosomes* and *mitochondria* which reproduces itself and carries the *genetic code.*

Dominance hierarchy: rank structuring of a primate group, usually based on winning and losing fights. For some purposes, the ranks within a subset of animals, such as the adult males, may be analyzed separately.

Dominant: expressed in the *phenotype* even when the organism is carrying only one copy of the underlying hereditary material (one copy of the responsible *gene*).

Dorsal: pertaining to the back of an animal or one of its parts; the opposite of *ventral.*

Dragon bones: the ancient Chinese term for fossils of various sorts that were collected and ground into medicines.

Drift: see *genetic drift.*

Dryopithecus: ape genus from Europe and dating to the mid- to late Miocene.

Dual-selection hypothesis: proposal that the canine tooth evolved under selection either as a weapon or for incisorlike functions.

Early *Homo:* general term referring collectively to *Homo habilis* and *Homo rudolfensis.*

Ecological niche: the set of resources and habitats exploited by a species.

Ecosystem: ecological system; the interacting community of all the organisms in an area and their physical environment, together with the flow of energy among its components.

Ecotone: the area where two ecological communities, or biomes (e.g., woodland and savanna), meet.

Emissary veins: veins that pass through the bones of the skull by means of small openings called *foramina.*

Encephalization quotient (EQ): in mammals, a number expressing observed brain size in a particular *species* relative to expected brain size calculated from body weight.

Endocast: a fossilized cast of the interior of a skull; may reveal much about brain size and shape.

Endogamy: selecting a mate from inside one's own group.

Energy efficiency hypothesis: proposal that the increased energy efficiency of *bipedal* walking brought about the selection of bipedalism.

Eoanthropus dawsoni: see *Piltdown man.*

Eocene: the geologic epoch extending from 58 to 35 million years BP.

Eosimias: probable basal *anthropoid* from the mid-*Eocene* of China.

Epicanthic fold: a fold of skin above the inner border of the eye; characteristic of Asiatic, some Native American, and Khoisan people.

Estrus: the period, usually around ovulation, of sexual *attractiveness* and activity by *primate* and other mammalian females.

Estrous cycle: cycle of periods of sexual *attractiveness* and activity of *primate* females; correlated with ovulation and the *menstrual cycle*, but with greater flexibility among *catarrhines*.

Ethnic group: a group of people perceived as sharing a common and distinctive culture.

Ethnographic analogy: an analogy between the ethnography of a society and the supposed ethnography of a prehistoric one.

Ethology: study of the social behavior of animal species in their natural environment.

Evolution: changes in the forms of organic species that have occurred throughout time since life first arose on earth.

Exogamy: among modern humans, the pattern of marrying (and mating) between individuals of different social groups.

Exons: segments of a *gene's DNA* that code for *protein* production.

External auditory meatus: auditory tube (ear) opening.

Extinction: the loss of a *species* when all its members die as a result of competition or climatic change.

Family: in human society, generally a unit marked by subsistence interdependence, sexual relationships among adults, and parent–offspring relationships.

Fauna: animal component of the ecosystem at a given place and time.

Faunal correlation: dating a site by the similarity of its animal fossils to those of another site that may carry a reliable absolute date.

Feedback: process in which a change in one component in a system affects other components, which in turn brings about changes in the first component.

Femur: thighbone.

Fish gorge: device for catching fish on a line using a moving part that opens at right angles and sticks in the fish's mouth.

Fission-track method: method of dating rocks from tracks left by the spontaneous splitting of uranium 238 atoms.

Fitness: individuals' relative degrees of success in surviving and reproducing, and thus in gaining genetic representation in succeeding generations.

Flakes: sharp-edged fragments struck from a stone; used as a cutting tool.

Flake tool: implement made from a flake struck from a stone.

Folivore: a leaf-eating animal (compare frugivore).

Foramen magnum: hole in the base of the skull through which the spinal cord passes.

Forensic anthropologists: physical anthropologists who apply their expertise to matters of law such as the identification of human remains.

Fossil: the remains of an organism, or direct evidence of its presence, preserved in rock. Generally only the hard parts of animals—teeth and bones—are preserved.

Fossil magnetism: naturally occurring property of rocks indicating the polarity of the earth's magnetic field when the sediments were laid down. By a comparison of the polarity of one layer with that of others, the age of a rock can, under certain conditions, be approximated.

Fossilization: the transformation of bones that occurs when they are buried under suitable circumstances. Certain mineral elements are dissolved and replaced by others. The form of the bone is effectively preserved.

Founder effect: typically, genetic difference between a newly founded, separated *population* and its parent group. The founding population is usually different because its *gene pool* is only a segment of the parent group's.

Founder principle: founders of a new colony, if few in number, will contain only a fraction of the total genetic variation of the parental *population* or *species*. The founder colony will therefore most likely differ genetically from the parent population.

Fovea: an area of the *anthropoid* retina that allows extremely detailed vision.

Frankfort plane: The line on the lateral view of a skull drawn from the lower rim of the orbit to the upper rim of the auditory meatus (ear hole).

Frenulum: the flap of skin that tethers the upper lip to the jaw in *prosimians*. It is reduced or absent in *anthropoids* and *tarsiers*.

Frontal bone: bone of the primate skull that constitutes the forehead and comes down around the eye sockets (orbits).

Frugivore: a fruit-eating animal.

Fusion–fission community: community of *primates* that splits into subgroups and reunites from time to time.

Gametes: reproductive *haploid* cells generated by *meiosis,* which fuse with *gametes* of the opposite sex in fertilization, in animals, eggs and sperm.

Gelada: species of terrestrial *monkey* related to *baboons,* found in the mountains of Ethiopia; *Theropithecus gelada.*

Gene flow: the transmission of *genes* between *populations,* which increases the variety of genes available to each and creates or maintains similarities in the genetic makeup of the populations.

Gene frequency: the number of times a gene occurs in proportion to the size of a *population.*

Gene pool: all of the *genes* of a *population* at a given time (summing genes within a *species* yields the species' gene pool).

Genes: primarily, functional units of the *chromosomes* in cell nuclei, controlling the inheritance of phenotypic traits; some genes also occur in *mitochondria.*

Generalized limbs: limbs that are not specialized in adaptation to a particular environment and allow a range of locomotion. Compare *specialization.*

Genetic code: the chemical code based on four *nucleotides,* carried by *DNA* and *RNA,* that specifies amino acids in sequence for protein synthesis.

Genetic drift: genetic changes in *populations* caused by random phenomena rather than by *natural selection.*

Genetic load: usually, the *recessive genes* in a *population* that are harmful when expressed in the rare *homozygous* condition.

Genetic swamping: the overrunning and absorption of a small *population* by a larger one; the *genes* of the minority are preserved but contribute little to the successors' physical characteristics.

Genome: the totality of the DNA unique to a particular organism or species.

Genotype: the genetic makeup of a plant or animal; the total information contained in all *genes* of the organism. (Compare with *phenotype.*)

Genus: *taxonomic* category composed of a group of *species* that are similar because of common ancestry.

Geology: study of the earth's physical formation, its nature, and its continuing development.

Gibbon: small, long-armed, tree-dwelling, brachiating *ape* of Southeast Asia.

Gigantopithecus: extinct giant *ape* found in Asia dating from *Pliocene* and *Pleistocene* epochs.

Glabella: anteriormost point on the frontal bone, usually between the brow ridges.

Glenoid fossa: another name for the *mandibular fossa.*

Gluteus medius: muscles of the hip; lateral stabilizers of the pelvis in modern humans.

Gluteus minimus: one of the muscles of the hip; a lateral stabilizer of the pelvis in modern humans.

Gorilla: the largest *ape;* a social, terrestrial, knuckle-walking vegetarian living in the rain forests and mountain forests of equatorial Africa.

Gracile: small, fine-boned, lightweight; lightly built.

Grade: arbitrarily defined level of evolutionary development (e.g., *prosimians* vs. *anthropoids*).

Gradualism: slow and steady evolutionary change in a lineage of plants or animals.

Gravettian: see *Perigordian.*

Grooming: cleaning and combing the fur, usually of another animal; an enjoyable pastime.

Group selection: theoretical model in which natural selection is presumed to operate not on the individual animal but on a social group as a unit.

Half-life: the time taken for half of any quantity of a radioactive element to decay to its fission products.

Hamadryas: a *species* of *baboon* adapted to the desert regions of Ethiopia.

Hamstring muscles: muscles of the hips and the back of the thigh; thigh extensors.

Hand ax: a bifacially flaked stone implement that characterized the *Acheulean industry.*

Haploid number: the number of *chromosomes* carried by *gametes;* one-half of the full count carried by somatic cells. (Compare with *diploid number.*)

Hardy–Weinberg theorem: formula that predicts the extent and nature of genetic change in a *population.*

Harem polygyny: in zoology, a group structure including one breeding male and multiple females; among humans, a structure involving one male and multiple wives and/or concubines.

Hemispherical asymmetry: the condition in which the two cerebral hemispheres differ in one or more dimensions. In most modern humans, the left hemisphere is somewhat larger than the right.

Hemoglobin: a protein found in *red blood cells* that carries oxygen through the circulatory system of vertebrates and some other animals.

Heritability: a property of phenotypic traits; the proportion of a trait's interindividual variance that is due to genetic variance.

Heterodont: having several different types of teeth (incisors, canines, etc.), each with a different function.

Heterozygous: having different versions of a *gene (alleles)* for a particular trait. (Compare with *homozygous;* see also *dominant.*)

Heuristic devices: devices that facilitate or stimulate further investigation and thought.

Home bases: camps where *hominid* groups gathered at evening for socializing, food sharing, and sleeping.

Home range: the area a *primate* group uses for foraging, sleeping, and so on in a year. (Compare with *territory.*)

Hominidae: the taxonomic family that includes *Homo sapiens* and ancestral species.

Hominids: living or fossil members of the human family *Hominidae.*

Hominines: members of the subfamily Homininae, which includes just one genus—*Homo.*

Hominization: the evolutionary transformation from ape to human.

Hominoidea (hominoids): superfamily of *Primates* that includes *apes* and humans.

Homo: a genus of the family *Hominidae,* subfamily Homininae; contains at least six species: *H. habilis, H. rudolfensis, H. erectus, H. heidelbergensis, H. neanderthalensis,* and *H. sapiens.*

Homo antecessor: proposed new *species* name for certain fossils from the site of Gran Dolina, Spain; *taxon* not recognized in this book.

Homo erectus: *hominid species* that inhabited much of the Old World between 1.9(?) million and at least 300,000 years BP; successor to "early *Homo.*"

Homo ergaster: *species* name given by some paleoanthropologists to certain African *fossils* regarded by most workers as being early *Homo erectus.* The authors of this book side with the majority.

Homo habilis: one of the two species of "early *Homo*"; inhabited East Africa 2.3 to 1.6 million years ago.

Homo heidelbergensis: successor to *Homo erectus,* first appearing about 800,000 to 600,000 years BP; ancestral to both *Homo sapiens* and the *Neandertals.*

Homologous chromosomes: *chromosomes* that are similar in shape, size, and sequence of *genes.*

Homo neanderthalensis: a *species* of humans that inhabited Europe and the Middle East from about 300,000 to 30,000 years BP. Descended from *Homo heidelbergensis,* the species' common name is usually spelled Neandertal.

Homo rudolfensis: one of the two *species* of "early *Homo*"; inhabited East Africa 2.4 to 1.6 million years ago.

Homo sapiens: among living *primates,* the scientific name for modern humans; members of the *species* first appeared about 130,000 years ago.

Homozygous: having identical version of a *gene (alleles)* for a particular trait. (Compare with *heterozygous.*)

Hybrid speciation: speciation through hybridization between two species.

Hyoid bone: a bone of the throat positioned just above the larynx and just below the mandible. The hyoid provides attachment for one of the muscles of the tongue and for certain muscles at the front of the neck.

Ignacius: a genus of the plesiadapiforms.

Iliac blade: the broad portion of the *ilium,* one of the bones of the pelvis.

Iliofemoral ligament: ligament that prevents backward movement of the trunk at the human hip.

Ilium: the hipbone, part of the *pelvis.*

Inbreeding: mating among related individuals.

Incest: legally or socially prohibited sexual relations between kin. How closely related individuals must be for mating to be considered incestuous differs from culture to culture.

Incest taboo: a sanction against committing incest, found in all human societies.

Inclusive fitness: the sum total of an organism's individual reproductive success (number of offspring) plus portions of the reproductive success of genetic kin.

Infanticide: the killing of infants.

Inferior: below or toward the tail.

Inion: midline point of the superior nuchal lines.

Interglacial: a period in which glaciers retreat and the climate warms.

Introns: segments of a *gene's DNA* that do not code for *protein* production (so-called noncoding *DNA*).

IQ tests: tests that supposedly measure an individual's "intelligence quotient." Many consider such tests flawed and of little value, particularly for cross-cultural comparisons.

Iron pyrite: a mineral substance (iron disulfide) that, when struck with flint, makes sparks that will start a fire.

Ischium: one of the bones of the pelvis.

Java man: see *Pithecanthropus.*

Kenyapithecus: a fossil *ape* from the middle *Miocene* of East Africa and a possible *hominid* ancestor.

Kin selection: the selection of characteristics (and their *genes*) that increase the probability of the survival and reproduction of close relatives.

Knuckle walking: *quadrupedal* walking on the knuckles of the hands and the soles of the feet, used on the ground by *bonobos, chimpanzees,* and *gorillas.*

Lambda: midline juncture of the sagittal and lambdoidal sutures.

Language: the cognitive aspect of human communication involving symbolic thinking structured by grammar.

Langur: slender, long-tailed Asian *monkey.*

Larynx: the voice box; the organ in the throat containing vocal cords, important in human *speech* production.

Laurel-leaf blade: *Upper Paleolithic* stone *artifact* so finely worked that it may have had an aesthetic or ritual function. Associated with *Solutrean* tool kits.

Leister: a three-pronged spear used for fishing.

Levallois technique: stone-knapping method in which a core is shaped to allow a *flake* of predetermined size and shape to be detached; originated about 250,000 years BP.

Life expectancy: the average age at death of individuals born into a particular *population.*

Limbic system: lower brain center that generates emotions and their expression.

Lingual: in the mouth, toward the tongue. (See also *buccal.*)

Linnaean classification: hierarchical classificatory system using a binomial terminology and based on morphological similarities and differences.

Lithic technology: stone-tool technology.

Locus: the position of a nuclear *gene* on a *chromosome;* each locus can carry only one *allele* of a gene.

Loris: a prosimian of India, Southeast Asia, and Africa that is small, solitary, *quadrupedal,* and slow moving.

Lothagam jaw: a mandibular fragment found at Lothagam in Kenya and dated about 5.6 mya.

Lower Paleolithic: the earliest part of the Old Stone Age, lasting from more than 2 million to about 200,000 years ago.

Lumbar curve: forward curvature of the vertebral column in the lower back that helps bring the hominid trunk over the hip joints.

Machine tools: tools used to make other tools, such as *burins.*

Macromutation: a large and genetically inherited change between parent and offspring.

Magdalenian: *Upper Paleolithic* culture existing in western Europe from about 16,500 to 11,000 years BP. Produced many *blade tools* and prototype harpoons.

Maglemosian: Mesolithic hunting-and-fishing culture of the north European plain (stretching from the UK to the Urals) with a composite microlithic culture.

Mammalia: class of four-legged vertebrates—including humans—having hair or fur, milk glands for suckling their young, and warm blood.

Mandible: the lower jaw.

Mandibular fossa: concave portion of the jaw joint; part of the temporal bone (also *glenoid fossa*).

Mandibular symphysis: the midline connecting the right and left halves of the lower jaw.

Manuports: unmodified stones that could not have occurred naturally at an archaeological site and must have been carried there; how manuports were used is unknown.

Masticatory apparatus: the entire apparatus involved in chewing: lips, jaws, teeth, tongue, and the associated musculature.

Mastoid process: bony projection of the temporal bone posterior to the *external auditory meatus.*

Mastoid region: the area around the mastoid process of the temporal bone.

Matrilineal kinship: kinship traced through the maternal line.

Mauer jaw: *fossil* mandible found at Mauer in Germany in 1907 and named *Homo heidelbergensis.*

Meiosis: cell division resulting in the formation of sex cells, each of which will have half the number of *chromosomes* present in the original cell (the *haploid number*).

Melanocyte: a kind of cell in the skin that produces pigment, giving the skin color.

Menstrual cycle: the interval (generally, monthly) from the end of one period of menstrual bleeding to the end of the next; especially characteristic of *catarrhine* females.

Mental region of mandible: the front, lower edge of the mandibular body.

Mesial: toward the anterior side of a tooth (i.e., toward the midline at the front of the jaw; see also *distal*).

Mesolithic: a Stone Age period recognizable at some European sites and characterized by the use of small stone tools called *microliths;* the Mesolithic followed the *Paleolithic* and preceded the *Neolithic.*

Microliths: small, geometrically shaped stone tools made from *flakes,* usually *Mesolithic.*

Microsatellites: short sequences of *DNA* believed to carry no functional code.

Microwear: the microscopic pattern of scratches, pits, and polish produced during the use of a stone tool.

Midden: a refuse heap or dung pile at an archaeological site in which artifacts and food remains may be preserved.

Middle Paleolithic: a period of stone-tool manufacture in the Old World (mainly Europe, Africa, and western Asia) that lasted from about 250,000 to 35,000 years BP.

Midfacial prognathism: forward protrusion of the upper jaw, the midface, and the nasal regions; characteristic of *Neandertals.*

Mimicry: phenomenon in which natural selection brings about the close resemblance of one species to another.

Miocene: the geologic epoch extending from 25 to 5 million years BP.

Mitochondria: granular or rod-shaped bodies in the cytoplasm of cells that function in the metabolism of fat and proteins. Probably of bacterial origin.

Mitosis: cell division in somatic cells; two identical *diploid* cells result.

Molars: grinding teeth, which bear many *cusps. Primate* molars have three to five cusps, depending on the *species;* premolars normally have two.

Molecular clocks: a variety of molecular measures for estimating the time of divergence of living *species* from their common ancestor.

Monkey: usually a small or medium-sized long-tailed arboreal, *quadrupedal,* vegetarian primate. The two groups are *New World monkeys* and *Old World monkeys.*

Monogamous: among humans, having only one spouse. (Compare with *polygamous.*)

Monogynous: in zoology, generally having only one mate. (Compare with *polygynous.*)

Monomorphic: both sexes showing the same trait (e.g., similar body size).

Monophyletic clade: a group of *species* sharing a common ancestor that would be included in the group.

Morotopithecus: an *ape* from East Africa that lived during the early *Miocene.*

Morphological pattern: the distinctive form of a *species;* those anatomical features common to members of

a species, which as a group distinguish them from other animals.

Morphology: the study of the form of organisms, especially external appearance.

Mosaic evolution: *evolution* of different parts of the body at different rates over long periods.

Mousterian industry: a *Middle Paleolithic* tool industry from Europe and the Middle East; primarily associated with *Neandertals.*

Mousterian of Acheulean tradition (MAT): a variety of the *Mousterian industry* that included very diverse tools, including numerous *hand axes;* associated with *Neandertals* in western Europe during the *Middle Paleolithic* period.

Movius line: geographic dividing line between the Acheulean tradition in the West and non-Acheulean lithic traditions in eastern and southeastern Asia.

mtDNA: genetic material found in the *mitochondria* of cells.

Multivariate analysis: method of analysis that makes it possible to compare two or more *populations* using a number of variable traits simultaneously.

Mutation: generally, a spontaneous change in the chemistry of a *gene* that can alter its phenotypic effect. The accumulation of such changes may contribute to the *evolution* of a new *species* of animal or plant. See also *point mutation.*

Nasion: midline juncture of the frontonasal and nasal sutures.

Nasoalveolar clivus: *anterior* edge of the premaxilla.

Natural selection: the principal mechanism of Darwinian evolutionary change, by which the individuals best adapted to the environment contribute more offspring to succeeding generations than others do. As more of such individuals' characteristics are incorporated into the *gene pool,* the characteristics of the *population* evolve.

Neandertals: (often spelled Neanderthal) members of the species *Homo neanderthalensis;* archaic humans who lived in Europe and the Middle East between 300,000 and 30,000 years ago.

Neolithic: relating to the New Stone Age; a late stage of stone-tool making that began about 10,000 years ago.

Neolithic revolution: revolutionary developments in human culture that took place between 15,000 and 10,000 years ago.

Neurons: nerve cells; the basic units of the nervous system.

New World monkeys: *monkeys* inhabiting the Americas.

Niche: precise environment and resource base of a *species* or *population.*

Nocturnal: active during the hours of darkness.

Nomadism: lifestyle involving continual traveling between different pastures or other resources.

Nuchal area: area of attachment of the muscles of the back of the neck, low on the occipital bone.

Nuclear family: a *family* group of two parents and their children.

Nucleic acid: a long, chainlike compound formed by a large number of *nucleotides;* present in all organisms in one or both of two forms: *DNA* and *RNA.*

Nucleotides: organic compounds consisting of bases, sugars, and phosphates; found in cells either free or as part of polynucleotide chains.

Nulliparous: never having given birth.

Occipital bun: a bunlike posterior projection of the occipital bone

Occipital condyles: pads of bone on the base of the skull that articulate with the uppermost vertebra.

Occipital torus: a ridge running side-to-side across the occipital bone at the back of a skull.

Occlusal plane: plane lying parallel to the biting surfaces of the teeth.

Occupation level (or **floor**): land surface occupied by prehistoric *hominids.*

Oldowan industry: earliest stone-tool tradition; appeared about 2.5 mya in Northeast Africa.

Old World monkeys: *monkeys* inhabiting Africa and Eurasia.

Oligocene: the geologic epoch extending from 35 to 25 million years BP.

Oligopithecines: late *Eocene anthropoids;* many have been collected from Egypt's Fayum Depression.

Omnivore: an animal that eats both meat and vegetation.

Omomyidae: one of the two families of *Eocene prosimians,* now extinct.

Opportunistic mating: mating done whenever and wherever the opportunity presents itself, and with whatever partner is available.

Opposable thumb: ability to hold thumb and index finger together in opposition, giving a *precision grip.*

Optically stimulated luminescence: method of dating sediments by stimulating them with intense light; such stimulation causes the sediments to release trapped electrons and thus measurable light.

Orangutan: tree-dwelling *ape* of Borneo and Sumatra. Has *prehensile* hands and feet for seizing and grasping; limbs articulated for reaching in any direction; and very long arms. Orangutans move on the ground rarely but are then *quadrupedal.*

Orbit: eye socket.

Order: a *taxonomic* rank. Humans belong to the order *Primates.*

Oreopithecus: *ape genus* from the mid- to late *Miocene* of Europe.

Osteodontokeratic culture: the culture of bone, tooth, and horn tools hypothesized by Raymond Dart for *A. africanus;* now largely dismissed.

Otavipithecus: a recently discovered *fossil ape* from the mid-*Miocene* of southern Africa.

Outbreeding: mating among unrelated individuals. (Compare with *inbreeding.*)

Pair bond: a psychological relationship between mates; thought to be marked by sexual faithfulness.

Palate: the bony plate separating the mouth from the nasal cavity. It is arched in humans and flat in *apes.*

Paleoanthropology: the study of the fossil and cultural remains and other evidence of humans' extinct ancestors.

Paleocene: the geologic epoch extending from 65 to 58 million years BP.

Paleolithic: relating to the Old Stone Age; the earliest stage of stone tool making, beginning about 2.5 million years ago.

Paleomagnetism: magnetism originally generated by the earth's magnetic field and preserved in rock. Past fluctuations in the intensity and direction of this field allow correlation between strata, a form of *relative dating* that can be used for *absolute dating* because the historic pattern of magnetic fluctuations and reversals is known and dated.

Paleontology: the study of the fossil remains and biology of organisms that lived in the past.

Parallel evolution: the evolution of similar but not identical adaptations in two or more lineages.

Paranthropus: *genus* of the Australopithecinae with robust characteristics.

Paranthropus aethiopicus: *species* of *Paranthropus* found in East Africa and dated 2.7–2.3 mya.

Paranthropus boisei: robust *species* of *Paranthropus* that lived in East Africa 2.3 to 1.3 million years ago.

Paranthropus robustus: *species* of *Paranthropus* from the Transvaal of South Africa dated between 2 and 1 mya.

Parapatric speciation: speciation among *populations* of sedentary organisms with adjacent ranges.

Parapithecus: a *primate* of the *Oligocene* epoch, from Egypt; probably a basal *anthropoid.*

Parental investment: any behavior toward offspring that improves the chance of the offspring's survival.

Parietal mastoid angle: angular connection between the parietal and temporal bones near the *mastoid process.*

Particulate inheritance: the transmission of hereditary characteristics by discrete units of genetic material; first proposed by Gregor Mendel (see also *genes*).

Pastoralism: a way of life, often nomadic, that involves herding domestic animals for milk and meat.

Patellar groove: groove separating the femoral condyles, particularly on the ventral aspect of the bone. The lateral lip of the patellar groove is an anterior projection from the lateral condyle that probably functions to prevent dislocation of the kneecap (patella).

Peking Man: traditional name for *Homo erectus* fossils from Zhoukoudian, near Beijing (Peking).

Pelvis: a bony structure forming a basinlike ring at the base of the vertebral column with which the legs articulate.

Periglacial: bordering a glacial region.

Perigordian: *Upper Paleolithic* culture of Western Europe dating 27,000 to 21,000 years BP.

Persistence hunting: hunting by chasing the prey until it stops, exhausted, when it can be killed.

Pharynx: the throat, above the *larynx.*

Phenetic classification: *taxonomy* based on physical similarities or differences between *species* or other taxa.

Phenotype: the observable characteristics of a plant or an animal; the expression of the *genotype.*

Phonation: the production of vowel sounds by the passage of air through the *larynx* and *pharynx.*

Phonemes: the smallest sound components of language.

Phyletic transformation: the conversion (mainly through *natural selection*) of an entire *species* into a new species (see *anagenesis*).

Phylogenetic classification: *taxonomy* that reflects evolutionary descent and is based on the pattern of primitive and derived traits; in traditional evolutionary classifications, traits may be given different weights.

Phylogeny: the evolutionary lineage of organisms; their evolutionary history.

Phylum: a major *taxonomic* rank. Humans are in the phylum *Chordata.*

Physical anthropologists: scientists who work in the field of human evolution and human variability.

Piltdown man: a "doctored" modern human skull and ape jaw "discovered" in 1911–1912 that was supposed to represent a very primitive human, *Eoanthropus dawsoni,* but was exposed as a hoax in 1953.

Pithecanthropus: the original *genus* name given by Eugene Dubois to *fossil* material from Java now classified as *Homo erectus.*

Platelets: minute blood cells associated with clotting.

Platycephalic: long, low-vaulted, and widest at the base; describes a skull.

Platyrrhines: an infraorder of the *anthropoids* that includes the *New World monkeys; species* have wide-spread round nostrils.

Pleistocene: geologic epoch that lasted from about 1.6 million to 10,000 years ago.

Pliocene: the geologic epoch extending from 5 to 1.6 million years BP.

Plio–Pleistocene: a combination of the last two epochs of the Cenozoic era; the Pliocene lasted from 5 to 1.6 million years BP and the Pleistocene from 1.6 million to 10,000 years BP.

Pneumatized: filled with air spaces.

Point mutation: usually the substitution of one *nucleotide* in a single *codon* of a *gene* that affects *protein* synthesis and *genotype*; gene *mutation.*

Polyandrous: a female having multiple male sexual partners (among humans, multiple husbands).

Polygamous: having many spouses. (Compare with *monogamous.*)

Polygenic traits: traits determined by more than one *gene.*

Polygynous: in zoology, tending to have regular sexual access to two or more females.

Polymerase chain reaction: technique for making an infinite number of copies of a *DNA* molecule from a single precursor; known as the PCR.

Polymorphism: the appearance of a gene in more than one form among individuals of a *population.*

Pondaungia: late *Eocene fossil* from Burma; possibly an *anthropoid.*

Population: usually, a local or breeding group; a group in which any two individuals have the potential of mating with each other.

Portable art: objects of art, such as small sculptures, that can be carried from place to place.

Positive feedback: process in which a positive change in one component of a system brings about changes in other components, which in turn bring about further positive changes in the first component.

Postcranial: behind the head (in quadrupeds) or below the head (in bipeds).

Posterior: back, or dorsal. In quadrupeds, the rear part of the body.

Postglenoid process: bony projection that bounds the mandibular fossa laterally and posteriorly.

Postorbital bar: a bar of bone running around the outside margin of the *orbits* of *prosimians.*

Potassium–argon dating: *chronometric dating* in which age is determined by measurement of the decay of radioactive potassium 40.

Power grip: a grip involving all fingers of the hand equally, as in grasping a baseball. (Compare with *precision grip.*)

Precision grip: a grip that involves opposing the tip of the thumb to the tips of the other fingers, allowing fine control of small objects. (Compare with *power grip.*)

Prehensile: adapted for grasping.

Primates: order of Mammals that includes *prosimians, monkeys, apes,* and humans.

Proceptivity: the aspect of female sexuality reflected by inviting copulation.

Proconsul: an *ape* from East Africa that lived during the early *Miocene* epoch.

Prognathic: having a protruding jaw.

Promiscuous: having multiple sexual partners.

Propliopithecus: an *Oligocene fossil* from Egypt believed to be a basal *catarrhine.*

Prosimians: a suborder of lower *primates* including lemurs and lorises.

Protein clock: a method for determining evolutionary relationships by using variations in the *proteins* of different living animal species to indicate the length of time since they diverged in their *evolution.* The method assumes a fairly constant rate of protein evolution, an assumption still open to some doubt.

Proteins: molecules composed of chains of *amino acids.*

Proteopithecus: a *genus* of late *Eocene anthropoids* from Africa.

Protoconid: see *cusps.*

Protoculture: learned patterns of behavior passed down the generations within a social group, not depending on symbols.

Punctuated equilibrium: the hypothesis that most species have long periods of stasis, interrupted by episodes of rapid evolutionary change and speciation by branching. (Compare with *gradualism.*)

Quadrupedal: moving on all four limbs.

Races: divisions of a *species,* usually based on physical or behavioral differences and less well marked than subspecies. Many anthropologists reject the concept of biological races of living humans.

Racism: the assumption of inherent superiority of certain *"races,"* and the consequent discrimination against others.

Ramapithecus: a *fossil ape* now subsumed within the genus *Sivapithecus;* thought to be an ancestor of the orangutan.

Ramus: the vertical portion of the *mandible,* as opposed to the mandibular body, which bears the teeth.

Rapid-replacement hypothesis: proposal that *populations* of *Homo sapiens* from Africa rapidly dispersed and displaced archaic humans on other continents.

Receptivity: the aspect of female sexuality reflected by cooperating in copulation.

Recessive: expressed only when the organism is carrying two copies of the underlying hereditary material (two copies of the responsible *gene*).

Reciprocal altruism: trading of apparently altruistic acts by different individuals at different times; a variety of *bioaltruism.*

Reconciliation: the act of restoring friendly relations.

Rectus femoris: one of the muscles that flexes the hominid thigh.

Red blood cells: vertebrate blood cells (corpuscles) lacking nuclei and containing *hemoglobin.*

Red ocher: powdered mineral and earth mixture used as a red pigment.

Regional-continuity hypothesis: proposal that *populations* of archaic humans throughout the Old World evolved more or less simultaneously into *Homo sapiens.*

Relative dating: estimating the age of geologic deposits (and the *fossils* in them) by determining their stratigraphic level in relation to that of other deposits whose relative or absolute age is known. (Compare with *absolute dating.*)

Replication: the capacity of *DNA* to generate copies of itself in the nucleus of a cell.

Reproductive success: the production of viable offspring that reproduce in turn; levels of reproductive success may differ between individuals.

Retromolar gap: the space between the M3 and the mandibular *ramus;* characteristic of Neandertals.

Rhinarium: the moist, hairless nose characteristic of all *prosimians* except *tarsiers,* and of most nonprimate mammals.

Rhodesian Man: the skeleton of an archaic human found at Kabwe in Zambia in 1921.

Ribonucleic acid: see *RNA.*

Ribosomes: cellular organelles that contribute to *protein* synthesis.

Rickets: a pathological condition involving curvature of the bones; caused by insufficient vitamin D.

RNA (ribonucleic acid): a compound found with *DNA* in cell nuclei and chemically close to DNA; transmits the *genetic code* from DNA to direct the production of *proteins.* May take two forms: messenger RNA (mRNA) or transfer RNA (tRNA).

Robust: heavy; heavily built.

Sacrum: the part of the vertebral column that articulates with the pelvis and forms the dorsal portion of the pelvic girdle.

Sagittal arc: the distance around a skull from defined points at the base to the front, around the median sagittal line.

Sagittal crest: a bony ridge that arises on the midline of the skull in response to extreme muscle development; typical of *gorillas* and *Paranthropus.*

Sagittal keeling: appearance of a slightly raised ridge running down the center of a skull; smaller than a *sagittal crest.*

Sagittal suture: the line of union joining the two main side bones of the braincase.

Sangoan industry: *Middle Paleolithic* tool industry from East and Central Africa; associated with *Homo heidelbergensis.*

Satellite DNA: tandem repetitions of *DNA* sequences that accumulate at certain locations on *chromosomes* and usually are noncoding.

Savanna: tropical or subtropical grassland, often with scattered trees (woodland savanna).

Sciatic notch: a deep indentation of the dorsal edge of the hominid *ilium.*

Scraper: a stone or bone tool for preparing hides and leather, used to scrape the fat and other tissues from the inner surface of the skin.

Secondary altriciality: the phenomenon of an infant's motor skills requiring a lengthy period of postnatal development, as opposed to its sensory systems, which are functional at birth or soon after; characteristic of *H. erectus* and later hominids. (See also *altricial).*

Secondary sites: archaeological sites in which the artifacts have been disturbed by natural forces and then redeposited.

Sectorial: evolved to cut fibrous material by shearing action.

Sedentism: a way of life marked by the lack of migratory movements and by the establishment of permanent habitations.

Seed-eating hypothesis: proposal that seed eating brought about a change in canine shape and body posture, which in turn led to bipedalism.

Selection: see *natural selection.*

Selective pressure: the influence exerted by the environment that promotes the maintenance of traits that facilitate survival in that environment and eliminates other, nonadaptive traits (see also *natural selection).*

Semicircular canals: fluid-filled canals of the inner ear that control balance and coordination.

Serum: the liquid remaining after blood has clotted.

Sex chromosomes: *chromosomes* carrying *genes* that control gender (femaleness or maleness).

Sex-linked trait: an inherited trait coded on the sex *chromosomes,* and thus having a special distribution related to sex.

Sex swellings: hormone-induced swellings on the hindquarters of certain primate females; generally correlated with ovulation.

Sexual dimorphism: characteristic anatomical (and behavioral) differences between the males and females of a *species.*

Sexual selection: a category including intrasexual competition for mates (usually aggressive and among males) and intersexual mate selection (usually of males by females).

Shaman: a priest of primitive religion who claims contact with spiritual forces.

Siamang: a large-bodied *gibbon* of Asia; formerly placed in its own *genus, Symphalangus,* it is now classified as a *species* of *Hylobates.*

Siamopithecus: late *Eocene anthropoid* from Thailand.

Sickle-cell anemia: a genetically caused disease that can be fatal, in which the *red blood corpuscles* carry insufficient oxygen.

Sinanthropus pekinensis: the original name given by Davidson Black to ancient *fossils* from Zhoukoudian, near Beijing. These remains are now classified as *Homo erectus.*

Sister groups: in *cladistics*, the groups resulting from a dichotomous evolutionary branching event; initially ranked as sister *species*, these groups may change rank because of subsequent branching, but must always maintain the same *taxonomic level*.

Sivapithecus: a genus of *Miocene apes* that includes *Ramapithecus;* probably ancestral to the *orangutan*.

Socialization: learning to live in a social group and to adapt to stable group behavior.

Sociobiology: science of the biological (especially genetic) basis of social behavior.

Socioecology: the connection between *species'* ecological relations and their social behaviors; also the study of this connection.

Solutrean: an *Upper Paleolithic* culture existing in western Europe between 21,000 and 16,500 years BP. Best known for its "laurel-leaf" blades.

Specialization: adaptation to a particular environment; may restrict an organism to that lifestyle.

Speciation: the production of new *species,* either through gradual transformation or the splitting or branching of existing species.

Species: following the *biological species* concept, a group of interbreeding natural *populations* that are reproductively isolated from other such groups.

Speech: communication by the human oral mode.

Sphenoid: a bone of complex shape in the floor of the skull.

Spheroids: spherical stone tools probably used as hammers or missiles or to pound food.

Splicing: the action of messenger *RNA* that removes *intron* information, leaving only information from *exons*.

Stabilizing natural selection: *natural selection* that operates during periods when the environment is stable and maintains the genetic and phenotypic status quo within a *population*.

Stasis: a period of evolutionary equilibrium or inactivity.

Stereoscopic vision: vision produced by two eyes with overlapping fields, giving a sense of depth and distance; most highly evolved in hunting animals and *primates*.

Stone Age: the earliest period in cultural evolution occurring from more than 2 million to 5,000 years ago. Recognizable periods are the *Paleolithic*, or Old Stone Age; the *Mesolithic*, or Middle Stone Age; and the *Neolithic*, or New Stone Age (see also *Lower Paleolithic, Middle Paleolithic,* and *Upper Paleolithic*).

Stone-knapping: stone flaking; generally, the production of flake and core tools by striking a stone module with a hammer stone or other object.

Strategy: in the special zoological sense, a complex of *adaptations* that brings about an effective and efficient means of reproduction or resource use (e.g., a species' reproductive strategy or feeding strategy). No conscious choice is implied.

Stratigraphy: the sequence of geologic strata, or rock layers, formed by materials deposited by water or wind; also, the study of this sequence.

Superfecundity: the universal tendency to produce more offspring than required to maintain a *population* of constant size; more than can possibly survive.

Superior pubic ramus: portion of the pubic bone that runs between the pubic symphysis and the acetabulum.

Superior: in anatomy, above or toward the head in humans.

Suprainiac fossa: a characteristic depression on the occipital bone of *Neandertals*.

Suspensory ape: a *fossil ape* with an apelike suspensory locomotor adaptation.

Sympathetic hunting magic: the use of rituals (and associated artifacts) that practitioners believed would ensure success and safety in the hunt.

Sympatric speciation: speciation among *populations* with the same or overlapping geographic ranges.

Syntax: the rules of structure in *language*.

Szalatavus: *Oligocene platyrrhine monkey* from Bolivia.

Taiga: northern coniferous forest bordering the tundra.

Talonid: distal, heel-like portion of lower molars.

Taphonomy: the scientific study of the conditions under which objects are preserved as *fossils*.

Tarsier: a small Asian *prosimian* with large eyes and a long tail.

Taxon: group (*species, genus*, etc.) in a formal system of nomenclature (plural, *taxa*).

Taxonomy: classification of plants or animals according to their relationships, and the ordering of these groups into hierarchies; taxonomic levels are ranks within these classifications, such as *species* or *genus*.

Temporomandibular joint: jaw joint.

Temporonuchal crest: bony crest running around the posterior and lateral edges of the braincase.

Terrestrial: adapted to living on the ground.

Territoriality: an animal's distinctive behavior toward and tendency to defend a recognizable area of land.

Territory: the area occupied and defended by individuals or groups of animals against *conspecifics*. (Compare with *home range*.)

Thermoluminescence: method of dating pottery and stone tools by heating them to release trapped electrons; the electrons produce measurable light.

Theropithecus oswaldi: an extinct *species* of *gelada baboon.*

Thorax: the region of the rib cage.

Tool kit: all the tools or implements used by a primitive culture; its technology. *Neandertals* had 60 or 70 kinds of known tools; *Cro-Magnons* had more than 100.

Toothcomb: a dental *specialization* of *prosimians* in which the lower front teeth are closely spaced and forwardly inclined.

Triangulation: in the context of anthropology, the process of interpreting the behavior of extinct *hominids* by using both *apes* and modern humans as analogue models.

True breeding (breeding true): situation in which the members of a genetic strain resemble each other in all important characters and show little variability.

Tuff: a rocklike substance formed from volcanic ash.

Tundra: treeless, low-vegetation arctic or subarctic plain, swampy in summer, with permanently frozen soil just beneath the surface.

Turnover pulse: the hypothesis that organisms periodically experience spurts of *speciation, extinction,* and dispersion in response to relatively rapid changes in the physical environment.

Tympanic plate: the cranial base surface of the tubular *external auditory meatus.*

Type specimen: the *fossil* specimen that serves as the basis for identifying all other individuals in a *species;* usually the original specimen to be found.

Unearned resources: resources that are outside a predator's range, but to which it nonetheless gains secondary access by preying on migratory herds moving between summer and winter pastures.

Uniformitarianism: the belief that the steady changes in the earth's crust that we see today were preceded by similar slow changes throughout geological time.

Upper Paleolithic: a period of stone-tool manufacture in the Old World that lasted from about 40,000 to 10,000 years BP; associated primarily with anatomically modern humans.

Veld (or veldt): South Africa's open savanna grassland, with few bushes or trees.

Ventral: pertaining to the belly side of an animal or one of its parts; the opposite of *dorsal.*

Venus figurines: small sculptures of women, probably fertility symbols or objects of veneration.

Vertebrata: a subphylum of the chordates containing all animals with backbones; comprising fishes, amphibians, reptiles, birds, and mammals.

Vibrissae: sensory whiskers present near the mouth of dogs and cats as well as *prosimians.*

Victoriapithecinae: extinct subfamily of the earliest *catarrhine monkeys.*

Visual predation theory: theory that early *primates* evolved as an adaptation to hunting insects by sight and stealth.

Wallace's line: deep ocean cleft separating Australasia (Sahul) from Asia (Sunda) geographically and faunally.

Weir: barrier or dam made of stones or sticks set out in a stream or river and used as a fish trap.

Wernicke's area: part of the human *cerebral cortex* essential in comprehension and production of meaningful speech.

White blood cells (leukocytes): vertebrate blood cells lacking *hemoglobin.*

Wide-knee stance: standing position in which the feet and knees are about as far apart as the hip joints.

Xenophobia: fear and hatred of strangers or outsiders.

Y–5 pattern: an arrangement of the cusps and grooves of the lower molars that is characteristic of living *hominoids.*

Zinjanthropus boisei: original name for the *australopithecine species* now called *Paranthropus boisei.*

Zygomatic arches: bony arches extending backwards from the cheekbone in higher *primates.*

Cited References and General Sources

Aiello, L., and C. Dean. *An Introduction to Human Evolutionary Anatomy.* Academic Press, 1990.

Aiello, L., and R. I. M. Dunbar. "Neocortex Size, Group Size, and the Evolution of Language." *Current Anthropology,* 34, 1993.

Aiello, L., and P. Wheeler. "The Expensive-Tissue Hypothesis." *Current Anthropology,* 36, 1995.

Aitken, M. J. *Science-Based Dating in Archaeology.* Longmans, 1990.

Allison, A. C. "Abnormal Haemoglobins and Erythrocyte Enzyme-Deficiency Traits," in G. A. Harrison, ed., *Genetical Variations in Human Populations.* Pergamon Press, 1960.

Alpagut, B., P. Andrews, M. Fortelius, J. Kappelman, I. Temizsoy, H. Celebi, and W. Lindsay. "A New Specimen of *Ankarapithecus meteai* from the Sinap Formation of Central Anatolia." *Nature,* 382, 1996.

Alroy, J. "Cope's Rule and the Dynamics of Body Mass Evolution in North American Fossil Mammals." *Science,* 280, 1998.

Arens, W. *The Man-Eating Myth.* Oxford University Press, 1979.

Arsuaga, J. L., I. Martinez, A. Garcia, J. M. Carretero, and E. Carbonell. "Three New Human Skulls from the Sima de los Huesos Middle Pleistocene Site in Sierra de Atapuerca, Spain." *Nature,* 362, 1993.

Arsuaga, J. L., I. Martinez, A. Garcia, and C. Lorenzo. "The Sima de los Huesos Crania (Sierra de Atapuerca, Spain). A Comparative Study." *Journal of Human Evolution,* 33, 1997a.

Arsuaga, J. L., I. Martinez, A. Garcia, J. M. Carretero, C. Lorenzo, N. Garcia, and A. I. Ortega. "Sima de los Huesos (Sierra de Atapuerca, Spain). The Site." *Journal of Human Evolution,* 33, 1997b.

Ascenzi, A., I. Biddittu, P. F. Cassoli, A. G. Segre, and E. Segre-Naldini. "A Calvarium of Late *Homo erectus* From Ceprano, Italy." *Journal of Human Evolution,* 31, 1996.

Aschoff, J., B. Gunther, and K. Kramer. *Energiehaushalt und Temperaturregulation.* Urban and Schwarzenberg, 1971.

Asfaw, B., T. White, O. Lovejoy, B. Latimer, S. Simpson, and G. Suwa. "*Australopithecus garhi:* A New Species of Early Hominid from Ethiopia." *Science,* 284, 1999.

Ayala, F. J. "The Mechanisms of Evolution." *Scientific American,* 234, no. 3, 1978.

Bada, J. L. "Aspartic Acid Racemization Ages of Californian Paleoindians." *American Antiquity,* 50, 1979.

Bahn, P. G. "Cannibalism or Ritual Dismemberment?" in S. Jones, R. Martin, and D. Pilbeam, eds., *The Cambridge Encyclopedia of Human Evolution.* Cambridge University Press, 1992.

Bailey, W. J. "Hominoid Trichotomy: A Molecular Overview." *Evolutionary Anthropology,* 2, 1993.

Baker, B. T. "Human Adaptations to the Physical Environment," in S. Jones, R. Martin, and D. Pilbeam, eds., *The Cambridge Encyclopedia of Human Evolution.* Cambridge University Press, 1992.

Baker, P. T. "Human Adaptability," in G. A. Harrison, J. M. Tanner, D. R. Pilbeam, and P. T. Baker, eds., *Human Biology: An Introduction to Human Evolution, Variation, Growth and Adaptability.* Oxford University Press, 1988.

Bartlett, T., R. Sussman, and J. Cheverud. "Infant Killing in Primates: A Review of Observed Cases with Specific Reference to the Sexual Selection Hypothesis." *American Anthropologist,* 95, 1993.

Beard, K. C., Tao Qi, M. R. Dawson, Banyue Wang, and Chuankuei Li. "A Diverse New Primate Fauna from Middle Eocene Fissure-Fillings in Southeastern China." *Nature,* 368, 1994.

Beard, K. C., Yongsheng Tong, M. R. Dawson, Jingwen Wang, and Xueshi Huang. "Earliest Complete Dentition of an Anthropoid Primate from the Late Middle Eocene of Shanxi Province, China." *Science,* 272, 1996.

Begun, D. R. "Relations among the Great Apes and Humans: New Interpretations Based on the Fossil Great Ape *Dryopithecus.*" *Yearbook of Physical Anthropology,* 37, 1994.

Begun, D., and A. Walker. "The Endocast," in A. Walker and R. Leakey, eds., *The Nariokotome Homo erectus Skeleton.* Harvard University Press, 1993.

Behrensmeyer, A. K., N. E. Todd, R. Potts, and G. E. McBrinn. "Late Pliocene Faunal Turnover in the Turkana Basin, Kenya and Ethiopia." *Science,* 278, 1997.

Bellomo, R. V. "Methods of Determining Early Hominid Behavioral Activities Associated with the Controlled Use of Fire at FxJj 20 Main, Koobi Fora, Kenya." *Journal of Human Evolution,* 27, 1994.

Beneviste, R. E., and G. J. Todaro. "Evolution of Type C Viral Genes: Evidence for an Asian Origin of Man." *Nature,* 261, 1976.

Berger, L. R., and P. V. Tobias. "A Chimpanzee-Like Tibia from Sterkfontein, South Africa and Its Implications for the Interpretation of Bipedalism in *Australopithecus africanus*." *Journal of Human Evolution*, 30, 1996.

Bermudez de Castro, J. M., J. L. Arsuaga, E. Carbonell, A. Rosas, I. Martinez, and M. Mosquera. "A Hominid from the Lower Pleistocene of Atapuerca, Spain: Possible Ancestor to Neandertals and Modern Humans." *Science*, 276, 1997.

Binford, L. R. *Bones: Ancient Men and Modern Myths.* Academic Press, 1981.

Binford, L. R. *Faunal Remains from Klasies River Mouth.* Academic Press, 1984.

Binford, L. R., and C. K. Ho. "Taphonomy at a Distance. Zhoukoudian, 'The Cave of Beijing Man'?" *Current Anthropology*, 26, 1985.

Binford, L. R., and N. M. Stone. "Zhoukoudian: A Closer Look." *Current Anthropology*, 27, 1986.

Bischoff, J. L., J. A. Fitzpatrick, L. Leon, J. L. Arsuaga, C. Falgueres, J. J. Bahain, and T. Bullen. "Geology and Preliminary Dating of the Hominid-Bearing Sedimentary Fill of the Sima de los Huesos Chamber, Cueva Mayor of the Sierra de Atapuerca, Burgos, Spain." *Journal of Human Evolution*, 33, 1997.

Blumenschine, R. J. "Percussion Marks, Tooth Marks, and Experimental Determinations of the Timing of Hominid and Carnivore Access to Long Bones at FLK *Zinjanthropus*, Olduvai Gorge, Tanzania." *Journal of Human Evolution*, 29, 1995.

Boag, P. T., and P. R. Grant. "Intense Natural Selection in a Population of Darwin's Finches (Geospizinae) in the Galapagos." *Science*, 214, 1981.

Boesch-Achermann, H., and C. Boesch. "Hominization in the Rainforest: The Chimpanzee's Piece of the Puzzle." *Evolutionary Anthropology*, 3, 1994.

Bordes, F. *A Tale of Two Caves.* Harper & Row, 1972.

Borja, C., M. Garcia-Pacheco, E. G. Olivares, G. Scheuenstuhl, and J. M. Lowenstein. "Immunospecificity of Albumin Detected in 1.6-Million-Year-Old Fossils from Venta Micena in Orce, Granada, Spain." *American Journal of Physical Anthropology*, 103, 1997.

Bowcock, A. M., A. Ruiz-Linares, J. Tomfohrde, E. Minch, J. R. Kidd, and L. L. Cavalli-Sforza. "High Resolution of Human Evolutionary Trees with Polymorphic Microsatellites." *Nature*, 368, 1994.

Brace, C. L. "A Nonracial Approach towards the Understanding of Human Diversity," in A. Montagu, ed., *The Concept of Race.* Free Press, 1964.

Braga, J., and C. Boesch. "Further Data about Venous Channels in South African Plio–Pleistocene Hominids." *Journal of Human Evolution*, 33, 1997.

Braidwood, R. *Prehistoric Men,* 7th ed. Scott, Foresman, 1967.

Brauer, G., and M. Schultz. "The Morphological Affinities of the Plio–Pleistocene Mandible from Dmanisi, Georgia." *Journal of Human Evolution*, 30, 1996.

Brauer, G., Y. Yokoyama, C. Falgueres, and E. Mbua. "Modern Human Origins Backdated." *Nature*, 386, 1997.

Breuil, Abbe H. *Four Hundred Centuries of Cave Art.* Centre d'Etudes et de Documentation Prehistoriques, 1952.

Bromage, T. G., F. Schrenk, and F. W. Zonneveld. "Paleoanthropology of the Malawi Rift: An Early Hominid Mandible from the Chiwondo Beds, Northern Malawi." *Journal of Human Evolution*, 28, 1995.

Broom, R. *Finding the Missing Link.* Watts, 1950.

Brose, D. S., and M. H. Wolpoff. "Early Upper Paleolithic Man and Late Middle Paleolithic Tools." *American Anthropologist*, 73, 1971.

Brothwell, D., and E. Higgs, eds. *Science in Archeology,* 2nd ed. Praeger, 1970.

Brown, B., A. Walker, C. V. Ward, and R. E. Leakey. "New *Australopithecus boisei* Calvaria from East Lake Turkana, Kenya." *American Journal of Physical Anthropology*, 91, 1993.

Brown, F. H. "Methods of Dating," in S. Jones, R. Martin, and D. Pilbeam, eds., *The Cambridge Encyclopedia of Human Evolution.* Cambridge University Press, 1992.

Brown, F., J. Harris, R. E. Leakey, and Alan Walker. "Early *Homo erectus* Skeleton from West Lake Turkana, Kenya." *Nature*, 316, 1985.

Brown, L. N. "Selection in a Population of House Mice Containing Mutant Individuals." *Journal of Mammalogy*, 46, 1965.

Brunet, B., A. Beauvilain, Y. Coppens, E. Heintz, A. H. E. Moutaye, and D. Pilbeam. "The First Australopithecine 2,500 Kilometres West of the Rift Valley (Chad)." *Nature*, 378, 1995.

Brunet, B., A. Beauvilain, Y. Coppens, E. Heintz, A. H. E. Moutaye, and D. Pilbeam. "*Australopithecus bahrelghazali*, une Nouvelle Espèce d'Hominide Ancien de la Région de Koro Toro (Tchad)." *Paleontology* (Academy of Sciences, Paris), 322, 1996.

Burckhardt F., and S. Smith. *The Correspondence of Charles Darwin.* Cambridge University Press, 1988.

Butzer, K. W. "Acheulean Occupation Sites at Torralba and Ambrona, Spain: Their Geology." *Science*, 150, no. 3704, 1965.

Butzer, K. W. *Environment and Archeology: An Ecological Approach to Prehistory.* Aldine–Atherton, 1971.

Butzer, K. W., and G. L. Isaac, eds. *After the Australopithecines: Stratigraphy, Ecology, and Culture Change in the Middle Pleistocene.* Mouton, 1975.

Byrne, R. *The Thinking Ape: Evolutionary Origins of Intelligence.* Oxford University Press, 1995.

Byrne, R. W. "Machiavellian Intelligence." *Evolutionary Anthropology*, 5, 1996.

Campbell, B. G., ed. *Sexual Selection and the Descent of Man, 1871–1971.* Aldine, 1972.

Campbell, B. G. *Human Ecology: The Story of Our Place in Nature from Prehistory to the Present.* Aldine de Gruyter, 1995.

Campbell, B. G. *Human Evolution,* 4th ed. Aldine, 1998.

Cann, R. L., M. Stoneking, and A. C. Wilson. "Mitochondrial DNA and Human Evolution." *Nature*, 325, 1987.

Carbonell, E., J. M. Bermudez de Castro., J. L. Arsuaga, J. C. Diez, A. Rosas, G. Cuenca-Bescos, R. Sala, M. Mosquera, and X. P. Rodriguez. "Lower Pleistocene Hominids and Artifacts from Atapuerca–TD6 (Spain)." *Science*, 269, 1995.

Cartmill, M. "Rethinking Primate Origins." *Science*, 184, 1974.

Cartmill, M. "New Views on Primate Origins." *Evolutionary Anthropology*, 1, 1992.

Cartmill, M. *A View to a Death in the Morning.* Harvard University Press, 1993.

Cavalli-Sforza, L. L., and W. F. Bodmer. *The Genetics of Human Populations.* Freeman, 1971.

Cavalli-Sforza, L. L., and F. Cavalli-Sforza. *The Great Human Diasporas.* Addison-Wesley, 1995.

Cavalli-Sforza, L. L., P. Menozzi, and A. Piazza. *The History and Geography of Human Genes.* Princeton University Press, 1994.

Chaimanee, Y., V. Suteethorn, J.-J. Jaeger, and S. Ducrocq. "A New Late Eocene Anthropoid Primate from Thailand." *Nature*, 385, 1997.

Chang, Kwang-chih. *The Archaeology of Ancient China.* Yale University Press, 1968.

Chapman, F. M. *Handbook of Birds of Eastern North America.* Dover, 1966.

Cheney, D. L. "Interactions and Relationships between Groups," in B. Smuts, D. Cheney, R. Seyfarth, R. Wangham, and T. Struhsaker, eds., *Primate Societies.* University of Chicago Press, 1987.

Cheney, D. L., and R. M. Seyfarth. *How Monkeys See the World.* University of Chicago Press, 1990.

Chivers, D. L., B. A. Wood, and A. Bilsborough, eds. *Food Acquisition and Processing in Primates.* Plenum Press, 1984.

Chu, J. Y., W. Huang, S. Q. Kuang, J. M. Wang, J. J. Xu, Z. T. Chu, Z. Q. Yang, K. Q. Lin, P. Li, M. Wu, Z. C. Geng, C. C. Tan, R. F. Du, and L. Jin. "Genetic Relationship of Populations in China." *Proceedings of the National Academy of Sciences*, 95, 1998.

Ciochon, R. L., and R. S. Corrucini. *New Interpretations of Ape and Human Ancestry.* Plenum Press, 1983.

Ciochon, R. L., and J. Fleagle, eds., *The Human Evolution Source Book.* Prentice Hall, 1993.

Clark, J. D. *The Prehistory of Africa.* Praeger, 1970.

Clark, J. G. D. *Prehistoric Europe: The Economic Basis.* Philosophical Library, 1952.

Clark, W. E. Le Gros. *The Antecedents of Man.* Edinburgh, 1959.

Clark, W. E. Le Gros. *Man-Apes or Ape-Men?* Holt, Rinehart & Winston, 1967.

Clarke, R. J., and P. V. Tobias. "Sterkfontein Member 2 Foot Bones of the Oldest South African Hominid." *Science*, 269, 1995.

Clottes, J., and D. Lewis-Williams. *The Shamans of Prehistory: Trance and Magic in the Painted Caves.* Abrams, 1999.

Cobb, S. "Brain Size." *Archives of Neurology, Chicago*, 12, 1965.

Coffing, K., C. Feibel, M. Leakey, and A. Walker. "Four-Million-Year-Old Hominids from East Lake Turkana, Kenya." *American Journal of Physical Anthropology*, 93, 1994.

Conkey, M. "Humans as Materialists and Symbolists: Image Making in the Upper Paleolithic," in D. T. Rasmussen, ed., *The Origin and Evolution of Humans and Humanness.* Jones & Bartlett, 1993.

Conroy, G. C. *Primate Evolution.* Norton, 1990.

Conroy, G. C. *Reconstructing Human Origins: A Modern Synthesis.* Norton, 1997.

Conroy, G. C., M. Pickford, B. Senut, and P. Mein. "Diamonds in the Desert: The Discovery of *Otavipithecus namibiensis*." *Evolutionary Anthropology*, 2, 1993.

Conroy, G. C., G. W. Weber, H. Seidler, P. V. Tobias, A. Kane, and B. Brunsden. "Endocranial Capacity in an Early Hominid Cranium from Sterkfontein, South Africa." *Science*, 280, 1998.

Convey, Curt. "Earth's Orbit and the Ice Ages." *Scientific American*, 250, 1984.

Coon, C. S., S. M. Garn, and J. B. Birdsell. *Races: A Study of the Problem of Race Formation in Man.* Charles Thomas, 1950.

Coon, C. S., and E. E. Hunt, Jr. *The Living Races of Man.* Knopf, 1965.

Coppens, Y. "East Side Story: The Origin of Humankind." *Scientific American*, 270, 1994.

Coppens, Y., F. Clark Howell, G. L. Isaac, and Richard E. F. Leakey, eds. *Earliest Man and Environments in the Lake Rudolf Basin.* University of Chicago Press, 1976.

Cronin, J. E. *South African Journal of Science*, 82, 1986.

Dahl, J. F. "Cyclic Perineal Swelling during the Intermenstrual Intervals of Captive Female Pygmy Chimpanzees (*Pan paniscus*)." *Journal of Human Evolution*, 15, 1986.

Daniel, G. A. *A Hundred and Fifty Years of Archaeology.* Duckworth, 1975.

Dart, R. *Adventures with the Missing Link.* Viking Press, 1959.

Darwin, C. R. *The Descent of Man and Selection in Relation to Sex.* John Murray, 1871.

Darwin, C. R. *On the Origin of Species* (facsimile of 1st ed.). Harvard University Press, 1966.

Darwin, F., ed. *The Life and Letters of Charles Darwin.* 2 vols. Basic Books, 1959.

Darwin, F., and A. C. Seward, eds. *More Letters of Charles Darwin.* 2 vols. John Murray, 1903.

Deacon, J. "South African Rock Art." *Evolutionary Anthropology*, 8, 1999.

Deacon, T. W. *The Symbolic Species: The Co-Evolution of Language and the Brain.* Norton, 1997.

Deevey, E. S. "The Human Population." *Scientific American*, 203, 1964.

Delgado, R. A. Jnr., and C. P. van Schaik. "The Behavioral Ecology and Conservation of the Orangutan (*Pongo pygmaeus*): A Tale of Two Islands." *Evolutionary Anthropology*, 9, 2000.

Delson, E., ed. *Ancestors: The Hard Evidence.* A. R. Liss, 1985.

de Lumley, H. "A Paleolithic Camp at Nice." *Scientific American,* 220, no. 5, 1969.

D'Errico, F., P. Villa, A. C. Pinto Llona, and R. Ruiz Idarraga. "A Middle Palaeolithic Origin of Music? Using Cave-Bear Bone Accumulations to Assess the Divje Babe I Bone 'Flute.'" *Antiquity,* 72, 1998.

DeVore, I., and K. R. L. Hall. "Baboon Ecology," in I. DeVore, ed., *Primate Behavior: Field Studies of Monkeys and Apes.* Holt, Rinehart and Winston, 1965.

De Vries, H. *Species and Varieties.* Open Court, 1905.

De Vries, H. *The Mutation Theory.* 2 vols. Open Court, 1909–1910.

Diamond, J. *Guns, Germs, and Steel.* Norton, 1997.

Dickson, D. B. *The Dawn of Belief.* University of Arizona Press, 1990.

Dillehay, T. D. "The Late Pleistocene Cultures of South America." *Evolutionary Anthropology,* 7, 1999.

Doran, D. M., and A. McNeilage. "Gorilla Ecology and Behavior." *Evolutionary Anthropology,* 6, 1998.

Dronkers, N. F. "A New Brain Region for Coordinating Speech Articulation." *Nature,* 384, 1996.

Duarte, C., J. Mauricio, P. B. Pettitt, P. Souto, E. Trinkhaus, H. van de Plicht, and J. Zilhao. "The Early Upper Paleolithic Human Skeleton from the Abrigo do Lagar Velho (Portugal) and Modern Human Emergence in Iberia." *Proceedings of the National Academy of Sciences,* 96, 1999.

Duchin, L. E. "The Evolution of Articulate Speech." *Journal of Human Evolution,* 19, 1990.

Dunbar, R. I. M. "Neocortex Size as a Constraint on Group Size in Primates." *Journal of Human Evolution,* 20, 1992.

Dunbar, R. I. M. "The Price of Being at the Top." *Nature,* 373, 1995.

Dunbar, R. I. M. "The Social Brain Hypothesis." *Evolutionary Anthropology,* 6, 1998.

Ebert, J. D. *Science and Creationism: A View from the National Academy of Sciences.* National Academy Press, 1984.

Eiseley, L. "Neandertal Man and the Dawn of Human Paleontology." *Quarterly Review of Biology,* 32, no. 4, 1957.

Eiseley, L. *Darwin's Century: Evolution and the Men Who Discovered It.* Doubleday, 1958.

Falk, D. *Braindance.* Henry Holt, 1992.

Feathers, J. K. "Luminescence Dating and Modern Human Origins." *Evolutionary Anthropology,* 5, 1996.

Fischman, J. "Putting a New Spin on the Birth of Human Birth." *Science,* 264, 1994.

Fisher, R. A. *The Genetical Theory of Natural Selection.* Clarendon Press, 1930.

Fleagle, J. G. *Primate Adaptation and Evolution.* Academic Press, 1988.

Fleagle, J. G., D. T. Rasmussen, S. Yirga, T. M. Bown, and F. E. Grine. "New Hominid Fossils from Fejej, Southern Ethiopia." *Journal of Human Evolution,* 21, 1991.

Fossey, D. *Gorillas in the Mist.* Houghton Mifflin, 1983.

Friday, A. E. "Human Evolution: The Evidence from DNA Sequencing," in S. Jones, R. Martin, and D. Pilbeam, eds., *The Cambridge Encyclopedia of Human Evolution.* Cambridge University Press, 1992.

Frison, G. C. "Modern People in the New World," in G. Burenhult, ed., *The First Humans: Human Origins and History to 10,000 BC.* HarperCollins, 1993.

Furuichi, T. "The Prolonged Estrus of Females and Factors Influencing Mating in a Wild Group of Bonobos (*Pan paniscus*) in Wamba, Zaire," in N. Itoigawa et al., eds., *Topics in Primatology: Vol. 2. Behavior, Ecology, and Conservation.* University of Tokyo Press, 1992.

Gabunia, L., and A. Vekua. "A Plio–Pleistocene Hominid from Dmanisi, East Georgia, Caucasus." *Nature,* 373, 1995.

Gabunia, L., and A. Vekua, D. Lordkipanidze, C. C. Swisher III, R. Ferring, A. Justus, M. Nioradze, M. Tvalchrelidze, S. C. Anton, G. Bosinski, O. Joris, M.-A. de Lumley, G. Majsuradze, and A. Mouskhelishvili. "Earliest Pleistocene Hominid Cranial Remains from Dmanisi, Republic of Georgia: Taxonomy, Geological Setting, and Age." *Science,* 288, 2000.

Gagneux, P., D. S. Woodruff, and C. Boesch. "Furtive Mating in Female Chimpanzees." *Nature,* 387, 1997.

Gardner, R. A., and B. T. Gardner. "Teaching Sign Language to a Chimpanzee." *Science,* 165, no. 3894, 1969.

Garn, S. M. *Human Races,* 2nd ed. Charles C. Thomas, 1965.

Gebo, D. L. "Climbing, Brachiation, and Terrestrial Quadrupedalism: Historical Precursors of Hominid Bipedalism." *American Journal of Physical Anthropology,* 101, 1996.

Gebo, D. L., L. MacLatchy, R. Kityo, A. Deino, J. Kingston, and D. Pilbeam. "A Hominoid Genus from the Early Miocene of Uganda." *Science,* 276, 1997.

Gee, H. "Box of Bones 'Clinches' Identity of Piltdown Palaeontology Hoaxer." *Nature,* 381, 1996.

Geschwind, N. "The Neural Basis of Language," in K. Salzinger and S. Salzinger, eds., *Research in Verbal Behavior and Some Neurophysiological Implications.* Academic Press, 1967.

Giacobini, G. *Hominidae: Proceedings of the Second International Congress of Human Paleontology, Turin, September–October 1987.* Jaca Book, 1989.

Gibbons, A. "Ideas on Human Origins Evolve at Anthropology Gathering." *Science,* 276, 1997.

Gibson, K. R. "Continuity Theories of Human Language Origins versus the Lieberman Model." *Language and Communication,* 14, 1994.

Gill, G. W. "The Beauty of Race and Races." *Anthropology Newsletter,* 39, no. 3, 1998.

Glover, I. C. "Tools and Cultures in Late Paleolithic Southeast Asia," in G. Burenhult, ed., *The First Humans: Human Origins and History to 10,000 BC.* HarperCollins, 1993.

Goodall, J. *The Chimpanzees of Gombe.* Harvard University Press, 1986.

Goodman, M. "Protein Sequencing and Immunological Specificity," in W. Luckett and F. Szalay, eds., *Phylogeny of the Primates.* Plenum, 1975.

Gore, R. "People Like Us." *National Geographic,* 198, 2000.

Gould, S. J. *The Mismeasure of Man.* Norton, 1981.

Gould, S. J. *Hen's Teeth and Horse's Toes: Further Reflections on Natural History.* Norton, 1983.

Gould, S. J. "Human Equality Is a Contingent Fact of History." *Natural History,* 93, 1984.

Gould, S. J. *Time's Arrow, Time's Cycle.* Harvard University Press, 1987.

Gould, S. J. *Full House.* Harmony Books, 1996.

Gouzoules, H., S. Gouzoules, and P. Marler. "Vocal Communication: A Vehicle for the Study of Social Relationships," in R. Rawlins and M. Kessler, eds., *The Cayo Santiago Macaques.* State University of New York Press, 1986.

Grant, V. *The Evolutionary Process,* 2nd ed. Columbia University Press, 1991.

Grayson, D. K. "Differential Mortality and the Donner Party Disaster." *Evolutionary Anthropology,* 2, 1993.

Greenfield, L. O. "Origin of the Human Canine: A New Solution to an Old Enigma." *Yearbook of Physical Anthropology,* 35, 1992.

Greenfield, P. M. "Language, Tools and Brain: The Ontogeny and Phylogeny of Hierarchically Organized Sequential Behavior." *Behavioral and Brain Sciences,* 14, 1991.

Grine, F. E. "Australopithecine Taxonomy and Phylogeny: Historical Background and Recent Interpretation," in R. L. Ciochon and J. G. Fleagle, eds., *The Human Evolution Source Book.* Prentice Hall, 1993.

Grine, F. E., B. Demes, W. L. Jungers, and T. M. Cole III. "Taxonomic Affinity of the Early *Homo* Cranium from Swartkrans, South Africa." *American Journal of Physical Anthropology,* 92, 1993.

Groves, C. P. *A Theory of Human and Primate Evolution.* Clarendon Press, 1989.

Grun, R., J. S. Brink, N. A. Spooner, L. Taylor, C. B. Stringer, R. G. Franciscus, and A. S. Murray. "Direct Dating of Florisbad Hominid." *Nature,* 382, 1996.

Haldane, J. B. S. *The Causes of Evolution.* Longmans, Green, 1932.

Hamilton, W. D. "The Genetical Evolution of Social Behavior, I." *Journal of Theoretical Biology,* 7, 1964.

Hammer, M. F. "A Recent Common Ancestry for Human Y Chromosomes." *Nature,* 378, 1995.

Hammer, M. F., and S. L. Zegura. "The Role of the Y Chromosome in Human Evolutionary Studies." *Evolutionary Anthropology,* 5, 1996.

Haraway, D. *Primate Visions.* Routledge, 1989.

Harris, J. W. K. "Cultural Beginnings: Plio–Pleistocene Archaeological Occurrences from the Afar, Ethiopia." *African Archaeological Review,* 1, 1983.

Harrison, T. "Cladistic Concepts and the Species Problem in Hominoid Evolution," in W. H. Kimbel and L. B. Martin, eds., *Species, Species Concepts, and Primate Evolution.* Plenum Press, 1993.

Hartwig-Scherer, S. "Body Weight Prediction in Early Fossil Hominids: Towards a Taxon-Independent Approach." *American Journal of Physical Anthropology,* 92, 1993.

Hausfater, G. *Dominance and Reproduction in Baboons (Papio cynocephalus).* S. Karger, 1975.

Hausfater, G., and S. Blaffer Hrdy, eds. *Infanticide: Comparative and Evolutionary Perspectives.* Aldine, 1984.

Hawkes, N. "'Missing Link' Ate Fruit and Leaves." *Times* (London), September 22, 1994.

Heltne, P. G., and L. A. Marquandt. *Understanding Chimpanzees.* Harvard University Press, 1989.

Henig, R. *The Monk in the Garden.* Houghton Mifflin, 2000.

Hill, A., and S. Ward. "Origin of the Hominidae: The Record of African Large Hominoid Evolution between 14 My and 4 My." *Yearbook of Physical Anthropology,* 31, 1988.

Hill, A., S. Ward, and B. Brown. "Anatomy and Age of the Lothagam Mandible." *Journal of Human Evolution,* 22, 1992.

Hockett, C. F. "The Origin of Speech." *Scientific American,* 203, no. 3, 1960.

Hohmann, G., and B. Fruth. "Field Observations on Meat Sharing among Bonobos (*Pan paniscus*)." *Folia Primatologica,* 60, 1993.

Holliday, T. W. "Postcranial Evidence of Cold Adaptation in European Neandertals." *American Journal of Physical Anthropology,* 104, 1997.

Holloway R. L. "The Casts of Fossil Hominid Brains." *Scientific American,* 231, 1974.

Hood, Dora. *Davidson Black: A Biography.* University of Toronto Press, 1971.

Hooton, E. A. *Up from the Ape.* Macmillan, 1946.

Howell, F. C. "European and Northwest African Middle Pleistocene Hominids." *Current Anthropology,* 1, 1960.

Howell, F. C. "Observations on the Earliest Phases of the European Lower Paleolithic." *American Anthropologist,* 68, no. 2, 1966.

Howell, F. C. "Recent Advances in Human Evolutionary Studies." *Quarterly Review of Biology,* 42, 1967.

Howells, W. "The Dispersion of Modern Humans," in S. Jones, R. Martin, and D. Pilbeam, eds., *The Cambridge Encyclopedia of Human Evolution.* Cambridge University Press, 1992.

Howells, W. *Getting Here.* Compass Press, 1993.

Howells, W. W. "*Homo erectus*—Who, When and Where: A Survey." *Yearbook of Physical Anthropology,* 23, 1980.

Hrdy, S. B. *The Langurs of Abu: Female and Male Strategies of Reproduction.* Harvard University Press, 1977.

Huffman, M. A., and R. Wrangham. "Diversity of Medicinal Plant Use by Chimpanzees in the Wild," in R. Wrangham et al., eds., *Chimpanzee Cultures.* Harvard University Press, 1994.

Hutchings, W. K., and L. W. Bruchert. "Spearthrower Performance: Ethnographic and Experimental Research." *Antiquity,* 71, 1997.

Huxley, J. *Evolution: The Modern Synthesis.* Allen & Unwin, 1942.

Huxley, T. H. *Man's Place in Nature.* University of Michigan Press, 1959. [Originally published 1863.]

Ingmanson, E. J. "Tool-Using Behavior in Wild *Pan paniscus:* Social and Ecological Considerations," in A. E. Russon et al., eds., *Reaching into Thought: The Minds of the Great Apes.* Cambridge University Press, 1996.

Isaac, G. L. "Studies of Early Culture in East Africa." *World Archaeology,* 1, no. 1, 1969.

Isaac, G. L. "The Diet of Early Man: Aspects of Archaeological Evidence from Lower and Middle Pleistocene Sites in Africa." *World Archaeology,* 2, no. 3, 1971.

Isaac, G. L., and Elizabeth R. McCown, eds. *Human Origins.* Staples Press, 1976.

Isbell, L. A., and T. P. Young. "The Evolution of Bipedalism in Hominids and Reduced Group Size in Chimpanzees: Alternative Responses to Decreasing Resource Availability." *Journal of Human Evolution,* 30, 1996.

Jablonski, N. G., and G. Chaplin. "The Origin of Hominid Bipedalism Re-examined." *Perspectives in Human Biology, 2/Archaeology in Oceania,* 27, 1992.

Jelinek, A. J. "The Lower Paleolithic: Current Evidence and Interpretations." *Annual Review of Anthropology,* 6, 1977.

Jellema, L. M., B. Latimer, and A. Walker. "The Rib Cage," in A. Walker and R. Leakey, eds., *The Nariokotome* Homo erectus *Skeleton.* Harvard University Press, 1993.

Jerison, H. J. *Evolution of the Brain and Intelligence.* Academic Press, 1973.

Jia, L., and Huang Weiwen. *The Story of Peking Man.* Oxford University Press, 1990.

Joblonski, D. "Body-Size Evolution in Cretaceous Molluscs and the Status of Cope's Rule." *Nature,* 385, 1997.

Johanson, D. C., and M. A. Edey. *Lucy: The Beginnings of Humankind.* Simon & Schuster, 1981.

Johanson, D. C., and B. Edgar. *From Lucy to Language.* Simon & Schuster, 1996.

Johanson, D. C., and T. D. White. "A Systematic Assessment of Early African Hominids." *Science,* 203, 1979.

Jolly, C. J. "The Seed-Eaters." *Man,* 5, no. 1, March 1970.

Jolly, C. J., and F. Plog. *Physical Anthropology and Archaeology.* McGraw-Hill, 1986.

Jolly, C. J., and R. White. *Physical Anthropology and Archaeology,* 5th ed. McGraw-Hill, 1995.

Jones, S. "Genetic Diversity in Humans," in S. Jones, R. Martin, and D. Pilbeam, eds., *The Cambridge Encyclopedia of Human Evolution.* Cambridge University Press, 1992a.

Jones, S. "The Evolutionary Future of Humankind," in S. Jones, R. Martin, and D. Pilbeam, eds., *The Cambridge Encyclopedia of Human Evolution.* Cambridge University Press, 1992b.

Jones, S., R. Martin, and D. Pilbeam, eds., *The Cambridge Encyclopedia of Human Evolution.* Cambridge University Press, 1992.

Ju-kang, Woo. "The Skull of Lantian Man." *Current Anthropology,* 7, no. 1, 1966.

Kappelman, J., G. C. Swisher, J. G. Fleagle, S. Yirga, T. M. Bown, and M. Feseha. "Age of *Australopithecus afarensis* from Fejej, Ethiopia." *Journal of Human Evolution,* 30, 1996.

Kay, R. F., M. Cartmill, and M. Balow. "The Hypoglossal Canal and the Origin of Human Vocal Behavior." *Proceedings of the National Academy of Sciences USA,* 95, 1998.

Kay, R. F., C. Ross, and B. A. Williams. "Anthropoid Origins." *Science,* 275, 1997.

Kay, R. F., J. G. M. Thewissen, and A. D. Yoder. "Cranial Anatomy of *Ignacius graybullianus* and the Affinities of the Plesiadapiformes." *American Journal of Physical Anthropology,* 89, 1992.

Keith, A. *A New Theory of Human Evolution.* Watts & Co., 1948.

Kelley, J. "Evolution of Apes," in S. Jones, R. Martin, and D. Pilbeam, eds., *The Cambridge Encyclopedia of Human Evolution,* Cambridge University Press, 1992.

Kennedy, K. A. R. "Paleoanthropology of South Asia." *Evolutionary Anthropology,* 8, 1999.

Kerr, R. A. "New Mammal Data Challenge Evolutionary Pulse Theory." *Science,* 273, 1996.

Kidd, R. S., P. O'Higgins, and C. E. Oxnard. "The OH8 Foot: A Reappraisal of the Functional Morphology of the Hindfoot Utilizing a Multivariate Analysis." *Journal of Human Evolution,* 31, 1996.

Kim, K. H. S., N. R. Relkin, K.-M. Lee, and J. Hirsch. "Distinct Cortical Areas Associated with Native and Second Languages." *Nature,* 388, 1997.

Kimbel, W. H., R. C. Walter, D. C. Johanson, K. E. Reed, J. L. Aronson, Z. Assefa, C. W. Marean, G. G. Eck, R. Bobe, E. Hovers, Y. Rak, C. Vondra, T. Yemane, D. York, Y. Chen, N. M. Evensen, and P. E. Smith. "Late Pliocene *Homo* and Oldowan Tools from the Hadar Formation (Kada Hadar Member), Ethiopia." *Journal of Human Evolution,* 31, 1996.

Kinsey, W. G., ed. *The Evolution of Human Behavior: Primate Models.* State University of New York Press, 1987.

Klein, R. G. *Man and Culture in the Late Pleistocene.* Chandler, 1969.

Klein, R. G. *The Human Career.* University of Chicago Press, 1989.

Klein, R. G. "The Archeology of Modern Human Origins." *Evolutionary Anthropology,* 1, 1992.

Klein, R. G. "Archaeology and the Evolution of Human Behavior." *Evolutionary Anthropology,* 9, 2000.

Kolata, G. "Mutant-Gene Study Alters Estimate of Risk to Women." *New York Times,* May 15, 1997.

Kolata, G. "Frequency of AIDS Resistant Gene and Progress of Black Plague from 1347 to 1352." *New York Times,* May 26, 1998.

Kramer, A. "A Critical Analysis of Claims for the Existence of Southeast Asian Australopithecines." *Journal of Human Evolution,* 26, 1994.

Krantz, G. S. "Brain Size and Hunting Ability in Earliest Man." *Current Anthropology,* 9, no. 5, 1966.

Kranzberg, M., and C. W. Pursell, Jr., eds. *Technology in Western Civilization,* vol. 1. Oxford University Press, 1967.

Krings, M., A. Stone, R. W. Schmitz, H. Krainitzki, M. Stoneking, and S. Paabo. "Neandertal DNA Sequences and the Origin of Modern Humans." *Cell,* 90, 1997.

Kummer, H. *Social Organization of Hamadryas Baboons.* University of Chicago Press, 1968.

Kummer, H. *In Quest of the Sacred Baboon.* Princeton University Press, 1995.

Kunzig, R. "Learning to Love Neandertals." *Discover,* 20, 1999.

Kurten, B. *Pleistocene Mammals of Europe.* Aldine, 1968.

Kurten, B. *The Ice Age.* Putnam's, 1972.

Kurten, B. *The Cave Bear Story.* Pantheon, 1977.

Lahr, M. M. "The Multiregional Model of Modern Human Origins: A Reassessment of Its Morphological Basis." *Journal of Human Evolution,* 26, 1994.

Lahr, M. M. "Patterns of Modern Human Diversification: Implications for Amerindian Origins." *Yearbook of Physical Anthropology,* 38, 1995.

Laitman, J. T., and R. C. Heimbuch. "The Basicranium of Plio–Pleistocene Hominids as an Indicator of Their Upper Respiratory Systems." *American Journal of Physical Anthropology,* 59, 1982.

Laitman, J. T., R. C. Heimbuch, and E. S. Crelin. "The Basicranium of Fossil Hominids as an Indicator of Their Upper Respiratory Systems." *American Journal of Physical Anthropology,* 51, 1979.

Laming, A. *Lascaux.* Penguin, 1959.

Lancaster, J. B. "Primate Communication Systems and the Emergence of Human Language," in P. C. Jay, ed., *Primates: Studies in Adaptation and Variability.* Holt, Rinehart & Winston, 1968.

Lancaster, J. B., and C. S. Lancaster. "Parental Investment: The Hominid Adaptation," in D. J. Ortner, ed., *How Humans Adapt: A Biocultural Odyssey.* Smithsonian Institute Press, 1983.

Laughlin, W. S. "Eskimos and Aleuts: Their Origins and Evolution." *Science,* 142, 1963.

Leakey, M. "The Dawn of Humans: The Farthest Horizon." *National Geographic,* 188, 1995.

Leakey, M. D. *Olduvai Gorge,* vol. 3. Cambridge University Press, 1971.

Leakey, M. G., et al. "New Hominin Genus from Eastern Africa Shows Diverse Middle Pliocene Lineages." *Nature,* 410, 2001.

Leakey, M., C. S. Feibel, I. McDougall, and A. Walker. "New Four-Million-Year-Old Hominid Species from Kanapoi and Allia Bay, Kenya." *Nature,* 376, 1995.

Leakey, M., and A. Walker. "Early Hominid Fossils from Africa." *Scientific American,* 276, 1997.

Lee, R. B. *Studies of the !Kung San and Their Neighbors.* Harvard University Press, 1976.

Lee, R. B., and I. DeVore, eds. *Man the Hunter.* Aldine, 1968.

Leonard, W. R., and M. L. Robertson. "Energetic Efficiency of Human Bipedality." *American Journal of Physical Anthropology,* 97, 1995.

Leroi-Gourhan, A. *Treasures of Prehistoric Art.* Abrams, 1967.

Leveque, F., A. Backer, and M. Guilbaud, eds. *Context of a Late Neandertal.* Prehistory Press, 1993.

Levin, J., and D. Suzuki. *The Secret of Life.* WGBH Boston, 1993.

Lewin, R. *Human Evolution: An Illustrated Introduction.* Blackwell Scientific Publications, 1993.

Lewis-Williams, J. D. *The Rock Art of Southern Africa.* Cambridge University Press, 1983.

Lewontin, R. *Human Diversity.* Scientific American Library, 1982.

Lieberman, D. E. "Sphenoid Shortening and the Evolution of Modern Human Cranial Shape." *Nature,* 393, 1998.

Lieberman, D. E., B. A. Wood, and D. R. Pilbeam. "Homoplasy and Early *Homo:* An Analysis of the Evolutionary Relationships of *H. habilis sensu stricto* and *H. rudolfensis.*" *Journal of Human Evolution,* 30, 1996.

Lieberman, P. *On the Origins of Language.* Macmillan, 1975.

Lieberman, P., E. S. Crelin, and D. H. Klatt. "Phonetic Ability and Related Anatomy of the Newborn and Adult Human, Neanderthal Man, and the Chimpanzee." *American Anthropologist,* 74, no. 3, 1972.

Littlefield, A., L. Lieberman, and L. T. Reynolds. "Redefining Race: The Potential Demise of a Concept in Physical Anthropology." *Current Anthropology,* 23, 1982.

Losos, J., K. I. Warheit, and T. W. Schoener. "Adaptive Differentiation Following Experimental Island Colonization in *Anolis* Lizards." *Nature,* 387, 1997.

Lovejoy, C. O., "The Origin of Man." *Science,* 211, no. 4480, 1981.

Lovejoy, C. O. "Evolution of Human Walking." *Scientific American,* 259, 1988.

Lovejoy, C. O. "Modeling Human Origins: Are We Sexy Because We're Smart, or Smart Because We're Sexy?" in D. T. Rasmussen, ed., *The Origin and Evolution of Humans and Humanness.* Jones & Bartlett, 1993.

Loy, J. D., and C. B. Peters, eds. *Understanding Behavior.* Oxford University Press, 1991.

Lyell, C. *Principles of Geology.* 3 vols. Murray, 1830–1833.

Lyell, C. *The Antiquity of Man.* Murray, 1863.

MacLarnon, A. "The Vertebral Canal," in A. Walker and R. Leakey, eds., *The Nariokotome* Homo erectus *Skeleton.* Harvard University Press, 1993.

Malthus, T. R. *Essay on the Principle of Population.* J. Johnson, 1798.

Marean, C. W., and Soo Yeun Kim. "Mousterian Large-Mammal Remains from Kobeh Cave." *Current Anthropology,* 39 (Supplement), 1998.

Maringer, J. *The Gods of Prehistoric Man.* Knopf, 1960.

Maringer, J., and H.-G. Bandi. *Art in the Ice Age.* Praeger, 1953.

Marks, J. "Black, White, Other." *Natural History,* 103, 1994.

Marks, J. *Human Biodiversity: Genes, Race and History.* Aldine de Gruyter, 1995.

Marshack, A. *The Roots of Civilization.* McGraw-Hill, 1972.

Martin, R. D. *Primate Origins and Evolution: A Phylogenetic Reconstruction.* Chapman & Hall, 1990.

Martin, R. D. "Primate Origins: Plugging the Gaps." *Nature,* 363, 1993.

Maynard Smith, J. "Bacteria Break the Antibiotic Bank." *Natural History,* 103, 1994.

Mayr, E. *Populations, Species and Evolution.* Harvard University Press, 1970.

Mayr, E. *The Growth of Biological Thought: Diversity, Evolution, and Inheritance.* Harvard University Press, 1982.

Mayr, E. *One Long Argument.* Harvard University Press, 1991.

Mayr, E. "What Is a Species, and What Is Not?" *Philosophy of Science,* 63, 1996.

McCrossin, M. L. "Bridging the Gap: Connecting the Origin of Bipedalism in Pliocene Hominidae with the Advent of Semiterrestrial Adaptations among African Miocene Hominoidea." Personal communication, 1997a.

McCrossin, M. L. "New Postcranial Remains of *Kenyapithecus* and Their Implications for Understanding the Origins of Hominoid Terrestriality." Unpublished conference paper abstracted in *American Journal of Physical Anthropology,* Suppl. 24, 1997b.

McGrew, W. C. *Chimpanzee Material Culture.* Cambridge University Press, 1992.

McHenry, H. M. "How Big Were Early Hominids?" *Evolutionary Anthropology,* 1, 1992.

McHenry, H. M. "Behavioral Ecological Implications of Early Hominid Body Size." *Journal of Human Evolution,* 27, 1994.

McHenry, H. M., and L. R. Berger. "Body Proportions in *Australopithecus afarensis* and *A. africanus* and the origin of the genus *Homo.*" *Journal of Human Evolution,* 35, 1998.

McKee, J. K. "Faunal Dating of the Taung Hominid Fossil Deposit." *Journal of Human Evolution,* 25, 1993.

McKie, R. "The People Eaters." *New Scientist,* 157, 1998.

Mellars, P., and C. Stringer, eds. *The Human Revolution.* Edinburgh University Press, 1989.

Melnick, D. J., and M. C. Pearl. "Cercopithecines in Multi-male Groups: Genetic Diversity and Population Structure," in B. Smuts, D. Cheney, R. Seyfarth, R. Wangham, and T. Struhsaker, eds., *Primate Societies.* University of Chicago Press, 1987.

Meltzer, D. J. "Pleistocene Peopling of the Americas." *Evolutionary Anthropology,* 1, 1993.

Meltzer, D. J. "Monte Verde and the Pleistocene Peopling of the Americas." *Science,* 276, 1997.

Mithen, S. *The Prehistory of the Mind.* Thames and Hudson, 1996.

Mivart, St. G. "On Lepilemur and Cheirogaleus and on the Zoological Rank of the Lemuroidea." *Proceedings of the Zoological Society, London,* 1873.

Molnar, S. *Human Variation,* 4th ed. Prentice Hall, 1998.

Montagu, A. *The Concept of Race.* Free Press, 1964.

Morgan, T. H. *Evolution and Adaptation.* Macmillan, 1903.

Morgan, T. H. *The Mechanism of Mendelian Heredity.* Constable, 1915.

Morgan, T. H. *The Physical Basis of Heredity.* Lippincott, 1919.

Morwood, M. J., P. B. O'Sullivan, F. Aziz, and A. Raza. "Fission-Track Ages of Stone Tools and Fossils on the East Indonesian Island of Flores." *Nature,* 392, 1998.

Moyá-Solà, S., and M. Kohler. "A *Dryopithecus* Skeleton and the Origins of Great-Ape Locomotion." *Nature,* 379, 1996.

Moyá-Solà, S., and M. Kohler. "The Orce Skull: Anatomy of a Mistake." *Journal of Human Evolution,* 33, 1997.

Muller, H. J. *Genetics, Medicine and Men.* Cornell University Press, Oxford University Press, 1947.

Mulvaney, D. J., and J. Gordon. *Aboriginal Man and Environment in Australia.* Australian National University Press, 1971.

Murrill, R. I. *Petralona Man.* Charles C. Thomas, 1981.

Myers, R. E. "Comparative Neurology of Vocalization and Speech," in S. L. Washburn and E. R. McCown, eds., *Human Evolution: Biosocial Perspectives.* Benjamin/Cummings, 1978.

Napier, J. "The Evolution of the Hand." *Scientific American,* 207, no. 6, 1962.

Napier, J. *The Roots of Mankind.* Smithsonian Institute Press, 1970.

Napier, J., and P. H. Napier. *Handbook of Living Primates.* Academic Press, 1967.

Nishida, T. *Chimpanzees of the Mahale Mountains.* University of Tokyo Press, 1990.

Nishida, T., and M. Hiraiwa-Hasegawa. "Chimpanzees and Bonobos: Cooperative Relationships among Males," in B. Smuts, D. Cheney, R. Seyfarth, R. Wangham, and T. Struhsaker, eds., *Primate Societies.* University of Chicago Press, 1987.

Nitecki, M. H., and D. V. Nitecki, eds. *Origins of Anatomically Modern Humans.* Plenum Press, 1994.

Numbers, R. L. *The Creationists.* Knopf, 1992.

Oakley, K. P. *Man the Tool-Maker,* 6th ed. Trustees of the British Museum (Natural History), 1972.

Oakley, K. P., B. G. Campbell, and T. I. Mollison. *Catalogue of Fossil Hominids.* 3 vols. Trustees of the British Museum (Natural History), 1967–1977.

O'Connell, J. R., and J. Allen. "When Did Humans First Arrive in Greater Australia and Why Is It Important to Know?" *Evolutionary Anthropology,* 6, 1998.

Orchinnikov, I. V., A. Gotherstrom, G. P. Romanova, V. M. Karitonov, K. Liden, and W. Goodwin. "Molecular Analysis of Neandertal DNA from the Northern Caucasus." *Nature,* 404, 2000.

Osborn, H. F. *Men of the Old Stone Age.* Scribner's, 1915.

Ovey, C. D., ed. "The Swanscombe Skull." *Occasional Papers of the Royal Anthropological Institute,* 20. London, 1964.

Oxnard, C. *The Order of Man.* Yale University Press, 1984.

Packer, C., D. A. Collins, A. Sindimwo, and J. Goodall. "Reproductive Constraints on Aggressive Competition in Female Baboons." *Nature,* 373, 1995.

Palmqvist, P. "A Critical Re-evaluation of the Evidence for the Presence of Hominids in Lower Pleistocene Times at Venta Micena, Southern Spain." *Journal of Human Evolution,* 33, 1997.

Palombit, R. "Dynamic Pair Bonds in Hylobatids: Implications Regarding Monogamous Social Systems." *Behaviour,* 128, 1994.

Parish, A. R. "Sex and Food Control in the 'Uncommon Chimpanzee': How Bonobo Females Overcame a Phylogenetic Legacy of Male Dominance." *Etiology and Sociobiology,* 15, 1994.

Passingham, R. L. *The Human Primate.* Freeman, 1982.

Patterson, B., A. K. Behrensmeyer, and W. D. Sill. "Geology of a New Pliocene Locality in Northwestern Kenya." *Nature,* 256, 1970.

Pei, W. C. "The Upper Cave Industry at Choukoutien." *Palaeontologia Sinica,* 9, 1939.

Petersen, S. E., P. T. Fox, M. I. Posner, M. Mintun, and M. E. Raichle. "Positron Emission Tomographic Studies of the Cortical Anatomy of Single-Word Processing." *Nature,* 331, 1988.

Pilbeam, D. "Middle Pleistocene Hominids," in K. W. Butzer and G. L. Isaac, eds., *After the Australopithecines.* Mouton, 1975.

Pilbeam, D. "Genetic and Morphological Records of the Hominoidea and Hominid Origins: A Synthesis." *Molecular Phylogenetics and Evolution,* 5, 1996.

Pinker, S. *The Language Instinct.* Morrow, 1994.

Pitts, M., and M. Roberts. *Fairweather Eden.* Fromm International, 1998.

Plavcan, J. M., and J. Kelley. "Evaluating the 'Dual Selection' Hypothesis of Canine Reduction." *American Journal of Physical Anthropology,* 99, 1996.

Pope, G. G. "Bamboo and Human Evolution." *Natural History,* 98, 1989.

Pope, G. G. "Ancient Asia's Cutting Edge." *Natural History,* 102, 1993.

Potts, R. *Early Hominid Activities at Olduvai.* Aldine de Gruyter, 1988.

Potts, R. "Archeological Interpretations of Early Hominid Behavior and Ecology," in D. T. Rasmussen, ed., *The Origin and Evolution of Humans and Humanness.* Jones & Bartlett, 1993.

Potts, R. *Humanity's Descent.* William Morrow, 1996.

Povinelli, D. J. "What Chimpanzees (Might) Know about the Mind," in R. Wraugham et al., eds., *Chimpanzee Cultures.* Harvard University Press, 1994.

Prescott, D. M. *Cells.* Jones & Bartlett, 1988.

Price, P. W. *Biological Evolution.* Saunders College Publishing, 1996.

Pusey, A., J. Williams, and J. Goodall. "The Influence of Dominance Rank on the Reproductive Success of Female Chimpanzees." *Science,* 277, 1997.

Rasmussen, D. T., and E. L. Simons. "Paleobiology of the Oligopithecines, the Earliest Known Anthropoid Primates." *International Journal of Primatology,* 13, 1992.

Raup, D. M. *Extinction: Bad Genes or Bad Luck?* Norton, 1991.

Reichard, U. "Extra-Pair Copulations in a Monogamous Gibbon (*Hylobates lar*)." *Ethology,* 100, 1995.

Relethford, J. H. "Hemispheric Difference in Human Skin Color." *American Journal of Physical Anthropology,* 104, 1997.

Richmond, B. G., and W. L. Jungers. "Size Variation and Sexual Dimorphism in *Australopithecus afarensis* and Living Hominoids." *Journal of Human Evolution,* 29, 1995.

Ridley, M. *Evolution,* 2nd ed. Blackwell Science, 1996.

Rightmire, G. P. *The Evolution of Homo erectus.* Cambridge University Press, 1990.

Rightmire, G. P. "*Homo erectus:* Ancestor or Evolutionary Side Branch?" *Evolutionary Anthropology,* 1, 1992.

Rightmire, G. P. "Variation among Early *Homo* Crania from Olduvai Gorge and the Koobi Fora Region." *American Journal of Physical Anthropology,* 90, 1993.

Rightmire, G. P. "The Human Cranium from Bodo, Ethiopia: Evidence for Speciation in the Middle Pleistocene?" *Journal of Human Evolution,* 31, 1996.

Rightmire, G. P. "Evidence from Facial Morphology for Similarity of Asian and African Representatives of *Homo erectus*." *American Journal of Physical Anthropology,* 106, 1998a.

Rightmire, G. P. "Human Evolution in the Middle Pleistocene: The Role of *Homo heidelbergensis*." *Evolutionary Anthropology,* 6, 1998b.

Roberts, M. B., C. B. Stringer, and S. A. Parfitt. "A Hominid Tibia from Middle Pleistocene Sediments at Boxgrove, UK." *Nature,* 369, 1994.

Roberts, N. "Climatic Change in the Past," in S. Jones et al., eds., *The Cambridge Encyclopedia of Human Evolution.* Cambridge University Press, 1992.

Roberts, R., G. Walsh, A. Murray, J. Olley, R. Jones, M. Morwood, C. Tuniz, E. Lawson, M. Macphail, D. Bowdery, and I. Naumann. "Luminescence Dating of Rock Art and Past Environments Using Mud-Wasp Nests in Northern Australia." *Nature,* 387, 1997.

Robins, A. H. *Biological Perspectives on Human Pigmentation.* Cambridge University Press, 1991.

Rodman, P. S., and J. C. Mitani. "Orangutans: Sexual Dimorphism in a Solitary Species," in B. Smuts, D. Cheney, R. Seyfarth, R. Wangham, and T. Struhsaker, eds., *Primate Societies.* University of Chicago Press, 1987.

Rogers, L. J., and G. Kaplan. "A New Form of Tool Use by Orang-Utans in Sabah, East Malaysia." *Folia Primatologica,* 63, 1994.

Rollefson, G., and I. Köhler-Rollefson. "Early Neolithic Exploitation Patterns in the Levant: Cultural Impact on the Environment." *Population and Environment,* 13, 1992.

Roosevelt, A. C., M. Lima da Costa, C. Lopes Machado, M. Michab, N. Mercier, H. Valladas, J. Feathers, W. Barnett, M. Imazio da Silveira, A. Henderson, J. Sliva, B. Chernoff, D. S. Reese, J. A. Holman, N. Toth, and K. Schick. "Paleoindian Cave Dwellers in the Amazon: The Peopling of the Americas." *Science,* 272, 1996.

Rose, L., and F. Marshall. "Meat Eating, Hominid Sociality, and Home Bases Revisited." *Current Anthropology,* 37, 1996.

Rosenberg, K. R. "The Evolution of Modern Human Childbirth." *Yearbook of Physical Anthropology,* 35, 1992.

Rosenberg, K. R., and W. Trevathan. "Bipedalism and Human Birth: The Obstetrical Dilemma Revisited." *Evolutionary Anthropology,* 4, 1995/96.

Ross, C., and M. Henneberg. "Basicranial Flexion, Relative Brain Size, and Facial Kyphosis in *Homo sapiens* and Some Fossil Hominids." *American Journal of Physical Anthropology,* 98, 1995.

Ruff, C. B. "Biomechanics of the Hip and Birth in Early *Homo.*" *American Journal of Physical Anthropology,* 98, 1995.

Ruff, C. B., E. Trinkaus, and T. W. Holliday. "Body Mass and Encephalization in Pleistocene *Homo.*" *Nature,* 387, 1997.

Sackett, J., "Human Antiquity and the Old Stone Age: The Nineteenth-Century Background to Paleoanthropology." *Evolutionary Anthropology,* 9, 2000.

Sarich, V. M. "Molecular Clocks," in S. Jones, R. Martin, and D. Pilbeam, eds., *The Cambridge Encyclopedia of Human Evolution,* Cambridge University Press, 1992.

Sarich, V. M., and J. E. Cronin. "Generation Length and Rates of Hominoid Molecular Evolution." *Nature,* 269, 1977.

Sarich, V. M., and A. C. Wilson. "Immunological Time Scale for Hominoid Evolution." *Science,* 158, 1967.

Savage-Rumbaugh, S. "Language Training of Apes," in S. Jones et al., eds., *The Cambridge Encyclopedia of Human Evolution.* Cambridge University Press, 1992.

Savage-Rumbaugh, S., and R. Lewin. "Ape at the Brink." *Discover,* 15, 1994.

Schaller, G. B. *Year of the Gorilla.* University of Chicago Press, 1964.

Schaller, G. B., and G. Lowther. "The Relevance of Carnivore Behavior to the Study of Early Hominids." *Southwestern Journal of Anthropology,* 25, no. 4 (University of New Mexico Press), 1969.

Schepartz, L. A. "Language and Modern Human Origins." *Yearbook of Physical Anthropology,* 36, 1993.

Schick, K. D., and N. Toth. *Making Silent Stones Speak.* Simon & Schuster, 1993.

Schrenk, F., T. G. Bromage, C. G. Betzler, U. Ring, and Y. M. Juwayeyi. "Oldest *Homo* and Pliocene Biogeography of the Malawi Rift." *Nature,* 365, 1993.

Schultz, A. H. "The Recent Hominoid Primates," in S. L. Washburn and P. C. Jay, eds., *Perspectives on Human Evolution 1.* Holt, Rinehart & Winston, 1968.

Schultz, A. H. *The Life of Primates.* Universe Books, 1969.

Schwartz, J. H. *Skeleton Keys.* Oxford University Press, 1995.

Semaw, S., P. Renne, J. W. K. Harris, C. S. Feibel, R. L. Bernor, N. Fesseha, and K. Mowbray. "2.5-Million-Year-Old Stone Tools from Gona, Ethiopia." *Nature,* 385, 1997.

Semenov, S. A. *Prehistoric Technology.* Cory, Adams & Mackay, 1964.

Senut, B. "New Ideas on the Origins of Hominid Locomotion," in T. Nishida, W. McGrew, P. Marler, M. Pickford, and F. de Waal, eds., *Topics in Primatology: Vol. 1. Human Origins.* University of Tokyo Press, 1992.

Senut, B., et al. "First Hominid from the Miocene (Lukeino Formation, Kenya)." *Comptes Rendus de l'Academie des Sciences Paris,* 332, 2001.

Seyfarth, R. M., D. L. Cheney, and P. Marler. "Monkey Responses to Three Different Alarm Calls: Evidence of Predator Classification and Semantic Communication." *Science,* 210, 1980.

Seyfarth, R. M., D. L. Cheney, and P. Marler. "Vervet Monkey Alarm Calls: Semantic Communication in a Free-Ranging Primate." *Animal Behavior,* 28, 1980.

Shanklin, E. *Anthropology and Race.* Wadsworth, 1994.

Shapiro, H. L. *Peking Man.* Simon & Schuster, 1974.

Shea, J. J. "Neandertal and Early Modern Human Behavioral Variability." *Current Anthropology,* 39 (Supplement), 1998.

Shipman, P. "Scavenging or Hunting in Early Hominids: Theoretical Framework and Tests." *American Anthropologist,* 88, 1986.

Shreeve, J. "Sunset on the Savanna." *Discover,* 17, 1996.

Sibley, C. G. "Times of Divergence," in S. Jones, R. Martin, and D. Pilbeam, eds., *The Cambridge Encyclopedia of Human Evolution.* Cambridge University Press, 1992.

Simons, E. L. *Primate Evolution.* Macmillan, 1972.

Simons, E. L. "The Fossil History of Primates," in S. Jones, R. Martin, and D. Pilbeam, eds., *The Cambridge Encyclopedia of Human Evolution.* Cambridge University Press, 1992.

Simons, E. L. "Egypt's Simian Spring." *Natural History,* 102, 1993.

Simons, E. L., and D. T. Rasmussen. "Skull of *Catopithecus browni,* an Early Tertiary Catarrhine." *American Journal of Physical Anthropology,* 100, 1996.

Simpson, G. G. *The Meaning of Evolution.* Oxford University Press, 1950.

Simpson, G. G. *The Major Features of Evolution.* Simon & Schuster, 1953.

Singer, M., and P. Berg. *Genes and Genomes.* University Science Books, 1991.

Skelton, R. R., and H. M. McHenry. "Evolutionary Relationships among Early Hominids." *Journal of Human Evolution,* 23, 1992.

Small, M. F. *Female Choices.* Cornell University Press, 1993.

Smith, B. D. "The Origins of Agriculture in the Americas." *Evolutionary Anthropology,* 3, 1994–95.

Smith, B. D. "The Initial Domestication of *Cucurbita pepo* in the Americas 10,000 Years Ago." *Science,* 276, 1997.

Smith, G. Elliot. "Neanderthal Man Not Our Ancestor." *Scientific American,* August 1928.

Smuts, B., D. L. Cheney, R. M. Seyfarth, R. W. Wrangham, and T. T. Struhsaker, eds., *Primate Societies.* University of Chicago Press, 1987.

Sohn, S., and M. H. Wolpoff. "Zuttiyeh Face: A View from the East." *American Journal of Physical Anthropology,* 91, 1993.

Solecki, R. S. *Shanidar: The First Flower People.* Knopf, 1971.

Spencer, F. *Piltdown: A Scientific Forgery.* Natural History Museum, London, and Oxford University Press, 1990.

Sponheimer, M., and J. A. Lee-Thorp. "Isotopic Evidence for the Diet of an Early Hominid, *Australopithecus africanus.*" *Science,* 283, 1999.

Spoor, F., B. Wood, and F. Zonneveld. "Implications of Early Hominid Labyrinthine Morphology for Evolution of Human Bipedal Locomotion." *Nature,* 369, 1994.

Stanford, C. B. "The Hunting Ecology of Wild Chimpanzees: Implications for the Evolutionary Ecology of Pliocene Hominids." *American Anthropologist,* 98, 1996.

Stanford, C. B. "The Social Behavior of Chimpanzees and Bonobos." *Current Anthropology,* 39, 1998.

Steudel, K. "Limb Morphology, Bipedal Gait, and the Energetics of Hominid Locomotion." *American Journal of Physical Anthropology,* 99, 1996.

Stewart, I. "Real Australopithecines Do Eat Meat." *New Scientist,* 134, 1992.

Stewart, K. I., and A. H. Harcourt. "Gorillas: Variation in Female Relationships," in B. Smuts, D. Cheney, R. Seyfarth, R. Wangham, and T. Struhsaker, eds., *Primate Societies.* University of Chicago Press, 1987.

Stoneking, M. "DNA and Recent Human Evolution." *Evolutionary Anthropology,* 2, 1993.

Strickberger, M. W. *Evolution,* 2nd ed. Jones and Bartlett, 1996.

Stringer, C. "New Views on Modern Human Origins," in D. T. Rasmussen, ed., *The Origin and Evolution of Humans and Humanness.* Jones & Bartlett, 1993.

Stringer, C. "A Metrical Study of the WLH-50 Calvaria." *Journal of Human Evolution,* 34, 1998.

Stringer, C., and P. Andrews. "Genetic and Fossil Evidence for the Origin of Modern Humans." *Science,* 239, 1988.

Stringer, C., and C. Gamble. *In Search of the Neandertals.* Thames & Hudson, 1993.

Stringer, C., J. J. Hublin, and B. Vandermeersch. "The Origin of Anatomically Modern Humans in Western Europe," in F. Smith and F. Spencer, eds., *The Origins of Modern Humans: A World Survey of the Fossil Evidence.* A. R. Liss, 1984.

Stringer, C., and R. McKie. *African Exodus.* Henry Holt, 1996.

Strum, S. C. *Almost Human: A Journey into the World of Baboons.* Elm Tree Books, 1987.

Sugiyama, Y. "On the Social Change of Hanuman Langurs (*Presbytis entellus*) in Their Natural Condition." *Primates,* 6, 1965.

Susman, R. L. "Fossil Evidence for Early Hominid Tool Use." *Science,* 265, 1994.

Susman, R. L., ed. *The Pygmy Chimpanzee: Evolutionary Biology and Behavior.* Plenum Press, 1984.

Sussman, R. W. "Primate Origins and the Evolution of Angiosperms." *American Journal of Primatology,* 23, 1991.

Suwa, G., T. D. White, and F. C. Howell. "Mandibular Postcanine Dentition from the Shungura Formation, Ethiopia: Crown Morphology, Taxonomic Allocations, and Plio–Pleistocene Hominid Evolution." *American Journal of Physical Anthropology,* 101, 1996.

Swisher, C. C., G. H. Curtis, T. Jacob, A. G. Getty, A. Suprijo, Widiasmoro. "Age of the Earliest Known Hominids in Java, Indonesia." *Science,* 263, 1994.

Swisher, C. C., W. J. Rink, S. C. Anton, H. P. Schwarcz, G. H. Curtis, A. Suprijo, Widiasmoro. "Latest *Homo erectus* of Java: Potential Contemporaneity with *Homo sapiens* in Southeast Asia." *Science,* 274, 1996.

Szalay, F. S., and E. Delson. *Evolutionary History of the Primates.* Academic Press, 1979.

Tacon, P. "Art of the Land," in G. Burenhult, ed., *The First Humans: Human Origins and History to 10,000 BC.* Harper San Francisco, 1993.

Tanner, N. M. *On Becoming Human.* Cambridge University Press, 1981.

Tattersall, I. *The Human Odyssey.* Prentice Hall, 1993.

Tattersall, I. *The Fossil Trail.* Oxford University Press, 1995a.

Tattersall, I. *The Last Neanderthal.* Macmillan, 1995b.

Tattersall, I. "Out of Africa Again … and Again?" *Scientific American,* 276, 1997.

Theunissen, B. *Eugene Dubois and the Ape-Man from Java.* Kluwer, 1989.

Thieme, H. "Lower Palaeolithic Hunting Spears from Germany." *Nature,* 385, 1997.

Tobias, P. V. *The Brain in Hominid Evolution.* Columbia University Press, 1971.

Tobias, P. V. *Hominid Evolution.* A. R. Liss, 1985.

Tobias, P. V. "The Brain of *Homo habilis:* A New Level of Organization in Cerebral Evolution." *Journal of Human Evolution,* 16, 1987.

Trevathan, W. *Human Birth: An Evolutionary Perspective.* Aldine de Gruyter, 1987.

Trevathan, W. "Fetal Emergence Patterns in Evolutionary Perspective." *American Anthropologist,* 90, 1988.

Trinkaus, E., and W. W. Howells. "The Neanderthals." *Scientific American,* 241, no. 6, 1979.

Trinkaus, E., and P. Shipman. *The Neandertals.* Knopf, 1993.

Trivers, R. "The Evolution of Reciprocal Altruism." *Quarterly Review of Biology,* 46, 1971.

Turnbaugh, W. A., R. Jurmain, H. Nelson, L. Kilgore. *Understanding Physical Anthropology and Archeology,* 6th ed. West, 1996.

Turner, A., and B. Wood. "Comparative Palaeontological Context for the Evolution of the Early Hominid Masticatory System." *Journal of Human Evolution,* 24, 1993.

Turner, C. G. II, and J. A. Turner. *Man Corn.* University of Utah Press, 1999.

Tuttle, R., ed. *The Functional and Evolutionary Biology of Primates.* Aldine-Atherton, 1972.

Ucko, P. J., and A. Rosenfeld. *Palaeolithic Cave Art.* McGraw-Hill, 1967.

van Schaik, C. P., E. A. Fox, and A. F. Sitompul. "Manufacture and Use of Tools in Wild Sumatran Orangutans." *Naturwissenschaften,* 83, 1996.

van Schaik, C. P., and J. A. R. A. M. van Hooff. "Toward an Understanding of the Orangutan's Social System," in W. C. McGrew et al., eds., *Great Ape Societies.* Cambridge University Press, 1996.

Venter, C., et al. "The Sequence of the Human Genome." *Science,* 291, 2001.

Villa, P. "Cannibalism in Prehistoric Europe." *Evolutionary Anthropology,* 1, 1992.

von Koenigswald, G. H. R. *Meeting Prehistoric Man.* Harper, 1956.

Vrba, E. S. "Ecological and Adaptive Changes Associated with Early Hominid Evolution," in R. L. Ciochon and J. G. Fleagle, eds., *The Human Evolution Source Book.* Prentice Hall, 1993a.

Vrba, E. S. "The Pulse That Produced Us." *Natural History,* 102, 1993b.

Vygotskii, L. S. *Mind in Society: The Development of Higher Psychological Processes.* Harvard University Press, 1978.

Waal, F. de. *Chimpanzee Politics: Power and Sex among Apes.* Harper & Row, 1982.

Waal, F. de. *Peacemaking among Primates.* Harvard University Press, 1989.

Waal, F. de, and F. Lanting. *Bonobo: The Forgotten Ape.* University of California Press, 1997.

Waddle, D. M. "Matrix Correlation Tests Support a Single Origin for Modern Humans." *Nature,* 368, 1994.

Walker, A. "Perspectives on the Nariokotome Discovery," in A. Walker and R. Leakey, eds., *The Nariokotome* Homo erectus *Skeleton.* Harvard University Press, 1993a.

Walker, A. "The Origin of the Genus *Homo,*" in D. T. Rasmussen, ed., *The Origin and Evolution of Humans and Humanness.* Jones & Bartlett, 1993b.

Walker, A., and R. E. Leakey, eds. *The Nariokotome* Homo erectus *Skeleton.* Harvard University Press, 1993.

Walker, A., R. E. Leakey, J. M. Harris, and F. H. Brown. "2.5 myr *Australopithecus boisei* from West of Lake Turkana, Kenya." *Nature,* 322, 1986.

Walker, A., and C. Ruff. "The Reconstruction of the Pelvis," in A. Walker and R. E. Leakey, eds., *The Nariokotome* Homo erectus *Skeleton.* Harvard University Press, 1993.

Wallace, A. R. *Darwinism: An Exposition of the Theory of Natural Selection.* Macmillan, 1889.

Wallace, A. R. *My Life: A Record of Events and Opinions.* 2 vols. Chapman & Hall, 1905.

Walsh, J. E. *Unraveling Piltdown.* Random House, 1996.

Wanpo, H., R. Ciochon, G. Yumin, R. Larick, F. Qiren, H. Schwarcz, C. Yonge, J. de Vos, and W. Rink. "Early *Homo* and Associated Artefacts from Asia." *Nature,* 378, 1995.

Ward, C. V., A. Walker, M. F. Teaford, and I. Odhiambo. "Partial Skeleton of *Proconsul nyanzae* from Mfangano Island, Kenya." *American Journal of Physical Anthropology,* 90, 1993.

Ward, N. "To People the World, Start with 500." *New York Times,* November 11, 1997.

Ward, R., and C. Stringer. "A Molecular Handle on the Neanderthals." *Nature,* 388, 1997.

Washburn, S. L. *Social Life of Early Man.* Aldine, 1961.

Washburn, S. L. "Behavior and Human Evolution," in S. L. Washburn, ed., *Classification and Human Evolution.* Aldine, 1963.

Washburn, S. L., and P. Dolhinow, eds. *Perspectives on Human Evolution.* 4 vols. Holt, Rinehart & Winston, 1968–1976.

Washburn, S. L., and R. Moore. *Ape into Man.* Little Brown, 1974.

Washburn, S. L., and S. C. Strum. "Concluding Comments," in S. L. Washburn and P. Dolhinow, eds., *Perspectives on Human Evolution,* vol. 2. Holt, Rinehart & Winston, 1972.

Watts, D. P. "Infanticide in Mountain Gorillas: New Cases and a Reconsideration of the Evidence." *Ethology,* 81, 1989.

Weidenreich, F. *Apes, Giants, and Man.* University of Chicago Press, 1946.

Weiner, J. *The Beak of the Finch.* Vintage Books, 1994.

Wells, H. G. "The Grisly Folk." Original 1921, reprinted in Wells's *Selected Short Stories.* Penguin, 1958.

Wheeler, P. "The Influence of Bipedalism on the Energy and Water Budgets of Early Hominids." *Journal of Human Evolution,* 21, 1991a.

Wheeler, P. "The Thermoregulatory Advantages of Hominid Bipedalism in Open Equatorial Environments: The Contribution of Increased Convective Heat Loss and Cutaneous Evaporative Cooling." *Journal of Human Evolution,* 21, 1991b.

Wheeler, P. "Human Ancestors Walked Tall, Stayed Cool." *Natural History,* 102, 1993.

White, F. J. "Activity Budgets, Feeding Behavior, and Habitat Use of Pygmy Chimpanzees at Lomako, Zaire." *American Journal of Primatology,* 26, 1992.

White, J. P. "The Settlement of Ancient Australia," in G. Burenhult, ed., *The First Humans: Human Origins and History to 10,000 BC.* HarperCollins, 1993.

White, T. D. *Prehistoric Cannibalism at Mancos 5MT-UMR–2346.* Princeton University Press, 1992.

White, T. D., D. C. Johanson, and W. H. Kimbel. "*Australopithecus africanus*: Its Phyletic Position Reconsidered." *South African Journal of Science,* 77, 1981.

White, T. D., G. Suwa, and B. Asfaw. "*Australopithecus ramidus*, a New Species of Early Hominid from Aramis, Ethiopia." *Nature,* 371, 1994.

White, T. D., G. Suwa, and B. Asfaw. "Corrigendum. *Australopithecus ramidus*" *Nature,* 375, 1995.

White, T. D., G. Suwa, W. K. Hart, R. C. Walter, G. WoldeGabriel, J. de Heinzelin, J. D. Clark, B. Asfaw, and E. Vrba. "New Discoveries of *Australopithecus* at Maka in Ethiopia." *Nature,* 366, 1993.

Wilford, J. N. "New Fossils Take Science Close to Dawn of Humans." *New York Times,* September 22, 1994.

Wilford, J. N. "Discovery of Flute Suggests Neanderthal Caves Echoed with Music." *New York Times,* October 29, 1996.

Wilford, J. N. "Evidence Indicates Humans Inhabited Siberia 300,000 Years Ago." *New York Times,* February 28, 1997a.

Wilford, J. N. "Fossil May Link Neanderthal and Modern Humans." *New York Times,* May 30, 1997b.

Willermet, C. M., and B. Hill. "Fuzzy Set Theory and Its Implications for Speciation Models," in G. A. Clark and C. M. Willermet, eds., *Conceptual Issues in Modern Human Origins Research.* Aldine de Gruyter, 1997.

Wilson, E. O. *On Human Nature.* Harvard University Press, 1978.

WoldeGabriel, G., T. D. White, G. Suwa, P. Renne, J. de Heinzelin, W. K. Hart, and G. Helken. "Ecological and Temporal Placement of Early Pliocene Hominids at Aramis, Ethiopia." *Nature,* 371, 1994.

Wolpoff, M. H. *Human Evolution,* 1996–1997 edition. McGraw-Hill, 1996.

Wood, B. A. "Origin and Evolution of the Genus *Homo*." *Nature,* 355, 1992.

Wood, B. A. "The Oldest Hominid Yet." *Nature,* 371, 1994.

Wood, B. A., L. Martin, and P. Andrews, eds. *Major Topics in Human and Primate Evolution.* Cambridge University Press, 1986.

Woodward, V. *Human Heredity and Society.* West, 1992.

Wrangham, R. W., W. C. McGrew, F. B. M. de Waal, and P. G. Heltme, eds. *Chimpanzee Cultures.* Harvard University Press, 1994.

Wrangham, R. W., and D. Peterson. *Demonic Males.* Houghton Mifflin, 1996.

Wu, Rukand, and Lin Shenglong. "Peking Man." *Scientific American,* 248, 1983.

Yamakoshi, G., and Y. Sugiyama. "Pestle-Pounding Behavior of Wild Chimpanzees at Bossou, Guinea: A Newly Observed Tool-Using Behavior." *Primates,* 36, 1995.

Credits

Photo Credits

Chapter 1

1: Mary Evans Picture Library; 4: William Buckland, *Reliquiae Diluvianae*, 1823.

Chapter 2

21: Corbis-Bettmann; 31: © Biophoto/Photo Researchers; 45: Science Source/Photo Researchers, Inc.

Chapter 3

49: © Shostak/AnthroPhoto, #3342; 57 (left): © Smucker/AnthroPhoto.

Chapter 4

75: David Haring/Duke University Primate Center; 83 (top left): © Wildlife Conservation Society, headquartered at the Bronx Zoo; 83 (top right): Arthur W. Ambler/National Audubon Society/Photo Researchers, Inc.; 83 (bottom left): © Sarah Blaffer Hrdy/AnthroPhoto, #7125; 83 (bottom right): Arthur W. Ambler/National Audubon Society/Photo Researchers, Inc.; 88 (top left): © D. J. Chivers/AnthroPhoto, #7114; 88 (top right): © Werner H. Muller/Peter Arnold, Inc.; 88 (bottom left): © Werner H. Muller/Peter Arnold, Inc.; 88 (bottom right): © D. J. Chivers/AnthroPhoto, #4331; 89 (top left): Michael Rougier; 89 (top right): Ralph Morse/Life Magazine © Time Inc.; 89 (bottom left): © Wildlife Conservation Society, headquartered at the Bronx Zoo; 89 (bottom right): © Richard Wrangham/AnthroPhoto, #3653; 92: © Fritz Goro; 99 (bottom right): From J. Napier and P. Napier, *A Handbook of Living Primates*. Copyright © 1967 by Academic Press Ltd. Reprinted by permission.

Chapter 5

109: Tom McHugh/Photo Researchers, Inc.; 114: © Richard Wrangham/AnthroPhoto, #6821; 116 (left): From *In the Shadow of Man* by Jane van Lawick-Goodall, © 1971 by Hugo van Lawick and Jane Goodall. Reprinted by permission of Houghton Mifflin Company and Hugo van Lawick; 116 (right): From *In the Shadow of Man* by Jane van Lawick-Goodall, © 1971 by Hugo van Lawick and Jane Goodall. Reprinted by permission of Houghton Mifflin Company and Hugo van Lawick; 118: © Irven DeVore/AnthroPhoto, #6784; 119: © Irven DeVore/AnthroPhoto, #7110; 121: © Joseph Popp/AnthroPhoto, #0293.

Chapter 6

129: Tom McHugh/Photo Researchers, Inc.; 134 (top): Zoological Society of San Diego; 137 (top): Dr. E. L. Simons/Duke University Primate Center; 140 (bottom): Natural History Museum Picture Library, London; 142: Salvador Moyá-Solà/Institut Paleontologic, Barcelona; 158: Dr. Geza Teleki; 159: Alison C. Hannah; 161: Reproduced with permission from Frans de Waal, (1989) *Peacemaking among Primates*.

Chapter 7

167: © David L. Brill, Atlanta; 172 (left): Don Johanson/Institute of Human Origins; 176: National Museums of Kenya; 179: © David L. Brill, Atlanta; 180 (top): Institute of Human Origins; 181: © David L. Brill, Atlanta; 183: John Reader/Science Source/Photo Researchers, Inc.; 186: Transvaal Museum, D.C., Panagos; 188: Des Bartlett/Photo Researchers, Inc.; 190: Alan Walker/National Museums of Kenya.

Chapter 8

197: John Reader/Science Source/Photo Researchers, Inc.; 203 (top left): Natural History Museum Picture Library, London; 203 (top right): Ronald J. Clark, University of Witwaterstrand; 203 (bottom left and right): © 1994 David L. Brill, Atlanta; 218: National Museums of Kenya; 220: Kathy D. Schick and Nicholas Toth, CRAFT Research Center, Indiana University (From Schick and Toth, 1993, p. 171).

Chapter 9

229: Courtesy of the Department Library Services, American Museum of Natural History, #335797; 233: Courtesy of the Department Library Service, American Museum of

Text and Illustration Credits

Chapter 1

Chapter 2

Chapter 3

Chapter 4

C. Jolly and S. Plog, 1986. Reprinted by permission of Mc-Graw-Hill Companies; Figure 4.5, p. 85: From *The Cambridge Encyclopedia of Human Evolution* by Steve Jones, Robert Martin, and David Pilbeam (Eds.), p. 24, 1992. Reprinted by permission of Cambridge University Press; Figure 4.9, p. 91: From *Primate Adaptation and Evolution* by John G. Fleagle, pp. 245–251, 1988. Copyright © 1988 Academic Press, Inc. Reprinted by permission of the publisher, author, and artist.

Chapter 5

Figure 5.1, p. 113: From *Primate Adaptation and Evolution* by John G. Fleagle, p. 57, 1988. Copyright © 1988 Academic Press, Inc. Reprinted by permission of the publisher, author, and artist; Figure 5.7, p. 123: From "Baboon Ecology," by I. DeVore and K. R. L. Hall, 1965. In I. DeVore (Ed.), *Primate Behavior: Field Studies of Monkeys and Apes*, Holt, Rinehart & Winston.

Chapter 6

Figure 6.1, p. 133: From *Reconstructing Human Origins: A Modern Synthesis* by Glenn C. Conroy. Copyright © 1997 by W. W. Norton & Company, Inc. Used by permission of W. W. Norton & Company, Inc.; Figure 6.7, p. 140: From *The Cambridge Encyclopedia of Human Evolution* by Steve Jones, Robert Martin, and David Pilbeam (Eds.), p. 224, 1992. Reprinted by permission of Cambridge University Press.

Chapter 7

Figure 7.7, p. 182: Redrawn from original drawings by Luba Dmytryk Gudz from *Lucy: The Beginnings of Humankind* by Donald C. Johanson and Maitland Edey, 1981, Simon & Schuster.

Chapter 8

Figure 8.4, p. 213: By Pete Wheeler from *Natural History*, 102(8), p. 66, 1993. Reprinted by permission of the author; Figure 8.5, p. 214: Adapted from "Evolution of Human Walking" by C. Owen Lovejoy, *Scientific American*, p. 125, November 1988, Vol. 259. Reprinted by permission of Carol Donner, the artist; Figure 8.8, p. 222: From *Olduvai Gorge*, Vol. III, 1971 by Mary Leakey. Reprinted by permission of Cambridge University Press; Figure 8.9, p. 223: From *Olduvai Gorge*, Vol. III, 1971 by Mary Leakey. Reprinted by permission of Cambridge University Press.

Chapter 9

Figure 9.6, p. 241: From *The Cambridge Encyclopedia of Human Evolution* by Steve Jones, Robert Martin, and David

Pilbeam (Eds.), p. 532, 1992. Reprinted by permission of Cambridge University Press; p. 244: From T. Harrison in *Species, Species Concepts, and Primate Evolution*, W. H. Kimbel and L. Martin, Eds., 1993. Reprinted by permission of the author and Kluwer Academic/Plenum Publishers; Figure 9.8, p. 246: "Climate Change in the Past" by N. Roberts, p. 175, from *The Cambridge Encyclopedia of Human Evolution* by Steve Jones, Robert Martin, and David Pilbeam (Eds.), 1992. Reprinted by permission of Cambridge University Press; Figure 9.9, p. 247: Redrawn by R. Freyman and N. Toth, pp. 232–233 from *Olduvai Gorge*, Vol. III © 1971 by Mary Leakey and Cambridge University Press. Reprinted with permission of the publishers; Figure 9.11, p. 251: From *The Cambridge Encyclopedia of Human Evolution* by Steve Jones, Robert Martin, and David Pilbeam (Eds.), p. 352, 1992. Reprinted by permission of Cambridge University Press and Joe LeMonnier from *Natural History*, October 1989, p. 50; Table 9.3, p. 254: Data from Aschoff et al. (1971), as reported by Aiello and Wheeler (1995). Reprinted by permission of the University of Chicago Press; Figure 9.12, p. 255: By L. C. Aiello and P. Wheeler from *Current Anthropology*, 36, no. 2, p. 204, April 1995. Reprinted by permission of the University of Chicago Press.

Chapter 10

Figure 10.5, p. 271: After Annick Peterson from *In Search of the Neandertals* by Christopher Stringer and Clive Gamble. © 1993 Christopher Stringer and Clive Gamble. Reprinted by permission of the publishers, Thames & Hudson.

Chapter 11

Figure 11.3, p. 303: Redrawn by permission from *The Old Stone Age* by Frances Bordes, © 1968 Frances Bordes, Weidenfeld & Nicolson publishers; Figure 11.4, p. 303: Redrawn by permission from *The Old Stone Age* by Frances Bordes, © 1968 Frances Bordes, Weidenfeld & Nicolson publishers; Figure 11.6, p. 314: Modified from "The Basicranium of Fossil Hominids as an Indicator of Their Upper Respiratory Systems" by J. Laitman, R. Heimbuch, and E. Crelin, 1979, *American Journal of Physical Anthropology*, 51. Copyright © 1979, John Wiley and Sons, Inc. Reprinted by permission of Wiley-Liss, Inc., a subsidiary of John Wiley and Sons, Inc.

Chapter 12

Figure 12.6 (right), p. 341: © Alexander Marshack.

Appendix

P. 357: From *Reconstructed Human Origins: A Modern Synthesis* by Glenn C. Conroy. Copyright © 1997 by W. W. Norton & Company, Inc. Reprinted by permission of W. W. Norton & Company, Inc.

Index